LORENZO MONACO

Marvin Eisenberg

PRINCETON UNIVERSITY PRESS

Published by Princeton University Press, 41 William Street,
Princeton, New Jersey 08540
In the United Kingdom: Princeton University Press,
Guildford, Surrey

Publication of this book has been aided by
a grant from The Millard Meiss Publication Fund of the College Art
Association of America

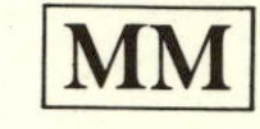

This book has been composed in Linotron Bembo type

Clothbound editions of Princeton University Press books
are printed on acid-free paper, and binding materials
are chosen for strength and durability. Paperbacks, although
satisfactory for personal collections, are not usually
suitable for library rebinding

Printed in the United States of America by Princeton
University Press, Princeton, New Jersey

Color illustrations printed by Garamond Pridemark Press,
Baltimore, Maryland

Library of Congress Cataloging-in-Publication Data
Eisenberg, Marvin
Lorenzo Monaco.
Bibliography: p.
Includes index.
1. Lorenzo, Monaco, 1370 or 71-1425—Criticism
and interpretation. 2. Lorenzo, Monaco, 1370
or 71-1425—Catalogues raisonnés. I. Title.
ND623.L77E35 1989 759.5 88-19559
ISBN 0-691-04042-7

for

Keiichi Hayano and Elizabeth Beatson

and

Frank and Elaine

Contents

Illustrations

PHOTOGRAPH credits and other acknowledgments are cited in parentheses. The credit Soprintendenza, Florence, refers to the Gabinetto Fotografico, Soprintendenza per i Beni Artistici e Storici per le Province di Firenze e Pistoia. Alinari, Anderson, and Brogi photographs are reproduced by courtesy of Alinari/Art Resource, New York.

COLORPLATES

BLACK-AND-WHITE ILLUSTRATIONS

Preface

Early in this century there appeared a cluster of monographs on Italian artists other than those who had been elevated by the Academies and by the Romantics to the rank of demigods. Within a decade the three major monastic painters of the Quattrocento were submitted for the first time to a comprehensive critical scrutiny, in books on Fra Angelico by Langton Douglas (1900) and Frieda Schottmüller (1911), on Fra Filippo Lippi by Henriette Mendelsohn (1909), and on Lorenzo Monaco by Osvald Sirén (1905). Their writings have continued to serve the student of earlier Florentine painting.

Following that initial monograph on Lorenzo Monaco, Sirén and other scholars expanded the painter's oeuvre in numerous articles, at times with less selectivity than in the pioneering book. Raimond van Marle (1927) largely reviewed the accumulated attributions, but he also made the first attempt to localize Don Lorenzo's artistic roots in the choir books of Santa Maria degli Angeli, using as a point of departure Paolo D'Ancona's seminal studies of Florentine miniature painting (1914). Vincenzo Golzio's appraisal of Lorenzo Monaco (1931) continued to depend on the corpus of works first defined by Sirén, while his principal concern was with the merging of styles in later Trecento Tuscan painting.

Two distinguished studies of Lorenzo Monaco appeared in the 1930s. By isolating a group of miniatures painted by the young monk in choir books for Santa Maria degli Angeli, Anna Maria Ciaranfi (1932) arrived at a more precise definition of Don Lorenzo's sources within the conglomerate Florentine stylistic idioms of the later Trecento. Georg Pudelko's classic essay (1938/39) provided an eloquent formalist interpretation that approached the work of Lorenzo Monaco both within Tuscan traditions and within the context of the International Style.

Evelyn Sandberg-Vavalà (1939), Hans Gronau (1950), and Federico Zeri (1964/65) cumulatively enlarged the corpus of Don Lorenzo's early works by reconstructing and attributing to him several important dispersed polyptychs. In my initial approach to the art of Lorenzo Monaco (1954), I accepted a more extensive body of juvenile works than I now believe is justified in defining an early style within the eclectic climate of later fourteenth-century painting. Mirella Levi D'Ancona, in an overview of the artist's development, rejected the reconstructions of his earliest activity as a panel painter (1958).

The background to the art of Lorenzo Monaco was clarified through the endeavors of Levi D'Ancona (1959), Luciano Bellosi (1965), and Miklós Boskovits (1972, 1975) to define aspects of the artistic environment of Florence in the later Trecento. In his encompassing study of Ghiberti, Richard Krautheimer (1956) posed fundamental questions with regard to the interchanges between sculpture and painting in the formation of late fourteenth and early fifteenth-century Florentine art, focussing on the stylistic convergences of Ghiberti and Lorenzo Monaco during their parallel careers in the first quarter of the Quattrocento. Krautheimer proffered the idea that the rediscovery of Ghiberti between 1895 and 1915 may be "best observed within the framework of the *art nouveau*" (1956, p. 26). Could the fact that in the same span of years the work of Lorenzo Monaco first received critical assessment be attributed in part to a sympathy with his linear harmonies and lyrical flights? In those same years Herbert Horne wrote his consummate book on Botticelli.

My intention in this monograph is twofold: first, to define within the context of Tuscan painting and sculpture a limited group of works that reveals the essential character of the art of Lorenzo Monaco; and second, to consider a large corpus of pictures that have been attributed to him, which range from works by assistants of varying talent who were active in his shop to those that do not have the ring of Don Lorenzo's formal language. The introductory essay treats only works that I believe were designed and in large part painted by Lorenzo Monaco, or for which he would seem to have provided the design and supervised the execution. I would hope that the general reader might gain from this essay a sense of the artist's identity as a maker of some of the most evocative images in later mediaeval painting. The general art-historical problems raised by these primarily autograph works are approached in the notes to the essay, while more localized questions with regard to the corpus of panels, miniatures, and frescoes attributed to Lorenzo Monaco are considered in the individual entries of the catalogue. My purpose will have been fulfilled if this comprehensive presentation of the artistic culture of Lorenzo Monaco were to serve as a foundation for reassessments by other methods and from other standpoints. Among the many aspects of this large body of material that are open to alternative approaches, I mention two of special import: first, my characterization of the formative years of Lorenzo Monaco within a contracted corpus of attributions, and secondly, my view of his mature work as Tuscan in essence, and only subordinately a manifestation of the International Style.

A BOOK long in preparation amasses large and varied debts to many persons and institutions. The late Evelyn Sandberg-Vavalà led me to Florence, to Lorenzo Monaco studies, and to the ebb and flow of connoisseurship. Gino Corti, with his unflagging enthusiasm and precision, corrected the transcriptions of previously published documents, transcribed others that had been cited or incompletely presented, and maintained a searching archival eye. The late Millard Meiss, a sympathetic friend and perceptive critic, was also a supportive sponsor during a term at the Institute for Advanced Study in Princeton.

For their assistance and courtesies, I record here my gratitude to a host of individuals: Umberto Baldini, Rev. Father Bruno Barnhart, Cam.O.S.B., the late Marchese Dott. Piero Bartolini Salimbeni Vivai, Marchesa Elena Bartolini Salimbeni Vivai Lenzoni, the late Luisa Becherucci, Luciano Bellosi, Giorgio Bonsanti, Angela Dillon Bussi, Keith Christiansen, the late Anna Maria Francini Ciaranfi, Mirella Levi D'Ancona, Doreta Dec, Anna Dobrzycka, Lola Faillant-Dumas, Franca Falletti, Creighton E. Gilbert, Michael Halls, Ann T. Lurie, Otto Manley, the late Luisa Marcucci, Mario Masserelli, Don Graziano Mengozzi, Cam.O.S.B., Piotr Michałowski, the late Ulrich Middeldorf, Victor H. Miesel, Agnieszka Morawinska, Peter Murray, Ottorino Nonfarmale, Rev. Padre Torello Nocioni, Vall.O.S.B., Pierre Rosenberg, Giuseppe Rosi, Rev. Padre Gerhard Ruf, o.f.m., Frances Spalding, Helena Stęszewska, Nadir Tronci, Don Lino Vigilucci, Cam.O.S.B., Roger B. Ward, Janus Wałek, Paul F. Watson, Susanna Weber, Nathan T. Whitman, Carolyn C. Wilson, and Bogna Wrońska. I am especially indebted to Susanna Pauli for her valiant assistance in Italy.

At the following centers of study the invaluable resources and the expertise of the staffs were made unstintingly available: the Kunsthistorisches Institut in Florence, the Biblioteca Berenson at Villa I Tatti, the Archivio di Stato in Florence, the Witt Library of the Courtauld Institute of Art, the Marquand Library and the Index of Christian Art of Princeton University, the Frick Art Reference Library, the Detroit Institute of Arts Research Library, and the Fine Arts Library of The University of Michigan. The staffs of two conservation laboratories in Florence provided detailed information on technical matters: the Laboratorio della Soprintendenza per i Beni Artistici e Storici per le Province di Firenze e Pistoia, and the Opificio delle Pietre Dure e Laboratori di Restauro.

Fellowships from the John Simon Guggenheim Foundation and the Horace H. Rackham School of Graduate Studies of The University of Michigan allowed periods of freedom from the demands of teaching and administration, and the Horace H. Rackham Publication Fund assisted in the acquisition of photographs and rights of publication. The color transparencies of works in Florence were made by Mario Quattrone, with the exception of the *Prophet* in the Biblioteca Laurenziana, which was photographed by Guido Sansoni. The diagram of the Bartolini Salimbeni Chapel was drawn by Michael Kent.

Joan C. Susskind was constantly watchful in typing the manuscript. Miriam Heins generously assisted in proofreading, and Alice Sunderland Wethey helped immeasurably in the preparation of the index. At the Princeton University Press, Tam Curry provided sensitive guidance as editor in knowing when to tighten and slacken the reins; Marilyn Campbell made many enlightening editorial suggestions; Julie Marvin adeptly undertook the final phase of editing; Susan Bishop brought form to the book with her fine vision and skilled hands; and Eric Van Tassel offered his humanism, in the several senses of that word.

And finally, I acknowledge the dedication of my students over the years who graciously permitted Lorenzo Monaco to become a household name.

Ann Arbor, Michigan *August 1987*

Lorenzo Monaco

Introductory Essay

In the work of Lorenzo Monaco traditional Christian imagery and elegant Late Gothic forms were infused with an ardent monastic devotion. For two decades prior to the emergence of Masaccio and Fra Angelico, the altarpieces, crucifixes, and miniatures by Lorenzo Monaco were the summit of painting in Florence, marking a departure from the persistent formulas of the late Trecento. Among contemporaries, Don Lorenzo's closest stylistic bond is with Ghiberti, for the extended creation of the North Door of the Baptistery both paralleled and influenced his development, and the sculptor and painter comparably assimilated elements of the International Style into inherently Tuscan idioms. Despite such formal analogies, divergent monastic and humanistic impulses underlay fundamental differences in their art. And in the same years that the work of Lorenzo Monaco reached a crest of impassioned fantasy and subtlety of line and color, Donatello was embodying the Florentine ethos in a rudely vigorous physical and psychological realism. The sacred characters of Don Lorenzo's images were stirred by forces outside themselves, unlike the growingly self-willed individuals who now occupied the niches at Orsanmichele, the Bell Tower, and the Cathedral, and who would soon populate the walls of the Brancacci Chapel. The final works of Lorenzo Monaco imply his recognition of the new primacy of the eye and quest for identity that were transforming Florentine art, but his career closed before the intensifying realism and humanism of the Renaissance could essentially modify a monastic art rooted in mediaeval liturgy, imagery, and style.

THE BIOGRAPHY

As with many early Italian artists, the life of Lorenzo Monaco is only meagerly recorded, and his status as a monk without civil ties makes his biography even more spare. We know that his secular name was Piero di Giovanni and that he had lived in the San Michele Visdomini parish of Florence before entering the Monastery of Santa Maria degli Angeli late in 1390.[1] After a year of novitiate in that major urban house of the Camaldolese Order, Lorenzo di Giovanni—his newly assumed monastic name—took simple vows and entered minor orders on the tenth of December 1391. His profession of solemn vows and ordination as subdeacon occurred in September of 1392. The theory that Don Lorenzo must have been at least twenty-one years of age in order to attain the clerical rank of subdeacon, which would place his birth no later than September 1371, has been repeated so often that it has taken on the guise of fact.[2] But this is a speculation based anachronistically on the prescriptions of Canon Law that were formulated by the Council of Trent, whereas in the time of Lorenzo Monaco the minimal age for professing solemn vows and ascending from minor to major orders was not legislated by firm rule.[3] Because the first works that can be securely ascribed to Don

Lorenzo's hand may be dated no earlier than the mid-1390s, and a distinctive personal style was rarely achieved at that time in the history of art until an artist had reached his twenties, it is reasonable to estimate that his date of birth was toward the middle of the 1370s.[4]

Lorenzo Monaco was ordained deacon in 1396, which was apparently the highest clerical level he was to attain, for the archives of Santa Maria degli Angeli possess no record of his ordination to full priesthood. By the mid-1390s Don Lorenzo's role within his monastic community would seem to have been that of a painter, although the first documented record of his work is in January 1399, when he received the first payment for an altarpiece commissioned for the second Ardinghelli Chapel at the Carmine in Florence.[5] The fact that no known work can be associated with this documentary evidence means that a crucial monument is missing from his early career. In these same later years of the 1390s Lorenzo took up residence outside Santa Maria degli Angeli, apparently to establish a workshop that was separate from the monastery's, where he had first practiced his craft as a painter of choir books and panels. Thus, at the very close of the century Lorenzo Monaco began to work independently as a panel painter and the master of a large and prolific workshop of both monastic and secular assistants. For the rest of his life he dwelled outside the monastery walls, but he never relinquished his monastic vocation.[6]

The few further documented notices of Lorenzo Monaco are largely records of payments for panel pictures and for miniatures in choir books, or for estimates of the value and quality of other painters' works—brief factual material that does little to enhance the conception either of his life or his art.[7] The altarpiece executed for San Bartolomeo at Monte Oliveto, now in the Accademia in Florence, dated 1410, is the sole work of Lorenzo's career that may be associated unequivocally with documented payments.[8] His most ambitious work on panel, the *Coronation of the Virgin* of 1414, now in the Uffizi but originally the high altarpiece at Santa Maria degli Angeli, bears his only signature. The long inscription on the frame proves that Lorenzo Monaco had remained a monk, though by this time he had lived outside the Camaldolese community for over a decade and a half, and also records that monastic assistants collaborated with him on the vast project. This dedicatory inscription, a rare acknowledgment of the combined effort of master and workshop, bespeaks the humility of a monastic artist and alerts us to the fact that the hands of assistants will often be discernible even in the major works of Lorenzo Monaco.

The continuing association of the painter and Santa Maria degli Angeli is attested to in 1415 when the monastery sold Lorenzo a house and garden directly across from the monastery.[9] The house apparently was used by the monk-painter as both residence and *bottega*. Buying and selling of property was not uncommon within a monastic community, nor did such transactions violate the solemn vow of poverty. As the document explicitly states, the house would revert to the monastery upon Lorenzo's death, so that in effect the sale was only a means of establishing individual ownership in the event some civil matter regarding the property should arise. There is another significance to this document, however. In the record of sale Don Lorenzo is called *dipintore da siene*, implying a connection with Siena if the obscure *siene* does in fact refer to the town. This ambiguous reference of as late as 1415 need not lead to the conclusion that Lorenzo Monaco was of Sienese origin. According to the agreement, whenever he would be absent from Florence, the monastery had the right to rent the house and turn the money over to him. Although these legalistic facts provoke unanswerable questions about Lorenzo's movements once he had emerged from the cloistered life of the monastery, this intractable document does not diminish the testimony of the painter's work that his principal artistic roots were in Florence rather than in Siena.

Of Don Lorenzo's three known estimates of other artists' works, one is notable in that the document preserves a unique example of his handwriting (Fig. 263).[10] Indeed, the disciplined elegance of his script suggests that at some time he could have worked as a scribe. Lorenzo's refined hand in the last entry on the page contrasts with the efficiently mechanical writing of the notary, the assertive strokes of the prior from the commissioning hospital, and the slovenly scrawl of Pietro Nelli, the painter whose work was under appraisal; the critical scrutiny of Lorenzo Monaco may have caused Pietro to falter on the first attempt to sign his name.

Numerous payments to Don Lorenzo are recorded between 1420 and 1422, but none of these documents may be securely linked to a surviving work.[11] And the archives have not yielded mention of the painter's final major project, the frescoes and altarpiece in the Bartolini Salimbeni Chapel at Santa Trinita. In a contract of March 1422, drawn up between the Corsini family and the Arte della Lana, an altarpiece was commissioned for the Duomo from either the *fratris de Angelis* or an equal or even better painter (*ydon et seu melioris pictoris*). Of the artists connected with Santa Maria degli Angeli only Lorenzo Monaco was sufficiently renowned to be cited in this anonymous way. The altarpiece for the Duomo still defies identification; it cannot be determined if Lorenzo or his peer finally received the commission.[12] The last document to come to light that mentions the name of Lorenzo Monaco is a final payment of August 1422 for the work on an apparently major altarpiece for the church of Sant'Egidio, a dependency of Santa Maria degli Angeli.[13] Once again, no surviving work by Lorenzo Monaco can be connected with certainty to the long series of payments that runs from 1420 to 1422, although the *Adoration of the Magi* in the Uffizi, a masterpiece of Lorenzo's later career, has been proposed with good reason.[14]

A retrospective entry in the ledger of monks at Santa Maria degli Angeli that records Don Lorenzo's progression from minor orders to the deaconate also notes his death on the twenty-fourth of May and his interment at the monastery; alas, the year was not inscribed.[15] From the evidence of style, however, it may be conjectured that Don Lorenzo's death occurred in 1423 or 1424, or alternatively, that his active career came to a close in those years.[16] The final works of Lorenzo Monaco and his shop evince the augmenting realism of the 1420s, intimating that his style might have been more significantly transformed had he painted longer into the decade and converged irresistibly with the maturing art of Masaccio and Fra Angelico.

The early Italian writers add little substance or color to this meager biography. Ghiberti does not mention Don Lorenzo, being concerned in the *Commentarii* only with his own artistic forebears or, among his contemporaries, with the defeated opponents in the competition of 1401. Nonetheless, the stylistic parallels between the two Lorenzos' works that are evident for nearly a quarter of a century make it virtually inevitable that the two men were acquainted and they indulged in direct artistic exchanges, with the path of influence leading largely from the sculptor to the painter. Vasari included a brief notice of Lorenzo Monaco in the *Lives*, but he afforded him little more than a paragraph, while longer passages extol the contemplative life and lavish praise on a monastic scribe and a book painter at Santa Maria degli Angeli.[17] Vasari's short list of ascriptions to Lorenzo Monaco served for nearly three centuries as the principal source for notices of the painter; even the early historians of the Camaldolese Order relied on his biography of Don Lorenzo, adding neither fact nor response to the account of the artist's life and work.[18] Toward the middle of the nineteenth century there began a critical evaluation of Lorenzo Monaco that would culminate some half a century later in the pathbreaking monograph by Osvald Sirén.[19]

SANTA MARIA DEGLI ANGELI

THE EARLY history of the Camaldolese is a shadowy one. According to tradition, the Order was founded at the beginning of the eleventh century by Saint Romuald, who fostered his ideas of a Benedictine reform in the monastery of Camaldoli, high up in the hills of the Casentino where Tuscany and the Romagna meet. His quest was a return to the pure monastic spirit of Saint Benedict and an unobstructed path to divine communion, to be achieved through a life of penitential austerity and isolation from the workaday world. Within this mystical, contemplative Order there flourished a scholarly and artistic tradition exemplified most notably in the early years of Camaldolese history by Gratian, the father of Canon Law, and by Guido d'Arezzo, who helped to formulate the modern system of musical notation.[20]

After the middle of the fourteenth century, with recovery from the ravages of the Black Death, the most thriving urban house of the Camaldolese in Tuscany was Santa Maria degli Angeli in Florence. At that time the original nucleus of the monastery, built only as recently as 1300, was expanded into a grand complex of three cloisters and made even more impressive by two adjacent dependencies, the hospital and chapel of Santa Maria Nuova and the church of Sant'Egidio (Fig. 262).[21] Steeped as the Camaldolese were in a tradition of mystical pietism and primitive monastic ideals, it was inevitable that Santa Maria degli Angeli should have become one of the Florentine strongholds of the Observance Movement, which arose at the end of the fourteenth century in rigorous defense against the growing tide of humanism. An order that could claim Saint Peter Damian,[22] who as early as the eleventh century had preached against the worldliness of the clergy in his demand for a spiritual reform, would be receptive to the conservative ideas of Giovanni Dominici, the most influential Dominican writer on the Observance. In fact, Dominici's major work, the *Lucula Noctis* of 1405, would be prompted by correspondence between the Camaldolese monk Giovanni da Samminiato, who entered Santa Maria degli Angeli in the early 1390s, and the humanist scholar Coluccio Salutati. Giovanni had written a letter to a disciple of Salutati in which he denounced the study of classical literature as a path to sin. Rather than the follower, Salutati himself answered the monk's denunciation, summarizing the humanist position in his reply. Giovanni da Samminiato, apparently finding neither himself nor any of his brothers at Santa Maria degli Angeli capable of refuting Salutati's close-grained arguments, sent the letter across Florence to Giovanni Dominici at the Dominican monastery of Santa Maria Novella. The *Lucula Noctis*, Dominici's response to Salutati, became an essential tract of the antihumanist viewpoint.[23] Unlike the mendicant Dominicans and Franciscans, the Camaldolese followed the Benedictine tendency to shun institutionalism so that in spite of their adherence to the strict tenets of the Observance, they never established an internal movement. The Camaldolese scholar Ambrogio Traversari, who came to Santa

Maria degli Angeli in 1400 and served as the General of the Order in the 1430s, supported the pietistic, conservative demands of the Observance and at the same time fostered Florentine humanism.[24]

During the last quarter of the Trecento there emerged at Santa Maria degli Angeli the most important monastic workshop of book and panel painters active in Florence before the generation of Fra Angelico at San Marco. From around 1370 until the early 1420s a corps of scribes and painters, monastic and secular, produced a series of liturgical choir books for use at the monastery and its dependent churches of Santa Maria Nuova and Sant'Egidio. With typically mediaeval collaboration, the making of these monumental books was shared by the scribes who wrote the musical notation and accompanying text, the illuminators of the lavishly ornamented initial letters and borders of pages, and the miniaturists who came along last to fill the blank fields of the letters with narrative scenes or with figures of prophets and saints appropriate to the liturgical text.[25] The style of these final additions, at times inserted only years after the writing, illumination, and dating of a book, rather than being essentially miniaturistic is rooted in the traditions of panel painting.

Among the artists at Santa Maria degli Angeli was a painter of both books and panels who has been distinguished with sufficient clarity to allow his identification as Don Silvestro dei Gherarducci, very likely that same Don Silvestro who was so enthusiastically lauded by Vasari in his life of Lorenzo Monaco.[26] Silvestro's figure of *Saint Mark* in a choir book of the 1370s from the Angeli scriptorium (Fig. 264) could have been conceived in full length, as if for the lateral of an altarpiece, and then reduced and accommodated to the oval of the initial *P*. The austerely simple forms—even the lion's tail has been disciplined—the assertive notes of coral red and green, and the gravity of expression seem foreign to the florid ornament and pale, variegated colors of the surrounding letter. Regardless of the reduced scale, Don Silvestro's *Mark* may be recognized as the immediate formal and spiritual heir to the august prophets and saints of Nardo di Cione (Fig. 265).

In his work on panel Don Silvestro's Cionesque inheritance is equally apparent, as a *Madonna of Humility* of the 1370s demonstrates, being based directly on a picture by Jacopo di Cione (cf. Figs. 266 and 267).[27] The dependence on the model is seen not only in the iconographic type but also in the rich embellishment of surfaces and in the shapes of drapery. The roots of this ornamentalism are in the traditions of Sienese painting, which had been transplanted earlier into Florentine art in the generation of Bernardo Daddi and then nurtured by subsequent Cionesque painters. But Don Silvestro's *Madonna of Humility* suggests a more direct linkage with Siena. The Child is closely akin to Ambrogio Lorenzetti's Infants, while the gracefully bowed angels' heads and the fluid figure of God the Father are lyrical accents reminiscent of Niccolò di Ser Sozzo and Luca di Tommè; Jacopo di Cione had imposed on these same elements the strict control of a vertical axis. Furthermore, in Don Silvestro's panel the brocaded draperies function as surface embellishment; in Jacopo's, the articulation of the ornamented textile with folds suggests the shapes of the body beneath. We do not know if Don Silvestro actually worked in the shop of Jacopo di Cione, where the modes of Orcagna and Nardo were perpetuated late into the century, or whether he came into direct contact with Sienese shops, or whether instead he gained his artistic education entirely at the Angeli through a more indirect tutelage. The latter seems more likely, for Don Silvestro—if he be the same one cited in the documents—entered the monastery at the age of nine and is unlikely to have been associated with a secular shop.[28] There is certainty, however, that in the second half of the Trecento the visual environment of Santa Maria degli Angeli was dominated by the preponderantly Orcagnesque and Cionesque panels on the altars of the monastery, providing a profoundly influential "schoolroom" for a monk-painter who would have celebrated his masses and said his Offices constantly in their presence.[29]

In contrast to the stylistic singularity of the *Saint Mark*, Don Silvestro's beautiful miniature of *Abraham and the Three Angels* (Fig. 268), painted in the last phase of his work in the 1390s, is more complex in its forms and more varied in reference to the traditions of Trecento painting. With Nardo's ritualistically formal art still as the matrix, the facial types and the heavily pocketed drapery now acknowledge the style of Spinello Aretino, while the knife-edged rocks, the types of trees, and the florid palette depend on the style of Agnolo Gaddi. Though a cloistered monk, Don Silvestro absorbed into his art the major stylistic modes of later fourteenth-century Tuscan painting. He and his monastic workshop, rather than comprising a distinctive "school," functioned as a catalyst for the various and often cognate modes of middle and later Trecento painting.[30]

THE EARLY MINIATURES AND THE ACCADEMIA *AGONY IN THE GARDEN*

IN THE spiritually conservative and artistically eclectic milieu of Santa Maria degli Angeli, Lorenzo Monaco began the life of a monk and painter in the 1390s. As the earliest evidence of his work is in book painting, Lorenzo's first instruction in the craft could have come in the monastic scriptorium under Don Simone and Don Silvestro dei Gherarducci. Indeed, Lorenzo's five miniatures of *Prophets* and *Saints* in choir books from Santa Maria degli Angeli, dated 1394, 1395, and 1396 (Florence, Biblioteca Laurenziana; Figs. 1-6), are direct descendants of a type exemplified by Don Silvestro's *Saint Mark*. Because the dates inscribed in these books are not necessarily the exact year of the work of the miniaturist, it is more informative to see the evolution of Lorenzo's miniatures within the half decade from 1395 to 1400.[31] In that span of years the figures of *Tobit* and *Saint Jerome* clearly precede the *Saint Romuald*, the *King David*, and the *Saint John the Evangelist*. The former's scale and placement in the field of the letter are unresolved, the line is less flexible, and the contrasts of light and dark lie as surface patterns rather than as a means of enhancing the plastic force of the figure. In contrast, the concerted linear rhythms and expressive tensions that bind the Saint John to his surrounding letter—the eagle lectern forms an elegant link—lead this miniature farthest from the more stolid forms of the later Trecento. The high seriousness and iconic dignity of Don Lorenzo's figures, their swarthy complexions, and the dominant colors of scarlet, coral red, rose, and bottle green shot with yellow pronounce a direct stylistic inheritance from the Cionesque tradition of panel painting (Fig. 270) rather than simple dependence on the more immediate model of Don Silvestro.[32] In turn, the Romuald and John of the Laurenziana choir book are the roots from which Lorenzo's own august saints of the *Coronation of the Virgin* for Santa Maria degli Angeli will have sprung a decade and a half in the future.

The first sure evidence of Lorenzo Monaco's work as a panel painter is from the last years of the Trecento, in a few pictures executed contemporarily with the choir book miniatures and not long before his departure from the monastery to establish his own workshop. As with his book painting,

Don Lorenzo's early training in the larger craft of the panel could also have been provided by Don Silvestro dei Gherarducci. If it is unfruitful, however, in any period in the history of art to seek the models for a fledgling artist's development in the work of a single master, it is doubly so in the late years of the Trecento when a complex interaction of the major Florentine painting shops prevailed, as Don Silvestro's work has demonstrated. In Florence the problem is compounded by the long survival of mid-Trecento traditions, the borrowing of types and motifs between shops, and the collaboration on commissions by masters from different workshops.[33] Moreover, the stratified and laborious techniques of tempera and fresco painting were conducive to the subdivision and protraction of work. And the skein of later Trecento painting is further tangled by the Giottesque revival, which was impelled both by a mixture of cultural nostalgia at a moment of renewed civic pride and by an urgent search for artistic inspiration in a period of lesser accomplishment.[34] The grafting of style onto style within this complex culture of later Trecento painting inevitably blurred the contour of individual artistic personality, so that in the study of this vast corpus of pictures the definition of stylistic idioms is frequently more productive than the attachment of specific names to individual works.

The *Agony in the Garden* (Figs. 7-14; Colorplates 1 and 2), painted by Lorenzo Monaco for Santa Maria degli Angeli in the last years of the Trecento, encompasses the range of choices the young painter confronted in the hybrid artistic environment of the waning century.[35] Burckhardt and Ruskin were prompted to attribute this large panel to Giotto, having discerned parallels in the format of the landscape and in the kneeling Christ with the fresco of the *Miracle of the Spring* at Assisi.[36] The impact of Giotto's art on Lorenzo's *Agony in the Garden*, however, would seem to come instead from a source with which he could more easily have had direct experience—the imposing *Stigmatization of Saint Francis* now in the Louvre, signed by Giotto but a collaborative effort of master and workshop.[37] Particularly influential were the precipitous landscape punctuated by heavily foliaged trees and the inclusion of narrative scenes beneath the principal icon. The intense convergence of Francis and the seraphic vision was recast by Lorenzo Monaco into the confrontation of Christ and the chalice-bearing angel. Saint Francis's most poignant "imitatio Christi," in a kind of typological reversal, had come now to inspire the imagery of the Agony in the Garden.[38]

In this process of garnering models, the impressionable young painter would also have referred to the major Orcagnesque works at Santa Maria degli Angeli wherein narrative subjects were elevated to the central position in an altarpiece.[39] The extensive panel of the *Agony in the Garden* permitted an inclusiveness and interaction of figures and setting more to be expected in the panoramic art of fresco painting. Placed against a simple wall surface in some quarter of Santa Maria degli Angeli, the *Agony in the Garden* must have conveyed the impression of a work of mural art. As in Spinello Aretino's frescoes at San Miniato and Agnolo Gaddi's at Santa Croce (Figs. 304 and 271), Lorenzo used the long, sloping diagonals of sharply stylized rock formations to shape distinctly separate spatial zones occupied by the praying Christ and the sleeping disciples.[40] Don Silvestro had made use of similar landscape elements in his *Abraham and the Angels* miniature (Fig. 268). And just as fully Gaddesque are the shapes of the trees with their clusters of light leaves silhouetted against dark masses of foliage. But the lessons of Orcagnesque painting and its Gerinesque offshoots persist in the conscious balance of the composition around an implied central axis, in the fixity of pose, the firmness of contour line, the sharp contrasts of light and dark on faces and drapery, and in facial types. The splendid palette concentrated in the group of sleeping disciples (Colorplate 1), which heralds Don Lorenzo's virtuosity as a colorist, is a textbook demonstration of two of the principal sources of his art. The light blue, yellow, and rose washed to pink is a key Gaddesque chord, while the more astringent combination of green, violet, and coral red is essentially Cionesque. The variety and precision of ornamentation in the gilded haloes of Christ and the Apostles are likewise indebted to the Orcagnesque and Cionesque traditions, which brought the craft to its highest complexity and refinement in Florentine Trecento painting. Finally, the assertive forms of later fourteenth-century Florentine sculpture, as in the *Madonna della Rosa* at Orsanmichele (Fig. 275), offered a more direct model than painting for the heavily accented folds radiating downward from the knees of Saint Peter and Saint James, which serve to stabilize the base of the composition.[41]

Beyond this web of derivations, to be expected of an art emerging in the waning years of the Trecento, the *Agony in the Garden* already conveys the intensely concentrated expressivity that will remain a distinctive aspect of Don Lorenzo's art, whereby all effects coalesce into a dramatic mood, and the painted image embodies a deeply contemplated spirituality. Bernard Berenson wrote: "It would seem as if in Lorenzo Monaco the ecstasy of the Orcagnas had flowered from half-hidden shoots into a rapture that surpassed theirs."[42] The rhythms of drapery, although still timid in contrast to the flux of line in Lorenzo's mature works, bind the disciples in their sleep and define a sympathetic response between the cloud-borne angel and the praying Christ. The stream of Kidron has its source in the cataract of Christ's mantle, while the hovering angel with the bitter cup impels a radiant path that reaches fullest intensity on the rocky slope and on the group of the sleeping Peter, James, and John. The halting diagonal ascent of this stony barrier and its sharp division of the pictorial field are a graphic metaphor of Christ's struggle between the human and divine aspects of His nature. Christ endures His travail in a dark and private zone; the somber blue mantle and light rose tunic contrast dramatically with the resonant coloration of the disciples' robes. The important note of violet in James's tunic, heightened by juxtaposition with his green mantle, is a subtle gloss on the tragic theme of the picture, as is the single palm tree that links Christ and the soaring angel. In James's mantle the sharply accented light dilutes the color from a deep forest green in the darks to a bottle green at the half light and then to a creamy white in the opaque highlight which clings like a shell to the surfaces of the heavy textile. These effects of light in the *Agony in the Garden* indicate that Lorenzo Monaco had looked closely at the art of Taddeo Gaddi in his *Annunciation to the Shepherds* (Fig. 273) in the Baroncelli Chapel at Santa Croce or the *Stigmatization of Saint Francis* in the Refectory. In those works of over half a century earlier, however, the contrasts of light and dark are more intense, and the sources of the dramatic illumination are concentrated in the annunciatory angel and the seraphic image of Christ. A closer parallel may be drawn between the lighted forms of Taddeo's John the Evangelist (Fig. 276) in the *Franciscan Tree* at Santa Croce and Lorenzo's Saint James. Resemblances such as these surely led Vasari to aver that Lorenzo Monaco was a pupil of Taddeo Gaddi. Befitting a sixteenth-century Mannerist, Vasari responded to the decorative and dramatic uses of light in the two painters' works and acutely discerned an artistic inheritance.

The effects of color and light and the scenic devices extend downward from the main panel to the two episodes of the predella. The *Betrayal of Christ* (Figs. 10, 12, and 14; Colorplate 2) is enacted in a

PLATE 1. Lorenzo Monaco, *Sleeping Apostles*, detail of the *Agony in the Garden*, Accademia, Florence.

PLATE 2. Lorenzo Monaco, *Betrayal of Christ*, predella of the *Agony in the Garden*, Accademia, Florence.

PLATE 3. Lorenzo Monaco, *Visitation*, Courtauld Institute Galleries, London.

PLATE 4. Lorenzo Monaco, *Prophet*, fol. 89v, Corale 3, Biblioteca Laurenziana, Florence.

darkened landscape that echoes Christ's somber enclave above. The dominant violet of Judas's mantle is identical to that of James's tunic in the *Agony*, while the golden yellow and coral red of Peter's robe are exactly replicated in the main panel and in the predella. The rocky masses framing off a space where Saint Peter attacks Malchas are a miniature reprise of the stagy landscape above. These obvious formal devices are also apparent in the conscious shaping of figures and setting to the demands of the elongated quatrefoil, a type of frame Lorenzo eventually employed with consummate skill in the six-panel predella of the *Coronation of the Virgin* for Santa Maria degli Angeli.[43] Judas's pose in the *Betrayal* is buttressed by the pointing Pharisee, and his, in turn, by the parallel rock formation. These bearded old men of the predella are the closest kin to *Saint Romuald* (Fig. 4), a miniature painted within the same half decade. In contrast to night in the *Betrayal*, the *Stripping of Christ* in the other predella panel (Fig. 11) is bathed in a soft light, with the approaching day implied in the uninterrupted area of gold against which the crest of Calvary and the staff of the cross are silhouetted. The rose color of Christ's half-fallen garment repeats the hue of the sleeping Saint John's mantle above and also of the Saint John tending the Virgin at the far left of the scene; a single note of color gently affirms the special bond between the two men. Hovering at the brink of the panel and locked into the lobe of the quatrefoil is the grieving Virgin, who foreshadows a series of pathetic women in Lorenzo's later art (Fig. 13).

The *Betrayal* and *Stripping of Christ* display at this early stage of Lorenzo's career his innate talent for lively and concise narration in which dramatic focal points and sequences of action are rendered with assurance and clarity. While both the *Agony in the Garden* and its predella already have the stamp of a distinctive artistic personality, these narrative scenes still remain dependent on Lorenzo's contemporaries, in particular Spinello Aretino's figural groups, such as the retinue of the Magi in a predella panel of the early 1380s (Fig. 277). Here, as in the predella of the *Agony in the Garden*, the principals of the scene are backed by dense clusters of overlapping figures whose intense gazes rivet attention on the central drama. Lunging poses and sequences of sharp contours propel the narrative across the picture plane. Yet nowhere in the art of Lorenzo's older contemporary is there so assured a rhythmic integration of figural, landscape, and framing elements as in the two predella panels beneath the *Agony in the Garden*. The clarity and trenchancy of the three episodes from Christ's Passion that comprise this earliest major panel painting by Lorenzo Monaco mark the work as an important contribution to the revival of narrative painting that was under way in the last decades of the Florentine Trecento.

The internal meaning of the *Agony in the Garden* may be comprehended only when this large devotional image is envisioned within a contemplative monastic environment.[44] The diminutive secular donor kneeling at the edge of a towering mystery reinforces the sense of communion with the icon. For a Camaldolese monk at Santa Maria degli Angeli, this impressive nocturne would not only have portrayed specific moments of Passiontide but would have conveyed the spirit and substance of Compline, the last Office of the day to which Saint Benedict himself had given the essential form. There is evidence for such an interpretation even beyond the pervasively crepuscular mood. The themes of Compline are night and sleep as figurative death, and trust in the protection of God and the angels from the enemies and dangers of the night. The visual corollaries of these concepts are the predominant role given the sleeping disciples, the widespread wings of the angel at the apex of the panel, recalling Psalm 90 in the liturgy of Compline—"under His feathers shalt thou trust"—and the encounter of Christ and His enemies within the scenes of the predella. A literal connection with the *Opus Dei* is the lion who lurks at the upper right, immediately above the sleeping Saint Peter (Fig. 7). At the beginning of Compline are the words from 1 Peter 5:8-9: "Brethren, be sober and watch: because your adversary the devil, as a roaring lion, goeth about seeking whom he may devour: whom resist ye, strong in faith." The specific function and location of Don Lorenzo's grand devotional icon at Santa Maria degli Angeli remain unknown, but it is certain that this three-part cycle of Christ's spiritual struggle and torment loomed throughout the liturgical year as a reminder of the Divine Office and as an embodiment of the dark events of Passiontide.

TWO EARLY MADONNAS

AN INSUPERABLE obstacle to establishing a cogent stylistic chronology of the emerging art of Lorenzo Monaco is the loss of the altarpiece he was commissioned to execute for the Ardinghelli Chapel at the Carmine in Florence in the very last years of the Trecento (see Documents 4A-4G). That first documented work by Don Lorenzo was created at the crucial moment of his departure from Santa Maria degli Angeli to establish a workshop outside the confines of the monastery. For over two decades an important activity of the workshop was the painting of images of the Madonna for both institutional and private devotions. Lorenzo Monaco seems to have provided designs for execution by workshop assistants from the outset of this prolific and continuous production of Madonnas, whereas he focussed his energies on a series of larger commissions.[45] This practice and the heterogeneity of the art of Lorenzo's formative years, compound the problems of attributing and dating the early Madonna panels. Nonetheless, for the purposes of this critical essay, two Madonnas—one in the Fitzwilliam Museum (Fig. 15) and the other in the Biblioteca Berenson (Fig. 16)—may serve to exemplify the beginnings in the workshop of Lorenzo Monaco of the production of modestly scaled devotional images, which had been a major activity of every later Trecento Tuscan master and his assistants.

In the large and inclusive *Agony in the Garden* the stylistic sources were discerned to be richly varied and intermingled. The Madonnas in Cambridge and at Villa I Tatti, by contrast, depend on more clearly definable prototypes, which eases the task of localizing the models to which Don Lorenzo was particularly drawn as he confronted the welter of Florentine Trecento idioms. The multiplicity of stylistic ingredients in the small cluster of early works attributable to Lorenzo Monaco reinforces the premise that his initial training as a painter was received in the eclectic artistic milieu of Santa Maria degli Angeli rather than with any one secular workshop.[46] The Fitzwilliam *Madonna Enthroned with Adoring Angels* pronounces a debt to Giotto with utmost clarity, making this beautiful panel, in spite of its diminutive size, as graphic a record of the Giottesque revival in later Trecento Florence as the grandly scaled *Agony in the Garden.* Quintessentially Giottesque are the ponderable forms and the evocation of space by a precisely constructed architecture. The Virgin and Child occupy the throne as securely as the three sleeping disciples inhabit their partitioned zone in the *Agony in the Garden.* By adapting the baldachin-like structure from the Ognissanti *Madonna*, Lorenzo emulated Giotto's device of enshrining the Virgin and Child within the strict and enveloping boundaries of the throne, even though he relinquished Giotto's airy side enclosures in favor of the deeply scooped arms that were a common feature of Trecento Florentine throne design.[47] Beyond the physical aspects of mass, weight, and space, Don Lorenzo also comprehended Giotto's capacity to transform the objective fact of the Virgin and Child into a moment of personal drama through an intense participation of witnessing figures. The hovering angel of the *Agony in the Garden* has now assumed the role of adoring guardian at either side of the throne. The rapt involvement of these two attendants, and of their slightly bowed counterparts who serve as finials above, infuses the image with the character of a finely poised tableau and recalls the unflinching gazes of saints and angels in Giotto's *Maestà*. At the same time, in the Fitzwilliam *Madonna* Lorenzo acknowledged the art of his contemporaries.[48] He had looked closely at Spinello Aretino's weighty, enthroned matriarchs and even adopted their facial types for the Virgin and Child. But nowhere in that prosaic master's art is there the delicate balance between spirit and substance captured by Don Lorenzo in this rare little icon in Cambridge. The sources of the palette are likewise varied: the clarion azure of the Virgin's mantle and the pink of the Child's acknowledge Agnolo Gaddi, while the steely blues shaded to mauves and pinks in the angels' robes, their soaring coral red wings, and the acidulous green floor are Cionesque.

The stylistic irresolution in these formative years of Don Lorenzo's art is pointedly demonstrated by a comparison between the Fitzwilliam *Madonna* and the *Madonna with Saints John the Baptist and Zenobius* in the Biblioteca Berenson (Fig. 16). While the similar segmentation of the area of the Virgin's mantle in each picture and the exact pitch of tension and rhythm in the mantles' double-piped borders give an inkling of a common authorship, the dissimilarities between the two pictures are most immediately apparent. In the Cambridge *Madonna* Don Lorenzo paid homage to Giotto and Spinello, but he also restated within the limited area of the panel the broadly drawn figures and circumscribed spaces of the *Agony in the Garden*; the mantles of the sleeping Saint James and the enthroned Virgin were cut from a very similar pattern. Regardless of its modest dimensions, the Fitzwilliam panel was not conceived as a work of predella scale. In the Berenson *Madonna* Don Lorenzo sought his formal vocabulary in the traditions of Cionesque painting, which ran counter to the Giottesque language of ponderable forms and rationally built spaces. The Virgin and Child reside high in the compositional field where they are sharply silhouetted against the gold ground.[49] Impinging exactly at the edges of the Virgin's mantle are the broad haloes of the two saints, which buttress the central figures afloat above a dais that provides only a shorthand version of enthronement. The suspended Virgin and Child, in opposition to the gravity-bound Cambridge Madonna, gain buoyancy from the calligraphic loops coursing along the lower hem of the Virgin's mantle, recalling the same flourishes in Christ's mantle in the *Agony in the Garden*. The Child takes on a dancing lightness from the upward sweep and shallow modelling of the mantle, much as the drapery forms lend a dreamy lyricism to the sleeping Saint John of the *Agony*. The facial features of the Baptist and Zenobius are drawn with the incisive line of the earlier miniatures for Santa Maria degli Angeli, but these standing figures, and in particular the Baptist, seem uneasy in their relationship to the fluid rhythms of the Virgin and Child. Do these saints betray the intervention of an assistant, or is Don Lorenzo himself as yet less competent with the full-length figure, unguided by the explicit shapes of an initial letter or a quatrefoil?

The sources of this vertical and planar composition are in Orcagnesque and Cionesque art, which we have observed to have been an important idiom in the visual environment of Santa Maria degli Angeli. Moreover, the color chord of violet, rose, vermilion, and an originally royal blue is Cionesque. The fundamentally different shapes of the heads and facial features in the Berenson and Fitzwilliam panels further demonstrate Don Lorenzo's vacillation between models at this early stage of his work. The long head and broad brow of the Cambridge Virgin are an inheritance from Spinello's sober matrons, while the rounded cranial structure, the short nose and pursed lips, and the gentle tilt of the head in the Berenson Madonna descend from the female type favored by Jacopo di Cione.[50] But Lorenzo Monaco did not reserve this physical type for an ingenuous Virgin, as is seen by comparing the sleeping Saint John of the *Agony in the Garden* (Fig. 9) or the Christ in the *Stripping* episode of its predella (Fig. 11).

There is also recollection of the type, for only a few years after the turn of the century, while Don Lorenzo was designing the Accademia *Man of Sorrows* (Fig. 18), there issued from his workshop a diminutive reduction of the central image of that imposing icon (Accademia Carrara, Bergamo; Fig. 136). The head of Christ has been transformed into the type of the *Agony in the Garden* predella scenes, as if this rounded shape were felt to convey a more personal drama. At the close of his career, in a kind of reminiscence often found in artists' later work, Lorenzo Monaco will return to the intimate scale of the Cambridge *Madonna* and the Bergamo *Man of Sorrows* when he paints his most interior masterpiece—the meditative diptych of the *Madonna of Humility* and *Saint Jerome in His Study* (Figs. 128 and 129).

THE ACCADEMIA *MAN OF SORROWS* AND THE EMPOLI *MADONNA OF HUMILITY*

In the *Man of Sorrows with Episodes and Emblems of the Passion* (Florence, Accademia; Figs. 18 and 19) Lorenzo Monaco turned for a second time to the large single-panel format, perhaps again for the liturgical use of Santa Maria degli Angeli. Although the inscribed date of 1404 establishes that this painting was completed at least half a decade after the *Agony in the Garden*, the stylistic connections between the two works and the vast size of the panel imply that the conception and execution could have occupied Don Lorenzo for a considerable time before that year. In rendering the theme he adhered closely to a long-established iconographic tradition.[51] The uniqueness of the *Man of Sorrows* lies in the sheer magnitude of the image, which stands as the most impressive Florentine icon since Orcagna's *Strozzi Altarpiece*; indeed, the closely bound group of Christ, the Virgin, and Saint John the Evangelist is a distant echo of the magnetic center of that great Dominican homily.[52] The morbid presence of the greenish gray corpus of Christ looms starkly against the blue and rose mantles, the parti-colored floor, and the warm aura cast by the broad expanse of gold ground. The mantles of the Virgin and Saint John, linked by the florid ornament of the sarcophagus,[53] compose a rhythmic opposition to the rigid "spine" of the picture, which ascends from the upright torso of Christ through the staff of the cross and then divides into the crossbar that leads to the framing verticals of the ladder and column at either side. An array of eucharistic symbolism is concentrated within this vertical axis: the pelican feeding its young with its own blood, the crown of thorns, the wounded torso, and the grape-laden vine of the sarcophagus, echoed in the richly berried halo of Christ. When illuminated by candlelight, the gilded chalice at the base of this symbolic axis would have provided a radiant link between the sacramental meaning of the image and the rite of the Mass. Silhouetted against the gold ground and floating above the head of Christ like the fragments of a dream are the synecdochic allusions to the episodes of His torment and death. Disembodied heads, hands, gestures, and objects tell the story of Christ's last hours with the concision and urgency found in the liturgy of Passiontide and in the pathetic, staccato texts of *laude* and the *Meditations*.[54] The spectral character of these upper reaches of the icon is amplified by contrast with the vividly material presence of the sarcophagus below, which is like a variation on the precise architectural forms of the Fitzwilliam *Madonna* (Fig. 15).

The directness of the progression from the *Agony in the Garden* to the *Man of Sorrows* is readily grasped from their proximity at the Accademia in Florence. The heads of the two Christs (Figs. 8 and 19) bear a close resemblance, but the modelling in the *Man of Sorrows* is more assured, and the line of the facial features and hair describes a more continuous rhythm. The group of Judas and Christ in the upper right above the crossbar in the *Man of Sorrows* has been enlarged from the *Betrayal* in the predella of the *Agony in the Garden*, even to the betrayer's black halo; and the passive Virgin of the *Stripping of Christ* has matured into a stoical server who both presents and supports her Son (Figs. 13 and 18). The pervasive dramatic lighting of the *Agony* now converges on the figure of the dead Christ. The two attendant mourners are reminiscent of the Christ and sleeping disciples of the *Agony in the Garden*, but Don Lorenzo has reinforced their physical substance by referring to Agnolo Gaddi's abundantly draped figures in the frescoes at Santa Croce (Fig. 282); the Evangelist, in fact, is the most Gaddesque moment in all of Lorenzo's art. In Agnolo's figure style, however, the conformations of drapery are determined by a static armature, while linear rhythms are treated as ornamental accessories reserved for the brief twirl of a cape or the tumble of a hem. Already in the *Agony in the Garden* there are intimations that Lorenzo Monaco was abandoning this later Trecento mode, although passages of continuous rhythm are still concentrated within discrete segments of the total composition; the triad of the sleeping Peter, James, and John are united by the legato flow of their mantles which resolves at the borders into a modestly ornamental calligraphy. In Don Lorenzo's work of these first years of the Quattrocento—the Accademia *Man of Sorrows* and the *Madonna with Saints John the Baptist and Nicholas* (Fig. 17), destroyed in Berlin in 1945—the rhythmic and calligraphic gestures of the style are no longer restricted to isolated passages but now begin to serve as the primary basis of compositional unity.

Although the place of the Berlin *Madonna* within the chronology of works painted in the first half-decade of the new century will be more apparent from the retrospective view of the Empoli *Madonna of Humility* of 1404 and the Monte Oliveto Altarpiece commissioned in 1407, there is reason now to establish the important role of this panel as a bridge between those immediately succeeding works and Lorenzo's earliest pictures.[55] No intermediate stages are known in the nearly half decade that separates the incunabular Berenson panel from the Berlin *Madonna*, a work that foreshadows essential elements of Don Lorenzo's mature style. The verticality and planarity of the Berenson *Madonna* are now intensified by the omission of the projecting dais and by the addition of a cloth of honor, reinforcing the axiality of the composition much as the cross functions in the *Man of Sorrows*. In the

Berenson panel a timid interplay of drapery provides only meager links between the parts of an additive composition; the Berlin *Madonna*, in contrast, is a game of rhythmic responses. The swinging arcs of the mantles impel a dialogue from center to sides, the angels cross their arms in a balletic variation of the interlocked hands of the Virgin and Child, and the cusped frame echoes the clustered haloes and the looping cascade of the Infant's mantle.

The network of rhythms that Don Lorenzo has begun to weave in the Berlin *Madonna* is similarly a fundamental stylistic aspect of the contemporary *Coronation of the Virgin* of 1401, by Spinello Aretino (Fig. 281). A continuous linear path courses through the two registers of the composition, with the nervous rhythms of the floating band of musical angels sounding an antiphonal response to the broader forms above. Spinello's *Coronation of the Virgin* comes at the end of a decade of work in which he seems to have undertaken a purposeful abandonment both of the gravely static Orcagnesque mode to which he had first strongly subscribed and of the Giottesque revival in which he had been so central a force.[56] In Spinello's *Annunciation* at San Francesco in Arezzo, painted at least half a decade earlier than the *Coronation of the Virgin*, the Gabriel (Fig. 283) floats onto the scene as if propelled by the swirl of his calligraphic mantle, the herald of a sacred mystery and of a new impulse toward dynamic and ornamental linearism in Florentine art.

The *Madonna of Humility with Four Saints* in the Museo della Collegiata in Empoli (Figs. 20 and 21) bears the same date as the *Man of Sorrows*, 1404, but in this work of intimate subject and more personal scale Don Lorenzo was freed from the dogmatic demands of the large devotional icon, which would seem to have been intended for a communal monastic use.[57] The proximity of the Berlin and the Empoli Madonnas is discernible on comparing the shape and tilt of the Virgin's head, the centrally parted coiffure, and the fall of the kerchief. The facial features in both of these images of the Virgin imply that Lorenzo Monaco turned more directly to Don Silvestro's *Madonna of Humility* (Fig. 267) than to the models provided previously by Spinello Aretino and Jacopo di Cione. The insistent shapes and dominant scale of the Virgin and Child, the loss of the central pinnacle, and the disjuncture in floor levels isolate the main panel of the Empoli altarpiece. This imbalance is redressed, however, by the calligraphic passages and chiastic repetition of lavender and rose in the draperies of the Baptist and Saint Peter, and the fixed gazes of Saints Donninus and Anthony Abbot toward the Madonna. In that the pairs of overlapping saints imply a shallow apsidal enclosure for the central image, the Empoli triptych modestly foreshadows the *Coronation of the Virgin*, which Don Lorenzo will complete exactly a decade later (Fig. 44). It was surely the master's intention in designing the four accompanying saints to evoke the illusion of continuity from the altarpiece to the worshipper by extending the feet in the left lateral and the cassock in the right beyond the edge of the marble floor, and by placing Saint Donninus's dog in front of the riser. At the root of such incidental illusionistic devices is Simone Martini's Uffizi *Annunciation*, in which fillet and drapery tumble beyond the confines of the platform and Saint Ansanus's assertive foot projects from his pedestal. Although the four saints of the Empoli triptych are surely Don Lorenzo's invention, in comparison with the finely wrought center panel their more reticent draughtsmanship betrays some degree of involvement of the workshop.

There are no uncertainties in the *Madonna of Humility*. In contrast to the angular Infant of the Berlin *Madonna*, who solely opposed the harmonies of the design, the more robust Child now in-scribes an arc as taut as a drawn bow, locking him to the Virgin's body and sparking an energy grounded in the ductile edges of the mantle, which cluster at the Virgin's extended knee and then fall to floor level in a restless course of swirls and loops. The darkening of the Virgin's blue mantle caused much of the interior modelling to be eradicated, lending the drapery more of the effect of a surfacy arabesque than was originally intended. Nonetheless, the stylistic path that leads from the lyrical sleepers of the *Agony in the Garden* (Fig. 7), through the rocking forms of the Virgin and Evangelist in the *Man of Sorrows* (Fig. 18), and the gentle interplay of shapes in the Berlin panel (Fig. 17) has been preparation for the Empoli *Madonna of Humility*, in which all rhythmic devices are now focussed and intensified within the boundaries of a compact unit. In the Empoli *Madonna* Lorenzo Monaco affirmed the direction of his style within the mainstream of Florentine painting and sculpture as it now emerged at this moment in mid-decade. Lorenzo Ghiberti had completed the competition relief late in 1402 and was now undertaking the designs of the earlier quatrefoils for the North Door of the Baptistery.[58] The pliant curve of Ghiberti's Annunciate Virgin (Fig. 284) and Don Lorenzo's arching Child in the Empoli *Madonna* convey a similarly studied awareness of rhythmic design; in contrast, the Gabriel in Ghiberti's relief is more closely related to Spinello's floating archangel (Fig. 283). Ghiberti's stylistic roots lay both in native Florentine sculptural traditions and in the art of the North European goldsmith,[59] whereas the evolution from the earliest works of Lorenzo Monaco to the Empoli triptych of 1404 has demonstrated an indigenous grounding in Tuscan painting and sculpture of the second half of the Trecento. Although there are no definable exchanges between the two Lorenzos at this moment in their careers, a line of influence from the sculptor to the painter will soon emerge. The hybrid Valencian translation of the International Style, imported into Florence in these first years of the Quattrocento through the return of Gherardo Starnina to his native soil, rather than suddenly and radically transforming the styles of Ghiberti and Lorenzo Monaco, as has been proposed, served instead to confirm and intensify their innate propensity for an ornamentally expressive linearism, which they had manifested from the inception of their art.[60]

THE MONTE OLIVETO ALTARPIECE

THE TECHNICAL and stylistic transformations within various segments of the altarpiece Lorenzo Monaco painted for the monastic church of San Bartolomeo a Monte Oliveto may be explained by the considerable time that elapsed between the commissioning of the work in 1407 and the inscribed date of 1410 (Figs. 22-28). The themes and general format of the altarpiece stem directly from late fourteenth-century Tuscan traditions: a full-length seated Madonna fills the central panel, paired saints stand in the laterals, and the Blessing Redeemer and Annunciation occupy the three pinnacles, elongated here by crowning ogival tympana.[61] In contrast to the usual Trecento mode of inserting bust-length prophets in roundels within the "mezzanine" between side panels and pinnacles, Lorenzo's eloquent Malachi and Isaiah, whose gestures and banderoles connect the Incarnation and the Advent, uncoil like tendrils to lace together the two registers of the altarpiece; they will shortly reappear in Lorenzo's work as miniatures enclosed by richly foliate initials. Their antecedents are the Isaiah and Ezekiel above Jacopo di Cione's *Coronation of the Virgin* of 1373, executed for the

Florentine Mint;[62] and they also recall Brunelleschi's impassioned *Prophets*, who defy the discipline of their quatrefoils on the Silver Altar in Pistoia (Fig. 295). The frame of the Monte Oliveto Altarpiece was overladen at some later date—most likely in the nineteenth century when it was common to gild the Gothic lily—with an outcropping of leafy ornament, a proliferation of niggling detail that vies with the internal decorative forms.

In the central panel of the *Madonna and Child* Don Lorenzo indulged in the most complex interweaving of line he had yet contrived. At the center of this web of folds stands the elegantly poised Child, whose bowed shape reciprocates the long arc of the Virgin's mantle; His gesture is nearer a salute than a benediction.[63] The rhythms that emerge in the center panel travel laterally through the mantles of the Baptist and Bartholomew to the left and Thaddeus to the right, but the simpler fall of Benedict's habit—he is depicted as an abbot in Camaldolese white—resists this lyrical tide to affirm his monastic sobriety. The boldly ornamented border of his cope contrasts with the simplicity of the habit and with the finely wrought decoration showered over the Virgin's tunic and cloth of honor, Bartholomew's mantle, and the floor plane. Don Lorenzo's Cionesque inheritance is still apparent in the refined ornamentation of the haloes and in the facial types of Benedict and Bartholomew who descend from Nardo's serious elders (Fig. 265). And in the subtle palette of the Monte Oliveto Altarpiece, with a prevalent chord of dark and light rose, azure and grayish blue, lilac, and white, Don Lorenzo would seem to be recalling the fresco art of Nardo di Cione. Only the glimpses of golden yellow in the lining of the Virgin's mantle and the notes of vermilion in the gesticulating prophets jar the muted tonality. Not until his later career will Lorenzo Monaco return to these tonal delicacies.

Beyond this variety of dependence on Cionesque traditions, there are other points of reference in the Monte Oliveto Altarpiece, which is the last of the painter's works in which a wide range of his stylistic sources may be so discretely isolated. As in the Empoli and Berlin *Madonna* panels, the set of the Virgin's head and the fall of her mantle continue to acknowledge Don Silvestro's model (Fig. 267). And Florentine sculpture has left its stamp on Don Lorenzo's forms; in conceiving the John the Baptist, he must have closely studied the drapery of Lorenzo di Giovanni d'Ambrogio's *Prophet* from the Porta della Mandorla (Fig. 296) or Niccolò Lamberti's *Saint Luke* from Orsanmichele.[64] In this process of culling models, Don Lorenzo also turned to the two major altarpieces Gherardo Starnina had executed in Florence soon after his return from Spain—the polyptych in Würzburg, completed around 1405, and the altarpiece for the Certosa at Galluzzo, probably completed by 1408 and certainly in the painter's shop for some time before that date. Starnina's impact on the Monte Oliveto Altarpiece is detectable in specific passages rather than overall conception. For example, Lorenzo's Saint Thaddeus (Fig. 24) is a conflation of Starnina's Andrew in Würzburg and the Magdalen in the fragment of the Certosa polyptych in East Berlin (Figs. 285 and 286); witness the studied character of the enveloping mantle, the broad beam of the figure, and the fullness of body implied in the heavy shelving of the drapery.[65] In Lorenzo's work the Child's mantle descends in sharp ridges that closely adhere to the contour of the leg, much as in Starnina's Saint Lawrence from the same Berlin panel (Fig. 286). Nowhere in Lorenzo's drapery forms, however, are the contrasts of dark recesses and lighted edges as staccato and aggressive, nor do the glance, gesture, and turn of body of his saints convey as active a response to a central icon.

In the zones of the Monte Oliveto Altarpiece that rise above the main register the technique and style of Lorenzo Monaco display a more distinctively personal character (Figs. 25-28). This is consistent with the tendency in early Italian painting for the marginalia of altarpieces—pinnacles and predellas—to be the vanguard of an artist's style, implying that in these subordinate areas he was less fettered by the force of tradition, which was more likely to prevail in the principal image. The palette of the three pinnacles, though an intentional reprise of the main register, has gained in luminosity; the genuflecting Gabriel is surrounded by incised rays, and his mantle is a continuous surface of finely milled gold. Along with such mechanical simulations of light, the lively hatching of the final layer of tempera and the gently highlighted edges of folds enhance the radiance of forms. The fluent technique of applying the last strokes of the tempera medium is matched by a new ductility of line, notably in the figure of the Annunciate Virgin (Fig. 26). Her drapery ascends without interruption from a pool of folds at the floor, and the black line used consistently in these earlier phases of Lorenzo's art to describe figural contours is here accentuated to serve as a strut for the delicately poised form. Although Ghiberti's Annunciate Virgin (Fig. 284) on the North Door stands rather than kneels, the parallel pleats arching through her tunic with the suppleness of a reed could have provided a model for Don Lorenzo's image.

THE PINNACLES of the Monte Oliveto Altarpiece are not as closely tied stylistically to the Madonna and saints in the main register as they are to a series of smaller works that were painted during the same years Don Lorenzo was occupied with this major commission. Four scenes from the Infancy of Christ, the splendid remnants of an unknown altarpiece, are scattered through museums in London, New York, and Altenburg; to assist in identification, these dispersed panels will be denoted here as the "Courtauld predella" (Figs. 29-32 and Colorplate 3). The type of horizontally elongated quatrefoil that frames each picture had been used previously in the predella of the *Agony in the Garden* (Figs. 10-11), where both figure and landscape began to submit to the rhythmic shape of the frame. In these scenes of Christ's Infancy—as the Lehman Collection *Nativity* shows with a special clarity—the accommodation is now complete. The kneeling Virgin's mantle responds to the cusped contour of the panel and, in turn, is answered by the ascending rocks, while the two right lobes of the frame, lamentably truncated, prompted the shapes of the transfixed Joseph and the radiant angel hovering above the awestruck shepherds. Contrasted with these curvilinear forms is the rigid manger shed, which is simply an extension from the angle of the quatrefoil.

Don Lorenzo referred directly to the work of Ghiberti in composing the "Courtauld predella," but the derivations are in the nature of individual motifs rather than dramatic means. We need only confront the predella and relief versions of the *Adoration of the Magi* (Figs. 31 and 291) to discern that the painter unfolded a simple tale across the surface of the panel, placing the figures against a slightly modified form of the traditional parapet and wing stage, while the sculptor constructed a complex drama in which the sophisticated convergence of the architectural setting forces attention on the Child. It is apparent, nonetheless, that Don Lorenzo had studied Ghiberti's reliefs closely. In the *Visitation* and *Nativity* the edge of the ground plane is fractured into a craggy shelf that appears to project from the quatrefoil, a device used consistently by Ghiberti in the competition panel and in the North Door. The pose of the old Magus in the Courtauld *Adoration* was adapted from Ghiberti's relief (Fig. 291), and the mantle of the Virgin in the Altenburg *Flight* and in the *Nativity* on the Door (Fig. 293) are cut from a very similar pattern.[66] In the Virgin of the London *Visitation* and the New York *Nativity*, elongated and highlighted ridges of drapery establish the axis of the figure, exactly as in the Annunciate of the Monte Oliveto pinnacle (Fig. 26) and Ghiberti's portal (Fig. 284). Here Don Lorenzo's line unfalteringly conveys dramatic nuances. The mellifluous group at the left of the *Visitation* is sharply interrupted by the taut yet resilient shapes of the Virgin which tell equally of her will and sympathy, and then resolve into the pliant forms of Saint Elizabeth's mantle.[67] To the far right, the slender arch and the half-hidden onlooker sound the final beats of the metrical pattern.

In this luminous predella, Lorenzo Monaco attained a unique mastery in the decorative and dramatic use of color. With the early *Agony in the Garden* (Colorplate 1), the duality of the palette, harking back to Agnolo Gaddi and to the Cionesques, was apparent, but now chromatic range and technique have become the painter's personal invention. Close perusal of the tempera surfaces reveals a lively brush in the act of painting (Colorplate 3); greens emerge from dark recesses of drapery to be transformed into yellow, a wine red is tempered to rose, violet is irradiated by streaks of yellow and light gray, and the interior folds of coral red, blue, and yellow draperies are aglow with a fine white hatching. The vibrant frieze of figures spread across the four panels is offset by the neutral grays, browns, and dusky greens of the setting; only the light-tipped rocks, the clusters of leaves, and the deferential palm in the *Flight into Egypt* share the radiance of the figures.[68] Each episode of the predella is lighted as an independent entity, with the limited accents of dark in the drapery folds punctuating the extended, lyrical band of variegated color. In the nocturnal fantasy of the *Nativity*, the Infant, the angelic glory above the Virgin, and the cloud-borne angel form three luminous points that are symbols not sources of light. Luminosity is a product of chromatic gradations within discrete passages of local color; light is not perceived as a pervasive and unifying "exterior influence."[69] For Lorenzo Monaco light was radiance and emanation, not illumination shed from a natural and singular source. While other painters of the early fifteenth century, notably Gentile da Fabriano in Italy and the Boucicaut Master and the Limbourgs in the North, prepared the way for the Renaissance preoccupation with light as a natural phenomenon perceived optically, Don Lorenzo maintained the mediaeval conception of light as an abstract metaphor of Christian mysteries, veering from that course only in his final works.[70]

THE PRAGUE-PARIS TRIPTYCH

THE YEAR 1408 inscribed on the wings of a triptych now divided between the National Gallery in Prague and the Louvre places it soon after the "Courtauld predella" and still within the span of years required to execute the Monte Oliveto Altarpiece.[71] The tableaux of the *Agony in the Garden* and the *Holy Women at the Tomb* (Fig. 33), visible when the wings were closed, rise and fall precipitously through the narrow confines of the two panels. The jutting cliffs and tightly interlocked group of sleeping disciples respond to the tense form of the praying Christ who appears transfixed by the cup-bearing angel hovering above; the ardor of His upward gaze recalls the awestruck Joseph in the Lehman *Nativity* (Fig. 30), or the praying *Prophet* from a monastic choir book (Fig. 65). Linear contours bind each element to the picture plane, securing the figures to their narrow shelves of space.

Over this steep lithic setting falls a subtly colorful cascade of draperies—silvery blue, bottle green, rose, lavender, golden yellow, and coral red—enclosed by the greenish gray cliffs. In the *Holy Women at the Tomb* the sarcophagus and lid obey no norms of perspective as did the tomb in the *Man of Sorrows* of 1404 (Fig. 18), but submit instead to the demands of a compositional logic. In contrast to the ascending path of the *Agony*, the scene of the *Holy Women* conveys descent, countered only by the modest gesture of the angel pointing upward to the risen Christ, abbreviated through a revision of the wings of the triptych to a cloud-borne fragment of drapery.

On opening these slender wings, their taut dialogue would have resolved into the dense company of keening mourners in the *Lamentation* who form a grieving chorus beneath the stark rock of Calvary (Figs. 34-37; Colorplate 6). Within the lancet-shaped panel Don Lorenzo attained an equipoise of narrative and icon. The empty cross rises triumphant, a bold foil to the fragile Christ below; his wounds have an immemorial echo in the dark crevasse below the looming rocks. To substantiate the martyrdom, Nicodemus and Joseph of Arimathaea stand aside to exhibit the crown of thorns, the nails, and the pincers as emblems of the Passion. And the tragic death is further confirmed by the opposition of the ashy corpus and pale violet shroud to the encircling palette of royal blue, bottle green, rose, and coral red. A grieving woman draped in shot colors of black and magenta and placed on the axis of the cross provides an epicenter for the figural group and an emblem of mourning. A silvery light picks out the spectrum of draperies and the gray forms of the barren, fractured landscape, beyond which rise the crystalline walls and towers of Jerusalem. Not since the narrative panels of Duccio's *Maestà* or of the Master of the Saint George Codex have the events of the Passion been told with so perfect a fusion of fervor and elegance.

With the Prague-Paris triptych, the most uniquely personal work he had yet created, Lorenzo Monaco's gift as a painter of devotional images emerged to the full. In this smaller panel format the emotive temperature of his art could rise higher than in the dissipating reaches of the early *Agony in the Garden* and the *Man of Sorrows*, while the intimate scale freed him from the conventional demands of the "public" altarpiece. It is in these three episodes of the Passion that Don Lorenzo crystallized both an individual and an essentially Florentine version of the International Style. This is also the moment when Ghiberti attained his fullest expression of the style in the *Agony in the Garden* on the North Door (Fig. 292) wherein every element of the design is drawn into a rhythm that encompasses the entire quatrefoil.[72] Lorenzo's Louvre *Agony* is a tightly woven version of Ghiberti's, but the forms are more schematic. The florid mantle of the mourner at the foreground of the Prague *Lamentation* suggests, moreover, the impact of Starnina; the isolation and higher dramatic pitch of this figure give the impression of a motif that has migrated from another context. There comes to mind the angelic choir of the Würzburg triptych (Fig. 294), painted soon after Starnina's return from Valencia in the first years of the new century, or the even more analogous seated mourner in the *Dormition of the Virgin* in Philadelphia.[73] The Empoli *Madonna of Humility* was a modest preparation for this moment of linear hyperbole. The ornamentalism of the style, however, continues to be achieved with linear convolution rather than surface embellishment. Don Lorenzo's Florentine heritage, compounded with the austerities of Camaldolese monasticism and his own contemplative spirit, imposed the exclusion of decorative or descriptive minutiae that would lessen the dramatic focus.[74] And as with Ghiberti, the scenic elements in narrative episodes are entirely at the service of the human drama; the picturesque discursiveness that characterizes most variants of the International Style, is eschewed. An art grounded in Florentine traditions could never diverge fully from the essentiality of Giotto.

AMONG the numerous images of the *Madonna of Humility* that issued from the workshop of Lorenzo Monaco in the wake of the Empoli triptych of 1404, two panels, one of 1405 in the Biblioteca Berenson (Fig. 38) and the other of 1407 in Stuttgart (Fig. 39), throw light on the complex nature of the painter's style at mid-decade. The Virgin in the Berenson panel could assume a role among the mourners of the Prague *Lamentation*, or could play the part of Saint Elizabeth in the Courtauld *Visitation*. But the sharp ridges that fan out from her raised knee are closer to Starnina's wiry accentuations (see Fig. 294) than to Lorenzo's more gently lighted edges of drapery folds. The long sweep of the Virgin's mantle is interrupted by her tense gesture, answered in the taut gathering of the Infant's mantle; the reciprocity of the Mother and Child in Empoli has been replaced with a nervous dialogue. In the Berenson *Madonna of Humility*, the "Courtauld predella," and the Prague-Paris triptych, Lorenzo Monaco vented an intimate emotionalism that will again prevail only in late works of his career.

In contrast to the unity of design and expression in the Berenson panel, the Stuttgart *Madonna of Humility* is a less cohesive work in which the painter seems to have been preoccupied with rendering the stuff of the mantle as a convincing sculptural mass. This intense concentration on a virtually separable passage of the picture could perhaps explain the workshop quality of the rigid folds in the Virgin's shawl and the mechanical conjuncture of her hand and the Child's foot. Nonetheless, the inscribed date of 1407 helps to localize a period of irresolution in Don Lorenzo's maturing art; the growing presence of sculptural mass in Florentine art seems to have challenged his primarily linear aesthetic.

THE METROPOLITAN MUSEUM *PROPHETS*

DURING this brief period of stylistic ambivalence, Lorenzo Monaco painted a group of panels that must be ranked among his most authoritative works—the four *Prophets* in the Metropolitan Museum of Art (Figs. 40-43 and Colorplate 5). These noble figures were published by Millard Meiss with a penetration and eloquence that would make extended comment seem redundant.[75] An aspect of the group that Meiss succinctly implied is worthy, however, of further analysis. The *Prophets* give clear evidence that around 1408 to 1410 Lorenzo Monaco found new sources of form and expression in the loges of the sculptors at work on the projects for the Duomo, just as Florentine Trecento sculpture and the art of Ghiberti had already provided him with influential models. There was no need to await the placement of Donatello's *Saint John the Evangelist* or Nanni di Banco's *Saint Luke* on the Cathedral façade in order for these works to exert their influence. Indeed, Lorenzo Monaco could well have seen Donatello's designs for the *Saint John* even before 1409, the year in which the actual carving of the upper portions of the figure was begun.[76] In Lorenzo's *Noah* (Fig. 42) the blousing of the tunic at the waist and the horizontal highlights suggestive of the creases of the paunch are unmistakably similar to Donatello's treatment of the same passage in his *Saint John* (Fig. 297), while the coiffures of both Donatello's *Evangelist* and Lorenzo's *Abraham* (Fig. 41) give the effect of tightly curled wigs capping their heads. Each of the four *Prophets* is strictly contained within a broadly based triangle that narrows to the shoulders and is crowned by a copiously bearded face, exactly the shape and sequence of the *Saint John* when the sculpture is viewed at the angle from which it was intended to be seen on the façade of the Duomo.[77] The coarse, weighty mantles and tunics of these ancient worthies, that fall from the knees into heavy ridges and deep pockets, recall the voluminous draperies of Nanni's *Saint Luke.*[78] Whereas the effect of Ghiberti's ductile bronze was felt in Don Lorenzo's works of this decade and will continue to be influential far into the painter's career, the *Prophets* are grounded in the lithic art of Donatello and Nanni di Banco. And one final sculptural analogy may be drawn, but here we are harder put to suggest that Don Lorenzo could have known either the design or the actual work. This is the Sienese Jacopo della Quercia's *Silvestri Madonna* in the Cathedral Museum at Ferrara (Fig. 298), begun in 1403 and completed by 1408.[79] The radiating folds at the Virgin's waist, the deep chevrons of her mantle at the thighs, which bring a sense of plastic dimension to the figure when it is viewed frontally, and the heavy knotting of the Child's sash, are elements of Lorenzo's vocabulary in the *Prophets* and in the Stuttgart *Madonna.* And perhaps more than coincidentally, the flexed pose of Quercia's Christ Child recalls the Infant in the Monte Oliveto Altarpiece.

Regardless of the difficulties in proving either the path or chronology of these influences, it is apparent that Lorenzo Monaco was impressed by the emergent monumentality in Tuscan sculpture. This was to be a brief attachment, for he chose instead to pursue the stylistic direction so movingly set in the Prague-Paris triptych of 1408. But while the powerful public sculptures that would arouse the Florentines to a pitch of civic pride had only momentarily inspired Don Lorenzo, the effect of Donatello's psychological vehemence would linger, confirming Lorenzo's own highly charged nature and deepening the passion of his Orcagnesque worthies. The spiritual force and gravity of mien in Lorenzo's *Abraham* and *Moses* were augmented within the emotional climate of Donatello's enrapt *Saint John.*[80]

Don Lorenzo's newly found sculptural emphasis in the *Prophets* did not impede his lavishing a sumptuous palette on the four figures. Separate notes of rose, azure, violet, and green are resoundingly struck in the draperies of *Abraham, Noah, Moses,* and *David.* These dominant areas of color are accented by yellow, dark salmon, and coral red mantle linings, grayish white and light blue shawls, and the striking combination of coral red and iron gray in Isaac's costume. Light green or pink platforms and grayish green benches touched with gold ornament complete this masterful assemblage of color. The plastic force conveyed by each of the "polychromed" figures is enhanced by the contradictory character of the settings in which flat gold grounds bluntly converge with the recessive platforms and benches. A strong illumination throws highlights on the roundings of shoulders and knees and carves deep pockets of darkness into drapery folds to further the illusion that these authoritative figures are in high relief. The point at which color as decoration and as dramatic means coincides is affectingly discerned in the figure of *Abraham.* As Millard Meiss observed, the shot effect of red and green in his tunic, a decorative device inherited from Gaddesque traditions of color, now serves, as do the intersecting halves of his mantle, to symbolize the old father's tragically conflicting loyalties.

THE *CORONATION OF THE VIRGIN* FOR SANTA MARIA DEGLI ANGELI

IN FEBRUARY of 1414 (O.S. 1413) Lorenzo Monaco inscribed his name on the most comprehensive and spectacular work of his career, the *Coronation of the Virgin* for the high altar of Santa Maria degli Angeli (Florence, Uffizi; Figs. 44-62; Frontispiece, and Colorplates 7-9). The inscription across the frame of the main panel records the collaboration of the master and his fellow monks, a testament to Lorenzo's affiliation with the monastery even though he had not resided there for well over a decade. In this vast altarpiece, as impressive in its breadth and inclusiveness as a Gothic portal, Lorenzo displayed the gamut of his art and enlarged the resplendent company of late mediaeval Florentine "showpieces"—Andrea Pisano's bronze doors for the Baptistery, Orcagna's Strozzi altarpiece and his tabernacle for Orsanmichele, and the dismembered San Piero Maggiore *Coronation* by Jacopo di Cione (Fig. 299), the most grandiose Trecento rendering of the subject.[81] As a means of unifying this sonorous choral celebration of the Virgin, Lorenzo abandoned the earlier Florentine convention in which the central group is framed off from the ranks of adorants, and he incorporated them instead into a single panoramic surface.[82] Nonetheless, the traditional subdivisions are still suggested by the elevated central arch, the crowning pinnacles, and the six-part predella, which falls into pairs below the implied sections of the *Coronation*. The unity of the tableau is finally regained through the encompassing sweep of star-studded arcs of graduated blue, Don Lorenzo's unique means of proclaiming the celestial realm of the ritual.[83] Floating above this empyreal symbol are the enthroned Virgin and Christ, a choir of angels, and three tiers of adoring saints. A baldachin, unmistakably inspired by Orcagna's tabernacle at Orsanmichele (Fig. 300), rises behind the throne, a metaphor of the Virgin as the Church, the new Solomon's temple.[84] The ribbed vaulting of the baldachin is repeated in the deep soffits of the frame which project far enough to create the effect of a continuous ceremonial canopy spread across the solemn gathering.[85] An angelic choir encircles the throne, cordoning off the sacred rite from the saintly witnesses to establish an enclave in which the festive event transpires.[86] This wreath of angels—an appropriate motif for the high altarpiece at Santa Maria degli Angeli—is completed by the three cloud-borne figures kneeling below the dais; two in that triad swing censers as though purifying an altar, but the third was virtually obliterated at some later time when a ciborium was attached to the panel, although a fragment of a portative organ still hints at the musical role of that lost angel. The enclosed zone occupied by Christ and the Virgin is further delimited and sanctified by the ornamental cloth of honor suspended between the forward piers of the baldachin.[87]

The truncated state and inept installation of the *Coronation of the Virgin* now conspire to blunt the viewer's response to this imposing edifice. Certainly there is justification for the removal of the nineteenth-century finials above the pilasters and heavy hoods over the pinnacles, but no measure has been taken to lend a sense of completion to the barren upper reaches of the altarpiece. Moreover, the towering structure is viewed across the short axis of the room and a wide skylight directly above creates a visually inappropriate environment. The *Coronation of the Virgin* may be envisioned on a candle-lit high altar in the reduced and shifting light of a church interior, where the gilded textures of the ornamented frame and haloes—not a pattern is repeated in a score of saints—and the broad unembellished gold grounds at the base and apex of the main panel and in the pinnacles would combine as a radiant setting for this colorful gathering. Contrary to the present onslaught of color, in which the reds and yellows are especially strident, a lowered lighting would balance the cool and warm ends of the spectrum and permit the most saturated hues to function, in the mode of mediaeval painting, as the deepest darks of a tonal progression.[88] The accents of yellow shot through the white and rose of the angels' robes would then convey the effect of a shimmering reflection of the Virgin and Christ. When the many Marian feasts were celebrated at Santa Maria degli Angeli throughout the liturgical year, white vestments and monastic habits would have been mirrored by the mantles of the Virgin and of the Blessing Redeemer above her, and by the Camaldolese garb of Benedict and Romuald, as the altarpiece and its setting coalesced into a sacred drama wherein the border between icon and ritual dissolved.

A tally of haloes reveals that more than twoscore saints and angels are gathered into the tableau of the *Coronation*. In this seemingly conscious display of elaborate and variegated aureoles, Lorenzo Monaco brought to its apogee the refined craft of incising, punching, and milling of gold leaf that traversed the Florentine generations of Taddeo Gaddi, and Andrea and Nardo di Cione. But within the dense assemblage the major linear rhythms and color chords are established in the central group of Christ and the Virgin, the six saints of the front rank, and the U-shaped group of five angels kneeling at the sides and beneath the dais of the throne. The frame pilasters and deeply indented consoles provide moorings for a festoon of calligraphic draperies, which gain in ornamental effect through contrast with the strictly parallel banding of the starry firmament below. A coherent progression from Don Lorenzo's previous work is apparent on comparing the Saint Romuald at the far right with the Annunciate Virgin in the Monte Oliveto Altarpiece (Fig. 26), which was completed in 1410 and must soon have been followed by the initial designs of the *Coronation* for Santa Maria degli Angeli. Now the rhythmic linear scheme provides a matrix for the deepened relief of drapery folds; calligraphic surfaces and modelled masses have been brought into equilibrium. The pendular folds and the long, arching axis of each figure inevitably recall Ghiberti's *Saint John the Baptist* (Fig. 301), completed for Orsanmichele in the same year as Don Lorenzo's *Coronation*.[89] Perhaps the closest parallel to Ghiberti's style in the *Saint John* is found in the Blessing Redeemer (Fig. 48) of the central pinnacle. The resolute arcs of the mantles accentuate the plane of the figure and at the same time begin to imply a flexible armature onto which the draperies have been wound. Comparison of this image with the central pinnacle of the Monte Oliveto Altarpiece (Fig. 27) confirms that Lorenzo Monaco has now relinquished the formulas of Trecento figure style still observable in the earlier work, where the bulky mantle gives no hint of an interior core.

Similarly, in the facial features of Lorenzo's company of saints (Fig. 46) line etches a rhythmic path from brow to nose to lips and beard, while the mass of the head is modelled in sharply accented lights and darks. And the complex linear network that binds the clusters of figures also defines both the plane and the contours of a sophisticated chromatic pattern (Frontispiece and Colorplate 7). With strict symmetry, the whites of Benedict's and Romuald's habits bracket the assemblage of saints and respond to the Virgin at the center, and the rose mantles of the Baptist and John the Evangelist enclose either side of the throne. The assertive notes of deep coral red in the lining of Peter's mantle and in Andrew's tunic provide both additional symmetry and a fraternal link. By way of relief from this overt balance, color is also organized contrapuntally; the yellow and blue of Saint Peter's mantle and tunic are repeated in reverse in Christ's costume, and the yellowish green of Andrew's mantle is reused only once in the entire panel—in the lining of the Virgin's robe.[90] This closely plotted chromatic scheme extends beyond the main register to the marginal elements, most evidently in the pinnacles where the areas of color have a nearly comparable breadth. The Virgin's white is quoted immediately above in the robe of the Blessing Redeemer in the central pinnacle, and the encircling seraphim assume the tawny coral red of the gold-brocaded cloth of honor on the throne below. Implicit diagonals ascend from Christ's ultramarine blue mantle lined in yellow to the Annunciate Virgin's identical palette, and from the deep rose and pink, and parti-colored wings of the censing angels up to the floating Gabriel.[91]

Light now assumes an even greater importance in Don Lorenzo's artistic language, accenting the convolutions of drapery and bringing harmony to a variegated palette. Though the individual elements of this inclusive assemblage are drawn with a steely brilliance, they are united by a complex interlocking of rhythms and by a decoratively unifying light. Both the main panel and the central pinnacle are lighted frontally, whereas the reversed light and dark of Gabriel and the Annunciate Virgin imply that they are illuminated by the Redeemer and from the tableau of the *Coronation* beneath. These luminous effects are achieved through a mature virtuosity in the handling of the tempera medium; the gradations of a local color are enlivened by a vibrant surface of hatched strokes, which enhance transparency and lighten the weight of luxuriant draperies. As a result of the harsh cleaning of the panel in the nineteenth century, this spirited *velatura* has survived mainly in the more resistant greens, yellows, and whites.

The descent from the spectacle of the *Coronation of the Virgin* to the intimate narratives of the predella is like passage from the public realm of communal rite into the enclosing privacy of the cloister. In these six masterful quatrefoils Lorenzo Monaco created a perfect amalgam of traditional iconographies, compositional invention, and monastic sentiment. The two central panels of the *Nativity* and *Adoration of the Magi* (Figs. 51 and 52), along with the *Annunciation* in the pinnacles (Figs. 59 and 60), foreshadow the *Coronation* as the last of the Joys of the Virgin. The ascent from the two Infancy scenes in the middle of the predella through the *Coronation* to Christ in Benediction at the crest establishes a theological axis within the altarpiece, recalling the insistent symbolic "spine" of the *Man of Sorrows* of 1404 (Fig. 18). In turn, a relationship between the Infancy scenes and the Benedictine episodes at either side (Figs. 49-58) is implied by the themes and gestures of adoration, reverence, and genuflection that pervade the six panels. The *Meditations on the Life of Christ* provided the source not only for the devotional type of *Nativity* in which the Virgin kneels in adoration but also for the radiant "multitude of angels" hovering above the manger.[92] The bond between the pair of scenes at the center and those at the sides has been strengthened by lending the old Magus in the *Adoration* the facial features and even the tonsure of the Saint Benedict in the monastic panels.

The four outer quatrefoils do not follow the order of Benedict's life but rather are paired according to thematic meaning, the two panels to the left conveying the saint's spiritual dedication and those to the right his miraculous works. For the *Death of Saint Benedict* (Fig. 49), at the far left, the huddled mourners in the Prague *Lamentation* have been recast in monastic guise. The ascent of Benedict's soul, observed only by the kneeling Maurus, describes an upward path to his effigy in the celestial company of the *Coronation*. Benedict's right to assist in that sacred event is affirmed by the adjoining

PLATE 8. Lorenzo Monaco, *Adoration of the Magi*, predella of the *Coronation of the Virgin*, Uffizi, Florence.

PLATE 7. Lorenzo Monaco, *Christ, the Virgin, and Angelic Choir*, detail of the *Coronation of the Virgin*, Uffizi, Florence.

PLATE 6. Lorenzo Monaco, *Lamentation*, National Gallery, Prague.

PLATE 5. Lorenzo Monaco, *Abraham*, Metropolitan Museum of Art, New York.

PLATE 9. Lorenzo Monaco, *Rescue of Saint Placidus and Saint Benedict's Visit to Saint Scholastica*, predella of the *Coronation of the Virgin*, Uffizi, Florence.

PLATE 10. Lorenzo Monaco, *Saint Nicholas Rescuing a Storm-tossed Ship*, Accademia, Florence.

PLATE 11. Lorenzo Monaco, *Visitation*, predella of the *Annunciation Altarpiece*, Bartolini Salimbeni Chapel, Santa Trinita, Florence.

PLATE 12. Lorenzo Monaco, *Annunciation*, detail of the *Annunciation with Four Saints*, Accademia, Florence.

predella panel (Fig. 50), which attests to his piety in the penitential Subiaco scene and to his concern for the spiritual life of his brothers as he recognizes that a devil had tempted a young monk from prayer. Within this single quatrefoil the two forms of Camaldolese devotion—hermitic and communal—are encompassed.

The pair of panels at the opposite end of the predella depict three of Benedict's miracles. At the far right, he resurrects a young monk who was killed by the force of the devil during the building of Monte Cassino (Fig. 58). The left segment of the adjacent panel (Fig. 57) represents Benedict instructing Maurus to rescue Placidus, whose imminent drowning has been revealed in a vision, and at the right is the poignant last encounter of Benedict and the dying Santa Scholastica, whose prayers were answered by a storm that forced her brother to remain longer at her convent. In the scenes at either end of the predella the figures enact a single episode within a space defined by the traditional parapet and wing architecture. The adjacent quatrefoils each contain three episodes that are enacted in exterior and interior settings separated by a sloping rocky formation, the same device that was used in the early *Agony in the Garden* (Fig. 7) and in the Paris wings (Fig. 33). In turn, the *Adoration* is related to the end panels by the similar general format of its architectural background. But here the three deep recesses of the arcade frame the participants and impel progression through the sacred ritual. That Don Lorenzo was conscious of these dual functions of the architecture and that he was exploring an inventive relationship of setting and narration, may be discerned in the pentimenti of the arch that encircles Joseph's halo; the final corrected placement functions to accentuate the sequence from Joseph, to the gift, to the oldest Magus enveloped in his reverential act.[93] Although the *Nativity* does not call for a developed architectural setting, the manger is emphasized by the intense lighting of the underside of the shed, which heightens the air of mystery and lends this primitive structure a place within the architectural sequence of the predella.

The Benedictine imagery of Don Lorenzo's *Coronation* predella, with literary roots in the *Dialogues of Gregory the Great* and the *Golden Legend*, depended on various models from Florentine Trecento painting.[94] The life of Saint Benedict had been most extensively depicted by Spinello Aretino in the frescoes of the 1380s at San Miniato, but even where the subjects are identical, Lorenzo adopted only isolated motifs from Spinello's cycle rather than entire compositions; this is most evident in the *Death of Saint Benedict* and the *Raising of the Young Monk* (Figs. 303 and 304). More influential were a variety of Orcagnesque works that could have been seen at Benedictine and Camaldolese foundations, for example, the *Rescue of Placidus* (Fig. 306) in the predella of the *Saint Bernard* altarpiece by the Master of the Rinuccini Chapel, originally at the Badia a Settimo.[95] Benedict, Maurus, and Placidus are all appropriately clothed here in black, whereas Lorenzo Monaco consistently garbed his Benedictines in Camaldolese white. The variants of the parapet and wing setting in Lorenzo's scenes of the *Death of Benedict*, the *Raising of the Young Monk*, and the *Adoration of the Magi* recall the use of that architectural convention by the shop of Nardo di Cione in the predella of the *Trinity* altarpiece of 1365 (Fig. 305), from Santa Maria degli Angeli. And the liveliest of Orcagnesque storytellers, Giovanni del Biondo, must also have inspired Don Lorenzo with the economy and clarity of his narration (Fig. 307).

Lorenzo Monaco transformed whatever elements he may have derived from Sienese narrative painting into an essentially Florentine idiom. When his episode of Benedict and Scholastica is compared with a panel from the *Beata Umiltà* altarpiece by a Lorenzettian painter (Fig. 308), we may detect a degree of resemblance in the figures of the nuns at table and in the type of foreshortened frontal architectural setting.[96] But in Lorenzo's predella the figures dominate the scene while the settings have the ancillary function of articulating the figural composition. Contrast between Florentine and Sienese modes may also be drawn in the differing functions of the color plane.[97] In the Lorenzettian altarpiece an assertive hue such as the coral red used in some of the architectural settings exists primarily as an element in a planar and ornamental assemblage of color, whereas in Don Lorenzo's predella the same intense hue serves as decorative passage and as reinforcement of the illusion of space. The range of reds in *Benedict's Visit to Scholastica* (Colorplate 9) progresses from the fullest saturation within interior space to a dilution toward white that simulates the effect of exterior light.

The line in the six quatrefoils of the *Coronation*, in contrast to that in the "Courtauld predella," is now more fluid, and the figures are more flexible in pose and action. The architecture and landscape have gained in substance and draw the eye beyond the ornate shapes of the frame into a world of stage-like spaces suffused with light. To enhance the illusion of space, the device of a figure entering or peering through a doorway which had been used earlier in the Courtauld *Visitation* (Fig. 29), is repeated frequently throughout the series, as in the memorable detail of the curious retainer in the *Adoration*, the servers of the Requiem in the *Death of Benedict*, or the small figure inserted into a doorway at the extreme right of the Scholastica episode.[98] At the same time, the rounded and rectilinear forms of the quatrefoil are reinforced by the parenthetical shapes of the horse and the Virgin at either edge of the *Adoration*, by the curve of the pond and the arched cell in the Maurus-Placidus episode, and by the shed in the *Nativity*. The fluid figural group of Maurus rescuing Placidus, which responds to the lobed shape of the frame, was foreshadowed from the outset of Don Lorenzo's art by the Peter and Malchas episode in the predella of the *Agony in the Garden* (Fig. 12).

The notes of royal blue, yellowish green, golden yellow, rose, and coral red, and the prevailing white in the monastic scenes, are a reprise of the palette in the *Coronation* above. This entire spectrum is concentrated in the *Adoration of the Magi*, where it is offset by the neutral tones of the pale green architecture and the browns and grays of the horse and stewards (Colorplate 8). Throughout the predella the distribution of lights and darks is determined by the decorative and expressive demands of each scene, rather than by an optically unified plan of illumination. Glimpses of dense forest tipped with points of light and the scintillant hailstorm of the Scholastica story provide a continuous backdrop to the shallow stages on which the episodes unfold. Within the magical world of these six quatrefoils fact and fancy intermingle. The convincing architectural forms of the Maurus and Placidus panel resolve into the artifice of rocks and water, an illogical world made to seem more real by the detail of a belfry or of a rope dangling from a ring—Marianne Moore's "imaginary gardens with real toads in them." The art of Lorenzo Monaco could best flourish in these marginal zones of his vast altarpiece for Santa Maria degli Angeli, for within the scope of predella and pinnacle he could exploit a style that was most expressive on an intimate scale. By expanding his supple line and iridescent palette to the grandiose size of the *Coronation of the Virgin* he met the demands of the commission but defied the inclinations of his spirit and vision.

The thematic plan of the *Coronation* altarpiece is completed by the ten Prophets in the pilasters who form a typological gloss on the New Testament subjects.[99] Noah, Abraham, Moses, and David—the same worthies who appear in the Metropolitan Museum's panels—are identifiable by their symbols, while an inscription on the frame beneath Daniel identifies that youthful prophet; the other five cannot be named with certainty. Although the pilaster figures were designed by Lorenzo, the quality of the execution is inconsistent, which indicates the assistance of the workshop and reminds us that the inscription on the frame records a collaboration of the master and his fellow monks. In contrast to the Magi of the predella, the *Abraham* and *Daniel* (Figs. 61 and 62) in the pilasters lack the flexibility of line, the rhythmic coordination of the parts of the figure, and the discipline of the brush as it applied the final highlights.

THE PILASTER figures of the *Coronation* altarpiece are important, nonetheless, in the study of a group of *Prophets* in the ornamented initial letters of a choir book from Santa Maria degli Angeli (Figs. 64-68; Colorplate 4). Although the book bears the date of 1409, the execution of the *Prophet* miniatures cannot be fixed so absolutely. Within the group of eight that are attributable to Lorenzo Monaco, there is a marked difference in style between the first four *Prophets* (fols. 35, 38v, 46v, and 65v) and the last four (fols. 86v, 89v, 93, and 96v). To demonstrate this distinction, the *Prophet* miniatures on folios 35 and 86v may be contrasted (Figs. 67 and 68). In the latter the modelling is enriched, facial features are more freely drawn, and an abundance of hatching suggests the play of light over drapery. Chronologically, the figures on the earlier folios of Corale 3 align with the prophets in the spandrels of the Monte Oliveto Altarpiece (Figs. 22 and 28), completed by 1410, while those on the later folios are closer to the marginal elements of the *Coronation of the Virgin*. Beyond this nuance of dating, the entire group of *Prophets* in this splendid book reveals, in contrast to Lorenzo's miniatures of the 1390s, a fuller accommodation of the figure to the contour and rhythm of the surrounding letter, similar to the integration of predella scenes within their quatrefoil frames. Like those earlier miniatures, however, the *Prophets* in Corale 3 are not miniaturistic in effect, but could be figures that have migrated from panel painting to the pages of a manuscript, passionate completions of the previous work of the scribe and illuminator.

On the same scale as Lorenzo's miniatures and small panels is a unique example of his draughtsmanship, the *Saint Benedict Enthroned* (Fig. 63), a pen drawing on paper in the collections of the Uffizi. Comparison of the long, descending path through the figure, or the fall of drapery from knees to ground, with the same elements in the *Annunciate Virgin* pinnacle of the *Coronation* (Fig. 60), places the drawing around 1415. A rapid and economical pen has captured the stern alertness of the face, the tension of the body beneath the cassock, and the illusion of an encompassing space defined by the partially sketched throne and the wedge shape of the book. The *Saint Benedict* is a descendant of Lorenzo's four seated *Prophets* in the Metropolitan Museum and again attests to the impact of Donatello, but now the *Saint Mark* at Orsanmichele, completed by 1413.[100] The intensity of Benedict's gaze, the turn of the head against the plane of the torso, and the response of drapery to the spiritual élan of the figure reveal that Lorenzo Monaco had once again been caught up in the expressive force of his greater compatriot.

On the reverse of the same sheet in the Uffizi is a drawing of *Six Kneeling Saints* (Fig. 176), which served as a model for a group of adorants of a *Coronation of the Virgin*. In the quality of draughtsmanship, these figures bear the same relationship to the *Saint Benedict* drawing as do the pilasters of the Uffizi *Coronation* to the other parts of that altarpiece; the line is halting, the construction of heads, arms, and hands is tentative, and the dark accents do not clarify the function of drapery or articulate the design. On the two sides of this sheet the differences between the hand of the master and of a close shop assistant are discernible, which makes the *Six Kneeling Saints* drawing particularly informative, for instead of being related to the Santa Maria degli Angeli *Coronation*, it is a preparatory study for a closely dependent altarpiece that was painted for the Monastery of San Benedetto outside Florence. Although that work surely was commissioned from Lorenzo Monaco and incorporates some essential changes in his art, the altarpiece reveals the extensive involvement of his workshop. The complex problem of the San Benedetto Altarpiece (Figs. 175, 178, and 180-189) is the subject of an extended essay in the catalogue.

THE CUTOUT CRUCIFIXES AND THE ACCADEMIA *ANNUNCIATION*

In the years immediately following the *Coronation of the Virgin* for Santa Maria degli Angeli, Lorenzo Monaco and his workshop produced numerous painted crucifixes in which the panel was cut along the contours of the cross and corpus. Although the cutout cross seems to have been devised first in Siena in the later Duecento, it was only in the generation of Lorenzo Monaco that this compelling type of devotional image gained a wide acceptance.[101] As with the monumental painted crosses that were produced in abundance in Tuscany from the twelfth to the early fourteenth centuries, the cutout cross, with the figure of Christ often greater than life size, served as a permanent church fixture, placed atop a choir screen or against an altar wall. In the smaller processional cross the front and back of the corpus of Christ were depicted in order to confront the observer with a fully rendered figure. By stripping away all of the marginal elements included in crucifixes of the Duecento and earlier Trecento—the terminals and apron with mourners and scenes of the Passion, and the crest with the Ascension—the dramatic core of the Crucifixion emerged in stark isolation; the image of the dead Christ came to simulate the physical existence of a work of sculpture. If from one standpoint the cutout cross manifests an intensifying quest for realistic presence in devotional art,[102] the type is also reminiscent of the images of Christ silhouetted against abstract reaches of "sky" in such monumental Florentine Trecento frescoes as the Orcagnesque *Crucifixion* in the refectory at Santo Spirito or the panoramic lunette by Andrea di Bonaiuto in the Spanish Chapel at Santa Maria Novella.[103] In the cutout crosses by Lorenzo Monaco the unrelieved concentration on the poignant figure is tempered by the fluidity of his style. Nowhere is this more apparent than in the processional cross in Santa Maria delle Vertighe at Monte San Savino (Fig. 71), the most beautiful of Don Lorenzo's cutout crosses, where the spiritual and corporeal burden of the "Christus Patiens" is lightened by the rhythmic flow of contour and the buoyant arabesque of the loincloth.

The most imposing of Lorenzo Monaco's crosses forms the central element of the *Crucifix with the Mourning Virgin and Saint John* in the Florentine church of San Giovannino dei Cavalieri (Figs. 70, and 73-76).[104] An eighteenth-century frescoed landscape on the rear wall of the sanctuary provides an anachronistic filmy backdrop for this severe group. Here Lorenzo continued the lineage of grave icons from his earlier years: the Saint James of the *Agony in the Garden* (Fig. 9), the sorrowing

Virgin in its predella (Fig. 13), and the potent triad of the *Man of Sorrows* (Fig. 18) are the ancestors of this mystical tableau. Their immediate contemporaries, however, are to be found in the *Coronation of the Virgin* of 1414, as may be demonstrated by comparing the mourning Virgin at San Giovannino with the Annunciate in the right pinnacle of the *Coronation* (Fig. 60). Although their costumes have been cut from the same cloth, the long slow curves of the Annunciate's mantle, which respond to the rising, rushing forms of Gabriel opposite and express her acquiescence to his message, are now stirred into restless, convoluted shapes by the surging grief of the Virgin. A vortex of drapery folds erupts from the torsion of her mouth and brow, and discharges below in a cascade of loops and ridges. In the *Coronation* the joys of the Virgin are pervasive; her sorrow is the emotive impulse of the San Giovannino *Crucifixion*.

When Lorenzo Monaco undertook this work he could have known in Ghiberti's studio the *Crucifixion* relief for the North Door (Fig. 309). If that composition did exert influence on him, however, he would not have been content with the treatment of a tragic subject in which "graceful melodiousness threatens to become the only aim."[105] Ghiberti's crescent angels are first and foremost decorative responses to the lobes of the quatrefoil or to the descending slopes of the mourners' mantles, and function secondarily as emblems of a universal grief. In the San Giovannino Virgin ornamental line, which now approaches the peak of intensity in the painter's style, has become the vehicle of a fervid religious pathos, an urgent calligraphy that would soon materialize Don Lorenzo's most intimate and dream-like fantasies.

WHEREAS descending line as an analogue of grief is the dominant motif of the San Giovannino *Crucifix* group, in the *Annunciation* in the Accademia in Florence (Figs. 77-81), of around 1418, every element contributes to an air of buoyancy and grace.[106] Turning from the potent icon at San Giovannino to the lyrical intimacy of the altarpiece recalls the earlier expressive antipodes of the *Man of Sorrows* and the Empoli triptych, (Figs. 18 and 21). The incisive contours of the cutout *Crucifixes* are now transformed into the finely wrought edges of the figures of the Virgin, the Gabriel, and the four accompanying saints, to the degree that they seem like appliqués over the continuous gold ground and the marbled pattern of the floor. The sharp recession of the dais from the picture plane is purposefully countered by the elusive patterns of draping and tooling in the blue-spangled cloth of honor that enfolds the figure of the Virgin and in the secondary cloth that sanctifies the clasped book lightly touched by her left hand. Her elongated, molten mantle flows from the dais to the very edge of the floor; the agitated forms of the kneeling angels at the base of the *Coronation of the Virgin* (Fig. 44) now merge with the broad and sober rhythms of the Annunciate and Mourning Virgins from the *Coronation* pinnacle and from San Giovannino dei Cavalieri (Figs. 60 and 75). But draperies are no longer as deeply modelled, and their calligraphic play is now concentrated into passages that alternate with quieter, less complicated areas. The dark outlining of the figure has been honed to the finest edge, or at times abandoned. And appropriate to this reduced assertiveness of forms is the lowered intensity of the palette; the clarion scheme of the *Coronation of the Virgin*, with its persisting echoes of Agnolo Gaddi, is now put aside. Although there are still notes of lapis blue, golden yellow, and coral red in the Virgin's mantle and in the cloak of Saint Proculus, they are set off against passages of lavender, pale blue, green washed to yellow, old rose, and dusky pink, a minor key concentrated in the figures of Gabriel and Catherine of Alexandria. The iron gray monastic garb of Saint Anthony and Saint Francis complements this muted palette, while their placement forms a chromatic chiasm within the lateral elements of the altarpiece. In his search for models earlier in his career, Lorenzo had turned to the Cionesque world of figures and color, and now he seems again to reminisce, as he had in the Monte Oliveto Altarpiece, on the subtle minor chords of Nardo's frescoes in the Strozzi Chapel at Santa Maria Novella. Less than half a decade after the completion of the *Coronation of the Virgin* for Santa Maria degli Angeli, Don Lorenzo has relinquished its enamelled brilliance.

Inevitably, Lorenzo's *Annunciation* brings to mind Simone Martini's altarpiece in the Uffizi, painted for the Cathedral of Siena; witness the pose of the Virgin as she shrinks from Gabriel's message, the concentration on the dramatic interplay of the two participants, the eloquent interval of gold that both separates and unites them, the legato contour of the Virgin's mantle, the sumptuous ceremonial cloth, and the rush of the angel's cloak. Yet, there are essential differences. Simone's *Annunciation* is an archetypally Sienese tour de force of embellished surfaces and interwoven patterns, while Don Lorenzo's picture is essentially Florentine, its ornamentation closely restricted and used only as accessory. The oblique roofed portico that houses the Virgin's throne is a direct quotation from the Giottesque vocabulary, with the small passage of tracery lending a churchly rather than domestic cast to the structure.[107] Recalling the pinnacle of his earlier *Coronation* (Fig. 59), Lorenzo Monaco has again adopted the type of hovering archangel that seems first to have been devised by Ambrogio Lorenzetti and then carried into the later fourteenth and early fifteenth century by Spinello Aretino and Ghiberti (Figs. 283 and 284).[108] The contrast between Don Lorenzo's cloud-borne Gabriels, however, defines the direction of his style in the few years that separate the *Coronation of the Virgin* from the *Annunciation*. The Gabriel of the *Coronation* is composed in profile; in the Accademia *Annunciation* he turns at a three-quarter angle, as if miraculously emerging from the gold ground. With the earlier Gabriel a rushing motion is conveyed by the upward surge of drapery, but at the same time is arrested by the strict pattern of line and firm alternations of light and dark. In the later, more attenuated Gabriel, movement springs from the taut armature of the figure; the churning cape becomes the wake of a line of force impelled by the prow-like contour of the body and the rays of light seem to emanate from an inner well of energy. In so shifting and transient an image contrasts of light and dark, and linear schemes may no longer be as strongly asserted as they are in the earlier panel. With this elegant, mercurial Gabriel sounding the keynote of the altarpiece, all other elements are drawn into sympathetic response: the elongated contrapposto of the Virgin's form resolves the thrust of the archangel, the paired saints turn in unison toward the central drama, and the Christ Logos in the roundel above provides the tableau with a radiant capstone.[109]

THE UFFIZI *ADORATION OF THE MAGI*

THE HEIGHTENED complexity and sophistication of the *Annunciation* altarpiece herald the last phase of Lorenzo Monaco's career. At the threshold of this final half-decade of activity is his most comprehensive narrative picture, the *Adoration of the Magi* in the Uffizi, executed early in the 1420s (Figs. 82-87; Colorplate 14).[110] While the Annunciation and Coronation of the Virgin frequently occupied the main position in Trecento altarpieces, only in the Quattrocento did the *Adoration of the Magi* assume a comparably important role. The subject offered an appropriate vehicle for the tastes of those patrons who subscribed to the aristocratic and exotic imagery of the International Style, and furthermore, provided a theme in which the early Renaissance painter could vent a passionate urge to record, often with anachronistic abandon, the varieties of peoples, places, and things. With Don Lorenzo's Uffizi altarpiece there began a lineage of Adorations of the Magi through each generation of fifteenth-century Florentine painting, until Leonardo's universally inclusive *Epiphany* announced a new epoch in the history of art.[111] In the later fifteenth century, Cosimo Rosselli sought to attune Don Lorenzo's altarpiece to Renaissance taste by extending the frame to a full rectangle and filling in the spandrels with an *Annunciation* and two *Prophets*, but he succeeded only in dwarfing the original Gothic gables and stifling the intervals of the frame that had complemented the airy openness of the main panel.[112] When we read away Rosselli's intrusions, it becomes evident that the three arches of the *Adoration* are crowned with the same flamboyant shapes that link the five arches of the Accademia *Annunciation*. There the series of steep arches accentuate the flatness of the abstract gold ground, whereas in the *Adoration* the broad rounded shapes invite the eye to traverse the picture plane and enter the most developed space Lorenzo Monaco had yet constructed. The visual path into this space is eased by the omission of decorative consoles at the junctures of the three arches, such as those in the *Annunciation* at Santa Trinita (Fig. 121). The narrative progresses diagonally across a ground plane occupied by three vividly differentiated groups of figures, punctuated by the deep penetration of the converging arches into the pictorial field.[113] By depicting the middle king in full length, a break from the progressive genuflection of the three figures found in his predella versions of the *Adoration*, Don Lorenzo establishes a discrete triangular unit that has a geometrical response in the group of the Virgin and Child, Joseph, and the kneeling old Magus, who is common to both units. The reverential pose of the kneeling figure echoes his counterpart in the *Adoration* predella of the Uffizi *Coronation* (Fig. 52), in contrast to the more explicit approach to the Child found in Lorenzo's other versions of the scene (Figs. 31, 126, and 185). Though the placement of the Virgin directly on a stony base implies a variant on the Madonna of Humility, the Mother and Child are at the crest of the tableau of adoration. At the far right, the swaying, interlocked shapes of animals, figures, and rocky outcroppings discharge a wave of energy that is gradually grounded in the dense gathering of standing retainers who provide a bridge to the Magi and Holy Family.[114] The three units of landscape and architecture encompassed by the arches are united by a long slope descending from upper right to lower left, in the same direction as the narrative, leading from the worldly kingdoms symbolized by the towered city to the manger that frames the Virgin and Child. Between these sacred and profane architectural parentheses is the scene of the Annunciation to the Shepherds—a variant on the same episode in Lorenzo's *Nativity* predellas (Figs. 30, 51, 94, and 125)—with the angel afloat beneath the Blessing Redeemer in the central gable.

An ambivalence of surface and depth prevails in the *Adoration of the Magi*; the nervous and fanciful game of silhouettes at the right (Fig. 87) offsets the precise construction and intersection of oblique architectural forms in the manger shed at the left (Fig. 83), an anticipation of the self-conscious demonstrations of perspective the optical realists will perform in the coming generations of Florentine painting.[115] The style of figures is equally dualistic. The wiry gold edges of costumes weave a restless filigree over a surface that in its linear brilliance seems as much in the realm of drawing as painting. But at the same time the draperies have become less convoluted and there is a new use of parallel vertical folds (Fig. 82). The thinner stuffs are pulled taut by a shoulder or an arm, as in the standing Magus or the pair of retainers in full length, which raises the tension of the figures to the same pitch as their rapt glances directed toward the Child. In the *Coronation of the Virgin* the unity of groups was achieved by the imposition of a decorative pattern, but now in the *Adoration* there is an evidently rising awareness that the internal energy and will of individual figures may motivate their alliance. The tight cluster of bystanders is aligned in a sequence of planes, the heads on the second and third rank alternating with those of the forefront (Fig. 86).

In these same years around 1420 Ghiberti was working in a similar style in such later reliefs for the North Door of the Baptistery as the *Way to Calvary* or the *Pentecost* (Figs. 311 and 314).[116] The rank of onlookers in the *Adoration* has the character of a relief inserted at the center, which suggests that Lorenzo Monaco could have incorporated a study of a passage from Ghiberti's plaques (Fig. 312). In contrast to their earlier styles, the sculptor and the painter now indulge in a more extreme elongation of the standing figure.[117] Beyond these parallels in the style and placement of figures, Don Lorenzo also seems to have borrowed figural elements from Ghiberti: both the Joseph and the oldest Magus of the *Adoration* may depend on the Socrates head among the *Prophets* of the door (Fig. 313); the retainer with the scimitar was at least in part inspired by the figure at the center of the *Pentecost* (Fig. 314); and the steward leading the hound is an adaptation of the soldier seen from the rear in the *Way to Calvary* (Fig. 311). In contrast to the elegant elongation of the standing figures, the hefty Child presages the type of young Hercules who will frequently enact the Infant in the first generation of Florentine Renaissance art.

In gathering this congeries of elements into the *Adoration*, Don Lorenzo taxed his capacity to design a coherent composition of panoramic breadth, although here, for the first time in his work, he introduced a consistent system of lighting, which is contradicted only at the far right where the lithe steward and his dog are illuminated by the radiant forms of the interlocking steed. It is the subtly orchestrated palette that finally unifies and casts a mesmerizing aura of fantasy over the discursive parts. The bright focal point provided by the coral red robes of the young Magus kneeling at the center, is echoed in less saturated tones at the sides of the composition in the manger shed and the awe-struck figure on horseback. The golden yellow of the seated Joseph and the steward, at the far left and right, form two further parentheses at the edges of the panel. Between these symmetrical points of color there evolves, from the old King across to the retainer with the sword, a resonant minor chord of rose, bottle green, violet, and lilac, all shot with yellow lights (Colorplate 14). The two figures draped in green, placed directly beneath the indentations of the frame, reinforce the divisions of the scene and provide further notes of chromatic symmetry. Intense accents of vermilion along the rear plane of heads contrast with the minor key of the foreplane, while the somber grayish brown landscape serves as a neutral backcloth to this subtle and intricate spectrum.

When the *Adoration of the Magi* is contrasted with a Trecento depiction of the subject by the Sienese Bartolo di Fredi (Fig. 315)—a rare example before the fifteenth century of the Epiphany in the central position of an altarpiece—it is evident that Don Lorenzo even in this richly inclusive picture, did not betray the essentially Florentine and monastic character of his art. Bartolo's *Adoration* is a tapestry of ornate costumes and trappings, bizarre processions, and topographical allusions to Siena.[118] The direct lineage from Bartolo's work will be to the cornucopian style of Gentile da Fabriano's Strozzi *Adoration* of 1423; the sumptuous world of "gold, silver, apes, and peacocks" was foreign to Lorenzo's spirit, rooted in traditions of Florentine and monastic reserve. Nor did his Florentine sense of narrative concentration permit him to introduce a competitive meandering subplot of the Journey of the Magi. This is not to deny that Lorenzo very likely referred to Bartolo's influential picture or to the same model books for descriptive details, in particular the fanciful headgear of the retinue that lends an air of oriental exoticism, or the grotesque blackamoor in Bartolo's Journey who is now ennobled at the center of the entourage.[119] But in Lorenzo's *Adoration* ornament and description are restricted to a few passages; the aristocratic tone of this fantastic assemblage is conveyed through elegant austerity rather than luxurious abundance.

Contemporaneously with the *Adoration of the Magi* Lorenzo Monaco produced a series of works on the intimate scale that permitted his compositional powers to flourish. The three pinnacles that crown Fra Angelico's *Descent from the Cross* at San Marco, depicting the *Resurrection of Christ*, the *Noli Me Tangere*, and the *Holy Women at the Tomb* (Figs. 88-91, and 316), reveal a skillful accommodation of the episodes to the steep triangular fields.[120] Here Lorenzo's pinnacles do not have the flamboyant contours of those above the Accademia *Annunciation* and the Uffizi *Adoration*. Instead, the severe rectilinearity of the three panels provides a foil to the rhythmic dialogue of drapery and landscape forms festooned across them. Although these pinnacles are in exact thematic and decorative accord with Angelico's composition beneath, a consideration of compositional balance and dramatic sequence raises the possibility that the *Noli Me Tangere* and the *Holy Women at the Tomb* may have been reversed in Don Lorenzo's original arrangement of the panels. Of the two events bracketing Christ's *Resurrection*, the design of the *Holy Women* impels movement to the right through the clustering of the mourners, the thrust of the outcropping, and the bridging sarcophagus lid. Conversely, the design of the *Noli Me Tangere* implies a closing bracket and a denouement in the arched shape of Christ's body and the downward slope of the landscape. This reversal of sequence would underscore the emblematic contrast of the closed sarcophagus at the center with the open ones immediately adjacent. The long descent and focussed lighting of drapery folds and the rhythmic play of the flinty landscape bring these ascetic and elegant panels into perfect stylistic accord with Don Lorenzo's panoramic *Adoration of the Magi*.

In the three panels of the predella in the Accademia in Florence, representing the *Nativity* at the center and scenes from the lives of Saints Nicholas and Onuphrius in the lateral panels (Figs. 92-95; Colorplate 10), the quatrefoil that Lorenzo had used in his earlier predellas was abandoned, marking the same shift from a Gothic to a Renaissance pictorial field that Ghiberti was effecting in these same years.[121] The extended metrical pattern of the predella is accentuated by the three oblique structures that directly recall the insistent forms of the manger shed and towered city of the Uffizi *Adoration*. The positions of the lateral panels have been interchanged at various times in their history at the Accademia, but in the more effective arrangement the Nicholas episode is placed to the left of the *Nativity* and the Onuphrius legend to the right, so that the shrine at Bari and the monastic church serve to bracket the three scenes rather than press in on the already compact design of the *Nativity*.

The stage for these fantasies is a steeply raked ground plane that ascends to a distant horizon and a blue sky, which now replace the gold ground or dense vegetation at the crest of Lorenzo's earlier outdoor scenes (Figs. 11 and 51). The *Nativity* is enacted on barren rock—the last tier of Calvary in the Prague *Lamentation* (Fig. 34) has been transformed into Bethlehem—over which the scene spreads concentrically, from the Child in the manger out to the towered and castellated wall. Whereas in his earlier *Nativity* panels (Figs. 30 and 51) Lorenzo had combined various literary and pictorial traditions, now in recounting the story he adhered closely to the imagery of the *Meditations on the Life of Christ*; the Child lies in the manger, covered only by a thin veil, and the ox and ass breathe their warmth over the newborn.[122] The shed stands as an independent structure, no longer combined with a cave, though the rocky outcropping immediately behind the kneeling Virgin could allude to that traditional feature of Nativity scenes.[123]

Don Lorenzo's narrative poetry has become a transcendent expression of lyrical and fantastic visions, imaginative flights nowhere surpassed in European art of the International Style. The scenes of the predella unfold as in the passage of a dream, where fragments of reality float in a vehicle of shifting light and incandescent color. In the *Onuphrius* panel the rapid alternations of the tangible and intangible, of substance and shadow, is the key to the mood of otherworldliness; the silvery light cast over the moonstruck wilderness reveals the jutting rocks and incisive architecture, and etches the evanescent forms of Onuphrius and the faithful Paphnutius.[124] In the *Saint Nicholas* episode the thrusting perspective of the prismatic shrine at Bari heightens the illusory character of the ship with its rainbow crew foundering in a sea of arabesques (Colorplate 10). Minute and cryptic figures posing around a bay of the jigsaw coast could migrate to a caprice by Callot. Reminiscing on the oblique architecture and the body of water in the Benedict and Scholastica predella (Fig. 57), Don Lorenzo now enlarges them into the dominant elements of the composition. The expressive tensions between these dimensional and patternistic sides of the picture recall the Uffizi *Adoration* in which the manger and the interlocking animals were comparably opposed. And as in that picture, the salient perspectives of an architectural element at the foreground and a distant towered city establish spatial boundaries within the composition.[125]

Even in creating this interior and unfettered imagery, Lorenzo turned to models from the Florentine visual environment, specifically to frescoes of the later Trecento at Santa Croce. For the scene of *Nicholas Rescuing a Storm-tossed Ship*, he reused virtually every element of a fresco by the Master of the Saint Nicholas Legend in the Castellani Chapel at Santa Croce (Fig. 319).[126] The prominent structure to the left in the fresco is now angled against the picture plane, an assuring response to the wind-swept ship, while the towered bays of the fresco have become an encircling sea. Reversals of scale and perspective are also employed, as they are in the composition at Santa Croce, with smaller buildings below and to the fore of larger structures that exist in an elusive middle distance.[127] In the *Onuphrius* panel (Fig. 95) a fragment of a church and the crest of a cliff emerge at the bottom of the picture plane to function as *repoussoirs* for the steeply raked landscape. The rocky outcroppings scattered over this forbidding wilderness define three stages on which the episodes of the legend are enacted: the encounter with Paphnutius, Onuphrius recounting his years of privation, and his death. For the landscape, Don Lorenzo appropriately adapted Agnolo Gaddi's Thebaid-like panorama superimposed on the *Discovery of the True Cross* in the choir at Santa Croce (Fig. 271), just as nearly a quarter of a century earlier he had used similar barren cliffs to isolate Christ from the sleeping disciples in Gethsemane (Fig. 7).[128]

At this most visionary moment of his art Lorenzo Monaco conjured up the chiaroscuro drawings of the *Visitation* and the *Journey of the Magi* in the Berlin Print Room (Figs. 96-98). Rather than being preparatory drawings for a panel or fresco, they would seem to exist solely as expressions of the artist's inmost fantasies. He recalls here his own earlier *Lamentation* (Fig. 34), but in a medium free of the finalities of tempera. A fluid pen and brush have shaped the forms from myriad hatchings poised on the surface of the parchment, a technique that perfectly conveys the impalpability of a vision. The characters play their roles on the narrowest shelves, which momentarily interrupt the precipitous ascent of the landscape.[129] Horses and riders, architecture, and cliffs are glimpsed in flashes of light edging the darkness as the spectral Magi rise up in their hectic journey, drawn by the star looming over the stalagmitic city.[130] Roger Fry saw in the landscape an evocation of "the long and weary journey of the three Kings, the mountain ranges they have surmounted, the seas they have crossed." He continues: "Nor were he [Lorenzo Monaco] tied to the exigencies of real structure could he give with quite such fantastic vehemence their gratified longing as they recognize again the star which they had lost sight of behind the mountains, nor in a convincingly realistic scene could the feathery pink clouds flushed with the coming dawn give so pure an abstract of the poetical quality of the idea."[131] In the privacy of a drawing Don Lorenzo had composed in retrospect the narrative prelude to his *Adoration of the Magi*. With the Berlin drawings, he joined a rarefied company of lyrical fantasists whose spirit is more of the East than the West, in the realm of the T'ang fresco and the Sung scroll, a domain Botticelli would enter three-quarters of a century later with the drawings for the *Divine Comedy*. There also come to mind Kenneth Clark's elegant phrases on a more distant fantasist: ". . . genius it was; that immediate access to some world outside our own, that perfectly clear conviction, which creates its own skill, that a thing must be thus and thus and not otherwise."[132]

A group of impassioned *Prophets* in a choir book in the Bargello (Cod. H 74), originally at Santa Maria Nuova, is from the same febrile moment of Lorenzo's art (Figs. 99-101). The awestruck old Magus in the Berlin *Journey* (Fig. 98) has his exact counterpart in the ecstatic *Prophets* on folio 63 with his stippled beard and highlighted brow. The roundel of *Isaiah* (Fig. 81) from the Accademia *Annunciation* was the clearest anticipation of these miniatures. Now the simplified field within the illuminated letter, which conveys the effect of a figure observed through an unobstructed opening, exactly parallels the abandonment of the quatrefoil in Don Lorenzo's predellas of this period.[133]

THE BARTOLINI SALIMBENI CHAPEL AT SANTA TRINITA

LORENZO MONACO devoted his final energies to the decoration of the Bartolini Salimbeni Chapel in the Florentine church of Santa Trinita (Figs. 102 and 103; diagram, p. 129). The altarpiece is the last in the series of his large works on panel that began over a quarter of a century earlier with the *Agony in the Garden* for Santa Maria degli Angeli and the lost polyptych for the Carmine; but the fresco program spread over the walls and vault of the chapel is the first he ever undertook.[134] Though the cycle is now little more than a shadow of the original, the Bartolini Salimbeni Chapel has remained an integral ensemble, even to the splendid grille, possibly the work of the Pistoiese Manfredo di Franco.[135] Through the accident of history, another complete decorative program, created more than sixty years later, is preserved at Santa Trinita: Ghirlandaio's Sassetti Chapel, where the life of Saint Francis is in part a pious excuse for recording the topography of Florence and the historical consciousness and pride of the patrons. The two chapels, separated by a few yards, form perfect termini to the traditions of Florentine Quattrocento painting.

The narrative program and symbolic allusions of the Bartolini Salimbeni Chapel may be grasped when the frescoes and altarpiece are considered as a unity, although from the standpoint of style, the altarpiece marks the furthest point of Lorenzo's artistic development. The layout of the frescoes evinces a continuing acknowledgment of the radical models for a mural program within a Gothic side chapel that Giotto had formulated at Santa Croce a century earlier. But as the altar wall of the Bartolini Chapel is not interrupted by the usual lancet window, Don Lorenzo gained a third lunette for the narrative cycle. On the three walls and in the zone above the entrance arch there unfolds the earlier and later life of the Virgin, with the altarpiece providing the link to the life of Christ in the *Annunciation* of the main panel and the Infancy cycle in the predella. The path through the life of the Virgin is initiated in the steep lunette at the upper left with the badly effaced double scene of *Joachim's Expulsion from the Temple* and the *Annunciation to Joachim* (Fig. 104). The story continues directly beneath in a broad rectangular register occupied by the *Meeting of Joachim and Anna at the Golden Portal* (Fig. 105). There follow the *Birth of the Virgin* and her *Presentation in the Temple* (Figs. 106 and 107), both scenes constricted within narrow strips of wall at either side and at exactly the level of the main panel of the altarpiece. The earlier life of the Virgin is completed by the *Betrothal* (Fig. 109) on the lower register of the right wall opposite the *Meeting of Joachim and Anna.* The cycle concludes within three lunettes that encompass the *Dormition of the Virgin* (Fig. 111) at the upper right, the *Assumption* (Fig. 112) over the entrance arch, and the *Miracle of the Snow* (Fig. 114) immediately above the altarpiece. In the four webs of the vault crowning the chapel are Old Testament heralds of the Virgin: *David, Malachi, Isaiah,* and *Micah* (Figs. 113, and 115-117).[136] Four saints on the soffits of the entrance arch complete this inclusive program: the *Baptist* and *Bartholomew* to the left, *John the Evangelist* and *Paul* to the right, each enshrined in an elaborately canopied niche (Figs. 103, 118-119, and 200).[137]

The dedication of the Bartolini Salimbeni Chapel to the Annunciate Virgin is confirmed by documentary and literary sources, as well as by the fact that the *Annunciation* is the central image of the altarpiece.[138] The document of 1407 (Document 18A) in which the supervision of the chapel is ceded by the family to the Arte del Cambio prescribes that masses be celebrated annually on the Feast of the Annunciation (March 25) and on another unspecified day in August, which could possibly have been the Feast of the Snow on the fifth day of that month or, more likely, the Feast of the Assumption of the Virgin on the fifteenth, both of which themes are depicted in the fresco program.[139] The implication of this document that Marian devotions in the chapel were not exclusively bound to the celebration of the Annunciation is substantiated by elements in the imagery of the frescoes and altarpiece that refer both to Mary's immaculate conception and to the virgin birth of Christ. In the *Meeting of Joachim and Anna* (Fig. 105), a floating angel sheds grace upon the parents of the Virgin to symbolize the purity of her conception.[140] The pivotal lunette of the chapel, at the crest of the altar wall, presents the *Miracle of the Snow* (Fig. 114), which is a graphic display of the Virgin's miraculous powers in the founding of Santa Maria Maggiore and of her purity as manifested in the snowfall.[141] Directly below this lunette, and linked to it by lofty pinnacles, is the *Annunciation* altarpiece where Mary's freedom from original sin is fulfilled in the immaculacy of Christ's birth.[142] The narrow frescoes of the *Birth of the Virgin* and the *Presentation in the Temple* (Figs. 106 and 107) that border the altarpiece and stand like pilasters beneath the *Miracle of the Snow*, enlarge the references to the Immaculate Conception of the Virgin and her dedication to a spiritual life.[143] Anna dominates the birth chamber and her gesture of benediction casts a liturgical solemnity over the event that is intensified by the figure seated at the lower right, who appears to be more sibyl than attendant (Fig. 108). The compelling presence of this meditative woman confers on her the role of a physical and thematic bridge between the *Birth of the Virgin* and the adjacent *Annunciation*.

In facing the challenge of a mural program for the first time, Lorenzo Monaco depended heavily on the array of Tuscan cycles he could observe at every turn. In fact, there is hardly a major Florentine fresco master of the previous century from whom he did not derive some element. For the setting of the *Expulsion of Joachim* he turned to both Taddeo and Agnolo Gaddi, adopting Agnolo's simplified structure in the Sacro Cingolo cycle at Prato,[144] but using Taddeo's raked angle as a means of heightening the emotional content of the scene (Fig. 320). The figures in this lunette, however, exclusively acknowledge Taddeo in their shape and dramatic urgency. From his *Tree of Bonaventura*, also at Santa Croce, Lorenzo borrowed figurative types and a vocabulary of ornament. It is but a short step from Taddeo's seated *Luke* and *John the Evangelist* with their scrolls to the four *Prophets* in the vault of the Bartolini Salimbeni Chapel (Figs. 113 and 276). And the ornate frame of Taddeo's fresco, made up of vegetal forms alternated with geometric motifs and busts of prophets and saints, provided a model for the borders of Don Lorenzo's frescoes, although in keeping with the decorative taste of the early Quattrocento he wove the plant forms into the cursive patterns of rinceaux.[145] The lavish ornamentation of the choir books for Santa Maria degli Angeli had now migrated to the realm of fresco.

The derivations from other masters, while never so extensive or literal as from Taddeo Gaddi, are nonetheless easily discovered, the *Meeting of Joachim and Anna* being particularly rich in references. In spite of differences in context, the craggy islet and the boat seem to have been modelled after a similar passage in the *Legend of the Prince of Marseille* in the Rinuccini Chapel at Santa Croce.[146] For this same backdrop various works outside Florence were also culled. Spinello Aretino's *Saint Ephisius* legends at the Camposanto in Pisa could have provided the arched bridge leading from the city gate.[147] The panoramic cityscape rising above Joachim and Anna recalls the dense clusters of more minutely described buildings in Antonio Veneziano's *Saint Raynerius* cycle in Pisa and Taddeo di Bartolo's *Life of the Virgin* in the Cappella de'Signori in Siena.[148] By incorporating such a variety of architectural forms into his view of Jerusalem, Lorenzo now brought a semblance of descriptive realism to his fanciful cities, in contrast to the indefinable forms towering over the Prague *Lamentation* (Fig. 34) and the Berlin *Visitation* (Fig. 96). The abrupt convergence of castellated wall and jagged rocks has the closest analogy in a late fourteenth-century relief on the silver altar from the Cathedral of Florence (Fig. 318). These impulsive shifts from architecture to rock formations, a device used with more decorative ease in Lorenzo's predella panels, foretell Filippo Lippi's quirky changes of scene in the frescoes at Prato a quarter of a century later. Although the only specific reference to the *Life of the Virgin* cycle in the Chiostro dei Morti at Santa Maria Novella, by a follower of Nardo di Cione, is the angel hovering above the embracing Joachim and Anna, the abbreviated compositions of the *Birth of the Virgin* and *Presentation in the Temple* in that cycle, each contained in the restricted space of a half lunette, foreshadow Lorenzo's comparably narrow versions of the same episodes.[149] Nardo's art, however, does directly underlie the focal figure in the Santa Trinita frescoes: the tragic Christ from the Strozzi Chapel at Santa Maria Novella (Fig. 321) provided the mold from which the Virgin in the *Miracle of the Snow* was cast.

In the four lunettes of the Bartolini Salimbeni Chapel the subject matter and the shape of the picture field induced relatively simple symmetrical compositions, but in the two rectangular zones reserved for the *Meeting of Joachim and Anna* and the *Betrothal of the Virgin*, Lorenzo was challenged with more complex problems of design. Regardless of the differences in theme, these panoramic scenes depend directly on compositional aspects of the Uffizi *Adoration* (Fig. 82), which had been brought to completion only shortly before. In the *Betrothal of the Virgin* the long frieze of figures is an extended repetition of the isocephalic cluster of retainers at the center of the *Adoration*.[150] The diagonal movement from right to left along this frieze is reinforced by the sequential organization of the architecture in three distinct planes, concluding in the oblique vaulted baldachin at the left, in which the converging arches focus attention on the Virgin as the principal character of the episode. But the insistent leftward progression of figures and architecture is resisted by the reversed turn of a head or glance, the bend of a figure whose action is masked through damage, by the attention to the young psalterer, and by the brooding face in the rear rank (Fig. 110), perhaps a rejected suitor, but so intentionally confronting us as to imply a clandestine self-portrait. The striking assemblage of arcades, diaphragm arches, and vaults (Fig. 110), suggestive of passage from the entrance to the sanctuary of a church, is an enlargement on the bravura construction of the manger shed in the Uffizi *Adoration* (Fig. 83).[151] Such games of architectural form have their beginnings in early Sienese art, vividly in the work of Pietro Lorenzetti, where the complex structure of an interior may verge on subordinating the narrative (Fig. 323). In Lorenzo's composition, however, the figures and architecture are concentrated and isolated into distinct horizontal bands, which bisect the pictorial field rather too bluntly.[152] The *Meeting of Joachim and Anna* is likewise a tripartite composition, in which the plot evolves from left to right, traversing the seascape and the rounded and rectangular segments of the city wall. When a position is taken at the threshold of the chapel, it becomes apparent that the carefully plotted sequences within these two facing frescoes were intended to suggest progression toward the altar wall and the climactic moment of the *Annunciation*. The frescoed consoles that splay out between the lower narrative register and the fictive marble dado (Fig. 103) further imply convergence. These various means of directing the observer's attention are subtly reinforced by the lighting system within the frescoes of the side walls, where Don Lorenzo attained the fullest optical consistency discernible in any of his works. As the altar wall is windowless, light enters the chapel from the interior of the church, which is the direction of illumination implied in the frescoes by the arrangement of lights and darks on the side walls (see Figs. 105 and 109). In spite of this intimation of interest in constructing a unified environment, Lorenzo Monaco continued to shun the cast shadow that would have conveyed a more developed concern for the pictorial simulation of light as a natural phenomenon.

Turning from broader aspects of design to particulars of figure style, resemblance to Don Lorenzo's works on panel are again apparent. The women attending Anna in the *Meeting of Joachim* or the bystander in the *Expulsion of Joachim* have their nearest kin in the *Holy Women at the Tomb* above Angelico's *Deposition* (Fig. 90). And several personages in the Uffizi *Adoration* have assumed new roles in the frescoes: the high priest and Joseph of the *Betrothal* seem to have emerged from the retinue of the Magi, but the deeper pockets of drapery and the stronger accents of light and dark make the frescoes more ponderable. Calligraphic flourishes are further diminished, enhancing the integration of the figure into a spatial environment.

Although Don Lorenzo's designs underlie the individual compositions of the cycle, the extensive involvement of assistants is apparent from the varying quality of specific figural passages. A comparison of the head of Joseph in the *Betrothal* and of Joachim in the *Expulsion and Annunciation* lunette (Fig. 198) points up the inarticulate rendering and shallow expression of the latter, betraying the hand of an assistant, as do the faltering angels of the *Dormition* and *Assumption*. But assignment of the work in the Bartolini Salimbeni Chapel to Don Lorenzo or to his workshop must remain inconclusive because of the extensively eroded condition, the inherently collaborative nature of fresco technique, and the fact that Lorenzo was working here in a less familiar and more summary medium than tempera, with which he could indulge in the finest nuances of his brush.[153] He would seem to have concentrated his efforts in patriarchal types such as the high priest in the *Betrothal* and the Prophets of the vault, who are like enlargements of his art in the choir book.[154] The head of *Micah* (Fig. 117) is among Don Lorenzo's most trenchant images, a distant but unmistakable descendant of Giotto's noble Moors in the *Fire Ordeal* of the Bardi Chapel (Fig. 322). In their zealous responses, quickened by the restless shapes of robes and banderoles, the four Prophets at the crest of the chapel are reminiscent of Ghiberti's Evangelists, Church Fathers, and Prophets of the North Door.[155] In contrast, the gravity-bound figure at the base of the *Birth of the Virgin* (Fig. 108) confirms that early in the third decade of the Quattrocento Don Lorenzo was intimating the monumentality of form that would shortly be fulfilled on the walls of the Brancacci Chapel. As late as mid-century, Fra Filippo and Castagno would continue to reflect upon this grave matron.[156]

Although the technical demands of fresco painting may have presented exceptional problems in composition, the diluted watercolor medium induced further exploration of the secondary palette that Lorenzo had come to favor in the larger panel paintings of the late 1410s and early 1420s—the Accademia *Annunciation* and the Uffizi *Adoration*. The fullest chromatic range is encompassed in the *Betrothal of the Virgin* (Colorplate 15), with its interweaving and alternation of wine red washed to rose and pink, golden yellow shaded to brown, aquamarine, and dark and light violet. The whites and grays in the Virgin's dress, in the turbans and scarves, and in the highlights of the architecture are a neutral foil to this harmonious minor chord. The tones of rose and gray that predominate in draperies and architecture throughout the frescoes are carried into the borders that frame the rinceaux and into the marbled veneers of the painted dado. In the midst of these tonal delicacies stands the altarpiece aglow with the opulence of tempera and gold.

The structural unity of the altarpiece and fresco program in the Bartolini Salimbeni Chapel is apparent upon traversing the grille and confronting the altar wall (Figs. 102 and 120). The base of the main panel, with its long unbroken inscription,[157] forms a continuous line with the lower borders of the first register of frescoes; the pilasters abut the narrow pictorial fields on the wall at either side, accentuating the verticality of these compositions; and the central pinnacle extends upward to the lower border of the lunette.[158] Intentional correspondences in shape bring visual unity to the entrance arch, the lunette of the altar wall, and the triple arches of the altarpiece. This close integration of panel and fresco reinforces the function of the altarpiece as a thematic link between the earlier and later life of the Virgin depicted on the walls. The narrative begins with the *Annunciation* (Fig. 121) in the main panel as an immediate sequel to the *Betrothal* on the right wall, then continues across the predella from the *Visitation* at the left through the *Nativity* and *Adoration of the Magi*, to conclude with a literal exit from "stage right" in the *Flight into Egypt* (Figs. 124-127). A formal correspondence between the frescoes and altarpiece is recognized in the repeated poses and colors of the paired attendants of Anna and the Virgin in the nearly contiguous *Meeting of Joachim and Anna* fresco and *Visitation* predella (Figs. 105 and 124, and Colorplate 11). In the pinnacles three Prophets in roundels, of whom only *Isaiah* at the center is identifiable, respond to the encounter below with an array of gestures and glances (Figs. 121 and 201).

With his close adherence to iconographic traditions, it is not unexpected that Don Lorenzo's most ambitious treatment of the theme of the Annunciation should depend directly on that Sienese prototype that had come to prevail in Tuscan painting of the Trecento, wherein the Virgin is seated in an open portico and the Gabriel genuflects in a forecourt.[159] A further debt to a Sienese source is the painter's adoption of Ambrogio Lorenzetti's innovative iconography in his *Annunciation* of 1344 in the Pinacoteca at Siena; the response of the Virgin to Gabriel's pronouncement is directed heavenward as she prepares to receive the dove of the Holy Spirit who descends on a shaft of light.[160] In the fresco cycle and altarpiece of the Bartolini Salimbeni Chapel central theological implications of the subjects have been conveyed: in the *Life of the Virgin* her Immaculate Conception and in the episode of the *Annunciation* the doctrine of the Incarnation.[161]

If the iconography of Don Lorenzo's *Annunciation* has revealed a clear acceptance of tradition, the rendering of the scene is rife with the stylistic contradictions that mark this last phase of his art—just as they did the beginnings—and that he will come to resolve only in the smaller panels painted at the same moment. The arabesques of Gabriel's mantle and the ornamental silhouette of the Virgin are restated in the rhythmic contours of the pinnacles which are similar in shape to the flamboyant framing of the Uffizi *Adoration* (Fig. 82). In the *Adoration*, however, the rounded arches did not impede passage into the scene, whereas here the pointed and heavily cusped arches form a decorative barrier against the complex spatial organization that presented the greatest challenge to Lorenzo in designing the picture. These crowning elements of the frame seem anachronistic, to the point that the interruptive placement of the consoles in relation to the heads of Gabriel and the Virgin convey a sense that the composition may first have been envisioned in a rectangular field, not unlike the two principal frescoes of the side walls.[162] Lorenzo's preoccupation with spatial effect is evident in the way the conventional pairing of portico and courtyard is surrounded by illusionistic devices. Behind the Virgin's bench a narrow corridor leads from the picture plane through an exit to some undefined

PLATE 13. Lorenzo Monaco, *Annunciate Virgin*, detail of the *Annunciation Altarpiece*, Bartolini Salimbeni Chapel, Santa Trinita, Florence.

PLATE 14. Lorenzo Monaco, *The Magi and Retinue*, detail of the *Adoration of the Magi*, Uffizi, Florence.

PLATE 15. Lorenzo Monaco, *Betrothal of the Virgin* (detail), Bartolini Salimbeni Chapel, Santa Trinita, Florence.

PLATE 16. Lorenzo Monaco, *Flight into Egypt*, predella of the *Annunciation Altarpiece*, Bartolini Salimbeni Chapel, Santa Trinita, Florence.

place, upper chambers are suggested in the ambiguous hints of architecture above the portico, and the single arch of the forecourt conveys the penetrability of the gold background.[163] The principal exercise in spatial illusion is in the progression through the central doorway to an inner room—as chaste and undomestic as a monk's cell—and thence to a garden. A stand of three trees framed by the doorway implies the *hortus conclusus* and, because of the placement of this detail exactly between Gabriel and the Virgin and below the seraphic vision, may also symbolize the Trinity.[164] A strictly patterned floor provides a continuous platform that ties the disparate spatial units of the composition. The rectilinearity of this architectural setting offsets, or better alienates, the florid lines concentrated in the Gabriel, who is like a visitor on foreign soil; his convoluted mantle and vaulting spread of wings would be more in harmony with the abstract realm of the Accademia *Annunciation*. The splendor of his wine-red and rose mantle and parti-colored wings and the brilliant accent of vermilion in the quartet of seraphim contrast sharply with the refined details of gold ornament clustered around the Virgin, a precious metaphor of the grace shed upon her (Colorplate 13). But the Virgin's connection with the world of the worshiper is gently implied by the slight tumble of her mantle over the edge of the floor, recalling Simone Martini's similarly momentary illusionistic device in the Uffizi *Annunciation*.

In the predella of the Bartolini Chapel altarpiece Lorenzo Monaco achieved the unity of style that had eluded him in the main panel and, to a lesser degree, in the frescoes, revealing once again that he materialized his vision most successfully in an intimate format. The painter's concern with spatial illusion and continuity is as apparent in the predella as in the *Annunciation* above. The *Nativity* and *Adoration* (Figs. 125 and 126) evolve on a continuous stage, with only a vertical band of painted gold filigree dividing the long central panel into its two episodes. The tilted ground plane runs through all four scenes, as does the dense forest backdrop, and in each of the panels there is a structure that amplifies the coherence of space. In the *Visitation* (Fig. 124) the extended oblique of the architecture defines a deep ground plane bracketed at the opposite side by a rocky mass, a spare means of building a stage that may have more than an accidental likeness to Donatello's relief of *Saint George Slaying the Dragon* from Orsanmichele (Fig. 325). Could the beckoning corridor at the right of the *Annunciation* also derive from Donatello's similar if more cerebral device in the *Saint George* relief? In the *Nativity*, as in the Accademia predella (Fig. 94), the shed is turned obliquely against the picture plane to form a container for the figures and the manger, which is constructed on another perspective. How fundamentally different this setting is from the manger sheds in the Lehman *Nativity* (Fig. 30) and in the predella of the Uffizi *Coronation* (Fig. 51), which were simply extensions of the central angle of the quatrefoil. In the *Adoration of the Magi* the rectangular frame and the stark parapet and wing architecture combine to shape a simple stage around the players. As in the *Coronation* predella of a decade earlier (Fig. 52), an onlooker appears at the gateway, but he now observes the mystery of the Epiphany from outside the pale, recalling Joseph's transfixed gaze toward the manger in the adjoining panel or the observer's glimpse of the inner room of the *Annunciation*. And finally among the devices to evoke space, the Virgin's dais and bench in the *Adoration* lead directly to the gushing trough in the *Flight* (Fig. 127). This depiction of the miraculous spring that provided the Holy Family with water in the wilderness also substantiates the corridor of land through which they pass.[165]

The figures in these four predella panels reveal a new simplicity that matches the unambiguous nature of the space. When the Holy Family and Magi of the *Coronation* and Bartolini Chapel predellas are compared, it is apparent that in the latter the interaction of figures is no longer imposed from without through a system of linear rhythms but now seems to evolve from an armature within each participant. Don Lorenzo had initiated this change in the *Blessing Redeemer* of the *Coronation* (Fig. 48), developing it further in the *Adoration of the Magi* (Fig. 86), as had Ghiberti in the later reliefs of the North Door (Fig. 311). Drapery contours respond with a new resiliency to the physical existence of the figure; they tauten with the reach of an arm or fold under the pressure of kneeling or leaning postures. The tempera medium is now more charged; the open brushwork weaves a lively pattern of hatched and stippled textures. Contrasts of light and dark heighten dramatic effect and lend tangibility to forms in an ample space. Throughout the Bartolini Salimbeni Chapel, but most emphatically in this masterful predella, Lorenzo Monaco displays an emerging sympathy with his more progressive contemporaries of the third decade of the Quattrocento in their quest for means of representing the essentials of visually perceived reality. At the beginning of his work as a painter in the last years of the Trecento, Don Lorenzo had been confronted by a comparable stylistic dichotomy in which the Giottesque revival had countered the realm of Cionesque abstraction with new dimensions of mass and space. Completing the circle, the Bartolini Chapel predella now provides the clearest testimony that the painter had begun to veer from the denials of gravity and the excursions into fantasy that had most fully captured his imagination less than half a decade earlier.[166]

Nonetheless, Don Lorenzo's decorative and dramatic power as a colorist are never more in evidence than in the four scenes of this final predella, one of the supreme inventions of his palette. In the *Visitation* (Colorplate 11), the elegant juxtaposition of blue and lavender in the robes of the Virgin and Elizabeth—a lingering echo of Duccio—is enclosed by intense notes of coral red in the thrusting wall and the attendant at the left. In the *Flight into Egypt* (Colorplate 16) at the opposite end of the predella, there is a similar contrast between the muted blue and gray of the Virgin and beast and the bright rose and golden yellow of the handmaid and Joseph. This continuous frieze of light-bathed color is silhouetted against the neutral grays and browns of the ground plane and rock forms, and the backdrop of forest-green trees touched by accents of yellow foliage. The mysteries of the Infancy cycle beckon "on a darkling plain." Light and color persist as vehicles of a private and rapturous spirituality.

In the same years he was occupied with the decoration of the Bartolini Salimbeni Chapel, Lorenzo Monaco painted a group of works that stands, along with the predella of the *Annunciation* altarpiece, as his last artistic testament. The diminutive panels of the *Madonna of Humility* and *Saint Jerome in His Study* (Figs. 128 and 129), which originally formed a diptych, are exhibited separately in Copenhagen and Amsterdam. Jerome stands in his study and gazes downward at the pleading lion, his hand poised to extract a thorn with a quill sharpener, as the blood streams from the wounded paw to the hem of his habit. Don Lorenzo cast Jerome in the role of a scholar-monk, with tonsure and cowl, accompanied by the shelves of books that symbolize his scholarship. The intersecting architectural forms of the study and the adjoining lectern, beneath which his cardinal's hat is suspended, recall the complex play of perspectives in the manger of the Uffizi *Adoration*; this wedgelike niche that frames Jerome is, in fact, among the painter's most sophisticated spatial inventions. Caught in a moment between thought and action, the saint could also be seen as pondering the concept of the Virgin's humility.[167] Mother and Child exist in the nonspatial realm of the adjoining panel, a domain that gains in abstractness by contrast with the insistent spatial devices of the saint's study. The rounded arch tooled into the gold ground encompasses the figures like an aureole to heighten the transcendental nature of their presence. The chromatic dialogue between the two panels reveals Lorenzo Monaco at the summit of his powers as a colorist. The asceticism of Jerome's brownish gray habit is relieved by the bright notes of vermilion and light and dark blue in the cardinal's hat and in the books aligned or scattered over the shelves and lectern. The salmon pink of the ground plane further alleviates the sobriety of Jerome's demeanor and garb. In a deft reversal of palette, the gray floor plane beneath the Virgin provides a foil for the clear azure of her mantle lined in golden yellow. This poignant diptych served the same needs of private devotion as did the Fitzwilliam *Madonna Enthroned* or the Prague-Paris triptych (Figs. 15, 33, and 34), intimately scaled works that were never intended for the scrutiny of the public eye, to which even Don Lorenzo's most deeply personal predella scenes had to submit.

While working on the reduced scale of predella and diptych, Lorenzo Monaco turned for the last time to the art of book painting. Among the miniatures in a choir book for Santa Maria Nuova, now in the Bargello (Cod. E 70), there is a figure of *Saint Anthony Abbot* (Fig. 131) in which the painter's hand may be recognized in spite of the eroded condition. His brush had never been more agile or suggestive in applying the tempera medium. The figure is a tissue of hatched and stippled strokes, made to seem even more fragile in being caught between the double crossbar of the letter. If the closest relative of *Saint Anthony* is the contemporary *Jerome* in Amsterdam, his ancestors are the *Jerome* and *Romuald* in the choir books painted for Santa Maria degli Angeli some thirty years before (Figs. 1 and 4). Those earliest of Don Lorenzo's works were impersonal icons wrought from external symbols and the trappings of old age. The inner life now stirring in the late image of *Saint Anthony* is an intimate summary of the artistic and spiritual growth of Lorenzo Monaco, on the threshold of an era in which painters and sculptors would probe ever more deeply into the physical and psychological existence of the individual. The pensive *Anthony*, the founder of monasticism, may stand as a spiritual self-portrait of the artist at the end of his work.

INFLUENCES AND ECHOES

DURING A CAREER that evolved over three decades, Lorenzo Monaco designed and was active in painting the major commissions and intimate works that have been the subject of this essay. Soon after his emergence from Santa Maria degli Angeli his newly founded workshop began the production of devotional pictures that continued unabated, while Don Lorenzo was primarily occupied with projects on a larger scale. As numerous works in Catalogue I reveal, the modulations in his personal style are mirrored concurrently in the host of Madonnas Enthroned, Madonnas of Humility, and cutout crucifixes that were the prevailing images turned out by the workshop, with the master's collaboration or as the independent effort of assistants.[168] This workshop activity must have ceased virtually upon Don Lorenzo's death, for no major or minor pictures in his distinctive style can be dated after the middle of the 1420s; the idiom of the shop, which had been a counterforce to conservative Trecento forms that survived deep into the new century, had become anachronistic. There is perhaps an intimation of the changing status of Lorenzo Monaco among Florentine painters in the document of 1422 (Document 17) that pointedly commissions a work for the Duomo from Don Lorenzo or from an equal or better painter. Strong confirmation that Lorenzo Monaco and his workshop were rapidly supplanted can be seen in the fact that in 1431 the Dominican Fra Angelico was commissioned to paint a *Last Judgment* for Santa Maria degli Angeli, a picture intended for a new oratory to be used in a Camaldolese celebration of singular importance—the naming of Ambrogio Traversari as Abbot General of the Order.[169]

A brief measure of the nature of Don Lorenzo's impact may be taken by observing a few works by Quattrocento painters who range from eclectic minor masters to major names in Renaissance art. The adoption of a rhythmic linearism toward the middle of the first decade of the century in the work of painters who had remained grounded in more stolid forms of the later Trecento was seen to be accountable to Ghiberti and Starnina as well as to Lorenzo Monaco. Nonetheless, there were conservative painters working far into the new century for whom the style of Lorenzo Monaco was the immediate source of transformation. This was true of Lorenzo di Niccolò in two versions of the *Madonna Enthroned* (Figs. 327 and 328). The earlier picture, from around 1400, is an additive assemblage of static segments, to which a mild fluttering in the Virgin's mantle adds a modicum of rhythmic play, whereas in the later work, dated 1412, a single pictorial gesture brings the Virgin and Child into a harmonious unity. The model was inevitably Don Lorenzo's Monte Oliveto Altarpiece, dated 1410 (Fig. 23), to which Lorenzo di Niccolò introduced a note of variation by reversing the arched shape of the Infant.[170]

An unusual and informative aspect of Don Lorenzo's influence is the literal copying of that same Monte Oliveto Altarpiece by the eclectic Andrea di Giusto. In composing the main register of a polyptych in Prato, dated 1435, Andrea looked back to Lorenzo's work of a quarter of a century earlier (cf. Figs. 22 and 329). But he caricatured the model into a papery insubstantiality and, with a small adjustment of features and symbols, Lorenzo's Saint Thaddeus assumed the role of Saint Margaret. Only slightly less direct a quotation is found in the *Nativity* at the center of the predella where Andrea combined two versions of the subject from different moments of Don Lorenzo's work—the predellas of the *Coronation of the Virgin* of 1414 and the *Annunciation* at Santa Trinita of nearly a decade later (Figs. 51 and 125)—while elsewhere in the narrative scenes there are literal adoptions from Fra Angelico.[171] This same ambivalence underlies the works of other minor masters. The lateral figures in the triptych by Francesco d'Antonio in the Fitzwilliam Museum (Fig. 330) descend directly from Starnina, whereas the central panel is yet another variation on the Monte Oliveto Altarpiece. In his frescoes of circa 1418 at Figline (Fig. 331) Francesco responded to the exactly contemporary Accademia *Annunciation* (Fig. 79), without capturing a trace of the ballon of Don Lorenzo's most lyrical panel. In the 1420s Francesco d'Antonio abandoned Lorenzo Monaco for other models, vacillating between the polarities of Gentile da Fabriano and Masaccio.[172] Stylistic heterogeneity also pervades the art of Giovanni dal Ponte and Parri Spinelli, but they are to be approached as rare individuals rather than minor eclectics; the rhythms and fantasy they discovered in the imagery of Lorenzo Monaco were reshaped into a heated expressionism.[173]

On ascending to the higher artistic plane of Masolino and Fra Angelico, we confront the unresolved questions with regard to their sources in the stylistic cultures of early Quattrocento Florence.[174] In varying degrees the art of Lorenzo Monaco is recognizable among the forces that shaped their styles. The calligraphic flourishes of Masolino's *Madonna of Humility* in Munich (Fig. 332), from no later than 1425, are an obvious recollection of Don Lorenzo's liveliest rhythms, a decorative linearism that only faintly veils Masolino's intensifying concern for ponderable form. With the fresco of the *Man of Sorrows* at Empoli (Fig. 333) Masolino acknowledged Don Lorenzo's potent icon of twenty years earlier (Fig. 18) and the pathos of the San Giovannino dei Cavalieri *Crucifixion* (Fig. 74), but the expressive vehicle has been decisively transformed from line into mass.[175]

The choir of angels that wreathes the Virgin and Child in Fra Angelico's first major altarpiece for San Domenico in Fiesole would seem to have been a conscious reminiscence of Don Lorenzo's *Coronation of the Virgin* at Santa Maria degli Angeli, and the fall of the Virgin's mantle is a moment of mellifluous linearism that will soon have little place in Angelico's formal idiom.[176] He would continue to quote from Lorenzo's works, for example, in the *Madonna Enthroned* at San Marco (Fig. 334), which is dependent on the Monte Oliveto Altarpiece and on later pictures by Lorenzo Monaco and his shop,[177] or in the central pinnacle of the Cortona polyptych (Fig. 335), which descends from the San Giovannino group. Angelico's use of color, however, was now inseparably bound to the shaping of palpable forms by minute gradations of light and shade; the refinement of the chiaroscuro technique suffuses three-dimensional mass with a translucence that is distinct from the intention and method of Lorenzo Monaco.[178] Light as an optically perceived phenomenon, tenuously implied in Don Lorenzo's later works, now definitively supplanted transcendental radiance. We may confirm Fra Angelico's mysteries with the eye and the hand, and his narratives, though inspired by the intimate predellas of Lorenzo Monaco, are enacted in Florentine cloisters and the Tuscan countryside rather than in the anonymous and timeless places where Don Lorenzo's stories occur. Finally, it is the architectonic coherence and spiritual serenity in the art of Fra Angelico that divulge a different interior life than was experienced by Lorenzo Monaco.

Although the artistic beginnings of Fra Filippo Lippi have been the source of a long-continuing debate, Don Lorenzo must be seen to have exerted essential and varied influences on the young Carmelite.[179] In contrast to the undisturbed modulations of Angelico's surfaces, Filippo intensified the vigorous hatching that had enlivened and illuminated Don Lorenzo's expressive forms. Fra Filippo, moreover, indulged in the juxtapositions of muted secondary and primary hues that mark the later technique of Lorenzo Monaco, though Lippi's impulse was toward a heightened physical presence. Even in his obvious reuse of those finely spun edges of drapery that had their most virtuosic elaboration in Don Lorenzo's Uffizi *Adoration of the Magi*, Fra Filippo adapted them to the illusion of a fuller substantiality of the figure in space.[180]

A clear if distant echo of Don Lorenzo's lyricism and fantasy, though transmuted by the forces of Quattrocento realism, resounded in the art of Sandro Botticelli. The convoluted and diaphanous Gabriel in his Uffizi *Annunciation* (Fig. 336) is alien to the rigorously perspectival environment, recalling the uneasy archangel of Don Lorenzo's Santa Trinita altarpiece (Fig. 121).[181] And as with the Accademia *Annunciation* (Fig. 79), the nexus of Botticelli's drama lies in the eloquent interval between the approaching Gabriel and the responding Virgin. The floating archangel in Don Lorenzo's rapturous image reverberates in the drawing of Beatrice in Canto VI of the *Paradiso* (Fig. 337), where Botticelli implied the most weightless of Annunciation iconographies for the climactic dialogue with Dante. Buoyant forms, stirred by a spiritual passion, materialize Lorenzo Monaco's sacred messenger and Botticelli's heavenly sphere.

NOTES

1. Don Lorenzo's passage through the novitiate, minor orders, and major orders from 1390 to 1396 is recorded in Documents 1A and 1B.

2. For example, Sirén, 1905, pp. 12-13; and van Marle, vol. 9, 1927, pp. 115-16.

3. Henriette Mendelsohn (p. 23) emphasized that before the Council of Trent there was no fixed age for the profession of solemn vows, referring to the study of Canon Law by J. B. Sägmüller (*Lehrbuch der katholischen Kirchenrechts*, Freiburg i.B., 1904, p. 736). Filippo Lippi professed solemn vows in June of 1421, at the age of fourteen or fifteen. Also see Marchini, 1975, p. 231. Although the focus is entirely on North European monastic practice, an informative study of the wide range of ages at the time of entrance into the novitiate is Dom U. Berlière, "Le recrutement dans les monastères bénédictins aux XIIIe et XIVe siècles," *Mémoires, Académie Royale de Belgique* (Classe des Lettres), ser. 2, 18, 1924, pp. 3-66, passim.

4. The attempt by Hans Gronau (p. 218, note 12) to establish Lorenzo's birth date circa 1367 was based on his view that the painter's death occurred by 1422 and his acceptance of Vasari's statement that he died at the age of fifty-five (see Note 17 below). This earlier birth date helped to accommodate Gronau's attribution to Lorenzo Monaco of a major altarpiece completed by 1387-88, the polyptych for the Nobili Chapel at Santa Maria degli Angeli. (See Catalogue II, Paris, Louvre, *Feast of Herod*. . . .)

5. See Documents 4A-4G. As Poggi noted (1904, pp. 200-201), the altarpiece by Lorenzo Monaco was for the second chapel established at the Carmine by Chiaro Ardinghelli, which was placed under the supervision of the Compagnia del Bigallo. Poggi dispelled a confusion begun by Milanesi (Vasari, vol. 2, 1878, p. 20, note 1; followed by Sirén, 1905, pp. 19-20 and p. 181, VII) that placed Don Lorenzo's altarpiece in the first Ardinghelli chapel at the Carmine, which was dedicated to the Annunciation and prescribed as the location of Chiaro Ardinghelli's tomb. Poggi observed (p. 201) that the second chapel was dedicated to Christ and the Virgin, and was under the patronage of Saints Nicholas, Martin, Margaret, and Catherine of Alexandria. Therefore, the subject of Lorenzo's lost Ardinghelli Chapel altarpiece was probably the Virgin and Child accompanied by the four patron saints and not the Annunciation, as was claimed by Milanesi and Sirén. For further documents on the second Ardinghelli Chapel, which record the installation of the altar and altarpiece by the artisan Nicolao ser Lari and paintings by Lorenzo di Salvi (apparently frescoes for the chapel), see Poggi, 1904, pp. 237-38. Don Lorenzo's altarpiece is noted in an inventory of 1437 which lists the contents of the Ardinghelli Chapel (Document 4F). The last notice of the altarpiece is in 1689 when it is mentioned as being in an oratory at the Carmine, having been moved there from the Ardinghelli Chapel, which was now under the patronage of the Marzichi family (Document 4G). It may be conjectured that the altarpiece was destroyed in the fire at the Carmine in 1771. The history of the two Ardinghelli Chapels is reviewed in Paatz, vol. 3, 1952, pp. 220-21 and 285-86, note 214; also noted is the continuing misidentification of the subject of Don Lorenzo's altarpiece as an Annunciation (p. 285, note 214, with bibliographical citations); further, see Procacci, 1932, p. 166.

Although there lacks conclusive proof, it is reasonable to believe that the "Piero di Giovanni," from the parish of San Michele Visdomini, who is listed in the Company of Painters in 1396 (Document 3), refers to Lorenzo Monaco. A "Piero di Giovanni" is again listed in the Company of Painters in 1402 (Document 6), years after Don Lorenzo had taken his monastic name, which is used in all of the known documents that relate to his activity as a painter. The awarding to Lorenzo Monaco of so important a commission as the Ardinghelli Chapel altarpiece at the moment of his emergence from Santa Maria degli Angeli suggests that a major panel such as the

Agony in the Garden (Fig. 7), which would seem to have been painted while he was still resident at the monastery, provided important evidence of his artistic competence. If the Carmine Polyptych (Figs. 215 and 217-23; Zeri, 1964/65, II, figs. 1-9 and 11) is accepted as the work of Lorenzo Monaco and did originate at the Carmine, this earliest major project by him would have provided further proof of his skill while still at Santa Maria degli Angeli, and would have been known to the Ardinghelli when Don Lorenzo was chosen to paint the altarpiece for their second family chapel at the Carmine (see Catalogue II, Florence, Accademia, *Saint Jerome; Saint John the Baptist . . .*).

See Note 17 for Vasari's notice of works by Lorenzo Monaco in the Ardinghelli Chapel at Santa Trinita in Florence.

6. The date of Lorenzo's departure from Santa Maria degli Angeli cannot be established with certainty, but must have occurred after February 26, 1396, when he was ordained deacon, and before the end of 1399. Appended to the document of 1391, the record of Lorenzo's entry into minor orders, is a note written in a different hand which reports that Lorenzo had left the monastery; only the first two numbers of the year are given (*partissi dì . . . di . . . 13 . . .*). In the first publication of the document the "13–" was omitted from the transcription (Sirén, 1905, p. 179). Mirella Levi D'Ancona proposed that Lorenzo left the monastery by May 5, 1398, as his name does not appear on a list of witnesses to a notarial document drawn up at the monastery on that date, whereas he is named on a comparable list in 1394 ("Some New Attributions," 1958, p. 175, note 2; see Document 2). In a later study, Levi D'Ancona hypothesised that Don Lorenzo left the monastery in 1396 (1961, p. 86). The first documented notice of Don Lorenzo's maintaining residence outside the monastery is in March of 1402, when he is recorded as being domiciled in the parish of San Bartolo del Corso (Document 5).

For evidence of the activity of monks and seculars in the workshop, see the discussion of the inscription on the *Coronation of the Virgin* for Santa Maria degli Angeli (p. 4) and Documents 16D and 16F. Wackernagel (Luchs trans., 1981, p. 307) observed an essential difference between the commissioning of works from Don Lorenzo and from Fra Angelico, noting that the cloistered Dominican artist let the business administrators of his conventual house negotiate outside commissions and settle subsequent financial accounts, while Don Lorenzo, who maintained his monastic status outside the cloister, was directly involved with commissions and payments, to the extent that he was permitted to live on the income from the production of his workshop. Baldini noted that documented payments to Fra Angelico were in effect directed to his religious community (1970, p. 83, 1423).

7. See Documents 7-10 and 12-17.

8. See Documents 8A and 8B.

9. See Document 11. Sirén (1905, p. 13) cited this document as proof that Lorenzo was born in Siena and had his artistic roots there. Pudelko adopted this conclusion and also repeated Milanesi's undocumented report that Lorenzo was in Rome in 1402 (1938/39, p. 237; Vasari, ed. Milanesi, vol. 2, 1878, p. 31). Without providing the source of information, Luisa Marcucci stated that the monks at Santa Maria degli Angeli were mostly Sienese (p. 137). Don Gregorio Farulli gives no indication of this in his early comprehensive history of Santa Maria degli Angeli (1710), citing more connections with Pisa and Arezzo than with Siena. Rosalba Amerio (col. 337) noted that a Piero di Giovanni appears in the civil registers of Siena for 1370/71; documentary reference is not provided.

10. See Document 12.

11. See Documents 16A-16G, and Catalogue I, Florence, Uffizi, *Adoration of the Magi*. I have found no documentary evidence to support Milanesi's claim that in 1417 Lorenzo Monaco painted the cover for a bier for the Florentine Compagnia di Gesù Pellegrino (Vasari, vol. 2, 1878, p. 32).

12. See Document 17. The repeated proposal that the *Saint Lawrence* altarpiece, attributed to the Maestro del Bambino Vispo, was executed to meet this commission has been convincingly dismissed by Waadenoijen in summoning evidence that the polyptych was located in the Certosa at Galluzzo (1974, p. 89). The tentative suggestion by Levi D'Ancona that the *Saint Lawrence* altarpiece from the Louvre, now in the Musée du Petit Palais at Avignon, may have been the work installed in the Duomo, did not reconcile the date of 1407 recorded for that altarpiece ("Matteo Torelli," 1958, pp. 254-55; see Catalogue II, Avignon, Musée du Petit Pa-

lais, *Saint Lawrence Enthroned, with Saints Ansanus and Margaret*).

13. See Document 16G.

14. See Catalogue I, Florence, Uffizi, *Adoration of the Magi*.

15. See Document 1B.

16. The deaths of monks and nuns were not recorded in the civil registers of Florence (*Libro dei Morti*); monastic ledgers contained such records (e.g., see Levi D'Ancona, 1962, p. 238, for the full date of the death of Don Silvestro dei Gherarducci, the major painter at Santa Maria degli Angeli in the generation before Lorenzo Monaco, who was also prior of the monastery at the time of his death in 1399).

For Don Lorenzo's works in the Bartolini Salimbeni Chapel at Santa Trinita, I propose a dating of circa 1422 to 1423, that is, immediately after the Uffizi *Adoration of the Magi*, which is very possibly the altarpiece for Saint'Egidio for which final payment was made in August 1422 (see Document 16G). The extensive involvement of the workshop in the execution of the fresco program at Santa Trinita, and the fact that Don Lorenzo left incomplete an altarpiece for the Sacristy-Chapel in that same church, may be indicative of his waning health or death, although this observation is speculative (see Catalogue I, Florence, Museo di San Marco, *Resurrection of Christ* . . .).

Levi D'Ancona (1962, p. 173) published from the *Ricordanze* of Santa Maria Nuova a notice of 1426 that lists the re-renting of a house "dove sta il Monacho," proposing therefrom that Don Lorenzo's death had occurred by that year (p. 171). In no other known document is Don Lorenzo referred to as "il Monacho." In 1415 he had purchased a house "a vita" across from Santa Maria degli Angeli (Document 11), which he apparently used as workshop and residence, and which was to revert to the ownership of the monastery at his death. As is indicated in Document 2, the renting of houses in Florence by the Monastery of Santa Maria degli Angeli was a sufficiently common practice to warrant specific mention in a general notarial act with regard to the appointment of legal proxies.

17. 1550/1568, Vasari, ed. Bettarini and Barocchi, Text, pp. 303-307. Vasari considered the art of Lorenzo Monaco to have its source in the style of Taddeo Gaddi and his tradition (p. 304 [1568]: ". . . questo monaco pittore, il quale tenne la maniera di Taddeo Gaddi e degl'altri suoi . . ."). In both versions of the *Vite*, Vasari reports that Don Lorenzo died at the age of fifty-five after long suffering from a severe abscess, but only in the edition of 1550 does he claim that the abscess was the result of the painter's habitual bending and leaning during his work ("Finalmente, per lo star chinato e col petto appoggiato, gli venne una postema crudele, la quale in lungo termine lo condusse al fine di sua vita di età d'anni LV." [p. 305]). In the *Vite* of 1568, Vasari states that Don Lorenzo was buried in the chapter house at Santa Maria degli Angeli, but he omits from this revised version the colorful report found in the 1550 edition, that Lorenzo Monaco was honored for his talent by the preservation of his hands as relics at the monastery (". . . e molto fu da essi stimato in vita et oggi dopo morte tengono i frati negli Agnoli le mani di esso come reliquie per memoria di lui"; ed. Bettarini and Barocchi, Text, pp. 304-305). In the 1568 version of the biography of Lorenzo Monaco, Vasari reports instead that a tabernacle at Santa Maria degli Angeli contains the right hands of Don Jacopo and Don Silvestro, Camaldolese of generations preceding Don Lorenzo, who were highly regarded for their ornamented choir books (for speculation on this matter by later editors of Vasari, see ed. Bettarini and Barocchi, Commentary, pp. 721-22). Righi and Landi observed (p. 397) that Vasari's omission of mention of Don Lorenzo's work as a miniaturist from the 1568 edition is consistent with his general disregard for the art of book illustration, unless it approached the character of monumental painting. Vasari does, however, praise the lavish choir books by Don Jacopo and Don Silvestro, reporting that Pope Leo X lauded their works to the extent that he would have acquired some for the use of Rome if they had not been so specifically in the service of the Camaldolese liturgy (ed. Bettarini and Barocchi, Text, p. 306).

Although there is documentary proof that Lorenzo Monaco was commissioned to paint an altarpiece for the second Ardinghelli Chapel at the Carmine (see Documents 4A-4G), Vasari claimed that he painted the frescoes and altarpiece for the Ardinghelli Chapel at Santa Trinita. The frescoes, now only in fragmentary state, are known to be the work of Giovanni Toscani (see Bellosi, 1966, pp. 50-51). For a comprehensive study of the problem of the altarpiece for the Ardinghelli Chapel at Santa Trinita, also the work of Giovanni Toscani, see Padoa Rizzo, pp. 5-10. Before Vasari, a few works were attributed to Don Lorenzo by Francesco Albertini, Antonio Billi, and the Anonimo Gaddiano (see Catalogue I, Florence, Uffizi, *Coronation of the Virgin*, and Santa Trinita, Bartolini Salimbeni Chapel, *Life of the Virgin*; also see the Appendix to the Catalogue). The appellation "Don Lorenzo Monaco" began with Vasari's 1568 edition of the *Vite*, where the title of the painter's biography is "Vita di Don Lorenzo Monaco degli Angeli di Firenze, Pittore," whereas in the 1550 edition the title is "Fra' Lorenzo degli Agnoli, Pittor fiorentino" (see Vasari, ed. Bettarini and Barocchi, Text, p. 303). Don Lorenzo Monaco or Don Lorenzo remained the standard forms of the painter's name until Gaye first omitted the monastic title, coining the name Lorenzo Monaco, which gradually became the more usual form of citation (see Catalogue I, Florence, Uffizi, *Coronation of the Virgin Altarpiece*, Literature, 1840).

18. See the Appendix to the Catalogue. For mention of Lorenzo Monaco by early writers on the history of the Camaldolese, see Agostino Fortunio, 1579, p. 126, and Don Gregorio Farulli, 1710, p. 31. The full texts of their brief notices on Lorenzo Monaco were published by Sirén (1905, pp. 180-81). There are no known documented bases for the statement by Fortunio that Don Lorenzo died in 1419, or Farulli's assertion that the painter's family name was Albizi [*sic*]. The only mention of Don Lorenzo in the *Annales Camaldulenses* (Mittarelli and Costadoni, pp. 190, and 278-79) is a brief quotation from Vasari with regard to a predecessor at Santa Maria degli Angeli—the scribe "Jacobus"—and a repetition of Fortunio's undocumented death date, misread however as 1429.

19. In 1844, Carlo Pini and Gaetano Milanesi wrote the first critical observations on the style of Lorenzo Monaco, focussing their brief remarks on a comparison with the work of Fra Angelico (Delécluze, p. 53, note 1, and p. 87, note 1). They singled out the *Coronation of the Virgin* for Santa Maria degli Angeli, which they saw at the Badia di San Pietro at Cerreto, as the touchstone of Lorenzo's work. The frescoes of the Bartolini Salimbeni Chapel at Santa Trinita were unknown to them, as the walls were still covered with a layer of whitewash. In 1861, A.-F. Rio (p. 323) characterized Don Lorenzo's art as part of a mystical trend that stood in opposition to Florentine naturalism of the first half of the fifteenth century. Rio associated Gentile da Fabriano and Fra Angelico with the same "école Mystique." Crowe and Cavalcaselle first brought the work of Lorenzo Monaco into the stream of fourteenth- and fifteenth-century Florentine painting (1864, vol. 1, pp. 551-56). For Roger Fry's early responses to Lorenzo Monaco, see below, Note 131. Adolfo Venturi's few but eloquent pages on Don Lorenzo concentrate on the ascetic monastic spirituality that pervades his traditional religious imagery (1911, pp. 3-19). Venturi refers to Sirén's recently published monograph and to the Berenson Lists of 1909 for the corpus of Don Lorenzo's works (p. 19, note 1).

Among J. A. Ramboux's notebook drawings of Italian paintings, executed from 1818 to 1822, and 1833 to 1843 (Städelsches Kunstinstitut, Frankfurt a.M.), there are eight sketches of works by Lorenzo Monaco or from his milieu: vol. IV, p. 117, *Nativity*, Pinacoteca Vaticana, Rome (Fig. 256); vol. V, p. 55, *Coronation of the Virgin*, National Gallery, London (center panel; then at Elmo, near Cerreto; Fig. 175); vol. V, p. 57, *Coronation of the Virgin*, Uffizi, Florence (then at the Badia di San Pietro, Cerreto; Fig. 44); vol. V, p. 58, *Saint Benedict* (upper half of figure), from the main panel of the Uffizi *Coronation* (Fig. 44); vol. V, p. 54, *Death of Saint Benedict*, from the predella of the Uffizi *Coronation* (Fig. 49); vol. V, p. 56, composite drawing, Kneeling Virgin from the *Nativity* and *Saint Benedict with Saint Scholastica*, from the predella of the Uffizi *Coronation* (Figs. 51 and 57); vol. V, p. 59, Holy Family and Magi from the *Adoration of the Magi*, predella of the Uffizi *Coronation* (Fig. 52); vol. VI, p. 32, *Madonna in Glory*, center panel of the triptych in the Pinacoteca Nazionale, Siena (Fig. 132).

20. Another Camaldolese who was notable in juridical history was Pope Gregory IX (1227-1241), the author of the *Decretals* (see Donati, p. 49). Prior to the generation of later fourteenth-century painters active at Santa Maria degli Angeli, there is no record of a significant artist in the Order. The most distinguished Camaldolese painter after Lorenzo Monaco was Bartolommeo della Gatta (1448-1502), who was mainly active in Arezzo after entering the Order (Mittarelli and Costadoni, p. 279).

21. Farulli (1710, pp. 2-7 and 19) records that the building of Santa Maria degli Angeli was approved by the Chapter at Camaldoli in 1295. He also relates that twenty-one monks died in the plague of 1348, leaving only seven survivors at the monastery. In

1378, during the papal Interdict and the Ciompi uprising, the monastery was sacked (see below, Note 25). In discussing the losses of liturgical books, Levi D'Ancona (1979, p. 461) states that Santa Maria degli Angeli was burned during the incursion of the late seventies, but Del Migliore (p. 332) reported that the monastery, although sacked, was saved from fire by a seemingly miraculous intervention: ". . . essendosi staccato un di quelli correndo per lo Monasterio cercando fuoco per abbruciarlo, e fu miracolo non seguisse, perchè quelli prima che' giugnesse ad una Lampana accesa in una di quelle Cappelle nascoste, ella da per se stessa si spense." For the sequential history of Santa Maria degli Angeli, see Paatz, vol. 3, 1952, pp. 107-110, and Savelli, pp. 7-12; for the interwoven histories of Santa Maria Nuova and Sant'Egidio, see Paatz, vol. 4, 1952, pp. 1-8. The debated question of the degree of social and economic decline and recovery in the aftermath of the Black Death is summarized, with ample bibliographical references, in Larner (pp. 237ff. and 376ff.) In a notarial act of 1394 (Document 2), forty monks are noted as constituting two thirds of the monastic population of Santa Maria degli Angeli.

22. Peter Damian wrote a life of Saint Romuald circa 1042 (for a modern edition, see Della Santa). The zealous spirit conveyed in Peter Damian's life of Romuald is eloquently characterized by Marvin Becker in *Mediaeval Italy, Constraints and Creativity*, Bloomington, 1981, pp. 71-73.

23. For the exchange between Giovanni da Samminiato and Salutati, see T. F. Rich, "Giovanni da Sanminiato and Coluccio Salutati," *Speculum* 11, 1936, pp. 386-90; for Salutati's response to Dominici's *Lucula Noctis*, see C. Trinkaus, *In Our Image and Likeness*, Chicago, 1970, vol. 1, p. 55, and vol. 2, pp. 555-62. Salutati's overarching "commitment to the task of orienting nascent Italian humanism toward Christian goals" has been investigated by Ronald Witt (*Hercules at the Crossroads, The Life, Works, and Thought of Coluccio Salutati*, Durham, North Carolina, 1983). P. O. Kristeller observed that while a number of monks showed interest in the ideas of Ficino and Pico in the later fifteenth century, two learned Camaldolese, Paolo Giustiniani and Pietro Querini, who had numerous contacts with the Florentine Platonists, were still "primarily concerned with religious reform rather than any particular brand of philosophy or scholarship (*Mediaeval Aspects of Renaissance Learning*, Durham, North Carolina, 1974, p. 113).

24. Traversari's intellectual and spiritual adaptability is approached in the following: Antal, pp. 347-48; Stinger, pp. 275-83. Drawing on his knowledge both of the social order and of pietistic movements in the later Middle Ages, Charles Trinkaus has suggested to me that the fact the Camaldolese did not formally organize an Observance may in part be accountable to the disdain felt by a monastic order that was essentially upper middle class and aristocratic for a movement considered to be attractive mainly to peasants and the lower social levels. In conversation, Charles Stinger expressed the view that there remains a need for investigation of the classes of society from which the various monastic orders drew their members.

25. For a rich corpus of illuminations and miniatures in Camaldolese choir books, see D'Ancona, 1914, vol. 1, pls. XXXII-L. The need for replenishment of choir books at Santa Maria degli Angeli as a result of losses incurred during the papal Interdict of 1376-78, is discussed by Levi D'Ancona (1979, pp. 461-62). Documented distinctions between the work of illuminators and miniaturists are cited by Salmi (1954, p. 19); Levi D'Ancona ("Matteo Torelli," 1958, p. 248, note 11); and Bellosi (1984, 310-312). Also see Catalogue I, Florence, Bargello, Cod. E 70; Biblioteca Laurenziana, Cod. Cor 3; and Documents 9A-9D.

26. The oeuvre of Don Silvestro dei Gherarducci was astutely reconstructed by Mirella Levi D'Ancona ("Don Silvestro," 1959); addenda to that original study were made in 1978, pp. 219-220, and 1979, pp. 466-68.

27. Don Silvestro's panel was for many years on loan to the Accademia Carrara in Bergamo from the Florentine Soprintendenza (no. 3161). For an excellent characterization of the work in relation to major stylistic trends of later Trecento Florentine painting, see Marcucci, pp. 136-37. Building on the foundation set by Levi D'Ancona, Miklós Boskovits enlarged the corpus of works by Don Silvestro, in particular his activity as a panel painter (1972, pp. 36-40, and 1975, pp. 421-26). In commenting on Marcucci's observations on Don Silvestro, Federico Zeri reinforced the important role his art played as a link between later Trecento Siena and Florence (1968, p. 75). An important case in point is the trip-

tych in the Herrington Collection, Indianapolis, attributed by Zeri to Don Silvestro ("Italian Primitives at Messrs Wildenstein," 1965, p. 255 and fig. 57); the triptych format is fundamentally Sienese, while the *Madonna of Humility* in the central panel is close to the model of Jacopo di Cione.

28. For the documentation of Don Silvestro's first association with Santa Maria degli Angeli, see Levi D'Ancona, "Don Silvestro," 1959, p. 8. The Sienese ingredient in Don Silvestro's style could also reflect association with another Camaldolese miniaturist, Don Simone, whose style is grounded in traditions of mid-Trecento Sienese painting (see Boskovits, 1972, pp. 40-42). Don Simone seems to have worked exclusively as a miniaturist, overlaying a Sienese stylistic matrix with the hybrid traits of the workshop at Santa Maria degli Angeli.

29. See Boskovits, 1972, p. 39. Another "severe" mode, the Gerinesque, was also favored in these same years at Santa Maria degli Angeli (see Note 44).

30. Levi D'Ancona first expressed doubt about the existence of a homogeneous Camaldolese style that could be denoted as the "School of Santa Maria degli Angeli" (1961, p. 82), a judgment that was confirmed by Boskovits (1972, p. 43). The artistic eclecticism at Santa Maria degli Angeli is a monastic parallel to the general condition of stylistic polyglotism that prevailed in Florentine painting at the close of the Trecento.

31. The fundamental study of Lorenzo Monaco as a miniaturist is by Anna Maria Ciaranfi (1932). For discussion of Don Lorenzo's early miniatures, see my Catalogue I entries under Florence, Biblioteca Laurenziana.

32. Levi D'Ancona has given undue stress, I believe, to Don Lorenzo's grounding in the style of Don Silvestro and of another miniaturist she has christened the "Maestro delle Canzoni" ("Don Silvestro," 1959, p. 37; 1979, p. 476). Boskovits likewise expressed doubt as to Lorenzo's dependence on the style of Don Silvestro (1972, p. 40). An important link between the Cionesque tradition and the work of Lorenzo Monaco is the style of Giovanni del Biondo, as seen, for example, in the two *Prophets* in the museum at Ponce in Puerto Rico (once part of the San Giovanni Valdarno *Coronation* altarpiece of circa 1370; see Shapley, 1966, figs. 83-84). These imposing figures exemplify the parallelism of painting and sculpture in the later Trecento (see Note 41).

33. Luisa Marcucci (p. 100) commented on the frequency of collaboration between masters of different workshops in the second half of the Trecento and noted several documented examples of such alliances (also see Boskovits, 1975, p. 209, note 33). While there is documentary evidence that masters as different in style as Niccolò di Pietro Gerini and Jacopo di Cione were associated with the important *Coronation of the Virgin* altarpieces for the Florentine Mint and for San Piero Maggiore, in both of these works the style of Jacopo di Cione prevails. Nonetheless, these associations between masters of independent workshops suggest the cross-movement of assistants, with a resultant migration and amalgamation of styles. The *Coronation of the Virgin* altarpiece for Santa Felicita (Berenson, 1963, vol. 1, pl. 386) exhibits a marked division among the hands of Spinello Aretino, Niccolò di Pietro Gerini, and Lorenzo di Niccolò (see Marcucci, pp. 109-110). The still elusive interchanges between the stylistic orbits of Lorenzo Monaco and the Master of the Straus Madonna are approached in Catalogue II, Florence, Accademia, *Saint Jerome; Saint John the Baptist. . . .*

34. The Giottesque revival in later Trecento Florentine painting has received suggestive attention from the following: Bellosi, "Da Spinello," 1965, pp. 22-25; White, 1966, pp. 373-76; Wilkins, pp. 83-84; Boskovits, 1975, pp. 87-92 and passim; B. Cole, 1980, pp. 12-35; Waadenoijen, 1983, p. 17, with further bibliography. Aspects of the Florentine intellectual climate in the later Trecento and early Quattrocento that were conducive to a revival of the art of Giotto have been studied by M. Baxandall, *Giotto and the Orators*, Oxford, 1971.

35. The kaleidoscopic variety of stylistic sources that have been suggested as essential in the formation of Don Lorenzo's early work indicates the numerous and intermingled traditions from which his art sprang in the waning years of the Trecento. Sirén and Pudelko believed that Lorenzo's roots were primarily Sienese (1905, p. 19; 1938/39, p. 237); Ciaranfi, emphasizing the variety of sources, was the first to single out the importance of Orcagnesque and Cionesque painting in Lorenzo's formation (1932, passim); Salvini considered the predominant influence to be from Agnolo Gaddi (1936, p. 176); Sandberg-Vavalà, finding the theories of Sienese

sources exaggerated, saw the painter's beginnings in the shop of Agnolo Gaddi, but also recognized a strong element of Cionesque form and color (1939, pp. 107-108); Levi D'Ancona at first stressed the Orcagnesque roots and later Trecento Florentine sculpture ("Some New Attributions," 1958, p. 187), but in a later study underscored the importance of Agnolo Gaddi (1961, p. 86); Amerio saw the essential source to be Orcagnesque, with admixtures of the styles of Spinello Aretino, Niccolò di Pietro Gerini, and Agnolo Gaddi (1964, col. 337); Bellosi considered the Giottesque bulk and intensifying dynamism of Spinello Aretino's art to be the principal influence ("Da Spinello," 1965, passim); Gronau, Zeri, and Boskovits focussed upon Agnolo Gaddi's impact (1950, p. 188; 1964/65, p. 558; 1975, pp. 132-35). Zeri also underscored the "rediscovery of the Giottesque" in Don Lorenzo's formation (1964/65, p. 8). The problem has been compounded by the continuing expansion of the corpus of Don Lorenzo's early works, an array of paintings, at times cognate, which grew out of the same varied soil that nurtured his first efforts as a miniaturist and panel painter. Through a cumulative process of attribution, some thirty-nine works have been credited to the hand of Lorenzo Monaco during his formative years in the late Trecento (in this tally, the various elements of a dispersed altarpiece are counted as a single work). For approaches to the diverse attributions to Don Lorenzo's early activity, see the following entries in Catalogue II: Florence, Accademia, *Saint Catherine of Alexandria*, and *Saint Caius*; Florence, Accademia, *Saint Jerome*; *Saint John the Baptist* . . . ; Paris, Louvre, *Feast of Herod*. . . .

36. Hans Gronau (p. 221) first noted Burckhardt's and Ruskin's observations on the *Agony in the Garden* (see Burckhardt, p. 154; and Ruskin, 1875-76, p. 39; in a retrospective comment [1889, p. 102], Ruskin accepted the verbal suggestion of Charles Murray that the panel, then in the Uffizi, is a work of Lorenzo Monaco; Ruskin especially admired the vivid narration of the two predella scenes).

37. For the Louvre *Stigmatization*, the earliest known location of which is the church of San Francesco in Pisa, see Fremantle, fig. 23. It is noteworthy that the principal narrative scene of this single-panel altarpiece is accompanied by narrative episodes beneath, in this case three in number, in contrast to the two scenes of the predella of Don Lorenzo's *Agony in the Garden*. Taddeo Gaddi's *Stigmatization* in the Fogg Art Museum, is an adaptation of the Louvre panel, but its cut-down state does not permit speculation as to whether narrative scenes ever existed below the principal image (see Ladis, p. 86 and fig. 3-1). For an intensive discussion of the Louvre *Stigmatization*, see J. Gardner, "The Louvre Stigmatization and the problem of the narrative Altarpiece," *Zeitschrift für Kunstgeschichte* 45, 1982, pp. 217-47.

38. The depiction of the *Stigmatization of Saint Francis* as the climactic "imitatio Christi" is approached by H. W. van Os ("The Earliest Altarpieces of St. Francis," *Francesco d'Assisi nella storia*, vol. 1, *Convegno di Studi, Secoli XIII-XV*, Istituto Storico dei Cappuccini, Rome, 1983, pp. 336-38). The *Agony in the Garden* and the *Stigmatization of Saint Francis* are juxtaposed in a pair of fourteenth-century Umbrian panels, probably at one time the wings of a portable triptych (*Mostra dei tesori segreti delle case fiorentine*, Florence, 1960, p. 10, nos. 12-13, and fig. 11). The events are also paired in the wings of a triptych in the Museo Horne, by a contemporary of Daddi (see Rossi, 1966, pp. 135-36, and fig. 21).

39. See Note 44.

40. Spinello's Benedictine cycle in the Sacristy at San Miniato and Agnolo's frescoes in the Choir at Santa Croce manifest the important revival of narrative mural art in Florence in the 1380s. Lorenzo's model for the stream of Kidron in the *Agony in the Garden*, with its outcroppings of bulrushes, may have come from another of Agnolo's cycles, the scene of the *Return of the Sticks and Stones* (Fig. 272; John the Evangelist cycle) in the Castellani Chapel at Santa Croce.

41. Offner (*Italian Primitives at Yale*, 1927, p. 21) and Levi D'Ancona ("Some New Attributions," 1958, p. 188, note 65) were the first to propose the importance of later Trecento Florentine sculpture in the formation of Don Lorenzo's style, but did not cite specific parallels. Interchanges between painting and sculpture in the late fourteenth century in Florence are considered by Boskovits (1975, pp. 89-93) and B. Cole (1980, pp. 72-80). G. Kreytenberg has noted the significant instance of the sculptor Piero di Giovanni Tedesco's dependence on the designs of several later Trecento Florentine painters in a group of statuettes for the Duomo (1981, p. 7, with further reference to his earlier investigations). The chevron

and cascade in the mantle of the sculptor's *Saint Paul* (Kreytenberg, fig. 8) bears the closest resemblance to the draperies of Christ in Lorenzo's *Agony in the Garden* (Fig. 7). John Pope-Hennessy (1969, p. 420) expressed doubt that the influence of sculpture on painting could at times have been a process whereby painters observed and drew from passages of sculptors' works in their search for new forms. I would submit, however, that the painters of the turn from Trecento to Quattrocento, saturated by Giottesque and Orcagnesque models but not as yet replenished by studies from life, would likely have found the emergent "culture" of sculptured works on the Florentine scene to be a fertile source of imagery. Given the additive character of design at this time, a painter would naturally merge traditionally received models with passages of sculpture that conveyed new conformations and energies (see below, Note 66). For an instructive study of the dialogue between sculpture and painting in Tuscan art of the Trecento and Quattrocento, see John White, 1967.

42. Berenson, 1970, p. 138.

43. Trecento precedents for the use of a quatrefoil frame with narrative predella scenes are discussed in Catalogue I, Florence, Accademia, *Agony in the Garden*.

44. For a more extensive analysis of the *Agony in the Garden* and its predella in relation to monastic liturgical use, see Eisenberg, 1984, pp. 275-89; note 13 provides a listing of the narrative altarpieces, from the traditions of the Cioni and Niccolò di Pietro Gerini, known to have been in use on the altars at Santa Maria degli Angeli in the late years of the Trecento. Reference is also made (note 10) to the conventual implication in the use of the wimple as part of the Virgin's costume in the *Stripping* episode.

45. The triptych in the Pinacoteca in Siena (Fig. 132) must also be included among the smaller works produced by Lorenzo Monaco and his workshop at the close of the century. The triptych demonstrates that even a work of intimate size may involve a significant degree of workshop collaboration (see Catalogue I, Siena, Pinacoteca Nazionale).

46. Miklós Boskovits (1975, pp. 106 and 124) has noted, however, in the formative works of the Master of Santa Verdiana, a secular painter, the "incertezze di un pittore ancora all'inizio della carriera." The earlier style of this painter, as reconstructed by Boskovits, vacillates between distinctive Gaddesque and Gerinesque idioms.

47. In the Bologna *Enthroned Madonna with Saints* (Fremantle, fig. 25), signed by Giotto, but a work of his shop, the throne does not have a protective baldachin and the arms are of the indented type that reappears in Florentine images of the enthroned Madonna throughout the Trecento (cf. Fremantle, figs. 142, 614, and 685). The baldachin type of throne back is found with sufficient frequency in the later Trecento to indicate that its use may be a further symptom of Giottesque revivalism (cf. Fremantle, fig. 45 and Boskovits, 1975, pl. III).

Precedents in the Florentine Trecento for the semicircular extension from the dais, found in the Fitzwilliam and Berenson panels, are noted by Hellmut Wohl (p. 80, note 3), in conjunction with a variation on the usage in the early Carnesecchi Tabernacle by Domenico Veneziano. A further and perhaps most immediate source is in the work of the Cionesque Giovanni Bonsi (Zeri, 1964, figs. 1 and 3; or Fremantle, figs. 436 and 445). The rounded extension will also appear in the Bologna *Madonna Enthroned* (Fig. 133), the Courtauld *Coronation of the Virgin* (Fig. 228), and the Assisi *Madonna of Humility* (Fig. 236). A polygonal version is seen in the Toledo *Madonna Enthroned* (Fig. 217) and an ornamental curvilinear variant in the work of the Master of the Straus Madonna (Fremantle, figs. 630 and 634).

48. Widely ranging opinions have been expressed with regard to the pictorial sources of the Fitzwilliam *Madonna* (see Catalogue I, Cambridge, Fitzwilliam Museum).

49. The prototype of this compositional format is the *Madonna* by Nardo di Cione from the New-York Historical Society, now on extended loan to the Metropolitan Museum of Art (see Meiss, 1951, fig. 11).

50. Spinello's characteristic facial types for the Virgin are exemplified by the *Madonna Enthroned* in the Museo Nazionale di San Matteo at Pisa and the triptych, dated 1391, in the Accademia in Florence (Fremantle, figs. 787 and 723). A close Cionesque comparison may be drawn with the *Madonna* in the Church of the Santi Apostoli in Florence (Fremantle, fig. 332). Pudelko proposed (1938/39, p. 238)

that the Fitzwilliam *Madonna* betrays some influence of Taddeo Gaddi's facial types, as well as Spinello's (cf. Ladis, fig. 24-1).

51. For the tradition of the subject in fourteenth-century Tuscan painting, see the entry in Catalogue I.

52. See Meiss, 1951, pp. 9-14, and fig. 1.

53. Although Pudelko (1938/39, p. 242, note 24) observed a similarity between this rinceau and the ornamentation on the altar in Ghiberti's *Sacrifice of Isaac* relief, there is a closer parallel with the borders of the Porta dei Canonici, completed by 1378 (see Kreytenberg, 1976, pp. 128-37; figs. 18a-c). Lorenzo introduced a modified rinceau in Christ's halo both at the center of the panel and in the abbreviated Betrayal at the upper right. This abundant vegetal ornamentation of haloes is initiated in the art of Taddeo Gaddi (e.g., see Ladis, fig. 19-3), again an explanation of Vasari's view that Don Lorenzo inherited the style of an earlier generation of Florentine painting (see Note 17).

54. The *lauda* of Jacopone da Todi, *Quando t'aliegre, omo d'altura*, offers the features of Christ as a sequence of dissected fragments (see F. Mancini, *Jacopone da Todi, Laude*, Rome-Bari, 1974, pp. 177-80, no. 61). In the *Meditationes Vitae Christi* the "Meditation on the Passion of the Lord" reads: ". . . in what battle is He tormented? You will hear (and see). One of them seizes Him, . . . another binds Him, another attacks Him, another scolds Him, another pushes Him, another blasphemes Him, another spits on Him, another beats Him, another walks around Him, another questions Him, . . . another accuses Him, another mocks Him, another blindfolds Him, another strikes His face, another goads Him, another leads Him to the column, another strips Him, another beats Him, . . . another screams, . . . another assaults Him, another scourges Him, another robes Him in purple to abuse Him, another places the crown of thorns, another gives Him the reed to hold, another madly takes it away to strike His thorn-covered head, another kneels mockingly, another salutes Him as king. These and many similar things were done to Him, not just by one but by many." (See *Meditations on the Life of Christ*, Ragusa and Green edition, p. 318.) For extensive analysis of the emblems of the Passion, see Berliner, pp. 35-152, and Suckale, pp. 177-208; Schiller (1972, pp. 207-15) presents a useful survey of the Man of Sorrows with the *Arma Christi*. The most recent comprehensive approach to the *Imago Pietatis* is H. Belting, *Das Bild und sein Publikum in Mittelalter, Form und Funktion früher Bildtafeln der Passion*, Berlin (West), 1981.

55. For the proposed date of 1401 or 1402, see Catalogue I, formerly Berlin, Kaiser-Friedrich-Museum, no. 1119. The *Madonna Enthroned* in the Pinacoteca Nazionale, Bologna (Fig. 133) would seem to be primarily a work of Don Lorenzo's shop, although certainly conceived under his supervision (see Catalogue I). The architecturally defined space of the Bologna *Madonna* suggests a contrast with the planarity of the Berlin panel similar to the comparison between the Fitzwilliam and Berenson Madonnas (Figs. 15 and 16).

56. The rhythmic dynamism in Spinello's art is already strongly manifested in the first years of the 1390s in the *Rout of the Pagans* fresco for the Camposanto in Pisa (Fremantle, fig. 727). In the art of Agnolo Gaddi the contrast between his *Coronation of the Virgin* panel in London, of circa 1380-1385, and his *Coronation* in Washington, of circa 1390 (see B. Cole, 1977, pls. 39 and 83), displays a change from an additive compositional method to a complex interweaving of rhythmic passages. By the mid-Trecento in Siena, Luca di Tommè had infused the linearism of Simone Martini with a bold expressivity (Fig. 280), which heralds Don Lorenzo's art of circa 1404, but by late century line had taken on the character of a self-conscious and playful ornamentalism in the hands of a little Sienese master such as Niccolò di Buonaccorso (see A. and E. Mongan, *European Paintings in The Timken Art Gallery*, San Diego, 1969, No. 4, *Madonna of Humility with Saints Catherine of Alexandria and Christopher*).

57. Although the provenance of the *Man of Sorrows* is unknown, its iconic formality contrasts with the more personal character of the contemporary Empoli *Madonna of Humility*, which suggests that this large panel, like the *Agony in the Garden*, was intended for a monastic environment. The relaxation of the style in the Empoli altarpiece implies a less dogmatic patronage and a more "public" function. Creighton Gilbert observed the influence of Dominican usage on pictorial style (review of S. Orlandi, *Beato Angelico*, in *Art Bulletin* 47, 1965, p. 274). While Frederick Antal (p. 317) proposed that the Camaldolese subscription to the Observance under-

lay the frequent representation of the Madonna of Humility by Lorenzo Monaco and his workshop—Ambrogio Traversari having denoted humility as the mother of all virtues—the subject was abundantly depicted by secular shops of the later Trecento in both Florence and Siena, and in particular by Andrea di Bartolo (see van Os, 1969, figs. 62-73). In Florence, the image of the Madonna of Humility accompanied by saints in separate lateral panels was significantly depicted in the workshop of Agnolo Gaddi and by the Master of Santa Verdiana (Fremantle, figs. 544 and 600). By the middle years of the first decade of the Quattrocento, the workshop of Lorenzo Monaco was engaged in the prolific production of small devotional images, which paralleled the larger commissions executed by the master and his assistants at various stages of stylistic development.

58. Throughout this essay, when referring to parallels between the styles of Ghiberti and Lorenzo Monaco, I have adopted the chronology of the reliefs on the North Door established by Richard Krautheimer (1956, pp. 113-134). The *Annunciation* may be dated around 1404 to 1407, that is, within the earliest group of reliefs. As Krautheimer explained in the preface to the second printing of his seminal book (1970, vol. 1, p. xvii), the "proposed sequence was intended to provide only loose *termini ante* and *ad quos* for larger groups rather than for single reliefs."

59. For a comprehensive review of theories regarding the Florentine and Northern influence on Ghiberti's formation, see Bellosi, Guiducci, Cardini, et al., in *Ghiberti, 'materia e ragionamenti,'* 1978, pp. 26-55. Also see Freytag, pp. 23-34, and Kreytenberg, 1980, pp. 59-78.

60. See Pudelko, 1938/39, pp. 238 and 242; Longhi, 1940, p. 184; and Paolucci, 1985, pp. 73-74. Pudelko's view that the *Annunciation* in the Accademia, Florence (Fig. 77), was painted around 1406 and brought to full expression the aspects of the International Style that had only been implied in Lorenzo's art with the Empoli triptych of 1404, gave a premature role to that important work, which should be dated no earlier than circa 1418. Krautheimer (1956, p. 82) proposed that Don Lorenzo's art assumed the characteristics of the International Style "without warning" around 1404, although he emphasized the importance of both continuity and change from Ghiberti's competition relief to the first quatrefoils for the North Door (p. 122). Most recently, Jeanne van Waadenoijen has theorized that the return of Gherardo Starnina from Spain to Florence around 1403 led directly and immediately to the calligraphic styles of Ghiberti and Lorenzo Monaco (1974, 1980, and 1983, pp. 26, 101, and passim). In contrast to this singular explanation of the emergent style of a major artistic personality, there is a greater likelihood that Starnina's importation of International Gothic forms from Valencia gave further impetus to a tendency that had already been evolving in Tuscan painting and sculpture before 1403. The impact of later Trecento Florentine sculpture and the survival of indigenous calligraphic traditions in late Trecento Sienese painting are not approached in Waadenoijen's studies.

Prompted by the earlier intuitions of Berti (1964, pp. 137-38, note 152) and Bellosi (1966, p. 75), Waadenoijen and Cornelia Seyre (1979) have independently allied the name of Starnina with a group of works attributed to the Maestro del Bambino Vispo. Two such influential works as the altarpiece in Würzburg and the dismembered polyptych from the Certosa at Galluzzo, which is scattered over numerous European museums (for confronted illustrations of the principal panels, see Berenson, 1963, vol. 1, pls. 475 and 476), must now be dated within the first decade of the Quattrocento rather than nearly twenty years later. While Seyre's arguments (pp. 116-20) in favor of assigning the Würzburg altarpiece to Starnina's workshop clearly point up the stylistic differences between that work and the Certosa polyptych, Waadenoijen's view seems preferable, namely, that the Würzburg altarpiece represents Starnina's art immediately after his return from Valencia and that a rapid transformation occurred in the following years.

The identification of Starnina with the Maestro del Bambino Vispo has aroused widely divergent reactions that are beyond my scope here to outline, except to note that opinion has recently weighed in favor of the theory (e.g., van Os, 1983, p. 75; Boskovits, 1985, p. 134; Paolucci, 1985, pp. 69-71 and 74). Waadenoijen's publications, in my view, do not sufficiently confront images in order to confirm her important attributions. For example, by juxtaposing the heads and passages of the habits of the Saint Benedict figures in Starnina's Carmine fresco of 1404 (Fig. 288) and in the Stockholm panel (Fig. 289), it becomes evident that they are painted by the same hand. Also noteworthy is the fact that in both the Carmine and Stockholm Benedicts their habits, rather than being the traditional black of the Benedictines, or the white of reformed orders, are painted in varying tones of blue—light and transparent in the fresco (see Meiss, 1970, p. 104) and a dark grayish blue in the panel—which to my knowledge, is rare, if not unique, in the depiction of Benedictine garb. Further supporting evidence for the early date of the Certosa polyptych may be found in the altarpiece in the Fitzwilliam Museum, Cambridge, signed by Francesco d'Antonio and dated 1415 (Fig. 330); the Saint Giovanni Gualberto is an unmistakable variant on the Benedict of the Certosa altarpiece, and the Saint Lawrence in the Cambridge triptych is only slightly less an echo of Starnina's Magdalen (Fig. 286). The Fitzwilliam triptych is an important clue to the fact that Starnina was most directly influential on the lesser painters in the milieu of Lorenzo Monaco, while his effect on Don Lorenzo himself, as will be seen in the Monte Oliveto Altarpiece of 1407 to 1410 (Fig. 22), or the Prague *Lamentation* of 1408 (Fig. 34), will be in Lorenzo's occasional adoption of a motif, or in his indulgence in moments of greater calligraphic abandon or of sharper contrasts in the lighting of drapery folds than was his wont. For comment on Starnina's direct impact on Bartolomeo di Fruosino, see Catalogue II, Avignon, Musée du Petit Palais, *Saint Lawrence Enthroned, with Saints Ansanus and Margaret.*

As Waadenoijen has noted (1983, pp. 69-70), after Starnina returned to the Florentine milieu, his style underwent a rapid transformation toward a quieter calligraphy and a more spacious pictorial environment, which may be demonstrated by comparing the Munich *Last Judgment* (Waadenoijen, 1983, fig. 18) or the Würzburg altarpiece with the Certosa polyptych or the serenely elegant *Madonna with Musical Angels* in the Getty Museum (Waadenoijen, fig. 24). The large production of pictures by Starnina's workshop and circle, both before his death no later than 1413 and for at least a decade after, raises questions of attribution and chronology that remain unresolved. Typically, the works produced following Starnina depended on different phases of his oeuvre and therefore vacillate between a restlessly calligraphic style and one of greater reserve (cf. *Madonna of the Girdle*, Prepositura, Stia, and *Madonna with Saints and Angels*, formerly Michelozzi Collection, Florence [Fremantle, fig. 933, and Seyre, fig. 150]). Well into the second quarter of the Quattrocento the voluminous and activated drapery forms of Starnina would be supercharged by the nervous sensibility of Parri Spinelli (see Fremantle, fig. 1127, and Bellosi and Bellini, figs. 57 and 61). An effective précis of the "Starnina question" is presented by L. Bellosi and G. Chelazzi Dini ("La pittura a Firenze al tempo della Porta Nord," in *Lorenzo Ghiberti, 'materia e ragionamenti,'* pp. 141-43).

61. A new prevalence of the ogival tympanum in the frames of Tuscan altarpieces of the first years of the fifteenth century was observed by Everett Fahy (1978, pp. 265 and 267). Don Lorenzo used this crowning shape for the pinnacles of several major works: *Annunciation*, Accademia, Florence (Fig. 77); *Adoration of the Magi*, Uffizi, Florence (Fig. 82); *Annunciation*, Bartolini Salimbeni Chapel, Santa Trinita, Florence (Fig. 120). Keith Christiansen has noted the appearance of the ogival (or "mixticurve") tympanum with a roundel in the center in Niccolò Lamberti's door frame at Orsanmichele (1410-1418), and the contemporaneous use of the type in the frames of altarpieces (1982, p. 28, and fig. 26). In the Monte Oliveto Altarpiece, Don Lorenzo implied the roundel by means of swirls of lightly tooled vegetal ornament, but in his later altarpieces the framed roundel with a painted tondo was adopted (Figs. 77, 81, and 120).

62. Berenson, 1963, vol. 1, pls. 229 and 231. Also, see the prophets in the "mezzanine" register of Lorenzo di Niccolò's *Coronation* altarpiece of 1402 in San Domenico, Cortona (Fremantle, fig. 807).

63. The origins and diffusion of the type of standing Christ Child in Italian painting and sculpture of the Trecento were investigated by Ishinabe (pp. 7-13).

64. For the placement and dating of the Porta della Mandorla *Prophet*, see Seymour, 1966, pp. 31-35. The Bargello *Saint Luke*, from the niche of the Magistrates and Notaries at Orsanmichele, is discussed and reproduced by Goldner (pp. 32-34 and pl. 18), who establishes 1406 as the date of completion of the *Saint Luke* and its niche. The voluminous draperies of the Thaddeus in Lorenzo's Monte Oliveto Altarpiece also recall the broad, apron-like expanse of the mantle of Saint Peter in Spinello Aretino's altarpiece at Quinto of 1393 (Fremantle, fig. 716).

65. See Notes 12 and 60. The Thaddeus could also have been inspired by the beautiful sheet of luxuriantly mantled saints in the Gabinetto Disegni e

Stampe of the Uffizi, initially published and attributed to Starnina by Bellosi and Bellini (pp. 26-28, no. 27, and fig. 43).

66. Krautheimer (1956, pp. 122-23) has dated the *Nativity* and *Adoration* in the years 1404-1407, within the first group of reliefs for the North Door. Even when beginning to focus on Ghiberti's designs for the reliefs of the North Door, Don Lorenzo continued to look closely at later Trecento Florentine sculpture, a source of influence graphically demonstrated by comparison of the saw-toothed rear contours of the mantles of the *Adoring Angels* for the façade of the Duomo in Florence, by Piero di Giovanni Tedesco (see Freytag, fig. 29), with the first attendant in the Altenburg *Flight into Egypt* (Fig. 32).

Don Lorenzo typically referred to various pictorial rather than literary sources in composing the Lehman Collection *Nativity* and the two later renderings of the subject in which essentially the same elements would appear (Figs. 51 and 125). As Christiansen has noted (1983, p. 4), the cave and the awestruck shepherds had been part of the pictorial imagery of the subject for more than a century before Lorenzo's panel. His citation of the *Revelations of Saint Bridget* (1370) as a textual source for the New York picture is correct insofar as the scene includes the naked, radiant Child lying on the ground, whereas the kneeling Virgin and the choir of angels had become part of the imagery of the Nativity before Bridget's vision (for a notable earlier Florentine example, see the panel by Bernardo Daddi in the predella of the San Pancrazio Altarpiece [Offner, sec. III, vol. III, 1930, pl. XIV[29]]). In the *Nativity* by Lorenzo Monaco in the Accademia, Florence (Fig. 94) there is a literal dependence on the description of the event in the *Meditations on the Life of Christ* (see Notes 122 and 123). Cornell (pp. 35-36 and 41-42) considered the influence of the *Meditations* on Nativity iconography as a distinct source and as an adumbration of Saint Bridget's vision.

In the depiction of all three of the Magi in poses of genuflection, the Courtauld *Adoration* and Don Lorenzo's subsequent predella panels of the subject (Figs. 52, 126, and 185) adhere to the textual description and to the manuscript illustrations of the scene in the *Meditations on the Life of Christ* (Ragusa and Green edition, p. 50 and figs. 38 and 39). Bartolo di Fredi had imbedded this same grouping of the kneeling Kings into his densely inclusive panel in the Siena Pinacoteca (Fig. 315), and also in a predella panel in the same collection (Torriti, p. 168). Don Lorenzo will diverge from the type in the late Uffizi *Adoration of the Magi* (Fig. 82). The motif of the oldest Magus approaching the Child, with the reverential intent to kiss His feet, was discussed by Kehrer (vol. 2, p. 192, note 2). Ghiberti's type of old Magus on the North Door will be quoted by Don Lorenzo in two subsequent predella panels (Figs. 126 and 185), but in two other versions of the *Adoration of the Magi* the kneeling figure will not explicitly approach the Child (Figs. 31 and 82).

For a suggestive iconographic and theological explication of the architecturally enclosed settings and the disposition of the participants in Don Lorenzo's four predella panels of the *Adoration of the Magi*, see Davisson, 1971, pp. 259-66. The emphasis given in this study to the painter's construction of a sacred, ecclesiastic precinct serves to confirm the monastic propensity for enclosure that is implied in the four predella versions of the Adoration theme. Essential to Davisson's discussion of the symbolic progression within Don Lorenzo's series of predella panels, however, is his adoption of von Fabriczy's novel proposal (Billi, 1891, p. 347, note 107) that the *Annunciation* altarpiece in the Bartolini Salimbeni Chapel at Santa Trinita may originally have been the work for the Ardinghelli Chapel at the Carmine, commissioned from Don Lorenzo in 1399 (Document 4B and Introductory Essay, Note 5; Catalogue I, Florence, Santa Trinita, Bartolini Salimbeni Chapel, *Life of the Virgin*).

67. Although the type of Visitation in which Saint Elizabeth kneels before the Virgin gained currency only in the early fifteenth century (see Schiller, vol. 1, 1971, p. 56), Taddeo Gaddi had already used this iconography by the 1330s in the frescoes of the Baroncelli Chapel at Santa Croce (Berenson, 1963, vol. 1, pl. 121; Ladis, p. 99, fig. 4b-2).

68. The miracle of the bending palm is from the Gospel of the Pseudo-Matthew, XX-XXI (M. R. James, *The Apocryphal New Testament*, Oxford, 1955, p. 75). Meiss (1967, vol. 1, pp, 239-40; vol. 2, figs. 763-67) noted the repeated occurrence of the motif in miniatures by the "Master of the Brussels Initials," an Italianate painter working in the last decade of the fourteenth and early years of the fifteenth century. For the iconographic tradition, see Schiller, vol. 1, 1971, pp. 118-19, and 121.

69. See Shearman, 1957, vol. 1, p. 5.

70. The "naturalization" of light in the service of Christian mysteries is discussed in a classic study by Millard Meiss (1945, pp. 43-68; republished in *The Painter's Choice*, New York, 1976, pp. 3-18). Meiss tentatively proposed that the Limbourgs' exploration of color modified by light could have influenced Lorenzo Monaco if the Northern painters were in Florence around 1405, but he also cautioned against a too-ready acceptance of the connection, seeing it instead as a matter of "independent though related innovations" drawing upon a common source in Trecento painting (1974, vol. 1, pp. 245-46).

The unexpected shadow cast by the shroud draped over the sarcophagus in the Louvre *Holy Women at the Tomb* (Fig. 33), observed by Keith Christiansen (1982, p. 72, note 21), has proved to be a later addition to the painted surface (see Catalogue I, Paris, Louvre, *Agony in the Garden* and *Holy Women at the Tomb*, Condition).

71. See Catalogue I, Prague, National Gallery, *Lamentation*. The depiction of a sequential narrative program within the small triptych format is rare, but there is a direct precedent in the Cionesque tradition (see Offner, ed. Maginnis, 1981, p. 35, and fig. 63, where the center panel with the Crucifixion is accompanied in the wings by four preceding Passion episodes).

72. Krautheimer implied a dating around 1407 for the *Agony in the Garden* of the North Door (1956, p. 124, and pl. 43). Andrew Martindale (1962) has observed the limited usefulness of the term "International Gothic Art" in defining Tuscan styles of the later fourteenth and early fifteenth centuries.

73. See Note 60. For the *Dormition* in the Johnson Collection, which Waadenoijen (1983, p. 60) justifiably considers to be from Starnina's workshop, see Berenson, 1963, vol. 1, pl. 470. As late as 1435, Bartolomeo di Fruosino adapted this foreground mourner to the role of an awestruck shepherd for a *Nativity* miniature in a choir book in the Opera del Duomo at Prato (Cor. C., fol. 9v; see Levi D'Ancona, 1961, fig. 17).

74. Several of the Madonnas produced at various moments in Don Lorenzo's workshop are elaborated with ornamental patterns that were probably included in order to satisfy the special taste of patrons (see Catalogue I, Lastra a Signa, San Martino a Gangalandi, *Madonna of Humility*).

75. Meiss, 1958. While these four Old Testament personages are not among the canonical Prophets, they may rightly be given that description in that they are all considered to prefigure Christ. Moreover, Abraham is specifically called a prophet in Genesis 20:7, as is Moses in Deuteronomy 34:10. This question of the correct general title for the four panels was first approached by Theodore Rousseau in a memorandum in the files of the Metropolitan Museum of Art, written at the time of acquisition of the pictures. G.-P. de Montebello's intensive analysis of the *Prophets* (1966), which enlarges on several aspects of Meiss's original study and raises additional technical questions, further limits the need for extended discussion in the present essay.

76. See Janson, p. 16. Meiss (1958, p. 196) noted that although there are similarities between Lorenzo's *Prophets* and Ghiberti's *Fathers* and *Evangelists* of the North Door, the heavy material and massive folds of the Prophets' draperies bring them closer to the style of Donatello and Nanni. Niccolò Lamberti's *Saint Mark* of 1409-1415 and Ciuffagni's *Saint Matthew* of 1410-1415, in the same series for the Duomo façade, retain more of the florid characteristics of the International Style than do Donatello's and Nanni's *Evangelists* or Don Lorenzo's Old Testament worthies (Goldner, pp. 42-52, and fig. 21; and Pope-Hennessy, 1972, figs. 81-82).

77. The importance of the angle of the observer's vision in Donatello's conception of the *Saint John* is discussed and graphically demonstrated by Seymour, 1966, p. 56, and fig. 6 (also see B. A. Bennett and D. G. Wilkins, *Donatello*, Oxford, 1984, figs. 61 and 62).

78. Seymour, 1966, pl. 12. The inclusive dates of Nanni's *Luke* are 1408-1415.

79. Seymour, 1973, pp. 31-32.

80. Indicative of their differing roles within the Florentine tradition, Lorenzo Monaco depicted *David* in the mediaeval guise of the old singer at the same moment Donatello was rendering him as a youth who would come to serve as a "civic-patriotic monument" (see Janson, pp. 4-7).

81. For a conclusive reconstruction of the San Piero Maggiore Altarpiece, see Offner and Steinweg, Sec. IV, vol. III, 1965, pp. 31-47; Jacopo's work is mentioned as a prototype of Don Lorenzo's *Coronation* for Santa Maria degli Angeli. Krautheimer (1956, p.

181) suggested that Ghiberti's panoramic *Meeting of Solomon and Sheba* on the East Door of the Baptistery recalls a type of early fifteenth-century Coronation of the Virgin composition, exemplified by Don Lorenzo's for Santa Maria degli Angeli.

82. The iconographic and compositional traditions in the depiction of the Coronation of the Virgin preceding Don Lorenzo's altarpiece for Santa Maria degli Angeli are considered in Catalogue I, Florence, Uffizi, *Coronation of the Virgin*.

83. Charles de Tolnay (1943, p. 93) identified the star-studded arcs as celestial spheres and the three angels in the foreground—two singing and one playing the organ—as translators of the harmony of a universal music. All of the angels are depicted with open mouths, however, suggesting an encircling choir. The celestial arcs, while in gradations of blue, may represent the theme from Revelation 4:3 of the throne of heaven with a "rainbow round about" (also see Ezekiel 1:28). In a *Coronation of the Virgin* in the National Gallery in Washington, by a predecessor of Paolo Veneziano, Christ and the Virgin are linked by a star-studded arch painted a graduated blue (Shapley, 1966, fig. 13).

84. For citation of literature on the uses of an ecclesiastical element as a metaphor of the "Virgin as the Church," see Eisenberg, 1966, p. 24, notes 27 and 28. The roundel of the bust-length Christ Child accompanied by floating angels, which approaches the effect of a *clipeus* within the gable of the baldachin, introduces a third guise of the Redeemer into the altarpiece, along with the Crowning and Blessing Christ.

85. A similar transition from a frame simulating a baldachin to a vaulted interior is found in the Cavalcanti *Annunciation* from Santa Maria Novella by Giovanni del Biondo, in the Accademia, Florence (see Offner and Steinweg, sec. IV, vol. V, pt. II, 1969, pl. XXV). For further discussion of the architectural aspects of this frame and of Lorenzo's for the Santa Maria degli Angeli altarpiece, see Catalogue I, Florence, Uffizi, *Coronation of the Virgin*.

86. Precedents for the angelic choir that encircles the throne are cited in the Catalogue entry on the *Coronation*.

87. Klesse (p. 393) observed that the brocaded pattern of this cloth of honor is also found identically in a work of Agnolo Gaddi's shop, in Don Lorenzo's Berlin *Madonna* (Fig. 17), and in the *Saint Lawrence* altarpiece at Avignon (Fig. 244).

88. The effect of modern gallery illumination on late mediaeval Italian painting has been discussed by John Shearman (1957, vol. 1, pp. v-vii). Sirén (1905, p. 79) described the quality of light required to see the Uffizi *Coronation* most effectively. For a general discussion of later Trecento and early Quattrocento color practice, see Ackerman, pp. 16-18.

89. The analysis of the *Saint John* is a pivotal aspect of Krautheimer's studies of Ghiberti (1956, pp. 71-85).

90. Shearman (1957, vol. 1, pp. 6-13) defines the contrast between "isochromatic" systems of symmetry and counterpoint, and presents a detailed analysis of the symmetrical and contrapuntal disposition of color in the Uffizi *Coronation* (vol. 2, pp. 70-71, note 28).

91. For Lorenzo's adoption of the type of floating angel, see p. 32 and Notes 108 and 109.

92. Ragusa and Green edition, 1961, p. 38. For further references to textual sources for Lorenzo's depictions of the *Nativity*, see Note 66.

93. John Pope-Hennessy, in comparing Lorenzo's *Adoration of the Magi* with Ghiberti's on the North Door, has noted the similarity between the sculptor's and the painter's methods of dividing the quadri-lobed pictorial field with upright architectural elements (1980, pp. 48-49, figs. 9 and 10). Ghiberti's setting, however, evokes a more sophisticated spatial environment than Don Lorenzo's simple winged stage, which depends more on Trecento models. As Pope-Hennessy observes, Ghiberti's scene is "on an altogether different level of psychological and visual complexity."

In Trecento representations of the Adoration of the Magi the event is almost invariably enacted in a landscape setting, with the shed and manger as architectural accessories. The few exceptions, in which an enclosing wall is introduced, are cited by Davisson (1971, p. 261). In the predella of the Linaiuoli Altarpiece, commissioned in 1433, Fra Angelico continued the use of the walled enclosure, but with a more complex spatial organization (Pope-Hennessy, 1974, pl. 29).

94. The *Second Book of the Dialogues of Gregory the Great,* which constitutes a life of Saint Benedict,

provides the most detailed story of his life and was the source, in turn, for the account in the *Golden Legend* (March 21). Sirén (1905, p. 83) claimed that Lorenzo Monaco depended on the latter source for the imagery of the Uffizi predella, but Kaftal (col. 173) and Dubler (p. 56) demonstrate that the *Dialogues of Gregory*, a popular text in monastic communities, provided a richer and more expressive body of biographical details that underlay the pictorial tradition. The following chapters in the *Second Book of Dialogues* are pertinent to Don Lorenzo's predella: chap. 37 (Death and Burial of Saint Benedict; Fig. 49); chaps. 1 and 4 (The Feeding of Benedict at Subiaco and the Temptation of the Young Monk from Prayer; Fig. 50); chaps. 7 and 33 (Maurus Rescuing Placidus at the Instruction of Saint Benedict and the Encounter of Benedict and Scholastica; Fig. 57); chap. 11 (Saint Benedict Raising the Young Monk Crushed by a Falling Wall; Fig. 58). For a standard modern edition of the *Dialogues* see Gregorii Magni, *Dialogi Libri IV*, ed. Umberto Moricca, Rome, 1924. A useful Latin and English edition is *The Life of Our Most Holy Father S. Benedict, being the Second Book of the Dialogues of S. Gregory the Great with the Rule of the Same Holy Patriarch*, Rome, 1895. An extensive bibliography of the literary sources is provided in an informative exhibition catalogue: Florence, *Iconografia di San Benedetto* . . . , 1982. In expressing the view that the Benedictine scenes within Don Lorenzo's *Coronation* predella are not in their original arrangement, Salvini and Traverso (p. 61) would seem to have been seeking a chronological rather than a thematic order within the series of four panels.

95. See Marcucci, pp. 94-96.

96. For a summary of the problems of reconstruction and attribution of the *Beata Umiltà* altarpiece, see Marcucci, pp. 153-57; I am unable to concur with the several proposals, noted by Marcucci (p. 155), that the work is Florentine rather than Sienese. I have adopted John White's terminology to describe the type of architectural setting (1967, p. 27, fig. 1).

97. The function of the color plane in late mediaeval and early Renaissance painting is approached by Shearman (1957, vol. 1, p. 4).

98. In Ghiberti's *Adoration of the Magi* on the North Door, Joseph plays the role of peering onlooker (Krautheimer, 1956, pl. 28). The device had been used earlier in Florentine painting by Maso di Banco in the *Dream of Constantine*, Bardi di Vernio Chapel, Santa Croce (Fremantle, fig. 259). In the context of his ecclesiastic interpretation of Don Lorenzo's four predella versions of the *Adoration of the Magi*, Davisson has interpreted the peeking figure as reinforcement of the sacred nature of the walled precinct and the ritualistic event (1971, p. 261; also see above, Note 66).

99. Sister Joan Braun, O.S.B., has suggested, in a seminar presentation, that the depiction of Prophets on the pilasters may have been inspired by the Proper of the Mass and the Responses in the Lessons for Matins of the Feast of Saint Benedict (March 21), where there is specific mention of Abraham, Moses, and David, and Saint Benedict is considered to be comparable to the Old Testament Prophets through his extraordinary deeds.

100. Janson, pp. 16-21, and pls. 6 and 7.

101. See Catalogue I, Florence, San Giovannino dei Cavalieri, *Crucifix with the Mourning Virgin and Saint John the Evangelist*. The earliest of Don Lorenzo's large cutout crosses would appear to be no. 3153 in the Accademia in Florence, from the years 1405 to 1410 (see Catalogue I).

102. Although a direct link with the new popularity of the cutout cross is not implied, it is suggestive that in Brunelleschi's second perspective picture, a view of the Piazza della Signoria, he heightened the illusionism of the demonstration by silhouetting the upper contours of the buildings rather than retaining the entire surface of the panel (see White, 1972, p. 117, and S. Y. Edgerton, Jr., *The Renaissance Rediscovery of Linear Perspective*, New York, 1975, p. 127, Diagram IX-2).

103. For the Santo Spirito fresco, see Offner, sec. IV, vol. I, 1962, pl. V[1]; for a detail of the Christ in Andrea di Bonaiuto's *Crucifixion*, see Fremantle, fig. 423. Don Lorenzo would have had close acquaintance with the boldly silhouetted Crucifix in the central panel of the *Trinity* altarpiece, from the workshop of Nardo di Cione, originally at Santa Maria degli Angeli (Accademia, Florence; Offner, sec. IV, vol. II, 1960, pl. XXVI).

104. The matter of shop intervention in this ensemble is discussed in Catalogue I, Florence, San Giovannino dei Cavalieri.

105. Krautheimer, 1956, p. 125. The iconographic

tradition of the Crucifixion with the Virgin and Saint John seated beneath the cross, and other versions of the subject from the workshop of Lorenzo Monaco, are noted in the entry in Catalogue I.

106. The reworked frame is a harsh intrusion (see Catalogue I, Florence, Accademia, no. 8458). For the *Isaiah* originally in the roundel of the right gable, see Catalogue I, New York, Richard L. Feigen Collection (Fig. 81). The intense presence of the *Isaiah* anticipates the miniatures in Cod. H 74 in the Bargello (Figs. 99-101).

107. E.g., Taddeo Gaddi, *Annunciation*, Fiesole, Museo Bandini (see Ladis, fig. 16-1). The cosmatesque inlays and leafy acroteria in Taddeo's more imposing structure may also imply an ecclesiastic setting.

108. The depiction of the floating or flying archangel in the iconography of the Annunciation was investigated by Robb, p. 487, note 35, and Meiss, 1941, pp. 55-56. For Meiss's subsequent observations on the motif, see Note 109.

109. I wish to convey my gratitude to Paul Watson for his permission to read the manuscript of a thoughtful paper on "Lorenzo Monaco and Franco-Flemish Illumination," which he presented at the Annual Meeting of the College Art Association of America, in January 1978. There he observed close parallels between Don Lorenzo's *Annunciation* and Jacquemart's miniature in the *Très Belles Heures de Jean de Berry* (p. 18), painted before 1402 (see Meiss, 1967, vol. 2, fig. 182), noting the similarities in the pose and placement of the floating Gabriel, in the expressive interval between the archangel and the Virgin, and in the extension of the Virgin's hand toward the book. It is noteworthy that Jacquemart, unlike Don Lorenzo, quoted Simone Martini's composition literally in the gesture of the Virgin's hand raised to her breast, with the index finger curling around the edge of the mantle. The pose of Jacquemart's Annunciate Virgin also recalls the emotionally charged response of Ambrogio Lorenzetti's Mary in the Montesiepi sinopia (see Meiss, 1970, pp. 80-81). As Meiss has observed (1967, vol. 1, p. 212), the soaring Gabriel with his arms crossed on his breast would seem to have been an invention of Ambrogio Lorenzetti, in a lost painting that had numerous and widespread recensions in several media. Could the parallels between Jacquemart's and Lorenzo's compositions be seen as a cognate relationship, both works dependent on varied Sienese traditions of Annunciation iconography?

Federico Zeri observed that in an *Annunciation* attributed to the Italo-Portuguese Alvaro Pirez in the Kisters Collection, Kreuzlingen, datable within the years 1430 to 1435, the painter referred to the figure of the Virgin in Lorenzo's Accademia *Annunciation*, while the Gabriel depended on Simone's Uffizi panel (1973, p. 364, and fig. 5; also see Fremantle, fig. 899). A deviation from Lorenzo's Annunciate Virgin is the shape of her right hand, which clutches the mantle in the gesture of a *Madonna Lactans*. The Kisters panel demonstrates the adaptation of earlier Sienese types to the imagery of the Annunciation.

110. The unresolved question of the provenance is approached in Catalogue I, Florence, Uffizi, *Adoration of the Magi*.

111. In his influential study of the Florentine Epiphany confraternity and festival Rab Hatfield (1970) provided the historical setting for a recurrent spectacle in the civic milieu that gave impetus to the depiction of the Adoration of the Magi as a principal theme in fifteenth-century Florentine painting. In 1390 a *Festa de'Magi* was held in Florence, which suggests that the *Compagnia de'Magi* was already in existence by that date. The *Compagnia* and its sponsorship of the *Festa de'Magi* seem to have been well established in Florence by 1417, when the confraternity is first mentioned in documents, no more than two or three years before Lorenzo Monaco painted his *Adoration* altarpiece. In a later study Hatfield (1976, p. 105) mentioned the prevalence of the "lateral" or processional Adoration in Florentine painting, until Botticelli's transformation of the composition into a central type, as in the Uffizi *Adoration* of the early 1470s. The "lateral" type would seem to have mirrored the splendid processions of the *Festa*.

112. As Cosimo Rosselli's unidentifiable Prophets hold scrolls inscribed with pseudo-Cufic script, they do not enlarge the typological commentary conveyed by Lorenzo's Isaiah and David (?) in the side pinnacles. The texts on their unfurled scrolls (for the transcriptions, see Catalogue I) are those chanted in the Gradual and Offertory of the First Vespers for the Feast of the Epiphany (January 6), each referring to the gifts presented to the Infant. On the Eucharistic implications of such scriptural references to the offerings of the Magi, see Hatfield, 1976, p. 42. Although I have not found a theological

explanation for the transposed Alpha and Omega on the Redeemer's book in the center pinnacle, the reversal occurs with sufficient frequency in Christological imagery—ranging from Paleochristian gems to Limoges enamels and Gothic stained glass—to imply a specific emblematic meaning (also see Fig. 205).

113. Monica Cämmerer-George (pp. 183-84) observed that Lorenzo's is the first depiction of the Adoration of the Magi in which the triple subdivision implied by the frame articulates a continuous scene spread across the panel. As Gentile da Fabriano's *Adoration of the Magi*, dated 1423, which employs the same principle of design, could have been conceived at exactly the time Lorenzo was executing his altarpiece, it is not possible to determine with finality whether Don Lorenzo's or Gentile's work has precedence in establishing this format. There is no reason to doubt that the two artists could have seen each other's work during preparatory stages. Panczenko (p. 64) proposes that Gentile's altarpiece for the Sacristy-Chapel at Santa Trinita was completed before Don Lorenzo's *Adoration* and shows direct, if limited, influences on the latter work.

114. A striking parallel to Lorenzo's game of surfacy shapes is found in two densely inclusive pages from the *Antiquités judaïques*, painted before 1416 for the Duc de Berry by an artist in the following of Jacquemart (see Meiss, 1967, vol. 2, fig. 683, and 1974, vol. 2, fig. 170). Animals and riders weave a similar pattern of interlocking silhouettes, bracketed by a tiered outcropping, while a figure with his back to the viewer functions as a *repoussoir*. Could Lorenzo have known a sketch of these virtuosic French miniatures, which seem so close to the art of tapestry in their panoramic variety and compositional registration? Here again, only a visual parallel may be suggested, as there is no conclusive evidence of Lorenzo's knowledge of transalpine art.

The precise tripartite division of Lorenzo's figural groups could also have been influenced by Starnina's elongated *Adoration of the Magi* in the museum at Douai, originally the central predella panel of the Certosa altarpiece of circa 1408 (see Note 12; Berenson, 1963, vol. 1, pl. 477). The group of animals and stewards at the left of the Douai panel bears some relationship to the passage at the extreme right of Don Lorenzo's composition. In the *Adoration of the Magi* from the workshop of Starnina, in the Nelson-Atkins Museum, Kansas City (Shapley, 1966, fig. 245), the closely gathered retinue and their varied Oriental headgear anticipate the central element of Lorenzo's composition.

115. Mariotto di Nardo, in turn, seems to have foreshadowed the converging obliques of the shed in Don Lorenzo's *Adoration* when he designed the architecture of his frescoed *Charity of Saint Nicholas* on a pilaster at Santa Maria Maggiore in Florence, painted no later than the 1390s (Fig. 310). Davisson also has noted the "analytical" character of the structure in the Uffizi *Adoration* (1971, p. 270). In the *Adoration* Don Lorenzo assertively employed the extreme oblique in the manger shed and the towered city, to adopt John White's terminology (1972, p. 27).

116. Krautheimer (1956, pp. 127-30) dates the last group of reliefs on the North Door, including the *Way to Calvary* and the *Pentecost*, circa 1416 to 1419.

117. The proportions of the standing attendant at the far left in Ghiberti's *Adoration* relief (ca. 1401; Fig. 291) are 1:5.25, while those of the retainer at the left of the *Pentecost* (ca. 1416-19; Fig. 314) are 1:6.5. Similarly, the change in proportion from Lorenzo's Saint Thaddeus (Fig. 24) of the Monte Oliveto Altarpiece of 1410 to the figure with the scimitar in the Uffizi *Adoration* (Fig. 82) is from 1:6 to 1:7. The proportion of the Gabriel in the pinnacle of the *Coronation* of 1414 (Fig. 59) is 1:6.3, whereas the Gabriel of the Accademia *Annunciation* (Fig. 79) is 1:7.2.

While I would suggest that the increased elongation of the figure in Lorenzo's later work, as in Ghiberti's final reliefs for the North Door, comes at the end of a gradually evolving internal process, Paul Watson, in the paper cited in Note 109, has proposed that such elongation in Lorenzo's work is a manifestation of a marked change in his style in the second and third decades of the century, the result of influence from Franco-Flemish miniatures (e.g., Boucicaut Master, *The Boucicaut Hours*, Paris, Musée Jacquemart-André, *The Marshal in Prayer before Saint Catherine*, fol. 38v; or Limbourg Brothers, *Belles Heures*, New York, The Cloisters, *Saint Catherine Refuses to Worship an Idol*, fol. 15v). Watson suggested tentatively that the Trenta Missal of around 1415, commissioned by a Lucchese family from a French miniaturist close to the Boucicaut Master, may provide more direct evidence of the influence of transalpine art on Lorenzo Monaco, particularly in aspects of figural elongation and the scale relationships of figure and setting (e.g., fol. 151v; Meiss, 1968, fig. 360).

Pudelko (1938/39, p. 247) suggested a parallelism between the calligraphic binding of figure and landscape in the Paris wings (Fig. 33) and the style of Broederlam in the Dijon altarpiece, implying that Lorenzo must have known Northern art by the first decade of the Quattrocento.

118. For a review of the debated dating of Bartolo di Fredi's *Adoration*, see Torriti, p. 165.

119. The orientalizing and other exotic elements in Lorenzo's *Adoration of the Magi* are discussed in Catalogue I, Florence, Uffizi, *Adoration of the Magi*.

120. The problem of the origin of the three pinnacles within an altarpiece apparently commissioned from Lorenzo Monaco by Palla Strozzi for the Sacristy-Chapel at Santa Trinita, a work later completed by Fra Angelico, is approached in Catalogue I, Florence, Museo di San Marco, *Resurrection of Christ. . . .*

For a recent study of the iconography of the floating risen Christ, see E. Cassee and K. Berserik, "The Iconography of the Resurrection: a re-examination of the risen Christ hovering above the tomb," *Burlington Magazine* 126, 1984, pp. 20-24.

Don Lorenzo's concentration on larger commissions at this late stage of his career—the Uffizi *Adoration of the Magi*, the altarpiece from the Sacristy-Chapel at Santa Trinita, and the frescoes and altarpiece in the Bartolini Salimbeni Chapel at Santa Trinita—may be inferred from the fact that numerous important Madonna panels from the early years of the 1420s display a significant degree of intervention of the workshop: e.g., Brooklyn Museum, *Madonna of Humility* (Fig. 147); National Gallery of Scotland, *Madonna Enthroned* (Fig. 158); Empoli, Museo della Collegiata, *Madonna Enthroned* (Fig. 156); Lugano, Thyssen-Bornemisza Foundation, *Madonna Enthroned* (Fig. 159); Tavèrnola, Parish Church, *Madonna Enthroned* (Fig. 160).

121. The composition of the final reliefs of the North Door—*Arrest of Christ, Flagellation, Way to Calvary, Pentecost*—resist the ornamental shapes of the quatrefoil, in contrast to such earlier reliefs as the *Nativity, Baptism of Christ, Christ in the Storm, Agony in the Garden, Crucifixion* (see Krautheimer, 1956, pls. 27, 32, 36, 43, 44, 47, 50, 52, 54). Krautheimer (p. 138) commented on Ghiberti's abandonment of the quatrefoil, first in the Siena Font and then in the East Door, as he met the illusionistic demands of pictorial relief. Bellosi (1977, p. 164) has drawn an analogy between Don Lorenzo's shift from quatrefoil to rectangle in his predella panels and the contemporary development from the complex Gothic polyptych to the rectangular pictorial field. The elongated octagonal panels of the predella for the *San Benedetto Altarpiece*, executed under Lorenzo's direction after 1415, could be seen as a transition from quatrefoil to rectangle (see Catalogue I, London, National Gallery). If the Carmine Polyptych (Figs. 215 and 217-23) is accepted as a work of Lorenzo Monaco, a reverse transformation from octagon to quatrefoil may be observed in the progression from the predella of that altarpiece to the two panels beneath the Accademia *Agony in the Garden* (Figs. 10 and 11); see Catalogue II, Florence, Accademia, *Saint Jerome; Saint John the Baptist. . . .*

The original alliance of this three-part predella with the altarpiece for Santa Trinita later completed by Fra Angelico, now in San Marco, is considered in Catalogue I, Florence, Museo di San Marco, *Resurrection of Christ. . . .*

122. *Meditations*, Ragusa and Green edition, p. 33.

123. In Lorenzo's two previous renditions of the *Nativity* (Figs. 30 and 51), he adopted the more common type of combined shed and cave, to which he later reverted in the *Nativity* of the predella of the *Annunciation* at Santa Trinita (Fig. 125). The outcropping, which I tentatively identify as an abbreviated allusion to the cave of the Nativity, has been identified as a well by D. Davisson (see Catalogue I, Florence, Museo di San Marco, *Resurrection of Christ . . .*).

124. In characterizing the light in the *Onuphrius* panel, Roth (p. 210, note 74) gave emphasis to the fact that Lorenzo did not intend to depict the naturalistic effect of moonlight. This observation may be confirmed by a comparison with the starlit *Gethsemane* on fol. 142v of the *Très Riches Heures* (see J. Longnon and R. Cazelles, *The "Très Riches Heures" of Jean, Duke of Berry*, New York, 1969, no. 107). In discussing Taddeo Gaddi's use of light effects in the Baroncelli Chapel at Santa Croce, Ladis (p. 31) has distinguished between the naturalistic depiction of nocturnal illumination and a spiritual light for which "darkness, not night, is its foil."

125. See Note 115.

126. For the Master of the Nicholas Legend, see Procacci, 1935, pp. 348-54. Around 1405 to 1410, Starnina introduced a similar coastal scene into the panel of the *Last Judgment* in the Alte Pinakothek, Munich (Berenson, 1963, vol. 1, pl. 469). Further evidence that at this point in his work Don Lorenzo was turning to earlier Florentine frescoes for models is the close similarity between the *Noli Me Tangere* pinnacle (Fig. 88) above Fra Angelico's San Marco *Deposition*, originally at Santa Trinita, and the fresco of the subject on the left wall of the Strozzi Chapel in that same church, which has been attributed by Offner to the Master of the Fabriano Altarpiece (sec. III, vol. VIII, 1958, pl. XLVII; identified as Puccio di Simone by Roberto Longhi ["Qualità e industria in Taddeo Gaddi ed altri-I," *Paragone* 10, no. 111, 1959, p. 9]).

127. Watson (see Note 109 above) has proposed that the precedent for Lorenzo's "skewing of space" is in Franco-Netherlandish miniatures (e.g., the Limbourgs, *Belles Heures*, fol. 97v; Meiss, 1974, vol. 2, fig. 472).

128. While suggesting that Lorenzo depended on Franco-Netherlandish miniatures in his conception of space and in the relationship of figure to setting, Watson also noted an indifference to the "intense but capricious realism" of Northern International Style artists. The barrenness of the rocky landscapes in Lorenzo's work is in diametric contrast to the depiction of an effulgent nature by the Boucicaut Master, or by Belbello and Giovannino de'Grassi in North Italy.

129. Not only did Lorenzo refer to his own earlier *Visitation* panel (Fig. 29), but he also seems to have turned again to a model in Trecento fresco painting—Taddeo Gaddi's *Visitation* in the Baroncelli Chapel at Santa Croce (Ladis, fig. 4b-4). The parallels between Don Lorenzo's drawing and Jacquemart's *Visitation* in the Brussels *Très Belles Heures de Jean de Berry* (Meiss, 1967, vol. 2, fig. 183) may be explained as a cognate relationship with a common root in Taddeo's fresco (also see Meiss, 1967, vol. 1, p. 237). Paul Barolsky has discerned that the textual source for the inclusion of a hilly landscape in depictions of the Visitation is Luke 1:39, "And Mary arose in those days and went into the hill country with haste . . ." (cited by Frederick Hartt, *History of Italian Renaissance Art*, 2d edition, New York, 1979, p. 217, with specific reference to Fra Angelico's predella scene beneath the Cortona *Annunciation*).

130. Among the analogies Paul Watson has drawn between Northern miniature traditions and the art of Lorenzo Monaco (see Note 109) is his depiction of the *Journey of the Magi* separate from the Adoration, which may be seen as equivalent to the independent episode of the *Meeting of the Magi* in the *Très Riches Heures* (see Meiss, 1974, vol. 2, fig. 471). The theme of the Magi transfixed by the star, depicted as an event distinct from the Adoration, had been used by Taddeo Gaddi in the Baroncelli Chapel at Santa Croce, where the star incorporates an apparition of the Christ Child (see Ladis, fig. 4b-7). Although there the Magi are not mounted, the literal rendering by Don Lorenzo and by Taddeo of Matthew 2:9-10 (". . . and, lo, the star, which they say in the east, /went before them . . . /When they saw the star, they rejoiced with exceeding great joy.") allies these images. Giovanni da Modena, working shortly after 1412 in the Bolognini Chapel at San Petronio, Bologna, produced an independent composition of the three Magi on horseback guided to their destination by the star (Volpe, 1983, fig. 228; also see Davisson, 1971, pp. 214-42). For a depiction of the subject in early Italian manuscript illustration, see the *Meditations on the Life of Christ* (Ragusa and Green edition, fig. 36).

In emphasizing the urgency and haste of the journey in the Berlin drawing, Don Lorenzo captured the spirit of the narrative in the *Golden Legend* (*The Epiphany*). In that text, however, the swiftness of the journey from the "bournes of the Orient to Jerusalem" is explained, according to one account, by the fact the Magi rode on dromedaries rather than horses (Jacobus da Voragine, *Golden Legend*, vol. 1, p. 86). Don Lorenzo acceded to this tradition by introducing a camel mounted by one of the retinue at the lower right in the Berlin drawing. The tiny fisherman discovered on a cliff at the bottom of the *Journey of the Magi* could be interpreted simply as a playful indulgence, but he may also be a marginal allusion to the theme of the "Divine Angler," a metaphor of Christ's triumph over the Devil (see F. P. Pickering, *Literature and Art in the Middle Ages*, Coral Gables, 1970, p. 269; I am grateful to Dan Ewing for this reference).

131. Florentine Lectures, VII, Transition to Quattrocento (Fry Papers, King's College Library, Cambridge), quoted in Frances Spalding, *Roger Fry, Art and Life*, Berkeley and Los Angeles, 1980, p. 72 (published with emendations in Fry, 1901, pp. 132-

33). Unfortunately, there is no trace of a copy of the *Journey of the Magi* that Spalding reports Fry made while in Berlin. Sirén commented upon Roger Fry's admiration of the Berlin drawings (1905, p. 102). Notebook entries and published work by Roger Fry from around the turn of the century further convey the depth of his attraction to the art of Lorenzo Monaco. In a notebook Fry kept on a trip to the Continent around October of 1899, during which he visited Berlin, there appears the heading "Raczynski Collection," followed by the entry: "Lorenzo Monaco. Early / strangely realistic in faces but strong Sienese line & already his tempera wonderful colour sense. Grey green architecture very simple & figures defile in front (its an anbetung of Kings) in green, red, blue, pink & yellow. Also pale mauve & yellow all put in with washes with great boldness & less hatching than Lippo himself." (Fry Papers, King's College Library, Cambridge, notebook 3, fol. 30.) The work described is the *Adoration of the Magi* now in the National Museum, Poznań (Fig. 185). On fol. 30v of the same notebook is a rapid pencil and pen sketch of the *Adoration* (further discussion of the panel in Fry, 1901, p. 131). In 1903, Roger Fry first attributed to Lorenzo Monaco the *Visitation* and *Adoration of the Magi* in the collection of Sir Hubert Parry (see Catalogue I, London, Courtauld Institute Galleries; Figs. 29 and 31, and Colorplate 3; also see D. Sutton, *Letters of Roger Fry*, vol. 1, London, 1972, p. 209, note 123[1] [for the caption to fig. 25, read *Visitation*]). In his study of the two panels in Gloucester, Fry made passing reference to the Raczyński *Adoration* he had recently seen in Berlin, considering it to be earlier in date. In 1905 Fry again visited Berlin, where he made the following notation: "Berlin. (from memory) / Herr von Kaufman Lorenzo Monaco 2 small pieces a monk (superb) & an adoration predella." (Fry Papers, King's College Library, Cambridge, notebook 13, fol. 11v.) The two pictures, once in the collection of Richard von Kaufmann, are the *Saint Jerome in His Study* in the Rijksmuseum (Fig. 129) and the *Nativity* in the Lehman Collection, Metropolitan Museum of Art (Fig. 30). Two years earlier Fry had published the Gambier-Parry companions to the *Nativity*; their connection would shortly be recognized by Osvald Sirén (1905, pp. 57-58). Roger Fry mentions in a letter to Vanessa Bell of August 5, 1916, that he "restored some old pictures" for Sirén and sold him "one of my Old Masters . . ." (Sutton, *Letters*, vol. 2, p. 400). I am deeply grateful to the executors of the Estate of the late Mrs. Pamela Diamand for permission to publish the above material from the notebooks of Roger Fry, and to Dr. M. A. Halls, Modern Archivist, King's College Library, Cambridge, who located and transcribed the appropriate passages.

132. "The Genius of Aubrey Beardsley," *New York Review of Books* 23, no. 20, Dec. 9, 1976, p. 50.

133. Cf., Figs. 92, 94, 95, and 124-127.

134. The frescoes once in the Convento delle Oblate, Florence, first attributed to Lorenzo Monaco by Berenson and Sirén, are the work of Mariotto di Nardo (see Catalogue II, Florence, Soprintendenza, Deposit, *Agony in the Garden; Christ and the Sleeping Disciples; The Man of Sorrows with an Abbreviated Passion Cycle*).

Luciano Bellosi (1979, p. 62, note 5) has expressed the view that the frescoes at Santa Trinita should be dated around 1420, that is, between the Accademia *Annunciation* and the Uffizi *Adoration of the Magi*, which he dates 1417? and 1422 respectively (for a fuller presentation of Bellosi's opinion, including a suggestion of documentary support, see Catalogue I, Florence, Santa Trinita, Bartolini Salimbeni Chapel, *Life of the Virgin*, History).

135. See E. Baccheschi and S. Levy, *Ferri battuti italiani*, Novara, 1981, p. 8, and pl. 4. For the problems surrounding the attribution of the grille, see Paatz, vol. 5, 1953, pp. 291, 356, note 223, and 358, note 228.

136. The texts of the scrolls held by the three Prophets of the vault are transcribed in Catalogue I, Florence, Santa Trinita, Bartolini Salimbeni Chapel, *Life of the Virgin*. Of the two Prophets who hold scrolls inscribed with texts from Isaiah, the elder would appear to be Isaiah, and the younger, Micah. The identification of the latter is based on the fact that the prophecies of Micah, as well as those of Isaiah, are associated typologically with the conception and advent of Christ (e.g., Micah 5:3). The lineage from David to the Virgin is implied in his placement within the vault web directly above the *Annunciation* on the altar.

137. The various types of fictive tabernacle used in the framing systems of Trecento and early Quattrocento Tuscan fresco cycles have been described and catalogued by A. T. Brown, (vol. 1, pp. 58-61, and vol. 2, pp. 341-51).

138. Document 18A. Here the dedication is cited as "intitolata nella Vergine Maria," whereas Benigno Davanzati (fol. 268) and Ildephonso di San Luigi (p. 268) transformed the words of the original document into "intitolata la Nunziata di Maria Vergine" (Davanzati) and "sotto la invocazione della Vergine annunziata dall'Angiolo" (San Luigi).

139. Document 18A. Ildephonso di San Luigi (p. 237), in a précis of the document, stated that the celebration prescribed for August is an Office of the Dead, but there is no indication of this in the actual text of the document. As the Feast of the Assumption (August 15) was of major importance among Marian celebrations, there is the strongest likelihood that the unspecified feast in August noted in the document was that annual liturgical event (see Note 141).

140. Two notable Florentine Trecento depictions of the *Meeting of Joachim and Anna* include the angel hovering over the couple: Bernardo Daddi, predella of the San Pancrazio Altarpiece (Offner, sec. III, vol. III, 1930, pl. XIV[25]); and follower of Nardo di Cione, Chapel of Saint Anne, Chiostro dei Morti, Santa Maria Novella (Offner, sec. IV, vol. II, 1960, pl. XIX). Neither Taddeo Gaddi in the Baroncelli Chapel nor Giovanni da Milano in the Rinuccini Chapel at Santa Croce depicted the angel above Joachim and Anna.

Although the inclusion of a seascape as a non-narrative element in the *Meeting of Joachim and Anna* does not, to my knowledge, have an iconographic precedent, I would propose conjecturally that it could serve as a metaphoric gloss on the Virgin's immaculacy, insofar as her role as *Stella Maris* was among the traditional fifteen emblems of the Immaculate Conception (for a resumé of the emblems, see Schiller, vol. 4, pt. 2, 1980, pp. 168-69; for the tradition of representing the star in the Madonna of Humility and its association with the *stella maris*, see van Os, 1969, p. 125). Ann Thurston Brown, in a seminar presentation, has suggested tentatively that the seascape with a boat sailing close to a rocky, towered islet in Lorenzo's *Meeting of Joachim and Anna* could be an oblique reference to the Benedictine legend of Helsinus, who was saved in a shipwreck off the coast of Normandy after invoking the name of Mary, on the condition that he faithfully celebrate the feast of the Immaculate Conception (for the legend, see Levi D'Ancona, 1957, pp. 12 and 58-59; fig. 30 illustrates a miniature from an early fifteenth-century Franciscan breviary in which the Meeting of Joachim and Anna is combined with a full rendering of the Helsinus story). A seascape with a towered islet crowns the Berlin *Journey of the Magi* (Fig. 97), a passage that may be both fanciful and symbolic of their widely ranging travels, or again conjecturally, a conflation of the *stella caeli* and *stella maris* that pointed the way for the three Kings and guided seafarers to a safe haven (van Os, 1969, p. 125, with reference to an early fifteenth-century Sienese tract on representations of the Virgin). Similar seascapes are found in a drawing of *Scenes from the Early Life of the Baptist* (Fig. 197) and in a *desco da parto* by Bartolomeo di Fruosino, dated 1428 (Fig. 324).

The two young boys crouching on the bank of the river at the lower left of the *Meeting of Joachim and Anna* defy conclusive interpretation. Do they represent the free play of the painter's imagination, comparable to the insertion of the fisherman into the cliffs of the Berlin *Journey of the Magi*? But that detail may also have been intended as a symbolic gloss (see Note 130). Kiel and Neri (p. 69) interpreted the idyllic motif of the two boys as a contrast to the austerity of the townscape and as a means of vitalizing the scene. For the transformation of the crouching boy into a "putto pissatore" on the reverse of the *desco da parto* by Bartolomeo di Fruosino, see Watson, pp. 4 and 7, and fig. 2; also see Levi D'Ancona, 1961, pp. 92-93, and Watson, fig. 5, for other versions of the type.

141. Given the centrality of the *Miracle of the Snow* lunette, the unspecified feast in August, cited in Document 18A, could possibly be a reference to the *Festum Nivis* (or *Maria ad Nives*) of August 5, which by the fourteenth century had assumed a liturgical usage outside of Rome (see J. Gardner, "Pope Nicholas IV and the decoration of Santa Maria Maggiore," *Zeitschrift für Kunstgeschichte* 36, 1973, p. 34). For the origins and diffusion of the liturgy of the *Festum Nivis* and the imagery of the Miracle of the Snow, see van Os, 1968. Of particular relevance to Don Lorenzo's fresco is van Os's analysis of the transformation from the Roman tradition of the Miracle of the Snow, where both Christ and the Virgin appear, to a type favored in Tuscany in which the Virgin is depicted alone (see pp. 10-24). Among representations in miniature painting, van Os illustrates (fig. 20) a reduced version by the Camaldolese book painter Don Simone, a member of the scrip-

torium at Santa Maria degli Angeli in the later Trecento. As was observed in Note 139, a more universally celebrated Marian feast that falls in August is that of the Assumption of the Virgin (August 15), the subject represented in the lunette over the entrance to the Bartolini Salimbeni Chapel (Fig. 112).

142. See Levi D'Ancona, 1957, pp. 36-38, for a discussion of later mediaeval theological ties between the themes of the Annunciation and the Immaculate Conception of the Virgin.

143. Levi D'Ancona (1957, p. 41) has noted that the Office of the Nativity of the Virgin served for the Feast of the Immaculate Conception until the late fifteenth century. For comment on Maculist and Immaculist controversies, particularly within the Carmelite Order, and on close thematic and visual associations of the Meeting of Joachim and Anna and the Birth of the Virgin, see J. Ruda, "Flemish Painting and the Early Renaissance in Florence: Questions of Influence," *Zeitschrift für Kunstgeschichte* 47, 1984, p. 223. A survey of the doctrine and diverse imagery of the Immaculate Conception may be found in Schiller, vol. 4, pt. 2, 1980, pp. 154-78; the Immaculist aspects of the theme of the Presentation of the Virgin in the Temple are treated on pp. 165-68.

The four *Saints* depicted on the soffit of the entrance arch would seem to be closely associated with the theological implications and the patronage of the chapel, as follows: the *Baptist* stands as the forerunner of Christ and as the son of Elizabeth, traditionally considered a kinswoman of the Virgin; *Bartholomew* was the onomastic saint and principal intercessor of the Bartolini Salimbeni family; *John the Evangelist* was entrusted with Mary by Christ; *Paul* gave emphasis to Christ's body as the vehicle of the Church and to the Virgin as the source of that body (Ephesians 1:22-23; Romans 1:3; II Timothy 2:8).

144. B. Cole, 1977, pl. 56.

145. The recently uncovered frescoed splays of the window in the Brancacci Chapel, at the Carmine, show some resemblance to the rinceau ornamentation of the Bartolini Chapel. This vegetal motif contrasts strongly with the classical fluted pilasters and dentil borders that enframe the narrative scenes.

146. Fremantle, fig. 387. The source of this combination of cityscape, rocky, towered coast, sea, and island would seem to be the Giottesque *Journey of the Magdalen* in the Magdalen Chapel of the Lower Church of San Francesco at Assisi (Sirén, 1917, vol. 2, pl. 77). An assemblage of comparable elements forms the seascape in the upper half of Jacquemart's *Flight into Egypt* in the *Très Belles Heures de Jean de Berry*, painted before 1402 (p. 106; Meiss, 1967, vol. 2, fig. 188). The panoramic view in this miniature has the character of a contrived insertion. Millard Meiss emphasized the influence of Simone Martini's and Ambrogio Lorenzetti's conceptions of landscape in this and related miniatures (1967, vol. 1, pp. 219-21), but sources in Giottesque as well as Sienese works at Assisi and in such Florentine images as those in the Rinuccini and Castellani Chapels at Santa Croce (Fig. 319) should be given further consideration in the process of migration of Tuscan landscape imagery to Northern artistic centers.

147. See van Marle, vol. 3, 1924, fig. 334.

148. Fremantle, fig. 474; and Borsook, pl. 72.

149. See Offner, sec. IV, vol. II, 1960, pls. XX and XXI. In light of Michael Mallory's definition of iconographical types in the Presentation of the Virgin (1964, pp. 533-34), Don Lorenzo may be seen to have combined the Florentine tradition of an exterior setting, where the parents of the Virgin stand together, with a variation on the polygonal architecture of Sienese usage.

150. The long frieze of figures and the contrary rhythms of the defeated suitors and playful children were depicted by Taddeo Gaddi at Santa Croce and Agnolo Gaddi at Prato (Ladis, fig. 41-11; and B. Cole, 1977, pl. 62). The extended isocephalic frieze was also used in a fresco of 1386, from the façade of the Loggia del Bigallo, painted by Niccolò di Pietro Gerini in collaboration with Ambrogio di Baldese (Berenson, 1963, vol. 1, pl. 365). The figural proportion of the standing Joseph in the *Betrothal* is 1:6, in contrast to a proportion of 1:7 for the retainer with the scimitar in the Uffizi *Adoration of the Magi* (Fig. 82), an indication of a significant movement away from decorative elongation (see Note 117). The figural proportion of 1:7 that prevails in the *Meeting of Joachim and Anna* implies either Don Lorenzo's vacillation between two canons or the intervention of an assistant who adhered to the elongations of the *Adoration of the Magi*. Certainly the total composition of the scene is the work of Don Lorenzo. A comparable ambivalence of figural pro-

portions is found in the predella of the *Annunciation* altarpiece of the chapel; in the *Visitation* (Fig. 124), an entirely autograph work, the proportions vary from 1:7 for the standing attendant at the far left to 1:6 for the figure of the Virgin.

151. In the restoration campaign of the 1960s, the fresco of the *Betrothal* was found to contain incisions that served as guidelines, and several pentimenti among those incisions, indicative of an adjustment in the perspective. Similar incised pentimenti are found even in the simple arcade of the *Adoration of the Magi*, in the predella of the Uffizi *Coronation of the Virgin* (Fig. 52). John White (1972, p. 104) has asserted that Don Lorenzo consistently used an "extreme oblique" perspective for distant towns and buildings, and a "foreshortened frontal" construction for "those buildings which fill the frame, particularly in fresco painting." But in the *Betrothal* at Santa Trinita, surely Don Lorenzo's most sophisticated indulgence in spatial effect, there is a combination of these types of perspective that indicates an attraction to illusionistic devices.

The progression from right to left, toward the figure of Mary and ultimately to the altar of the chapel, apparently necessitated a change from the usual placement of the Virgin to the priest's left. This reversal of position required that the ring be put on Mary's left hand in order to give the figure full visibility. Alternately, Lorenzo could have been incorporating an earlier mediaeval practice, prevalent in Rome and Latin countries, of placing the betrothal ring on the left hand (see H. Leclercq, "Anneaux," in *Dictionnaire d'archéologie chrétienne et de liturgie*, ed. F. Cabrol and H. Leclercq, vol. 1, pt. 2, Paris, 1924, col. 2179; also see R. Corso, "Anello," in *Enciclopedia italiana*, vol. 3, Rome, 1929, p. 243, for folkloric distinctions between the use of the left and right hand for betrothal and marriage rings). The traditional position of the Virgin's free arm—in this case her right—across the body, was adapted by Lorenzo to a graceful gesture of gathering up a fall of drapery.

152. The influence on the composition of the method of laying the intonaco is discussed in the entry on the chapel in Catalogue I (Condition and Technique).

153. Documents 16D-F refer to painters who would seem to have been active in the shop of Lorenzo Monaco in the early 1420s. The head of Joachim (Fig. 198) suggests the intervention of Bartolomeo di Fruosino, whose presence is not as immediately detectable elsewhere in the cycle, though he very possibly contributed the various heads in the octagonal frames of the decorative borders (Figs. 104 and 111). The figure of the Virgin in the *Assumption* lunette (Fig. 112), a fresco that was probably not designed and surely not executed by Don Lorenzo, is reminiscent of the same figure in the miniature of the *Death and Assumption of the Virgin* (fol. 54v, Cod. F 72, Bargello), which Levi D'Ancona has attributed to Bartolomeo di Fruosino (1961, pp. 84 and 93; see D'Ancona, vol. 1, 1914, pl. XLIV). That Bartolomeo was still collaborating with Lorenzo Monaco in the early 1420s is substantiated by the fact, first discerned by Levi D'Ancona (1961, pp. 84 and 92), that he was responsible for at least two of the *Prophet* roundels in the altarpiece of the chapel (see Catalogue I, Florence, Santa Trinita; and Catalogue II, Avignon, Musée du Petit Palais, *Saint Lawrence Enthroned, with Saints Ansanus and Margaret*).

154. For an excellent colorplate of the head of the priest in the *Betrothal*, see Meiss, 1970, p. 105.

155. Krautheimer (1956, pp. 124-25 and 131) dated the *Evangelists* and *Church Fathers* circa 1413 and the *Prophets*, for the most part, after 1415.

156. See Lippi's *Funeral of Saint Stephen* in the Cathedral at Prato (Marchini, 1975, fig. 115) and Castagno's *Crucifixion* at Sant'Apollonia, Florence (Horster, p. 176, and pls. 35 and 37; Horster noted the relationship between the crouching figures in Don Lorenzo's and Castagno's frescoes). Berenson implied that Fra Filippo may have assisted Lorenzo Monaco in painting the Bartolini Chapel cycle (1932/33, p. 56). Amerio (1964, col. 340) singled out the *Prophets* in the vault of the Bartolini Chapel as heralds of the growing palpability in Florentine painting.

Antal (pp. 324 and 353, note 102) observed that the virtually contemporary commissioning by the Arte del Cambio of the fresco cycle from Don Lorenzo and the *Saint Matthew* for Orsanmichele from Ghiberti was indicative of the tastes of an "upper-middle-class" guild that remained essentially conservative but nonetheless sought a style that was moderately progressive. Krautheimer (1956, pp. 88-89 and 92), however, envisioned Ghiberti's *Matthew* as a major pronouncement of a new classicism in his style, a work with which the sculptor "fell in with the young *avant-garde* movement of the incipient Renaissance." In Krautheimer's view (1956, pp. 92 and 127), this fundamental shift in style was already evident in the latest reliefs for the North Door. Don Lorenzo's widening sympathies with the new trends of the 1420s did not reach that stage of development.

157. As in his previous inscriptions, Lorenzo continued here to use the Gothic majuscule at the same moment that Gentile da Fabriano and Masaccio were adopting the Roman capital (see Covi, pp. 5-6). By the later 1420s, Ambrogio Traversari was exerting effort for the adoption of a classicizing humanistic script in the books produced by the Angeli scriptorium (see Stinger, pp. 275-76.)

158. Gardner von Teuffel (1982, p. 5) has observed that the rectangular frescoed border, into which the altarpiece is directly set, virtually establishes a second framing system.

159. The gradual resolution of this form of setting for the two principal participants in the Annunciation is discussed by Robb, pp. 485-88, and Spencer, p. 274. In a cut miniature of the *Annunciation* in the British Museum, Don Silvestro dei Gherarducci combined the "portico" setting with the floating angel, a conflation of two basically Sienese types (Boskovits, 1975, pl. 80).

160. See Torriti, fig. 124. H. W. van Os (1969, pp. 48-57) has extensively analyzed the doctrinal and liturgical aspects of Ambrogio's *Annunciation*.

161. The inscription on the frame (see Catalogue I entry on the *Annunciation* altarpiece) is from Luke 1:28-29: "Hail, thou that art highly favoured, the Lord is with thee: blessed art thou among women. / And when she saw him, she was troubled at his saying, and cast in her mind what [manner of salutation this should be]." It is noteworthy that Don Lorenzo's Accademia and Santa Trinita *Annunciation* altarpieces manifest iconographical differences that parallel the two versions of the subject by Simone Martini and Ambrogio Lorenzetti (Uffizi, and Pinacoteca, Siena). In an *Annunciation* miniature (fol. 24v, Cod. F 72, Bargello), painted in the mid-1420s, Bartolomeo di Fruosino introduced the soaring Gabriel of Don Lorenzo's Accademia altarpiece into an image that is otherwise closer to the Santa Trinita *Annunciation* (Levi D'Ancona, 1961, p. 93, and fig. 16).

162. The source of these punctuating consoles in Orcagna's Strozzi Altarpiece at Santa Maria Novella was observed by Gardner von Teuffel (1982, p. 6). Cämmerer-George (p. 183) noted the interruptive placement of the consoles in Don Lorenzo's *Annunciation*.

163. There is a distinct similarity between the upper zones of architecture in the *Annunciation* and in the Manley Collection *Scenes from the Early Life of the Baptist* (Fig. 197).

164. For symbolic allusions to the Trinity in scenes of the *Annunciation*, see Panofsky, vol. 1, p. 132. Rather than depicting the commonly found domestic *thalamus Virginis* as the inner chamber (see Robb, p. 489 and fig. 9), Don Lorenzo constructed an unoccupied space between the portico and the view into the garden. In the *Annunciation* by the Master of Santa Verdiana in the Kisters Collection in Kreuzlingen, of around 1410, there is a close juxtaposition of the descending dove and a triple-barred window in the bedchamber of the Virgin (Boskovits, 1967, fig. 25).

165. The literary source of the miraculous spring is Pseudo-Matthew 20 (see Panofsky, vol. 1, p. 89). For the iconographic tradition, see Schiller, vol. 1, 1971, pp. 118 and 123. Both the bending palm (see Note 68) and the miraculous spring are depicted in a window at Orsanmichele that represents the *Rest on the Flight into Egypt*, the normative context for the spring (see Boskovits, 1975, p. 407, and fig. 96; attributed to Niccolò di Pietro Gerini and dated 1395-1405).

Mirella Levi D'Ancona ("Some New Attributions," 1958, p. 178) has proposed that the central group of Lorenzo's *Flight into Egypt* was influenced by Gentile da Fabriano's panel in the predella of the Uffizi *Adoration of the Magi* of 1423 and, conversely, that the nocturnal illumination of Gentile's *Nativity* panel in that same predella was inspired by Lorenzo's various *Nativity* scenes (e.g., Figs. 30 and 51). Although the silhouette and gait of the ass and the tightly swaddled Infant do exhibit similarities in the two *Flight into Egypt* panels, Lorenzo's Virgin is woven into a game of decorative responses with the Joseph, the female attendant, and the palm, while Gentile's Mother and Child impel the forward movement of the drama. In Lorenzo's Altenburg and Santa Trinita panels (Figs. 32 and 127) the painter followed an iconographic tradition in which the Virgin is placed frontally, whereas Gentile adopted an alternative version in which her position reinforces the lateral course of the action. As Levi D'Ancona proposes, the nocturnal environment of Gentile's *Nativity* predella could, in general terms, reflect Don Lorenzo's several versions of the episode; the angelic illumination of the awakened shepherd would surely seem to have a source in such panels (e.g., Figs. 51 and 95). The mergence of supernatural effect and optical realism in the lighting system of Gentile's *Nativity* is, of course, distinct from the art of Lorenzo Monaco.

166. Luciano Bellosi dated the Bartolini Salimbeni Chapel around 1420, rather than among Lorenzo's final works, but he discerned in the frescoes the growing accommodation of the painter's style to the new modes of the 1420s (*Maestri*, 1965, [p. 6], and in *Ghiberti, 'materia e ragionamenti,'* 1978, p. 149).

167. In an investigation of the iconography of Saint Jerome in early Italian art, Bernhard Ridderbos (pp. 15-40) traces the representation of Saint Jerome in his study, including the pairing of the Saint with the wounded lion. As Ridderbos observes (p. 37), the taming of the lion through removal of the thorn is a symbol for the conquering of the devil's temptations of the flesh and diversions from intellectual and spiritual pursuits. Clifton Olds has suggested to me that the combination of Jerome in his study with the image of the Madonna, rather than deriving from any specific textual source in the Latin Father's writings, reflects his perpetual concern with the virginity of Mary. For the citation of Jerome's writings as evidence of the Virgin's immaculacy, see Levi D'Ancona, 1957, p. 70. A Sienese diptych of the later fourteenth century in the Johnson Collection, Philadelphia, combines the image of Jerome in his study with the Madonna of Humility (*Johnson Collection*, 1966, pp. 71-72 and 93 [illus.]); the parallel with Lorenzo's Copenhagen-Amsterdam diptych was noted independently by Longhi (1965, p. 15, no. 29) and Olsen (1965, p. 54).

168. A limited number of models underlie these works, with variations in iconographic type or quantity of ornamentation apparently conforming to the requirements of the patron. There is no documentary evidence as to whether this large workshop production was maintained in part as a stock of pictures, as opposed to works executed according to specific commissions. For comment on works painted without commission, see B. Cole, "The Interior Decoration of the Palazzo Datini in Prato," *Mitteilungen des Kunsthistorischen Institutes in Florenz* 13, 1967, p. 61, note 2, and idem, 1980, p. xx; Gilbert, 1977, pp. 21 and 28, note 75; van Os, 1974, p. 21. See the following for workshop practices: Wackernagel, Luchs trans., 1981, pp. 308-310; Boskovits, 1975, pp. 159-88. Clusters of works produced in Don Lorenzo's shop under the supervision of a shop assistant or group of assistants with distinguishable stylistic traits are discussed in the following entries in Catalogue I: Florence, Accademia, no. 470, *Madonna and Child with Four Saints* (1408); London, National Gallery, San Benedetto Altarpiece; Pisa, Sant'Ermete, *Madonna of Humility with Eight Angels* (1415); Prato, Galleria Comunale, *Madonna Enthroned, with Four Saints*; Toledo, Museum of Art, *Madonna of Humility*.

The large body of works painted at various phases in the activity of Don Lorenzo's shop, that has been ascribed by Mirella Levi D'Ancona to Matteo Torelli is, in my view, not the production of a single artistic personality; the attributions are cited in individual entries in Catalogues I and II, and range through the Siena triptych (Fig. 132), the *eglomisé* Turin *Madonna* (Fig. 140), the *Annunciation* formerly in the Féron-Stoclet Collection in Brussels (Fig. 157), a large share of the frescoes of the Bartolini Salimbeni Chapel at Santa Trinita (e.g., Figs. 104, 105), the *Saint Lawrence* altarpiece in Avignon (Fig. 244), the Amsterdam *Madonna Enthroned* (Fig. 237) and *Head of the Virgin* (Fig. 235), and numerous miniatures in choir books from Santa Maria degli Angeli and Santa Maria Nuova. For discussion of the proposed reconstruction of Matteo Torelli as a painter of panels and miniatures, see Catalogue I, Florence, Bargello, Cod. E 70.

Bartolomeo di Fruosino came under the direct influence of Don Lorenzo and participated in the activity of his shop, but his work as miniaturist and panel painter is sufficiently distinctive to permit his being considered an individual master (see Note 153, and Catalogue II, Avignon, Musée du Petit Palais, *Saint Lawrence Enthroned, with Saints Ansanus and Margaret*).

169. The *Last Judgment* is in the Museo di San Marco (see Baldini, 1970, pp. 83 and 92; Pope-Hennessy, 1974, p. 192 and fig. 2, with reference to Orlandi, p. 29). By the mid-1420s the workshop at San Marco, under Angelico's supervision, was adding miniatures to initial letters of the choir books at

Santa Maria degli Angeli that had been left incomplete (see Catalogue I, Florence, Biblioteca Laurenziana, Cod. Cor. 3). Antal (p. 338) interpreted this interchange as a "typical sign of the times, a symbol of the transference of leadership once again from the more secluded Benedictines to the more active Dominicans."

170. The *Coronation of the Virgin* altarpieces by Lorenzo di Niccolò in San Domenico, Cortona, and Santa Croce, Florence, dated 1402 and 1410 respectively, manifest the transformation in the painter's style during the first decade of the century (see Eisenberg, 1966, p. 16, and figs. 7 and 8; B. Cole, 1980, pp. 52-55, and figs. 33 and 34). Fahy (1978, p. 379) suggests that the change in style from the Cortona to the Santa Croce altarpieces "reflects the milieu of Ghiberti and the younger Renaissance artists at Florence" and proposes that the latter work, dated 1410, anticipates Don Lorenzo's *Coronation of the Virgin* for Santa Maria degli Angeli, dated 1414. The figure of Christ in Lorenzo di Niccolò's Santa Croce altarpiece would seem more predictive of the *Coronation of the Virgin* in London (Fig. 175), produced in Don Lorenzo's shop after 1415, thereby helping to confirm the retardataire nature of the figure style in a work that is at the same time progressive in the conception of space.

The augmentation of calligraphic line in the style of Mariotto di Nardo during the first decade of the century is discussed by Boskovits (1968, p. 22). The voluminously draped *Coronation of the Virgin* by Mariotto in the Acton Collection, Florence, a work of around 1415 that bears the apocryphal date of 1431, was, in fact, at one time attributed to Lorenzo Monaco (Milanesi, 1883, p. 13, no. 50; see Eisenberg, 1966, p. 23, note 18, Boskovits, 1975, p. 394, and Fremantle, fig. 956).

171. The Prato altarpiece was painted for the reformed Benedictine monastery of the Olivetani alle Sacca, which explains the white habit of Saint Benedict and his transposition to a more central location than he holds in Don Lorenzo's model (see G. Datini, *Musei di Prato, Musei d'Italia—Meraviglie d'Italia*, vol. 1, Bologna, 1972, p. 17, and M. Boskovits, "Due secoli di pittura murale a Prato: aggiunte e precisazioni," *Arte illustrata* 3, 25/26, 1970, p. 45, note 30). Whereas Andrea di Giusto depended on Don Lorenzo's Monte Oliveto Altarpiece for composition and figural types, the lavishly ornamented haloes are modified adaptations from the *Coronation of the Virgin* from Santa Maria degli Angeli (cf. Fig. 46). Wohl (p. 67, and pl. 20) has noted Andrea's subsequent use of the Prato composition of the Madonna and Child in a panel in the Accademia in Florence, but with a lightly veiled Child tending toward the more advanced model of Domenico Veneziano's nude Infant in the Carnesecchi Tabernacle (Wohl, pl. 6), whose pose and gesture in turn continue to echo Don Lorenzo's Monte Oliveto Altarpiece.

The fact that the *Naming of Saint John the Baptist* in the predella of the Prato altarpiece is a nearly exact copy of Fra Angelico's panel in the Museo di San Marco establishes a date before 1435 for that work (see Pope-Hennessy, 1974, p. 196, citing earlier notices by Salmi). So committed a copyist as Bicci di Lorenzo did not produce any literal replicas of works by Lorenzo Monaco, although in Bicci's *Annunciation* in the Walters Art Gallery, Baltimore, there are evident adaptations of elements from the Santa Trinita altarpiece and, as Zeri has noted, from the *Annunciation* formerly in the Féron-Stoclet Collection, Brussels (1976, vol. 1, p. 32).

172. For the probable identification of Francesco d'Antonio with the "Francesco Fiorentino" cited by Vasari as a pupil of Lorenzo Monaco, see Sirén, 1905, p. 162, and Colnaghi, 1928, p. 105. Roberto Longhi firmly localized the dating of the frescoes in Figline (1940, p. 186, note 24). Francesco's dependence on Don Lorenzo's style and his subsequent adoptions of the idioms of Masolino, Masaccio, and Gentile da Fabriano were summarized by Curtis Shell (1965, pp. 467-69; note 12 provides the essential literature on Francesco d'Antonio). For notices of Francesco's adaptation of Don Lorenzo's *Lamentation* of 1408, see Catalogue I, Prague, National Gallery, Literature, 1946, Meiss; 1965, Shell. The direct quotations from Starnina in the Fitzwilliam triptych are proposed in Note 60 above.

The transformations in the style of Rossello di Jacopo Franchi also demonstrate the process of an eclectic painter drawing upon models from several generations of masters, ranging from the later Trecento, through Ghiberti and Lorenzo Monaco, to Masaccio and Filippo Lippi (see the documented study by Peters). The miniature of *Saint Stephen Enthroned* (Fig. 326; Museo dell'Opera del Duomo, Prato, Cod. D, fol. 48v), of the late 1420s, displays Rossello's continuing dependence on Don Lorenzo's work, recalling directly the early *Madonna* in Cambridge (Fig. 15), the London *Coronation of the*

Virgin (Fig. 175), and the drawing of *Saint Benedict* in the Uffizi (Fig. 63). The attribution to Rossello of this large miniature, virtually of predella scale, is concurred with by Ciatti (p. 516) and Peters (pp. 84-85).

173. Curtis Shell's work of 1958 remains the most comprehensive statement on the art of Giovanni dal Ponte. Luciano Bellosi has more recently raised the issue of Starnina's influence on his style (Bellosi and Bellini, p. xix). The literature on Parri Spinelli is recorded in Bellosi and Bellini, pp. 36-47; in addition, see M. J. Zucker, "Parri Spinelli: Aretine Painter of the Fifteenth Century," Ph.D. diss., Columbia University, 1973.

174. For a panoramic characterization of the complex stylistic cultures that underlay Masolino's emerging art, see Micheletti, pp. 7-14. Contrasting theories with regard to Angelico's beginnings are found in the approach of John Pope-Hennessy, who has left the question open, but tentatively conjectured that his first training might have occurred in the workshop of Ambrogio di Baldese (1974, p. 5), and in Diane Cole Ahl's view that Angelico's earliest artistic experience was in the workshop of Lorenzo Monaco (1980, pp. 367-68). Miklós Boskovits (1976, p. 45 and passim) discounts the importance of Don Lorenzo's influence on Angelico and views his beginnings as strongly eclectic, but already indicative of an innovative vision.

175. The direct influence of the composition of Don Lorenzo's Accademia *Man of Sorrows* was first observed by Henrik Lindberg (vol. 1, pp. 122-23; the works are confronted in vol. 2, pls. 40 and 41). Paul Joannides has noted the reversed quotation of the Virgin in the Santa Trinita *Betrothal* fresco in Masolino's destroyed predella panel of the same subject ("A Masolino Partially Reconstructed," *Source* 4, 4, 1985, p. 3 and fig. 1). In that lost panel Masolino introduced an extended arcade similar to that in the *Adoration of the Magi* in Poznań (Fig. 185), but with a consistent lighting from the left in contrast to the decoratively symmetrical system of lighting in the earlier panel. Millard Meiss described and illustrated the "diffuse luminosity" of Masolino's frescoes in Sant'Agostino at Empoli of 1424, noting the influence of Starnina's and Don Lorenzo's concern for the effect of light on objects (1970, p. 107; colorplates, pp. 110-11).

176. Observing the "principle of circularity" in the angelic choir, Pope-Hennessy (1974, p. 11) defined its source in Ghiberti, specifically in the sculptor's design for the *Assumption of the Virgin* window for the Duomo in Florence (also see Catalogue I, Florence, Uffizi, *Coronation of the Virgin*).

A more active calligraphy emerges in certain works by Fra Angelico's shop in which there is also the inclusion of elaborately decorated textiles as backdrops (see Pope-Hennessy, 1974, figs. 53, 54, 55, and 86). These works apparently would have met the taste of patrons who continued to favor the rhythmic linearism of Lorenzo Monaco and the surface embellishments of Gentile da Fabriano.

177. The relationship of the San Marco *Madonna* to the Monte Oliveto Altarpiece has been characterized by Pope-Hennessy as "one of iconography rather than style" (1974, p. 13). In later versions of the *Madonna Enthroned* by Don Lorenzo and his workshop, for which the Monte Oliveto Altarpiece was the model, there is a clear anticipation of Angelico's San Marco panel in the convincing space and in the shift from the gracefully arched to the erect pose of the Child (e.g., Museo della Collegiata, Empoli, and Thyssen-Bornemisza Foundation, Lugano, Figs. 156 and 159).

178. As Pope-Hennessy observed, the quality of translucence distinguishes Angelico's rendering of surfaces even among his earliest pictures (1974, p. 12; plates 8-9, and figs. 7-8; also see p. 40). Limpid pinks and light blues are omnipresent notes in Angelico's palette that would seem to stem more directly from Agnolo Gaddi than from Don Lorenzo. Moreover, Angelico's subtly graduated chiaroscuro precludes the juxtaposition of variegated colors and the hatching of surfaces that are inherent to Don Lorenzo's technique.

179. The recent investigations of Fra Filippo's earliest style by Jeffrey Ruda (see p. 76 for reference to his preceding studies, and pp. 1-9 for an historiographic review) have broken new ground in the definition of the painter's roots and subsequent development, and have, in my view, decisively countered the traditional conception of his strictly Masaccesque beginnings. See Notes 131 and 156 above for observations by Roger Fry and Bernard Berenson that indicate awareness of a stylistic progression from Don Lorenzo to Fra Filippo. While I believe there is insufficient evidence to support Berenson's guarded proposal that Fra Filippo may have assisted

Lorenzo Monaco in the fresco cycle at Santa Trinita, the conjecture points up an aspect of stylistic continuity, notably in the favoring of a secondary palette.

180. In the Introductory Essay (p. 39) I have noted the parallel between Don Lorenzo's and Fra Filippo's precipitous shifts from architecture to landscape in narrative scenes, whether of fresco or predella scale. Also see Ruda, p. 129, note 19, for further comment on continuity from Don Lorenzo's predellas to the style of Fra Filippo. Curtis Shell gave eloquent expression to the balance between line and mass in Lippi's style ("The Early Style of Fra Filippo Lippi and the Prato Master," *Art Bulletin* 43, 1961, p. 200). In Lippi's Uffizi *Coronation of the Virgin*, painted for Sant'Ambrogio in Florence, he shifted the firmamental arcs of Don Lorenzo's *Coronation* altarpiece for Santa Maria degli Angeli from the base to the crest of the composition (see Marchini, 1975, fig. 21).

181. Herbert Horne first commented on Botticelli's inheritance from Lorenzo Monaco: "It is this quality of line [of Lorenzo Monaco], like a strain of the blood which reasserts itself in an after-generation, that recurs with a new significance, and a finer power of expression, in the paintings of Botticelli." (*Alessandro Filipepi, Commonly called Sandro Botticelli, Painter of Florence*, London, 1908, p. 10).

Offner (*Studies*, 1927, p. 2, and *Italian Primitives at Yale*, 1927, pp. 21-22) and Pudelko (1938/39, p. 81) observed the lyrical, non-monumental strain in Florentine painting and Don Lorenzo's place in its progression. In Botticelli's fresco from San Martino della Scala and a panel in the Pushkin Museum, Moscow, the Annunciatory Gabriels are reversions to the floating type found in Don Lorenzo's Accademia *Annunciation* (Fig. 77; see R.W. Lightbown, *Sandro Botticelli*, London, 1978, vol. 1, pls. 24 and 47). The lineage from Lorenzo Monaco to the generation of Botticelli is further indicated by the revival of the cutout crucifix late in the century, a type that earlier had passed directly from Don Lorenzo's generation to that of Fra Angelico (see Shapley, 1966, figs. 326 and 327; Pope-Hennessy, 1974, fig. 62; Cole Ahl, 1980, fig. 10).

The monumental forms of Andrea del Castagno are totally divergent from the style of Lorenzo Monaco, but Andrea's two contemplative *Crucifixion* frescoes, both originally at Santa Maria degli Angeli, betray a spiritual inheritance from the earlier master (see Horster, pls. 17 and 109, and Note 156 above).

Catalogue

METHOD OF THE CATALOGUE

THE CATALOGUE is arranged in two parts: I. Works by Lorenzo Monaco and His Workshop; II. Other Works Ascribed to Lorenzo Monaco. In both sections the individual works are presented in alphabetical order by city, and within the geographical heading, again alphabetically, by gallery or collection, and church. Catalogue I includes the limited group of works by Lorenzo Monaco discussed in the Introductory Essay that bear the stamp of the painter's technique and style at the moments of his fullest mastery and thereby provide the bases for attribution. A symbol (§) precedes each catalogue entry for works approached in the Introductory Essay. Catalogue I also includes those works that I consider to have been painted collaboratively in the workshop at various moments during the career of Lorenzo Monaco. Although the master provided the design for a number of these pictures, the execution reveals a significant intervention of assistants. The illustrations of works that are primarily by Lorenzo Monaco are arranged in the order of their presentation in the Introductory Essay, while those that I ascribe to the collaborative activity of the workshop are as often as possible presented in clusters that are intended to demonstrate stylistic affinities.

The range of quality in the work of Don Lorenzo's shop is extremely wide, indicating that although he was largely responsible for most of the major commissions, a corps of painters in his employ was producing devotional images in great quantity, either under the master's supervision or independently. I have chosen to cast so wide a net in Catalogue I in order to provide a corpus of works that represents a particular idiom of Florentine painting. Because the working methods of a late mediaeval *bottega* were highly stratified, the search for a nucleus of autograph works best avoids, I believe, the atomization of the artistic milieu and the stylistic modality formulated by the master in the context of his workshop.

Detailed comment on condition is restricted to those works for which there is a technical report or in which a significant change from the original state is visible. If a report on condition or conservation may be found in a readily accessible publication, that source is cited and the information is presented here in abbreviated form. The literature on each work is arranged chronologically in order to provide a cumulative sequence of critical opinion before indulging in comment. The complete titles for abbreviated citations of sources may be found in the bibliography at the end of the book. If a work has been thoroughly catalogued in a modern and conveniently available publication, the full history and literature are not repeated. Figure numbers are included in bibliographical citations when the painting is not reproduced in this monograph or when the earlier illustration records a different state than the photograph published here. Entries in biographical dictionaries, encyclopedias, and exhibition catalogues are noted when they contain a contribution to the critical literature. The initial appearance of a work in a museum's catalogue is cited; subsequent editions are noted if the attribution has been changed, new information is provided, or the catalogue has entered the standard literature. My position on the attribution of works that were once components of an altarpiece but are now dispersed, or on groups of closely related shop works, is presented within the entry for one element of the group, with cross-referral to the others.

Catalogue II includes works ascribed to Lorenzo Monaco that I do not believe were produced either by him or within the stylistic "culture" of his shop, or are by painters who came under his influence but exhibit a distinct individuality. These works may be, at one extreme, mediocre efforts that display superficially adopted traits of Don Lorenzo's style or, conversely, works of a superior quality that represent a significantly different stylistic idiom from that of Lorenzo Monaco within the hybrid language of later Trecento and early Quattrocento painting in Florence. This is the case, in particular, with many of the works that have been assigned to the early activity of the painter. I have sought to convey my vacillating stand on certain of these attributions. The rubric "imitator of," which is attached to numerous works in Catalogue II, is used when Don Lorenzo's influence appears to be of primary importance, but there is a sufficient admixture of other stylistic strains to indicate that a work did not issue from the shop of Lorenzo Monaco.

The citation of literature in Catalogue II begins with the initial published attribution of a work to Lorenzo Monaco, where the earlier literature is almost invariably recorded, but previous literature may be cited if it contains a significant alternative attribution. When a work in Catalogue II is not reproduced, reference is made wherever possible to a published illustration or photographic source.

An appendix to the catalogue lists the unknown works that have been ascribed to Lorenzo Monaco in documents and pre-nineteenth-century literary sources.

A final word regards miniatures by Don Lorenzo and his workshop. Whether they remain in their original books or have been detached, the miniatures are approached from a stylistic standpoint; the individual choir books are not treated in codical or liturgical terms. Bibliographies and summaries of attributions for the miniatures in choir books were thoroughly recorded by Mirella Levi D'Ancona ("Some New Attributions," 1958, pp. 188-91), who has also provided a liturgical index of the twenty choir books from Santa Maria degli Angeli, now in the Biblioteca Laurenziana (1978, pp. 215-16). In the present catalogue, the only citations of opinions prior to 1958 are those of Anna Maria Ciaranfi (1932), who published the fundamental study of Lorenzo Monaco as a miniaturist. Levi D'Ancona's encyclopedic study of manuscript painting at Santa Maria degli Angeli, now in preparation, should provide a definitive corpus.

I
LORENZO MONACO AND HIS WORKSHOP

ALTENBURG, Staatliches Lindenau-Museum, no. 23

Crucifixion with Saints Francis, Benedict, and Romuald

FIG. 173

Panel: 56 x 42 cm.

CONDITION: The panel has been slightly trimmed along the lower side and bottom edges, resulting in a loss of small areas of the saints' habits.

HISTORY: Acquired in Rome in 1845 by Dr. E. Braun, as a work of Spinello Aretino. The panel entered the Altenburg collections in that same year.

LITERATURE: 1848, von Quandt and Schulz, no. 121: Spinello Aretino // 1897, Schmarsow, p. 176: Spinello Aretino // 1898, Becker, no. 23: Spinello Aretino // 1905, Sirén, p. 42: Lorenzo Monaco, 1403-1405 // 1909, Berenson, p. 152: LM, early // 1915, Becker, revision of 1898 catalogue, p. 31, no. 23: LM // 1927, van Marle, vol. 9, pp. 148-49: LM, 1408-1412 // 1929, Suida, p. 392: LM // 1932, Berenson, p. 298: deletes "early" (1963, vol. 1, p. 117) // 1938/39, Pudelko, p. 248, note 35: LM, about 1404 // 1955, Gabelentz, p. 52: LM // 1961, Oertel, pp. 130-131: LM, ca. 1414 // 1975, Boskovits, p. 337: LM, 1410-15.

COMMENT: The Altenburg *Crucifixion* links the autograph work of Lorenzo Monaco of around 1410, notably the four *Prophets* (Figs. 40-43) in the Metropolitan Museum, New York, with a shop tradition that had its climax in the San Benedetto Altarpiece of the years 1415-20 (see Catalogue I, London, National Gallery). The figures of Benedict and Romuald have the bulky presence of the *Prophets* and of the Stuttgart *Madonna* (Fig. 39), and also show a degree of kinship with the transfixed Joseph in the Metropolitan Museum *Nativity* (Fig. 30). Although Lorenzo abandoned these palpable forms by the time he designed the *Coronation of the Virgin* of 1414 for Santa Maria degli Angeli, they persisted in some works largely by his shop. The intervention of an assistant in the Altenburg panel is apparent in the sharply angular and inorganic passages in the draperies of Benedict and Romuald and in the intractable line and abrupt modelling of facial features. There may be discernible here the same hand that first assisted Don Lorenzo in the upper zones of the *Man of Sorrows* (Fig. 18) of 1404, that subsequently executed the Munich *Saint Peter* (Fig. 172), the Saint John in the San Giovannino dei Cavalieri group (Fig. 76), and the Yale *Crucifixion* (Fig. 174), and that would be extensively responsible for the painting of the San Benedetto Altarpiece. Although separated by at least half a decade, there is a clear stylistic continuity from the Benedict and Romuald of the Altenburg panel to the Romuald of the London *Coronation* (Fig. 175) who again exhibits the harsh angularity that jars the principal rhythm of the figure, and the coarse rendering of the face. The figure of Christ in the Altenburg panel helps to establish a dating around 1410; the compact proportions of the body are closer to *Crucifix* no. 3153 (Fig. 69) in the Accademia, Florence, than to the elongated forms in the crosses produced by Don Lorenzo and his shop after 1415 (e.g., Florence, San Giovannino dei Cavalieri, Fig. 70). The opaque stuff of the loincloth is further indication of an earlier date.

The Altenburg *Crucifixion with Saints* signals the debt owed by Lorenzo Monaco and his workshop to the tradition of grave and richly bearded patriarchs established by Nardo di Cione in the mid-Trecento. Don Lorenzo's first addition to that lineage was the noble miniature of *Romuald* (Fig. 4) in a choir book of the mid-1390s (see Catalogue I, Florence, Biblioteca Laurenziana, Cod. Cor. 8, fol. 76). The Altenburg Benedict and Romuald are his spiritual and physical heirs. This intensely contemplative icon is exceptional in the equal importance given the patron saints of the Camaldolese and the Franciscans, which raises the possibility that the image was not painted specifically for Camaldolese use. By 1410 Lorenzo Monaco had directed a workshop outside the walls of Santa Maria degli Angeli for at least a decade, so that the monastic alliance in the Altenburg panel could have been formed at the request of a secular patron whose family in some way served both Orders. For a late work of Lorenzo Monaco and his shop in which Franciscan imagery prevails, see Catalogue I, Fiesole, Museo Bandini. [ca. 1410]

§ ALTENBURG, Staatliches Lindenau-Museum, no. 90

Flight into Egypt

FIG. 32

Panel: 20 x 32.3 cm. (without modern additions)

CONDITION: See Oertel, 1961, p. 132. The quatrefoil has been somewhat truncated. With the exception of the bottom center and lower right, all of the angles and lobes reveal small additions of wood and repainting to substitute in part for the losses. With these additions, the dimensions are 21.2 x 35.5 cm. The haloes have been regilded. A coarsely retouched loss at the tip of the Virgin's nose modifies the contour and facial expression.

HISTORY: In the collection of Bernhard von Lindenau by 1848; bequeathed to the Duchy of Sachsen-Altenburg in 1854.

LITERATURE: 1848, von Quandt and Schulz, no. 31: Sienese school, mid-fourteenth century // 1870, J. A. Crowe and G. B. Cavalcaselle, *Geschichte der italienischen Malerei*, ed. M. Jordan, vol. 3, Leipzig, p. 377: probably by Lorenzo Monaco rather than from the Sienese school // 1896, Berenson, p. 119: LM, early // 1897, Schmarsow, p. 161: credits Hermann Hettner with first attributing the work to Lorenzo, but no reference is provided // 1898, Schmarsow, p. 509: LM // 1898, Becker, no. 90: LM // 1902, Frizzoni, p. 290: LM; establishes connection of the *Flight* with the *Nativity* in the von Kaufmann Collection in Berlin (now New York, Lehman-Metropolitan) // 1905, Sirén, pp. 57 and 59: LM, 1408-1412; first observes the relationship of the *Flight* and the von Kaufmann *Nativity* with the Gambier-Parry *Visitation* and *Adoration of the Magi* (now London, Courtauld Institute Galleries) // 1909, Berenson, p. 152: omits the qualification of "early" (1932, p. 298; 1963, vol. 1, p. 117) // 1927, van Marle, vol. 9, p. 168: LM; inferior work of the painter's old age // 1929, Suida, p. 392: LM // 1937/38, Sandberg-Vavalà, pp. 34-38: LM; earlier than *Coronation* predella of 1413 // 1938/39, Pudelko, p. 77, note 5: LM, ca. 1405 // 1961, Oertel, pp. 131-32, color illus. pl. 51: LM, ca. 1405 // 1966, Castelfranchi Vegas, pl. 83 (in color): LM, 1410-20 // 1975, Boskovits, p. 337: LM, 1405-1410.

COMMENT: See Catalogue I, London, Courtauld Institute Galleries, *Visitation* and *Adoration of the Magi*; and New York, Metropolitan Museum of Art, *Nativity*. [ca. 1407-1408]

§ AMSTERDAM, Rijksmuseum, no. A 3976

Saint Jerome in His Study

FIGS. 129, 130

Panel: 23 x 18 cm. (including engaged frame)

CONDITION: The gold ground at the right has been abraded and partially repainted, effacing the original crackle. A similarly coarse restoration was imposed on the lower left and upper right segments of the halo.

HISTORY: Costabili Collection, Ferrara, by 1872; Richard von Kaufmann Collection, Berlin, 1885; acquired by Otto Lanz, Amsterdam, 1917. After the Second World War the panel came under the protection of the Dienst voor's Rijks Verspreide Kunstvoorwerpen, and in 1960 was transferred to the collections of the Rijksmuseum.

LITERATURE: 1872, *Catalogo de'quadri di varie scuole pittoriche nella Galleria Costabili in Ferrara*, Ferrara, p. 7, no. 59: attribution uncertain; perhaps a Florentine work in the manner of Andrea del Castagno (the picture does not appear in the 1838 catalogue of the Costabili Collection [*Descrizione della Quadreria Costabili*, Ferrara]) // 1885, Catalogue of Costabili sale, Milan, April 27, no. 19: school of Murano // 1889, Harck, p. 206: tentatively Lorenzo Monaco // 1896, Berenson, p. 119: LM (1932, p. 298) // 1902, Frizzoni, p. 290: LM // 1905, Sirén, pp. 95-96: LM, 1418; connects panel with the *Madonna of Humility* in the Thorvaldsens Museum, Copenhagen // 1917, Friedländer, no. 4: LM // 1927, van Marle, vol. 9, p. 150: LM, around 1408 // 1929, Suida, p. 293: LM // 1934, Amsterdam, *Italiaansche Kunst*, p. 88, no. 241: LM // 1938/39, Pudelko, p. 78, note 9: LM, after 1414 // 1941, Degenhart, p. 35: the luminosity and refinement of color reveal Don Lorenzo's connection with art of miniature painting // 1963, Berenson, vol. 1, p. 117: connection with the Thorvaldsens *Madonna* mentioned with question mark // 1965, Bellosi, *Maestri*, [p. 6]: LM, shortly before 1422 // 1965, Gore, p. 17, no. 29: rejects van Marle's dating of work around 1408, and implies agreement with Sirén's placement late in Lorenzo's career // 1965, Murray, p. 284: LM, before 1413 // 1974, van Os and Prakken, pp. 68-70 (entry by Saskia Bos):

agrees with van Marle's early dating ca. 1408, because of close stylistic connections with *Nativity* in the Lehman Collection; provides further bibliography and short essay on the iconography of Saint Jerome in his study // 1975, Boskovits; p. 337: LM, 1415-20 // 1976, Amsterdam, *Rijksmuseum*, p. 393: LM.

COMMENT: For the companion panel, see Catalogue I, Copenhagen, Thorvaldsens Museum, *Madonna of Humility*. The early dating proposed by van Marle (1927) and supported more recently by Bos (1974) is not tenable, given the stylistic analogies between the *Saint Jerome* and the predella of the *Annunciation* in the Bartolini Salimbeni Chapel at Santa Trinita. Comparison of the female attendant in the *Flight into Egypt* (Fig. 127) with the *Jerome* demonstrates the contemporaneity of these works. In addition, the stippled technique used in both the head of Jerome and the lion is found identically in Lorenzo's miniatures and drawings of the late 1410s and early 1420s (e.g., Bargello, Cod. H 74, Fig. 101; *Journey of the Magi*, Berlin, Print Room, Figs. 96-97). [ca. 1422-23]

AMSTERDAM, Rijksmuseum, no. A 4006

Stigmatization of Saint Francis
FIG. 190

Panel: 67.5 x 53.3 cm. (painted surface)

CONDITION: In generally good condition, excepting a crudely repainted vertical crack through the landscape and the head of Saint Francis. For a fuller report, see van Os and Prakken, 1974, p. 70, no. 35; for comment on the frame, see below.

HISTORY: Neither the source nor the date of acquisition by Otto Lanz of Amsterdam is known. At the end of the Second World War the picture came under the protection of the Dienst voor's Rijks Verspreide Kunstvoorwerpen and in 1960 was transferred to the collections of the Rijksmuseum.

LITERATURE: 1927, van Marle, vol. 9, p. 150: Lorenzo Monaco, after 1408, but before *Coronation* of 1413 // 1929, Suida, p. 392: LM // 1932, Berenson, p. 298: LM (1963, vol. 1, p. 117) // 1932, Amsterdam, *Italiaansche Kunst*, p. 88, no. 240: LM // 1938/39, Pudelko, p. 78, note 9: between 1414 and end of Don Lorenzo's career; first to associate the panel with the *Funeral of Saint Francis* in the Pallavicini Collection, Rome // 1941, Degenhart, p. 35: LM; with high technical refinement, reaches a summit of the International Style // 1945, Brandi, no. 68: LM; suggests connection with the *Funeral of Saint Francis* in Pallavicini Collection; an independent observation (confirming Pudelko's earlier proposal) // 1959, Zeri, no. 281: LM, implying a late date because of connection with Pallavicini panel // 1974, van Os and Prakken, p. 70, no. 35 (entry by S. Bos): LM, implying a late date; further bibliography // 1975, Boskovits, p. 337: LM, 1420-25 // 1976, Amsterdam, *Rijksmuseum*, p. 393: LM // 1979, Bellosi, pp. 63-65: LM in latest style; integrates with *Crucifixion*, Museo Bandini, Fiesole and Pallavicini *Funeral of Saint Francis*.

COMMENT: The composition is by Lorenzo Monaco, but the execution is by a close associate in the shop. The drawing of the head and cowl of Saint Francis does not convey the rhythmic pulse of Lorenzo's hand, and the folds radiating from the knee are merely mechanically correct and fail to reinforce the ascending tension of the figure. The formulaic neutrality of the rocky masses is recognized when they are compared with landscapes in Lorenzo's predella panel with *Scenes from the Life of Saint Onuphrius* (Florence, Accademia; Fig. 95), or in the pinnacles above Fra Angelico's *Deposition* in the Museo di San Marco (Fig. 90), where the shapes and lighting of the landscape give resonance to the drama and echo the springing energy of the figures. Nonetheless, that the painter of the Amsterdam panel was among Lorenzo's most talented associates is proved by comparing the scene with its companion, the *Funeral of Saint Francis* (Fig. 191) in the Pallavicini Collection, Rome, which Cesare Brandi (1945) fittingly assigned to an assistant, in part because of the schematic drawing of the figures.

In spite of obvious inadequacies in execution, the Rome panel and its more worthy counterpart in Amsterdam, along with the *Funeral of a Bishop Saint in Nice* (Fig. 193), perhaps by the same hand again using a design by the master, form a cluster of works that represent Don Lorenzo's most advanced representation of space. The Rijksmuseum and Pallavicini panels may be dated in the last years of his career, around 1422-23. Federico Zeri (1959) justifiably cast doubt on the possibility that the two panels were part of a predella. Saskia Bos's opinion that the frame of the Amsterdam panel is original (1974, van

Os and Prakken), is countered by Luciano Bellosi's (1979, pp. 63-65) integration of the Amsterdam and Pallavicini panels with the *Crucifixion* in the Museo Bandini in Fiesole, which has exactly the same frame ornament as the panel in Rome (see Figs. 191 and 192). (Also see Catalogue I, Rome, Pallavicini Collection, *Funeral of Saint Francis*; Fiesole, Museo Bandini, *Crucifixion with the Virgin and Saints John the Evangelist and Francis*; and Nice, Musée des Beaux-Arts, *Funeral of a Bishop Saint*.) [ca. 1422-23]

BERGAMO, Accademia Carrara, no. 918 (Morelli Collection, no. 6)

The Man of Sorrows
FIG. 136

Panel: 33.4 x 22.9 cm.

CONDITION: The four edges of the panel have been cut, resulting in the loss of segments of the cusping and an unknown extent of the front of the sarcophagus. The surface reveals one long vertical crack to the left of center and some superficial scratches. A heavy crackle pervades the gold ground, which shows some crude repair, being especially disruptive in the halo ornamentation above the left shoulder of Christ. For further comment on condition, see Zeri and Rossi, p. 68. The photograph provided by the Accademia Carrara for Fig. 136 cuts fractionally beyond the present edges of the panel and thereby removes a small remnant of the front of the sarcophagus and the top edge of the cross, which is framed in by a truncated cusp (cf. Zeri and Rossi, ill. on p. 69).

HISTORY: Bequest of Sen. Giovanni Morelli to the Accademia Carrara, 1891.

LITERATURE: 1892, Frizzoni, p. 3: Lorenzo Monaco // 1896, Berenson, p. 119: LM (1932, p. 298; 1963, vol. 1, p. 117) // 1897, Frizzoni, pp. 82-83: LM // 1905, Sirén, p. 39: LM; closest in style to Empoli triptych of 1404, for which it was perhaps once the central pinnacle // 1927, van Marle, vol. 9, p. 176: shop of LM // 1929, Suida, p. 392: LM // 1938/39, Pudelko, p. 242, note 24: LM, related to the *Man of Sorrows* of 1404; refutes Sirén's association of the panel with the Empoli triptych // 1955, Ottino della Chiesa, p. 14 (1967 ed., p. 12): LM // 1975, Boskovits, p. 338: LM, 1405-1410 // 1979, Rossi, p. 26, no. 918: LM // 1986, Zeri and Rossi, p. 68: LM, ca. 1405; possibly with the intervention of a pupil or follower in the studio, working from the master's design, indicated by the rather mechanical and summary execution and the dry calligraphy; suggest stylistic connections with the *Madonna of Humility* in New York (Fig. 141) and the *Crucifixion* in Seattle (Fig. 137), and strong resemblance to the *Saint Lawrence* altarpiece in Avignon (Fig. 244); note another version of the subject by Don Lorenzo, formerly in the Van Gelder Collection, Brussels (q.v., Catalogue I).

COMMENT: On first response, the Bergamo panel would seem simply to be a minuscule offshoot from the *Man of Sorrows* of 1404 (Fig. 18). Certainly the design was adapted from that work, or perhaps even provided by Don Lorenzo, but the rigid drawing, observed by Zeri and Rossi (1986), and the imprecise workmanship of the punched and milled halo imply execution by an assistant in the workshop. The Bergamo panel, however, is valuable evidence of transition in the art of Lorenzo Monaco at the turn of the century. Stylistically, the work faces in two directions, forward to the great icon of 1404, which would have occupied Don Lorenzo for a considerable time before that inscribed date, and retrospectively to the *Agony in the Garden* and its predella (Figs. 7-14), and to the early *Madonna* in the Berenson Collection (Fig. 16). Along with the advancements of mid-decade, recollection of those works of the last years of the Trecento is discerned in the rounded cranial structure of the Christ, the conformation of the overlapping arm and hand, and the temperate modelling and lighting of the torso.

As Zeri and Rossi noted, the loss of the original contour of the panel permits only speculation as to its function. The likelihood, however, is that the work was either an independent devotional image or was accompanied by an adjoining panel, in which case the subject customarily would have been the Madonna and Child. The Man of Sorrows, whether alone or as part of a diptych, was a more popular devotional image in Trecento Siena than in Florence (see *Madonna and Man of Sorrows*, Museo Horne, Florence, no. 55-56; Meiss, 1967, vol. 2, figs. 631 and 632: workshop of Barna). [1400-1405]

§ BERLIN, Kaiser-Friedrich-Museum, no. 1119 (formerly)

Madonna and Child with Saints John the Baptist and Nicholas
FIG. 17

Panel: 90 x 49 cm.
Inscription: ANNO DNI M.CCC.

HISTORY: The panel entered the Berlin collections in 1821 as part of the Solly bequest. It was among the works lost in the fire at Flakturm Friedrichshain in 1945 (see Roditi, 1949, p. 312 and Norris, 1952, p. 344). According to Sirén (1905, p. 29), the gold ground and haloes were regilded and the inscription was also reworked.

LITERATURE: 1830, *Verzeichnis der Gemälde-Sammlung des königlichen Museum zu Berlin*, Berlin, no. 26: Florentine school, related to Giotto // 1891, *Beschreibendes Verzeichnis der Gemälde*, Berlin, no. 1119: around 1400, and presumably the work of Jacopo di Maestro Franchi (i.e., Rossello di Jacopo Franchi) // 1896, Berenson, p. 119: LM, an early work (1909, p. 152; 1932, p. 298) // 1905, Sirén, p. 28: LM, in a group of works ranging from 1398-1408 // 1909, Posse, p. 28, no. 1119: LM // 1927, van Marle, vol. 9, p. 118: the earliest dated work by LM, the inscription read as 1400 // 1929, Suida, p. 392: LM // 1938/39, Pudelko, p. 238: LM, 1400-1405 // 1950, Gronau, p. 221: LM, around 1400 // 1958, Levi D'Ancona, "Some New Attributions," p. 185, note 44: an attribution to Lorenzo Monaco implied, but the repainted inscription prevents its use in building the chronology // 1963, Berenson, vol. 1, p. 117: LM, destroyed // 1975, Boskovits, p. 242, note 200 and p. 338: LM, 1395-1400.

COMMENT: From the evidence of a photograph and Sirén's report (1905), the inscription on the dais was restored, with the addition of a period to close the truncated date, but there is no reason to doubt the authenticity of the fragment that remained after the reworking. The blank space on the dais is not sufficient to contain a date in the 1390s written in Roman numerals. As the Berlin *Madonna* is from the same period in which Lorenzo Monaco was executing the *Man of Sorrows* in the Accademia in Florence, dated 1404, but is less developed in its calligraphic linearism than the Empoli *Madonna of Humility*, also of 1404, a date circa 1402 would seem appropriate, and in its Roman form would fit the allotted space satisfactorily.

The clustering of angels at either side of the enthroned Virgin and Child—the third in each group is limned by a partial halo—is an indigenous Sienese motif that had gained wide currency in later Trecento Florentine shops: see Fremantle, figs. 553, 677, 680, and 723. The common workshop practice of using a standard model for various saints is demonstrated by the closely similar lineaments of the figures of Nicholas in the Berlin *Madonna* and the Siena triptych (Fig. 132), and of Zenobius in the Berenson *Madonna* (Fig. 16).

The only record of the palette of the destroyed Berlin *Madonna* is in color notes published in the catalogue of the Kaiser-Friedrich-Museum (1909 and 1913 editions) and in Sirén's description (1905) in which he observed that the color scheme was adopted from Agnolo Gaddi. [ca. 1402]

BERLIN, Kaiser-Friedrich-Museum, no. 1123A (formerly)

Madonna of Humility
FIG. 161

Predella: *Man of Sorrows*; *Mourning Virgin* and *Saint John the Evangelist*

Panel: 148 x 76 cm.

HISTORY: The panel entered the Berlin collections in 1903 as a gift from the Florentine art market. First listed among the pictures destroyed in 1945 in the fire at Flakturm Friedrichshain, it was later reported that the picture had survived (see Roditi, 1949, p. 312; Norris, 1952, p. 338, note 8, erroneously described as a Madonna Enthroned), although no indication was given as to its whereabouts.

LITERATURE: 1903, Douglas and Strong ed. of Crowe and Cavalcaselle, vol. 2, p. 303, note 1: refer to a small *Madonna* of the Humility type in Berlin; Lorenzo Monaco // 1904, *Beschreibendes Verzeichnis der Gemälde*, Berlin, no. 1123A: Lorenzo Monaco // 1905, Sirén, p. 168: shop of LM; by the same hand are the following: Loeser *Madonna* (now Brooklyn), Toscanelli *Madonna* (now Kansas City), Louvre *Madonna*, and the *Saints* laterals in Empoli // 1927, van Marle, vol. 9, p. 176: shop of LM // 1932, Berenson, p. 298: LM, in great part // 1938/39, Pudelko, p. 76, note 2: not wholly by Don Lorenzo's hand, but from the workshop // 1963, Berenson, vol. 1, p. 117: listed as destroyed in 1945 // 1975, Boskovits, p. 338: LM, 1415-20; listed as destroyed.

COMMENT: Sirén's grouping of the Berlin *Madonna of Humility* and the other pictures mentioned above (1905) as the work of a single shop hand is not convincing. The picture was produced in Don Lorenzo's workshop around 1418-20 by an assistant who was unable to bring coherence to a sequence of calligraphic forms; witness the passages of the mantle that fall from the knees to the floor. The atypical features of the Virgin imply a considerable later revision. The *Madonna of Humility* in the Nelson-Atkins Museum of Art, Kansas City (Fig. 145) includes a similar predella, a type Preiser (pp. 226-27) has discerned to be Sienese in origin. See Catalogue I, The Hague, *Madonna Enthroned*. [ca. 1418-20]

§ BERLIN-DAHLEM, Staatliche Museen, Kupferstichkabinett, nos. KdZ 608 and KdZ 609

Visitation; and *Journey of the Magi*
FIGS. 96-98

Parchment: 26.3 x 19 cm. (no. 608); 25.9 x 18.2 cm. (no. 609)
Technique: Pen and brush with bister, colored washes, and tempera

HISTORY: The provenances are unknown. Information may be written on the matting beneath the drawings, but detachment of the parchment sheets is not advisable from a technical standpoint.

LITERATURE: 1902, Loeser, p. 349: Lorenzo Monaco // 1905, Sirén, pp. 100-102: LM, between 1418 and 1422 // 1909, Berenson, p. 152: LM; described as miniatures (1932, p. 298; 1963, vol. 1, p. 117) // 1910, *Zeichnungen alter Meister im Kupferstichkabinett der K. Museen zu Berlin*, vol. 1, Berlin, no. 3: LM; only the *Visitation* listed and reproduced; the *Journey* mentioned within the same entry // 1927, van Marle, vol. 9, pp. 144-45: LM, around 1408 // 1929, Suida, p. 392: LM // 1930, London, *Italian Art 1200-1900*, no. 428, 1 and 2; 1931, London, *Commemorative Catalogue*, vol. 1, nos. 610 and 611; vol. 2, pl. 205: LM // 1931, Popham, nos. 8 and 9: LM // 1938/39 Pudelko, p. 78: LM, around 1420 // 1968, Degenhart and Schmitt, pt. 1, vol. 2, pp. 271-74, nos. 171, 172; and vol. 4, pls. 197a and 197b: LM, 1423-24, at the time of predella of the *Annunciation* in the Bartolini Chapel at Santa Trinita; provide further bibliography and technical analysis // 1970, Fossi Todorow, p. 83, and pls. 18 and 19, in color: LM, around 1420, at the time of the Uffizi *Adoration* // 1975, Boskovits, p. 339: LM, ca. 1415-20 // 1975, Eisler, p. 163, the *Journey of the Magi* reproduced in color: LM, ca. 1420; epitomizes the forceful refinement of the International Style // 1978, Bellosi and Bellini, p. xviii: the *Visitation* perhaps from first decade of the century, and the *Journey* a work of Lorenzo's late style.

COMMENT: As Degenhart and Schmitt (1968) noted, the Berlin drawings must be of the type mentioned by Vasari in the 1568 edition of the *Vite* (Bettarini and Barocchi, Text, p. 307): "Nel nostro libro de' disegni ho di mano di don Lorenzo le Virtù teologiche, fatte di chiaroscuro con buon disegno e bella e graziosa maniera, intantoché sono per avventura migliori che i disegni di qualsivoglia altro maestro di que' tempi." There should also be added Baldinucci's report that Lorenzo drew customarily in chiaroscuro (1686, p. 94): "Ebbe Don Lorenzo Monaco, oltre ad una buona practica nell'inventare una franchezza, e correzione di disegno si fatta, che al certo superò ogn'altro stato fino al suo tempo; usò per ordinario di disegnare in chiaro scuro, costume assai usato in quell'età." There survive several Trecento drawings with the same chiaroscuro effect, but there is no exact precedent for Lorenzo's technique. Notable are the following: *The Man of Sorrows*, Schmid Collection, Vienna (Degenhart and Schmitt, 1968, pt. 1, vol. 1, no. 23; vol. 3, pl. 48a: attributed to a Tuscan artist in the third decade of the fourteenth century); *Saint Francis Kneeling at the Cross and Other Figures*, Woodner Collection (G. R. Goldner, *Master Drawings from the Woodner Collection*, Malibu, 1983, p. 14, no. 1, illus.: Taddeo Gaddi, or his circle; Degenhart and Schmitt, pt. 1, vol. 1, no. 25; vol. 3, pl. 50: Florentine, ca. 1340); *Martyrdom of San Miniato*, Pierpont Morgan Library, New York (Degenhart and Schmitt, pt. 1, vol. 1, no. 30; vol. 3, pl. 58c: circle of Bernardo Daddi; or preferably, Fossi Todorow, 1970, p. 81 and pl. V: Master in the Orcagna circle, ca. 1350-75; Boskovits, 1975, p. 291 and fig. 314: Cenni di Francesco, 1380-85). The chiaroscuro effect seems also to have attracted painters working in both tempera and fresco in the aftermath of Lorenzo Monaco, as in the following: Giovanni Toscani, *Pietà*, the reverse of the triptych in the gallery of the Spedale degli Innocenti (Bellosi, 1977, p. 233, and pl. 49; ca. 1415-20); Parri Spinelli, *The Routing of Maxentius*, detached fresco, Museum, Arezzo; attributed to Giovanni dal Ponte, *Studies of Apostles and Allegorical Figures*, Lehman Collection, Metropolitan Museum of Art (G. Szabó, 1983, no. 8, with discussion of the possibility that this is the sheet of "Theological Virtues" owned by Vasari and attributed by him to Lorenzo Monaco; Ragghianti Collobi [vol. 1, p. 41], identifies the figures as *Temperance*, *Hope*, and *Justice*, and proposes that the contemporaneity of Giovanni dal Ponte and Lorenzo Monaco, the later completion of the figures, and evidence of a lost early mounting, make it plausible that this is the drawing to which Vasari refers).

To place the Berlin *Visitation* in the first decade of the century (van Marle, 1927; and Bellosi, 1978) would demand closer formal analogies with the *Visitation* in the Courtauld Institute Galleries, or with the *Lamentation* in Prague, dated 1408. While there are basic similarities, inevitable in the continuities of a master's work, the technique and style of the *Visitation* are characteristic of the last phase of Don Lorenzo's art. The hatched line both models form and quickens expression and, given the subject, there need not be expected the hectic urgency of line of the *Journey of the Magi*, the absence of which suggests to Bellosi that the drawings are not from the same period of Lorenzo's activity. Degenhart and Schmitt (1968) rightly discern the closest technical and stylistic affinities of the Berlin *Visitation* with the predella of the Santa Trinita *Annunciation*. Neither Berlin drawing is imaginable in Lorenzo's evolution without the sequence of works leading to his latest style in the early 1420s. As in the Santa Trinita predella, the figure style of the Berlin *Visitation* signals the abandonment of the decorative arabesque and the reinforcement of the figure's existence in space.

Degenhart and Schmitt published a drawing on parchment of *Scenes from the Early Life of the Baptist* (Fig. 197) in the collection of Otto Manley in Scarsdale, New York, in which they observed specific connections with the style of Lorenzo Monaco (pt. 1, vol. 2, pp. 298-300, no. 198 and vol. 4, pl. 217a). Whereas they found the closest similarity in composition to the *desco da parto* (Fig. 324) in the New-York Historical Society, dated 1428, which has subsequently been attributed to Bartolomeo di Fruosino (Boskovits, 1972, p. 58, note 55; Watson, 1974, pp. 4-9), Degenhart and Schmitt also observed the relationship of the Manley sheet to the Berlin drawings. They further proposed that the drawing in Scarsdale was based on a lost composition by Lorenzo Monaco, but did not rule out the possibility that it could have formed a third piece along with the Berlin pair, although not brought to completion. Parallels with the *Birth of the Virgin* (Fig. 106) in the Bartolini Salimbeni Chapel at Santa Trinita were also observed. The Manley sheet is virtually identical in dimensions with the Berlin drawings. Boskovits (1975, p. 354) attributed the drawing to Lorenzo Monaco and proposed a dating from 1400 to 1405. Bellosi likewise mentioned the Manley drawing (1978), stressing however its connection with the Berlin *Visitation* and the Santa Trinita frescoes. At the crest of the drawing and of the *desco* is a seascape with towered islets and ships at full sail, recalling a similar device in Don Lorenzo's *Meeting of Joachim and Anna* (Fig. 105) in the Bartolini Chapel cycle and in the Berlin *Journey of the Magi*. Moreover, the Manley *Scenes of the Baptist* and the Berlin *Visitation* are framed by an illusionistic molding, a feature not included in the *Journey*. There can be little doubt that Bartolomeo di Fruosino, in his crudely vigorous later style, used the Manley drawing as a model for the *desco da parto* of 1428, transforming the *Birth of the Baptist* into a secular scene in a birth chamber. This required the omission of the episode of the Naming of the Baptist in the anteroom, which Bartolomeo chose simply to stack with bearers of gifts. The *desco da parto* therefore indicates a date before 1428 for the Manley drawing. Although the connections between that sheet and the Berlin *Visitation* and Santa Trinita frescoes are obvious, the tendency of the figure style toward a greater monumentality and stockier proportions than in these later works would at first seem to prevent an outright attribution to Lorenzo Monaco. But on closer examination the proportions are found to be the same as those of the Joseph in the Santa Trinita *Betrothal* (Fig. 109), that is, 1:5.5 (see the Introductory Essay, Notes 117 and 150). The fact that the drawing was left incomplete, its chiaroscuro surfaces never rendered, could imply that in this late work Lorenzo was moving a further step toward stylistic trends of the 1420s, as was the case with the frescoes and altarpiece of the Bartolini Salimbeni Chapel. In the frescoes it is a peripheral element—the seated attendant in the *Birth of the Virgin* (Fig. 108)—that gives the strongest evidence of the painter's urge toward greater plastic force; there is a close parallel between that figure and the seated Zacharias in the Manley sheet, just as he is anticipated by the attendant kneeling behind the Virgin in the Berlin *Visitation* (Fig. 96). If the completion of the Manley drawing in a chiaroscuro technique was ever intended, the mass of the figure conveyed by the schematic line drawing would have been countered by the contrasts of light and dark and by the hatched surfaces. A further parallel may be drawn between the Virgin standing behind the bed in the Scarsdale drawing and the hovering Virgin of the *Miracle of the Snow* (Fig. 114) in the Santa Trinita frescoes. Could this beautiful and rare sheet be one of the final efforts of Lorenzo Monaco and testimony that had his career continued he would have come into fuller harmony with the generation of Masaccio? [ca. 1422-23]

BERLIN-DAHLEM, Staatliche Museen, Kupferstichkabinett, no. min. 1231

God the Father with Globe and Scepter

Cut miniature from a choir book
Parchment: 34.5 x 31.3 cm.

HISTORY: From the von Nagler Collection, 1835; see below, 1978, Levi D'Ancona.

LITERATURE: 1931, Wescher, p. 91, and fig. 77: school of the Angeli, 1410-20, tending toward Lorenzo Monaco, but of lesser quality; the source of the figure is the *David* in Cassel (now Metropolitan Museum, New York) // 1975, Boskovits, p. 339, and fig. 445: LM, 1395-1400; identifies as King David // 1978, Levi D'Ancona, p. 219: identifies the provenance as fol. 63, Cod. Cor. 1, Biblioteca Laurenziana; attributes to Matteo Torelli.

COMMENT: The style is a conglomeration of traits from Lorenzo's miniatures of the 1390s and, as Wescher recognized, the more mature work from the first decade of the fifteenth century. An earlier and less assured effort, possibly by the same assistant to Lorenzo Monaco, is the *Moses* on fol. 89 of Corale 13 in the Laurenziana (see Levi D'Ancona, "Some New Attributions," 1958, fig. 25). [1405-1410]

BERLIN-DAHLEM, Staatliche Museen, Kupferstichkabinett, no. min. 1239

Saint John the Baptist

FIG. 204

Cut miniature from a choir book
Parchment: 31.4 x 31.7 cm.

HISTORY: From the von Nagler Collection, 1835; see below, 1978, Levi D'Ancona.

LITERATURE: 1931, Wescher, p. 91: school of the Angeli, 1410-20; tending toward Lorenzo Monaco, but of lesser quality // 1965, Bellosi, "Da Spinello," p. 39: LM // 1970, González-Palacios, p. 30, and fig. 28a: shop of LM // 1975, Boskovits, p. 339: LM, 1395-1400 // 1978, Levi D'Ancona, p. 229: identifies the provenance as fol. 102, Cod. Cor. 8, Biblioteca Laurenziana; LM.

COMMENT: The Berlin *Baptist* miniature was executed by a scriptorium assistant, perhaps on Lorenzo's design. The same hand, faltering in draughtsmanship and favoring attenuated forms may also have been responsible for the *Christ in Glory* miniature in Berlin (no. 1240) and the *Saint Paul* on fol. 163 of Corale 8 in the Laurenziana (Figs. 205 and 203). In its elongations and hardness of line the Berlin miniature displays some resemblance to the figure of the Baptist in the *Madonna* at the Biblioteca Berenson (Fig. 16). [ca. 1398-1400]

BERLIN-DAHLEM, Staatliche Museen, Kupferstichkabinett, no. min. 1240

Christ in Glory

FIG. 205

Cut miniature from a choir book
Parchment: 34.3 x 30.2 cm.
Inscription: ΩA

HISTORY: From the von Nagler Collection, 1835; see below, 1978, Levi D'Ancona.

LITERATURE: 1929, Wescher, p. 99: tentatively attributed to Lorenzo Monaco // 1930, Toesca, p. 40, and fig. 25: LM // 1931, Wescher, p. 90, and fig. 74: LM // 1932, Berenson, p. 298: LM (1963, vol. 1, p. 117) // 1965, Bellosi, "Da Spinello," p. 39: LM // 1975, Boskovits, p. 339: LM, 1395-1400 // 1978, Levi D'Ancona, p. 219: identifies the provenance as fol. 102, Cod. Cor. 1, Biblioteca Laurenziana; attributes to Matteo Torelli.

COMMENT: While Lorenzo Monaco very likely provided the design for this miniature, the execution was left to an assistant. The draughtsmanship is tentative and brittle, and the expression lacks the gravity of Don Lorenzo's early miniatures, recalling characteristics of the *Saint Paul* (Fig. 203) on fol. 163 of Corale 8 in the Laurenziana (after 1395) and the *Saint John the Baptist* in Berlin (Fig. 204). For the reversed inscription, see the Introductory Essay, Note 12. [ca. 1400]

BOLOGNA, Pinacoteca Nazionale, no. 501

Madonna Enthroned, with Four Angels
FIG. 133

Panel: 127 x 74.5 cm.

CONDITION: Cutting of the upper and lower edges of the panel resulted in truncation of the arched gold ground and of the kneeling angels and semicircular projection of the dais. The cropped wings, haloes, and drapery of the lower pair of angels are indications that the panel was also reduced in width by several centimeters. These losses could have occurred when the panel was inserted into a heavy Victorian frame that is recorded in earlier photographs of the picture (Alinari 37999). A mild cleaning of the panel in 1966 revealed that the paint film is in exceptionally good state.

HISTORY: Acquired by the Bologna Pinacoteca in 1894. The provenance is unknown.

LITERATURE: 1899, Guadagnini, p. 95, no. 501: Bolognese school // 1904, Toesca, pp. 171-72: Lorenzo Monaco, before 1410, that is, before the Monte Oliveto Altarpiece // 1905, Sirén, p. 165: by an assistant of Lorenzo Monaco also responsible for the *Agony in the Garden* in the Accademia, Florence, and the Vecchietti *Madonna*, Bibbiena (now Assisi) // 1909, Baldani, p. 458: Vitale da Bologna // 1927, van Marle, vol. 9, p. 172: follower of LM, comparable to the *Madonna of Humility* in the Cook Collection, Richmond (now Toledo Museum of Art); in an addendum (p. 589), changes attribution to include the panel among early works of Lorenzo // 1931, Mauceri, p. 15, no. 501: LM // 1932, Berenson, p. 298: LM, early (1963, vol. 1, p. 117) // 1938/39, Pudelko, p. 76, note 2: shop of LM, around 1413 // 1950, Gronau, p. 221 and note 27: early work of Lorenzo Monaco that would fit well physically and stylistically as the center panel above the "Nobili predella" (Louvre) of the late 1380s // 1957, Eisenberg, p. 50: LM, from the last decade of the century // 1958, Levi D'Ancona, "Some New Attributions," p. 184, note 40: possibly by the same follower of Lorenzo Monaco who painted the London *Coronation of the Virgin*; may be dated in same period as the Monte Oliveto Altarpiece, or later // 1964/65, Zeri, p. 11: Lorenzo Monaco following on the San Gaggio polyptych of the mid-1390s; part of a group of works in which here and there one begins to notice, alongside the master's hand, the hand of pupils and assistants // 1965, Bellosi "Da Spinello," p. 40: LM, showing impact of the early style of Ghiberti // 1967, Emiliani, pp. 168-69: LM // 1975, Boskovits, p. 339: LM, 1400-1405.

COMMENT: The Bologna *Madonna* provides important evidence that Lorenzo Monaco had already turned over major commissions to associates by the early years of the Quattrocento, thereby absorbing strains from cognate stylistic cultures into the formal language of his shop. The picture represents a process of migration from the intensely Cionesque environment of the shop responsible for the San Gaggio Altarpiece (see Catalogue II, Florence, Accademia, *Saint Catherine of Alexandria* and *Saint Caius*, or the Cloisters *Intercession*, Figs. 227, 229, and 234). The frieze of leafy bosses along the riser of the dais, which may have been derived from that milieu (cf. Figs. 133 and 228), has a source, as Zeri noted, in works of the Cionesque Giovanni Bonsi (1964, p. 226, and figs. 1 and 3; or Fremantle, figs. 436 and 445). But the painter of the Bologna panel has been more recently steeped in such major autograph works by Lorenzo Monaco as the *Agony in the Garden* and the *Man of Sorrows*, both in the Accademia, Florence (Figs. 7 and 18). The radial folds of the Virgin's mantle, descending to the broad calligraphy of the border, recall comparable passages in the *Agony*, although in that work the light and dark system is organic to the structure of the draperies rather than a schematic overlay. The painter of the Bologna *Madonna*, working under the close supervision of Lorenzo Monaco, may have assisted in the execution of the upper passages of the *Man of Sorrows*, dated 1404. The hard contours, the brusque handling of the tempera medium, the swarthy flesh tones, and the ungraduated contrasts of light and dark in the Bologna panel recall the Denial and Betrayal of Christ at the crest of that vast icon, while the facial type of the woman accosting Saint Peter in the *Man of Sorrows* is closely akin to the attendant angels in the Bologna *Madonna.* The still hesitant rhythms and the sense of a bulky Trecento core underlying the individual figures, prevent dating the Bologna panel as late as or later than the Monte Oliveto Altarpiece (completed in 1410), as Levi D'Ancona proposed (1958). Nonetheless, her observation that the Bologna *Madonna* may be the work of the same assistant who at least a decade later was closely involved with the London *Coronation of the Virgin* (Fig. 175) establishes an important connection, given the traits of metallic hardness and stylization in both works. In spite of the constriction and steep verticality of the Bologna *Madonna*, effects that were exaggerated by the trimming of the panel, the deep recession of the throne and dais shows a continuing concern for spatial illusion implied in the landscape of Lorenzo's *Agony in the Garden* and explicitly conveyed by the scenographic throne of the *Madonna* in Cambridge (Fig. 15). A throne remarkably close in format to that in the Bologna *Madonna* is found in a Florentine drawing of 1427 for the *Life and Fioretti of Saint Francis* (Degenhart and Schmitt, 1968, pt. 1, vol. 4, pl. 199b). For the proposed stylistic development of the work of the assistant who was largely responsible for the Bologna *Madonna*, see Catalogue I, London, National Gallery, San Benedetto Altarpiece. [ca. 1405]

BROOKLYN (New York), Brooklyn Museum, no. 34.842

Madonna of Humility

FIG. 147

Panel: 83.9 x 47.2 cm. (including engaged inner molding)

CONDITION: The Virgin's mantle has suffered extensive deterioration and repainting, most visibly in the area of the raised knee. The gold ground was defaced when rays were unskillfully incised at a later date. A split in the panel has invaded the halo and head of the Madonna, while the two fissures at either side of the panel are openings in the seams of joined planks. The base and spiral colonnettes of the frame are a later addition and the original wood gable has been stripped of its ornamental surface. The Medicean coat of arms at the center of the platform beneath the Virgin and Child is a later addition.

HISTORY: Loeser Collection, Florence; [Volpi, Florence]; George Gray Barnard, New York; Frank Lusk Babbott, Brooklyn, 1916; gift to the Brooklyn Museum, 1934, from Mary Babbott Ladd, Lydia Babbott Stokes, and Dr. Frank L. Babbott, Jr.

LITERATURE: 1905, Sirén, p. 168: shop of Lorenzo Monaco; the best and earliest of a series of panels by the same hand that painted Madonnas in the Louvre, the Toscanelli Collection (now Kansas City), and the Kaiser-Friedrich-Museum // 1917, Sirén and Brockwell, no. 13: LM, a late work, ca. 1420 // 1927, van Marle, vol. 9, p. 176: workshop of LM (cited as in Loeser Collection; on p. 130 attributes the Babbott *Madonna* to Lorenzo Monaco, around 1405) // 1932, Berenson, p. 298: LM, in part (1963, vol. 1, p. 117) // 1932, Berenson, "Quadri senza casa," p. 34 (1970, p. 141): the draperies are by Lorenzo Monaco and the faces by an assistant // 1934, Platt and Price, no. 4: LM // 1938/39, Pudelko, p. 76, note 2: LM, after 1413 // 1972, Fredericksen and Zeri, p. 111: LM // 1975, Boskovits, p. 350: LM, 1415-20 // 1982, Fahy, p. 241: LM, 1415.

COMMENT: The Brooklyn panel was designed and largely executed by Lorenzo Monaco at the time of his work on the Uffizi *Adoration of the Magi*, as a comparison with the seated Virgin in that picture demonstrates (Fig. 83); a continuous line descending from head to torso is resolved into extended, flat folds edged with a double line and dot border. The hefty proportions of the Child and the lighted ridges of His mantle are also identical in the Brooklyn and Uffizi panels. Sirén (1905) singled the picture out for special praise and later (1917) proposed a more satisfactory dating of around 1420. The lesser quality in the execution of the faces, observed by Berenson (1932, "Quadri"), suggests the intervention of an assistant even in this superior work from Lorenzo's later career. Everett Fahy observed (1982) that the same cartoon was probably used for the Brooklyn, Philadelphia, and Toledo versions of the *Madonna of Humility* (Figs. 148 and 149), an alliance that is particularly apparent in the type of Infant. Of this group, however, only the Brooklyn panel displays a satisfactory proportional relationship of the Virgin and Child and a coherence of design worthy of Don Lorenzo's hand. [ca. 1420]

BRUSSELS, Féron-Stoclet Collection (formerly)

Annunciation

FIG. 157

Panel: 136 x 98 cm. (painted surface)

Inscription: (On the book) AD TE LEVAVI OCLOS MEOS Q H (ab) ITAS Ī CELIS. ECCE SICUT OCULI SERVORUM Ī MANIBUS (Psalms 123:1)

CONDITION: At an unknown date the panel was squared off with approximately triangular inserts at both upper corners, as a means of accommodating the picture to a rectangular outer frame (see van Marle, vol. 9, 1927, fig. 80). In 1983, the picture underwent extensive conservation measures (the present anonymous owner has requested that the location of this technical work not be divulged). Of particular importance was the partial removal of discolored varnishes from the ultramarine blue of the Virgin's mantle, and the repair of several vertical splits in the panel, the most serious of which is at the lower left, midway in the figure of Gabriel. The gold ground and haloes have suffered considerable losses.

HISTORY: Fornari Collection, Fabriano; Adolphe Stoclet Collection (Féron-Stoclet), Brussels; private collection. The tentative proposal by Berenson that the provenance is the Carmine in Florence is without basis (see the Introductory Essay, Note 5).

LITERATURE: 1908, Angelelli, p. 34: attributed to Francesco di Gentile, with reservation // 1909, Berenson, "Un nuovo Lorenzo Monaco," pp. 3-4: although not typical, one of Lorenzo's most beautiful works; compares with the *Annunciation* in the Accademia, Florence; an early work, perhaps from the altarpiece painted for the Carmine in 1399 // 1909, Sirén, "Opere sconosciute," pp. 35-36: around 1413, comparable to the Virgin in the Uffizi *Coronation* of that year and to the *Madonna* in the Masson Collection (now National Gallery, Washington), also dated 1413 // 1922, A. Venturi, p. 163: shop of LM; lacks the master's usual quality // 1927, van Marle, vol. 9, pp. 124-26: LM, ca. 1400; possibly from the Carmine // 1929, Suida, p. 392: LM // 1932, Berenson, p. 298: LM // 1935, Paris, *Exposition*, p. 141, no. 213: LM // 1936, Robb, p. 519, note 134: LM, 1398-1400; employs a Northern iconography // 1938/39, Pudelko, p. 242: LM, 1403-1404; refutes the Carmine provenance // 1956, Salles and Lion-Goldschmidt, pp. 72-77, colorplate on p. 73: LM; provide further bibliography // 1958, Levi D'Ancona, "Matteo Torelli," pp. 252 and 255-57: Matteo Torelli; a later work in the period of the Bartolini Chapel at Santa Trinita; possibly the center panel of a triptych in which the Empoli *Saints* were the laterals // 1963, Berenson, vol. 1, p. 117: LM, 1398-1400? // 1975, Boskovits, pp. 339-40: LM, 1410-15.

COMMENT: The *Annunciation* was likely to have been accompanied originally by side panels with standing saints, in a type of ensemble that would have more closely resembled altarpieces by the Master of Santa Verdiana (Fremantle, figs. 601-603 and 612) than the *Annunciation* by Lorenzo Monaco in the Accademia, Florence (Fig. 77). Regardless of its distance in time, a direct model for the former Féron-Stoclet *Annunciation* could have been the panel by Taddeo Gaddi in the Museo Bandini, Fiesole (Ladis, fig. 16-1). The *Annunciation* and the Empoli *Saints* (Figs. 154-155) are by the same workshop associate of Lorenzo Monaco, but physical evidence proves that they were not part of the same altarpiece. In the *Annunciation* the outlines of consoles at the spring of the arch are located 91 cm. from the bottom of the painted surface, whereas in each of the Empoli laterals the distance is 61 cm. In addition, double lines run horizontally along the surface of the platform in the *Annunciation*, but in the *Saints* panels the lines are drawn on the riser.

For further discussion, see Catalogue I, Prato, Galleria Comunale, *Madonna and Child Enthroned, with Four Saints*. [ca. 1420-22]

BRUSSELS, Van Gelder Collection (formerly)

The Man of Sorrows

Panel: 64 x 34.3 cm.

HISTORY: M. L. Gruner, as Taddeo Gaddi; Rev. John Fuller Russell, 1885, as school of Giotto; Charles Butler; [Charles Butler Collection sale, Christie's, May 25-26, 1911, no. 32, Florentine school]; Henry Wagner; [Henry Wagner Collection sale, Christie's, January 16, 1925, no. 70, Taddeo Gaddi]; [Lilienfeld]; M. van Gelder, Brussels, 1934, as Lorenzo Monaco; William van Gelder, Brussels (Uccle); [Duc de Brissac and Other Collections sale, Christie's, May 14, 1971, no. 13, Lorenzo Monaco (to "Wall")]; private collection, New York, according to Zeri and Rossi, p. 68 (further information on whereabouts not available).

LITERATURE: 1934, Amsterdam, *Italiaansche Kunst*, p. 88, no. 242: Lorenzo Monaco // 1934/35, van Marle, p. 304, and fig. 22: LM // 1938/39, Pudelko, p. 242, note 24: LM; related to the *Man of Sorrows* of 1404 in the Accademia, Florence // 1970, González-Palacios, p. 34, and fig. 36: LM, in a late phase of his work; the features recall the Toulouse *Crucifix* // 1975, Boskovits, p. 349: LM, 1415-20 // 1986, Zeri and Rossi, p. 68: LM.

COMMENT: See Catalogue I, Toledo (Ohio), Toledo Museum of Art, *Madonna of Humility*. [ca. 1418-20]

BUDAPEST, Museum of Fine Arts, no. 1089

Crucifix

FIG. 164

Panel (cutout): 146 x 84 cm.

CONDITION: The paint surface in the areas of the face and torso has suffered extensive scoring, which in part appears to be an intentional defacement. The almost totally obliterated left hand of Christ has been crudely repainted and the skull at the base is not contemporary with the corpus.

HISTORY: Bought in Venice in 1893 and entered the collections of the Museum of Fine Arts, Budapest, in that same year.

LITERATURE: 1927, van Marle, vol. 9, p. 168, note 3: Lorenzo Monaco // 1929, Suida, p. 392: LM // 1932, Berenson, p. 298: LM // 1937, *Catalogue, Museum of Fine Arts*, Budapest, p. 150, no. 1089: the first attribution to Lorenzo Monaco in the official museum catalogue, revising the ascription to the Tuscan school of the fourteenth or fifteenth century proposed in earlier editions // 1963, Berenson, vol. 1, p. 117, and pl. 458: LM // 1968, Pigler, p. 394: LM // 1969, Boskovits, no. 1 (detail illustration in color): LM, close in time to the *Madonna of Humility* in the National Gallery, Washington, dated 1413 // 1975, Boskovits, p. 340: LM, 1420-25.

COMMENT: The coarse application of the tempera medium, most apparent in the rendering of the hair, the flat, unrhythmic drawing of the head, and the summary tooling of the halo indicate extensive collaboration of the shop working on a standard design by Lorenzo Monaco. Of the series of cutout crosses by Lorenzo Monaco and his workshop, the San Giovannino dei Cavalieri *Crucifix* (Fig. 70) of around 1415 shows the closest parallels in proportion and detail. [ca. 1415]

§ CAMBRIDGE, Fitzwilliam Museum, no. 555

Madonna Enthroned

FIG. 15

Panel: 32.4 x 21.2 cm. (painted surface)

CONDITION: Described as follows in Goodison and Robertson, 1967, p. 90: The whole surface has suffered in some degree, with repaired local damages to the drapery of the Child and of the right-hand angel, to the gold work in the haloes and round the edges of the background; the lower left-hand corner renewed; some rubbing of the angels' wings. Cleaned 1954.

HISTORY: Fricca Collection; bought, probably by Charles Butler, in Florence, 1883; bought by the Fitzwilliam Museum from Charles Butler in 1893.

LITERATURE: 1884, Exhibition, *Old Masters*, Royal Academy, London, no. 223: Justus of Padua, ca. 1330-1400 // 1902, Earp, p. 72: Florentine School, ca. 1350-75 // 1905, Sirén, "Tre Madonnine," pp. 245-48: Lorenzo Monaco, in his early style around 1400 to 1403 // 1912, Cockerell, pp. xiv and 112, no. 555: LM // 1927, van Marle, vol. 9, p. 118: LM, 1395-1400 // 1928, Longhi, p. 38, note 2: LM; showing that the Master of the Straus Madonna began in a circle close to him // 1929, Suida, p. 392: LM // 1930, London, *Italian Art 1200-1900*, no. 69; 1931, London, *Commemorative Catalogue*, vol. 1, no. 46; vol. 2, pl. 20: LM; early work // 1932, Berenson, p. 298: LM, early (1963, vol. 1, p. 117) // 1938/39, Pudelko, pp. 237-38: LM; recalling both Spinello Aretino and Taddeo Gaddi // 1950, Gronau, p. 221: LM; an early work that indicates his debt to Giotto and predicts his intimate paintings of the Madonna and Child in the early fifteenth century // 1965, Bellosi, *Maestri* [p. 7] and pl. 2 (color): LM; important as an indication of the Florentine roots of his style // 1965, Bellosi, "Da Spinello," p. 29: LM, beginning of the fifteenth century; once formed a diptych with a *Crucifixion* panel in the Musei Civici, Pesaro; the style suggests connections with Spinello Aretino and the idiom of the Master of the Straus Madonna

// 1967, Goodison and Robertson, pp. 90-91, no. 555: LM, implying the acceptance of a dating ca. 1400-1403; further bibliography // 1975, Boskovits, p. 340: LM, 1395-1400.

COMMENT: The proposal by Bellosi (1965) that the Cambridge *Madonna* and a *Crucifixion* in Pesaro (Fig. 249) were once joined as a diptych presents difficulties because of contradictions in figure style and ornamental detail. The Pesaro panel would seem to be the work of a minor Tuscan painter whose principal model was Spinello Aretino.

The ornamental patterns of the haloes in the Cambridge panel are not found elsewhere in works by Lorenzo Monaco or his shop, but the Virgin's halo has a close replica in the *Crucifixion* formerly in the Galleria Ferroni, Florence (Fig. 240), which I believe is by a Cionesque painter who worked close to the milieu of the Master of the Straus Madonna. As Longhi first noted (1928), the Fitzwilliam panel shares aspects of that unidentified master's style, which was formulated contemporarily with the early work of Lorenzo Monaco and sprang from comparable sources. For further comment, see Catalogue II, Florence, Accademia, *Saint Jerome*; *Saint John the Baptist*. . . . [1395-1400]

CLEVELAND, Cleveland Museum of Art, no. 49.536

Prophet
FIG. 207

Cut miniature from a choir book
Parchment: 16.7 x 13.5 cm. (size of sheet)

HISTORY: Simkovitch Collection, New York; Cleveland Museum, 1949.

LITERATURE: 1950, Milliken, pp. 44-45: Lorenzo Monaco, between 1409 and 1413, the years of the choir book miniatures in the Laurenziana and Bargello // 1958, Levi D'Ancona, "Some New Attributions," pp. 177 and 181, and fig. 8: probably executed by Matteo Torelli under supervision of LM; from later period of the shop, 1415-22 // 1963, Cleveland, *Gothic Art*, p. 184, no. 64: LM or Matteo Torelli, 1409-1413 // 1971, Pillsbury, no. 45: Matteo Torelli // 1975, Boskovits, p. 340: LM, 1405-1410.

COMMENT: The Cleveland miniature was designed and executed by an assistant of Lorenzo Monaco who used as model a miniature by the master such as that on fol. 86v of Corale 3 in the Laurenziana, which dates from the second phase of his activity in the choir book, around 1414 (Fig. 68). The schematic and tentative drawing, the flatness of forms, and the naive contours, mark the Cleveland *Prophet* as a shop work, while the brilliance of execution of the illuminated letter points up the relative insubstantiality of the miniaturist's effort. A stylistic parallel is detectable between this miniature and the Prophets (Fig. 62) in the pilasters of the *Coronation of the Virgin* in the Uffizi, which are largely the work of Don Lorenzo's assistants. For comment with regard to attributions of miniatures to Matteo Torelli, see Catalogue I, Florence, Bargello, Cod. E 70. [ca. 1415]

§ COPENHAGEN, Thorvaldsens Museum, no. 1

Madonna of Humility
FIG. 128

Panel: 22.8 x 17.8 cm. (including original frame)

CONDITION: The paint surface is abraded and pitted, with especially disruptive losses in the faces of the Virgin and Child. The gold ground has suffered extensive disintegration.

HISTORY: Bequeathed to the Danish state by Thorvaldsen in 1844; in the Thorvaldsens Museum since its inception in 1848.

LITERATURE: 1852, catalogue, *Thorvaldsens Museum*, Copenhagen, p. 43, no. 1: Florentine, fourteenth or fifteenth century // 1905, Sirén, pp. 95-97: Lorenzo Monaco, 1418; connects the panel with *Saint Jerome* in the Rijksmuseum (then in the von Kaufmann Collection, Berlin) // 1909, Berenson, p. 152: LM (1932, p. 298; 1963, vol. 1, p. 117) // 1910, Krohn, p. 16: LM // 1927, van Marle, vol. 9, p. 130: LM, around 1405, that is, earlier than the Amsterdam *Saint Jerome in His Study*, which is of around 1408 // 1929, Suida, p. 392: LM // 1938/39, Pudelko, p. 77: LM, around 1415 // 1961, Olsen, p. 69: LM; with further bibliography // 1965, Bellosi, *Maestri*, [p. 6]: LM, shortly before 1422 // 1965, Gore, p. 17, no. 30: LM, later than the *Madonna* of 1413 in the Contini-Bonacossi Collection (Washington, National Gallery); the panel is described as a predella and as part of a diptych, of which the other half is the Rijksmuseum *Saint Jerome* // 1965, Murray, p. 284: LM, before 1413 // 1965, Olsen, pp. 52-55: LM, shortly after 1415 // 1975, Boskovits, p. 340: LM, 1415-20.

COMMENT: For the companion panel, see Catalogue I, Amsterdam, Rijksmuseum, *Saint Jerome in His Study*.

Although the intimately scaled Madonna of Humility of the *Lactans* type gained a special popularity in later Trecento Siena (van Os, 1969, pp. 118-22), Don Lorenzo could also have encountered the type in a work by his immediate predecessor at Santa Maria degli Angeli, Don Silvestro dei Gherarducci—the *Nursing Madonna of Humility* formerly in the De Clemente collection in Florence (Offner, ed. Maginnis, *Corpus*, 1981, fig. 58). In addition to the Copenhagen *Madonna*, there are three other Madonnas of Humility of the *Lactans* type among the known works of Lorenzo Monaco and his shop: Paris (Fig. 144), Kansas City (Fig. 145), and Pisa (Fig. 146). The picture in Copenhagen differs markedly from these examples in that Don Lorenzo combined here the *Glykophilousa* and *Lactans* types (see Shorr, 1954, Types 6 and 9) and depicted the Child in a standing rather than seated position. The use of the standing Child is common in representations of the *Glykophilousa* (*Affettuosa*) type of Madonna. The unusual motif of the Child nursing in a standing position had been used in the 1390s in a *Madonna of Humility* by Agnolo Gaddi (Shorr, 1954, Type 10, Florence 11). Examples from Lorenzo's workshop of the standing Child in the Madonna of Humility, preceding the Copenhagen picture, are the panels formerly in Berlin (Fig. 161; ca. 1418-20) and formerly in the Schaeffer Galleries, New York (Fig. 195; ca. 1420). [ca. 1422-23]

CRACOW, National Museum, Czartoryski Collection, no. XII-187

Saints Catherine of Alexandria and John the Baptist

FIG. 153

Panel: 64 x 41 cm.

CONDITION: The panel is cut at the bottom, shortening the figures by nearly a quarter of their original height. In a restoration completed in 1987, scattered abrasions, largely in the lower areas of the panel, were inpainted and a darkened varnish was removed. The original *velatura* was found to be in good state. The gold ground has suffered numerous losses, but the ornamented haloes are largely intact.

HISTORY: Władysław Czartoryski Collection; probably acquired in Paris in the mid-nineteenth century.

LITERATURE: 1914, *Galeria obrazów, Katalog tymczasowy*, Cracow, no. 44: Florentine, fifteenth century // 1915, Logan Berenson, p. 2: school of Lorenzo Monaco. // 1918, Gerevich, pp. 24-26: Sassetta // 1927, van Marle, vol. 9, p. 590: school of LM // 1939, Pope-Hennessy, pp. 185 and 203, note 139: refutes Gerevich's attribution to Sassetta; ascribes to LM // 1958, Levi D'Ancona, "Matteo Torelli," p. 253: Matteo Torelli // 1960, Różycka-Bryzek, pp. 213-15: imitator of LM; the same painter as the Empoli panels // 1961, Cracow, *Peinture italienne*, pp. 54-55, no. 35: imitator of LM, first half of the fifteenth century; Levi D'Ancona's attribution to Torelli is refuted; the *Saint Catherine* is modelled after the same saint in the Prato altarpiece, attributed to LM; the *Saint John* is related to the same figure in the Empoli triptych // 1975, Boskovits, p. 340: LM, 1410-15; quotes Zeri's verbal observation that the panel may have been the left lateral of the Edinburgh *Madonna Enthroned*.

COMMENT: See the following in Catalogue I: Edinburgh, National Gallery of Scotland, *Madonna and Child Enthroned*; Empoli, Museo della Collegiata, *Saints John the Evangelist and Catherine of Alexandria, Saint John the Baptist and a Bishop Saint*; Prato, Galleria Comunale, *Madonna and Child, and Four Saints*. [ca. 1418]

DETROIT, Detroit Institute of Arts, no. 37.133

Pentecost

FIG. 208

Parchment: 24.1 x 24.1 cm.

HISTORY: Gift of W. R. Valentiner, 1937.

LITERATURE: 1944, Valentiner, pp. 32-34: Lorenzo Monaco, before 1409 // 1944, *Catalogue of Paintings, The Detroit Institute of Arts*, p. 80, no. 621: LM // 1958, Levi D'Ancona, "Matteo Torelli," pp. 252 and 254: Matteo Torelli, 1413-20; close to miniatures in Bargello Cod. E 70 // 1968, Degenhart and Schmitt, pt. 1, vol. 2, p. 28, and fig. 387: circle of LM; review the tradition of Florentine Pentecost representations from the mid-Trecento to the early Quattrocento // 1975, Boskovits, p. 340: LM, 1410-15; the heads in the borders are by Bartolomeo di Fruosino.

COMMENT: The Detroit *Pentecost* was designed by Lorenzo Monaco and executed by a shop assistant, around 1420. Levi D'Ancona's (1958) comparison with miniatures in Cod. E 70 in the Bargello is persuasive, although I am unable to accept the attribution to Torelli (see Catalogue I, Florence, Bargello, Cod. E 70). The Virgin of the Detroit miniature is closely related to the *Madonna and Child* on fol. 74v of the Bargello choir book (Fig. 210). The rude draughtsmanship and undisciplined brushwork of the *Pentecost* prevent its consideration as an autograph work of Lorenzo Monaco. More significantly, however, the miniature reveals the impact on Lorenzo's shop of Ghiberti's work around 1418, specifically the *Pentecost* of the North Door (Krautheimer, 1956, pl. 54). The two figures standing below are direct but reversed reflections of Ghiberti's central figure with the scimitar in the relief (Fig. 314), and the dense clustering of heads recalls Ghiberti's group at either side of the Virgin. There are similar parallels between Ghiberti's latest works for the North Door and Don Lorenzo's *Adoration of the Magi* in the Uffizi (see the Introductory Essay, p. 34). The heads in the frame of the Detroit miniature are rightly ascribed to Bartolomeo di Fruosino (Boskovits, 1975). [ca. 1420]

EDINBURGH, National Gallery of Scotland, no. 2271

Madonna and Child Enthroned
FIG. 158

Panel: 101.6 x 62.3 cm.

Inscription: (Christ Child) EGO SUM V

CONDITION: The picture was restored in 1965 at the National Gallery of Scotland. The gold ground adjacent to the Child's head and in an area at the center of the floor reveals extensive repair. Details of the lions' heads of the faldstool have been strengthened. The fragment of drapery on the left border was discovered during the restoration. For a fuller report, see Brigstocke, 1978, p. 71.

HISTORY: William Drury-Lowe, Locko Park, Derbyshire, probably bought in Italy, 1840-65; by descent to Lt.-Col. J. Packe-Drury-Lowe; Capt. P.J.B. Drury-Lowe; [Sotheby's, London, March 24, 1965, no. 56]; [Thos. Agnew & Sons, London]; National Gallery of Scotland 1965.

LITERATURE: 1884, *Winter Exhibition of Old Masters*, Royal Academy, London, no. 224: Lorenzo Monaco // 1901, Richter, no. 25: LM // 1905, Sirén, p. 190: doubts the attribution to LM // 1953, *Works of Art from Midland Houses*, Birmingham City Art Gallery, no. 164 // 1967, Baxandall, pp. 6-7: LM, the fuller modelling of the Christ Child implies an influence on Fra Angelico // 1970, Thompson and Brigstocke, pp. 51-52, no. 2271: late work, designed by Don Lorenzo and probably executed with workshop assistance; provide additional bibliography; the fragment of crimson drapery at the left evidently belonged to a subsidiary figure, suggesting that the *Madonna and Child* formed the center panel of an altarpiece // 1975, Boskovits, p. 341: LM, 1410-15; cites Zeri's verbal opinion that the *Saints* wing in Cracow may have formed the left lateral of the same altarpiece // 1978, Brigstocke, pp. 71-72: LM and workshop, ca. 1418-20 (accepting my dating proposed *in litteris*).

COMMENT: The Edinburgh *Madonna* was designed by Lorenzo Monaco and executed by the shop contemporarily with a major work of around 1418—the *Annunciation* in the Accademia in Florence (Fig. 77). Don Lorenzo's forms now assume their fullest attenuation, with the ductus long and unbroken. The six-petaled pattern in the halo of the Edinburgh Virgin, found in no other *Madonna* by the master or his shop, is a variant of the halo of Gabriel in the *Annunciation*. The intervention of the workshop in the Edinburgh panel is detectable in the coarseness of the tempera technique and the summary character of facial features. The discovery of a fragment of drapery on the left border of the panel rules out the alliance of the Cracow *Saints* (Fig. 153) with the *Madonna* (see Boskovits, 1975).

A similar lion-headed faldstool was used in the *Madonna Enthroned* at Empoli (Fig. 156), but by a different hand in the workshop. A nearly identical stool appears in the *Madonna and Saints* altarpiece (Fig. 330) by Francesco d'Antonio in the Fitzwilliam Museum, dated 1415, at a moment when the painter appears to have been under the direct tutelage of Lorenzo Monaco, but also significantly influenced by Starnina (see Longhi, 1940, p. 186, note 24; and the Introductory Essay, Note 60). [ca. 1418]

§ EMPOLI, Museo della Collegiata di Sant'Andrea, no. 2

Madonna of Humility with Saints Donninus, John the Baptist, Peter, and Anthony Abbot
FIGS. 20, 21

Panel: (Overall) 157 x 205 cm.; (center panel) 127 x 78 cm.; (lateral panels) 157 x 62.8 cm.
Inscribed date: 1404
Inscriptions: (Center base) AVE.MARIA.GRATIA. PLENA.DNS.TECUM.ANO DI.M.CCCCIIII. // (lateral bases) S.DOMNINUS.M. / S.IONES BAPSTA. // S.PETRUS.APOSTOLUS. / S.AMTONIUS.ABB. [*sic*]

CONDITION: An Alinari photograph of 1929 (no. 42376) shows the triptych with modern spiral colonnettes and capitals that mask the divisions between the central and lateral panels, extensive losses in the frame moldings, and scattered abrasions to the gold ground. In a subsequent restoration, the date of which I have not found, the colonnettes were removed, damaged segments of the frame were replaced, and small patches of abraded gold leaf were filled, largely in the area above the head of the Virgin. Scattered liftings of the paint film were secured and losses in the Child's hair repainted. The triptych was cleaned and mildly restored at the Gabinetto dei Restauri in Florence in the early 1950s. The names of the saints, inscribed on the bases of the lateral panels, are badly abraded (transcriptions above are adapted from Paolucci, 1985, p. 72).

HISTORY: From the suppressed church of San Donnino, near Empoli; in the gallery of the Collegiata since its inception in 1860.

LITERATURE: 1864, Crowe and Cavalcaselle, vol. 1, p. 552: Lorenzo Monaco // 1878, Vasari, ed. Milanesi, vol. 2, p. 31: LM // 1896, Berenson, p. 119: LM (1932, p. 298; 1963, vol. 1, p. 117) // 1899, Carocci, p. 6: LM // 1905, Sirén, p. 38, pl. 7 (showing the spiral colonnettes): LM // 1906, Giglioli, p. 70: LM // 1927, van Marle, vol. 9, p. 126: LM; Saint Donninus is misnamed Saint Julian // 1929, Suida, p. 392: LM // 1931, Golzio, p. 33: LM // 1933/34, Gamba, p. 154: entirely by the hand of a close follower of LM // 1938/39, Pudelko, p. 238: LM // 1947, Procacci, pp. 48-49, no. 47: LM // 1956, Baldini, p. 10, no. 2: LM // 1970, González-Palacios, pp. 32-33: LM // 1975, Boskovits, p. 341: LM // 1985, Paolucci, pp. 72-74: LM; provides additional bibliography, including inventories of 1863 and 1894; detail of the Madonna and Child in color, p. 73.

COMMENT: Sirén's (1905) proposal that the Bergamo *Man of Sorrows* (Fig. 136) was the central pinnacle is not acceptable from a stylistic standpoint, and because of a disparity in dimensions; the width of the horizontal frame molding above the *Madonna* panel is 43 cm., whereas that of the Bergamo panel is only 23 cm. The proposal by González-Palacios (1970) that the Lehman (Metropolitan Museum) *Crucifixion* (Fig. 135) served as the central pinnacle of the Empoli triptych demonstrates the stylistic compatibility of these works, but presents physical obstacles. Although the width of the New York *Crucifixion* (41.9 cm., including the modern lateral frame moldings) could be satisfactorily accommodated above the truncated gable of the central panel (43.5 cm.), the frame moldings of the Empoli altarpiece and the original segments in the frame of the *Crucifixion* have significantly different profiles. A combination of painted gable surfaces, as at Empoli, with the surviving original pastiglia ornament in the gable of the Lehman Collection panel would be contradictory, and to my knowledge, unprecedented. Nonetheless, enlarging on González-Palacios's perceptive stylistic grouping, I would further propose that the same shop assistant, working under the close supervision of Lorenzo Monaco, who intervened in the painting of the lateral panels at Empoli and the Lehman Collection *Crucifixion*, was also responsible for the *Madonna and Saints* of 1408 in the Accademia, Florence, and the *Madonna of Humility* in the Pushkin Museum, Moscow (Figs. 138 and 142).

The type of Child who is closely bonded to the Virgin's shoulder and torso, which Don Lorenzo devised in the Empoli *Madonna of Humility*, was repeated with slight variations in the Berenson and Stuttgart *Madonna of Humility* panels of 1405 and 1407 (Figs. 38 and 39), and in several shop works produced in these same middle years of the first decade: Lastra a Signa (Florence), San Martino a Gangalandi (Fig. 139); Moscow, Pushkin Museum (Fig. 142); New York, Metropolitan Museum of Art (Fig. 141). [1404]

EMPOLI, Museo della Collegiata di Sant'Andrea, no. 21

Saints John the Evangelist and Catherine of Alexandria; and *Saint John the Baptist and a Bishop Saint* (Augustine?)

FIGS. 154-155

Pinnacles: (Left) *Moses*; (right) *Prophet*

Panel: 132 x 54 cm. (each panel, from bottom of painted surface to crest of pinnacle)
Inscription: (Baptist) ECCE AGNUS DEI. ECCE

CONDITION: Both panels show scattered areas of harsh repainting, apparently with an oil medium. Wood strips at the base of the panels are modern additions. Restoration measures were undertaken in 1938 by Vittorio Granchi (Paolucci, 1985, p. 76).

HISTORY: From the Collegiata di Sant'Andrea in Empoli; in the gallery of the Collegiata since its inception in 1860 (for further conjectural history, see Paolucci, 1985, p. 75). Since 1956 the panels have been exhibited as the laterals of a triptych, along with the *Madonna Enthroned* (formerly no. 72).

LITERATURE: 1899, Carocci, p. 7, no. 21: Lorenzo Monaco // 1905, Sirén, p. 168: by the same shop assistant of Lorenzo who painted the Madonnas in the Loeser Collection (now Brooklyn), the Louvre, the Toscanelli Collection (now Kansas City), and Berlin no. 1123A (now destroyed) // 1906, Giglioli, p. 74: LM // 1927, van Marle, vol. 9, p. 176: shop of LM // 1932, Berenson, p. 298: LM // 1933, Florence, *Mostra del Tesoro*, p. 116, nos. 276 and 277: style of LM // 1933/34, Gamba, p. 154: school of Lorenzo Monaco // 1940, Longhi, p. 188, note 25: triptych from the school of LM; the figures in the trefoils of the pinnacles are attributed to Paolo Schiavo // 1947, Procacci, p. 38, nos. 33-34: school of LM; not certain that the *Madonna Enthroned* (no. 72) in the Collegiata formed the central panel // 1956, Baldini, p. 15, no. 21: the recomposed triptych, including the two laterals and *Madonna Enthroned* (no. 72), formerly attributed to Lorenzo, are rather by a close follower, perhaps the same one who painted the polyptych in the gallery at Prato // 1958, Levi D'Ancona, "Matteo Torelli," p. 253: Torelli // 1963, Berenson, vol. 1, p. 118: shop of LM; connects with the *Madonna Enthroned* // 1975, Boskovits, p. 341: LM, 1420-25 // 1984, Bellosi, p. 309: largely by Paolo Schiavo // 1985, Paolucci, pp. 75-77 (figs. on pp. 75 and 77 do not show the original risers of the platform): workshop of LM, 1420s, with the possible intervention of Paolo Schiavo in the figures of the saints, as well as in the trefoils of the pinnacles; the laterals and the *Madonna Enthroned* form an integral triptych; further bibliography.

COMMENT: For discussion of the proposed physical and stylistic relationship of these panels, see the following in Catalogue I: Empoli, Museo della Collegiata, *Madonna Enthroned*, and Brussels (formerly), Féron-Stoclet Collection, *Annunciation*. The place of the works within the traditions of Lorenzo's shop is discussed in Catalogue I, Prato, Galleria Comunale, *Madonna Enthroned with Four Saints*. Longhi's (1940) attribution of the trefoils in the pinnacles to Paolo Schiavo is definitive, but I am unable to concur with Bellosi's and Paolucci's detection of the same hand in the figures of the four saints. [ca. 1420-22]

EMPOLI, Museo della Collegiata di Sant'Andrea, no. 21 (formerly no. 72)

Madonna Enthroned

FIG. 156

Panel: 101 x 58.5 cm. (painted surface)

CONDITION: The panel was reduced in size at some point in its history, which truncated the dais and the crest of the cloth of honor. Excepting some visible fissures at the base of the panel and small losses of paint in the Virgin's scarf and the Child's tunic, the picture is in sound condition. The panel underwent restoration by Gaetano Lo Vullo in 1935 and a further mild restoration was undertaken around 1960.

HISTORY: From the Collegiata di Sant'Andrea in Empoli, where the panel may have been in the third chapel to the right, integrated into a seventeenth-century canvas depicting Saints Andrew and John the Baptist (Paolucci, 1983, pp. 75-76). The panel is known to have been in the Museo della Collegiata by 1933, when it was included in the *Mostra del Tesoro di Firenze Sacra* (see below). Since 1956, the panel has been exhibited as the center of a triptych, along with the *Saints* laterals (no. 21).

LITERATURE: 1933, Florence, *Mostra del Tesoro*, p. 116, no. 278: Florentine school, first half of the fifteenth century // 1933/34, Gamba, p. 154: school of Lorenzo Monaco // 1936, Berenson, p. 256: shop of

LM // 1940, Longhi, p. 188, note 25: triptych from school of LM // 1947, Procacci, p. 37, no. 32: LM; the connection with the *Saints* laterals (no. 21) is not certain // 1956, Baldini, p. 15, no. 72: forms a triptych with the Empoli *Saints*; by a close follower of LM, perhaps the same one who painted a polyptych in the Galleria Comunale in Prato // 1958, Levi D'Ancona, "Matteo Torelli," p. 256, note 26: Matteo Torelli; from the same period as the Empoli *Saints*, but not from the same altarpiece // 1963, Berenson, vol. 1, p. 118: LM, shop; forms a triptych with Empoli 21 // 1975, Boskovits, p. 341: LM, 1420-25 // 1984, Bellosi, p. 309: largely by Paolo Schiavo // 1985, Paolucci, pp. 75-77: workshop of LM, 1420s; forms an integral triptych with the lateral panels (no. 21).

COMMENT: There is sufficient internal evidence to prove that the *Madonna Enthroned* did not form a triptych with the two laterals (no. 21) in the Museo della Collegiata. The downward gaze of the two Saints John suggests that the panel to which the Empoli *Saints* were originally attached would have been either a Madonna of Humility, with the Child placed low in the picture field, or an Annunciation, in which the genuflecting or alighting Gabriel and the seated Virgin formed a low center of attention. Moreover, the arches of the *Madonna* and the *Saints* panels spring at different heights, measuring from the bottom of the painted surfaces of each panel (at 75 cm. in the *Madonna* and at 61 cm. in the laterals). As Baldini (1956) suggested, however, the *Madonna Enthroned* and the *Saints* panels do come from the same late moment in the work of the assistant in Don Lorenzo's shop whose hand is first discernible in the altarpiece at Prato. For the series of works produced by that assistant, from around 1415 to the early 1420s, see Catalogue I, Prato, Galleria Comunale, *Madonna Enthroned, with Four Saints.* [ca. 1420-22]

FIESOLE, Museo Bandini, no. III.37

Crucifixion with the Virgin and Saints John the Evangelist and Francis
FIG. 192

Panel: 123 x 55 cm. (including engaged frame)

CONDITION: The panel was restored in the early 1950s, with the following interventions: extensive repainting of the figure of the Virgin was removed, leaving the gesso ground exposed; the paint film was cleaned and the gold ground secured; deteriorated areas of wood in the frame were refurbished.

HISTORY: From the Oratorio di Sant'Ansano (around 1910).

LITERATURE: 1905, Sirén, p. 102: Lorenzo Monaco, 1418-22 // 1909, Berenson, p. 152: LM // 1927, van Marle, vol. 9, pp. 243 and 589: Andrea di Giusto, revising the prior attribution to Lorenzo Monaco (p. 168, note 3) // 1929, Suida, p. 392: LM // 1932, Berenson, p. 298: LM, late work (1963, vol. 1, p. 118) // 1933, Giglioli, pp. 241-42: LM school // 1938/39, Pudelko, p. 248, note 35: LM // 1955, Baldini, p. 82: LM // 1975, Boskovits, p. 341: LM, 1415-20 // 1979, Bellosi, pp. 63-65: LM; a late work; see below for reconstruction // 1981, Bandera Viani, pp. 30-31: LM; fig. 80 before restoration; figs. 79 and 81 in color, after restoration.

COMMENT: Luciano Bellosi (1979) has convincingly proposed that the Bandini *Crucifixion* formed the center panel of a triptych in which the laterals were the *Stigmatization of Saint Francis* in the Rijksmuseum, Amsterdam, and the *Funeral of Saint Francis* in the Pallavicini Collection in Rome (Figs. 190-191). Bellosi records (note 6) that Roberto Longhi had earlier perceived a relationship among the three panels. Even in the title of his article ("Un trittico molto insolito"), Bellosi indicated his awareness of the unusual nature of the triptych, but he mustered sufficient physical evidence (frame carpentry and ornament, halo patterns, overall dimensions) to make the connection secure. In his study he noted that all aspects of the dimensions had not yet been checked. The integration of the panels may be further affirmed by the fact that the spring of the arch in the Fiesole panel comes at 55 cm. from the bottom of the painted surface, while in the Pallavicini and Rijksmuseum panels the spring of the flatter arches is at approximately 53 cm. Study of the backs of the three panels for possible evidence of connecting battens or other physical alliances has not as yet been undertaken.

Bellosi considers the reintegrated triptych to be an entirely autograph work of Lorenzo Monaco, whereas in my discussion of the *Stigmatization* and the *Funeral of Saint Francis* (see Catalogue I, Amsterdam, Rijksmuseum), I propose that there is shop intervention in both works, although the Amsterdam panel is clearly of finer quality and was painted under the direct supervision of Lorenzo Monaco. The Fiesole *Crucifixion* is also in part a product of the late workshop, the collaboration being especially perceptible in the figures beneath the cross. Saint Francis's cassock is drawn with a mechanical line that recalls the Pallavicini panel, and the raised hand of the Evangelist is an unthinkable detail in a work in which Don Lorenzo's own brush prevailed. The Saint John, in fact, with his squarish head and paunchy midriff, appears to be an emigré from Starnina's milieu.

Regardless of the extensive involvement of the workshop, this reintegrated triptych is among the works of the early 1420s that define the direction of Don Lorenzo's latest style. As Bellosi implies, we are brought to a new and final phase of the painter's work. Just as spatial effects are a primary aspect of the Amsterdam and Rome panels, in the Fiesole *Crucifixion* the gold ground seems to open up as "sky" behind the isolated silhouette of Christ; we are reminded of the anachronistic gold ground in the Santa Trinita *Annunciation* (Fig. 121), and there are analogous stylistic directions in Don Lorenzo's intimate late masterpiece of *Saint Jerome in His Study* (Fig. 129). It is in the upper zone of the Fiesole panel that the personal involvement of Lorenzo Monaco is most evident. The modelling of the torso of Christ heightens the physical presence of the figure, differing subtly from the more abstract use of light and dark in the cutout crosses (cf. Fig. 72). An intensified physicality is also conveyed by the organic connection between the drooping head and the torsion of the shoulders and arms. These qualities of realism make the roulade of the loincloth seem to be an habitual gesture. If the immediate precursors of this Christ are the cutout crosses by Don Lorenzo and his workshop, the wooden *Crucifix* by Donatello at Santa Croce also stands in its background. The path is direct to the *Crucifixion* by Giovanni Toscani in a pinnacle for the Ardinghelli Chapel altarpiece at Santa Trinita, of circa 1423 to 1424, in which the stylistic and emotive worlds of Lorenzo Monaco, Masolino, and the early Masaccio converged (Padoa Rizzo, fig. 2). [ca. 1422-23]

FIESOLE, San Domenico

Saints Catherine of Alexandria, Agnes, Mary Magdalen, Lucy, and *Two Female Saints*

Pilasters of the *Madonna Enthroned and Four Saints* by Fra Angelico

Panel: 50.5 x 10.2 cm. (each panel)

CONDITION: Beginning in the early 1970s, the entire altarpiece was restored by the Laboratorio dei Restauri of the Florentine Soprintendenza (for preliminary notice of the restoration, see U. Baldini and P. dal Poggetto, *Firenze Restaura, Guida alla Mostra*, Florence, 1972, p. 25). The six pilaster panels are in good condition, except for the considerable losses in the gold grounds (cf. Pope-Hennessy, 1974, fig. 1, and Baldini, 1977, figs. 236-37).

HISTORY: The panels were inserted at an unknown date into the pilasters of the frame constructed in 1501, when Lorenzo di Credi imposed Renaissance revisions on Fra Angelico's Gothic altarpiece (see Baldini, 1977, p. 236, and figs. 225 and 236-37). Baldini (1977, p. 240, note 5) observed that as all of the saints are female their original location could possibly have been in an altarpiece located at a convent.

LITERATURE: 1908, Cruttwell, p. 112: Lorenzo Monaco // 1911, A. Venturi, vol. 7, pt. 1, p. 40: by a pupil of LM; added later to Angelico's altarpiece // 1952, Pope-Hennessy, p. 166: Rossello di Jacopo Franchi // 1953, Salmi, p. 13: follower of LM // 1963, Berenson, vol. 1, p. 13: Rossello di Jacopo Franchi // 1970, Baldini, p. 89: follower of LM, possibly originally intended for the altarpiece // 1974, Pope-Hennessy, pp. 189-90, fig. 1: reviews the uncertain history of the replacement of Fra Angelico's original pilaster panels; does not attribute the pilaster figures // 1975, Boskovits, p. 341: LM, 1400-1405 // 1977, Baldini, p. 236: LM.

COMMENT: The pilaster figures are late works from the shop of Lorenzo Monaco. The elongated proportions, in particular of the Magdalen and Catherine, recall the saints in the pilasters of the *Annunciation* in the Bartolini Salimbeni Chapel at Santa Trinita (Fig. 202), although the quality of the Fiesole figures is considerably higher. The six saints panels most closely approach the figure style of Lorenzo Monaco in the Accademia *Annunciation* (Fig. 77) and the Uffizi *Adoration of the Magi* (Fig. 82). [ca. 1418-20]

§ FLORENCE, Accademia, no. 438

Agony in the Garden

FIGS. 7-14; COLORPLATES 1 AND 2

Predella: *Betrayal of Christ; Stripping of Christ*

Panel: 189 x 108 cm. (main panel unframed); 26.5 x 50.5 cm. (each predella panel, including engaged quatrefoil frame)

CONDITION: Restoration was undertaken in 1957 by Messrs. Lo Vullo, Lumini, and Toschi for the Gabinetto dei Restauri of the Florentine Soprintendenza. Damage to the surface and old repaint, apparently of the late nineteenth or early twentieth century, were discovered along a crack running from the ear of Christ to the bottom of the panel, in Saint James's mantle, and along the top of each predella panel. The areas of repaint and a varnish that lent an exaggeratedly dark tonality were removed, and damage to the surface was inpainted. The predella was only lightly cleaned and retouched. An overburdening nineteenth-century frame was removed, and now the panel is exhibited unframed, excepting the original quatrefoils of the predella which had been slightly cut at either end and coarsely regilded, probably when the work was repainted and varnished.

HISTORY: With the suppression of religious orders in 1810, the panel was transferred from Santa Maria degli Angeli, first to San Marco and then to the Accademia. By 1814 it was in the Uffizi, remaining there until 1919 when it was returned to the Accademia. The statement by Crowe and Cavalcaselle (1864) that the provenance is the Ardinghelli Chapel at Santa Maria del Carmine in Florence is without foundation (see the Introductory Essay, Note 5), as is Rigoni's notice (1891, p. 82) that the panel came from the suppressed convent of the Annalena.

LITERATURE: 1810, "Inventario degli oggetti di Belle Arti estratti dalle chiese e conventi soppressi nel 1808 e 1810, e raccolti nel Convento di San Marco," MS., library of the Galleria dell'Accademia, Florence, p. 36, no. 802: Giotto // 1825, "Giornale delle robe venute nella Real Galleria, 1784-1825," MS., Uffizi, p. 101: Giotto // 1855, Burckhardt, p. 154: praised the panel as a work by Giotto // 1860, *Catalogue de la R. Galerie de Florence*, vol. 2, p. 2, no. 4: Giotto // 1864, Crowe and Cavalcaselle, vol. 1, p. 342, note 3: Giottesque, late fourteenth century; for the Carmine // 1875-76, Ruskin, pp. 39-42 (1899, p. 102): cites the altarpiece twice, first as a work of Giotto, and in an afterthought as possibly by Lorenzo Monaco (Gronau, 1950, p. 221, noted Ruskin's discussion of the *Agony* as a work by Giotto, but not the later revision of the attribution) // 1883, Crowe and Cavalcaselle, vol. 2, p. 344, note 1: LM, early // 1891, Rigoni, p. 82: Giotto? // 1895, Schmarsow, p. 124: LM // 1904, Toesca, pp. 172-74: believed his to be the initial attribution to LM; around 1404-1410, that is, between the Empoli and Monte Oliveto Altarpieces // 1905, Sirén, p. 164: school of LM, by the same hand as the Bologna and Vecchietti (now Assisi) Madonnas // 1907, Pieraccini, p. 100, no. 8: LM // 1927, van Marle, vol. 9, p. 60: school of LM // 1929, Suida, p. 392: school of LM // 1931, Golzio, p. 60: a pupil of Lorenzo // 1932, Berenson, p. 298: LM, early, with assistance in the predella // 1936, Procacci, p. 40, no. 438: LM // 1938/39, Pudelko, p. 237, note 8: LM, early // 1939, Sandberg-Vavalà, p. 106: LM, but the dark coloring raises some doubt as to the attribution // 1950, Gronau, p. 218: LM, around 1395 // 1958, Baldini, pp. 20-22, no. 6: a succinct report on the restoration // 1958, "Some New Attributions," Levi D'Ancona, p. 185: LM, early style, but the predella by an assistant // 1963, Berenson, vol. 1, p. 118: LM, early // 1965, Bellosi, "Da Spinello," pp. 36 and 39: LM, late 1390s // 1975, Boskovits, p. 343: LM, 1395-1400 // 1979, Florence, *Uffizi*, p. 346, no. P922: LM, 1395-1400 // 1984, Eisenberg, pp. 275-89 // 1987, Bonsanti, p. 90; colorplate, p. 78: LM.

COMMENT: Although Don Lorenzo's use of a quatrefoil frame around a narrative scene had important precedents in Florentine painting and sculpture, for example, Taddeo Gaddi's series of panels for the Sacristy cupboard at Santa Croce and Andrea Pisano's doors of the Baptistery, the introduction of the quatrefoil into a predella seems rather to have a Sienese origin. A notable example is the dispersed predella by Luca di Tommè that once stood beneath the *Madonna and Saints* (no. 51) in the Pinacoteca, Siena (see Zeri, 1958, pp. 3-10; Fehm, 1986, pp. 76-79). The central quatrefoil in that predella is of the elongated type adopted by Lorenzo Monaco. For a discussion of the use of the quatrefoil in Sienese predellas, see Preiser, pp. 145ff. In the series of *Saint Lucy* episodes in the Metropolitan Museum, New York, by the Pistoiese painter Cristiani the lobes of the elongated quatrefoils are flamboyant rather than rounded (see Zeri, 1971, pp. 40-41). A close parallel to Lorenzo's predella panels for the *Agony in the Garden*, both in the shape of the quatrefoil and the types and arrangement of figures and landscape, is the socle relief of the *Martyrdom of Saint James* by the Lamberti workshop (ca. 1414 to 1416) on the niche of the Furriers' Guild at Orsanmichele (Fig. 274). George Goldner (pp. 66-74) has demonstrated relationships between the Lamberti socle relief and the *Martyrdom of Saint James* in the Louvre (Fig. 216), attributed to the workshop of Agnolo Gaddi and to Lorenzo Monaco, which is from the predella of the Nobili Chapel altarpiece of 1388 from Santa Maria degli Angeli. In the relief, however, the forms of the landscape and their relationship to the figures are closer to Lorenzo's *Agony* predella, with an added derivation from Ghiberti of the rocky shelf that provides a stage for the narrative. Pope-Hennessy (1980, p. 64) has noted the proximity of the decapitated saint, the projecting rocks, and the diagonal cliffs to Ghiberti's style, suggesting the possibility that he provided the model for the Orsanmichele relief. The three sloping cliffs in the background resemble even more closely Don Lorenzo's landscape forms and, in general, later Trecento settings.

A fragment of an *Agony in the Garden* in the Kestner Museum in Hannover (No. 165) is a variation on Lorenzo's three sleeping disciples, the Saint Peter being the most dependent on the model. I would tentatively attribute the panel to the milieu of Alvaro Pirez.

As Pope-Hennessy has observed, in the *Agony in the Garden* window of 1443 for the Florentine Duomo, Ghiberti apparently turned to Don Lorenzo's composition for the figural elements (1980, pp. 63-64 and fig. 23). Ironically, in this late work the sculptor quoted the painter's panel of the late 1390s more closely than his own relief of the same subject on the North Door of the Baptistery. [1395-1400]

§ FLORENCE, Accademia, no. 467

The Man of Sorrows with the Virgin, Saint John the Evangelist, and Episodes and Emblems of the Passion

FIGS. 18, 19

Panel: 268 x 170 cm. (including engaged frame)
Inscribed date: 1404 (ABANNO SUE INCARNATIONIS. M.CCCC.IIII)

CONDITION: The picture surface is in exceptionally sound condition. There are a few small areas of damage and old repair in the body of Christ and in the gold ground, slight blistering in the Virgin's mantle, and an unthreatening vertical crack through the head of Christ in the *Betrayal* at the upper right. The frame is original (see Cämmerer-George, p. 190).

HISTORY: The coats of arms at either end of the inscription at the base of the panel have defied identification. The panel was acquired in 1871 from a Cav. Carovana by the English painter and art dealer William Blundell Spence, a resident of Florence (see J. Fleming, "Art Dealing in the Risorgimento, II and III," *Burlington Magazine* 121, 1979, pp. 492-508 and 568-80). Spence sold the panel to the Uffizi in 1886, where it remained until 1919 when it was transferred to the Accademia.

LITERATURE: 1886, letter of December 11 from W. B. Spence to Sir Frederick Burton, Director of the National Gallery, London: Lorenzo Monaco; in "wonderful condition" // 1888, Rigoni, p. 121, no. 1318: by an unknown painter of the fifteenth century // 1896, Berenson, p. 152: LM (1932, p. 299; 1963, vol. 1, p. 118) // 1901, Pieraccini, p. 104, no. 40: LM // 1905, Sirén, p. 37: LM, related to the Oblate frescoes, which he attributes to Lorenzo // 1927, van Marle, vol. 9, p. 126: LM; a repetition of his work at the Oblate // 1929, Suida, p. 392: LM // 1931, Golzio, pp. 31 and 60: a school work, the hardness of the style and the lack of passion preventing an attribution to the master; depends on the Oblate fresco // 1936, Procacci, p. 40, no. 467: LM // 1938/39, Pudelko, p. 238: LM // 1965, Bellosi, *Maestri*, [p. 4] and pl. 3, in color: LM // 1975, Boskovits, p. 343: LM // 1979, Florence, *Uffizi*, p. 347, no. P923: LM // 1987, Bonsanti, p. 90; colorplate, p. 82: LM.

COMMENT: The design and execution of this extensive work are essentially by Lorenzo Monaco, but the upper portions of the panel reveal the intervention of the shop, which is especially evident when the heads of Christ, the Virgin, and Saint John are compared with the heads of Judas and Christ in the abbreviated *Betrayal* above the crossbar. Lorenzo's brush modelled with fine gradations of light and dark within a taut linear framework, whereas the assistant's line is flaccid, the brushwork coarse, and the forms flat and virtually unmodelled. The same schematizing hand could have been closely involved with the *Madonna Enthroned* (Fig. 133) in Bologna of around 1405 and eventually the San Benedetto Altarpiece (see Catalogue I, London, National Gallery).

There are several comprehensive Tuscan representations of the Man of Sorrows with episodes and emblems of the Passion that immediately preceded Don Lorenzo's imposing icon and on which he could have depended in assembling its multifarious imagery: e.g., circle of Bartolo di Fredi, San Gimignano, Sant'Agostino (L. Venturi, 1944, fig. 11); circle of the Master of the Straus Madonna, Valiana (Pratovecchio), San Romolo (Boskovits, 1975, fig. 466, and *Arte nel Aretino*, Florence, 1974, figs. 97-101); Mariotto di Nardo, Florence, Soprintendenza (Deposit), from the former Convento delle Oblate (see Catalogue II); circle of Mariotto di Nardo?, San Giovanni Valdarno, San Lorenzo (*Arte nel Aretino*, fig. 118). The Christ, Virgin, and Saint John in Don Lorenzo's panel have prototypes in Tuscan images of the Lamentation, the Pietà, and the Entombment; see for example, Taddeo Gaddi and workshop, Yale University Art Gallery (Ladis, fig. 62-1); Master of Santa Verdiana, formerly Oxford, Grissel Collection (Boskovits, 1967, fig. 24; see also, Antal, p. 226, note 141); Giovanni da Milano, Florence, Accademia, dated 1365 (Fremantle, fig. 378). Within the series of images noted above, it is in the fresco at San Giovanni Valdarno that the relationship of the Virgin and Saint John to the Man of Sorrows most resembles that in Don Lorenzo's central group. Furthermore, the rinceau bordering the lower edge of the fresco and running directly below the sarcophagus is reminiscent of the symbolically motivated ornament on the sarcophagus in the Accademia panel. The sinopia of Mariotto's *Man of Sorrows* from the Convento delle Oblate (Florence, Sopr. Gab. Fot. 113205) includes pyxes and a chalice similar to the cluster of liturgical objects at the base of Don Lorenzo's panel, but in the completed fresco these were omitted, to be replaced by the veil of Veronica draped over the front of the sarcophagus. A striking and virtually contemporary variant on Don Lorenzo's large icon is the horizontal panel of the *Man of Sorrows with the Virgin, Magdalen, and Episodes and Emblems of the Passion* by the Master of the Straus Madonna (Accademia, Florence, Sopr. Gab. Fot. 376062; see Mosco, pp. 122-23 [entry by R. Protopisani], reproduced in color). [1404]

§ FLORENCE, Accademia, no. 468

Monte Oliveto Altarpiece: Madonna Enthroned, with Saints Bartholomew, John the Baptist, Thaddeus, and Benedict

FIGS. 22-28

Pinnacles: *Blessing Redeemer; Annunciation*
Spandrels: *Malachi*; *Isaiah*

Panel: (Overall) 277 x 235 cm.; (center panel) 154 x 84 cm.; (side panels) 122 x 80.5 cm.
Inscribed date: 1410; Documented dates: 1407 and 1411 (see Documents 8A and 8B)
Inscriptions: (Center base) AVE GRATIA PLENA DOMINUS TECUM . . . MCCCCX;
(lateral bases) S. BARTOLOMEUS APL̄ / S. JOHES BA // S. THADEUS APL̄ / S. BENEDICTUS AB;
(Christ Child) EGO SUM VIA V; (center pinnacle) AΩ;
(left spandrel) ECCE EGO MICTO AN (Malachi 3:1);
(right spandrel) ECCE VIRGO CŌCI (Isaiah 7:14);
(Benedict's book) PASSIONIBŪ XR̄I P PATIĒTIAM PARTECIPEMUR UT REGNI EĪ MEREAMUR ĒS
(conclusion of Prologue to the *Rule*)

CONDITION: The only significant blemish on the panel surfaces is abrasion and staining of the gold grounds around the Prophets in the spandrels of the middle register. The leafy outcroppings on the arched frames abutting the consoles of the pinnacles and above the ogival tympana at the crest of the altarpiece are not original ornament. Segments of the finials, spiral colonnettes, and cusps of the frame are modern replacements.

HISTORY: Commissioned for the Benedictine monastic church of San Bartolomeo at Monte Oliveto (outside the Porta San Frediano, Florence). Payments for work on the altarpiece were made to Lorenzo Monaco in July 1407 and June 1411 (see Documents 8A and 8B). The altarpiece was brought from San Bartolomeo to the Uffizi collections in 1867 (Rigoni, 1888, p. 124), where it remained until the mid-1950s. After being in deposit for several years at Palazzo Pitti, it was put on exhibition in 1961 at the Museo dell'Antica Casa Fiorentina in Palazzo Davanzati. After several subsequent years in the deposit of the Soprintendenza, the altarpiece has been in the collections of the Accademia since 1976.

LITERATURE: 1846, Vasari, ed. Marchese, Pini, and Milanesi, p. 211: Lorenzo Monaco, from San Piero Scheraggio; seen in the subterranean oratory at Monte Oliveto // 1864, Crowe and Cavalcaselle, vol. 1, p. 551: LM // 1878, Vasari, ed. Milanesi, p. 20, note 3, and p. 31: LM; in the sacristy of San Bartolomeo at Monte Oliveto // 1888, Rigoni, p. 124, no. 1331: LM // 1896, Berenson, p. 119 (1932, p. 299; 1963, vol. 1, p. 118): LM // 1903, Poggi, p. 58: publishes documents of 1406 (now corrected to 1407) and 1411 recording the commission and payment // 1905, Sirén, pp. 45-47, 172, and 182: republishes the documents; doubts that the altarpiece had a predella; cites a work in Prato by Andrea di Giusto closely based on the Monte Oliveto altarpiece, although the predella shows more the influence of Fra Angelico // 1927, van Marle, vol. 9, pp. 133-34 and 243: contrasts the style with miniatures from the same years; notes Andrea di Giusto's version // 1931, Golzio, pp. 37-38: notes milder color and Sienese character of the work // 1938/39, Pudelko, p. 247: characterizes style as academic // 1948, Sandberg-Vavalà, pp. 95-97: fullest gothicism in the pinnacles // 1958, Levi D'Ancona, "Some New Attributions," pp. 176 and 183: a fundamental work in establishing LM chronology // 1970, Berti, p. 215, no. 236 // 1975, Boskovits, p. 346 // 1982, Florence, *Iconografia di San Benedetto*, pp. 99-100, no. 33 // 1987, Bonsanti, p. 90; colorplate, p. 81.

COMMENT: Marchese, Pini and Milanesi's conjecture (1846; repeated by Milanesi in 1878) that the altarpiece was the one seen by Richa (1775, vol. 2, p. 15) at San Piero Scheraggio was later invalidated by Poggi's (1903) discovery of the documents of commission and payment, which connect it with San Bartolomeo. Van Marle's (1927) distinctions between Don Lorenzo's panel and miniature styles around 1410 is based on an attribution to him of those miniatures in Corale 3 at the Laurenziana which are most certainly not by the hand of Lorenzo Monaco, nor from his workshop. [1407-1411]

Note: For Andrea di Giusto's version and its modifications, see the Introductory Essay, p. 46 and Fig. 329. In the Church of Corpus Christi in New York City there is a modern adaptation of the Monte Oliveto Altarpiece that also incorporates elements of Don Lorenzo's Accademia *Annunciation* (for the history of this pastiche, see Frick Art Reference Library, file 707-9Q).

FLORENCE, Accademia, no. 470

Madonna and Child with Saints Catherine of Alexandria, John the Baptist, Peter, and an Unidentified Female Saint

FIG. 138

Panel: 89 x 49 cm. (painted surface)
Inscribed date: 1408 (A.D.M.CCCCVIII)

CONDITION: The gold ground is extensively eroded. Crude repair to the damaged paint film extends down the fall of Saint Peter's mantle to the riser of the dais, where the last numbers of the date are abraded. The panel was mildly restored in 1978. The frame is a nineteenth-century addition.

HISTORY: Acquired in Padua by Cav. Toscanelli, Pontedera, near Pisa; Uffizi, 1883; Accademia, 1933.

LITERATURE: 1883, G. Milanesi, p. 12, no. 47: Cennino Cennini (following the apocryphal inscription on the frame) // 1885, Crowe and Cavalcaselle, vol. 2, p. 338: follower of Lorenzo Monaco // 1891, Rigoni, p. 89, no. 42: anonymous Tuscan, fifteenth century // 1901, Pieraccini, p. 105, no. 42: anonymous fourteenth century, implying that the inscribed date is not authentic // 1905, Sirén, pp. 47-48: Lorenzo Monaco, in the period of the Monte Oliveto Altarpiece // 1909, Berenson, p. 153: LM; gives the correct museum number, but identifies the subject as the Madonna with the Baptist and Paul (1932, p. 299; 1963, vol. 1, p. 118) // 1927, van Marle, vol. 9, p. 134: LM // 1929, Suida, p. 392: LM // 1931, Golzio, p. 63: tentatively attributes to LM // 1936, Procacci, p. 38: LM and shop // 1938/39, Pudelko, p. 76: LM, corresponding with the Prato altarpiece // 1939, Sandberg-Vavalà, p. 108: LM, in a formative Giottesque period // 1975, Boskovits, p. 343: LM // 1979, Florence, *Uffizi*, p. 347, no. P924: LM // 1987, Bonsanti, p. 94: LM.

COMMENT: The base of the later frame bears the apocryphal inscription (CEÑUS.DE.ANDR̄E.CENNI.ME.PINXIT). The panel is the work of a competent but academic assistant who used as models the Empoli *Madonna of Humility* (Fig. 21) of 1404 and the Monte Oliveto Altarpiece (Fig. 22), dated 1410 but commissioned in 1407. Pudelko's (1938/39) description of the style as miniaturistic is confirmed by the highly keyed and flowery palette, recalling the *Prophets* of Corale 3 in the Laurenziana (Colorplate

4). The hand of the painter of the Accademia *Madonna* of 1408, an assistant working under the close supervision of Lorenzo Monaco, is visible in varying degrees of intervention in the following works: the four saints in the laterals of the Empoli triptych of 1404 (Fig. 20); the *Crucifixion* (Fig. 135) in the Metropolitan Museum of Art, New York; the *Crucifixion* (Fig. 137), dated 1408, in the Seattle Art Museum; the *Madonna of Humility* (Fig. 142) in the Pushkin Museum, Moscow (see the individual entries in Catalogue I). [1408]

FLORENCE, Accademia, nos. 2141, 2140, 2169

Crucifixion with the Lance and Sponge; Mourning Virgin; and *Mourning Saint John the Evangelist*

FIGS. 167, 168, 170

Panel: 50.5 x 27 cm.; 48.5 x 26 cm. (original panel surface); 48.5 x 26 cm. (original panel surface)
Inscription: (Cross) ĪÑRĪ

CONDITION: The three panels, now extensively transformed, were in the pinnacles of an altarpiece. The original ogival shape of the *Crucifixion* panel is still visible, beginning at the crossbar and inscribing either side of the pelican at the crest. The panels with the Virgin and Saint John were revised to a rococo contour, but the original vertical edges of the panels are readily discernible, in particular where the rocky outcroppings were enlarged in a generalized technique, possibly by the same hand that repainted the Virgin's drapery from the knees to the hem. The grounds of the three panels were repaired with gold paint in lieu of leaf gold.

HISTORY: The panels were transferred from the Florentine church of San Jacopo sopr'Arno to the Accademia in 1867. As Vasari (ed. Milanesi, vol. 2, 1878, p. 21), echoed by later writers, mentions an altarpiece by Lorenzo Monaco in the church, it may be conjectured that the three Accademia panels are fragments of that work (see the Appendix). Judging from the eighteenth-century shapes imposed on the Virgin and Saint John pinnacles, there is a likelihood that these panels were revised in the period when San Jacopo sopr'Arno was transformed into one of the prime examples of the Tuscan rococo (see Paatz, vol. 2, 1941, pp. 387-88). At various times since 1867 the panels have been in the collections of the Uffizi and San Marco, as well as the Accademia.

LITERATURE: 1864, Crowe and Cavalcaselle, vol. 1, p. 555: Lorenzo Monaco // 1869, *Catalogue de la R. Galerie de Florence*, nos. 16 bis: LM // 1878, Vasari, ed. Milanesi, vol. 2, p. 21, note 2: first proposed that the panels were part of the altarpiece at San Jacopo sopr'Arno mentioned by Vasari // 1896, Berenson, p. 119: LM; in the Uffizi deposit (1932, p. 299; 1963, vol. 1, p. 118) // 1905, Sirén, p. 43: LM, 1403-1405 // 1927, Van Marle, vol. 9, pp. 168 and 177, note 1: LM and school // 1931, Golzio, p. 47: LM, around 1414 // 1938/39, Pudelko, p. 248, note 35: LM, ca. 1410 // 1941, Paatz, vol. 2, pp. 393-94: review various locations since the 1860s // 1951, Procacci, p. 42: LM; from the church of San Jacopo de'Barbetti (sopr'Arno) // 1975, Boskovits, p. 343: LM, 1405-1410 // 1987, Bonsanti, p. 94; colorplates, pp. 92-93: LM.

COMMENT: The inarticulate relationship of torso and hands in the figure of the Virgin and the technical coarseness in the use of the tempera medium throughout the three panels indicate the work of a shop assistant based on Don Lorenzo's designs. The dependence of the figure of Christ and the Virgin on the same elements of the San Giovannino dei Cavalieri group (Fig. 74) helps to localize the Accademia pinnacles around 1415. The lance and sponge appear on either side of Christ in Don Lorenzo's *Man of Sorrows with Episodes and Emblems of the Passion* (Fig. 18) of 1404 and they accompany the empty cross in a miniature on folio 129 of Corale 10 in the Laurenziana, produced in the scriptorium at Santa Maria degli Angeli. Antal (p. 348, note 40, citing Emile Mâle) noted the relationship between the imagery of the lance and sponge in the Accademia panel and liturgical texts of the fourteenth century. [ca. 1415]

§ FLORENCE, Accademia, no. 3153

Crucifix

FIG. 69

Panel (cutout): 184 x 194 cm.

CONDITION: The state of the cross prior to a restoration of 1930 is recorded in the photograph reproduced here (Florence, Sopr. Gab. Fot. 5515). In that intervention an open panel seam across the corpus and fissures in the head and left arm were repaired and scattered losses in the tempera surface repainted. At an undocumented time between 1968 and 1984, further minor repairs were made, which are recorded in an ineffective photograph of the cross (Florence, Sopr. Gab. Fot. 367048). The superscription (I.N.R.I) now attached to the staff is not an original element of the cross.

HISTORY: From the Arcispedale di Santa Maria Nuova, 1900.

LITERATURE: 1905, Sirén, p. 89: Lorenzo Monaco // 1927, van Marle, vol. 9, p. 177: LM school // 1931, Golzio, p. 62: LM school // 1932, Berenson, p. 299: LM (1963, vol. 1, p. 118) //1936, Procacci, p. 42, no. 3153: LM // 1955, Eisenberg, p. 49, note 3: LM shop // 1961, Levi D'Ancona, p. 90: LM, ca. 1410 // 1975, Boskovits, p. 344: LM, 1405-1410 // 1987, Bonsanti, p. 89 (listed as No. 3147): LM.

COMMENT: The Accademia *Crucifix* is the first in the series of large cutout crosses produced by Lorenzo Monaco and his workshop. A dating within the half decade 1405-1410 would seem most satisfactory, judging from the closely related rendering of the torso in the *Man of Sorrows* (Fig. 18) of 1404 and the similar play of light and the soft hair textures of the Monte Oliveto Altarpiece (Figs. 22-28), executed from 1407-1410, analogies cited by Levi D'Ancona (1961). The close connection with the latter work is also discerned in the tonality of the grayish olive green of the corpus and in the arabesques of the loincloth, which recall the play of Gabriel's mantle in the left pinnacle (Fig. 25). The stocky proportions, in contrast to the more attenuated Christ of the later San Giuseppe, San Giovannino dei Cavalieri, and Monte San Savino crucifixes (Figs. 165, 70, and 71) relate the Accademia Christ to the saints of the Monte Oliveto Altarpiece. In Accademia 3153 and the San Giuseppe *Crucifix*, the next in the sequence of cutout crosses, Lorenzo continued to use a rich vegetal ornamentation of Christ's halo as he had done in the *Man of Sorrows* of 1404, but now translating the punched and incised patterns into gilded gesso relief.

For discussion of the tradition of the cutout cross, see Catalogue I, Florence, San Giovannino dei Cavalieri, *Crucifix with the Mourning Virgin and Saint John the Evangelist* (see also, Catalogue I, Florence, Museo Horne). [1405-1410]

§ FLORENCE, Accademia, no. 8458

Annunciation with Saints Catherine of Alexandria, Anthony Abbot, Proculus, and Francis of Assisi

FIGS. 77-80; COLORPLATE 12

Pinnacles (roundels): (center) *Christ Logos*; (lateral; see below, Condition and History)

Panel: (overall) 2.06 x 2.31 cm.; (center panel) 129.5 x 102 cm.; (lateral panels) 109 x 64.5 cm.; (center roundel) 32.5 cm.; (lateral roundels) 19 cm.

CONDITION: The pinnacle of the central panel is in nearly original state, although regilded, but those above the lateral panels have been crudely reworked and regilded. The center roundel is from the original altarpiece; the frame is engaged. For many years the roundels in the lateral pinnacles, having lost their bust-length Prophets, were filled with angels from the workshop of Bernardo Daddi, once elements of the San Pancrazio Altarpiece (see Fig. 77; also see below, Cohn, 1957; Marcucci [p. 37] notes that the angel roundels are no longer inserted in the pinnacles). Exposed seams between the center and side panels indicate that slender colonnettes and consoles originally masked these divisions. The base inscribed with the saints' names is modern. The painted and gilded surfaces of the panels, although in need of cleaning, are in an excellent state.

HISTORY: The earliest certain location of the altarpiece is the Badia Fiorentina, from whence it was transferred to the Accademia in 1812 (also see below, 1951, Procacci, and Comment). For the *Isaiah* originally in the roundel of the right gable, see Catalogue I, New York, Richard L. Feigen Collection.

LITERATURE: 1677, Bocchi, ed. Cinelli, p. 389: (under San Procolo) ". . . una Nunziata dipinta sul legno nel 1409 . . ." (see Paatz, vol. 4, 1952, pp. 694 and 700, note 31; associate the Accademia *Annunciation* with this citation of 1677 and the following one of 1794) // 1794, Follini and Rastrelli, vol. 5, p. 142: (under San Procolo) ". . . una Nunziata dipinta da incerto sul legno nel 1409 . . ." // 1795, Lanzi, p. 16: Giotto (in the Badia); considered to be the Annunciation by Giotto in the Badia mentioned by Vasari (see Vasari, ed. Milanesi, vol. 1, 1878, p. 373) // 1817, C. Colzi, "Descrizione . . . R. Accademia delle Belle Arti," MS., Soprintendenza alle Gallerie, Florence, p. 28: Giotto // 1844, Delécluze, ed. Pini and Milanesi, p. 54: Lorenzo Monaco // 1847, *Description de l'Imp. et R. Académie des Beaux-Arts de Florence*, 7th ed., Florence, p. 11: LM // 1859, G. Masselli, "Catalogo descritivo e storico delle pitture antiche che si conservano nelle sale della Fiorentina Accademia delle Belle Arti," MS., Soprintendenza alle Gallerie, Florence, no. 74: LM // 1864, Crowe and Cavalcaselle, vol. 1, p. 554: LM (in the 1883 ed., vol. 2, p. 340, the authors repeat Lanzi's mistaken identification with the work mentioned by Vasari) // 1896, Berenson, p. 119, LM (1932, p. 299; 1963, vol. 1, p. 118) // 1905, Sirén, pp. 53-56: LM, ca. 1408-1409; shows direct Sienese influence; suggests the predella may have been made up of the *Visitation* and *Adoration of the Magi* (now London, Courtauld Institute Galleries), the *Nativity* (now New York, Lehman Collection, Metropolitan Museum), and the *Flight into Egypt* (Altenburg) // 1927, van Marle, vol. 9, p. 150: LM, ca. 1408; denies Sirén's association of the predella series with the *Annunciation* // 1929, Suida, p. 392: LM // 1931, Golzio, p. 42: LM, ca. 1410 // 1938/39, Pudelko, p. 242: LM, around 1406 // 1940, Paatz, vol. 1, p. 315, note 144 and p. 316, note 151: see above, 1677 // 1951, Procacci, p. 44, no. 8458: LM; the altarpiece may be from San Procolo because of the presence of that saint in the right wing; denies the association of the altarpiece with the Annunciation, a work in fresco, mentioned by Vasari in the Badia and attributed by him to Giotto; it may be presumed that at the time of the suppression of San Procolo in 1788 its works of art were transferred to the patronal foundation of the Badia Fiorentina // 1956, Eisenberg, pp. 333-35: LM, accepting the reported dating of 1409; integrates into the right pinnacle a lost roundel of the *Prophet Isaiah*, once in the Artaud de Montor Collection in Paris (now Richard L. Feigen Collection, New York) // 1957, Cohn, pp. 176-78: attributes the two roundels with angels in the side pinnacles to Bernardo Daddi and traces their source to the San Pancrazio altarpiece // 1961, Levi D'Ancona, p. 93: LM, ca. 1414 // 1965, Bellosi, *Maestri*, [p. 6]: LM, ca. 1415 // 1975, Boskovits, p. 344: LM, 1410-15 // 1976, Eisenberg (*in litteris*), cited in *Toledo Museum of Art, European Paintings*, p. 99: LM, 1418-20 // 1984, Bellosi, p. 313, note 25: LM, 1415-20 // 1987, Bonsanti, p. 94, with colorplate: LM.

COMMENT: A contradiction in hagiography raises doubt that the Florentine church of San Procolo was the original source of the altarpiece. The titular saint of that church was the sixth-century Proculus the bishop, invariably represented as a mature man in clerical garb, whereas the Proculus in the altarpiece is the youthful knight of the fourth century, a different personage in the catalogue of saints (see Kaftal, 1952, cols. 857-62, and figs. 966 and 972).

Sirén's attempt to associate a four-part predella with the Accademia *Annunciation* is discussed under Catalogue I, London, Courtauld Institute Galleries, *Visitation* and *Adoration of the Magi*. [ca. 1418]

Note: The *Annunciation* has "inspired" several modern copyists. A panel in the Arnot Collection in London (Witt Library photograph, dated 1928) is a reduced version of the center panel, with the half-length Christ Logos transferred from the central roundel to the gabled apex of the panel. Two panels once in the Demandolx-Dedons Collection in Marseille (Hôtel Drouot, June 19, 1956, no. 30) are modern copies of the Saint Catherine and Saint Proculus from the Accademia altarpiece (see Boskovits, 1975, p. 352: Lorenzo Monaco, 1410-1415). Finally, in the Church of Corpus Christi in New York City there is a modern altarpiece that combines elements of the Monte Oliveto polyptych, dated 1410, and the *Annunciation* (see Frick Art Reference Library, file 707-9Q).

§ FLORENCE, Accademia, nos. 8617, 8616, 8615

Saint Nicholas Rescuing a Storm-tossed Ship; Nativity; Legend of Saint Onuphrius

FIGS. 92-95; COLORPLATE 10

Panel: 24 x 57 cm.; 23.5 x 61.2 cm.; 24 x 57 cm.
(including original engaged moldings)

CONDITION: Wood strips, added at some later date, surround the gilded cyma moldings, which are apparently the original engaged frames, judging from the small segments of tempera that overlap the gold leaf (e.g., the crest of the church behind the seated Onuphrius and the contours of rock forms and architectural details throughout the three panels). Only the *Nativity* shows significant deterioration, visible in areas of loss or of coarse repainting in the facial features, hands, and draperies of the Virgin and Joseph, and in the body of the ox. A close examination of the surface of the Onuphrius panel has disproved the statement that the feathery trees surrounding the rocky outcroppings at the center and left of the landscape are later additions (see Bellosi, in *Ghiberti, 'materia e ragionamenti,'* 1978, pp. 147-49, quoting an observation by Roberto Longhi).

HISTORY: The conjectural source of the predella is discussed in relation to the problems that surround the *Descent from the Cross* by Fra Angelico, with pinnacles by Lorenzo Monaco, from the Sacristy-Chapel at Santa Trinita (see Catalogue I, Florence, Museo di San Marco, *Resurrection, Noli Me Tangere,* and *Holy Women at the Tomb*). Giovanni Masselli (MS., Sopr. alle Gallerie, Florence, *Galleria di Piccoli Quadri dell'Accademia,* 1859, p. 151, nos. 182 and 183; p. 154, no. 187) recorded that the predella is "forse proveniente dal convento delle Monache di S. Onofrio, detto di Fuligno." This tentative proposal cannot be confirmed. There is some evidence that the *Nativity* was at one time separated from the other two elements of the predella. In the 1846 edition of Vasari (Marchese, Pini, and Milanesi, p. 217), it was noted that a *Nativity* by Lorenzo Monaco served as the center panel in a predella by Fra Angelico on the altar of the Compagnia di San Luca at the Santissima Annunziata, and that the *Nativity* panel was the most damaged part of the predella. The Cappella di San Luca predella is the series of Cosmas and Damian panels now in the Museo di San Marco, first attributed to Zanobi Strozzi by van Marle (vol. 10, 1928, p. 182) and more recently by Pope-Hennessy (1974, p. 211). Strozzi's predella may originally have included two further scenes from the Cosmas and Damian legends and a wider center panel of the Pietà (Pope-Hennessy, p. 211). The unframed height of 20 cm. of the San Marco panels would have permitted the integration of Lorenzo's *Nativity* (framed height, 23.5 cm.), in order to reestablish a predella that had lost three of its original members. The fact that of the three Accademia panels only the *Nativity* shows significant damage and repair may help to support this tentative history, the panel apparently having been exposed to more public use and change of location than the *Nicholas* and *Onuphrius* scenes. The three panels are listed together for the first time in the 1854 catalogue of the Accademia (*Description de l'Imp. et R. Académie des Beaux-Arts*, Florence, p. 29, no. 21: attributed to Lorenzo Monaco; the Saint Nicholas panel is described as an episode from the life of Saint Martin). For many years the three panels served as a predella beneath Don Lorenzo's *Annunciation* in the Accademia (Fig. 77; see below, Sirén, 1905 and Paris, *Exposition . . . ,* 1935).

LITERATURE: 1854 and 1859, see above // 1864, Crowe and Cavalcaselle, vol. 1, p. 554, note 1: LM; identify the Nicholas episode as Saint Martin // 1896, Berenson, p. 119: LM (1932, p. 299; 1963, vol. 1, p. 118) // 1905, Sirén, pp. 97-100: LM, 1418-22; notes the incorrect use of the panels as a predella to the Accademia *Annunciation*; revises the Saint Martin identification to Nicholas // 1927, van Marle, vol. 9, pp. 142-43: LM, ca. 1408 //1929, Suida, p. 392: LM // 1930, Golzio, pp. 47-48: LM, ca. 1413 // 1935, Paris *Exposition . . . Cimabue à Tiepolo*, p. 141, no. 312: *Nativity* and *Legend of Onuphrius* exhibited; noted as the predella of the Accademia *Annunciation* // 1938/39, Pudelko, p. 78: LM, ca. 1420; once formed the predella of Fra Angelico's *Descent from the Cross* at San Marco // 1951, Procacci, pp. 43-44: LM; the provenance is unknown // 1955, Berti, p. 42: once the predella of Angelico's *Deposition* // 1962, Vienna, *Europäische Kunst*, p. 103, no. 33 // 1966, Cämmerer-George, p. 187: the predella was originally part of the altarpiece for the Strozzi Sacristy-Chapel at Santa Trinita // 1970, Baldini, p. 100: formed the predella of Angelico's *Deposition* // 1974, Pope-Hennessy, p. 211: cites Pudelko's opinion that the provenance is the San Marco altarpiece // 1975, Boskovits, p. 344: LM, 1420-25, from the San Marco *Deposition* // 1975, Davisson, pp. 320-22: from the San Marco *Deposition* // 1978, Bellosi, in *Ghiberti, 'materia e ragionamenti,'* pp. 147-49: LM, 1422-25; from the San Marco *Deposition* // 1981, Cole Ahl, p. 142: denies the connection with Fra Angelico's altarpiece // 1987, Bonsanti, p. 94; colorplate of *Onuphrius* panel, p. 92: LM, from Santa Trinita.

COMMENT: There is not an exact precedent, to my knowledge, for Lorenzo's depiction of the Nativity within a fully walled precinct. In Franco-Netherlandish miniatures of the late fourteenth and early fifteenth centuries, Nativities abound in which a wicker or picket fence encloses the manager (e.g., Meiss, 1967, vol. 2, figs. 8, 91, 184, 259, 332). Broad analogies could be drawn, of course, with the Upper Rhenish *Paradise Garden* in Frankfurt, of circa 1420, where the crenellated wall symbolizes Mary's virginity (see C. Glaser, *Die altdeutsche Malerei*, Munich, 1924, fig. 59). The crenellated wall is found in settings of the Adoration of the Magi in the Trecento and Quattrocento, but the wall does not circumscribe the scene (see Introductory Essay, Note 93). Passion scenes enclosed by a wall or fence appear in Northern manuscript painting, as in the *Hours of Charles the Noble* in the Cleveland Museum, ca. 1400-1408, a collaborative Italian and Franco-Netherlandish work (see Wixom, figs. 31 and 37). A miniature from the Boucicaut workshop, ca. 1412-14, depicts the Garden of Eden surrounded by a high octagonal wall (Meiss, 1974, vol. 2, fig. 168).

In the Introductory Essay (p. 36) I propose that the outcropping at the base of the encircling wall and immediately behind the kneeling Virgin, may be intended as a reference to a cave. The tradition of representing the subterranean caves in Bethlehem, which were the site of the Nativity and the Epiphany, is approached by G. von der Osten ("Der Blick in die Geburtshöhle," *Kölner Domblatt*, 23-24, 1964, pp. 346-58; cited by Schiller, vol. 1, 1971, p. 78, note 96). Charles de Tolnay (1956, p. 164) proposed that the dark cavern introduced into luminous scenes of the Nativity and Epiphany symbolized conquest over the forces of night and death, citing the following depictions: Botticelli, *Nativity*, Washington, National Gallery (Shapley, 1966, fig. 333); Roger van der Weyden, *Nativity*, Bladelin Altarpiece, and *Epiphany*, Columba Altarpiece.

Although several full-length effigies of Saint Onuphrius are known in Tuscan Trecento painting (see Offner, sec. III, vol. VIII, 1958, p. 120; and Kaftal, cols. 777-81), the composite narrative of the encounter between Onuphrius and Paphnutius represented in Don Lorenzo's predella panel is preceded only by Traini's two episodes in the *Thebaid* fresco of the Camposanto in Pisa. The tradition of Thebaid imagery has been investigated by Ellen Callmann (1975, pp. 3-22; fig. 1 includes the Onuphrius-Paphnutius episodes in the Pisan fresco). Pudelko (1938/39, p. 78, note 10) observed that Lorenzo's rendering of the naked, prostrate Onuphrius depended on an antique model as adapted in Ghiberti's North Door. Pudelko's reference, although unspecified, was to the fallen youth in the *Expulsion*, which was possibly modelled after a hunter in an Hippolytus sarcophagus (Krautheimer, 1956, p. 283, and fig. 35). Krautheimer (p. 127) dated the *Expulsion* relief circa 1414-16. A Spanish predella panel of the third quarter of the fourteenth century, which C. R. Post tentatively attributed to Jaime Serra (*A History of Spanish Painting*, vol. 2, Cambridge, Mass., 1930, p. 246, and fig. 158), shows a degree of resemblance to Traini's fresco and Lorenzo's predella panel in the use of steep rock formations as a device to partition the eight episodes from the life of Saint Onuphrius. [ca. 1420-22]

§ FLORENCE, Bargello (Museo Nazionale, Cod. E. 70)

Martyred Female Saint; Bishop Saint; Saint Anthony Abbot; Madonna and Child; and *Christ in Judgment*

FIGS. 131, 210

Miniatures in an Antiphonary (Common of Saints), fols. 15, 41v, 52v, 74v, and 84v
Parchment: 50 x 34.5 cm. (size of page)

HISTORY: From the Galleria dell'Arcispedale di Santa Maria Nuova, by 1898 (see the following entry, Cod. H 74).

LITERATURE: 1932, Ciaranfi, pp. 495-96, figs. 13-16: Lorenzo Monaco, 1413-22 // 1958, Levi D'Ancona, "Some New Attributions," pp. 181-82 and 190: attributes fols. 41v, 52v, and 74v to LM, at the time of the Uffizi *Adoration of the Magi* (1420-22); seven miniatures in the book are given to Matteo Torelli, who was paid for work in a "Comune dei Santi" in 1413 // 1958, Levi D'Ancona, "Matteo Torelli," p. 247: repeats the ascription of three miniatures to LM; the remaining seven to Matteo Torelli // 1972, Boskovits, pp. 44-45: denies the attributions to Matteo Torelli, considering the greater number of miniatures to be the autograph work of LM // 1975, Boskovits, p. 345: attributes eight miniatures to LM, including fols. 41v and 52v; 1405-1410 // 1984, Bellosi, p. 311, and figs. 19 and 20: 52v (cited as 41v) and 84v to LM, in last years and freer style; refutes all attributions to Matteo Torelli.

COMMENT: Only the *Saint Anthony* (fol. 52v) was designed and executed by Lorenzo Monaco. The *Bishop Saint* on fol. 41v (Ciaranfi, fig. 15) is Lorenzo's design but the miniature was painted by an assistant in a brittle technique. The *Madonna and Child* (fol. 74v) is also a work of the shop that conveys none of the interior intimacy of Lorenzo's later images of the Virgin and Child (cf. *Flight into Egypt*, Santa Trinita, and *Madonna of Humility*, Thorvaldsens Museum [Figs. 127 and 128]). The figure of the Virgin on fol. 74v is closely related to her counterpart in the *Pentecost* miniature in the Detroit Institute of Arts (Fig. 208), which Levi D'Ancona has attributed to Matteo Torelli (1958, "Matteo Torelli," pp.

252 and 254) but is, I believe, more satisfactorily labelled as a later work of Don Lorenzo's shop. The *Martyred Female Saint* (fol. 15; Ciaranfi, 1932, fig. 13) would seem to be by the same hand. The painter active in Cod. E 70 may also have executed on Lorenzo's design the predella panel of the *Funeral of a Bishop Saint* in Nice (Fig. 193). The *Christ in Judgment* (fol. 84v), which reveals damage similar to that on fol. 52v, appears to be based on Don Lorenzo's design, but was painted by an assistant in a summary technique. The composition is distinctly related to the miniature in the Lehman Collection (see Catalogue II, New York, Metropolitan Museum of Art).

The cornerstone of Mirella Levi D'Ancona's reconstruction of the oeuvre of Matteo Torelli are the documented payments to him in 1413 for "7 mini di pennello" in Cod. E 70 ("Matteo Torelli," 1958, pp. 247-49). On the basis of this notice, she attributed seven of the ten miniatures in the choir book to Matteo Torelli and the remaining three to Lorenzo Monaco. With this starting point, a large corpus of attributions of miniatures and panel paintings was assigned to Torelli (see the Introductory Essay, Note 168). The first published analytical challenge to Levi D'Ancona's extensive building of Matteo Torelli is a recent study by Luciano Bellosi (1984, pp. 310-312 and pp. 313-14, notes 21-32). As he observes, the use of Cod. E 70 as a foundation is tenuous on two principal counts: first, the documentary notice records seven "mini" (illuminations) while there are ten illuminated initials that frame miniatures; and secondly, the date of 1413 is too early by nearly a decade for the miniatures in the choir book. Bellosi's further documentary citations support his reasonable conclusion that Matteo Torelli was a prolific illuminator of choir books rather than a miniaturist and panel painter. Central documentation regards a choir book (Gradual) in the Museo dell'Opera del Duomo, Prato (Cor. D), in which the division of work between Rossello di Jacopo Franchi as miniaturist and Matteo Torelli as illuminator is specifically differentiated (Bellosi, 1984, p. 312, citing Marchini's earlier publication of documents; also see Ciatti, p. 516). Carol T. Peters (pp. 12-13 and 335-36) paid special attention to the division in professional nomenclature for Matteo Torelli as illuminator and Rossello di Jacopo Franchi as painter (miniaturist) in the Prato Gradual (p. 335, document 22b: "Uscita di denari data a chartolaio e al miniatore e a dipintore per lo graduale"). The same distinction is found in the documentation of work by Rossello and Matteo for the Bigallo (Peters, pp. 332-33 and 336). Throughout the abundant documentary record of Matteo Torelli's life and artistic activity (Levi D'Ancona, 1962, pp. 188-91), he is consistently cited as "miniatore," with "dipintore" used in a single document of 1426, which does not involve an artistic commission.

Further evidence of the distinction between illuminators and miniaturists is found in documents with regard to Lorenzo Monaco (Documents 9A-9D). Payments to Don Lorenzo for work cited as "per miniatura di penello" (9A), "per mini" (9B), and ". . . miniare di penello" (9C), are distinguished from payments "per fighure che fecie ne'mini . . ." (9D). As Documents 9A-9D cannot be associated with a known manuscript, there is not a definitive answer as to whether these payments for illuminations and miniatures were for the personal work of Don Lorenzo or for that of assistants in the workshop, although there is a greater likelihood that at this advanced date in the painter's career (1412-13), the ornamentation of initials was undertaken by assistants. In the Missal for the dedication of the church of Sant'Egidio (San Marco, Inv. 557), with important miniatures by Bartolomeo di Fruosino, the colophon (fol. 70) records that "Pictor Bartholomeus ornat." [ca. 1422-23]

§ FLORENCE, Bargello (Museo Nazionale, Cod. H 74)

Thirty-two *Prophets*

FIGS. 99-101

Miniatures in a Gradual (Sunday Diurnal), fols. 3v, 4v*, 8v*, 15, 18*, 21*, 23, 25*, 27v, 30, 33, 63*, 67, 68v*, 70v*, 72v*, 79v, 90, 92v, 95v*, 98v, 101v*, 107v*, 118v, 122v, 125v*, 131, 134*, 153v*, 156v*, 160, 163

Parchment: 52.5 x 36.5 cm. (size of page)

HISTORY: Chapel of the hospital of Santa Maria Nuova; probably then used by around 1420 in the church of Sant'Egidio (later named Santa Maria e Sant'Egidio), adjoining the hospital (see Paatz, vol. 4, 1952, pp. 1-6). In the Marchese, Pini, and Milanesi edition of Vasari (p. 215), the editors report seeing Cod. H 74 in the sacristy of the church in 1845, where they noted a total of nine important choir books executed by various hands (see Vasari, *Vite*, ed. Bettarini and Barocchi, Commentary, p. 715). Around 1865, the choir books were exhibited in the newly established Galleria dell'Arcispedale di Santa Maria Nuova. By 1898, they were transferred to the Museo Nazionale (Ridolfi, pp. 150-51 and 185-86).

LITERATURE: 1932, Ciaranfi, pp. 379-83, and figs. 3-10: all miniatures by Lorenzo Monaco, except fols. 79v, 90, 92v, and 122v, which are by an immediate pupil; 1412-13 // 1958, Levi D'Ancona, "Some New Attributions," pp. 181-82 and 190-91: nine of the thirty-eight miniatures by followers of Don Lorenzo (lists folios), among whom is Bartolomeo di Fruosino; ca. 1423-24, recalling the style of the predella of the Santa Trinita *Annunciation*; the cut miniature of a *Prophet* in the Rosenwald Collection, National Gallery, Washington, is probably from the same book // 1961, Levi D'Ancona, pp. 84 and 91: miniatures on fols. 11 and 129v (new 128) to Bartolomeo di Fruosino // 1963, Berenson, vol. 1, p. 119: mainly by LM // 1975, Boskovits, p. 345: all miniatures by LM, 1405-1410 // 1984, Bellosi, pp. 308 and 312, note 4: LM, later period; various figures in the vegetal ornament by the "Maestro del Codice Squarcialupi."

COMMENT: The thirty-two miniatures of *Prophets* listed above were all produced either by Lorenzo Monaco or under his supervision. Sixteen folio numbers have been marked here with a (*) to accentuate those miniatures which stand, in my view, at the highest level of quality and are therefore likely to be fully autograph works by Don Lorenzo. But this demarcation is meant suggestively, not as a watertight division between the work of master and shop, which would be an unrealistic quest in the study of choir books at this late stage of Don Lorenzo's career, when he was occupied with several major commissions. Not listed above are fols. 104, 110, and 113, on which the miniatures of *Prophets* are too damaged to permit an ascription beyond "style of Lorenzo Monaco." The *Resurrection of Christ* on fol. 3v, the only narrative miniature in the book, is a workshop adaptation of Don Lorenzo's composition for the center pinnacle of Fra Angelico's *Descent from the Cross* at San Marco (Fig. 89) and of an earlier design for a choir book miniature (see Catalogue I, Florence, Biblioteca Laurenziana, Cod. Cor. 3). To Levi D'Ancona's attribution of the *Prophets* on fols. 11 and 129v (new 128) to Bartolomeo di Fruosino, I would tentatively add fol. 150v. (The numbering of the folios replaces the older system used by Paolo D'Ancona [vol. 2, 1914, pp. 138-41]; also see Catalogue I, Washington, National Gallery of Art, *Prophet*.) [ca. 1420-22]

§ FLORENCE, Biblioteca Berenson

Madonna with Saints John the Baptist and Zenobius

FIG. 16

Panel: 89 x 48 cm. (including engaged frame)

CONDITION: The paint and gold surfaces were damaged in transport during the Second World War. An extensive area of loss at the upper right of the Virgin's halo has been weakly repaired and there are areas of coarse repainting, most visible in the Baptist's mantle and on the surface of the circular projection of the dais.

HISTORY: There is no record of the provenance of the panel, nor of the date it was acquired by Bernard Berenson.

LITERATURE: 1932, Berenson, p. 299: Lorenzo Monaco, an early work (1963, vol. 1, p. 119) // 1939, Sandberg-Vavalà, p. 108: LM, from his formative Giottesque period // 1938/39, Pudelko, p. 238, note 12: LM, between the triptych in Siena and the Berlin *Madonna* of shortly after 1400 // 1950, Gronau, p. 221: LM, ca. 1400 // 1954, Eisenberg, p. 102: LM, 1390-95 // 1962, Russoli, no. XXXI (in color): LM // 1975, Boskovits, p. 346: LM, 1395-1400.

COMMENT: The type of the Berenson *Madonna*, with the Virgin and Child afloat above a dais and accompanied by confronted saints, is derived from a Cionesque format (cf. *Madonna and Saints with the Nativity and Crucifixion*, Ottawa, National Gallery of Canada; Fremantle, fig. 331). The frequent depiction of a comparable type in Siena, particularly in the work of Paolo di Giovanni Fei (cf., Mallory, 1976, figs. 46 and 95), does not confirm Pudelko's view (1938/39, p. 238) that a Sienese model was the direct source of the Berenson panel. Emphasis should also be given to Daddesque and subsequent Cionesque traditions as catalysts of the Sienese influence on Florentine art.

The fact that the Infant in the Berenson panel has a virtually exact replica in the *Madonna with Four Saints*, formerly in the Larderel Collection in Leghorn (Fig. 226), is important evidence of direct borrowings between later Trecento workshops, in this case, an exchange between Don Lorenzo and the prolific and influential milieu of the Master of the Straus Madonna. For further discussion of this borrowing, see Catalogue II, formerly Leghorn, Larderel Collection, *Madonna with Four Saints*. [1395-1400]

§ FLORENCE, Biblioteca Berenson

Madonna of Humility
FIG. 38

Panel: 78 x 41 cm. (including engaged frame)
Inscribed date: 1405 (AVE MARIA AD.M.CCCCV)

CONDITION: There is some repainting in the Virgin's mantle and a damaged passage running vertically from her right brow to the scarf at her neck is still visible through the crude repair. The cupid and vine ornamentation of the upper frame is modern, and segments of the heavy, carved cusps and of the base of the frame have been replaced. For the state of the panel prior to the modern restorations, see Sirén, 1904, illus. on p. 443, or Frick Art Reference Library, photo. 707-8.

HISTORY: Osvald Sirén, Stockholm, until 1904 or 1905; Cav. Aldo Noseda, Milan, until the mid-1920s; Bernard Berenson, Florence.

LITERATURE: 1903, Crowe and Cavalcaselle, vol. 2, p. 302, note 1: Lorenzo Monaco, with the date read as 1404 // 1904, Sirén, "Italian Pictures in Sweden," p. 439: LM // 1905, Sirén, p. 38: LM // 1908, Suida, p. 305 (1929, p. 329): LM // 1909, Berenson, p. 153: LM (1932, p. 299; 1963, vol. 1, p. 119) // 1924, Lazareff, p. 126: LM // 1927, van Marle, vol. 9, p. 126: LM // 1932, Berenson, "Quadri senza casa," p. 32 (1970, p. 141): LM // 1938/39, Pudelko, p. 238: LM, related in style to the *Madonna of Humility* in the Metropolitan Museum and Moscow // 1962, Russoli, no. XXXII (in color): LM // 1975, Boskovits, p. 346: LM.

COMMENT: The herculean right arm of the Child reaching to grasp the Virgin's mantle contrasts with the generally refined drawing and possibly predicts the quest for sculptural form that will shortly occupy Don Lorenzo. The crossed wrapping of the Child's mantle will be reused in the *Abraham* of the New York *Prophet* series (Fig. 41), which are the foremost examples of a sculptural ingredient in Lorenzo's style. The *Madonna of Humility* of 1405 and the Prague *Lamentation* of 1408 (Fig. 34) with its companion panels in Paris are among the intimate works from the first years of Lorenzo's maturity that foretell the deeply personal devotional imagery of his later years, most notably the Copenhagen *Madonna of Humility* and the Amsterdam *Saint Jerome*, which were once joined as a diptych (Figs. 128 and 129). [1405]

§ FLORENCE, Biblioteca Laurenziana, Cod. Cor. 1

Saint John the Evangelist
FIG. 5

Miniature in an Antiphonary, fol. 33
Parchment: 70 x 48 cm. (size of page)
Inscribed date of book: 1396 (fol. 28: COMPLETUM EST HOC OPUS ANNO DNI MCCCLXXXXVI)

HISTORY: From Santa Maria degli Angeli (A 7), between 1809 and 1810.

LITERATURE: 1932, Ciaranfi, p. 301, note 1: fol. 33 is close to Lorenzo Monaco, but without his finesse; comparable to a *Moses* in Laurenziana, Cor. 13, fol. 89 // 1958, Levi D'Ancona, "Some New Attributions," pp. 184 and 188: LM, possibly between 1396 and 1398; fol. 86 (*Ascension of Christ*) is by a follower of Agnolo Gaddi // 1965, Bellosi, "Da Spinello," p. 39: LM, as is fol. 86 // 1975, Boskovits, p. 341: LM in fols. 33 and 86; 1396 // 1978, Levi D'Ancona, p. 220: *Ascension* (fol. 86) attributed to Matteo Torelli // 1979, Levi D'Ancona, p. 471, and figs. 3 and 4: the *John the Evangelist* compared with an earlier version, also attributed to Don Lorenzo, in Bargello, Cod. C 71 (q.v., Cat. II).

COMMENT: In the *Ascension* on fol. 86 (Fig. 243), the group of the Virgin and Disciples shows close affinities with the style of Don Silvestro dei Gherarducci (Fig. 268). [ca. 1396-98]

§ FLORENCE, Biblioteca Laurenziana, Cod. Cor. 3

Eight Prophets
FIGS. 64-68; COLORPLATE 4

Miniatures in a Gradual (Sunday Diurnal), fols. 35, 38v, 46v, 65v, 86v, 89v, 93, 96v
Parchment: 67 x 48 cm. (size of page)
Inscribed date of book: 1409 (fol. 3: ANNO DOMINI MCCCCIX COMPLETUM EST HOC OPUS)

HISTORY: From Santa Maria degli Angeli (C.c.I), between 1809 and 1810.

LITERATURE: 1932, Ciaranfi, pp. 302-316, and figs. 7-20: attributes the eight *Prophets* to Lorenzo Monaco; accepts the date of 1409 for the entire group // 1958, Levi D'Ancona, "Some New Attributions," pp. 180-81, note 26, and 188-89: attributes the *Prophets* to LM; dates them 1422-23, seeing a connection with the Santa Trinita frescoes in the handling of light; reviews the wide range of opinions on the attribution of the narrative miniatures // 1958, Levi D'Ancona, "Matteo Torelli," p. 254: the *Pentecost* on fol. 80v was probably begun by Don Lorenzo and completed much later by Zanobi Strozzi // 1963, Berenson, vol. 1, p. 118: the eight *Prophets* by LM // 1964, Orlandi, pp. 11-12: narrative miniatures designed by LM, with Fra Angelico in his earliest style seen in draperies and certain heads // 1972, Boskovits, pp. 50, 59, note 60, and 60, note 70: attributes to LM seven *Prophets* and one narrative miniature fol. 27v (Levi D'Ancona, 1958, fig. 3, to Matteo Torelli); excludes fol. 89v; Don Lorenzo was also probably responsible for the preliminary design of some narrative miniatures completed by Zanobi Strozzi (especially fol. 1v: *Resurrection of Christ*) // 1975, Boskovits, pp. 341-42: repeats the above attributions (1972) and assigns the date of 1409 to Don Lorenzo's miniatures; marginal figures are by Bartolomeo di Fruosino // 1978, Levi D'Ancona, pp. 225-26: miniatures in the book, which is dated 1409, were painted by Lorenzo Monaco, Zanobi Strozzi, Matteo Torelli, and others; a cut miniature in the Woodner Collection, representing the *Procession of the Holy Innocents* and attributed to Zanobi Strozzi, was originally on fol. 31 of Corale 3 // 1984, Bellosi, pp. 307-309: the eight *Prophets* and a miniature of *Saints Mary Magdalen, Peter, and John the Evangelist at the Tomb* (fol. 27v) by Don Lorenzo; *Resurrection* (fol. 1v) designed by him; illuminations and other ornamentation by the "Maestro del Codice Squarcialupi."

COMMENT: The two phases of execution of the eight *Prophets*—the first four circa 1410, the second circa 1414—are discussed in the Introductory Essay (p. 29). Among the narrative miniatures, the *Resurrection* (fol. 1v; see Ciaranfi, 1932, fig. 7) was apparently designed by Lorenzo Monaco, but left unfinished. The same composition, with minor variations, was reused in the early 1420s, becoming the center pinnacle above Fra Angelico's *Descent from the Cross* (Fig. 89), and by a miniaturist in the workshop of Don Lorenzo in Cod. H 74 in the Bargello (fol. 3v). Work on the *Resurrection* miniature in Cor. 3 was apparently resumed in the next generation, in the Dominican milieu of Fra Angelico at San Marco. With more developed manifestations of space, the Risen Christ now opposes the planarity of the gold ground and the lid of the sarcophagus is rendered in a finely graduated chiaroscuro, with the heavy decorative bosses enhancing the quality of three-dimensionality, in contrast to the planar figure of Christ in the San Marco pinnacle and the miniature of Cod. H 74; in short, Don Lorenzo's original design would seem to have been brought up to date in the completed miniature. The *Pentecost* on fol. 80v (Salmi, 1954, colorplate 40) points up the change in style when it is confronted with the cut miniature of the same subject in the Detroit Institute of Arts (Fig. 208), designed by Lorenzo Monaco and executed in his workshop circa 1420. There are evident parallels, but the miniature in Cor. 3 gives evidence of being entirely the work of the new generation; the continuous space that unifies the lower and upper areas of the scene, the dominance of the coffered barrel vault enclosing the Virgin and apostles, and the minutely graduated lighting of draperies are all indicative of a new vision.

Pope-Hennessy (1974, pp. 223-24) lists the narrative miniatures of Cor. 3, reviews the various ascriptions, and contests attributions to Fra Angelico. In a search for the original manuscript sources of dispersed miniatures cut from the choir books of Santa Maria degli Angeli, Levi D'Ancona (1978, p. 226) has concluded through a probing liturgical and textual analysis that the missing fol. 59 of Laurenziana Cor. 3 would originally have contained a miniature of the Ascension of Christ, within an initial V for the incipit of the Introit ("Viri Galilei . . ."). I would propose that the miniature is that reproduced in *Christie's Year in Review 1980* (p. 103, with colorplate), attributed to the Florentine School, ca. 1420. The *Ascension* within a letter V would appear to have been designed by Bartolomeo di Fruosino under the supervision of Lorenzo Monaco, and painted in the milieu of Fra Angelico, whereas the figures in the leafy swirls of the initial and in the surrounding frame were designed and painted by Bartolomeo. Boskovits (*in litteris*, 1976; quoted in *The Hatvany Collection*, Christie's, London, June 24, 1980, no. 2) proposed that the border of the *Ascension* miniature is by Bartolomeo di Fruosino, but the main figural group was painted by Zanobi Strozzi on Don Lorenzo's design. [ca. 1410, fols. 35-65v; ca. 1414, fols. 86v-96v]

§ FLORENCE, Biblioteca Laurenziana, Cod. Cor. 5

Saint Jerome; and *Tobit*

FIGS. 1, 2

Miniatures in an Antiphonary, fols. 138 and 20
Parchment: 71.5 x 50 cm. (size of page)
Inscribed date of book: 1394 (fol. 35: COMPLETUM EST HOC OPUS ANNO DNI MCCCLXXXXIIII)

HISTORY: From Santa Maria degli Angeli (10'g), between 1809 and 1810.

LITERATURE: 1932, Ciaranfi, pp. 291-301: fol. 138, Lorenzo Monaco; fol. 20, which shows the strong influence of Sienese color, is considered close to but not by Don Lorenzo // 1958, Levi D'Ancona, "Some New Attributions," pp. 185 and 189: LM, 1394-96, not long before the *Agony in the Garden* in the Accademia, Florence; fol. 105 (*Saint Michael Defeating the Demons*) given tentatively to Matteo Torelli // 1963, Berenson, vol. 1, p. 118: *Jerome* to LM, ca. 1394 // 1965, Bellosi, "Da Spinello," p. 39: fol. 105 (*Saint Michael*) to LM, as well as fols. 20 and 138 // 1975, Boskovits, p. 342: all three miniatures by LM, 1394.

COMMENT: Although the *Saint Michael* miniature reflects the influence of Don Lorenzo's early work, as seen in the predella of the *Agony in the Garden* (Figs. 10-11), it does not appear to have been produced in his immediate milieu. [ca. 1395]

§ FLORENCE, Biblioteca Laurenziana, Cod. Cor. 8

King David; Saint Romuald; and *Saint Paul*

FIGS. 3, 4, 6, 203

Miniatures in an Antiphonary, fols. 34, 76, and 163
Parchment: 69 x 48.5 cm. (size of page)
Inscribed date of book: 1395 (fol. 158v: A.D. MCCCLXXXXV. COMPLETUM EST HOC OPUS)

HISTORY: From Santa Maria degli Angeli (H8), between 1809 and 1810.

LITERATURE: 1932, Ciaranfi, pp. 301-302: attributes the *David* and *Romuald* to Lorenzo Monaco, acknowledging that Berenson had already recognized the painter's hand in the *Romuald* (1932, p. 299, called *Benedict*); a smaller figure of *Saint Romuald in Glory* (fol. 97v) and a *Saint Paul* (fol. 163) are deemed far lower in quality and less likely to be by LM // 1958, Levi D'Ancona, "Some New Attributions," pp. 187 and 189: ascribes fols. 34 and 76 to LM, fol. 163 to an assistant in the shop // 1961, Levi D'Ancona, pp. 83 and 86: ascribes the *Saint Paul* to Bartolomeo di Fruosino, possibly 1396 // 1963, Berenson, vol. 1, p. 118: LM, ca. 1395 // 1965, Bellosi, "Da Spinello," p. 39: all miniatures by LM // 1965, Bellosi, *Maestri*, [p. 4]: LM, after 1395 // 1975, Boskovits, p. 342: all miniatures by LM; 1395.

COMMENT: In contrast to the assured design and refined execution of the *David* and *Romuald*, the *Saint Paul* betrays the hand of an assistant in the uncertain relationship of the figure to the surrounding letter and in the relative crudity of the draughtsmanship. The tiny medallion of *Romuald in Glory* (fol. 97v) is little more than a decorative accent in the splendidly ornamented letter, perhaps even the momentary indulgence of the illuminator. [ca. 1396-98]

FLORENCE, Museo Horne, no. 97

Crucifix

FIG. 163

Panel (cutout, painted on front and back): 65.5 x 43.5 cm.

CONDITION: The features are blurred by abrasion and darkened varnish. There is an intrusive loss in the panel between the knees at the hem of the loincloth. Although considerably abraded, the painted surface of the reverse of the cross is intact (see Alinari/Brogi no. 20672). The *Crucifix* appears truncated as a result of the loss of the crest above the crossbar.

HISTORY: There is no record of the provenance of the cross or the date it was acquired by Herbert Horne.

LITERATURE: 1909, Sirén, p. 35: Lorenzo Monaco // 1921, Gamba, p. 35, no. 97: LM // 1927, van Marle, vol. 9, p. 168, note 3: LM // 1929, Suida, p. 392: LM // 1929, Sandberg-Vavalà, p. 905: LM; reproduces obverse and reverse (fig. 572, a-b); the cutout type of cross was initiated by Don Lorenzo // 1931, Golzio, p. 63: LM; similar to that in San Giovanni della Calza // 1932, Berenson, p. 299: LM (1963, vol. 1, p. 119) // 1961, Gamba, p. 54: LM // 1966,

Rossi, p. 139: LM school // 1975, Boskovits, p. 345: LM, 1400-1405.

COMMENT: In this small processional cross the coarse use of the tempera medium and the assemblage of elements from several phases of Lorenzo's style indicate the work of a shop assistant. The rounded cranial shape and tooled pattern of the halo have the closest parallel in the Christ of the *Betrayal* (Fig. 10), in the predella of Lorenzo's early *Agony in the Garden*, and there are also recollections of the Bergamo *Man of Sorrows* (Fig. 136). The assertive rendering of the rib cage depends on Lorenzo's Christ in the *Man of Sorrows* (Fig. 18) of 1404, whereas the calligraphy of the loincloth most closely approximates Lorenzo's *Crucifix* (no. 3153) in the Accademia, Florence (Fig. 69). A dating within the years 1405-1410 is appropriate for the Horne panel. Of incidental interest is the fact that this cross is the only one by Don Lorenzo or his shop in which the Christ is depicted without the crown of thorns. [1405-1410]

FLORENCE, Museo dell'Opera di Santa Croce

Saint James Enthroned
FIG. 171

Panel: 160 x 95 cm. (painted surface)
Inscribed date: 1408 (. . . [illegible] MCCCCVIII)

CONDITION: As the pre-restoration photograph reveals, the painted surface above the throne has been totally effaced. On the section of wood inserted at the top to accommodate the panel to an old but unrelated frame there are two finials that seem to be fragments of some demolished picture. The panel was restored in 1960 by Giuseppe Rosi, at the Gabinetto dei Restauri in Florence, at which time all later additions were removed and the date of 1408 was discovered on the dais of the throne. The panel, engulfed in the flood of November 4, 1966, was transported for restoration first to the Limonaia of the Pitti Palace and then to the Opificio delle Pietre Dure e Laboratori di Restauro at the Fortezza da Basso, where it has remained. The paint film, gold ground, and gesso, which are in relatively good condition, have been detached from the damaged wood support and await transfer to a new panel. A vertical split, visible in Fig. 171, now runs upward through the book to the shoulder of the figure, the result of further splitting of the flood-damaged wood support.

HISTORY: This may be the panel that Don Gregorio Farulli saw in Santa Croce and attributed to Lorenzo Monaco, without identifying the subject (1710, p. 31). The picture was at Santa Croce by no later than 1842, the year in which Fantozzi described it (see below).

LITERATURE: 1842, Fantozzi, p. 205: among the pictures in the monastery of Santa Croce, refers to an *Eternal Father Enthroned* with a predella panel of *Death on a Horse* beneath; no attribution offered // 1905, Sirén, p. 88: Lorenzo Monaco, contemporary with the Uffizi *Coronation of the Virgin* // 1927, van Marle, vol. 9, p. 172: shop of LM // 1929, Suida, p. 392: LM // 1931, Golzio, p. 63: LM // 1932, Berenson, p. 299: LM (1963, vol. 1, p. 119) // 1938/39, Pudelko, p. 77: LM, soon after 1415 // 1967, Bellosi, p. 87, figs. 24 and 25 (show the panel before the restoration of 1960 and covered with protective rice paper in transit to the Limonaia): provisionally attributed to LM; notes the frame is not original // 1975, Boskovits, p. 346: LM // 1983, Waadenoijen, p. 80: LM, influenced by Starnina.

COMMENT: The *Saint James Enthroned* was painted by an assistant from a design by Lorenzo Monaco. The superficial rendering and exaggerated swarthiness of facial features, the dry symmetry of the coiffure, the bold separation of elements of the palette, and the wayward calligraphy of the mantle indicate shop intervention. There need only be compared the drapery forms of the Prague *Lamentation* (Fig. 34) of the same year to point up the inorganic character of the *Saint James*. Nonetheless, the painter used as his model Lorenzo's calligraphic style of around 1408 rather than the more sculptural forms that tempered the play of line in works such as the *Prophets* (Figs. 40-43) in the Metropolitan Museum or the *Madonna of Humility* (Fig. 39) in Stuttgart, dated 1407 (also see, Munich, Alte Pinakothek, *Saint Peter* [Fig. 172]). But the *Saint James* clearly evinces the impact of Starnina (Waadenoijen, 1983), in passages where the calligraphy has taken on an existence independent of the figure, in the exaggerated lighting of the edges of drapery folds, and in the high key of the palette (see Figs. 285 and 294; also see, Catalogue II, Avignon, Musée du Petit Palais, *Saint Lawrence Enthroned*). An important early Florentine ancestor of the *Saint James* is the *John the Baptist Enthroned* at

Christ Church, Oxford (Byam Shaw, pl. 1). For the predella panel noted by Fantozzi (1842), see Catalogue II, Florence, Santa Croce (predella of high altarpiece), *Death Riding a Bull*. [1408]

§ FLORENCE, Museo di San Marco

Resurrection of Christ; Noli Me Tangere; and *Holy Women at the Tomb*
FIGS. 88-91, 316

Pinnacles of Fra Angelico's *Descent from the Cross*

Panel: 106 x 71.5 cm. (*Resurrection*); 101.5 x 67.5 cm. (including engaged frame moldings and full extent of painted surfaces behind foliate ornament)

CONDITION: The three panels are exceptionally well preserved. The heavy foliate frame ornaments are modern additions, which mask the lowest areas of rocky landscape in each pinnacle.

HISTORY: As the provenance would seem to be the Sacristy-Chapel at Santa Trinita, the history of the three panels cannot be separated from various hypotheses with regard to Fra Angelico's *Descent from the Cross* (see below, *Literature* and *Comment*). The entire altarpiece was moved from Santa Trinita to the Galleria dell'Accademia in 1810 (no. 166), where it remained until 1919, when it was transferred to the Museo di San Marco (inventory, Soprintendenza, Florence, after 1920, no. 1870).

LITERATURE: 1844, Delécluze, ed. Pini and Milanesi, p. 87, note 1: first attribute to Lorenzo Monaco the three pinnacles of Fra Angelico's San Marco *Descent from the Cross*, then in the Accademia, Florence // 1854, Marchese, vol. 1, p. 275: LM // 1864, Crowe and Cavalcaselle, vol. 1, p. 554, note 5: LM // 1896, Berenson, p. 119: LM (1932, p. 299; 1963, vol. 1, p. 119) // 1900, Douglas, pp. 80-82: incongruous scenes taken from some altarpiece by Lorenzo Monaco // 1905, Sirén, pp. 111-12: LM, 1418-22; considers the panels to have been added to Angelico's *Deposition* early in the nineteenth century // 1927, van Marle, vol. 9, p. 150: LM, ca. 1408 // 1928, van Marle, vol. 10, pp. 52-53: Lorenzo's pinnacles were part of an altarpiece inherited by Fra Angelico, who continued the work on the main panel around 1425 // 1929, Suida, p. 392: LM // 1930, Golzio, p. 48: LM, ca. 1414 // 1938, Wackernagel, p. 138 (Luchs trans., 1981, p. 132): Lorenzo's pinnacles were part of the original altarpiece adapted by Fra Angelico, revealing modification in the direction of the uninterrupted pictorial field of Renaissance altarpieces // 1938/39, Pudelko, p. 78: although the three pinnacles are not specifically mentioned, implies their relationship to Lorenzo's *Nativity, Nicholas*, and *Onuphrius* panels in the Accademia, which formed the predella to Angelico's *Deposition* altarpiece; ca. 1420 // 1953, Paatz, vol. 5, pp. 309 and 380-81: LM, ca. 1410(?) // 1955, Florence, *Mostra dell'Angelico* (Berti), p. 42: Lorenzo's pinnacles and the Accademia predella were executed before 1425; Angelico continued work some years later on the *Deposition* begun by Don Lorenzo // 1964, Orlandi, p. 46: hypothesizes that the altarpiece was commissioned from Lorenzo Monaco by Palla Strozzi, but only the woodwork and the pinnacles were completed at the time of the painter's death; pinnacles should be dated ca. 1423-25 // 1966, Cämmerer-George, pp. 187-88: Lorenzo painted the pinnacles and predella (Accademia 8615-17) before 1425; the question remains as to whether his main panel ever existed or was re-used by Angelico, adapting the composition to the arched shapes // 1974, Pope-Hennessy, p. 210: the three pinnacles, part of the original altarpiece for the Sacristy at Santa Trinita, were painted by Lorenzo Monaco before 1424-25; at a later date (early 1440s) Angelico resumed work on the altarpiece which Don Lorenzo had left unfinished at his death // 1975, Boskovits, p. 346: LM, 1420-25; along with the Accademia predella (nos. 8615-17), the pinnacles are original parts of the *Deposition* altarpiece at San Marco // 1975, Davisson, pp. 320-23: considers the three pinnacles, the Accademia predella, and the pilasters to be the original elements of an altarpiece commissioned from Lorenzo Monaco for the Sacristy-Chapel at Santa Trinita; the main subject of the altarpiece is hypothesized to have been a Madonna and Child with standing figures of Saints Nicholas and Onuphrius; the frame was then partially adopted by Fra Angelico for the *Descent from the Cross*; fig. 11 shows the predella in an appropriate arrangement, with the Nicholas and Onuphrius scenes to the left and right, respectively // 1978, Bellosi, in *Ghiberti, 'materia e ragionamenti,'* pp. 147-49: LM, ca. 1422-25; the pinnacles and Accademia predella were original parts of the altarpiece completed by Fra Angelico // 1981, Cole Ahl, p. 141: Lorenzo's altarpiece, including the three pinnacles and, presumably, the theme of the Deposition in the main panel, was brought to completion by Fra Angelico in the early 1430s // 1982, Christiansen, pp. 25 and 72-73: Fra Angelico adopted Lorenzo's frame for the *Deposition*; Lorenzo's work for the Strozzi must be dated before 1418 // 1984, Jones, pp. 31 and 37-38: Lorenzo's altarpiece was intended for the main sacristy; the predella was not used for the *Deposition*.

COMMENT: Until the main panel of Fra Angelico's *Descent from the Cross* is submitted to a thorough technical analysis and the entire framing system is dismantled in order to permit study of the carpentry, theories as to stages in the formation of the altarpiece must continue to be hypothetical. Nonetheless, there is sufficient internal evidence of coordination between Don Lorenzo's pinnacles and Fra Angelico's *Deposition* to counter the views of Douglas (1900) and Sirén (1905) that the pinnacles are later additions, miscellaneous fragments of some dismembered altarpiece by Lorenzo Monaco. The beginnings of a theoretical history would seem to have been in the years just before 1420 with an hypothesized commission from Palla Strozzi to Lorenzo Monaco for an altarpiece for the Sacristy-Chapel at Santa Trinita (Orlandi, 1964). Keith Christiansen's alternative proposal (1982, p. 72, note 24) that the altarpiece was commissioned by Nofri Strozzi from Lorenzo Monaco before 1418 and was left incomplete because of the patron's death early in that year is less satisfactory as the three pinnacles would seem to have been painted no earlier than 1420. That no payments for an altarpiece for the Sacristy-Chapel other than Gentile's *Adoration* are known between 1418 and 1423 need not be taken as conclusive proof that the commission was given to Lorenzo Monaco before 1418. With the intention from the outset to erect a double chapel, necessitating two altars, it would seem reasonable that two altarpieces be commissioned with subjects portraying the extreme moments in the life of Christ.

While it is generally agreed that Gentile's *Adoration of the Magi* stood on the altar of the major sacristy (D. Cole, 1977, p. 224; Christiansen, 1982, p. 25), and that Fra Angelico's altarpiece hung above an altar in the adjacent minor sacristy (for a plan, see Jones, 1984, fig. 1), the question remains as to whether the altarpiece originally commissioned from Lorenzo Monaco, eventually to be completed by Fra Angelico, was intended for the principal or secondary altar. Darrell Davisson's view (1975, p. 320) that Don Lorenzo's altarpiece was meant for the main altar has been substantiated in a recent study by Roger Jones (1984, pp. 37-38), although their conceptions of the altarpiece do not coincide. Jones observed that in Fra Angelico's *Deposition* the light falls from the left, which suggests that the circular window on the left wall of the minor sacristy would have been the source of illumination for the altarpiece. Applying the observation of J. P. Hills (1976, p. 261), that the light in Lorenzo Monaco's pinnacles falls principally from the right, Jones proposes that the altarpiece commissioned from Don Lorenzo was intended for the altar of the main sacristy, where the light enters from the right. There would seem to be no equally cogent explanation for the disparity between the lighting systems of the main register and the pinnacles. Jones's proposal gains further credence from the fact that the light also falls from the right in the two side panels of the predella that seems originally to have been intended for Don Lorenzo's altarpiece (Figs. 92 and 95; see Catalogue I, *Saint Nicholas Rescuing a Storm-tossed Ship . . .*).

Davisson's theory (1975) that Lorenzo's original altarpiece was completed and represented a Madonna and Child with Saints Onuphrius and Nicholas is problematic from several standpoints. As Cole Ahl has noted (1981, p. 142, note 26), the *Resurrection, Noli Me Tangere*, and *Holy Women at the Tomb* are not appropriate subject matter for the crowning elements of a Madonna and saints composition. Davisson's conclusion from a passage in Richa that pictures of Saints Onuphrius and Nicholas existed in the Sacristy-Chapel at Santa Trinita is based on a doubtful reading of Richa's text, which does not mention actual images of the two saints (see Porçal, p. 474). Finally, as Christiansen notes (1982, p. 72), three areas of panel of equal dimension would not have been meant to accommodate a Madonna and saints composition. Christiansen's observation should be slightly revised to read "nearly equal," as Lorenzo's *Resurrection* pinnacle spans a central segment of the main panel wider than the sides by 5 cm. This seemingly minor disparity in dimensions will be useful evidence in later discussion of the predella of Don Lorenzo's altarpiece.

As the carpentry would have been executed before the process of painting had begun, it may be theorized that Lorenzo Monaco carried the fully constructed Strozzi Altarpiece to partial completion before his death. Internal physical and stylistic evidence from the altarpiece eventually completed by

Fra Angelico suggests a next step in this hypothetical reconstruction. Without technical study of the strata beneath the present paint surface it cannot be determined whether the main panel on which Angelico painted the *Deposition* is the original wood and follows the composition commissioned from Lorenzo Monaco and left incomplete by him. Nonetheless, Angelico's image, while implying an uninterrupted rectangular pictorial field, contains sufficient accommodations to the three arches to indicate that the design was established in relation to crowning pinnacles, for example, the parallel contours of the frame and the tunic of Joseph of Arimathaea, the dense gathering of the cross and ladders into the constricted zone of the central arch, and the symmetrically balanced groups of floating angels. The heavy, modern foliate frames invade the main panel deeply enough to mask the ends of the Hebrew superscription on the cross. But a close inspection of the surface of the main panel just beyond the three arches—a narrow space between the pinnacles and *Deposition* permits a scant glimpse—reveals that Angelico's landscape does not continue upward to a horizontal contour, which is contrary to what Sirén reported Supino had observed (1905, p. 111; the neutral surface above the main panel shown in colorplates 12 and 13 of Baldini's *Angelico*, 1970, is not an indication that the frame had been removed, but is simply a masking out of Lorenzo's pinnacles in order to illustrate only the *Deposition*; cf. D. Cole, 1977, p. 223, note 1).

The elements of the San Marco altarpiece that most obviously conflict with Lorenzo's pinnacles from a physical standpoint, and that would be out of tune with any altarpiece by him, are the pilasters and base. The deeply recessed and heavily framed fields reserved for the standing saints of the pilasters and the insistent wedge-shaped subdivisions of the inscribed base are unknown in the carpentry of Lorenzo's altarpieces, notably, the nearly contemporary *Annunciation* in the Bartolini Salimbeni Chapel at Santa Trinita, executed within the same half decade as the hypothesized commission for the Sacristy-Chapel. Such visual evidence permits the conjecture that Fra Angelico, on inheriting the altarpiece begun by Lorenzo Monaco, removed the original pilasters and the base of the frame, replacing them with elements of greater plastic force that were consistent with his optically sophisticated rendering of the saints on pedestals which are adjusted in their perspective to the viewer's angle of vision. The width and weight of the pilasters dwarf the pinnacles and lend them the alien appearance that troubled Douglas and Sirén. There remains the problem of reconciling the dominant pilasters of the San Marco altarpiece with the modest planar ones in Don Lorenzo's Santa Trinita *Annunciation* (Fig. 202).

The three inscriptions on the base, first noted by Beissel (pp. 54-56) and subsequently recorded by Pope-Hennessy (1974, p. 210), D. Cole (1977, p. 220), and most recently in *Beato Angelico, Miscellanea di studi*, Rome, 1984, p. 385, have never been precisely analyzed with regard to their textual and liturgical sources. The inscriptions are as follows: (center) ESTIMATUS SUM CUM DESCENDENTIBUS IN LACUM; (proper right) PLANGENT EUM QUASI UNIGENITUM QUIA INOCENS; (proper left) ECCE QUOMODO MORITUR IUSTUS ET NEMO PERCIPIT CORDE. While the scriptural sources are, respectively, Psalms 87:5, Zachariah 12:10, and Isaiah 57:1, the two lateral inscriptions on the altarpiece vary from the original texts, which are as follows: (Zachariah) Et plangent eum planctu quasi super unigenitum, Et dolebunt super eum . . . ; (Isaiah) Iustus perit, Et non est qui recogitet in corde suo. The explanation for this considerable disparity between the scriptural texts and two of the inscriptions on the altarpiece is that all three are quotations from an antiphon and responses in the Divine Office for Holy Saturday: ESTIMATUS SUM . . . (Resp. 8, Matins, Nocturn 3); PLANGENT EUM . . . (Ant. 2, Lauds); ECCE QUOMODO . . . (Resp. 3, Matins, Nocturn 2; the source of this last inscription in the Divine Office was noted by Beissel, who did not, however, connect the other two inscriptions with the liturgy; Cole noted the scriptural sources and that all are used in the Divine Office for Holy Saturday, but did not comment on the extensive changes from scriptural to liturgical texts). The responsorial texts in the Divine Office are frequently adaptations of the original scriptural passages. It is fitting, therefore, that Fra Angelico, a monastic painter, would have turned to the Office for the inscriptions, as it is a source in which he was perpetually steeped. That the inscriptions are from the generation of Fra Angelico seems certain from the fact they are in Roman capitals rather than the Gothic majuscules consistently used by Lorenzo Monaco (e.g., Uffizi *Coronation of the Virgin* [Fig. 44] and Santa Trinita *Annunciation* [Fig. 121]; see Covi, pp. 2-6).

Creighton Gilbert (*in litteris*, 1976) has offered

perceptive observations on the appropriateness of the three inscriptions in relation to the dramatic dialogue between the scene of the *Deposition* and the three pinnacles. At the center the theme of descent conveyed by the text ("I am counted with them that go down into the pit") and embodied in the *Descent from the Cross* is contrasted with the *Resurrection* in the pinnacle directly above. The inscription to the left ("They shall mourn for him as for an only son, for he is innocent") is enacted by the mourning women above and then answered by the *Noli Me Tangere*, thereby conveying once again the "polarity of death and life," as Gilbert observed. Directly above the inscription in the right segment of the plinth ("See how the just one dies and no one takes it to heart.") the male bystanders display the crown of thorns and the nails, while in the pinnacle the angel points to the empty tomb; the instruments of Christ's martyrdom are contrasted with the triumph over death. It is also noteworthy that the scriptural source (Isaiah 57:1; see above) does not include the idea of presentation, whereas the response in the Divine Office begins with the word "Ecce," just as in Angelico's *Deposition* the crown and nails are presented for inspection. Although these thematic harmonies and contrasts of inscription and image explain the reversal of the chronological order in the pinnacles—the Noli Me Tangere more normally standing to the right of the Holy Women at the Tomb, in a left to right reading order—there is a compositional disharmony in the placement of the lateral pinnacles, as I have discussed in the Introductory Essay (p. 35), raising the possibility that when Angelico revised Don Lorenzo's altarpiece he may have transposed the *Noli Me Tangere* and *Holy Women at the Tomb* in order better to integrate these inherited elements into a thematic program newly devised for the reworked altarpiece. The wedge-shaped moldings that rise through the spandrels of the arches are such strong echoes of the projecting elements of the base that they would seem to be one further revision of the original carpentry, undertaken by Angelico as a means of enhancing the structural and visual unity of the base and pinnacles of the altarpiece. A now-dismembered polyptych by Don Silvestro dei Gherarducci, possibly from Santa Maria degli Angeli, could have provided Lorenzo Monaco with a model for an altarpiece with Passion episodes in the pinnacles (see Catalogue I, Florence, Uffizi, *Coronation of the Virgin*). In Miklós Boskovits's reconstruction of Don Silvestro's altarpiece (1972, p. 37) he proposes that the *Noli Me Tangere* (London, National Gallery) was placed over the main register as a left lateral pinnacle (also see 1975, figs. 269-73). As the right pinnacle is lost, this suggested placement of the *Noli Me Tangere* may possibly be based on the arrangement of the San Marco pinnacles.

That the three Accademia panels (Figs. 92, 94, 95) were to serve as the predella of Lorenzo's original altarpiece would seem certain from physical and iconographic standpoints. The three inscribed segments of the base of Angelico's altarpiece, which measure 60, 62.5, and 60 cm. respectively, with the additional width of the intervals, very likely approximate the dimensions of Lorenzo's original frame. These widths would have accommodated the three predella panels, which have respective widths of 57, 61.2, and 57 cm., including their surviving engaged moldings. The differences in the horizontal dimensions of the center and side panels of the predella are comparable to the differences both in the widths of the center and side pinnacles and in the central and lateral fields of the continuous main panel. Thematically, the presence of scenes from the lives of Saints Onuphrius and Nicholas would have been appropriate in an altarpiece destined for the major sacristy, which was consecrated to Nofri Strozzi's patron saint and to the patron of his deceased son Niccolò (died 1411; for the consecration, see Orlandi, 1966, pp. 45-46). Davisson observed (pp. 325-28) that the imagery of water in both the *Nicholas* and *Onuphrius* panels possibly refers to Nofri's seafaring days and to the nurturing spring in the life of Saint Onuphrius. But Jones (p. 31) has mustered a series of historical objections to Davisson's proposal that the well at Santa Trinita was a further basis for the imagery of water in the predella. Moreover, the outcropping to the left of the Nativity scene, which Davisson identifies as a well (p. 328, note 103), may instead be a cave (see Catalogue I, Florence, Accademia, *Saint Nicholas Rescuing a Storm-tossed Ship* . . .). The choice of a rocky promontory, with its inevitable evocation of Calvary, for the site of the Nativity could possibly further support the hypothesis that Don Lorenzo's central predella panel was intended to lie below the post-Passion episodes in the pinnacles. From the standpoint of color, the *Nativity* forms the apex of a reversed chromatic triangle with its base aloft in the three pinnacles. The dominant note is an intense coral red in the robes of the kneeling Magdalen of the left pinnacle and the Holy

Woman in full profile in the right pinnacle. Fra Angelico reused this strong chromatic motif in the kneeling Magdalen (observed by Gilbert, *in litteris*, 1976), in her male counterpart, and in the front angels of the two floating clusters. The color has a brilliant restatement in the encircling wall of the *Nativity*. I would concur, nonetheless, with Jones's view (p. 38, note 64) that Angelico rejected the predella because neither Nofri nor Niccolò, nor their onomastic saints, appear in the *Deposition*, and the minor sacristy that was to receive the altarpiece was not dedicated to those saints.

The refractory questions remain as to whether Lorenzo Monaco left the altarpiece for the major sacristy incomplete, and if so, for what reason. Cämmerer-George (p. 187) tentatively proposed that Lorenzo Monaco completed the altarpiece and that the main register was expunged in 1434, during the events leading to the exile of Palla Strozzi, because of the inclusion of Strozzi portraits (for further comment, see Christiansen, 1972, p. 24, and Jones, 1984, pp. 38-39). The limning even of clandestine portraits would seem to run counter to the nature of Don Lorenzo's religious pictures; among all the visages of the *Adoration of the Magi* and the frescoes of the Bartolini Salimbeni Chapel there is none so individualized as to suggest an historical personage. As Lorenzo's undertaking of the project is devoid of documentary proof, but rather is assumed from the internal evidence of the *Deposition* altarpiece in its present state, an approach to the question may be made from the standpoint of Lorenzo's activities at this stage of his career. In the late 1410s and early 1420s he was committed to important commissions, and his shop was at the peak of activity. The *Adoration of the Magi* of circa 1420-1422, which may have been a more extensive work before its Renaissance revisions, made large demands. Although the design and execution of the frescoes and altarpiece for the Bartolini Salimbeni Chapel at Santa Trinita appear to be from the years 1422-23, Lorenzo could already have been faced by that commission shortly after 1420, which challenged him with the unfamiliar technique of fresco painting. For an artist attuned to panel painting and best able to exploit his talent on an intimate scale, it would seem reasonable that Lorenzo Monaco, having established the format of the Sacristy altarpiece, turned first to the peripheral elements of pinnacles and predella, with the intention of completing later the more demanding central scene. The proliferation of commissions and his death before mid-decade could thus permit the theory that the altarpiece for the Sacristy-Chapel at Santa Trinita was left unfinished, to be inherited by Fra Angelico and transformed in the completion. Whether Angelico was guided by Don Lorenzo's composition of the main panel remains a moot question, although from the evidence of the *Deposition* this would not seem to be the case. An alternative conjecture is that Palla Strozzi may have suspended the project when he discerned Don Lorenzo's work to be retardataire in the face of Gentile da Fabriano's *Adoration of the Magi*, the conception of which Palla could have known in preparatory drawings by 1421, or even as early as 1420 (for the date of Gentile's commission, see Christiansen, 1982, p. 97). Regardless of the fundamental differences in the nature of the optical realism of the altarpieces by Gentile and Angelico, the eventual pairing of these progressive works would have achieved a degree of visual consistency and a sense of subscription to a new art, which would have been less the case had Don Lorenzo's been the pendant work. If Palla Strozzi did indeed make such a decision, the modest accessions to a new style in Lorenzo's *Annunciation* altarpiece in the Bartolini Salimbeni Chapel at Santa Trinita, painted contemporarily with Gentile's *Adoration of the Magi*, would have confirmed his judgment. Moreover, could the antitheses of Gentile's *Adoration* and Don Lorenzo's representation of the same theme, probably for Sant'Egidio, have further prompted the decision? A comparable proposal has been expressed by Russell Panczenko (p. 29), to the effect that Palla Strozzi's initial choice of Lorenzo Monaco was premised on the patron's close affiliation with Ghiberti and his recognition that the styles of the sculptor and painter had run parallel courses in the first fifteen years of the century. With the marked changes in Ghiberti's art in the early 1420s and the arrival of Gentile da Fabriano on the Florentine scene, Palla would have been cognizant of the degree to which Don Lorenzo was not part of a new artistic wave. [ca. 1420-22]

FLORENCE, Museo dello Spedale degli Innocenti, no. 248

The Man of Sorrows

FIG. 169

Fresco (detached): 51 x 66 cm. (original surface; with new support, 68 x 80 cm.)

CONDITION: There is extensive rubbing and loss of intonaco in the lower areas of the face, throughout the upper torso and arms, and in the background. The fresco fragment was transferred to a new surface at the Gabinetto dei Restauri in Florence between 1967 and 1968.

HISTORY: The only record of the *Man of Sorrows* before it was deposited at some unknown date among the detached fresco fragments in the Refectory at Ognissanti, is a label on the frame which lists the work as no. 715 in the 1918 Inventory of the Museo di San Marco. Around 1960, the fragment was transferred from Ognissanti to its present location.

LITERATURE: 1932, Berenson, p. 300: Lorenzo Monaco (1963, vol. 1, p. 119) // 1935, Calamandrei, p. 6, no. 4: Florentine school, fourteenth century // 1952, Paatz, vol. 4, p. 430: anonymous fourteenth century // 1955, Eisenberg, pp. 46-49: LM, ca. 1415 // 1975, Boskovits, p. 346: LM, 1405-1410 // 1977, Bellosi, p. 263: LM shop, 1415-20.

COMMENT: The open and rapid brushwork suggests a dating around 1422-23, close to the frescoes at Santa Trinita. The lack of relationship between the head and the coarsely drawn and ill-proportioned body is indicative of workshop collaboration. As Bellosi observed (1977), the facial type bears a close resemblance to the cutout *Crucifix* at the Convento di Santa Marta in Florence (Fig. 72). [ca. 1422-23]

§ FLORENCE, Uffizi, no. 466

Adoration of the Magi
FIGS. 82-87; COLORPLATE 14

Pinnacles: (Center) *Blessing Redeemer*; (left) *Isaiah*; (right) *David*?
Spandrels (by Cosimo Rosselli): *Annunciation*; two unidentifiable *Prophets*

Panel: (Overall) 155 x 183 cm.; (painted surface of main panel) 113 x 166 cm.
Inscriptions: (Center pinnacle) AΩ ; (left pinnacle) OM̄S . D . SABA . VEN . AUR (Isaiah 60:6); (right pinnacle) REGES . THARSIS . ET . ĪSULE (Psalms 71:10)

CONDITION: Although the paint film is notably well preserved, the panel is in need of cleaning to free the surface of old and darkened varnishes. A cleaning at an unknown date destroyed some areas of the *velatura*, especially in the reddish hues. There is extensive patching of the original gilding, in the main panel above the manger shed and throughout the three pinnacles. Only the framing of the ogival pinnacles and the three arches is original (see Cämmerer-George, p. 184: citing my mistaken view that the converging arches were originally ornamented with consoles). The inner molding along the sides and bottom was probably added in the later fifteenth century when the spandrels were filled. The outer strip molding appears to be of a later date (see Comment below).

HISTORY: The provenance is uncertain (see Comment). In the later fifteenth century the figures in the spandrels, attributable to Cosimo Rosselli, were added in order to accommodate the altarpiece to the Renaissance taste for rectangular framing systems. The *Adoration* is listed in 1810 in an inventory of works at San Marco (MS., Sopr. alle Gallerie, Florence, Inventario di San Marco, no. 564, ascribed to Fra Angelico). In that same year the picture was transferred to the Accademia, where it remained until 1844, when it was moved to the Uffizi (MS., Sopr. alle Gallerie, Florence, 1844, Catalogo generale del 1825, supplemento, no. 2392, Lorenzo Monaco).

LITERATURE: 1846, Vasari, ed. Marchese, Pini, and Milanesi, vol. 2, p. 216: Lorenzo Monaco // 1855, Burckhardt, p. 185: among LM's major works // 1864, Crowe and Cavalcaselle, vol. 1, p. 555, note 1: "a pretty picture" by LM; the figures in the pinnacles and spandrels are attributed to Cosimo Rosselli // 1878, Vasari, ed. Milanesi, vol. 2, p. 28: LM // 1891, Rigoni, p. 88: LM; the first appearance in the official catalogue of the Uffizi (in all subsequent editions) // 1895, Lafenestre and Richtenberger, p. 8: commissioned from LM by the Signoria of Florence for the church of Santa Lucia dei Magnoli; tentatively identify the pointing figure at the right as Donato Acciaiuoli // 1896, Berenson, p. 119: LM; the *Annunciation* and *Prophets* in the spandrels are by Cosimo Rosselli // 1905, Sirén, pp. 104-11: a touchstone of LM's career, ca. 1420-22; perhaps for Sant'Egidio // 1921, A. Lorenzoni, *Cosimo Rosselli*, Florence, p. 49: spandrels by Cosimo Rosselli // 1927, van Marle, vol. 9, pp. 151-53: LM, from the years before the *Coronation* of 1414 // 1929, Suida, p. 392: LM // 1929, van Marle, vol. 11, p. 616, note 1: spandrels by Cosimo Rosselli // 1931, Golzio, p. 49: LM, in later style // 1932, Berenson, p. 299: LM, a later work // 1938/39, Pudelko, p. 78: LM, ca. 1420 // 1948, Sandberg-Vavalà, p. 101: LM, from last years // 1958, Levi D'Ancona, "Some New Attributions," p. 179: LM, 1420-22 // 1963, Berenson, vol. 1, p. 118, and vol. 2, pl. 1021 (illustrates a *Prophet* by Cosimo Rosselli) // 1975, Boskovits, p. 344: LM, 1420-25 // 1979, Florence, *Uffizi*, p. 347, no. P296: LM, 1421-22 // 1979, Bellosi, p. 61: almost certainly the altarpiece for Sant'Egidio, 1421-22.

COMMENT: The proposal that Santa Lucia dei Magnoli was the original location of the altarpiece is without documented evidence (Lafenestre and Richtenberger, 1895). Although there is no conclusive proof of the proposal first made by Sirén (1905) that the altarpiece for Sant'Egidio referred to in Documents 16A-16G is the Uffizi *Adoration of the Magi*, the importance of that work and its stylistic localization within the years 1420 to 1422 make a strong case for the theory. Davisson (1971, p. 272) has proposed that the *Adoration* could have been painted between 1418 and 1421, or soon thereafter, in commemoration of the sojourn of Pope Martin V in Florence, during which he officiated at the rededication of the rebuilt church at Sant'Egidio. If indeed the *Adoration of the Magi* was located in Sant'Egidio, the altarpiece may have been reduced in size and complexity and shaped to Renaissance taste at the time it was replaced by an unidentified work of Baldovinetti or by the *Adoration of the Shepherds* of Hugo van der Goes, now in the Uffizi (for a review of the hypothesized sequence of altarpieces for the high altar of Sant'Egidio, see Paatz, vol. 4, 1952, pp. 24-25, and 51, notes 96a-98). Levi D'Ancona (1962, p. 171) considers that only Document 16G refers to the Sant'Egidio altarpiece, and that the other documents in the sequence could possibly be connected with the San Benedetto Altarpiece (see Catalogue I, London, National Gallery). However, the total sums of payments match in Documents 16F and 16G, which indicates that the entire sequence has to do with a single project. In its reference to the wood, gessoing, and painting of the Sant'Egidio altarpiece, Document 16G would seem to be a cumulative account of the project, with the implication that the preparation of the panel was undertaken in Don Lorenzo's workshop without the collaboration of an independent carpenter. The large sum of 182 florins paid to Lorenzo Monaco (see Documents 16A-16G, Digest) is indicative of the size of the altarpiece, its central location in a major Florentine church, and the eminence of the painter at this moment of his career. For the early altarpiece in the Ardinghelli Chapel at the Carmine, his first documented commission, Don Lorenzo had received 55 florins, and for the Monte Oliveto Altarpiece little more than 10 florins (see Documents 4C-E and 8A-8B).

The broadly painted figures in the three pinnacles and the imprecise craftsmanship of the aureoles in the main panel are indicative of varying levels of workshop assistance in this late commission. It is noteworthy that at least two assistants are named in the documents for the Sant'Egidio altarpiece (see Documents 16D-F, and Digest). Although there is no evidence that the *Adoration of the Magi* originally included a predella and pilasters, as in Gentile da Fabriano's Strozzi *Adoration of the Magi* of 1423 for Santa Trinita, such accessory elements may have been removed when the frame was revised. The introduction of the spandrel figures in order to establish a rectangular upper contour, raises the possibility that these revisions of the altarpiece had also included a classicizing cornice and pilasters, which are found in several Renaissance remodellings of Gothic altarpieces (e.g., workshop of Giotto, *Coronation of the Virgin*, Baroncelli Chapel, Santa Croce; Taddeo Gaddi, *Madonna and Saints*, Metropolitan Museum of Art, New York and San Martino a Mensola [Ladis, figs. 4b-1, 14-1, and 51-1]; for a list of Gothic altarpieces "modernized" in the fifteenth century, see Offner, sec. III, vol. V, 1947, p. 88, note 10). If such additions to the frame of Lorenzo's *Adoration* were made in the later fifteenth century and then removed in more recent times, the present outer strip molding which circumscribes the altarpiece would seem to be modern. This stark edge would hardly have been acceptable to later Quattrocento taste.

Soulier (p. 166) observed that Lorenzo's "orientalism" in the *Adoration of the Magi* involves more specific ethnic differentiations than Gentile's Strozzi *Adoration*. Soulier also noted in Lorenzo's panel the important use of pseudo-Cufic lettering on the costumes of the standing Magus and the adjacent equerry, who is placed virtually at the center of the composition. A variety of detailed "Oriental" headgear had already appeared in Florentine painting in such mid-Trecento works as Giovanni del Biondo's *San Giovanni Gualberto* altarpiece (Offner and Steinweg, sec. IV, vol. V, p. II, 1969, pl. I[2]) and Andrea di Bonaiuto's Spanish Chapel frescoes (Meiss, 1951, figs. 38 and 51). Closer in time to Don Lorenzo's

Uffizi panel is the *Adoration* predella beneath Pietro di Miniato's Prato *Coronation of the Virgin*, documented 1412, where there is a similarly compressed group of retainers bracketed by steep orientalizing hats (Fremantle, fig. 825). In the *Adoration of the Magi* at the center of the predella of Giovanni del Biondo's polyptych in the Rinuccini Chapel at Santa Croce, dated 1379, a blackamoor appears at the end of the retinue of the Magi (Fremantle, fig. 489). The depiction of Asian and African elements in the work of Lorenzo Monaco was mentioned by Goetz (pp. 55-56), who identified the high, pointed headgear in the Uffizi *Adoration* as a North African *qalansuwah*. Olschki (pp. 97 and 105-106) noted the introduction of exotic Asiatic types particularly in images of the Adoration of the Magi, suggesting that the presence of Asiatic peoples within Italian urban milieus in the later fourteenth and fifteenth centuries may explain this usage. Lorenzo's inclusion of a black personage in the retinue of the Uffizi *Adoration* who is placed in close physical proximity to royalty rather than playing the usual menial role of groom, was noted by Kehrer (vol. 2, p. 224, note 3) and by Devisse and Mollat (vol. 2, pp. 111-12). Mark (pp. 47-48) commented that Lorenzo juxtaposed differing individuals of African origin in the retinue, one light and the other dark in complexion, also noting (p. 49) the depiction of an African type in the figure riding a camel in the drawing of the *Journey of the Magi* in Berlin (Fig. 97). [ca. 1420-22]

§ FLORENCE, Uffizi, no. 885

Coronation of the Virgin Altarpiece

FIGS. 44-62; 177, 179; FRONTISPIECE; COLORPLATES 7-9

Main panel: *Coronation of the Virgin*. Saints: (Left to right) (front rank) Benedict, Peter, John the Baptist // John the Evangelist, Andrew, Romuald; (second rank) Stephen, Paul, James Major, Matthew // Lawrence, Bartholomew, Zenobius, Giovanni Gualberto; (third rank) Crowned Saint, Anthony Abbot, Bishop Saint // Turbaned Saint, Monk Saint, Warrior Saint

Pinnacles: (center) *Blessing Redeemer*; (lateral) *Annunciation*

Predella: (Left to right) *Death of Saint Benedict; Saint Benedict in the Sacro Speco and a Young Monk Tempted from Prayer; Nativity; Adoration of the Magi; Saint Maurus Rescuing Saint Placidus and The Visit of Saint Benedict to Saint Scholastica; Saint Benedict Raises a Young Monk*

Pilasters: (Reading downward) (left) *Prophet, Noah, Abraham, David, Prophet*; (right) *Prophet, Moses, Prophet, Daniel, Prophet*

Panel: (Overall) 512 x 450 cm.; (painted surface of main panel) 248 x 372 cm.; (painted surface of center pinnacle) 85.5 x 57 cm.; (painted surface of lateral pinnacles) 83 x 60.5 cm.; (painted surface of each predella panel) 31.7 x 53.3 cm.; (painted surface of each full-length pilaster panel) 36.5 x 11 cm.

Inscribed signature and date: 1413 (n.s. 1414); for signature, see Inscriptions.

Inscriptions: (Frame of main panel) HEC . TABULA . FACTA . EST . PRO . ANIMA . ZENOBII . CECCHI . FRASCHE . ET . SUŌ . IN . RECOMPENSATIONĒ . UNIUS . ALTERĪ . TABULE . PER . EUM . IN . HOC[TEMPLO POSITA EST PER OPERAM LA]URENTII . JOH̄IS . E . SUŌ . MONAC̄I . HUĪ . ORDINIS . QUI . EAM . DEPINXIT . A̅N̅O . D̅N̅I̅ . M . CCCC . XIII . MĒSE . FEBR̄ . TP̄ORE . DŌNI . MATH̄I . PRIORIS . H̄ . MONASTER̄.

(Pinnacles) AVE MARIA GRATIA PL // ENA DN̄S TECUM BENEDI // CTA TU IN MULIERIBUS (Luke 1:28-29)

(Pilasters) (left) DAVID PPHA; (right) DANIEL PPHA

(Saint Benedict) AUSCULTA O FILI P̄CPTA MAGR̄I ET INCLINA AUREM CORDIS TUĪ ET A̅M̅ONITIONĒ PII P̅R̅I̅S LIBENT̄ EXCIPE ET EFFICACIT̄ COMPLE. UT A . . . (Incipit of Prologue to the *Rule*)

(Saint Paul) AD ROMANOS

(Saint Matthew) (L)IB̄ GR̄ATŌNIS IH̄U XR̄I FILII DD̄ FILII ABRAĀ (Incipit of the Gospel of Matthew)

(Saint John the Evangelist) IN PRINCIPIO ERAT V . . . BŪ ET V̄BUM ERAT APŪ DEŪ ET DEUS (Incipit of the Gospel of John)

CONDITION: The altarpiece was restored by Ettore Franchi in the early 1860s, shortly before being placed on exhibition in the Uffizi. The restoration apparently involved cleaning of the paint surfaces, some retouching, and a refurbishing of the frame, including the addition of ornamental details. This is probably when a neutral tone was added to the lower center of the main panel where a ciborium had once been attached at the cost of the central organ-playing angel. The outline of that ruined figure can still be detected, but the painted surface was irretrievably damaged. The only significant traces of repainting in the altarpiece are along the vertical seams of the main panel, most noticeably through the figure of the Virgin and down to the hand of the censing angel. As was usual with nineteenth-century restoration, soda was used as a solvent, which stripped the paint film of the final brush strokes (*velatura*) and the original varnish. This loss of refined brushwork, abetted by the passage of time, is most detectable in the lake colors—for example, in the light rose of Christ's sleeve and the darker rose of the Baptist's mantle—but less apparent in the sturdier, more resistant greens, yellows, and whites. The predella shows the same effects of the nineteenth-century overcleaning and some retouching, most visibly in the Joseph, the Virgin's face, and the ox and ass of the *Nativity*. There is no firm record of when the *Death of Saint Benedict* (Fig. 49) was damaged and repaired, but the state of the lower central area is poor in an Alinari photograph of 1929 (no. 46202), and considerably improved as seen in Fig. 49, from a photograph of around 1960. According to a verbal report received at the Soprintendenza alle Gallerie in Florence (1960), during the Second World War, while the altarpiece was in deposit at Torre a Cona, outside Florence, billeted troops who were using the predella as a mess table, spilled hot soup, which damaged areas at the far right of the *Death of Saint Benedict* and, ironically, the *Feeding of Saint Benedict at the Sacro Speco* (Fig. 50). The frame moldings and the inscription on the frame of the main panel are restored in the section where a tabernacle once impinged (TEMPLO through OPERAM LA). The frame preserves the essential format of the original, although there are extensive replacements of wood in the pilasters and numerous regilded areas. In 1956 the nineteenth-century hoods over the pinnacles, elongated finials, and foliate crockets above the main panel were removed (Berenson, 1963, vol. 1, pl. 448).

HISTORY: Sixteenth-century sources mention the altarpiece in its original location on the high altar of Santa Maria degli Angeli (see below). In the late sixteenth century it was replaced by a *Coronation of the Virgin*, documented 1593, by Alessandro Allori, now in the Accademia, Florence (no. 3171). In the mid-nineteenth century (see below, 1840 and 1846) the *Coronation* was discovered at the Badia di San Pietro at Cerreto, near Certaldo in the Val d'Elsa. In 1864 the altarpiece was transferred to the Uffizi, where it has been continuously exhibited.

LITERATURE: Ca. 1516-30, Antonio Billi (Strozziano), p. 361: "Frate Lorenzo, frate negli Agnoli di Firenze. Costui dipinse in detto luogo la tavola dell'altare maggiore in detta chiesa con grande ornamento lavorata . . ."; (Petrei), p. 326: "Fra Lorenzo frate negli Agnioli, dipinse la tavola dello altare maggiore di decta chiesa . . ." // ca. 1537-42, Anonimo Gaddiano, p. 77: "Fra Lorenzo pittore, frate delli Agnoli di Firenze, fece nella chiesa di detti frati la tavola dell'altare maggiore lavorata con grande hornamento . . ." // 1550, Vasari, ed. Bettarini and Barocchi, Text, p. 304: "Nelli Agnoli di Fiorenza fece la tavola dello altar maggiore finita nel MCCCCXIII" // 1568, Vasari, ed. Bettarini and Barocchi, Text, p. 304: "Le prime opere di questo monaco pittore . . . furono nel suo monasterio degli Agnoli, dove, oltre molte altre cose, dipinse la tavola dell'altar maggiore che ancor oggi nella loro chiesa si vede, la quale fu posta su finita del tutto, come per lettere scritte da basso nel fornimento si può vedere, l'anno 1413." // 1579, Fortunio, p. 126: "Templum tabulis primus exornavit & Angelorum & Sancti Benedicti" // 1677, Bocchi, ed. Cinelli, p. 492: (Chiesa degli Angioli) "Entrando poi in Chiesa vi è la tavola dell'altar maggiore di mano d'Alessandro Allori ov è un Assunta, e prima ve n'era una di mano di D. Lorenzo del quale una simile alla Cappella degli Alberti ancora si vede" (this last mentioned work is the *Coronation* altarpiece, which had been moved to Santa Maria degli Angeli from the monastery of San Benedetto fuori della Porta a Pinti; see Catalogue I, London, National Gallery) // 1684, Del Migliore, p. 330: (Monastero degli Angeli) "Vi si vede un'Incoronazione all'altare d'Alessandro Allori Padre di Christofano Bronzino famoso dipintore, la quale v'è in vece d'una Tavola, in cui rappresentavasi il medesimo Misterio dell'Incoronazione di nostra Donna, per di mano di quel D. Lorenzo Monaco, del quale il Vasari scrive la Vita." // 1686, Baldinucci, vol. 2, p. 94: ". . . dipinse la tavola dell'Altar maggiore di suo Monastero, la quale vedeasi nello stesso luogo circa al fine del passato secolo, e poi ne fu levata per dar luogo a moderna pittura . . ." // 1710, Farulli, p. 31: "L'anno 1413 a tempera dipinse la tavola dell'Altar maggiore di questo venerabile luogo . . ." // 1840, Gaye, p. 433: "E qui parlando di pitture ignote mi giova avvertire che una delle più belle opere, atte a caratterizare il principio del secolo XV, fu trovata da me nella chiesa di Cerreto. . . . È questa tavola stupenda un lavoro di Lorenzo Monaco, intatta e . . . perfettamente conservata; È questa, se non sbaglio, la tavola che ornava già l'altar maggiore della chiesa degli Angeli." (Gaye also describes the subject matter and records the inscription, leaving a blank where the letters had been effaced.) // 1846, Vasari, ed. Marchese, Pini, and Milanesi, p. 211, note 1: report having seen the *Coronation* in 1840 at the Badia of San Pietro at Cerreto // 1855, Burckhardt, p. 185: mentions that Lorenzo's principal work is the *Coronation of the Virgin* at the Badia of Cerreto // 1864, Crowe and Cavalcaselle, vol. 1, pp. 552-53: mention the *Coronation* of 1413 at the abbey at Ceretto; in the 1883 edition, vol. 2, p. 337, the *Coronation*, by then in the Uffizi, is judged to be of finer quality than the other version at Certaldo (now London, National Gallery) // 1878, Vasari, ed. Milanesi, vol. 2, p. 18, note 4: Milanesi reports he had first seen the *Coronation* in 1830, which would precede Gaye's discovery // 1881, *Catalogo della R. Galleria di Firenze*, Florence, p. 122, no. 1309: the restoration in the early 1860s by Ettore Franchi is noted // 1896, Berenson, p. 119 (1932, p. 299; 1963, vol. 1, p. 118) // 1905, Sirén, pp. 76-87 // 1927, van Marle, vol. 9, pp. 160-62: considers the *Coronation* to be the last major altarpiece by Lorenzo Monaco, postdating the *Adoration of the Magi* in the Uffizi and the frescoes and altarpiece of the Bartolini Salimbeni Chapel at Santa Trinita // 1931, Golzio, pp. 44-46: essentially Florentine in its vigorous expression // 1938/39, Pudelko, p. 247: the *Coronation* a summary of the various Florentine sources of Lorenzo's style // 1948, Sandberg-Vavalà, pp. 97-101: emphasizes Don Lorenzo's mastery in the predella // 1958, Levi D'Ancona, "Some New Attributions," passim // 1960, Salvini and Traverso, pp. 61-65 // 1968, Degenhart and Schmitt: see Catalogue I, Florence, Uffizi, Gabinetto Disegni e Stampe, no. 11 E. // 1979, Florence, *Uffizi*, p. 347, no. P925 // 1983, Gardner von Teuffel, p. 326.

COMMENT: A search for information on the secular patrons of the altarpiece cited in the inscription has brought no result, nor can there be determined the subject or artist of the altarpiece that was replaced by Lorenzo's *Coronation of the Virgin* (. . . UNIUS ALTERĪ TABULE . . .). For the modified replica of the Santa Maria degli Angeli *Coronation* executed for the monastery of San Benedetto fuori della Porta a Pinti, see Catalogue I, London, National Gallery.

The variations in the types of Coronation of the Virgin in Florentine Trecento painting are surveyed in Offner, sec. III, vol. V, 1947, pp. 248-50. From the second quarter of the century through the generations of Cionesque painters the prevalent type of Coronation of the Virgin polyptych represented the saintly witnesses in multi-tiered clusters kneeling and standing at either side of the central group of Christ and the Virgin: e.g., Giotto workshop, Baroncelli Chapel, Santa Croce (Ladis, fig. 11, attributed to Giotto); Jacopo di Cione, San Piero Maggiore altarpiece, London, National Gallery (Fig. 299); Giovanni del Biondo, San Giovanni Valdarno, Santa Maria delle Grazie (Offner and Steinweg, sec. IV, vol. IV, pt. I, 1967, pl. XXXI). Late in the Trecento and in the first years of the Quattrocento, the principal type incorporated a reduced number of saints, at times as few as two pairs, all in standing positions: e.g., Spinello Aretino, Niccolò di Pietro Gerini, and Lorenzo di Niccolò, Florence, Accademia, dated 1401 (Berenson, 1963, vol. 1, pl. 386); Lorenzo di Niccolò, Cortona, San Domenico, dated 1402 (Fremantle, fig. 807); Mariotto di Nardo, Minneapolis Institute of Arts and J. Paul Getty Museum, Malibu, dated 1408 (Berenson, 1963, vol. 1, pl. 520); Pietro di Miniato, Prato, Galleria Comunale, documented 1412 (Berenson, 1963, vol. 1, pl. 399). These turn-of-the-century Florentine Coronation altarpieces reveal an essential structural difference from Lorenzo's work for Santa Maria degli Angeli in that their broad main registers are divided by frames, so that the saintly witnesses are physically separated from the central icon. From this standpoint, these altarpieces do not reveal a significant change from Jacopo di Cione's compartmentalized panel for San Piero Maggiore or even from the earlier Giottesque altarpiece in the Baroncelli Chapel at Santa Croce.

A notable exception is the *Coronation of the Virgin* by Giovanni del Biondo (Fig. 302) in the Cathedral at Fiesole (property of the Museo Bandini), dated 1373, to my knowledge the earliest rendering of the panoramic type of Coronation on an uninterrupted main register, which results in the unification of the witnesses and the central event (independently observed by Cämmerer-George, p. 181; see Offner and Steinweg, sec. IV, vol. IV, pt. I, 1967, p. 125). The Fiesole altarpiece serves, therefore, as an important transition between Jacopo di Cione's San Piero Maggiore altarpiece, completed only two years earlier, and Don Lorenzo's for Santa Maria degli Angeli. From Jacopo came the galaxy of witnesses and the central unit of figures enshrined by a throne and baldachin, whereas Giovanni del Biondo's unified pictorial field provided the single prototype for Lorenzo's construction of the main panel. But Lorenzo Monaco also reacted against Jacopo di Cione's central icon, in which a broad cloth of honor negates the spaciousness of the architecture and silhouettes the figures against an abstract ground. Lorenzo's architecture does not admit such a barrier and, in fact, the cusped arches at the back of the baldachin frame the rear plane of the angelic choir. Don Lorenzo's convincing spatial effects indicate a direct awareness of the elaborate structures that are such salient features in works of Spinello Aretino, for example, the *Madonna and Saints* in the Museo Diocesano or the *Annunciation* in San Francesco, both in Arezzo (Fremantle, figs. 715 and 721). Nonetheless, a dichotomy between surface and space persists in Lorenzo's work, for the architecture is more backdrop than container and the entire unit of figures, throne, and baldachin levitates above a starry firmament, indicating that the painter had not abandoned the illusion of suspension that was a hallmark of mid-Trecento Florentine painting, where his deepest stylistic roots are once again discerned.

Along with his references to Jacopo di Cione's broad tableau and enthroned Virgin and Christ, and to the unified pictorial field of Giovanni del Biondo, Lorenzo Monaco seems also to have turned to these earlier painters' works in designing the framing system for the Santa Maria degli Angeli *Coronation*, the most architecturally developed frame he and his collaborating carpenters ever devised. As Cämmerer-George has noted (1966, pp. 181-82), the three arches over the main panel are in actuality a series of canopies that recalls the projecting frames of Jacopo di Cione's *Crucifixion* in the National Gallery in London and Giovanni del Biondo's Cavalcanti *Annunciation* in the Accademia, Florence (Offner and Steinweg, sec. IV, vol. III, 1965, pl. IV; and sec. IV, vol. V, 1969, pl. XXV). The interiors of the canopies over Jacopo's and Giovanni's altarpieces were originally simple, star-studded vaults, whereas Don Lorenzo treated the interior surfaces as fully groined vaults, enhancing thereby the ecclesiastical character of the setting for the sacred rite (see Cämmerer-George, pl. 33). In all of these canopied works the framing systems take on the guise of sheltering enclosures and at the same time strengthen the bond between the realms of the icon and the observer. Granted the additions to Lorenzo's frame (Berenson, 1963, vol. 1, pl. 448), fabricated in the nineteenth century and now removed, were strongly Victorian in their gothicism; nonetheless, the analogy with the Cavalcanti altarpiece suggests that projecting hoods would appropriately cap the three pinnacles and equalize the architectural character of the frame on all three registers. Further evidence for the original framing system of the three pinnacles in the Santa Maria degli Angeli altarpiece may be found in the recently restored *Coronation of the Virgin* of 1402, by Lorenzo di Niccolò, which Lorenzo Monaco would have seen at San Marco, long before its transfer by the Medici to San Domenico in Cortona (Fremantle, fig. 807). The flat ogival tympana used as pinnacles in several of Don Lorenzo's major altarpieces would not have provided an appropriate complement in shape or weight to the architectonic framing of the main register of the altarpiece (see the Introductory Essay, note 61). In her study of structural developments in Trecento and early Quattrocento Florentine framing systems, Christa Gardner von Teuffel noted (1983, p. 326) that the arches suspended over the main panel of the Uffizi *Coronation* were "inserted only after the painting process had been virtually completed." An incised line on the panel surface was now used to establish the matching contours of painted image and frame, indicating that the collaboration of painter, carpenter, and gilder continued until nearly the completion of a large, complex altarpiece.

The question remains whether Lorenzo's frame for the Santa Maria degli Angeli *Coronation* was his initial reminiscence of the aggressively structural frames in works by Jacopo di Cione and Giovanni del Biondo. In the document of 1398 (Document 4A) the woodworker Andrea di Giovanni is recorded as receiving a payment for a panel with a ciborium and other accoutrements (. . . *cum civorio et aliis fornimentis* . . .) for the second Ardinghelli Chapel at the Carmine. As the word "ciborium" may refer both to a container for the host and to a baldachin, could this document be the specification of the type of elaborate framing system used earlier in the Cionesque tradition, to be echoed and sophisticated in the *Coronation* altarpiece for the high altar of Santa Maria degli Angeli?

According to a reconstruction proposed cumulatively by Zeri (1968, pp. 75-76) and Boskovits (1972, pp. 36-38; 1975, figs. 269-73), there may have been an earlier *Coronation of the Virgin* at Santa Maria degli Angeli, by Don Silvestro dei Gherarducci. Two panels of *Kneeling Saints* would have been the laterals of this divided type of polyptych, with a *Crucifixion* and *Noli Me Tangere*, and by implication a third Passion scene, in the pinnacles, and a *Man of Sorrows* at the center of the predella. To my knowledge, such an extensive depiction of the Passion along with the festive theme of the Coronation of the Virgin would be unique, although there are important examples in which the central pinnacle represents the Crucifixion or Trinity (e.g., Giovanni del Biondo, Fiesole [Fig. 302], and San Giovanni Valdarno [Offner and Steinweg, sec. IV, vol. IV, pt. I, 1967, pl. XXXI]; Lorenzo di Niccolò, Cortona [Fremantle, fig. 807]). It is noteworthy that in Giovanni del Biondo's Cavalcanti *Annunciation* (Offner and Steinweg, sec. IV, vol. V, pt. II, 1969, pl. XXV) three Passion episodes occupy the pinnacles, and a Man of Sorrows is at the center of the predella.

Within Tuscan painting the inclusion of an angelic choir around a throne is Sienese in origin, but by the later Trecento the device was common in Florentine painting; see, for example, Agnolo Gaddi, *Madonna Enthroned, with Saints*, National Gallery, Washington (Shapley, 1979, vol. 2, pl. 134), or Spinello Aretino, *Madonna Enthroned, with Saints*, dated 1391, Accademia, Florence (Fremantle, fig. 723). Don Lorenzo's device of placing angels under the arches of the baldachin, which lends the effect of intimate participation in the ritual, is found earlier in the *Coronation of the Virgin* in the Bargello, by the Master of the Saint George Codex (Berenson, 1963, vol. 1, pl. 109). In Bernardo Daddi's San Pancrazio altarpiece a choir of saints and angels forms a half circle around the enthroned Madonna, heightening the suggestion of a sacred precinct (Berenson, 1963, vol. 1, pl. 177). In the first decade of the Quattrocento, Starnina continued to adopt the motif of an encircling angelic choir as a means to reinforce the ritualistic isolation of the enthroned Virgin and Child (e.g., Martin von Wagner Museum, Würzburg, and Getty Museum, Malibu; Waadenoijen, 1983, figs. 16 and 24).

The versicles and responses in the liturgy of the Mass and the Offices for the Feast of the Assumption of the Virgin (August 15), incorporating the theme of the Coronation of the Virgin, which was never officially established as a feast, refer persistently to the jubilant angelic choir. The migration of the angelic company from Assumption to Coronation imagery is exemplified by Giovanni del Biondo's *Coronation of the Virgin*, in the Cathedral at Fiesole, where a choir of thirteen angels occupies the entire foreground of the panel (Fig. 302). Robert (col. 55) noted the emphasis given to the theme of angels in Camaldolese liturgy when the praises of Christ and the Virgin are sung. Pope-Hennessy (1980, p. 47) has proposed the influence on Lorenzo Monaco of Ghiberti's *Assumption* window in the Duomo of Florence, specifically with regard to the convincing spatial environment formed by the angelic choir (for the debated attribution of the window, which dates from 1404 to 1405, see *Ghiberti, 'materia e ragionamenti,'* p. 144). [1414]

§ FLORENCE, Uffizi, Gabinetto Disegni e Stampe, No. 11 E.

Six Kneeling Saints (recto); and *Saint Benedict Enthroned* (verso)

FIGS. 63, 176

Paper: 245 x 175 mm.
Technique: (Recto) silverpoint and pen; (verso) reed pen, on reddish tinted paper

CONDITION: The silverpoint underdrawing on the recto is considerably rubbed. On the verso a silverpoint sketch of what appears to be a Madonna and Child, at the level of Benedict's shoulder, has been rubbed nearly to invisibility.

HISTORY: For the provenance and notices in the Uffizi inventory and index of 1784 and 1793, see Bellosi and Bellini, 1978, p. 28.

LITERATURE: 1849, Ramirez di Montalvo, no. 9: Stefano Fiorentino // 1881, Ferri, p. 5: Agnolo Gaddi // 1890, Ferri, p. 93: Lorenzo Monaco // 1905, Sirén, pp. 64-65: LM; the *Six Saints* is a study for the left panel in the National Gallery London; observes the superior quality of the *Enthroned Benedict* // 1927, van Marle, vol. 9, pp. 163-64: LM; the *Saint Benedict* is probably a rough draft for the central panel of an altarpiece for which the wings of *Kneeling Saints* in London were the side elements // 1929, Suida, p. 392: LM; mentions only the recto // 1938, Berenson, vol. 2, p. 158, no. 1391A: LM // 1940, Oertel, pp. 252-53: LM; the *Saint Benedict* was the original idea for the center of an altarpiece commissioned from Lorenzo, the freshness and rapidity of the technique suggesting the immediacy of a new idea; the *Kneeling Saints* is based on the Uffizi *Coronation*, but is also closely related to the left panel of the London *Coronation* altarpiece, although originally intended for an altarpiece with Saint Benedict as the principal theme // 1951, Davies, p. 240 (1961, p. 307): LM; the *Adoring Saints* seems to be a study for the London panel, but the figure of *Saint Benedict* "seems irrelevant" // 1968, Degenhart and Schmitt, pt. 1, vol. 2, pp. 269-71, no. 170; and vol. 4, pls. 196c and 196d: LM; see a summary of their theories under London, National Gallery, San Benedetto Altarpiece // 1970, Fossi Todorow, p. 68: LM // 1975, Boskovits, p. 344: LM, 1410-15 // 1978, Bellosi and Bellini, pp. 28-29, no. 28: LM; summarize earlier opinions; additional bibliography // 1982, Florence, *Iconografia di San Benedetto*, p. 111, no. 42 // 1984, Bellosi, p. 311: drawing for London *Coronation* proves that the altarpiece postdates that for Santa Maria degli Angeli.

COMMENT: See Catalogue I, London, National Gallery, San Benedetto Altarpiece. A miniature of the *Enthroned Saint Benedict with Eight Saints* by Don Silvestro dei Gherarducci, in the Gulbenkian Foundation in Lisbon, shows some resemblances to Lorenzo's drawing in the figure of the saint and the design of the throne; see Kaftal, fig. 180, citing Offner's attribution to the Master of the Cionesque Humility; attributed to Don Silvestro by Boskovits, 1975, p. 423; also see Offner, ed. Maginnis, 1981, p. 32: Don Silvestro dei Gherarducci (Master of the Cionesque Humility). [ca. 1415]

FLORENCE, Uffizi, Gabinetto Disegni e Stampe, nos. 179 E. and 180 E.

Two Studies of the *Virgin and Child* (probably for an Adoration of the Magi)

FIGS. 211, 212

Paper: 105 x 63 mm. (179 E.); 103 x 62 mm. (180 E.)
Technique: Reed pen and brown ink

HISTORY: For the provenance, an early reproduction (1778), and notices in the Uffizi inventory and index of 1784 and 1793, see Bellosi and Bellini, 1978, pp. 29-30.

LITERATURE: 1849, Ramirez di Montalvo, nos. 13 and 14: Agnolo Gaddi // 1881, Ferri, p. 13 (1890, p. 86): anonymous Florentine, fifteenth century // 1905, Sirén, p. 58, note 1: Lorenzo Monaco, before 1414 // 1908, Toesca, p. 254, note 4: probably not by LM // 1929, Suida, p. 392: LM // 1968, Degenhart and Schmitt, pt. 1, vol. 2, p. 269, nos. 168 and 169; vol. 4, pls. 196a and 196b: LM, first years of the fifteenth century; provide further technical information // 1975, Boskovits, p. 344: LM, 1405-1410 // 1978, Bellosi and Bellini, pp. 29-30, nos. 29 and 30, and figs. 46 and 47: anonymous Florentine, close to LM; with extensive bibliography.

COMMENT: The two studies of the *Virgin and Child* may be tentatively proposed as pages of sketchbooks used in Don Lorenzo's shop. Bellini (1978) justly removes the drawings from the autograph works of Lorenzo, observing the rigid and conventional drawing technique. The two studies should be differentiated in date, 179 E. having closer affinities to the ponderable forms of Don Lorenzo's *Prophets* in the Metropolitan Museum, New York, of circa 1408-1410 (Figs. 40-43), whereas 180 E. is more reminiscent of his later works, such as the *Annunciation* (Fig. 77) and the *Adoration of the Magi* (Fig. 82). [ca. 1408-1410 (179 E.); ca. 1418-20 (180 E.)]

§ FLORENCE, San Giovannino dei Cavalieri

Crucifix with the Mourning Virgin and Saint John the Evangelist

FIGS. 70, 73-76

Panel (cutout): 416 x 221 cm. (crucifix); 166 x 118 cm. (Virgin); 161 x 117 cm. (Saint John)

CONDITION: The group of panels was restored in 1955 by the Florentine Gabinetto dei Restauri. Some areas of loss in the left sleeve, the lower edges of the mantle, and the hands of Saint John required inpainting. The gesturing hand of the Virgin, a later addition, was replaced by a neutrally contoured and toned panel. The scrolled superscription in Roman capitals is a later repainting.

HISTORY: This would seem to be the work in the church of the Romiti di Camaldoli (San Salvatore), then outside Florence, which Vasari (1550) attributed to Lorenzo Monaco. In the 1568 edition of the *Vite*, Vasari mentioned both the church and Don Lorenzo's panels in the past tense (see below, 1550/1568). San Salvatore di Camaldoli was the seat of the Maltese Order of Camaldolese until 1552, when the Order was transferred to the Celestine monastery in Florence, formerly called San Piero Murrone, but in 1551 renamed San Giovannino dei Cavalieri (di Malta). It is probable that the panels were moved into Florence at that time, as the abandonment of San Salvatore di Camaldoli occurred in 1552, whereas the adjoining monastery had been destroyed in 1529 (see Paatz, vol. 2, 1941, pp. 300-301, and vol. 5, 1953, pp. 41-42). Fantozzi (1842) first noted the location of the panels as San Giovannino dei Cavalieri.

LITERATURE: 1550/1568, Vasari, ed. Bettarini and Barocchi, p. 305 (1550): ". . . et in Camaldoli di Fiorenza un Crocifisso in tavola et un San Giovanni"; p. 305 (1568): ". . . et in Firenze nella chiesa de'Romiti pur di Camaldoli (che oggi, essendo rovinata insieme col monasterio, ha rilasciato solamente il nome a quella parte di là d'Arno che dal nome di quel santo luogo si chiama Camaldoli) oltre a molte altre cose fece un Crucifisso in tavola et un S. Giovanni che furono tenuti bellissimi" // 1686, Baldinucci, vol. 2, p. 94: ". . . e nella Chiesa de'Romiti di Camaldoli . . . dipinse un Crocifisso sopra a tavola, ed un San Giovanni . . ." // 1710, Farulli, p. 31: lists as by Lorenzo Monaco "una tavola in S. Salvadore di Camaldoli" // 1761, Richa, vol. 9, p. 147: repeats Baldinucci's notice. // 1842, Fantozzi, p. 447: mentions a Crucifix with the Virgin and Saint John in San Giovannino, but does not attribute the work, indicating only that it is by a better artist than Gherardini, who painted the frescoes behind // 1878, Vasari, ed. Milanesi, vol. 2, p. 21, note 5: states without substantiation that the panels perished in the destruction of the church [*sic*] and monastery of San Salvatore, but makes no mention of works at San Giovannino // 1905, Sirén, pp. 90-91: Lorenzo Monaco, ca. 1415-17; tentatively identifies with the work cited by Vasari // 1905, Chiappelli, p. 39: style of LM // 1909, Berenson, p. 153: LM (1932, p. 299; 1963, vol. 1, p. 119) // 1927, van Marle, vol. 9, pp. 149-50: LM, ca. 1410 // 1929, Suida, p. 392: LM // 1931, Golzio, p. 48: LM, ca. 1413 // 1933, Florence, *Mostra del Tesoro*, p. 87, nos. 965-67: LM // 1933/34, Gamba, p. 154: LM // 1935 Paris, *Exposition*, no. 31: LM // 1938/39, Pudelko, p. 248: LM, a late work // 1941, Paatz, vol. 2, pp. 311 and 317, note 39: the San Giovannino group is identified with that mentioned by Vasari at San Salvatore di Camaldoli; transferred in the sixteenth century // 1975, Boskovits, p. 342: LM, 1410-15 // 1979, Bellosi, p. 61: certainly the work noted by Vasari // 1984, Bellosi, p. 312, note 4: datable 1408-1414.

COMMENT: For the sequence of cutout crosses by Lorenzo Monaco preceding that at San Giovannino, see Catalogue I, Florence, San Giuseppe. Virtually contemporary is the *Crucifix* in Santa Maria delle Vertighe at Monte San Savino, while that at the Convento di Santa Marta in Florence follows by less than half a decade (Figs. 71, 72). The inadequacies of design and execution of the mourning Saint John the Evangelist are discussed in relation to a cluster of shop works centered around the San Benedetto Altarpiece (see Catalogue I, London, National Gallery).

In a study of a *Crucifix* in the Museo Diocesano at Cortona, Maginnis (1981) demonstrated that the type of cutout cross was already in use in the generation of Pietro Lorenzetti and perhaps even by the later Duecento. Baldini (1952, p. 255) observed that two Florentine cutout crosses of the earlier fourteenth century are reductions from the full Duecento type with apron and terminals, which is also the case with the *Crucifix* by Segna di Bonaventura in the Pushkin Museum, Moscow (Stubblebine, vol. 1, p. 132, and vol. 2, fig. 313). As Boskovits has observed (1975, pp. 101 and 228, note 79; pl. 101), in the cross attributed to Pietro Nelli in San Pietro a Ripoli (Bagno a Ripoli), of around 1380-85, the considerable extensions of the panel surface beyond the painted contours of the corpus and loincloth indicate that the work was reduced to a cutout type at a later date, perhaps around 1399 in conjunction with the activities of the confraternity of the Bianchi, given the apparent addition of the two white-clad suppliants in areas of the panel at the base of the cross (also see Tartuferi, 1984, fig. 4). Boskovits notes, however, that the San Pietro a Ripoli cross has also been considered to have been originally of the cutout type (M. Lisner, *Holzkruzifixe in Florenz und in der Toskana von der Zeit um 1300*, Munich, 1970, p. 11). The *Crucifix* in Santa Lucia al Borghetto, Tavarnelle Val di Pesa, attributed by Boskovits to Jacopo del Casentino, was cut out and deprived of its terminals, possibly in the early fifteenth century (1984, p. 306, and pl. 131). On the high altar of San Michele at Rovezzano, near Florence, is a cutout cross dated 1400, in a later Trecento Florentine style with some reminiscences of Lorenzo di Bicci in the facial type (see A. Conti et al, *I dintorni di Firenze*, Florence, 1983, p. 104, fig. 151). If the date and place of invention of the cutout cross are still uncertain, the type seems to have gained currency in the shop of Lorenzo Monaco during the first quarter of the fifteenth century, which led to the transformation of panels into the cutout type, for example, the work by Jacopo del Casentino mentioned above. Charles Seymour and Hanns Swarzenski suggested that the silhouetted form served as a transition between the sculptured crucifix and the painted Crucifixion scene in the early Quattrocento (p. 141, note 16), a view also expressed by Antal (p. 318). The cutout crucifix as an isolated image or in a grouped composition persisted through several generations after Lorenzo Monaco. A *Crucifix* from the mid-1420s in the Museo di San Marco, attributed to Fra Angelico, reveals the impact of Masaccio's new anatomical realism in the *Trinity* fresco (Cole Ahl, 1980, pp. 370-71, and fig. 10) or in Donatello's wood *Crucifix* at Santa Croce of circa 1412 (Janson, pl. 3). Directly dependent on the San Giovannino ensemble is Fra Angelico's *Christ on the Cross Adored by Saints Nicholas and Francis* at San Niccolò del Ceppo, Florence (Baldini, 1977, figs. 242-43). In turn, the cutout *Crucifix with Saints Jerome, Francis, and Mary Magdalen* at San Gaetano in Florence, attributed by Marchini to the school of Filippo Lippi (1975, figs. 208-209), depends on Angelico's model. In Notre Dame, Indiana, and Portland, Oregon, cutout crucifixes attributed to Cosimo Rosselli and Botticelli demonstrate the survival of the type into the last years of the Quattrocento (Shapley, 1966, figs. 326 and 327). The seated *Mourning Virgin* and *Saint John the Evangelist* by Giovanni di Paolo from the Oratorio della Compagnia dei SS. Giovannino, Gennaro, e Bernardino in Siena, of circa 1450, were cut from a Crucifixion panel at some unknown time, in obvious emulation of Lorenzo's San Giovannino group (see C. Brandi, *Giovanni di Paolo*, Florence 1947, figs. 51 and 52).

Lorenzo Monaco and his workshop adopted several times the iconography of the Crucifixion in which the Virgin and Saint John are seated on the ground beneath the cross. A reduced version of the San Giovannino group in an unidentified private collection was noted by Bellosi and attributed to the Maestro del Codice Squarcialupi (1984, p. 309, and fig. 17; see Catalogue II, Avignon, Musée du Petit Palais). The other examples of the iconographic type, but not cutout panels, are in the Lehman Collection, Metropolitan Museum, New York (Fig. 135), in New Haven (Fig. 174), and in the Accademia, Florence (Figs. 167-68 and 170). The Lehman Collection panel issued from Don Lorenzo's workshop around the middle of the first decade of the Quattrocento, predating both the San Giovannino group and Ghiberti's *Crucifixion* relief on the North Door (Fig. 309), which Krautheimer localized within the years 1407 to 1413 (1956, pp. 124-25). Could the sculptor's work have prompted Don Lorenzo, within whose shop the cutout cross had already been produced several times (e.g., Figs. 69 and 163), to extend the technique to an entire Crucifixion group? The image of the Crucifixion with the mourning Virgin and Saint John seated on the ground had migrated from Siena to Florence as early as the generation of Bernardo Daddi and was widely represented there by the later Trecento (see Krautheimer, 1956, p. 217). Dorothy Shorr (1940, p. 68) noted that the type may be allied in concept to the Madonna of Humility and also to the Adoration of the Magi in which the Virgin is seated directly on the ground, a variant that Lorenzo Monaco incorporated into his major panel in the Uffizi (Fig. 82). The Madonna of Humility had come to the fore as a theme within Don Lorenzo's workshop during the same early years of the century in which the Lehman panel may be dated. The persistent presence of sloping and sharply profiled rocks as backdrop to the Virgin and Saint John in Don Lorenzo's images of the Crucifixion implies that he was adopting an essentially Sienese means of intensifying the emotional bond between the two mourners and the Christ on the cross. There is no more trenchant example of this device than is found in the *Crucifixion* predella panel by Luca di Tommè in the Pinacoteca Vaticana (Fehm, pl. 12), a work, in fact, long attributed to Lorenzo Monaco. An expressive link between Luca and Don Lorenzo may also be discerned in the head of the mourning Virgin in the Sienese painter's *Crucifixion* in the Museo Nazionale, Pisa (Meiss, 1963, fig. 8). [ca. 1415]

FLORENCE, San Giuseppe

Crucifix

FIGS. 165, 166

Panel (cutout): 308 x 226 cm. (without later superscription)

CONDITION: The *Crucifix* was damaged in the flood of November 1966. Restoration work, for which there is no documentation, was undertaken by the Opificio delle Pietre Dure e Laboratori di Restauro at the Fortezza da Basso in Florence between 1966 and 1976, when the cross was returned to San Giuseppe. The fissures in the paint and gesso across the armpit and breast, visible before the flood damage (see Florence, Sopr. Gab. Fot. 115317) have been repaired and inpainted. Lighter passages of the staff are areas of inpainting. The superscription in Roman capitals does not appear to be contemporary with the cross and corpus.

HISTORY: Sirén's publication in 1905 is the first record of the work.

LITERATURE: 1905, Sirén, pp. 89 and 188: Lorenzo Monaco, 1412-17 // 1909, Berenson, p. 153 (1932, p. 299; 1963, vol. 1, p. 119) // 1927, van Marle, vol. 9, p. 168, note 3: LM // 1929, Suida, p. 392: LM // 1931, Golzio, p. 63: LM school // 1941, Paatz, vol. 2, pp. 366 and 368: style of LM // 1967, Shearman, p. 28: reports the partial submersion of the cross in the flood of November 1966 // 1975, Boskovits, p. 342: LM, 1405–1410.

COMMENT: In overall design the San Giuseppe *Crucifix* ranks in quality with that at San Giovannino dei Cavalieri (Fig. 70), but the unusually coarse brushwork and the summary drawing of the features indicate haste in production and imply the collaboration of the shop. The stocky proportions of the figure, the complex folding of the loincloth, and the raised gilded rinceau of the halo bring the San Giuseppe *Crucifix* into alliance with that in the Accademia (No. 3153) in Florence (Fig. 69). In both these works the bleeding palms of Christ are exposed, whereas in Don Lorenzo's subsequent crosses the hands close around the wounds. A second cutout *Crucifix* at San Giuseppe, once in the nearby church of Santa Maria della Croce a Tempio, which van Marle (1927, p. 177, note 1) attributed to the school of Lorenzo Monaco, is not related to his style. For further comment on the sequence of cutout crosses, see Catalogue I, Florence, Accademia, *Crucifix*, no. 3153, and Florence, San Giovannino dei Cavalieri, *Crucifix with the Mourning Virgin and Saint John the Evangelist*. [ca. 1410]

§ FLORENCE, Santa Marta, Convento

Crucifix

FIG. 72

Panel (cutout): 319 x 223 cm.
Inscription: (Cross) ĪNRĪ

CONDITION: Structural repairs to the panel and minor areas of inpainting were undertaken in the early 1950s by the Gabinetto dei Restauri in Florence. The conservators were Giuseppe Rosi and Alfio Del Serra. (See Sopr. Gab. Fot. 67693.)

HISTORY: There is no record of previous ownership, nor of when the cross became the property of the Convent of Santa Marta.

LITERATURE: 1955, Baldini, "Note brevi," pp. 81-82: Lorenzo Monaco, 1415-20 // 1955, Baldini, *Mostra . . . VIII esposizione*, p. 17, no. 6 // 1975, Boskovits, p. 343: LM, 1410-15.

COMMENT: Baldini (1955, "Note brevi") suggested persuasively that the *Crucifix* reveals a greater maturity than the Christ of the San Giovannino dei Cavalieri group (Fig. 70) and is most satisfactorily compared with the style of the Uffizi *Adoration of the Magi* (Fig. 82). The tempered rhythms of the loincloth, the clear division between three-dimensional and calligraphic form, and the lessened accentuation of light and dark localize the Santa Marta panel around 1420. The features of the Christ are drawn with a degree of individualization also observed in the central group of retainers of the Uffizi *Adoration*, notably the figure behind the standing Magus. Baldini discerned an analogy between the Santa Marta panel and the Christ of the *Crucifixion* (Fig. 192) in the Museo Bandini, Fiesole. [ca. 1420]

§ FLORENCE, Santa Trinita, Bartolini Salimbeni Chapel

Life of the Virgin

FIGS: 102-119, 198-200, COLORPLATE 15; DIAGRAM, p. 129

Fresco: (Dimensions of chapel, H x W x D) 9 x 5.28 x 4.1 m.; (dimensions of side-wall rectangular frescoes) 210 x 330 cm.
Inscriptions (Prophets in the vault; see the diagram of the chapel): (Micah) ECCE VIRGO CON(cipiet) (Isaiah 7:14); (Isaiah) EGREDIETUR VIRGA DE(radice Jesse) (Isaiah 11:1); (Malachi) ECCE EGO MICTO AN(gel) UM MEUM (Malachi 3:1)

CONDITION AND TECHNIQUE: In 1961-62 the Gabinetto dei Restauri of the Florentine Soprintendenza undertook the restoration of the frescoes, with Giuseppe Rosi as director of the campaign. This abbreviated report on condition and technique is derived from conversations with him after the completion of the project. A separate publication of

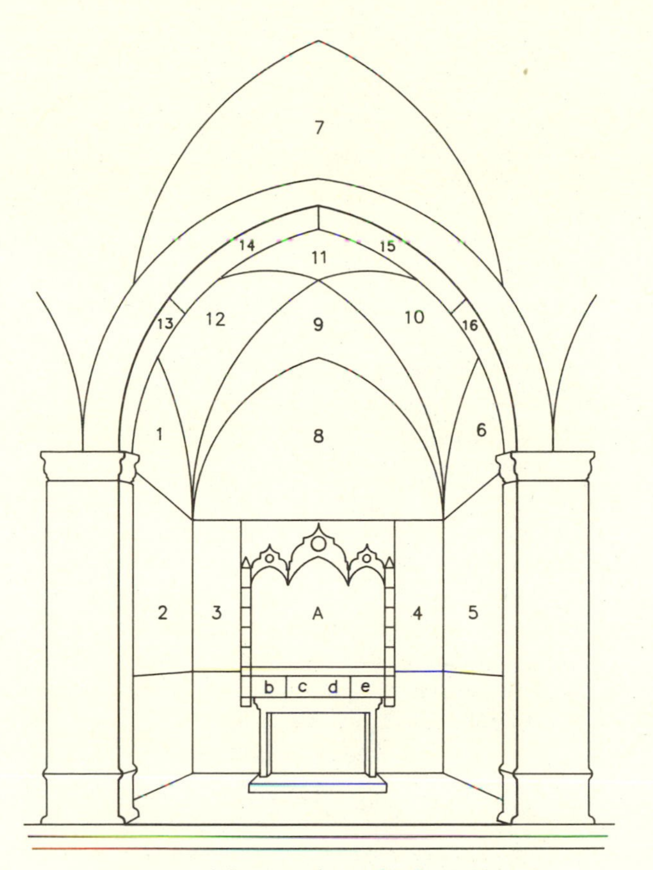

Diagram of the Bartolini Salimbeni Chapel,
Santa Trinita

KEY

1. Expulsion of Joachim, Annunciation to Joachim (Fig. 104)
2. Meeting of Joachim and Anna (Fig. 105)
3. Birth of the Virgin (Fig. 106)
4. Presentation of the Virgin (Fig. 107)
5. Betrothal of the Virgin (Fig. 109)
6. Dormition of the Virgin (Fig. 111)
7. Assumption of the Virgin (Fig. 112)
8. Miracle of the Snow (Fig. 114)
9. David (Fig. 115)
10. Isaiah (Fig. 113)
11. Malachi (Fig. 116)
12. Micah (Fig. 117)
13. Saint Bartholomew (Fig. 118)
14. Saint John the Baptist (Fig. 119)
15. Saint John the Evangelist (Fig. 103)
16. Saint Paul (Fig. 103)

A. Annunciation (Fig. 121)
b. Visitation (Fig. 124)
c. Nativity (Fig. 125)
d. Adoration of the Magi (Fig. 126)
e. Flight into Egypt (Fig. 127)

the restorations in the chapel was apparently planned but not completed.

Two fundamental problems faced the conservator, the first of which was the accumulation and solidification of salts and mold over the surface of the walls, which had virtually obliterated large areas of the mural cycle. The condition had developed over the years through normal seepage and was then accelerated by the weakening of the outer walls of Santa Trinita during the detonation of explosives in the immediate area in 1944. The second problem was encountered in the restorations completed by Augusto Burchi in 1887, in which he undertook the removal of the whitewash that had covered the walls of the chapel since the early eighteenth century. Burchi occasionally did not remove the whitewash, but painted it with passages of his own devising: the roulade of drapery beyond the lowered knee of *Malachi* (Fig. 116) would seem to be one of his remaining inventions, or an inept original addition. Large sections of the dado that were relatively intact after the removal of the whitewash were unnecessarily repainted in order to make them consistent with areas of the dado Burchi had to invent. Also, in gouging out the rays of haloes which had been choked by whitewash, he coarsened numerous segments of the frescoes.

The restoration campaign brought to light various aspects of Lorenzo Monaco's fresco technique. The few sinopie that were uncovered (Figs. 104 and 114) were rapidly and broadly sketched in reds and blacks, an indication that small drawings had provided the models for the frescoes. One passage of sinopia, unrelated to the scene depicted, seems to have been simply a moment of practice with facial types (Fig. 199). Some *spolveri* were found, but are restricted to architecture or decorative detail (Fig. 200). Eve Borsook (pp. xxxv–vi) has noted a similarly limited early use of *spolveri* by Starnina in the ciboria of the Chapel of San Girolamo at the Carmine, and by Masaccio in the dentil frieze of the *Trinity* fresco. There are few traces of the unmodulated blue background, which typically had been painted *a secco* over a reddish ground; the omnipresence of this exposed ground color augments the pinkish tonality of the chapel.

The method of applying the intonaco reveals that Lorenzo and his workshop were not particularly adept in fresco technique, nor comfortable with a major mural commission. In general, the segments of intonaco were illogically applied, with cuts sometimes bisecting haloes and traversing the middle of a hand; in the *Meeting of Joachim and Anna* the ends of Anna's fingers, added *a secco*, have not survived the passage of time. The contours of figures were rarely followed in laying the intonaco; in the *Betrothal of the Virgin* the heads were painted on broad, shallow patches, which partially explains the exaggerated isocephalism in the composition. The extensive destruction of the *Miracle of the Snow* is largely a result of the fact the intonaco was laid in numerous segments. The crudely frescoed bands that decorate the ribs of the vault, possibly executed in an earlier period of work in the chapel (see below), clash with the refined rinceau borders of the frescoes. The tessellated border of the steep lunette of the *Assumption of the Virgin* (Diagram, 7; Fig. 112) is not found elsewhere in the chapel and the vegetal ornament that frames the web above the lunette is a coarse later invention (for a categorized description of the ornamental system of the chapel, see Brown, vol. 1, p. 61; vol. 2, pp. 162, 209, 236, 246, 258, 298, 313, 329, 332, and 350).

Close examination of the walls and the strata of the frescoes during the restoration campaign of 1961-62 produced important structural and pictorial evidence. First, there was originally a splayed lancet window in the altar wall, located about one-half meter to the right of center, which extended upward into the lunette-shaped area of the wall (see Saalman, p. 30 and pl. II; acknowledgment is made of the work of Hannelore Glasser and Berta Leggeri during the restoration campaign). The window was filled in, apparently at the time the fresco cycle was undertaken, in order to gain an uninterrupted surface for the *Miracle of the Snow* located directly above the altarpiece. A second discovery during the restoration campaign, the result of the study of strata behind the *Meeting of Joachim and Anna*, was a complete fresco and its sinopia by Spinello Aretino. The fresco by Lorenzo Monaco was detached to reveal Spinello's *Marriage of Saint Catherine, with Six Witnessing Saints*, in which the triptych format suggests a frescoed altarpiece (Fig. 317). Spinello's fresco, its nearly complete sinopia, and a fragment of a coarsely painted dado were detached, mounted on a new support, and are now displayed in the adjoining chapel (Cappella Sercialli).

There are clear indications in Spinello's uncovered fresco that Lorenzo Monaco respected this earlier work, which his own commission, undertaken some three decades later, required that he obliterate. An unsuccessful attempt was first made to detach the entire fresco, followed by the decision to detach specific passages before covering over Spinello's work in its entirety (see De Benedictis, p. 55). The hammer blows (*martellinatura*) that pock the surface of Spinello's fresco as a means of lending firm adhesion to the new layer of intonaco were struck in a relatively even pattern rather than at random. In addition, valiant but unsuccessful attempts were made to remove from Spinello's work the entire figure of the Christ Child and the heads of the Virgin, Saint Catherine, and Saint Bartholomew, as the chisel marks or strict zones of obliteration around these passages indicate. The fact that of the five male saints depicted in the fresco it was the head of Bartholomew (to the Virgin's right) that Don Lorenzo most apparently sought to preserve, could have been an act of homage not only to Spinello's fresco but to a principal patron saint of the Bartolini Salimbeni family.

In a conversation of May 1985, Giuseppe Rosi informed me that the frescoes are again in urgent need of conservation measures. Through a process of chemical change, induced in large part by the increased acid content in the atmosphere of the city, areas of the already fragile intonaco are being gradually transformed from calcium carbonate into calcium sulfate (gesso). This sulfation of the intonaco has virtually obliterated the *Birth of the Virgin* and the *Presentation in the Temple*, which had been brought to a fairly visible state in the restoration campaign of the early 1960s (Figs. 106 and 107). As the *Meeting of Joachim and Anna*, the only section of the narrative cycle that was detached during the restoration, does not show these effects of sulfation, it is reasonable to assume that all of the frescoes would profit from detachment, in spite of the inevitably diminished liveliness of the intonaco that results from this process.

HISTORY: A search of the archives of the Bartolini Salimbeni family, with the assistance of Gino Corti and with the gracious permission of the late Marchese Dott. Piero Bartolini Salimbeni Vivai, disclosed no mention of the chapel at any point in its history (also see Sirén, 1905, p. 113, note 1). A valuable source of information on the chapel is the study of the Bartolini Salimbeni family by Ildephonso di San Luigi (see Literature, 1786) who records that the family had already assumed the patronage of the chapel by 1363, but not until 1405 was there a decision to undertake a program of decoration. San Luigi, of course, was unaware of the fresco by Spinello Aretino, datable in the early 1390s, on the left wall of the chapel (see above, Condition and Technique). The important role given in that image to Saint Bartholomew implies that the family had commissioned the fresco, paying homage to their patron saint, but its self-sufficiency as a simulated altarpiece in fresco suggests that the Bartolini Salimbeni did not intend a full-scale narrative program. In 1405 the brothers Salimbene and Bartolomeo Bartolini Salimbeni joined to "terminare, abellire, ornare, e finalmente dotare la loro Cappella gentilizia . . ." (p. 237). In May of 1407 the brothers ceded the supervision of the chapel to the Arte del Cambio, with which they had close association as a family of bankers (Document 18A). In addition to the use of the chapel for daily masses, festive masses were celebrated annually on the day of the Annunciation and on an unspecified day in August (see Document 18A, and the Introductory Essay, Note 141). Luciano Bellosi has noted the records of annual payments by the Bartolini Salimbeni family for the celebration of the Mass of the Annunciation in the chapel (1979, p. 62, note 5; citing the archival source), and hypothesized that the reduction from the usual sum of 6 florins to 4 florins in 1420, and the return thereafter to the regular amount, may be explained by the fact that the chapel could not be used fully because of the encumbrance of work in progress on the fresco program. A puzzling issue is raised by a document of March 1434 (or 1435) in which the governing body of the Arte del Cambio indicates that the decoration of the chapel is not sufficiently completed to allow the celebration of mass (Document 18B). This document does not specifically refer to the fresco program, so that the reference could be to some decorative additions that were commissioned during the decade and a half that elapsed between the period of work on the chapel by Lorenzo Monaco and his shop and the document of the mid-1430s. The last mention of the frescoes before their obliteration is in the Cinelli edition of Bocchi (1677, p. 191). Apparently by 1740 the frescoes were hidden under a layer of whitewash, judging from the fact that Don Benigno Davanzati, in his history of Santa Trinita of that year, describes the altarpiece in detail, but pointedly notes that from the outset the chapel was little prized, as is indicated by the absence of pictures and ornament ("Benvero è, che dalla sua prima erezione in qua è stata poco considerata, vedendosi meschina di pitture e di ornamenti . . . ," p. 268). In 1784 the Bartolini Salimbeni family added marble ornamentation to the interior of the chapel (see the dedicatory inscription in Nocioni, p. 36). By 1887 the whitewash had been removed and the extensive restoration completed by Augusto Burchi (see inscription in Nocioni, pp. 36-37). The restoration campaign of 1961-62 is the last step in the chronology.

The figure of *Saint Bartholomew* in the soffit of the entrance arch (Figs. 102 and 118) is fully visible on first entering the church through the right side aisle, a positioning that could have been determined by his role as a principal patron of the Bartolini Salimbeni family.

LITERATURE: Ca. 1516-30, Billi, (Strozziano), p. 361: "Et in S.[a] Trinita . . . La cappella de'Bartolini in detta chiesa dove è lo Sponsalitio di Nostra Donna"; (Petrei), pp. 326-27: ". . . et in s.[ta] Trinita . . . la cappella de Bartolini in detta chiesa dove dipinse lo Sponsalitio di nostra Donna" // ca. 1537-42, Anonimo Gaddiano, p. 77: "Et in detta chiesa anchora dipinse la cappella de Bartolini dove fece lo sponzalizio di Nostra Donna." // 1550, Vasari, ed. Bettarini and Barocchi, Text, p. 305: ". . . in detto luogo lavorò la cappella de' Bartolini" // 1568, Vasari, ed. Bettarini and Barocchi, Text, p. 305: ". . . e nella detta chiesa di S. Trinita la capella de' Bartolini" // 1579, Fortunio, p. 126: "Deinde pinxit ad Templum Sanctae Trinitatis Sacellum Bartholinorum . . ." // 1677, Bocchi, ed. Cinelli, p. 191: (under Santa Trinita) "Cappella degli Ardinghelli nella quale è una Vergine Annunziata di mano di D. Lorenzo; è vaga nel suo genere per esser di quei tempi così è anche dipinta a fresco tutta la Cappella, come la Cappella de'Bartolini ancora" (see Introductory Essay, Note 17) // 1710, Farulli, p. 31: ". . . in Santa Trinita dipinse la Cappella degli Ardinghelli . . . e quella de'Bartolini . . ." // 1740, Davanzati, fols. 268 and 274: mentions only the altarpiece; see quotation above under History // 1755, Richa, vol. 3, p. 163: "Finalmente vengono due Cappelle una de'-Bartolini, l'altra degli Ardinghelli, ambedue erano state dipinte a fresco da Don Lorenzo Monaco Camaldolense . . . ma queste cappelle si veggono inoggi imbiancate, essendo solamente rimaste sull'altare due tavole del medesimo Pittore" // 1786, Ildephonso di San Luigi, p. 237 (under Salimbene II Bartolini Salimbeni): "Fu uomo di gran prudenza, e saviezza, e di singolare pietà, come dimostrè nell'unirsi con Bartolommeo suo fratello l'anno 1405, a terminare, abellire, ornare, e finalmente dotare la loro Cappella gentilizia, posta nella Chiesa di S. Trinita; siccome meglio diremo sotto il nome di esso Bartolommeo"; pp. 268-69 (under Bartolommeo Bartolini Salimbeni): "Di Bartolommeo si rende ancora memorabile la pietà, esso dimostrata spezialmente in due occasioni; la prima nel miglior riattamento della Cappella antica gentilizia, che ha la famiglia fin dall'anno 1363 (*Mem. dell'Archivio di S. Trinita*) nella Chiesa di S. Trinita, mentre nell'anno 1405, per ordine della Repubblica, si restaurò, ed abellì, la Chiesa medesima. Questa cappella, che resta a man ritta, è sotto la invocazione della Vergine annunziata dall'Angiolo, della quale si vede la Tavola dipinta da D. Lorenzo Monaco degli Angeli, che ritenne sempre la maniera di Taddeo Gaddi suo maestro. Or nella detta occasione, dopo aver ridotta in miglior forma detta Cappella, Bartolommeo e Salimbene suo fratello la dotarono, e quindi per Contratto rogato da Ser Cristofano da Laterina, sotto dì Maggio 1407, convennero insieme co'Consoli dell'Arte del Cambio, di cedere ad essa Arte un podere con terre annesse, in luogo detto, *Alla Strada*, nel popolo di S. Piero a Ponti, accomandando agli stessi Consoli la vigilanza, e la cura dell'ufiziatura perpetua della Cappella medesima, con una Messa quotidiana, ed una festa solenne il dì della Nunziata, ed un ufizio annuale de'Morti colle rendite di detti affetti, e colla giunta, che ogni rimanente de'frutti servisse per ornare la stessa Cappella; della quale, in caso di inosservanza di dette cose, si dà la soprantendenza a'Capitano d'Orsanmichele" // 1840, Gaye, p. 433 (describing the *Coronation of the Virgin* from Santa Maria degli Angeli, then at Cerreto): ". . . fra quattro storie della vita di S. Benedetto stanno, sul gradino in mezzo presepio e l'adorazione de'tre Magi, tutte bellissime e quest'ultima simile affatto alla medesima rappresentazione sul quadro dello stesso pittore in Sta. Trinita" // 1842, Fantozzi, p. 570: mentions only the *Annunciation* by Lorenzo Monaco // 1848, Rosini, opp. p. 160: publishes an engraving of a detail from the *Adoration of the Magi* in the predella of the altarpiece // 1864, Crowe and Cavalcaselle, vol. 1, p. 555: mention only the *Annunciation* (1883, vol. 2, p. 341: mention the altarpiece and the fact the frescoes are whitewashed) // 1887, Castellazzi, pp. 43-46: discusses mainly the patronage of the chapel, basing the material largely on the work of Ildephonso di San Luigi // 1896 (1903 ed.), Crowe and Cavalcaselle, vol. 2, p. 300: mention both the altarpiece and the frescoes, which they note have been recently uncovered // 1896, Berenson, p. 119: mentions both the altarpiece and the frescoes (1909, p. 153; 1932, p. 300) // 1898, Tarani, p. 23: the entire chapel was painted by Don Lorenzo, who it is said was a descendant of the Bartolini family; p. 25: records the attribution of the grille to Manfredi di Franco da Pistoia // 1905, Sirén, pp. 113-31: places both the frescoes and the altarpiece at the end of Lorenzo's career, around 1420-24; whereas the *Annunciation* seems somewhat less mature than the frescoes, the composition of the scene and the figure style of the predella suggest a later date; the illegible state of the lunette on the altar wall led to a tentative identification of the subject as an event from the life of San Frediano // 1927, van Marle, vol. 9, pp. 154-60: LM, after 1408 and before 1413 // 1929, Suida, p. 392: LM // 1931, Golzio, pp. 49-54: the final work of LM, the *Annunciation* probably later than the frescoes, indicated by the more advanced spatial representation // 1932/33, Berenson, p. 56: the color of Filippo Lippi's first works virtually allows the observation that he was inspired by having assisted Lorenzo Monaco on the work in the Bartolini Chapel // 1938, Botto, p. 18: no new documentation has come forth on either the patronage or decoration of the chapel // 1938/39, Pudelko, p. 248: LM's final works, ca. 1422-25 / 1953, Paatz, vol. 5, pp. 291 and 256-57: probably 1422-25; the altar wall lunette is identified as the *Miracle of the Snow* // 1958, Levi D'Ancona, "Some New Attributions," pp. 178-80: the frescoes of the *Birth of the Virgin* and *Marriage* are LM's masterpieces; the frescoes may be dated 1422-23 and the altarpiece 1423-24, the climbing roses and morning glories in Gentile's *Adoration of the Magi* of 1423 providing the *terminus post quem* for LM's altarpiece; excepting the *Birth* and *Marriage*, the frescoes are for the most part by Matteo Torelli // 1959, Sandberg-Vavalà, pp. 222-47: illuminating visual analyses of the frescoes and altarpiece; the nearest precedent for the transparency of the color is in the frescoes of Nardo di Cione at Santa Maria Novella; the predella of the altarpiece is singled out for praise // 1963, Berenson, vol. 1, p. 119: LM, 1422-25 // 1965, Bellosi, *Maestri* [p. 7]: LM, ca. 1420 // 1968, Procacci, p. 39, fig. 10: reproduces a detail of the Spinello Aretino fresco found beneath Lorenzo's *Meeting of Joachim and Anna*, using it as an example of an unsuccessful early attempt at detachment // 1970, Meiss, p. 105: colorplate of the high priest in the *Marriage of the Virgin* // 1975, Boskovits, p. 343: LM, 1420-25 // 1979, Bellosi, p. 62, note 5: the fresco program should be dated around 1420, between the Accademia *Annunciation* of circa 1417 and the Uffizi *Adoration of the Magi* of

1422 (see History above) // 1980, Nocioni, pp. 34-37: records all of the inscriptions in the chapel that refer to the patronage and restoration of the decorative program // 1982, Gardner von Teuffel, pp. 1-9: comprehensive observations on the visual and structural integration of the fresco cycle and altarpiece // 1984, De Benedictis, pp. 55 and 59; figs. 50-52: hypothesizes the commissioning of Spinello's work by Bartolomeo Bartolini Salimbeni, before 1390; observations on technical history of Spinello's fresco; Don Lorenzo's cycle ca. 1420-22.

COMMENT: The Introductory Essay cites the numerous references made by Lorenzo Monaco to earlier fresco programs, regardless of subject matter, in composing the murals at Santa Trinita. Cycles devoted specifically to the life of the Virgin were Taddeo Gaddi's in the Baroncelli Chapel at Santa Croce, the Saint Anne Chapel in the Chiostro dei Morti at Santa Maria Novella by a follower of Nardo di Cione, and Agnolo Gaddi's program in the Cappella del Sacro Cingolo in the Cathedral of Prato. Don Lorenzo's sources were essentially Florentine, and at this stage of artistic maturity, derivations were limited to occasional passages. In spite of the profusion of imagery of the life of the Virgin in Sienese art of the Trecento and early Quattrocento, only in two instances in the Santa Trinita cycle did Lorenzo turn to Sienese traditions for models. We have already noted that his depiction of the *Presentation of the Virgin* is a conflation of Florentine and Sienese types and that in the *Betrothal of the Virgin* the "game" of architectural forms is strongly reminiscent of the Sienese predilection for complex structural assemblages (p. 40 and p. 69, Note 149). The assertive division of the *Betrothal* into figural and architectural strata is, in fact, the most clearly Sienese aspect of the Bartolini Chapel cycle. In Florentine depictions of the scene, the settings are obliquely placed porticoes and extended walls that serve as flat backdrops for the dense figural friezes (Ladis, 1982, fig. 4a-11; B. Cole, 1977, pl. 62). Lorenzo Monaco abandoned this simple courtyard setting to suggest, even if ambiguously, the entrance, nave, and sanctuary of a church. He could find models for this complex architectural apparatus in such Sienese *Betrothals* as the now fragmentary frescoes of 1411 attributed to Gualtieri di Giovanni in the Sacristy of Siena Cathedral (V. Lusini, *Il Duomo di Siena*, vol. 1, Siena, 1911, illus. p. 287) or the prototypical scenes from the life of the Virgin on the façade of the Scala Hospital (see M. Eisenberg, "The First Altarpiece for the 'Cappella de'Signori' of the Palazzo Pubblico in Siena . . . ," *Burlington Magazine* 108, March, 1981, p. 136, and figs. 10-13). Although the specific architectural forms in these Sienese examples are not similar to those in the Santa Trinita *Betrothal*, as can be seen from the fragmentary evidence of Gualtieri's frescoes or a late recension on panel by Sano di Pietro (Eisenberg, fig. 12), the prominence of the architecture in the Santa Trinita fresco and its contradictory effect of articulating and competing with the drama is essentially a Sienese device, unknown in Florentine Trecento versions of the subject (also see, Kiel and Neri, p. 69). At the same time, Lorenzo's processional figure composition remained indigenously Florentine, in contrast to the axial placement of the priest, Joseph, and the Virgin found consistently in Sienese images of the Betrothal.

A depiction of the *Miracle of the Snow*, similar in narrative elements and composition to Don Lorenzo's fresco at Santa Trinita, is among the stained-glass windows of the Virgin cycle at Orsanmichele, designed and executed in the first years of the fifteenth century (see Cohn, 1959, pp. 8-9, and fig. 8). Gaetano Milanesi (Vasari, vol. 2, 1878, p. 31) began a tradition of associating Don Lorenzo's name with windows at Orsanmichele when he noted, without offering documentary evidence, that in 1409 the painter had provided designs for Niccolò della Magna. Van Straelen's (pp. 37-38 and 43) attribution to Lorenzo Monaco of the *Annunciation to Joachim* window was prompted by Milanesi's notice, which she accepted as a documented fact. In subsequent studies van Straelen's opinions have been the basis for attribution (Marchini, 1955, pp. 35 and 228, and Boskovits, 1975, p. 343). Herbert Horne, who is credited by Boskovits with the publication of the document of 1409, cited instead a decree of 1397-98 for the decoration of Orsanmichele ("A Commentary upon Vasari's Life of Jacopo dal Casentino," *Rivista d'arte* 6, 1909, pp. 168-69; also see Marchini, 1955, p. 229, note 50). The recent cleaning of the extensively restored *Annunciation to Joachim* window (north wall, center window) would seem to confirm Don Lorenzo's participation in the design and the accuracy of Milanesi's undocumented citation. The voluminous drapery of Joachim recalls the mantles of the New York *Proph-*

ets (Figs. 40-43), which would place the design of the window circa 1408-1410 (Sopr. Gab. Fot. 351901 and 351906).

For the likely presence of Bartolomeo di Fruosino in the collaborative execution of the fresco program at Santa Trinita, see the Introductory Essay, Note 153. [ca. 1422-23]

§ FLORENCE, Santa Trinita, Bartolini Salimbeni Chapel

Annunciation Altarpiece

FIGS. 120-127, 201-202; COLORPLATES 11, 13, 16; DIAGRAM p. 129

Main panel: *Annunciation*
Predella: (Left to right) *Visitation; Nativity; Adoration of the Magi; Flight into Egypt*
Pilasters: (Reading downward) (left) *Saints Stephen, Jerome, Anthony Abbot*, and *Scholastica*; (right) *Saints Augustine, Bonaventura, Bernard*(?), and *Francis*
Pinnacles (roundels): Three *Prophets* (center: *Isaiah* [ECCE VIRGO])

Panel: (Overall) 300 x 274 cm.; (predella) 24.5 x 94 cm. (center, painted surface), 24.5 x 45.5 cm. (sides, painted surface); (pilasters) 31 x 10.5 cm. (painted surface of each panel)
Inscription: (Frame of main panel) AVE. GRATIA. PLENA. DÑS. TECUM. BENEDICTA TU IN MULIERIB̄. QUE CUM AUDISSET TURBATA Ē INS̄MONE EĪ. ET COGITABAT QUALIS (Luke 1:28-29)

CONDITION: In 1961-62, the Gabinetto dei Restauri of the Florentine Soprintendenza undertook the restoration of the *Annunciation Altarpiece*. The conservator was Mario Di Prete. Heavy incrustations of candle grease, soilage, and old varnish were removed from all of the tempera and gilded surfaces. Major vertical fissures at the center of the panel and to the far right were sealed, but left visible in the restored state (Fig. 122). The vines that entwined the three slender tree trunks at the center of the *Annunciation* proved to be later additions. The original lateral consoles beneath the arches of the frame, which provided a transition to the pilasters, had been removed at an unknown date. Modern finials were removed from the frame. All restored gold leaf was stripped from the frames of the predella and pilasters, leaving only the original gilding on the three pinnacles and the bands that border the inscription. The ungilded elements of the frame, which are in large part recent replacements, were given a neutral tone. In order to preserve a physical record of the altarpiece before and after restoration, a small patch of the main panel was left untouched, adjacent to the second panel reading upward in the right pilaster. Recently, the fissures noted above have reopened and await further conservation measures.

HISTORY: See Florence, Santa Trinita, Bartolini Salimbeni Chapel, *Life of the Virgin* (fresco cycle).

LITERATURE: See as above.

COMMENT: The main panel and the predella of the Bartolini Chapel altarpiece rank among the major works of Lorenzo Monaco's career, but the three roundels in the pinnacles and the eight pilaster figures are not from his hand. To confirm this observation, one need only compare the consummately designed and executed predella with the other marginal elements of the altarpiece. The dour, rugged expressiveness of the *Prophet* roundels is indicative of the presence of Bartolomeo di Fruosino, if not in design then certainly in execution, as Levi D'Ancona first observed (1961, pp. 81 and 92), crediting him only with the lateral roundels, although I believe that he is also responsible for painting the central figure of *Isaiah* (Fig. 201). Note the resemblance of his features and coarse hair texture to the two images of *Saint Egidius* on fols. 11v and 35v of a missal at San Marco (Inv. 557), signed and dated 1421 (fol. 11v, Levi D'Ancona, 1961, fig. 2; fol. 35v, Fig. 248). The standing saints in the pilasters are exaggeratedly elongated and summary in the rendering of features and hands, but here an attribution of both design and execution to Bartolomeo di Fruosino is conceivable through several comparisons: the faces of *Saint Anthony Abbot* (Fig. 202, upper left) and *Isaiah* of the center roundel; the extreme elongation and ineffectual hands in Bartolomeo's *desco da parto* of 1428 (Fig. 324); the *Bishop Saint* on fol. 141v of Cod. F 72 in the Bargello (Levi D'Ancona, 1961, p. 84, to Bartolomeo di Fruosino; D'Ancona, vol. 1, 1914, pl. 46).

The blank surfaces in the top framed segment of each pilaster are exactly the size of the panels aligned below, which suggests that two further saints once occupied these positions. Slight traces of pigment on the halo of *Saint Stephen* indicate where two emblematic stones were originally painted.

Lorenzo Monaco's adoption of a long-established Sienese iconography for the Santa Trinita *Annunciation* is noted in the Introductory Essay (p. 42).

John Spencer observed in his iconographic study of the Annunciation (p. 274) that Florentine Trecento painters veered from the Sienese type, which features an open courtyard and covered portico, by extending the canopy of the portico over both the Virgin and Gabriel. Only with Lorenzo's Santa Trinita altarpiece, Spencer proposed, did the "correct" Sienese type reappear in the Florentine tradition. A notable exception to these observations, by an artist who has been shown repeatedly to have had a significant influence on Lorenzo Monaco, is the Cavalcanti *Annunciation* by Giovanni del Biondo of circa 1385, originally in Santa Maria Novella (Offner and Steinweg, sec. IV, vol. V, 1969, pl. XXV[2]). Here the Gabriel genuflects at the threshold that separates an open courtyard from the vaulted portico sheltering the seated Virgin. It would seem more than coincidental that the lofty extension of Gabriel's wings and the position of the Virgin's hands are virtually identical with these same elements in the Santa Trinita panel. The distinctiveness of the Cavalcanti Altarpiece and its likely role in the formulation of Lorenzo's imagery are conveyed by comparison with the *Annunciation* of circa 1375 in the Museo dello Spedale degli Innocenti (Offner and Steinweg, sec. IV, vol. V, 1969, pl. XXIV), where Giovanni del Biondo used the normative Florentine canopied enclosure over the Gabriel; here neither the archangel nor the Virgin bears a trace of resemblance to Lorenzo's figures (also see Bellosi, 1977, p. 232).

In a study of the program in the Bartolini Salimbeni Chapel, Christa Gardner von Teuffel noted that the figure composition and the format of the frame in Lorenzo's *Annunciation* have a source in the Sienese tradition, specifically in Simone Martini's *Annunciation* of 1333, where Gabriel, the seraphic Holy spirit (Simone) or Christ Logos (Lorenzo), and the Virgin are similarly distributed beneath the three arches (1982, p. 5). As Gardner von Teuffel also observed, for the nineteenth-century replacement of Simone's frame, a model was provided by the frame of Don Lorenzo's *Annunciation*. Although Lorenzo surely had referred to Simone's picture in designing the altarpiece at Santa Trinita, the broad arches in his work differ from the steep ones of Simone's altarpiece. This variance may be explained by Don Lorenzo's intention to integrate the *Annunciation* into the design of the fresco cycle, which required that the central arch of the altarpiece approximate the shape of the lunette with the *Miracle of the Snow* immediately above (Fig. 102).

Neither the Sienese iconographical source nor the parallels with the format of Simone's altarpiece, however, lessen the realization that Lorenzo's late *Annunciation* also emerged both from an internal evolution and from Florentine prototypes. The broad, uninterrupted panel surface capped by deeply descending arches had already been used in his *Adoration of the Magi* of circa 1420-22 (Fig. 82), in the *Annunciation* of circa 1418 (Fig. 77), and in the *Coronation of the Virgin* of 1414 (Fig. 44). At this late stage of his career, he of course would have found models in his own work, at the same time he viewed Simone's *Annunciation* with reverence (see Gardner von Teuffel, 1982, p. 5, note 15; the original frame of Simone's altarpiece had been modified as early as 1420). Perhaps the deepest homage that Don Lorenzo paid was to a work more immediately within his artistic milieu, the beautiful *Annunciation* of the 1390s by the Master of the Straus Madonna (Fig. 278), whose circle was so important a cognate culture during the early phase of Lorenzo's work (see Sandberg-Vavalà, 1959, p. 243). The elegant rectilinears, the refined ornamentation of surfaces, the patterned floors, and the beckoning glimpses through windows, doors, and passages inseparably link the two works. The poses and gestures of Don Lorenzo's Gabriel and Virgin are evident variations on that earlier work. Finally, it is the spatial amplitude of the two panels that establishes their underlying accord and that also betrays the arched frame in Lorenzo's altarpiece as an anachronistic invasion of a finely tuned geometry. A decade later, in the Cortona *Annunciation*, Fra Angelico will have banished Gothic intrusions from his classically ordered design (Pope-Hennessy, 1974, pl. 18).

The questions that surround the attribution of the drawing of *Scenes from the Early Life of the Baptist* (Fig. 197) in the Otto Manley Collection in Scarsdale, which have been considered in relation to Lorenzo's late drawing of the *Visitation* and the Santa Trinita frescoes (see Catalogue I, Berlin, Staatliche Museen, Kupferstichkabinett), may also be approached in connection with the *Annunciation*. Similarities between the sophisticated architectural settings are apparent; to the right of the portico housing the Annunciate Virgin and the birth chamber of the Baptist is a narrow passage—one parallel and the other perpendicular to the picture plane—which implies a zone beyond the principal space. The ceilings of the portico and the bedroom are barrel vaulted, but in the drawing there is no suggestion of the articulating transverse ribs; the same barrel vault covers the chamber in Don Lorenzo's fresco of the *Birth of the Virgin* (Fig. 106). Above both roof lines are partially walled terraces, masked in the altarpiece by the encroaching frame. A similar terrace appears in the *Birth of the Virgin*, though nearly obliterated by damage to the wall surface. These links with the frescoes and altarpiece of the Bartolini Salimbeni Chapel further ally the important Manley drawing with the later work of Lorenzo Monaco. [ca. 1422-23]

THE HAGUE, Rijksdienst Beeldende Kunst, no. NK 1488

Madonna Enthroned

FIG. 162

Panel: 124 x 71 cm. (painted surface)

CONDITION: The gold ground is severely abraded and in some areas coarsely restored. For a detailed report, see van Os and Prakken, 1974, p. 71.

HISTORY: Ciampolini Collection, Florence (1886); Joseph Spiridon Collection, Paris; [Spiridon sale, Cassirer and Helbing, Berlin, May 31, 1929, no. 44]; [D. A. Hoogendijk, Amsterdam]; Dienst voor's Rijks Verspreide Kunstvoorwerpen, The Hague; Rijksmuseum Het Catharijneconvent (formerly Archiepiscopal Museum), Utrecht, until 1976.

LITERATURE: 1909, Sirén, p. 36: Lorenzo Monaco // 1927, van Marle, vol. 9, p. 165: LM, in a period considerably later than the *Coronation of the Virgin* of 1413 // 1929, O. Fischel, *Die Sammlung Joseph Spiridon, Paris*, Berlin, no. 44: LM // 1929, Suida, p. 392: LM // 1932, Berenson, "Quadri senza casa," p. 32 (1970, p. 141): the draperies are by Lorenzo Monaco, but the faces are by the same Fra Giovanni da Vallombrosa who executed the *Madonna of Humility* at Sant'Ermete, Pisa (Fig. 146) // 1934, Amsterdam, *Italiaansche Kunst*, p. 88, no. 238: LM // 1974, van Os and Prakken, pp. 71-72: LM school, 1415-25; additional bibliography // 1975, Boskovits, p. 355: LM, 1410-15.

COMMENT: The disproportionate elongation of the torso and the mechanical pleating of the draperies reveal the hand of an assistant who has taken as one of several models Lorenzo's Virgin and Child from the Monte Oliveto Altarpiece, completed in 1410 (Accademia, Florence; Fig. 22). The lavishly brocaded patterns that ornament the Virgin's tunic, the cloth of honor, and the floor covering ally the panel with a cluster of shop works that display a decorative embellishment to which the master himself never subscribed (for further comment, see Catalogue I, Lastra a Signa, San Martino a Gangalandi). The brocaded patterns are virtually identical in the *Madonna of Humility* in the Nelson-Atkins Museum of Art, Kansas City (Fig. 145; also, see Klesse, pp. 221 and 464). A *Madonna of Humility* once in the Kaiser-Friedrich-Museum (Fig. 161) is by the same hand as the *Madonna* in The Hague. In both works the Child is cast from the same mold and the peculiar ascending loops at the hem of the mantle are similarly naive calligraphic motifs. The fall of the Virgin's mantle from the knees and cushion to the floor is a direct reference to the *Annunciation* at the Accademia, Florence (Fig. 79), executed by Don Lorenzo around 1418. The panel in The Hague and the former Berlin picture may be dated, therefore, around 1418-20, and are the works of a shop assistant who combined elements from different phases of the master's style. [ca. 1418-20]

KANSAS CITY, Nelson-Atkins Museum of Art, no. 40-40

Madonna of Humility

FIG. 145

Predella: *Man of Sorrows; Mourning Virgin* and *Saint John the Evangelist*

Panel: 112.6 x 66 cm. (including predella)

CONDITION: The tempera surface is in notably good state, but the upper areas of the gold ground have developed a heavy crackle. The predella, although a separate piece of wood attached to the main panel, would seem to be an original element of the picture, judging by the fact that the black and red painting of the lower series of dentils continues into the outer frame moulding at the top of the predella. Moreover, there are identical patterns of deterioration on the contiguous edges of the main panel and the predella. (Curatorial information, 1984)

HISTORY: Toscanelli Collection, Pontedera, near Pisa, until 1883; Edouard Aynard, Lyon, until 1913; [Hoentshell]; W.P. Bloch, London; [Wildenstein, New York]; Nelson Gallery, 1940.

LITERATURE: 1883, Milanesi, p. 27, no. 205: Jacopo

di Mino del Pellicciaio // 1905, Reinach, vol. 1, p. 196: Jacopo di Mino, but quotes an unpublished attribution to Lorenzo Monaco by Berenson // 1905, Sirén, p. 168: shop of Lorenzo Monaco, by the same assistant who painted the Loeser (now Brooklyn), Louvre, and Berlin Madonna of Humility panels, and the Empoli *Saints* // 1913, *Collection Edouard Aynard*, Galerie Georges Petit, Paris, December 1-4, no. 55, p. 70: LM // 1929, Suida, p. 392; LM // 1932, Berenson, "Quadri senza casa," p. 32 (1970, p. 141): LM, around 1410; the angels and the figures in the predella are not by Don Lorenzo // 1938/39, Pudelko, p. 76, note 2: LM, after 1413 // 1963, Berenson, vol. 1, p. 119: LM // 1972, Fredericksen and Zeri, p. 111: LM // 1975, Boskovits, p. 347: LM, 1415-20.

COMMENT: The picture was produced by an assistant in the workshop who apparently accommodated a normally more austere style to a patron's desire for ornamental embellishment. The brocaded patterns on the Virgin's mantle and on the floor are repeated identically in the *Madonna Enthroned* in The Hague (Fig. 162), which suggests the use of the same decorative motifs by assistants in the shop who were engaged in the production of Madonnas of an elaborate guise (see Klesse, pp. 221 and 464). A complex interplay of drapery forms in Don Lorenzo's Accademia *Annunciation* (Fig. 79) of circa 1418 provided the principal stylistic vocabulary for the talented assistant who painted the Kansas City panel within the years 1418 to 1420. The *Madonna of Humility* in the Thorvaldsens Museum, Copenhagen (Fig. 128), a late work by Lorenzo Monaco, exhibits the sort of unembellished matrix the master provided his collaborators in a shop that reached a peak of activity around 1420. For an earlier shop work that exemplifies this decorative mode, see Catalogue I, Lastra a Signa (Florence), San Martino a Gangalandi. The Child in the Kansas City panel and in the *Madonna* at Sant'Ermete, Pisa (Fig. 146), dated 1415, are variants of the same model. The angels supporting the cloth of honor and the three roundels of the predella are by the hand of a lesser painter, such as the one who was later assigned the pilaster figures in the *Annunciation* of the Bartolini Salimbeni Chapel at Santa Trinita (Fig. 202; Bartolomeo di Fruosino?). The *Man of Sorrows* in the central roundel of the predella echoes an earlier image from Don Lorenzo's workshop, the panel in Bergamo (Fig. 136). A similar predella is found in the *Madonna of Humility* formerly in the Kaiser-Friedrich-Museum, Berlin (Fig. 161), a type that Preiser (pp. 226-27) localized as Sienese in origin. [ca. 1418-20].

LASTRA A SIGNA (Florence), San Martino a Gangalandi, Piccolo Museo Parrocchiale

Madonna of Humility
FIG. 139

Panel: 84 x 49 cm.

CONDITION: There are extensive cracks and some areas of repainting in the Virgin's mantle. The gold background shows abrasion and patching, and the crest of the arched panel is cut away.

HISTORY: The panel was permanently transferred around 1980 from the church of San Romolo a Settimo to the nearby church of San Martino a Gangalandi. There is no record of the provenance of the panel or when it was installed in San Romolo a Settimo.

LITERATURE: 1927, van Marle, vol. 9, p. 130: Lorenzo Monaco, around 1405 // 1929, Suida, p. 392: LM // 1932, Berenson, p. 300: LM, in great part (1963, vol. 1, p. 119) // 1933, Florence, *Mostra del Tesoro*, p. 129, no. 256: LM (erroneously described as a Madonna Enthroned) // 1933/34, Gamba, p. 154: early work of Lorenzo Monaco // 1933, Middeldorf, p. 196: LM // 1938/39, Pudelko, p. 240: LM, around 1405 // 1961, Rossi, p. 44, no. 333: LM // 1966, Castelfranchi Vegas, pl. 82 (in color): LM, first decade of the fifteenth century // 1975, Boskovits, p. 346: LM, 1405-1410.

COMMENT: The former San Romolo a Settimo *Madonna of Humility* is an immediate echo of the cursive style of Don Lorenzo's Empoli *Madonna* of 1404 (Fig. 21). The assistant who executed the work around 1405, probably to satisfy the florid taste of a patron, created the first in a series of shop works by various hands that are marked by a degree of embellishment that is foreign to Lorenzo's personal idiom. For other examples of this ornamental mode, from a later phase of workshop activity, see Catalogue I, Kansas City, Nelson-Atkins Museum (Fig. 145), and The Hague, Rijksdienst . . . (Fig. 162). Klesse (p. 428) noted in the San Romolo panel the exact resemblance of the brocaded cloth of honor to the patterns beneath the lateral saints in the Monte

Oliveto Altarpiece of 1407-1410 (Fig. 24). [ca. 1405]

§ LONDON, Courtauld Institute Galleries, no. 32 (Gambier-Parry Collection, no. 122)

Visitation; and *Adoration of the Magi*

FIGS. 29, 31; COLORPLATE 3

Panel: 20.5 x 32.3 cm.; 21 x 33.3 cm. (painted surface)

CONDITION: The frames are considerably truncated, with only a lobe and angle remaining in each quatrefoil. Below the kneeling Magus and the Virgin in the *Adoration* there is an area of damage that has been coarsely repaired.

HISTORY: James Dennistoun, Edinburgh, until 1855; [Dennistoun sale, Christie's, June 14, 1855, no. 9, as Taddeo Gaddi; sale catalogue reprinted in J. Dennistoun, *Memoirs of the Dukes of Urbino* (1851), ed. E. Hutton (London, 1909), p. 20]; W. Davenport Bromley; [Davenport Bromley sale, Christie's, June 12, 1863, nos. 14 and 15: Giottino]; Thomas Gambier Parry, Highnam Court, Gloucester; Courtauld Institute, University of London, 1966, bequest of Mark Gambier-Parry.

LITERATURE: 1854, Waagen, vol. 3, p. 281: school of Giotto, in disagreement with Dennistoun's ascription to Taddeo Gaddi // 1903, Fry, pp. 126-31: Lorenzo Monaco, among the finest and latest works by the painter; the *Adoration*, however, shows the intervention of a shop assistant, particularly in the head of the second king; a link with the art of Masolino and Masaccio // 1905, Sirén, pp. 57-58: LM, 1408-1412; relates the two panels to the von Kaufmann (now New York, Lehman-Metropolitan) *Nativity* and the Altenburg *Flight into Egypt*, which had previously been associated by Frizzoni (1902, p. 290); the four panels once formed the predella of the *Annunciation* in the Accademia, Florence // 1909, Berenson, p. 153: LM (1932, p. 300; 1963, vol 1, p. 119) // 1927, van Marle, vol. 9, p. 150, note 1, and pp. 166-68: inferior works of Lorenzo's old age; denies Sirén's proposal that the panels formed the predella of the Accademia *Annunciation* // 1929, Suida, p. 392: LM // 1930, London, *Italian Art 1200-1900*, no. 70 (1 and 2); 1931, London, *Commemorative Catalogue*, vol. 1, no. 49 (1 and 2): LM; late work // 1937/38, Sandberg-Vavalà, pp. 34-38: LM, before 1413 and, tentatively supporting Sirén's theory, possibly once formed part of a predella for the Accademia *Annunciation* // 1938/39, Pudelko, p. 77, note 5: LM, ca. 1405; denies a connection with the *Annunciation* // 1961, Oertel, pp. 131-32: LM, ca. 1405 // 1967, Blunt, *Provisional Catalogue*, pp. 39-40: LM, from the middle period of his work, ca. 1405 // 1967, Blunt, "History," p. 115: LM // 1975, Boskovits, p. 347: LM, 1405-1410.

COMMENT: Sirén's (1905) proposal that the four panels of the "Courtauld predella" were once part of the Accademia *Annunciation* (Fig. 77) is disproved by contradictions of style and dimension. The four quatrefoils would have spanned less than two thirds of the width of the *Annunciation*, although missing elements in the series could of course be hypothesized. But the same four subjects comprise the complete predella of the late *Annunciation* (Fig. 120) at Santa Trinita, extending to the full width of the main panel. The "Courtauld predella" is in closest stylistic accord with the Monte Oliveto Altarpiece (Accademia, Florence) of 1407-1410 (Fig. 22), although a more extensive series of panels would be needed to span that work. The fact that Andrea di Giusto's literal copy of the Monte Oliveto Altarpiece (Prato, Galleria Comunale, dated 1435; Fig. 329) incorporates a predella based on his adaptations of both Lorenzo's later style and the work of Fra Angelico, implies that the triptych of 1407-1410 was never accompanied by a predella.

Fry (1903) discerned the hand of an assistant in the *Adoration* and Sirén (1905) saw the intervention of the shop in the von Kaufmann *Nativity*, but the Altenburg *Flight into Egypt* (Fig. 32) would seem to present the strongest evidence of collaboration. The curiously enlarged figure of Joseph appears to stand apart from the physical types and rhythmic coherence of the other elements of the predella.

See Catalogue I, Altenburg, Staatliches Lindenau-Museum, *Flight into Egypt*; and New York, Metropolitan Museum of Art (Robert Lehman Collection), *Nativity*. [ca. 1407-1408]

LONDON, National Gallery

San Benedetto Altarpiece

FIGS. 175, 178, 182-184, 187

Center panel: *Coronation of the Virgin* (no. 1897), 217 x 115 cm.

Left panel: *Adoring Saints* (no. 215), 181.5 x 105 cm.

Right panel: *Adoring Saints* (no. 216), 179 x 101.5 cm.
Predella panels: *Saint Benedict Admitting Saints Maurus and Placidus into the Benedictine Order* (no. 2862), 28.5 x 38.5 cm.; *Saint Maurus Rescuing Saint Placidus and the Visit of Saint Benedict to Saint Scholastica* (no. 4062), 28.5 x 52 cm.; *Death of Saint Benedict* (anonymous loan), 28.5 x 52 cm.

Inscriptions: transcribed in Davies, 1961, pp. 238-39.

CONDITION: The *Coronation* and *Adoring Saints* originally formed a single panel surface. When the panel was divided into three parts at some unknown date, various losses were incurred at the outer edges of the *Adoring Saints* panels where the original frame had impinged and on the inner vertical edges where the continuous panel was severed. The panels are now joined in a modern frame, the losses between the three parts filled in with neutral strips. Each of the separated predella panels originally formed approximately one half of an elongated octagon. No. 2862 is completed by the *Scenes in the Life of Saint Benedict* (Fig. 186) in the Pinacoteca Vaticana, while no. 4062 and the panel on anonymous loan to the National Gallery formed one continuous surface. The panels were all rigorously cleaned in the 1940s. For a detailed report on the physical connections and the condition of the panels, see Davies, 1961, pp. 305-12. Conti (p. 13) proposed that the damage to the lower edges of the London *Coronation* and the heavy crackle and losses of *velatura* in all of the predella panels could possibly be explained by the fact the altarpiece was in the Alberti Chapel at Santa Maria degli Angeli at the time of the major flood of 1557 (for the location of the chapel, see Paatz, vol. 3, 1952, pp. 109 and 113[plan]).

HISTORY: The *Coronation of the Virgin* is surely the altarpiece that Vasari declared was originally located at the Camaldolese monastery of San Benedetto fuori della Porta a Pinti, outside Florence (Vasari, ed. Bettarini and Barocchi, 1550/1568, p. 304; cited only in the 1568 edition). Vasari saw the altarpiece in the Alberti Chapel at Santa Maria degli Angeli in Florence whence it had been transferred after the destruction of San Benedetto during the siege of the city in 1529-30, and where it was still located in 1792 (Follini and Rastrelli, p. 84). There is no record of the date of its removal or dismemberment. The early history and subsequent peregrinations of elements of the San Benedetto Altarpiece in London are presented in detail by Davies (1961, pp. 308 and 311-12).

LITERATURE: Literature relevant to the Comment below is cited here; for a more complete bibliography, see Davies, 1961, pp. 305-312. 1905, Sirén, pp. 63-68: denies the connection between the *Saints* laterals and the *Coronation* panel, first proposed by Crowe and Cavalcaselle (1864, vol. 1, p. 554); the *Coronation* considered a coarse work, possibly by an assistant to Lorenzo Monaco; the side panels, by Don Lorenzo, are from the years 1408-1412, that is, before the Uffizi *Coronation*; a drawing of *Kneeling Saints* in the Uffizi is identified as a preparatory study for the left panel in London; the Vatican *Benedict* panel and another with scenes from the saint's life, then in the collection of Henry Wagner in London (now National Gallery, no. 2862) are connected with the *Adoring Saints* panels // 1927, van Marle, vol. 9, p. 164: confirms Sirén's opinion that the London *Coronation* and *Saints* panels do not go together, and that the *Coronation* is probably not by Don Lorenzo; accepts Sirén's connection of the Vatican and Wagner predella panels with the London laterals, but a date considerably later than 1413 is proposed // 1938/39, Pudelko, pp. 247-48: partially reconstructs the San Benedetto Altarpiece, including the following elements: in the main register and predella, all of the London panels listed above; for the right pinnacle, a *Virgin Annunciate* then in the Liechtenstein Collection in Vienna (now Pasadena, Norton Simon Museum); as pilaster figures, four small panels of *Saints* in Braunschweig; in the spandrel between the *Adoring Saints* and the *Annunciation* pinnacle a small tondo of "St. Cyprianus," once in the Artaud de Montor Collection (now New York, Richard L. Feigen Collection); a date around 1415 is suggested, that is, after the Uffizi *Coronation* of 1414; assistance of pupils is recognized from the fact that the execution of some parts of the altarpiece is not as meticulous as in other works by Lorenzo Monaco // 1949, Davies, pp. 202-210: the three main panels in London are published for the first time since the recent cleaning, which proved conclusively that they once formed a single, continuous surface; the only accessory parts that can be convincingly associated with the main panels are the Benedictine scenes of the predella; the San Benedetto Altarpiece was painted by Lorenzo Monaco after and in imitation of the *Coronation* of 1414 for Santa Maria degli Angeli // 1951, Davies, pp. 238-43: see 1961 edition // 1958, D'Ancona, "Some New Attributions," p. 180, note 25: the London *Coronation* and *Adoring Saints*, and the Benedictine predella panels are by a "copyist" working in the 1420s; the predella scenes may be by Matteo Torelli and the Liechtenstein *Annunciate Virgin* seems more surely to be by him; Pudelko's connection of that panel with the altarpiece is mentioned, but is neither confirmed nor refuted; p. 184, note 40: the same follower may earlier have painted the *Madonna* in Bologna // 1961, Davies, pp. 305-312; repeats the reconstruction proposed in 1949, with a fuller history and technical analysis of the component panels; identifies the *Adoring Saints*; the *Coronation* and *Saints*, although by Don Lorenzo, are lesser works than the Uffizi *Coronation*, to be expected when the differences in destination are considered; the quality of the *Saints* is not as high as that of the *Coronation* panel; the execution of the predella panels is found to be rather weak so that it is "uncertain if they are by Lorenzo Monaco (of predella quality) or by an assistant in his studio" // 1963, Berenson, vol. 1, p. 120: LM // 1965, Bellosi, *Maestri*, p. 6: LM; the caricaturistic aspect of the faces indicates influence of the Maestro del Bambino Vispo // 1975, Boskovits, p. 348: LM, 1410-15 // 1978, Bellosi and Bellini, p. 29: LM, after the *Coronation* of 1414 in the Uffizi (repeated by Bellosi, 1984, p. 311).

COMMENT: The problems of reconstruction, attribution, and chronology of the San Benedetto Altarpiece involve the following works in addition to the panels in the National Gallery, London: Rome, Pinacoteca Vaticana, *Scenes from the Life of Saint Benedict* (Fig. 186); Pasadena, Norton Simon Museum, *Annunciate Virgin* (Fig. 180); Poznań, National Museum, *Adoration of the Magi* (Fig. 185); Florence, Uffizi, Gabinetto Disegni e Stampe, *Six Kneeling Saints* (Fig. 176), and *Saint Benedict Enthroned* (Fig. 63). The technical information and the literature on these works are presented under the individual entries (Catalogue I); the present essay incorporates all of the elements I believe must be included in a consideration of the San Benedetto Altarpiece.

Pudelkos's (1938) and Davies's (1949) integrations of the monastic predella scenes with the three sections of the main panel are the only firmly established reconstructions of the San Benedetto Altarpiece. Pudelko's proposal that the former Artaud de Montor "Cyprianus" (Isaiah) and the Braunschweig *Saints* once formed part of the altarpiece is refuted elsewhere in the catalogue (see Catalogue I, Florence, Accademia, *Annunciation with Four Saints*; and Catalogue II, Braunschweig, Herzog Anton-Ulrich-Museum, *Saints Stephen, Lawrence . . .*). Pudelko's passing suggestion that the Liechtenstein *Virgin Annunciate* (now Pasadena, Norton Simon Museum) once formed the right pinnacle of the altarpiece has gained only limited acceptance, but the connection is demonstrable by physical and stylistic comparisons. Once the reduction from the original size of the Norton Simon panel is taken into account, it is found that the pinnacle has the identical vertical scale relationship to the right side of the London *Coronation* (i.e., 1:2.5) as does the *Annunciate Virgin* pinnacle within the Uffizi *Coronation*. The integration of the Norton Simon panel with the San Benedetto Altarpiece is further confirmed by resemblances to the London panels in details of ornament and setting and in the handling of space. The haloes of the *Annunciate Virgin* and of the adoring angels of the London *Coronation* are identical, and their diadems are similar in ornamentation and in the mode of lacing them to the hair. The Virgin's mantle is bordered with the same trapezoidal meander that embellishes the robes of Christ, the Virgin, and the Baptist in the London panels. Details of anatomy are also identical; the Virgin's upraised hand is a reversed replica of the right hand of the Virgin in the *Coronation*, and the shapes of her nose, mouth, and chin, and the strictly curled locks of hair are repeated in the kneeling angels. The space in the *Annunciate Virgin* panel and the London *Coronation* is achieved by the same architectural means; the tilted dais and the embracing shapes of the throne create a spacious container for the figures, just as do the precisely drawn sections of wall, vault, and platform in the Norton Simon pinnacle. Likewise, the moldings that border these architectural props are identical, with parallel thick and thin lines used to simulate the concave and convex arcs of the cyma recta. The figure style presents further confirmation; the placement of the *Annunciate Virgin* and the fall of her mantle respond harmoniously to the Christ of the *Coronation*, and the sharply accented pockets of drapery are cut from the same cloth. The color chord of the blue mantle lined in salmon pink shot with lavender would have provided a resonant answer to the enthroned Christ and the censer-swinging angel at the lower left of the *Coronation*. With the unmistakable analogies between the San Benedetto *Coronation* and the altarpiece for Santa Maria degli Angeli, it is virtually certain that the remaining pinnacles of the dispersed work would have represented Gabriel at the left and a Blessing Redeemer in the center, directly above the rite of the Coronation.

The two side elements of the predella of the San Benedetto *Coronation* have been definitively integrated with the main register and correspondences of subject matter with the predella of the Uffizi *Coronation* have been noted (Davies, 1949 and 1961). While the episode of the Sacro Speco is omitted from the San Benedetto predella, the scene of *Admitting Maurus and Placidus into the Order* is gained. In this way, each of the two side predella panels begins with an aspect of the lives of Maurus and Placidus (Figs. 183 and 184). But now in the San Benedetto Altarpiece the order of the monastic scenes across the two long octagons is chronological, in contrast to the thematic arrangement found in the four quatrefoils of the Uffizi *Coronation* (see the Introductory Essay, p. 26 and Note 94).

There still remains the question of the central panel of the predella. I propose that the *Adoration of the Magi* in the National Museum in Poznań, considerably altered from the original size and shape, once held that position (Figs. 185, 188, 189). In the predella of the Uffizi *Coronation* the two central panels depict the Nativity and the Adoration of the Magi, and the remaining pairs of quatrefoils narrate events from the life of Saint Benedict (Fig. 44). Since the narrative content of the two predellas is found to be as analogous as other elements of the polyptych, it may be assumed that the center of the San Benedetto predella would also have been devoted to the Infancy of Christ. If the Poznań *Adoration* did serve as the central panel, the Nativity would have had to be omitted. It is fitting that the Epiphany be chosen for a single, elongated panel surface, for the episode invites horizontal extension as the tableau progresses in a narrative crescendo from the retinue, thence to the Magi, and finally to the Holy Family. In fact, of the four known predella versions of the *Adoration of the Magi* attributed to Lorenzo Monaco, the panel in Poznań gives by far the most extended role to the courtly retinue. The unusual omission of haloes from the two younger Magi would seem to have been prompted by the need to allow the arcade to progress rightward without impediment. This same elongated format and central placement of the Adoration was used by Lorenzo di Niccolò in the predella for the *Coronation of the Virgin* of 1402 in San Domenico, Cortona (Berenson, 1963, vol. 1, pl. 394), and by Pietro di Miniato in the upper register of the double predella beneath his *Coronation of the Virgin* in the Galleria Comunale in Prato (documented 1412; Fremantle, fig. 821). The symbolic aptness of the Adoration of the Magi as a marginal accompaniment to the Coronation of the Virgin was observed by Davisson (1971, p. 20): "For as Mary is made the Queen of Heaven with the 'crown of life,' the kings exchange their worldly crowns for the eternal crown by a similar expression of their humility." In the predella of the altarpiece in the Rinuccini Chapel at Santa Croce, Giovanni del Biondo introduced a long central panel that incorporates the Adoration of the Shepherds and Journey of the Magi (Berenson, 1963, vol. 1, pl. 300). One further example of the type, which may have had an indirect but significant influence on Don Lorenzo's Poznań *Adoration*, is a predella panel of around 1370 by Bartolo di Fredi in the Pinacoteca, Siena (Torriti, p. 168). In each of these predellas the center panel is accompanied by pairs of scenes at either side which depict episodes from the lives of the saints represented in the main register of the altarpiece. Lorenzo Monaco could also have known Starnina's elongated *Adoration of the Magi*, now in the Museum in Douai, originally the center of the predella in the Certosa polyptych, painted around 1408 (see Berenson, 1963, vol. 1, pl. 477; for a reconstruction of the predella, see Volpe, pp. 347-55; for the attribution to Starnina and the early dating of circa 1408, see Waadenoijen, 1974, p. 89).

As with the two long side panels of the predella, there is evidence that the Poznań *Adoration* once had the form of an octagonal painted surface on a rectangular panel. Cutting the left end of the panel weakened the compositional function of the tiered rock formation but did not entirely obliterate all trace of the original diagonal corners. Small triangular areas, which still remained at the corners after the cutting, were painted in to simulate a continuation of the original tempera surface, thereby imposing a rectangular shape on the left end of the picture (Fig. 188). This was exactly the means used to square off the four panels that made up the two long side elements of the predella (London and Vatican). But the right end of the Poznań panel shows no evidence of diagonal corners and must therefore have been cut back to a point beyond them, squaring off that end of the originally polygonal pictorial field. The tiny fragment of rock that still juts forth at the lower right corner may indicate that a fuller parenthesis of landscape and architecture originally enclosed this end of the scene (Fig. 189). Indeed, it is likely that the *Adoration* was once bracketed at both ends by the same rising shelves of rock that are used to subdivide the monastic scenes of the predella. These revisions of the Poznań panel drastically reduced the original width, but left the height (29.5 cm.) unchanged. This vertical dimension matches to within a centimeter the four panels that made up the sides of the predella, which in turn vary slightly in their heights. But the present width of the *Adoration* (85.5 cm.) is not satisfactory, being about 20 cm. shorter than the side elements of the predella. This discrepancy may largely be explained by taking into account the total loss of the original right end and the truncation of the left. At least 10.5 cm. were lost through the cutting away of about one half of the diagonal corners of the left side and the total removal of those at the right, an estimate based on the fact that the diagonal corners of the Saint Benedict panels are 7 cm. in width. By adding this approximate loss (10.5 cm.) to the present width of the panel (85.5 cm.), the regained length is 96 cm., or only 8 cm. less than the maximum width of the monastic panels (104 cm.). That remaining amount would have been occupied by a more extensive setting of architecture and rock forms, which provided the seated Virgin with less constricting quarters. Further evidence of the extensive reduction of the original width of the panel is the fact that on the back there remains the impression of a central vertical batten, which now lies 50 cm. from the right end of the reverse and 35.5 cm. from the left. The combined widths of the three elongated predella panels, surely once of equal length, plus the spaces allotted for the frame intervals, would have satisfactorily filled the predella area beneath the continuous surface of the main panel. It is impossible to determine the exact original width of the main panel because of the loss incurred when it was divided into three parts. The present width as reconstructed is 334 cm., whereas the total width of the three predella panels, assuming they were of equal length, would have been approximately 312 cm. (i.e., 3 x 104 cm.), thus leaving at least 22 cm. to be apportioned in the four intervals of the frame.

Along with the thematic and physical connections of the Poznań *Adoration*, the Benedict panels, and the main register, there are numerous stylistic affinities. The major obstacle to stylistic comparison is overcome once it is considered that the participants in the Epiphany must wear more decorative raiment than the simple habits appropriate to the monastic episodes. Nonetheless, shapes of drapery folding could hardly be more closely mirrored than in the cascading mantle carried by the attendant of the youngest Magus and the monastic *cucullus* offered by Saint Benedict in the *Investiture* scene, or in the arabesques repeated so frequently in the robes of genuflecting figures, although in the Poznań panel line is more resilient and the application of the tempera more refined, implying some degree of personal involvement or close supervision by Lorenzo Monaco. The kneeling pose, omnipresent in the predella, is a motif established above in the main register both in the front line of adoring saints and in the semicircle of angels. A less insistent sequence of shapes descends through the seated, voluminously robed figures of the *Annunciate Virgin* of the pinnacle, the Christ of the *Coronation*, and the Virgin of the *Adoration*. There are also close resemblances of face and gesture between the Poznań *Adoration* and other parts of the altarpiece: the profiles of the two younger Magi and the comparably elegant monk in the right foreground of the scene of *Investiture*; the pensive figure who heads the cluster of monks in that same episode and the first attendant in the *Adoration*; the crossed hands of the youngest Magus and those of the Virgin in the *Coronation*. It is inevitable that the same palette would not be used for the *Adoration* and for the monastic episodes, but in spite of the dissimilarities in hue, a light tonality suffuses all of the panels and binds them into a chromatic unity. The same consistency is discerned in the method of constructing space, with the series of scenes punctuated by arches springing diagonally from posts rooted at the picture plane. Decoratively clustered groups of figures are threaded through this series of arches and along a ground plane, which is further articulated by receding architecture and landscape. The dualistic lighting system of the Poznań *Adoration* provides links to the other elements of the predella and to the *Coronation* panel above, and reinforces the proposed central position. While the figures are lighted from the left, as in the London predella panels, the purposeful reversal of illumination in the extended arcade mimics the opposed lighting of the kneeling angels and of the embracing sides of the throne in the London *Coronation* (also see the Introductory Essay, Note 175).

Two further physical aspects of the Poznań *Ado-*

ration help to ally it with the San Benedetto predella. First, the punched ornament of the haloes is the same throughout the Poznań, London, and Vatican panels, although the craftsmanship is notably finer in the haloes of the *Adoration*. Finally, in all of the predella panels the obvious crackle is a consistent network of uneven rectangles, longer on the vertical axis (see Conti's speculation in Condition section above). Evidence of continuity in the wood grain within the predella is lacking since all three panels have been reduced in width to a greater or lesser degree and the original intervals remain indeterminate.

As the range of conflicting opinions suggests, difficult and interrelated questions of attribution and chronology surround the San Benedetto Altarpiece. Inevitably, the *Coronation* of 1414 for Santa Maria degli Angeli must serve as the touchstone and, differences of design aside, a comparison of the two works confirms the marked superiority of that central project of Lorenzo Monaco's career. One need only juxtapose details of heads and passages of drapery in the groups of adoring saints to point up the refinement of modelling and the resiliency of line in the work of 1414 in contrast to the mechanical hardness of facial features, the formulaic draping of cloth, and the brusque handling of the tempera in the London panels (cf. Figs. 178 and 179). The ornamenting of haloes, so resplendent and varied in the Uffizi *Coronation*, is here more modest in the decorative vocabulary and workmanship. But within the London *Coronation* itself, as Martin Davies observed (1961, p. 307), there are differences in quality, the central group of the enthroned Christ and Virgin being more refined in linear rhythms and in craftsmanship than the adoring saints, a contrast comparable to that observed between the central and lateral segments of the predella. Perhaps there is recognizable here, particularly in the panels of *Adoring Saints*, the aggressive brush of the assistant who earlier executed the upper figures of the *Man of Sorrows* of 1404 in the Accademia in Florence (Fig. 18), the *Madonna* in Bologna (Fig. 133) (as Mirella Levi D'Ancona first proposed; 1958), and the Saint John in the San Giovannino dei Cavalieri *Crucifixion* group (Fig. 76). The same assistant or group in the workshop may also have been responsible for the *Crucifixion with Saints Benedict and Romuald* in Altenburg (Fig. 173) and the *Crucifixion* in the Yale University Art Gallery (Fig. 174). Further confirmation of the important role of the workshop in the San Benedetto Altarpiece was provided by a technical study of the modelling in the mantle of the Virgin in the Norton Simon panel (Muller, 1978, pp. 10 and 16, note 5). The sharp division between highlights and middle tones in this panel were deemed atypical of Lorenzo's autograph works. These same unmodulated contrasts and the absence of the master's luminosity are likewise characteristic of the other elements of the San Benedetto Altarpiece.

Two drawings on a single sheet in the Gabinetto Disegni e Stampe of the Uffizi provide substantial evidence for the approximate date of the San Benedetto Altarpiece and its relationship to the *Coronation of the Virgin* from Santa Maria degli Angeli. Degenhart and Schmitt, building on the theories of van Marle and Oertel (q.v., Catalogue I, Florence, Uffizi, Gabinetto Disegni e Stampe, 11 E., Literature, 1927, 1940, and 1968) have demonstrated from several standpoints that the two-sided drawing, representing *Six Kneeling Saints* on the recto and the *Enthroned Saint Benedict* on the verso, reveals the stages of conception and execution of the San Benedetto Altarpiece. The *Saint Benedict* (Fig. 63), drawn directly in rapid strokes of the reed pen, was Lorenzo Monaco's initial idea for the center of the altarpiece, a fitting theme for the Camaldolese monastery of San Benedetto. The *Kneeling Saints* (Fig. 176) still echoes the Uffizi altarpiece in the use of celestial arcs beneath, but the front row of saints is identical in personage, placement, and drapery style to the left panel of the London *Coronation*; the arcs would be abandoned in favor of a continuous patterned floor. Unlike the spontaneous drawing of the *Saint Benedict*, the *Kneeling Saints*, being adapted from an already existing model, were drawn first in a sketchy silverpoint outline and then completed with a less fluent pen. The inclusion of Saint Benedict in the group implies that the idea for the new altarpiece had been changed from one with the saint at the center into a Coronation of the Virgin. One important element of the *Saint Benedict* drawing, however, survives in the completed project: the throne is essentially the same as that in the London *Coronation*.

Degenhart and Schmitt's cogent theories may be advanced a step farther with the proposal that the differences in quality between the two sides of the Uffizi sheet—the *Saint Benedict Enthroned* being an autograph work by Lorenzo and the *Kneeling Saints* a less effective production of the shop—indicate that the master turned over much of the project for San Benedetto to an assistant once the commission became a version of his work already on the high altar at Santa Maria degli Angeli. The qualitative differences between the two drawings are recognized on comparing the assurance of contour and modelling line in the *Saint Benedict* with the timid and even faltering draughtsmanship of the *Kneeling Saints*, or the penetrating gaze of the former with the cursory features of the latter. The shift of Benedict's discipline and book in Lorenzo's drawing shows an idea taking shape on the paper. The San Benedetto *Coronation* may be seen then to rely on an authoritative model, but also to incorporate the transformations formulated in preparatory drawings. In the *Kneeling Saints* drawing and the London panel (no. 215) Saint Matthew is in a place of honor, the first at the right in the front row. Davies (1961, p. 308, quoting Moreni) noted that the monastery of San Benedetto had been briefly dedicated to Matthew, which could provide further evidence that the altarpiece was from the outset intended for San Benedetto. The placement of Matthew could be considered a continuing homage to the original patron. In the Uffizi *Coronation*, Matthew is placed in the second tier of saints.

Regardless of inadequacies in the quality of the San Benedetto *Coronation*, the work stands as a major embodiment of advances in spatial representation within the culture of Lorenzo Monaco's shop, reflective of the master's impulse. The continuous patterned floor in the main register provides a foundation for the participants in the tableau and for the tilted dais at the center. There is, however, a contradiction to this spatial recession in the traditional method of stacking tier on tier of figures that cling as groups to the picture plane and counter the inward path of the eye. The diminished size of the Christ and Virgin at the center in relation to the lateral saints intensifies the illusion of a focal group placed at a greater distance from the observer. In the Uffizi *Coronation* the central and lateral elements are on the same scale, which reinforces the planarity of the composition. With the London panel the eye is led into the sacred enclave by the draperies of the kneeling angels which overlap the edge of the patterned floor, an illusionistic device that appears in the Norton Simon *Annunciate Virgin* and had been anticipated a decade earlier in the Isaac of the New York *Abraham* (Fig. 41). The London *Coronation* clearly manifests within the painter's milieu an augmented concern for pictorial space.

It is in the peripheral components of the San Benedetto Altarpiece rather than in the main panel that a consistent representation of space has been achieved. In contrast to the setting for the Annunciate Virgin in the pinnacle of the *Coronation* of 1414 (Fig. 60), which is a conventional assemblage of bench and abbreviated portico, the Annunciate Virgin from the right pinnacle of the San Benedetto Altarpiece (Fig. 180) is enclosed in a coherently defined structure, with continuation of the architectural space implied in the truncated barrel vault. In the predella of the San Benedetto Altarpiece there is a comparable enhancement of space. In the London version of the *Rescue of Placidus and Benedict's Visit to Scholastica* the separate zones of the narrative are joined by a continuous ground plane and by the directional thrusts of architecture and landscape, the same devices that bind the episodes of the *Legend of Onuphrius* panel in the Accademia in Florence (Fig. 95). In the Placidus-Scholastica panel (Fig. 57) of the 1414 *Coronation* the composition is more additive, the lobes of the quatrefoil being used to clarify the segments of the composition and at the same time strengthen the calligraphic unity of the image. Consistent with this augmented concern for space in the San Benedetto Altarpiece is the abandonment of the quatrefoil in favor of a shape that removes the barrier between the observer and the picture (see the Introductory Essay, Note 121). Obliques recede deeply and rapidly, and the frontal surfaces of buildings are no longer so securely bound to the picture plane (cf. Figs. 57 and 184); the housing of solids within voids has gained in sophistication, although the fulfillment of this deepening concern for space in the art of Lorenzo Monaco will be attained in his works of the early 1420s, such as the Uffizi *Adoration of the Magi* and the frescoes and altarpiece at Santa Trinita. Just as in the Norton Simon *Annunciate Virgin* pinnacle, the figures of the San Benedetto predella are contained within spaces that are securely established by architectural members, for example, the barrel-vaulted refectory in the Placidus-Scholastica scene. The spatial realism of the predella is enhanced by the frequent depiction of principal figures in three-quarter view, whereas the profile is more commonly found in the predella of the 1414 *Coronation*; the two Saint Benedicts in each of the Placidus-Scholastica panels exemplify the difference. And in what would seem to be a conscious rejection of the persistent Trecento formula of the parapet and wing setting in the *Death of Saint Benedict*—a device used in the predella of 1414—in the London version the bier lies diagonally against the picture plane, while the numerous exits and entrances suggest the labyrinthine passages of a monastery (cf. Figs. 49 and 187). The consistency in the spatial innovations of the San Benedetto predella and one surviving pinnacle, and the degree to which they provide a bridge to Lorenzo's later style, lead to the conclusion that the master was more involved with the design of the marginal elements of the altarpiece, where he continued to develop his art on the scale he had always found most comfortable, one that freed him from the conventions of the large icon.

Although the evidence is clear that the San Benedetto Altarpiece was produced after the *Coronation of the Virgin* of 1414, there remains the question of a more exact chronological placement in relation to the principal autograph works of Lorenzo Monaco. If, as I believe, the *Saint Benedict* drawing in Florence was the original idea for the center of the altarpiece, by establishing a date for that drawing, a *terminus post quem* for the San Benedetto Altarpiece could be surmised. A date around 1415 would seem to be most satisfactory for the *Saint Benedict*, that is, after the *Coronation* for Santa Maria degli Angeli and contemporary with the *Crucifixion* group at San Giovannino dei Cavalieri. Benedict's cassock and the mourning Virgin's mantle are from the same moment in Lorenzo's art (see Figs. 63 and 75); note the deep trenching of the drapery along the torso and the radiation of the folds downward from the knee, flattening to an arabesque at the floor. It was observed, in turn, that the mourning Virgin at San Giovannino dei Cavalieri is a direct offshoot from the Annunciate Virgin (Fig. 60) in the right pinnacle of the *Coronation* of 1414.

By combining the evidence that the *Saint Benedict* drawing would seem to date no earlier than 1415 with the fact that the London *Coronation* and its allied elements anticipate an even more evolved space, a dating for the San Benedetto Altarpiece between 1415 and 1420 would seem most appropriate. Even in his *Annunciation* of around 1418 (Fig. 79), where the calligraphy and silhouette comprise the dominant effects, Lorenzo Monaco contrasted an insistent surface linearism with the oblique thrust of the Virgin's dais and the turn of Gabriel at three-quarter angle to the flat expanse of gold ground. Could this figure of the archangel give some hint of the image in the lost left pinnacle of the San Benedetto *Coronation*? Surely that Gabriel would not have been shown in strict profile, as he appears in the altarpiece of 1414 (Fig. 59). It is in these same years (late 1410s) that the so-called Master of 1419 was joining the elements of altarpieces with a continuous and patterned ground plane, another modest but fundamental indicator of the impulse of Florentine art toward the spatial realism that would preoccupy the artists of the second quarter of the century (see *European Paintings before 1500*, The Cleveland Museum of Art, 1974, pp. 89-91, figs. 33b and c). Much of the design and execution of the San Benedetto Altarpiece were assigned by Lorenzo Monaco to his shop collaborators, but the work announces the master's direction within the currents of Florentine art on the threshold of the Renaissance. [1415-20)

Note: John Shearman kindly brought to my attention a Master of Arts Report, written under his direction at the Courtauld Institute of Art, in which documentary material transcribed in an eighteenth-century source is interpreted as supportive evidence that the San Benedetto Altarpiece was executed before that of 1414 from Santa Maria degli Angeli (M.-L. Frawley, "Lorenzo Monaco and His Patrons," University of London, 1975); as this essay is not released, comment would not be appropriate.

LONDON, National Gallery, no. 5224

Saint Benedict in the Sacro Speco at Subiaco
(fragment)
FIG. 196

Panel: 29 x 26 cm. (excluding gilded and painted borders)

CONDITION: The entire surface of the panel is heavily abraded. The decorative border at the top and the inscription at the bottom were added at some later date over areas of the original panel (for further technical analysis see Davies, 1961, p. 314).

HISTORY: [Bottenwieser, Berlin]; [Thos Agnew & Sons, London]; Lord Rothermere, 1927; presented to the National Gallery by Viscount Rothermere, 1940.

LITERATURE: 1930, London, *Exhibition of Italian Art*, no. 68; 1931, London, *Commemorative Catalogue*, no. 47: Lorenzo Monaco // 1932, Berenson, p. 300: LM, a late work // 1951, Davies, p. 244: (see 1961 ed.) // 1958, Levi D'Ancona, "Matteo Torelli," p. 258: not by LM; perhaps part of the predella of the London *Coronation of the Virgin* // 1961, Davies, pp. 313-14: much in the style of Lorenzo, but not certainly or even probably by his hand; clearly not connected with the London *Coronation* predella; additional bibliography // 1963, Berenson, vol. 1, p. 120: LM; a repainted fragment // 1975, Boskovits, p. 348: LM, 1415-20.

COMMENT: The style of the *Sacro Speco* fragment is closely related to the scenes from the predella of the San Benedetto *Coronation of the Virgin*, but Davies (1961) justly denied that the panel was ever part of that altarpiece. Further supporting Davies's opinion is the fact that the pattern of the crackle in the *Sacro Speco* panel is distinctly different from that found throughout the panels of the San Benedetto predella (see Catalogue I, London, National Gallery, San Benedetto Altarpiece).

The exact parallelism in the elements of the London fragment to the left half of Taddeo Gaddi's fresco in the Refectory at Santa Croce representing the *Priest at the Easter Meal Receiving Word from an Angel of Saint Benedict's Hunger in the Wilderness* (Ladis, fig. 23-26), makes it virtually certain that the lost segment of the London panel depicted this same episode in Benedict's life (see Davies, 1961, p. 314). The theme is not included in the predellas of the *Coronation* altarpieces for Santa Maria degli Angeli and San Benedetto. [1415-20]

LUGANO, Thyssen-Bornemisza Foundation, no. 167 D

Madonna Enthroned, with Six Angels
FIG. 159

Panel: 147.3 x 82.5 cm. (painted surface and gable)

CONDITION: The picture was restored by Mario Modestini in the early 1960s and lightly cleaned by Marco Grassi early in 1982. Older photographs show an unornamented truncated gable. The gilded scrollwork now on the surface of this original gable is modern, as are the base and two-level pilasters of the frame.

HISTORY: Private collection, Florence, 1887; James Young, Kellie on the Clyde, Scotland; Mrs. J. Walker (Miss Young), Limefield, West Calder, Midlothian, Scotland; Miss Alice M. Thom, Glasgow; [Knoedler & Co., New York]; Heinemann Collection, New York; Thyssen-Bornemisza Foundation, 1981.

LITERATURE: 1958, *Connoisseur*, 142, no. 573, p. lxv (illus.): Lorenzo Monaco // 1962, *The Arts of Man*, Dallas Museum of Fine Arts, no. 45: LM // 1975, Boskovits, p. 349: LM, 1410-15 // 1983, Pope-Hennessy, p. 12; pl. XII, in color: LM, not long after 1410.

COMMENT: As John Pope-Hennessy suggests (1983), the imposing size of the Thyssen-Bornemisza panel indicates that it was originally the center element of a pentaptych, with lateral panels probably occupied by paired saints, as in the Monte Oliveto Altarpiece, dated 1410 (Fig. 22). Should panels come to light that were likely to have been the laterals of the altarpiece, the measurement in the Lugano panel of 101.6 cm. from the base of the painted surface to the springing of the arch would be useful evidence in an attempted reconstruction. Although the Monte Oliveto Altarpiece was the model for the type of polyptych, more than a decade separates it from the Thyssen-Bornemisza *Madonna*. Roberto Longhi (*in litteris*, 1956) recognized the characteristics that mark the panel in Lugano as a late work, but I am unable to concur with his unqualified attribution to Lorenzo Monaco. The picture was designed by him, but the execution was the work of the shop. The draughtsmanship has none of the brilliance of the Annunciate Virgin in the Santa Trinita altarpiece (Figs. 121 and 123) or of the *Adoration of the Magi* (Figs. 82 and 84), autograph works that provide standards of judgment. The long contour of the left side of the Virgin's mantle is hesitant and unresolved, the brushwork is coarse, as the textures of hair especially reveal, and the mannered angels caricature Lorenzo's types. The angular pose of the angel at the left of the throne recalls the monk with the censer in the Pallavicini *Funeral of Saint Francis* (Fig. 191), a late work of the shop. Further alliances of the Lugano picture with the later productions of Lorenzo's workshop are the high key of the color and the ungraduated shifts from dark to light, effects that are concentrated in the brilliant coral red of the tunics worn by the full-length angels and in the Child's rose and pink mantle. These passages of intense and unintegrated color recall the palette of the *Annunciation* formerly in the Féron-Stoclet Collection, Brussels, and contrast with the finely modulated palette that is a hallmark of the later phase of Don Lorenzo's work (see Colorplate 14).

Regardless of the intervention of the workshop in the execution of the *Madonna Enthroned*, the conception of the picture is fundamental evidence of Don Lorenzo's deepening interest in the illusion of space that came to be fulfilled in the frescoes and altarpiece of the Bartolini Salimbeni Chapel at Santa Trinita. It was again a work that was partially designed and largely executed by the shop—the San Benedetto Altarpiece (London, National Gallery), of around 1415 to 1420—that first clearly augured this trend in Don Lorenzo's style. As with the work in the Bartolini Chapel, the calligraphy in the Lugano picture is modestly active; the primary shapes of the Child's mantle are now columnar and his pose is erect (cf. Fig. 22). How much more unified is this design than that of the *Madonna of Humility* of 1413 (Fig. 143), where the contrast between the flowing forms of the Virgin and the rectilinears of the Child seem to have arisen from the opposing wills of master and pupil. A further comparison, with the *Madonna Enthroned* in Edinburgh (Fig. 158), demonstrates the change away from a predominantly calligraphic style that occurred around the turn of the decade. As Longhi recognized, the Thyssen-Bornemisza picture brings Don Lorenzo's Madonna compositions to their farthest point of development; it is a short path to Angelico's San Marco *Madonna Enthroned* (Fig. 334) or to the *Madonna Enthroned* by Masolino, originally the center panel of the Carnesecchi triptych at Santa Maria Maggiore in Florence (Micheletti, pl. 19). [ca. 1422-23]

§ MONTE SAN SAVINO, Santa Maria delle Vertighe

Crucifix

FIG. 71

Panel (cutout, painted on front and back): 127 x 84 cm.

CONDITION: A deep fissure runs through the upper left arm of Christ and into the adjoining areas of the halo, where the losses of gold leaf have been crudely patched. The truncated top of the staff implies the loss of an inscribed crest. On the reverse of the cross, the back of Christ's head and the adjoining areas of the staff and crossbar are totally effaced, but otherwise the painted surface is intact (see Florence, Sopr. Gab. Fot. 169241).

HISTORY: After the destruction of the Camaldolese monastery of San Benedetto fuori della Porta a Pinti during the siege of Florence from 1529 to 1530, the title of the foundation was transferred to Santa Maria delle Vertighe. The monks from San Benedetto moved there with "tutti i mobili" (see Farulli, 1710, pp. 201 and 286); the *Crucifix* could have been transferred from Florence to Monte San Savino at that time.

LITERATURE: 1922, Salmi, p. 359: Lorenzo Monaco // 1950, Moriondo, p. 83, no. 253: LM // 1955, Baldini, p. 81: LM; confirms the attribution of the *Crucifix* at the Convento di Santa Marta, Florence // 1955, Eisenberg, pp. 45-46: LM, 1415-20 // 1963, Berenson, vol. 1, p. 120: LM // 1965, Bellosi, *Maestri*, [p. 6] and pl. 8 (in color): LM; the most beautiful of his cutout crosses // 1970, Bellosi, et al., *L'Arte in Valdichiana*, p. 19, no. 23: LM, 1415-20; additional bibliography // 1975, Boskovits, p. 349: LM, 1410-15.

COMMENT: In the proportions of the corpus, the tempered depiction of anatomical detail, and the configurations of the loincloth, the Monte San Savino processional cross is most closely allied with the Christ in the San Giovannino dei Cavalieri *Crucifixion* group (Fig. 70) of circa 1415. The contrast between the refined handling of the tempera medium and the coarse, even slovenly, ornamentation of the gilded halo is an indicator of the degrees of collaboration and competence of shop assistants in the extensive production of this type of cutout cross. [ca. 1415]

MOSCOW, Pushkin State Museum of Fine Arts, no. 144

Madonna of Humility

FIG. 142

Canvas, transferred from panel: 74 x 50 cm. (painted surface)

CONDITION: The painted surface has been ineptly restored and the gold ground renewed, perhaps in 1889 when the picture was transferred from panel to canvas. The base of the modern frame is inscribed with the fictitious date of 1400 (AVE MARIA GRATIA PLENA. AMCCCC).

HISTORY: Palazzo Strozzi, Florence, unknown date; D. A. Homiakov Collection, Moscow; Rumiantzev Museum, Moscow, 1901; Pushkin State Museum of Fine Arts, Moscow, since 1924.

LITERATURE: 1905, Sirén, p. 190: reports word of a *Madonna* in Moscow attributed to Lorenzo Monaco // 1924, Lazareff, pp. 124-26: LM, around 1400, about the time of the *Madonna* in Berlin (now destroyed); the inscribed date is not original; shows Lorenzo's essentially Florentine root; close in style to the Fischer *Madonna of Humility* (now Metropolitan Museum, New York) // 1927, van Marle, vol. 9, p. 130: LM // 1929, Suida, p. 392: LM // 1932, Berenson, p. 300: LM, early (1963, vol. 1, p. 120: 1400) // 1938/39, Pudelko, p. 238, note 13: LM, from the time of the Empoli *Madonna* of 1404; related in style to the *Madonna of Humility* in the Metropolitan Museum // 1975, Boskovits, p. 349: LM, 1405-1410 // 1975, Fremantle, p. 639: LM, 1400.

COMMENT: The Moscow *Madonna* would appear to be the work of the same assistant to Lorenzo Monaco, under his close supervision, who painted the *Madonna with Four Saints* (Fig. 138) in the Accademia, Florence, dated 1408. Comparable aspects of the two works are the light and flowery palettes and the facial types of the Child and angels. In rendering the upper half of the figure of the Virgin, the painter of the Moscow panel depended on Don Lorenzo's Monte Oliveto Altarpiece (Fig. 23), dated 1410, which was still in the studio when this assistant was at work on the Accademia, Moscow, and other allied pictures. The less competent painter of the Metropolitan Museum's *Madonna of Humility* (Fig. 141) adopted closely similar models for the Child and for the adoring angels. [ca. 1408-1410]

MUNICH, Alte Pinakothek, no. L.970

Saint Peter

FIG. 172

Panel: 53.5 x 39.8 cm. (painted surface)

CONDITION: Losses in the paint surface have obliterated the right end of the bench and the lower right folds of the mantle. Much of the original gold ground has disintegrated. Areas of the mantle and tunic were inpainted when the panel was restored in Munich around 1960. Given the closeness in size and format to the four *Prophets* (Figs. 40-43) in the Metropolitan Museum, New York, it seems likely, as Federico Zeri suggested (1971, p. 63), that a strip of panel was removed below, which would have contained the riser of the platform. Fig. 172 records the state of the picture after the intervention of 1960.

HISTORY: The late Adelheid Freifrau von Lotzbeck informed me (*in litteris*, 1956) that the panel came into the possession of her husband's family in the mid-nineteenth century. Since the late 1950s the picture has been on long-term loan to the Munich gallery from the Lotzbeck Collection at Nannhofen, near Augsburg.

LITERATURE: 1896, Berenson, p. 119: Lorenzo Monaco // 1905, Sirén, pp. 43-44: LM, ca. 1403-1405; associated with a *David* in Cassel (now Metropolitan Museum, New York) // 1909, Berenson, p. 153: LM, an early work (omitted from 1932 and 1963 editions) // 1927, van Marle, vol. 9, p. 168, note 3: LM // 1929, Suida, p. 392: LM // 1938/39, Pudelko, p. 238, note 13: LM; mentioned with the *David*, formerly at Cassel; later than 1405, the Berenson *Madonna of Humility* serving as comparison // 1958, Meiss, pp. 192 and 195-96: by a weaker hand in Lorenzo's shop; probably not from the same series as the four Metropolitan panels, although the possibility must still be considered // 1966, Montebello, p. 167: possibly by Lorenzo Monaco // 1971, Zeri pp. 62-66: appears to be slightly inferior in quality to the four panels in the Metropolitan Museum, which could be due to the participation of the workshop, although it is difficult to be precise about the quality of a picture in such a rubbed and repainted state // 1975, Boskovits, p. 349: LM, 1405-1410. // 1975, Kultzen, p. 66, no. L.970: LM; from the same series as the four New York panels; ca. 1410 (1983, Munich, pp. 299-300).

COMMENT: For a discussion of the relationship between the *Saint Peter* and the four Old Testament panels, see Catalogue I, New York, Metropolitan Museum of Art, *Abraham, Noah, Moses*, and *David*. The *Saint Peter* is not so restored as to mask the quality of the original work, which is inferior to that of the four *Prophets*; the shapes of the mantle from shoulder to floor on the left side of the figure are fully intact and the area of the head is virtually free of damage or restoration. But the drapery is flaccid and lacks the physical substance that amplifies the psychological force of the Metropolitan's figures, where, to use Susanne Langer's phrase from another context, "every line is composition." A telling contrast may be drawn between the blousing of the tunic at the waist in the *Noah* (Fig. 42) and the *Saint Peter*. The hard drawing and mechanical modelling of the face and hair recall works by assistants in Lorenzo's shop ranging from the Bologna *Madonna Enthroned* (Fig. 133) to the London *Coronation of the Virgin* (Fig. 175) and the Altenburg *Crucifixion* (Fig. 173). The lack of structural accents of light and dark would seem to be the result of artistic reticence rather than, as Zeri has proposed (1971, p. 63), an indication that the *Saint Peter,* with the light falling on him centrally and evenly, was located somewhere in the middle of the ensemble while the more intensely lighted New York figures were at either side. The odd emergence of the toes directly on the axis of the figure recalls a similar quirk in the Saint John the Evangelist of the *Crucifixion* at San Giovannino dei Cavalieri (Fig. 76), the element of that impressive group that betrays the lesser talent of an assistant. [ca. 1408-1410]

NEW HAVEN, Yale University Art Gallery, James Jackson Jarves Collection, no. 1871.24

Crucifixion with God the Father, the Mourning Virgin, and Saint John the Evangelist

FIG. 174

Panel: 64.9 x 37 cm.
Inscriptions: (Cross) INRI; (God the Father) AΩ

CONDITION: The *Crucifixion* was among the group of early Italian panels in the Yale collection submitted to rigorous cleaning and removal of repaint in the late 1960s. For a report on the condition, see Seymour, 1970, p. 163.

HISTORY: James Jackson Jarves Collection, Florence; acquired by Yale University in 1871.

LITERATURE: 1860, Jarves, p. 43: Giotto // 1868, Sturgis, p. 33: Giotto // 1905, Perkins, p. 76: school of Bartolo di Fredi // 1905, Sirén, pp. 91 and 189: Lorenzo Monaco, not before 1415 // 1908/1909, Sirén, p. 325: latest and finest of Don Lorenzo's *Crucifixion* panels // 1916, Sirén, pp. 67-69: LM // 1927, Offner, *Italian Primitives at Yale*, pp. 5 and 21-22: LM // 1927, van Marle, vol. 9, pp. 147-48: LM, around 1413 // 1929, Suida, p. 392: LM // 1931, L. Venturi, pl. 142: LM, 1412-15 // 1932, Berenson, p. 300: LM (1963, vol. 1, p. 120) // 1938/39, Pudelko, p. 248, note 35: LM, 1415-20 // 1970, Seymour, pp. 163-65: close follower of Lorenzo Monaco, ca. 1410-15?; additional bibliography // 1972, Fredericksen and Zeri, p. 111: LM // 1975, Boskovits, p. 350: LM, 1400-1405.

COMMENT: The Yale *Crucifixion* was designed and executed by a distinctive assistant in the shop of Lorenzo Monaco soon after 1415, following Lorenzo's deeply pathetic *Crucifixion* group at San Giovannino dei Cavalieri, Florence (Fig. 74). The forceful bulk and closed contours of the Virgin and Saint John in the Yale panel imply the involvement of the hand that a half decade earlier had executed the *Crucifixion* in Altenburg (Fig. 173). Morphological similarities help strengthen the connection: the facial features of the mourning Virgin are closely akin to those of the transfixed Saint Francis and the elongated right hand of the Virgin has a virtual replica in that of Saint Benedict. The attenuation of the corpus in the Yale panel and the elaborate arabesques of Christ's loincloth and of the mantle of God the Father above suggest a date around 1415 to 1420. The hovering God the Father foreshadows the figures afloat in the pinnacles of Lorenzo's *Adoration of the Magi* in the Uffizi (Fig. 82), peripheral elements that are largely the work of a shop assistant.

As Charles Seymour observed (1970), the bulk and monumentality of the figures and the composition of the Yale panel predict the ponderability and spatial realism of Florentine painting in the 1420s. These are the characteristics that also mark the San Benedetto Altarpiece (e.g., Fig. 175), produced between 1415 and 1420, where the intensification of spatial illusion is a progressive aspect of the work (see Catalogue I, London, National Gallery). An earlier, less impassioned model for the Yale panel is the *Crucifixion* (Fig. 135) in the Lehman Collection, Metropolitan Museum, New York, produced in Don Lorenzo's shop around 1405 to 1408. Conversely, the Yale panel could well have been the model for the *Crucifixion* miniature (Padua, Biblioteca Capitolare, MS. B29, fol. 157v), which Degenhart and Schmitt have attributed to the shop of Lorenzo Monaco (pt. 1, vol. 2, p. 281, fig. 389f), but which I believe is a characteristic work of Bartolomeo di Fruosino, after 1420. For discussion of Don Lorenzo's use of the iconography of the Crucifixion with the mourning Virgin and Saint John the Evangelist seated beneath the cross, see Catalogue I, Florence, San Giovannino dei Cavalieri. [1415-20]

§ NEW YORK, Richard L. Feigen Collection

Isaiah

FIG. 81

Panel (rounded): 19.5 cm.
Inscription: ECCE V̄IGO C̄OCIP

CONDITION: The detachment of the roundel from the original frame and its insertion into a frame that

Isaiah, from [Artaud de Montor], *Peintres primitifs* . . . , no. 51, fig. 17.

masked the edges of the panel surface, resulted in the abrasion of a narrow strip of the circumference. Small exposed patches of blue in the features, in the scroll, and in the deep coral red robe indicate that the image was painted on a blue ground. With the exception of these small losses in the paint film and some abrasion in the gold ground, the panel is in excellent state.

HISTORY: The roundel was originally located in the right pinnacle of the *Annunciation* in the Accademia, Florence (Fig. 77). It is mentioned in 1843, in the Artaud de Montor Collection in Paris (see below), and was sold there in 1851 (Schroth, sale catalogue, January 16 and 17, no. 51; as Cimabue). Evidence that the mid-nineteenth-century lithographic reproduction of the *Isaiah* (see accompanying illustration) was made from the panel in its modern frame is the truncated final letter P of the inscription, whereas the letter is complete in the actual panel. There was no trace of the roundel from the time of sale in 1851 until its recent emergence at Sotheby's, London (*Old Master Paintings*, July 8, 1987, no. 20, with facing colorplate; as Lorenzo Monaco). On the reverse of the frame liner, a nineteenth-century addition, are painted block letters that faintly read Angelico, an indication that at some time after the sale of 1851, an owner had begun to arrive at a more appropriate stylistic localization of the roundel.

LITERATURE: 1843, Artaud de Montor, no. 51, fig. 17: Cimabue; identified as Saint Cyprian; the inscription on the scroll is read as "ECCE IMAGO DNI CIP" // 1851, sale catalogue, Schroth, Paris, January 16 and 17, no. 51: Cimabue // 1898, Schmarsow, p. 502: Antonio Veneziano; corrected the reading of the inscription to "ECCE VIRGO CONCIP," but adhered to the identification as Saint Cyprian // 1905, Sirén, p. 44: Lorenzo Monaco, ca. 1406; identified as Isaiah // 1938/39, Pudelko, p. 248, note 33: LM, but repeats the earlier identification as Saint Cyprian; proposes that the roundel formed part of the San Benedetto *Coronation of the Virgin* altarpiece // 1956, Eisenberg, pp. 333-35: LM, ca. 1409; establishes the original location in the right pinnacle of the Accademia *Annunciation* // 1964, Previtali, pp. 231-32: discusses the formation of the Artaud de Montor Collection and the numerous attributions to Cimabue // 1975, Boskovits, p. 352: LM, 1410-15.

COMMENT: See Catalogue I, Florence, Accademia, *Annunciation with Saints Catherine of Alexandria, Anthony Abbot, Proculus, and Francis of Assisi.* [ca. 1418]

NEW YORK, Metropolitan Museum of Art, no. 09.91

Madonna of Humility with Two Angels

FIG. 141

Panel: 89.6 x 56.2 cm.

CONDITION: The following report was provided by the museum's conservation laboratory. Cleaning of the picture in 1984 revealed extensive abrasion. The final modelling has been broken through everywhere except in the two angels, which are the best preserved areas of the picture. The flesh has in many places been reduced to the green preparation. There is a large loss in the lower center of the picture of approximately 12 by 3 inches. The gold is in good state.

HISTORY: [Dealer, Dover, England]; Victor G. Fischer, Washington, D.C., by 1909; Metropolitan Museum purchase, 1909.

LITERATURE: 1905, Sirén, pp. 36-37: Lorenzo Monaco, no later than 1403; close to the *Madonna and Saints* in Berlin (now destroyed) // 1909, Berenson, p. 154: LM, early (1932, p. 300; 1963, vol. 1, p. 120) // 1924, Lazareff, p. 124: accepts Sirén's dating and compares it with a *Madonna of Humility* in the Rumiantzev Museum in Moscow (now Pushkin Museum) // 1927, van Marle, vol. 9, p. 134: LM, between the Berenson *Madonna* of 1405 and the Monte Oliveto Altarpiece of 1406-1410 (now Accademia, Florence) // 1929, Suida, p. 392: LM // 1937, R. Offner (verbally): shop of Lorenzo Monaco // 1938/39, Pudelko, p. 238, note 13: LM, shortly before 1405; related to the *Madonna of Humility* panels in the Berenson Collection and Moscow // 1940, Wehle, p. 18: LM, 1400-1406 // 1966, Montebello, pp. 165-66: LM; close in style and technique to the *Prophets* in the Metropolitan Museum; the seemingly lesser quality is a matter of condition // 1971, Zeri, pp. 67-68: LM workshop, between 1405 and 1410; about the time of a *Crucifixion* in the Seattle Art Museum, dated 1408; the design is likely to be by Lorenzo, but the execution is by an assistant, apparently the same artist who painted the *Saint Lawrence* altarpiece and predella in the Louvre (now Avignon) and Vatican; additional bibliography // 1972, Fredericksen and Zeri, p. 111: LM // 1975, Boskovits, p. 350: LM, 1400-1405.

COMMENT: The *Madonna of Humility* provides an instructive demonstration of the stratified evolution of an image commonly produced in the workshop of Lorenzo Monaco. The model for the composition is Don Lorenzo's *Madonna of Humility* in Empoli (Fig. 21), dated 1404, but there are more direct connections with the cluster of works centered in the *Madonna with Four Saints* in the Accademia, Florence (Fig. 138), which includes the *Madonna of Humility* in Moscow (Fig. 142; cited by Lazareff, 1924). The high-keyed palette of the New York panel is also apparent in the *Madonna* of 1408. Pudelko (1938/39) observed that in Madonnas by Lorenzo Monaco and his shop from the years 1405 to 1408 the Virgin frequently wears a kerchief over her mantle. The heavily encrusted cuffs of the Virgin's double sleeve have the closest parallel in the Stuttgart *Madonna of Humility* of 1407 (Fig. 39). The floating, ribboned angels were a stock motif that appeared in several variants in works from the shop of Lorenzo Monaco and from cognate milieus (Figs. 142, 152, 225, 236, and 255). The sense of an inorganic assemblage of elements conveyed by the New York panel, although partially to be explained by the poor condition, is primarily the result of a process of garnering and combining motifs.

Federico Zeri's revealing observation (1971, p. 67) of an alliance between the Metropolitan Museum *Madonna* and the *Saint Lawrence* altarpiece of 1407, now in Avignon (Fig. 244), raises the possibility that the stylized and additive character of the New York picture could be clues to the intervention of Bartolomeo di Fruosino, to whom I reservedly attribute the Avignon triptych (see Catalogue II, Avignon, Musée du Petit Palais, *Saint Lawrence Enthroned, with Saints Ansanus and Margaret*). The tentativeness of my approach both to the New York *Madonna of Humility* and to the Avignon triptych is implied by the inclusion of the former in Catalogue I. [ca. 1408-1410]

Note: A modern copy of the upper half of the *Madonna of Humility* is the central image of a tondo formerly in the collection of the Earl of Southesk that appeared some years ago at Sotheby's, London (July 20, 1955, no. 46; present location unknown; first mentioned by Everett Fahy, 1967, p. 134, note 30; Frick Art Reference Library, photo no. 707-9N). Fahy attributed the two adoring angels, one at either side of the Virgin and Child, to the "Master of Marradi," a follower of Domenico Ghirlandaio, and proposed that the two angels were added to a work of Lorenzo Monaco in the later fifteenth century. It would seem, instead, that the center of the original tondo either had been left incomplete in the later Quattrocento or had suffered sufficient damage to necessitate its total replacement, which led to the partial and anachronistic copy of the New York *Madonna of Humility*. Evidence of this proposed history is the truncation of the angels' wings by the oversized disc halo of the Virgin and the obliteration of their praying hands by the impinging contours of the Virgin and Child. The direction of the angels' gazes implies an original center of attention at a lower point in the circular pictorial field.

§ NEW YORK, Metropolitan Museum of Art, nos. 65.14.1-4

Abraham; Noah; Moses; and *David*

FIGS. 40-43; COLORPLATE 5

Panel: 58.4 x 42.2 cm.; 58.4 x 43.1.; 57.8 x 45.1 cm.; 56.5 x 43.1 cm. (painted surface)

CONDITION: The state of preservation is notably fine, with the exception of the deteriorated and patched gold ground of the *Noah*. The *Abraham, Noah*, and *Moses* were at one time forced into wide rectangular frames, which invaded a large area of each panel surface. Evidence of this intrusion are vertical abrasions that extend through the paint film and gold leaf at either side of the benches and continue upward and across the rectangular perimeters of the crudely painted half spandrels, now correctly masked by modern frames. The separate history of the *David* (see below) is demonstrated physically in that the panel is the only one of the set that has been cut to an arched shape and cradled; the three other panels reveal the natural lateral bowing of the wood.

HISTORY: *Abraham, Noah,* and *Moses*: Biondi Collection, Florence, until 1841; [sold at George, Paris, March 12-13, 1841, no. 8, as attributed to Beato Angelico]; Chalandon Collection, La Grange Blanche, Trévoux, near Lyon; [Wildenstein and Co., New York, after 1958 to 1965]. *David*: Wallis Collection, Florence, until 1847; [sold at Heberle, Berlin, May 24, 1895, no. 61]; Königliche Gemäldegalerie, Cassel, by 1903; [A. S. Drey, Munich, 1929]; Solomon R. Guggenheim, New York, 1929; [sold at Sotheby's, London, June 27, 1962, no. 14]; [Wildenstein and Co., New York, 1962-65]. For more detailed information on the provenance of the four panels, see Zeri, 1971, pp. 66-67; and Meiss, 1958, p. 192, note 9.

LITERATURE: Only the principal notices and the literature relevant to the Comment below are cited here; for a complete bibliography and record of opinions, see Zeri, 1971, pp. 62-66. 1903, *Kurzes Verzeichnis der Gemälde in der königlichen Galerie zu Cassel*, no. 4772: the *David* ascribed to Lorenzo Monaco // 1905, Sirén, pp. 43-44: the *David* attributed to Don Lorenzo and associated with a *Saint Peter* in the Lotzbeck Collection at Nannhofen, near Munich; a dating around 1403 to 1406 is proposed; possibly parts of the altarpiece Lorenzo is said by Vasari to have painted for the Fioravanti Chapel in San Piero Maggiore // 1909, Berenson, pp. 152 and 154: LM; the three Chalandon panels described as each representing a saint and a prophet // 1927, van Marle, vol. 9, pp. 165 and 168, note 3: LM; the *David* is noted separately and dated after 1413 // 1929, Suida, p. 392: LM // 1931, Golzio, p. 34: the Cassel *David* by LM, around 1405 // 1932, Berenson, "Quadri senza casa," pp. 30-31 (1970, p. 140): the *David* is dated between 1405 and 1410 // 1938/39, Pudelko, p. 238, note 13: the *David* ascribed to Lorenzo and mentioned along with the *Saint Peter* in the Lotzbeck Collection; dates them both later than 1405, the Berenson *Madonna of Humility* serving as comparison // 1958, Meiss, pp. 191-96: LM, around 1410-12; extensive discussion of the four panels from stylistic and iconographic standpoints; the connection with the *Saint Peter* is tentatively denied; hypothesizes the original arrangement of the four panels (see Comment below); in a later addendum notes the location of the *David* in the Guggenheim Collection, New York (Meiss, 1958, letter to the editor, "Four Panels by Lorenzo Monaco," p. 359) // 1963, Berenson, vol. 1, p. 120: LM, 1405-1410 (restored to lists after omission from 1932 and 1936 editions) // 1966, Montebello, pp. 155-68: LM, around 1406; related in style and technique to the *Madonna of Humility* in the Metropolitan Museum, also ascribed to Lorenzo; enlarges on Meiss's hypotheses as to the original function // 1971, Zeri, pp. 62-67: LM, around 1410 or a little earlier; Meiss's proposal as to the arrangement of the panels is confirmed; suggests that the Lotzbeck *Saint Peter* (Munich) was part of the group // 1972, Fredericksen and Zeri, p. 111: LM // 1975, Boskovits, p. 350: LM, 1405-1410.

COMMENT: Sirén's (1905) unfounded suggestion that the *David* and the Lotzbeck *Saint Peter* (and by extension the other three panels) were intended for the Fioravanti Chapel at San Piero Maggiore is justly refuted by Zeri (1971, p. 62).

The two persistent and interdependent questions with regard to the Metropolitan Museum panels are, first, the acceptability of the Nannhofen (now Munich) *Saint Peter* (Fig. 172) as a fifth element and, secondly, the original arrangement and function of the group of images. The Munich panel has suffered extensive damage and restoration, but there are sufficient areas still intact to demonstrate that the quality does not reach the level of the New York panels, an indication of workshop intervention, possibly using Don Lorenzo's design (for fuller discussion of the panel, see Catalogue I, Munich, Alte Pinakothek, *Saint Peter*). The proposal by Zeri (1971, p. 63) that the *Saint Peter*, which he attributes to Lorenzo Monaco, held a central position in the ensemble, with the Old Testament figures at the sides, raises doubts that the lesser work of an assistant would have been given the central location in a complex of panels while the work of the master would occupy a secondary position. On the other hand, it is unlikely in Christian usage that so central a New Testament personage as Saint Peter would hold a subordinate position in relation to Old Testament figures. Therefore, Meiss's conditional denial that the *Saint Peter* ever formed part of the group remains, in my view, a reasonable stand (1958, p. 196). He left the question open by suggesting the possibility that the program was based on a correlation of Apostles and Old Testament figures, although the resultant uniquely vast size of the work would pose problems. One small but telling inconsistency between the Metropolitan series and the *Saint Peter* that has not been noted is the absence in the latter panel of the dentil ornamentation that runs beneath the cornice of the benches in all four New York panels. This ornamental detail did not escape the notice of an assistant of Fra Angelico in his rendering of the bench in a drawing of *David* in the British Museum that was apparently inspired by Lorenzo's panel of the same subject, as Meiss observed (p. 195 and fig. 11). The dissimilarity between the pattern in the halo of Moses and those of the other prophets is noted by Zeri (1971). A possible explanation for the difference is that the simpler and smaller detail in Moses's halo allowed emphasis on the rays that emanate from his head (Exodus 34:29-35). The punched ornamentation of the halo in the Munich *Saint Peter* is unlike that in the four New York panels, although the simple patterns are closest in type to those of the *Moses*.

If the original format and use of the four Prophets continues to be uncertain, Meiss's proposal of an arrangement by pairs on two registers—*Moses* and *Abraham* placed above *Noah* and *David*—would seem the most satisfactory. As Meiss observed, the differing perspectives of the benches within these two pairs was an intentional adjustment to the viewer's level and angle of sight; the floors of the upper pair are pink and in the lower pair green; and, finally, the light falls from the right on the *Moses* and *Noah*, and from the left on *Abraham* and *David*, implying that they were located at either side of a central element from which they received physical and spiritual illumination, perhaps a figure of Christ. The roles of the four Old Testament figures as heralds of Christ are more explicit and consistent than their individual typological associations with Saint Peter. Among the ten Old Testament figures in the pilasters of Don Lorenzo's *Coronation of the Virgin* of 1414 (Fig. 44), painted for Santa Maria degli Angeli, the same four worthies of the Metropolitan series reappear, but now as minuscule witnesses to a spectacular Christian mystery.

Millard Meiss observed in a letter of 1964 addressed to the Metropolitan Museum of Art (mentioned by Zeri, 1971, p. 67) that the Vallombrosan Order venerated Old Testament personages who are represented several times in their church of Santa Trinita in Florence. In Baldovinetti's frescoes in the four webs of the chancel vault the identical group of Noah, Abraham, Moses, and David form an integral unit. Meiss had noted (1958, p. 195) that there is a series of the same four figures by Cosimo Rosselli in the Accademia in Florence, again lacking an original context. Procacci's oral proposal (Meiss, letter, 1958) that Don Lorenzo's four panels could have provided an appropriate imagery in the courtroom of the Mercanzia is attractive, but there is no evidence to substantiate the idea. Equally conjectural is my proposal that the four panels could once have been inserted into the doors of a custodial, enclosing a work either of sculpture or of painting. An alliance of the *Prophets* with sculpture could perhaps explain in part Don Lorenzo's brief enhancement of the three-dimensionality of form at this moment in his development. The unusual thinness of the three uncradled panels (average dimension, 1.7 cm.), which may be their original state, could possibly indicate that a lighter weight was desirable for the attachment of the panels to the movable framework of a custodial. [ca. 1408-1410]

§ NEW YORK, Metropolitan Museum of Art (Robert Lehman Collection), no. 1975.1.66

Nativity

FIG. 30

Panel: 21 x 30 cm.

CONDITION: The original quatrefoil is truncated at the sides and bottom of the panel. A narrow strip along the right edge of the painted surface was retouched in order to accommodate the loss of the lobes and angle of the quatrefoil.

HISTORY: Richard von Kaufmann Collection, Berlin, by 1902; [von Kaufmann sale, Cassirer-Helbing, Berlin, December 4, 1917, no.5]; Frank Channing Smith, Jr., Worcester, Mass., 1921; Robert Lehman Collection, New York.

LITERATURE: 1902, Frizzoni, pp. 290 and 292: Lorenzo Monaco; establishes the connection of the *Nativity* with the *Flight into Egypt* in Altenburg // 1905, Sirén, p. 57: LM, probably with shop assistance; associates the *Nativity* and *Flight* with the Gambier-

Parry (now London, Courtauld Institute Galleries) *Visitation* and *Adoration of the Magi* // 1909, Berenson, p. 152: LM // 1917, Friedländer, no. 5: LM // 1927, van Marle, vol. 9, pp. 166-68: LM, but an inferior work of the painter's old age // 1929, Suida, p. 392: LM // 1931, L. Venturi, pl. 143: LM, ca. 1408 // 1932, Berenson, p. 301: LM, a late work // 1937/38, Sandberg-Vavalà, pp. 34-38: LM, before 1413; an eloquent visual analysis // 1938/39, Pudelko, p. 77: LM, ca. 1405 // 1957, Sterling, Laclotte, pp. 22-23, no. 28: LM, ca. 1405-1410; consider the *Nativity* the finest part of the predella // 1963, Berenson, vol. 1, p. 120: LM, omits the late dating // 1975, Szabó, p. 27, and fig. 21 (color): LM, shortly before 1413 // 1975, Boskovits, p. 350: LM, 1405-1410 // 1980, Hibbard, p. 228, and fig. 390 (color): LM, before 1413 // 1983, Christiansen, pp. 4-5, and fig. 1 (colorplate): LM, ca. 1405.

COMMENT: See Catalogue I, London, Courtauld Institute Galleries, *Visitation* and *Adoration of the Magi*; and Altenburg, Staatliches Lindenau-Museum, *Flight into Egypt*. [ca. 1407-1408]

NEW YORK, Metropolitan Museum of Art (Robert Lehman Collection), no. 1975.1.67

Crucifixion with the Virgin and Saint John the Evangelist

FIG. 135

Panel: 55.9 x 31.7 cm. (painted surface)
Inscription: (Cross) ĪN̄R̄Ī

CONDITION: A conservation report of 1978 records that the side and bottom frame moldings are modern and that much of the original pastiglia detail in the gable has been lost. The gold ground, in particular at the left, is considerably damaged, and there are small losses throughout the painted surface, most extensively in the face of the Saint John. Losses in the Virgin's blue mantle were inpainted. An earlier restoration report (1958), describes the gable as original but regilded, and notes damage to the rocky ground at the base of the cross.

HISTORY: Bardini Collection, Florence, until 1902; [sold at Christie's, London, May 27, 1902, no. 627, as Spinello Aretino]; Charles Loeser, Florence; Robert Lehman Collection, New York, 1958.

LITERATURE: 1905, Sirén, p. 42: Lorenzo Monaco, ca. 1405 // 1908/1909, Sirén, p. 325: the mourning Virgin lacks the expressivity of the later Jarves (Yale University) panel // 1909, Berenson, p. 153: LM (1932, p. 299; 1963, vol. 1, p. 120) // 1927, van Marle, vol. 9, p. 145: LM, 1408-1412 // 1929, Suida, p. 392: LM // 1938/39, Pudelko, p. 148, note 35: LM, ca. 1406 // 1959, Cincinnati, *Lehman Collection*, p. 17, no. 64: LM // 1965, Bellosi, *Maestri*, [p. 6]: LM, shortly after 1404 // 1970, González-Palacios, p. 33: LM; once formed the central pinnacle above the *Madonna of Humility with Four Saints* in Empoli, dated 1404; the gable is a later addition // 1975, Szabó, pp. 26-27, colorplate no. 32: LM; close to the Empoli triptych of 1404 and to the *Crucifixion* in the Jarves Collection // 1975, Boskovits, p. 350: LM, 1405-1410 // 1985, Paolucci, p. 74: accepts the proposal that the *Crucifixion* was originally the central pinnacle of the Empoli triptych.

COMMENT: The Lehman *Crucifixion* was painted by a workshop assistant of Lorenzo Monaco working from the master's design. The coarsely handled tempera and the perfunctory rendering of hands and facial features mark the intervention of the shop. Don Lorenzo's dependence on assistants in the vast production of devotional images within his workshop would even extend to the figure of Saint John in the impressive cutout group at San Giovannino dei Cavalieri (Fig. 76).

See Catalogue I, Empoli, Museo della Collegiata, *Madonna of Humility with Four Saints*, for comment on González-Palacios's proposed reconstruction (1970); Florence, Accademia, no. 470, *Madonna and Child with Four Saints*, 1408, for a group of works apparently by the same assistant to Lorenzo Monaco who intervened in the painting of the Lehman *Crucifixion*. For discussion of sources of the iconography of the Crucifixion with the mourning Virgin and Saint John the Evangelist seated beneath the cross, and the representation in works by Lorenzo Monaco and his shop, see Catalogue I, Florence, San Giovannino dei Cavalieri. [ca. 1405-1408]

NEW YORK, Schaeffer Galleries (formerly)

Madonna in Glory with Six Saints

FIG. 195

Pinnacle: *Blessing Redeemer*

Panel: 50 x 28.5 cm. (painted surface); 77 x 36.9 cm. (framed; later base and inscription)

HISTORY: Crespi Collection, Milan; [Crespi sale, Georges Petit, Paris, June 4, 1914, no. 30]; Count Avolgi; Herman Heilbuth, Copenhagen; [sold Trotti, Paris, 1932]; [Katz, Dieren]; George Rasmussen; [Charpentier sale, Paris, June 1, 1951, no. 15]; [Schaeffer Galleries, New York].

LITERATURE: 1900, A. Venturi, p. 120: Lorenzo Monaco // 1905, Sirén, p. 165: by a gifted pupil of Don Lorenzo, working with the master in his last years // 1909, Berenson, p. 153: LM // 1920, Madsen, no. 6: LM // 1927, van Marle, vol. 9, p. 130: LM, around 1405 // 1929, Suida, p. 392: LM // 1938/39, Pudelko, p. 77: LM, around 1415 // 1975, Boskovits, p. 350: LM, 1415-20.

COMMENT: In noting the miniaturistic character of the panel, Sirén (1905) defined its distinction from works by Lorenzo Monaco. Comparison with an autograph work such as the *Madonna of Humility* in the Thorvaldsens Museum (Fig. 128) proves that even when creating a work of intimate size Don Lorenzo's conception and form were not within the scale of a miniaturist's vision. The painter of the *Madonna with Six Saints* borrowed the idea of the ring of figures from the cordon of angels in the *Coronation of the Virgin* of 1414 (Fig. 44), but the style is closer to Don Lorenzo's work of around 1420, notably the seafarers on the foundering ship in the *Saint Nicholas* predella in the Accademia, Florence (Fig. 92).

For the iconographic type, see Catalogue I, Vaduz, Liechtenstein Collection, *Madonna in Glory with Two Angels*; and Copenhagen, Thorvaldsens Museum, *Madonna of Humility*. [ca. 1420-22]

Note: A *Madonna of Humility* in the Abbazia della Trinità at Cava dei Tirreni (Campania), first attributed to Lorenzo Monaco by Boskovits (1975, p. 340, ca. 1415-20; noted as repainted; Naples, Sopr. Gab. Fot. 10307) combines the type of Virgin and Child in the former Schaeffer panel with the brocaded floor pattern of the Kansas City and The Hague *Madonna* panels (Figs. 145 and 162).

NICE, Musée des Beaux-Arts Jules Chéret, no. 162

Funeral of a Bishop Saint

FIG. 193

Panel: 29 x 44 cm. (including engaged quatrefoil)

CONDITION: The panel was restored in 1956 on the occasion of the exhibition *De Giotto à Bellini* in Paris.

HISTORY: The picture was bequeathed to the museum in Nice in the mid-nineteenth century by the Niçois watercolorist, Hercule Trachel. In 1949 the panel was stolen from the Musée des Beaux-Arts, along with a sketch by Delacroix, but was recovered soon after. Since 1977 the panel has been provisionally exhibited at the Musée Masséna, in the Palais Masséna, the administrative seat of the Musées de la Ville de Nice.

LITERATURE: 1923, Reinach, vol. 6, p. 142: Lorenzo Monaco // 1925, A. Venturi, "Un prezioso frammento sconosciuto di Filippo Lippi," *L'Arte* 28, pp. 174-76 (reprinted in A. Venturi, *Studi del vero*, pp. 25-28): Fra Filippo Lippi, at the beginning of his career // 1928, van Marle, vol. 10, p. 417, note 1: LM // 1932, Berenson, p. 300: LM, late (1963, vol. 1, p. 120) // 1932/33, Berenson, p. 66, note 12: mentions that he had attributed the work to Lorenzo Monaco years before Venturi's publication; panel confirms the view that Lorenzo Monaco influenced Lippi's early development // 1938/39, Pudelko, p. 78, note 9: LM, from the phase beginning in 1414 // 1949, Pittaluga, p. 223: LM, late work // 1956, Laclotte, p. 65, no. 91: LM, in the latest stage of the career, after the frescoes in Santa Trinita, as indicated by the classical quietude of the scene and the interest in three-dimensionality // 1975, Boskovits, p. 351: LM, 1415-20.

COMMENT: The design is by Lorenzo Monaco, but the execution was left to a close shop associate, which can be discerned by comparing the rigid and generalized draughtsmanship of draperies and facial features with Don Lorenzo's predella for the *Annunciation* in the Bartolini Salimbeni Chapel at Santa Trinita, the measure of quality in his later style (Fig. 126). The painter of the Nice panel may be the same associate who executed from Don Lorenzo's design, but at a less skillful moment, the *Funeral of Saint Francis* in the Pallavicini Collection, Rome (Fig. 191). The quatrefoil framing of the Nice panel is an anachronism in conjunction with the advanced representation of enclosed space. The original context of the panel is unknown, but it would appear to have been part of a conservative work that at the same time incorporated the spatial factor of Lorenzo's later style. As Laclotte (1956) proposed, Don Lorenzo absorbed the conceptions of dimensionality that were a central stylistic issue of the 1420s. To this extent, Adolfo Venturi's attribution to Fra Filippo Lippi, while not acceptable, indicates his recognition of the progressive aspects of the image. For further comment, see Catalogue I, Amsterdam, Rijksmuseum, *Stigmatization of Saint Francis*. The same painter may have executed miniatures in Corale E 70 in the Bargello (Fig. 210). [ca. 1422-23]

PARIS, Louvre, no. 1315

Madonna of Humility
FIG. 144

Panel: 93 x 54 cm. (painted surface)

CONDITION: The Virgin's features are abraded, and her mantle, from the knees to the floor, is heavily varnished and partially repainted. The extensive crackling of the paint film and gold leaf has coarsened the surface of the picture. The entire frame is a later addition, so that the coats of arms, including the Alberti, on the ornate base do not help to determine the provenance.

HISTORY: Campana Collection, Rome, by 1858; acquired by the French Government in 1861; Musée Napoléon III (Campana Collection), 1863; Louvre, 1864 (see Vertova, 1977, p. 165).

LITERATURE: 1858, *Cataloghi del Museo Campana*, Rome, p. 13, no. 108: Orcagna // 1862, Cornu, p. 27, no. 108: Orcagna // 1863, Reiset, p. 17, no. 26: school of Giotto (attribution repeated in subsequent catalogues: 1878, Tauzia, p. 125, no. 195; 1913, de Ricci, p. 67, no. 1315) // 1883, Crowe and Cavalcaselle, vol. 2, p. 347: Lorenzo Monaco // 1903, Toesca, pp. 225-26: close to the Monte Oliveto Altarpiece of 1410, but a late work, foreshadowing Masolino and Fra Angelico // 1905, Sirén, p. 168: LM workshop; by the same hand as the *Madonna* panels in the Loeser Collection (now Brooklyn), the Toscanelli Collection (now Kansas City), and Berlin // 1926, Hautecoeur, p. 76, no. 1315: Lorenzo Monaco // 1927, van Marle, vol. 9, p. 134: LM, close to the Monte Oliveto Altarpiece of 1410 // 1929, Suida, p. 392: LM // 1932, Berenson, p. 300: LM, in great part; the Eternal Father in the gable by another hand (1963, vol. 1, p. 120) // 1938/39, Pudelko, p. 76, note 2: workshop of LM; after 1413 // 1975, Boskovits, p. 351: LM, 1410-15.

COMMENT: The Louvre *Madonna of Humility* was designed by Lorenzo Monaco around 1415, at the time of the *Crucifix with the Virgin and Saint John the Evangelist* at San Giovannino dei Cavalieri in Florence. Comparison of the fluctuant contour of the Virgin's mantle with the Mourning Virgin in the San Giovannino group (Fig. 75) confirms their contemporaneity. But the mechanical line of the Virgin's sleeve, the passages of indeterminate rhythm, visible through the heavy varnish and repaint, and the stilted fold of drapery falling from the Child's raised knee suggest the involvement of an assistant, perhaps the one who collaborated in the Saint John the Evangelist from the San Giovannino group (Fig. 76). As is proposed in the discussion of that work, this may be the same shop associate who was extensively responsible for the execution of the San Benedetto Altarpiece (see Catalogue I, London, National Gallery). [ca. 1415]

§ PARIS, Louvre, no. 1348A

Agony in the Garden; and *Holy Women at the Tomb*
FIG. 33

Pinnacles: (Left) *Angel offering chalice*; (right) *Resurrected Christ*

Panel: 66 x 26.5 cm.
Inscribed date: 1408 (ANNO.DÑI. M.CCCCVIII)

CONDITION: Apparently because of extensive woodworm damage, both panels were reduced in thickness and the upper contours were changed from an arched to a rectilinear shape, which obliterated most of the figure of the risen Christ and all evidence of the inner faces of the wings. The revision explains the disparity between the contours of the Louvre wings and the pointed arch of the *Lamentation* in Prague (Fig. 34), which was the center panel of the original triptych. Trimming of the edges of the two wings reduced their width and truncated the angel with the chalice. The wings and the oblong panels with the inscribed date of 1408 are framed with a decorative molding. A detailed report on the transformation of the two joined panels was published by Olga Pujmanová ("Italian Primitives," 1977, p. 539).

The Louvre wings were lightly cleaned in 1947 and the backs of the panels disinfested in 1979. From a technical examination undertaken in 1956 in the Laboratoire du Musée du Louvre (Institut Mainini), which included radiographic, ultraviolet, and infrared studies, it was discerned that the shroud draped over the sarcophagus in the *Holy Women at the Tomb* was originally wider, but was narrowed and a cast shadow added at an unknown date. This area of the painted surface had apparently disintegrated to a degree, the result of a breach in the seam of the finely woven fabric between the panel and gesso, which was also the case with an area of the sleeping disciples in the *Agony in the Garden*, extending horizontally from below the knee of Saint Peter to the edge of the adjacent taut mantle. These repainted areas are visible on close sight examination of the painted surface, particularly the shadow of the shroud, which is painted in an inappropriately heavy impasto that interrupts the natural crackle. The minute shadows beneath the swirls of the mantle at the base of the *Agony in the Garden* would seem to be original, although they do not appear in the *Holy Women at the Tomb* or in the Prague *Lamentation.*

HISTORY: The two panels, once the outer faces of the wings of a triptych of which the *Lamentation* in the National Gallery, Prague, was the central panel, were revised and joined probably at the beginning of the eighteenth century. A label with the attribution "Gentile da Fabbriano" [*sic*] affixed to the back and crossing the seam between the two panels, dates from that time (see Pujmanová, fig. 5); Musée de Cluny, Paris, by 1861; Louvre, 1896.

LITERATURE: 1861, Sommerard, p. 101, no. 710: Gentile da Fabriano // 1864, Crowe and Cavalcaselle, vol. 1, p. 552, note 2: Lorenzo Monaco, an "exquisite work . . . from his finest period" // 1878, Vasari, ed. Milanesi, vol. 2, p. 31: LM // 1883, Sommerard, p. 133, no. 1667: LM // 1896, Berenson, p. 119: LM (1909, p. 154; 1932, p. 300; 1963, vol. 1, p. 120) // 1905, Sirén, pp. 61-63: LM; originally the wings of a triptych, with the Madonna and Child probably the central subject // 1926, Hautecoeur, p. 76, no. 1348A: LM; reported that the central panel, which he left unidentified as to subject, remained in the Cluny Museum // 1927, van Marle, vol. 9, p. 142: LM, miniaturistic in style // 1929, Suida, p. 392: LM // 1938/39, Pudelko, p. 242: LM // 1946, Meiss, pp. 14-15: LM; tentatively proposed that the panels were the wings of a triptych of which the central element was the *Lamentation* at Konopiště (now National Gallery, Prague) // 1965, Bellosi, *Maestri*, [pp. 6-7] and pl. 5 (color): LM, showing a close parallel to the style of Ghiberti // 1975, Boskovits, p. 351: LM // 1977, Pujmanová, *Umění*, pp. 35-43 // 1977, Pujmanová, "Italian Primitives," pp. 536 and 539: LM; with a technical analysis that provides a closer physical integration with the *Lamentation* in Prague.

COMMENT: See Catalogue I, Prague, National Gallery, *Lamentation.*

In designing the *Holy Women at the Tomb*, Lorenzo Monaco may have referred to a miniature of the same subject that Levi D'Ancona ("Matteo Torelli," 1958, p. 247, note 10) first observed to be related to the style of Don Silvestro dei Gherarducci (Paris; Louvre; Fig. 269). She later attributed the cut miniature to Torelli and identified its provenance as fol. 3, Cod. Cor. 1, Biblioteca Laurenziana (1978, p. 218). I am unable to concur with Levi D'Ancona's view that the Louvre miniature is close in style to that on fol. 27v of Cod. Cor. 3 in the Laurenziana, which she also attributes to Torelli (1958, "Matteo Torelli," p. 247, note 10, and fig. 11). The landscape and drapery of the Laurenziana miniature are not drawn with the same incisive mastery found in the Louvre miniature, and the facial types are unrelated. Sirén (1905, p. 73) attributed the miniature in Paris to the school of Lorenzo Monaco. [1408]

PARIS, Musée Marmottan (Wildenstein Collection, no. 14)

God the Father, with the Crucifix

FIG. 206

Cut miniature from a choir book
Parchment: 25.5 x 23.5 cm. (size of sheet)

HISTORY: Wildenstein Collection, Paris; Musée Marmottan, 1980.

LITERATURE: 1926, *Exposition du livre italien*, Bibliothèque Nationale, Paris, no. 181: Tuscan school, fourteenth century // 1958, Levi D'Ancona, "Some New Attributions," p. 183, and fig. 12: Lorenzo Monaco, around 1410, contemporary with the Monte Oliveto Altarpiece // 1972, Boskovits, p. 47: LM, with the collaboration of Bartolomeo di Fruosino // 1975, Boskovits, p. 352: LM, 1410-15; the heads in the border by Bartolomeo di Fruosino // (n.d., after 1980), *Académie des Beaux-Arts, La Collection Wildenstein.* Musée Marmottan, Paris: LM, ca. 1406-1410; surrounding heads by Bartolomeo di Fruosino.

COMMENT: The *God the Father, with the Crucifix* is, in my view, the only completed miniature by Lorenzo Monaco that does not represent a prophet in half length. The execution, however, lacks the virtuosity in the handling of the tempera and in the rhythms of drapery to be found in Don Lorenzo's contemporary miniatures (see Figs. 64-68) or in his predella figures that are nearly on the same scale (see Figs. 29-32). The blandness of the figure of Christ on the cross is untypical and the drawing of the lower border of the Eternal's mantle lacks the spring of draperies in the pinnacles of the Monte Oliveto Altarpiece (Figs. 25-27) or in the "Courtauld predella" (Figs. 29 and 30), which suggests the involvement of an assistant in the completion of the miniature. Nonetheless, the rendering of the head and gesture of God the Father places this work among Don Lorenzo's most expressive images. Parallels with the Blessing Redeemer (Fig. 48) in the central pinnacle of the *Coronation of the Virgin* of 1414 for Santa Maria degli Angeli, imply an approximate dating between the Monte Oliveto Altarpiece (1410) and that subsequent major project. To confirm the primarily autograph caliber of the Musée Marmottan miniature, one need only compare the nearly identical image of the *Trinity* on fol. 101v of Cod. E 70 in the Bargello (Levi D'Ancona, "Some New Attributions," 1958, fig. 13: attributed to Matteo Torelli). The heads by Bartolomeo di Fruosino in the border of the Paris miniature are intrusive. [1410-15]

PASADENA, Norton Simon Museum, no. M.73.5.p

Annunciate Virgin

FIGS. 180, 181

Panel: 80 x 45 cm.

CONDITION: The painted surface, which is in excellent state, shows evidence the panel was originally wider and higher. The uneven levels of the springing points of the arch and the confusion in the space that results from truncation of the barrel vault indicate that the panel was cut down by about three cm. on the right side and that the crown of the arch was originally higher.

HISTORY: The panel was the right pinnacle of the *Coronation of the Virgin* altarpiece for the monastery of San Benedetto, near Florence (see Catalogue I, London, National Gallery, San Benedetto Altarpiece). Acquired in Florence in 1894 for the collection of the Prince of Liechtenstein (Mödling); [Thos. Agnew & Sons, London, 1959]; Norton Simon, 1962.

LITERATURE: 1908, Suida, "Beiträge," p. 305: Lorenzo Monaco (1929, p. 392) // 1927, van Marle, vol. 9, p. 160: from the period of Lorenzo's Bartolini Chapel *Annunciation*, before 1413 // 1932, Berenson, p. 301: LM (1963, vol. 1, p. 121) // 1938/39, Pudelko, p. 247: LM, between the Uffizi *Coronation* of 1414 and the late works; proposes that the panel was a pinnacle of the San Benedetto *Coronation of the Virgin* altarpiece // 1948, Lucerne, *Meisterwerke*, p. 8, no. 34: LM // 1958, Levi D'Ancona, "Some New Attributions," p. 180, note 25: apparently by Matteo Torelli // 1958, Levi D'Ancona, "Matteo Torelli," p. 257 and note 29: repeats the ascription to Matteo Torelli; implies that the connection with the San Benedetto Altarpiece is convincing, although the other parts of that work are not attributed to Torelli // 1960, London, *Italian Art and Britain*, p. 107, no. 283: LM // 1967, Vertova, p. 206: LM; from the San Benedetto *Coronation*, ca. 1415 // 1975, Boskovits, p. 349: LM, 1410-15 // 1978, Muller, pp. 10 and 16, note 5: painted by a closer follower of Lorenzo Monaco, implying that the design is by the master // 1980, Pasadena, *Selected Paintings*, p. 22, illustrated in color.

COMMENT: See Catalogue I, London, National Gallery, San Benedetto Altarpiece. [1415-20]

PESCIA, Museo Civico

Madonna and Child with Saints Peter and Sebastian

FIG. 134

Predella: *Saint James Major; Mourning Virgin; Man of Sorrows; Mourning Saint John the Evangelist; Saint Catherine of Alexandria*

Panel: 149 x 179 cm. (including predella)

CONDITION: The extensive abrasion of the paint surface has weakened the facial features of the Virgin and Child and Saint Sebastian, and the left half of the Virgin's face is feebly repainted. The predella has been shortened by a few centimeters at each end, enough to obliterate half of the geometrical forms that bracketed the roundels.

HISTORY: The coats of arms on the predella, an original element of the altarpiece, are of the Canigiani family, which indicates that the triptych was originally painted for a Pescian patron; names of members of that family appear several times in the later Trecento in lists of civil officials of the town (see I. Orsini, *Storia delle monete della repubblica fiorentina*, Florence, 1760, pp. 166ff; also, C. Bernardini, *Memorie sparse della città di Pescia*, Pescia, 1899, pp. 108ff). On the plinth beneath the predella a badly rubbed inscription records the civil regime at Pescia of Filippo Tornabuoni in the mid-1460s: TEMPORE REGIMINIS PHILIPPI PPI . . . TORNABUONIS V ET PO . . . PISCIE MCCCCLXIIII ET MCCCCLXV. The dates indicate the plinth is a later addition. The altarpiece is apparently the work referred to in the inventory of 1786 of the Palazzo Pretorio in Pescia (MS., Biblioteca Comunale, Pescia: "Nell'ingresso un quadro incassato nel muro esprimente la SSma Vergine e due altre figure in tavola antica . . .").

LITERATURE: 1905, Stiavelli, p. 61, no. 10: lists but does not attribute the altarpiece // 1938/39, Pudelko, p. 237, note 8: Lorenzo Monaco, an early work related to the *Agony in the Garden* in the Accademia, Florence // 1957, Eisenberg, pp. 49-52: LM, early, with closest resemblances to the Accademia *Agony* // 1958, Levi D'Ancona, "Some New Attributions," p. 187: denies the attribution to Lorenzo; the flat schematization in the drapery is more in keeping with the style of Matteo Torelli // 1959, Levi D'Ancona, "Letter," p. 128: Matteo Torelli, after 1403, on the basis of similarities to an illumination considered to be documented work of the miniaturist (Bargello, Cod. E 70, fol. 64; illustrated in D'Ancona, 1914, pl. 43) // 1968, *Guida del Museo Civico*, Pescia, p. 4: LM school // 1970, González-Palacios, pp. 28 and 30: LM; the Saint Sebastian closely resembles the Saint Stephen in a panel in the Musée Jacquemart-André, Paris // 1973, Preiser, pp. 226-27: the predella with tondi is Sienese in type // 1975, Boskovits, p. 352: LM, 1395-1400.

COMMENT: Contrary to my previously published attribution of the Pescia triptych to Lorenzo Monaco (1957), I now reservedly consider the work to be a product of his shop, a reflection of the central surviving early work by the master—the *Agony in the Garden* in the Accademia, Florence, of the late 1390s. Comparison of the facial type of the Saint Peter with the Christ of the *Agony* (Fig. 8), or of the Saint Sebastian with the young centurion with the shield in the predella scene of the *Stripping of Christ* (Fig. 11) confirms the morphological parallels between these works. But even through the badly abraded surface there can be detected an ineptness in drawing, a schematic reduction of forms, and a lack of craftsmanship in the ornamentation of the gold—all observed by Mirella Levi D'Ancona in her initial rejection of my attribution to Lorenzo Monaco (1958)—which mark the hand of the painter as a relatively provincial one, perhaps even an imitator rather than a direct associate of Don Lorenzo. Levi D'Ancona's denial of any connection between the vocabulary of ornament here and in Lorenzo's work is contradicted, however, by comparison with the haloes in the Accademia *Man of Sorrows* (Fig. 18) of 1404. I am unable to accept her subsequent attribution of the triptych to Matteo Torelli (1959). The similarity between the Child in the Pescia triptych and the Amsterdam *Madonna Enthroned* (Fig. 237) is one of type rather than of morphology and is not sufficient evidence of the identity of artistic hands, which I originally proposed and Levi D'Ancona also suggested in order to prove that both works must be by Torelli. Again in contradiction of my earlier opinion, I now see the shortened predella to be an original part of the altarpiece; the Man of Sorrows in the center roundel parallels the Bergamo panel of the same subject (Fig. 136). The depiction of Saints Peter and Sebastian in the main register and Saints James Major and Catherine in the predella is probably to be explained as a joining of martyred apostles and saints.

In its reflection of antecedent traditions of Trecento painting, the Pescia triptych has particular significance as a product of the earliest stylistic milieu dominated by Lorenzo Monaco. The type of altarpiece, with its imposing three-quarter-length figures reminiscent of a format employed by the shops of Giotto, Maso di Banco, and Bernardo Daddi, is symptomatic of the Giottesque revival of the later Trecento. Dependence on the art of Jacopo di Cione, whose work was an essential model for Lorenzo Monaco in his formative years, is recognized in a comparison of the Pescia Saint Peter with the *Saint Peter* by Jacopo at Oxford (see Byam Shaw, pl. 8). The color chord of rose, vermilion, golden yellow, and dark green is characteristically Cionesque. The multiple sources of the altarpiece were further defined by Preiser (1973), who traced the predella type to Siena. There is, however, a close Florentine precursor to the Pescia predella in the long predella with five medallions by Giovanni del Biondo in the Guidetti Chapel in Santa Felicita, Florence (Offner and Steinweg, sec. IV, vol. V, pt. I, 1967, pl. XXII[3]). [ca. 1400]

PHILADELPHIA, John G. Johnson Collection, no. J.10

Madonna of Humility
FIG. 148

Panel: 83.2 x 50.3 cm. (painted surface)
Inscription: (Christ Child) EGO SUM LUX MU.

CONDITION: The darkening and abrasion in the surface of the Virgin's mantle have obscured all definition of the drawing of the figure. A vertical fissure extending the length of the panel particularly disrupts the features of the Child. The frame, including the cusped arch and inscribed base, is not original.

HISTORY: John G. Johnson purchased the panel in 1908, on the recommendation of Osvald Sirén. The place of purchase is unknown. Since 1933, located in the Philadelphia Museum of Art.

LITERATURE: 1909, Sirén, p. 36: Lorenzo Monaco; a late work // 1913, Berenson, p. 8: LM, in great part // 1927, van Marle, vol. 9, p. 130: LM, after 1405 // 1929, Suida, p. 392: LM // 1932, Berenson, p. 301: LM, in great part (1963, vol. 1, p. 120) // 1941, *Johnson Collection*, p. 9: LM // 1966, *Johnson Collection*, p. 44: LM // 1972, Fredericksen and Zeri, p. 111: LM // 1975, Boskovits, p. 341: LM, 1405-1410.

COMMENT: See Catalogue I, Brooklyn (New York), Brooklyn Museum, *Madonna of Humility*. [ca. 1418-20]

PISA, Sant'Ermete

Madonna of Humility with Eight Angels
FIG. 146

Panel: 142.2 x 106.6 cm. (painted surface)
Inscribed date: 1415 (A.D.M. CCCCXV)
Inscription: HOC.OP.FECIT.FIERI.IACH . . . HOS . . . DE. VETRATA.P.REMEDIO ANIME SUE.Ē.SUORUM

CONDITION: The panel was restored in the late 1950s by conservators at the Museo Nazionale di San Matteo, Pisa. The following additions, apparently from the eighteenth century, were removed: heavy repainting in oil, particularly in the lower areas of the Virgin's mantle; a false date of 1412 at the lower right; a blue ground studded with gold stars; heavy gilded crowns attached to the haloes of the Virgin and Child. The removal of repaint from the background and floor areas uncovered a badly abraded gold ground, the original date of 1415, and the partially effaced inscription recording the donor's commission. Losses of paint, gold leaf, and gesso, that were particularly severe in the heads and haloes of the angels to the far right, were repaired in a neutral tone. Extensively damaged areas running vertically from the feet of the Child to the border of the Virgin's mantle were inpainted. The series of holes still visible in the haloes of the Virgin and Child were the points of attachment of the florid crowns.

HISTORY: No record exists of when the panel was placed in the church of Sant'Ermete, but there is the remote possibility that this could be one of the two works by Lorenzo Monaco mentioned by Grassi in the second quarter of the nineteenth century as being in the church of San Michele in Borgo, Pisa (1837, p. 137). Grassi's description of each work as a Madonna with various saints would seem to preclude a reference to the panel now at Sant'Ermete, but the Madonna could have been accompanied by side panels, and Grassi did emphasize that one of the two pictures was quite damaged by a poor repainting. Without describing the subject, Vasari (1550 and 1568) mentioned some panels by Lorenzo Monaco in the monastery of San Michele, Pisa (see Appendix). He attributed a Madonna with Saints Peter, John the Baptist, Francis, and Ranieri, with three predella panels beneath, to a Pisan pupil of Don Lorenzo. This work, dated 1415, was seen by Vasari in the Maggiolini Chapel in San Francesco, Pisa (Vasari, ed. Bettarini and Barocchi, Text, p. 307).

LITERATURE: 1912, Giolli, p. 28: Lorenzo Monaco // 1914/15, Sirén, p. 108: LM, 1412 // 1927, van Marle, vol. 9, p. 154, and fig. 103 (shows the condition before restoration and the false date of 1412); the extreme mediocrity of the central figure raises the possibility the picture is a school work, but the angels are so close to the *Coronation* in the Uffizi that the attribution to Lorenzo must be retained; the inscribed date is not original // 1929, Suida, p. 392: LM // 1932, Berenson, "Quadri senza casa," p. 34 (1970, p. 141): the execution seems to have been left to Fra Giovanni da Vallombrosa, who may also have helped Don Lorenzo with the Spiridon *Madonna* (now The Hague) // 1938/39, Pudelko, p. 77: LM, contemporary with the Santa Trinita *Annunciation* (i.e., 1422-25) // 1963, Berenson, vol. 1, p. 120: LM, 1412 // 1965, Bellosi, *Maestri*, [p. 6]: LM, 1415 // 1975, Boskovits, p. 352: LM, 1412.

COMMENT: The large size and dense enclosure of the Sant'Ermete *Madonna of Humility* would seem to indicate that it was once the center of a compound altarpiece, perhaps similar in format to Don Lorenzo's triptych of 1404 in Empoli (Fig. 20). The two *Saints* laterals, also in Empoli (Figs. 154-155), while not compatible in physical details or style, provide the closest approximation to the appearance of such accompanying elements, the gazes of two of the saints being directed toward a figure placed low at the center.

The Sant'Ermete panel was produced in Don Lorenzo's shop contemporarily with the *Crucifixion* (Fig. 74) at San Giovannino dei Cavalieri and during the final stages in the conception of the San Benedetto Altarpiece (Fig. 175). The closest stylistic analogies may be drawn with the mourning Saint John (Fig. 76) from the San Giovannino group, a figure of considerably lesser caliber than the Virgin and Christ. The lower areas of the mantle in the Pisa *Madonna* are equally mechanical in the virtually symmetrical arrangement, and the calligraphic contours hovering above the ground plane seem in conflict with the gravity of the matronly Virgin. Specific details of the Sant'Ermete *Madonna* reveal an assistant's exaggerations of the style and technique of Lorenzo Monaco. The accented edges of folds in the angels' sleeves and along the blousing of the tunics are a caricature of the master's use of light and recall the same exaggeration in the *Saint James Enthroned* at Santa Croce (Fig. 171), a work likely to be by the same assistant. Pictures for which this associate in Don Lorenzo's shop would seem to have been entirely or in part responsible are listed in the discussion of the San Benedetto Altarpiece (Catalogue I, London, National Gallery). [1415]

POZNAŃ, National Museum, no. MO 21

Adoration of the Magi
FIGS. 185, 188, 189

Panel: 29.5 x 85.5 cm.

CONDITION: As the painted surface reveals, the panel is reduced in length at both ends and the scene was originally enclosed by a long, octagonal frame that covered the angles of a rectangular panel. The corners at the left end of the panel show traces of a diagonal beard where the edges of that frame once impinged; the painted surfaces of these exposed angles are clearly later additions. At certain points the vertical rock form extends beyond the present limit of the painted surface. A faint streak of gold paint along the left end of the painted surface indicates that a later frame was retouched while containing the panel. A band of white paint crudely applied to the left edge suggests an attempt to lend completeness to this truncated end of the panel. Areas of repainting are readily visible at the base of the ascending rock form to the left, in the mantle of the camel groom, and in the distorting loss in the neck of the second Magus. The *velatura* is inconsistently preserved, which may have prompted Roger Fry's comment on the lack of hatching in comparison with Filippo Lippi's technique (see the Introductory Essay, Note 131; also see Conti, p. 13).

HISTORY: The *Adoration of the Magi* held the central position in the predella of the *Coronation of the Virgin* altarpiece in the monastery of San Benedetto fuori della Porta a Pinti, outside Florence (see Catalogue I, London, National Gallery, San Benedetto Altarpiece, History and Comment). The name "Böhm" inscribed on the reverse of the panel reveals that the *Adoration* was once owned by Josef Daniel Böhm, a Viennese *marchand-amateur*, who began a collection of Italian pictures in 1823-24, after initial visits to Italy in 1821 and 1822. The *Adoration* was bought from Böhm by Samuel von Festetics of Vienna, probably in the 1830s or 1840s, when the latter began his own collection (see T. von Frimmel, *Lexikon der wiener Gemäldesammlungen*, vol. 1, Munich, 1913, pp. 189-97 [on Böhm] and 352-89 [on von Festetics]). The panel was purchased in 1863 by Count Atanazy Raczyński of Berlin, from the property of his late son-in-law, Samuel von Festetics, who had died in 1859. The Raczyński Collection was housed in the later nineteenth century in the Königliche National-Galerie, Berlin. In 1903 the Raczyński Collection became part of the provincial Kaiser-Friedrich-Museum in Posen, renamed the Wielkopolskie Muzeum in 1919, and the Muzeum Narodowe w Poznaniu (National Museum in Poznań) in 1950. (I am deeply grateful to Piotr Michałowski of the Department of European Painting in the National Museum in Poznań for providing information on the nineteenth-century history of the panel before its purchase in 1863 by Count Raczyński and for clarification of the earlier phases of the National Museum.)

LITERATURE: 1866, Raczyński no. 66: Spinello Aretino // 1883, Crowe and Cavalcaselle, vol. 2, p. 346: Lorenzo Monaco // 1886, von Donop, p. 19, no. 42: probably Spinello Aretino // 1896, Berenson, p. 119: LM. // 1903, Fry, p. 127: LM; precedes the *Adoration* in the Parry Collection (now London, Courtauld Institute Galleries) // 1905, Sirèn, pp. 92-94: LM, around 1415-17; in Raczińsky Collection, Posen // 1927, van Marle, vol. 9, p. 153: LM, contemporary with the Uffizi *Adoration of the Magi*, which precedes the *Coronation of the Virgin* of 1413 // 1929, Suida, p. 392: LM // 1931, Golzio, p. 36: by the pupil of Lorenzo who executed some miniatures in Corali 3 and 8 in the Laurenziana // 1932, Berenson, p. 301: LM, a late work (1963, vol. 1, p. 120) // 1956, Krautheimer, p. 81: LM, noting resemblances to Ghiberti's style on the North Door around 1404 to 1407 // 1957, Białostocki and Walicki, p. 465: LM, ca. 1414; with extensive bibliography // 1961, Cracow, *Peinture italienne*, pp. 53-54, no. 34: LM, with additional bibliography // 1962, Różycka-Bryzek, p. 117: LM // 1975, Boskovits, p. 352: LM, 1405-1410 // 1981, A. Dobrzycka, in Poznań, *Muzeum Narodowe*, p. 73: LM; recent bibliography.

COMMENT: See Catalogue I, London, National Gallery, San Benedetto Altarpiece. [1415-20]

§ PRAGUE, National Gallery, no. 428

Lamentation

FIGS. 34-37; COLORPLATE 6

Panel: 67 x 28.5 cm.
Inscription: (Cross) I.N.R.I.

CONDITION: A skillful cleaning in the mid-1940s disclosed the nearly perfect preservation of the paint film. For discussion of the slight revisions of the panel, see Olga Pujmanová, "Italian Primitives," 1977, p. 539. The trimming of the side edges of the panel obliterated any trace that may have survived of points of attachment to adjoining wings.

HISTORY: The panel was originally the center of a triptych, dismembered at an unknown date (see Comment below). The *Lamentation* was likely to have been part of the collection formed before 1805 by the Marchese Tommaso degli Obizzi at his castle, Catajo, near Padua (see Meiss, 1946, p. 1). The collection was willed in 1805 to Ercole III, Duke of Modena, and passed through generations of Este heirs down to Archduke Franz Ferdinand. The archduke transferred the major part of the Obizzi collection to Vienna in 1896 and shortly thereafter to the castle at Konopiště, near Prague. The *Lamentation* was part of the Konopiště Collections. During the German occupation of Czechoslovakia, the collection was taken to Austria and then returned in 1945. In that same year the *Lamentation* entered the inventory of the National Gallery in Prague. Affixed to the back of the panel is a small sheet of paper on which lines in praise of Andrea del Verrocchio are written in a nineteenth-century hand, an indication of an earlier attribution.

LITERATURE: 1946, Meiss, pp. 14-15: Lorenzo Monaco, with the tentative proposal that the panel once formed a triptych along with the *Agony in the Garden* and *Holy Women at the Tomb* in the Louvre; a copy of the *Lamentation* in Narbonne is cited, along with Berenson's (1932, p. 12) attribution of that work to Andrea di Giusto // 1949, *Národní Galerie*, Prague, p. 62, no. 406: LM // 1963, Berenson, vol. 1, p. 120: LM // 1965, Shell, p. 468, and fig. 12: the Narbonne panel is cited as an adaptation of the Prague *Lamentation*, with admixtures of the styles of Masolino and Masaccio; confirms Longhi's attribution of the Narbonne panel to Francesco d'Antonio (1940, p. 187, note 24) // 1975, Boskovits, p. 352: LM, 1408 // 1977, Pujmanová, *Umění*, pp. 35-43 // 1977, Pujmanová, "Italian Primitives," pp. 536 and 539: LM; technical analysis establishes a closer physical integration with the panels in Paris.

COMMENT: See Catalogue I, Paris, Louvre, *Agony in the Garden* and *Holy Women at the Tomb*. Meiss's tentative proposal (1946) that the *Lamentation* and the two Louvre panels formed the center and lateral elements of a triptych was premised on compatibility of style, subject matter, halo patterns, and dimensions, but the disparity in contour between the tops of the wings and of the main panel remained troublesome. Now the alliance of the three panels has been confirmed through the acute physical analysis undertaken by Olga Pujmanová (1977). In her view, the Prague *Lamentation* fully expresses the International Style, whereas the wings in Paris are still largely in the spirit of the fourteenth century. This seeming variation between the wings and center panel may instead be accountable to the constrictive narrowness of the lancet-shaped wings, which precludes the presence of so florid a figure as the mourner at the center of the *Lamentation*, and to the fact that the Louvre panels have not been afforded the degree of cleaning that released the nuances of color and rhythm of the panel in Prague.

The various iconographic elements of the *Lamentation* have precedents in earlier Florentine painting. Meiss (1951, p. 145) defined the theme of the Virgin seated on the ground in the Lamentation and in the Pietà as a *Vesperbild* with a polar relationship to the Madonna of Humility. A direct antecedent to Lorenzo's treatment of the Lamentation enacted below the cross is the panel in a tabernacle by Pacino di Bonaguida, (Offner, sec. III, vol. VI, 1956, pl. XLI), although in that work neither the towered cityscape nor the sarcophagus is included. Pacino incorporated the nails and the crown of thorns as emblems still attached to the cross. A panel in the Ashmolean Museum, attributed to the Master of the Dominican Effigies (A 677), is an example from the mid-Trecento in Florence of a Lamentation beneath the cross in which Joseph of Arimathaea and Nicodemus exhibit the crown of thorns and the nails (see Lloyd, pl. 77). For a discussion of the symbols of the crown and nails in relation to the Lamentation and the Last Judgment, see Offner, sec. III, vol. VI, 1956, p. 139, note 4, and D. Denny, "Notes on the Avignon Pietà," *Speculum*, 44, 1969, p. 223, note 51 (cites the Ashmolean panel). The foreground of the panel by Pacino mentioned above is a craggy shelf, as in Lorenzo's Prague and Louvre panels (see Tolnay, 1956, p. 161, for an interpretation of this device as a means to lift a sacred event to a more elevated plane; Lorenzo's Louvre panels are cited as a precedent).

The *Lamentation* by the Master of the Saint George Codex in The Cloisters, New York, displays several similarities to Lorenzo's panel in Prague: the sarcophagus is included; the principal feature of the landscape is a steep, tiered rock formation; the cross is planted on an outcropping, with the blood of Christ flowing at the base; Joseph of Arimathaea and Nicodemus stand as onlookers behind the cluster of mourners; Saint John the Evangelist lifts Christ's hand (see Howett, figs. 1 and 2). [1408]

PRATO, Galleria Comunale, no. 7

Madonna Enthroned, with Saints Catherine of Alexandria, Benedict, Giovanni Gualberto, and Agatha

FIG. 152

Panel: (Overall) 157 x 214.5 cm.; (center panel, painted surface) 132 x 69 cm.; (laterals, painted surface) 143 x 64.5 cm.

Inscriptions: (Christ Child) EGO SUM VIA VERITAS ET VITA; (Saint Benedict) PASSIONIB XRI P PATIENTIAM PARTICIPEMUR UT. R. . . . (Conclusion of Prologue to the *Rule*); (Lateral bases) S̄CA KATERINA.V / S̄CS BENEDICTUS ABB // S̄CS JOHS GUALBERTUS / S̄CA AGATA.V

CONDITION: A photograph of unknown date (Florence, Sopr. Gab. Fot. 1716; Fremantle, fig. 772) records the state of the Prato altarpiece before extensive additions were made to the frame and shows the triangular area of wood added to the severely truncated center panel. This modern addition was in turn cut down to fit the new frame and then ineptly painted in order to suggest the completion of the Gothic throne back. The altarpiece was fitted with a new frame, which integrates the original three bases and the roundels above the pairs of saints in the laterals. All of the frame cusps are modern.

HISTORY: Badia degli Olivetani di San Bartolomeo alle Sacca, near Prato (suppressed in 1784); Collegio Cicognini, Prato; sold to the city of Prato in 1870.

LITERATURE: 1864, Crowe and Cavalcaselle, vol. 1, p. 556, note 1: ascribed to Lorenzo Monaco; then in the Collegio Cicognini // 1888, Guasti, pp. 33-34; no. 4: LM // 1896, Berenson, p. 258: LM, early (1932, p. 301; 1963, vol. 1, p. 120)// 1905, Sirén, pp. 50-53: shows a new contact with the art of Siena; LM, around 1408-1412 // 1927, van Marle, vol. 9, p. 126: LM, around 1404 // 1929, Suida, p. 392: LM // 1931, Golzio, pp. 38-39: LM, after 1410; shows lessened Sienese character of Lorenzo's style // 1938/39, Pudelko, pp. 247 and 248, note 33: LM, immediately following the Monte Oliveto Altarpiece of 1406-1410; the Loeser *Blessing Christ* (now London, private collection) may have been the central pinnacle // 1956, Baldini, p. 15: by a close follower of Don Lorenzo, perhaps the same one who painted a recomposed polyptych at Empoli (nos. 72 and 21) // 1958, Marchini, pp. 17-18: by a follower working in the earlier style of Don Lorenzo, with his approval; a comparable style seen in nos. 72 and 21 of the Museo della Collegiata at Empoli // 1958, Levi D'Ancona, "Matteo Torelli," p. 249: LM, 1408-1410 // 1975, Boskovits, p. 352: LM, 1410-15 // 1982 Florence, *Iconografia di San Benedetto*, pp. 101-102, no. 34: the Olivetan provenance explains the white habit worn by Saint Benedict // 1984, Bellosi, p. 309: largely by Francesco d'Antonio.

COMMENT: The Prato altarpiece demonstrates the working method of a primary assistant in Lorenzo Monaco's shop who used as a basic model the polyptych for San Bartolomeo at Monte Oliveto (Accademia, Florence; Fig. 22), dated 1410. Parallels with that work are the "saluting" Child composed on a long arc, the grave Saint Benedict, and the apron-like arrangement of the mantle of Saint Catherine. The format of the three panels at Prato, with the deeply indented consoles implying a pentaptych, suggests further reliance on the same source. In the Prato altarpiece, however, the style of Lorenzo Monaco at the end of the first decade of the Quattrocento is overlaid with characteristics of his *Coronation of the Virgin* of 1414. The planar and calligraphic mantle of Christ in that work (Fig. 44) provided the matrix on which the lower half of the Prato Madonna was composed. Gone are the extended flat folds and the double layering of mantle and tunic of the Monte Oliveto Madonna of 1410, replaced by serpentine contours that define an incisive silhouette. A date after the Monte Oliveto Altarpiece and during the designing of the *Coronation*, around 1412-14, would seem appropriate for the Prato altarpiece. Along with the hybrid character of the style, there are other aspects of the work that mark it as a product of Lorenzo's shop. The mildness of the drawing, particularly of the saints in the laterals, lends these standing figures a papery insubstantiality. The drawing of their features is even more summary than in the Madonna of the center panel, which suggests that the execution of this large shop work involved the intervention of assistants of varying degrees of competence. The hand of Francesco d'Antonio (Bellosi, 1984) is ruled out by comparison with his signed and dated triptych in the Fitzwilliam Museum (1415; Fig. 330). The similarity of calligraphic passages in the fall of the Virgin's mantle is a matter of reference to established models in the workshop.

Sirén (1905) recognized that the enthroned Madonna in the central panel of the Prato altarpiece is directly dependent on a Sienese model. Previously, in the Monte Oliveto Altarpiece, Lorenzo had quoted the type of Sienese standing Christ Child, and now, whether through direct reference or intermediary works, there is a literal reuse in the Prato Madonna of the frontal pose and central clasping of the mantle found early in Simone Martini's *Maestà* fresco in the Palazzo Pubblico in Siena. The adoption at this moment in the activity of Don Lorenzo's workshop of an indigenously Sienese motif could possibly help in the interpretation of the document of 1415, which notes elliptically the painter's Sienese connection and implies that he is absent from his residence in Florence with sufficient frequency to necessitate an arrangement for the rental of his house (see Document 11 and the Introductory Essay, Note 9).

Umberto Baldini's suggestion (1956) that the follower of Lorenzo Monaco who painted the Prato altarpiece was also responsible for the *Madonna Enthroned* and two *Saints* laterals in Empoli (Figs. 154-156) was the key to the reconstruction of a cohesive group of works that spans an extended period in the activity of Don Lorenzo's shop. As the entries on the Empoli panels in Catalogue I indicate, I do not believe that they were originally part of the same altarpiece. Mirella Levi D'Ancona (1958), although considering the Prato altarpiece to be an autograph work of Lorenzo Monaco, first recognized that a group of pictures dependent on it includes not only the panels in Empoli but works in Cracow (Fig. 153), Houston (Fig. 257), and Brussels (Fig. 157), to all of which she attached the name of Matteo Torelli (for the panels in the Museum of Fine Arts, Houston, see Catalogue II). The Catherine of the Cracow panel is a conflation of the same saint and the Agatha of the Prato altarpiece, while the immediate model for the Baptist is in the Empoli triptych of 1404 (Fig. 20; noted in Cracow, 1961, p. 54). But the variegated secondary palette of the Cracow Catherine, evident from the recent restoration, and the elongated proportions of the Catherine and Baptist bring the panel into closest alliance with Don Lorenzo's Accademia *Annunciation* of around 1418 (Fig. 77). During his activity in the workshop of Lorenzo Monaco in the early 1420s the painter of the Prato altarpiece would seem to have designed and executed the *Annunciation*, formerly in the Féron-Stoclet Collection in Brussels, and the closely related panels in Empoli, a continuity discerned cumulatively by Baldini and Levi D'Ancona. The Prato and Empoli Catherines show a clear descendance and the latter figure is an unmistakable relative of the Annunciate Virgin (see Figs. 152, 154, and 156). In turn, the Annunciate Virgin and the Empoli *Madonna* display close stylistic parallels. Confirming the proximity of these two works is the identical ornamental detail in the borders of the mantles and the unusual application of a star on both shoulders of the Virgin. The rhythms of the Prato Virgin's draperies persist in the Empoli panel, but the bowed shape of the Child has been supplanted by the columnar forms that will migrate into the art of Fra Angelico (also see Catalogue I, Lugano, Thyssen-Bornemisza Foundation, *Madonna Enthroned*).

The wiry elegance of Don Lorenzo's *Adoration of the Magi* (Fig. 82) provided the stylistic mode for the "Prato painter" in this later group of works. Witness the three Magi and the pair of full-length figures to their right in comparison with the Gabriel of the *Annunciation* or the Bishop Saint in the right lateral at Empoli. The sequence of works initiating in the Prato altarpiece demonstrates an evolving process whereby a close associate of Lorenzo Monaco accommodated his style to successive stages of the master's development. An aspect of the former Brussels *Annunciation* and the works in Empoli that confirms their relationship and at the same time decisively differentiates them from the later autograph work of Lorenzo Monaco, however, is the high chromatic key, concentrated in such passages as the intense coral red of Gabriel's mantle and wings, and the robe of Saint Catherine. The subtly graduated colors in the wings of the archangel in the Santa Trinita *Annunciation*, painted by Lorenzo Monaco within the same half decade, are the creation of a divergent sensibility. [ca. 1412-14]

ROME, Galleria Pallavicini, no. 281

Funeral of Saint Francis

FIG. 191

Panel: 73.3 x 57.9 cm. (framed); 68.5 x 53.3 cm. (painted surface)

CONDITION: A fissure running the entire vertical length of the panel noticeably disrupts the figure with the aspergill and the lower area of Saint Francis's cassock. For a detailed report, see Zeri, 1959, p. 164.

HISTORY: In the collections at Casa Pallavicini, Rome, by 1856.

LITERATURE: 1856, T. Minardi, *Descrizione, misura, e stima . . .*, MS., Archive of Casa Pallavicini, Rome, vol. A.5.26.7, p. 28, no. 202: school of Giotto (cited by Zeri, 1959) // 1905, Sirén, p. 168: assistant of Lorenzo Monaco // 1927, van Marle, vol. 9, p. 162; Lorenzo Monaco; related in style to the predella scenes of the *Coronation of the Virgin* of 1413 // 1932, Berenson, p. 301: LM, studio (1963, vol. 1, p. 121) // 1932, De Benedetti, p. 145: LM // 1938/39, Pudelko, p. 78, note 9: LM; allies the panel with the *Stigmatization of Saint Francis* in Amsterdam; from the period between 1414 and the end of Lorenzo's career // 1945, Brandi, no. 68: the shop of Lorenzo Monaco was probably involved in the execution, indicated by a certain crudeness in the palette and a summary quality in the rendering of detail; proposes a connection with the *Stigmatization* in the Lanz Collection, Amsterdam, an independent observation that confirms Pudelko's earlier notice // 1959, Zeri, pp. 164-65: designed and mainly executed by Lorenzo in his later style; some figures show the hand of a pupil, perhaps the same one who painted the *Saint Lawrence* triptych in the Louvre (now Avignon) and its predella (Vatican, Pinacoteca); further bibliography // 1965, Russoli, p. 142: LM and pupils, ca. 1420 // 1974, S. Bos, in van Os and Prakken, p. 70, no. 35: discusses in relation to the Amsterdam *Saint Francis* // 1975, Boskovits, p. 353: LM, 1420-25. // 1979, Bellosi, pp. 63-65: LM in latest style; integrates with *Crucifixion*, Museo Bandini, Fiesole and *Stigmatization of Saint Francis*, Rijksmuseum, Amsterdam.

COMMENT: The overlapping and isocephalism of the cluster of monks recall Don Lorenzo's figural groupings, notably in the Uffizi *Adoration of the Magi* (Fig. 82) and the *Betrothal of the Virgin* at Santa Trinita (Fig. 109). Among the monks in the *Funeral* one peers out at the left who is a counterpart to the glowering figure amidst the rear rank of onlookers in the *Betrothal* fresco. For further comment on the picture in relation to its companion panels and its place in the context of Lorenzo's later style, see Catalogue I, Amsterdam, Rijksmuseum, *Stigmatization of Saint Francis*; Fiesole, Museo Bandini, *Crucifixion with the Virgin and Saints John the Evangelist and Francis*. [ca. 1422-23]

ROME, Pinacoteca Vaticana, no. 193

A Young Monk Tempted from Prayer, and Saint Benedict Raises a Young Monk
FIG. 186

Panel: 30 x 65 cm.

CONDITION: The Vatican picture and that in the National Gallery, London, of *Saint Benedict Admitting Saints Maurus and Placidus into the Order* (Fig. 183), were originally elements of a single, elongated rectangular panel framed as an octagon. After the original frame was removed, probably when the scenes were severed, the unpainted corners at the right in the Vatican panel and at the left in the London fragment were painted in, to square off the images. These four triangular patches remain clearly visible. The picture surface has suffered extensive abrasion and fracturing of the paint film.

HISTORY: Predella of the *Coronation of the Virgin* altarpiece, San Benedetto fuori della Porta a Pinti, outside Florence (for the history of the altarpiece until the later eighteenth century, see Catalogue I, London, National Gallery, San Benedetto Altarpiece); Biblioteca Apostolica, Vatican, Rome, 1837(?); Museo Sacro, Biblioteca Apostolica, until 1908; Pinacoteca Vaticana, since 1908.

LITERATURE: 1905, Sirén, pp. 67-68: Lorenzo Monaco; part of the predella of a Coronation of the Virgin of which the side panels are in London, National Gallery // 1906, Sirén, "Notizie critiche," p. 335: repeats earlier opinion // 1906, Perkins, p. 123: LM // 1909, Berenson, p. 154: LM (1932, p. 301; 1963, vol. 1, p. 121) // 1913, *Guida della Pinacoteca Vaticana*, p. 30, no. 68: LM // 1915, Biagi, p. 230: LM; reports that the panel has been recently cleaned // 1927, van Marle, vol. 9, p. 164: LM, considerably later than 1413; possibly part of an altarpiece with an hypothesized central panel of Saint Benedict and the side panels of *Kneeling Saints* in the National Gallery, London // 1929, Suida, p. 392: LM // 1938/39, Pudelko, p. 247, note 32: LM // 1951, Davies, p. 242 (see 1961 ed.) // 1961, Davies, p. 310: either by LM, of predella quality, or by an assistant in the studio; from the predella of the San Benedetto *Coronation of the Virgin* altarpiece // 1963, Berenson, vol. 1, p. 121: records the connection with the London predella // 1975, Boskovits, p. 353: LM, 1410-15 // 1981, Mancinelli and Nahmad, p. 18, no. 11: LM, ca. 1410.

COMMENT: See Catalogue I, London, National Gallery, San Benedetto Altarpiece. [1415-20]

SCARSDALE (New York), Otto Manley Collection

Scenes from the Early Life of John the Baptist
FIG. 197

Parchment: 25.8 x 19.1 cm.
Technique: Brown ink, and brown and rose pencil

HISTORY: The drawing bears the marks of two collectors: (to left of basin) Jonathan Richardson (Lugt 2184); (lower left corner) Theodore Lippert (Lugt 1377). There is no available information on the subsequent history of the drawing.

LITERATURE: 1968, Degenhart and Schmitt, pt. 1, vol. 2, pp. 298-300, no. 198; vol. 4, pl. 217a: Florentine, 1425-30 // 1974, Watson, p. 8, note 15: beginning of the fifteenth century; an important iconographic model for the *desco da parto* by Bartolomeo di Fruosino in the New-York Historical Society // 1975, Boskovits, p. 354: Lorenzo Monaco, 1400-1405 // 1978, Bellosi and Bellini, p. xviii: recalls Don Lorenzo's *Visitation* drawing in Berlin and the frescoes of the Bartolini Salimbeni Chapel at Santa Trinita.

COMMENT: The drawing is discussed in relation to the Berlin *Visitation* and the fresco cycle and altarpiece at Santa Trinita (see Catalogue I, Berlin-Dahlem, Staatliche Museen, Kupferstichkabinett, *Visitation*; and Florence, Santa Trinita, Bartolini Salimbeni Chapel, *Life of the Virgin* and *Annunciation* altarpiece). [ca. 1422-23]

SEATTLE (Washington), Seattle Art Museum, Kress Collection, no. 61.158

Crucifixion with the Virgin and Saint John the Evangelist
FIG. 137

Panel: 125.7 x 59.7 cm. (with engaged frame)
Inscribed date: 1408 (AVE MARIA GRATIA PL MCCCCVIII)
Inscription: (Cross) ĪÑR̄Ī

CONDITION: Virtually the entire gold ground has developed an obtrusive crackle, but the condition is not precarious.

HISTORY: Charles Butler, London, by 1885, ascribed

to Cennino Cennini; [Wildenstein and Co., New York]; Samuel Kress, New York, 1949; Seattle Art Museum, 1952.

LITERATURE: 1952, Suida, p. 14: Lorenzo Monaco // 1963, Berenson, vol. 1, p. 121: studio of LM // 1966, Shapley, p. 90: follower of LM // 1972, Fredericksen and Zeri, p. 111: LM // 1975, Boskovits, p. 354: LM.

COMMENT: See Catalogue I, Florence, Accademia, *Madonna and Child with Four Saints* (no. 470). [1408]

SIENA, Pinacoteca Nazionale, no. 157

Madonna and Child in Glory, with Saints John the Baptist and Nicholas
FIG. 132

Pinnacles: (Center) *Bishop Saint* (Augustine?); (wings) *Annunciation*

Panel: 60 x 45 cm. (overall dimensions of triptych)
Inscription: (Baptist) ECCE AN

CONDITION: The triptych was restored in 1981 by Martino Oberto, revealing the excellent condition of the paint film.

HISTORY: In the collections of the Istituto di Belle Arti in Siena by 1842.

LITERATURE: 1842, Pini, p. 6, no. 61: by an unknown painter // 1903, Olcott-Heywood, p. 391: in the manner of Lorenzo Monaco // 1905, Sirén, pp. 31-32: LM, in the early years of the Quattrocento, demonstrating the importance of Sienese art in the formation of his style // 1906, Schubring, p. 174: denies the attribution to Lorenzo, proposing instead the circle of Taddeo di Bartolo // 1909, Berenson, p. 154: LM, early (1932, p. 301; 1963, vol. 1, p. 121) // 1927, van Marle, vol. 9, pp. 130-31: LM, 1405-1408 // 1928, Perkins, p. 160: by a close follower and contemporary of Lorenzo // 1928, Longhi, p. 38, note 2: LM; indicates that the Master of the Straus Madonna began in a circle close to him // 1929, Suida, p. 392: LM // 1931, Golzio, p. 32: LM; shows the influence of Fei and anticipates the delicacy of Angelico // 1933, Brandi, p. 341, no. 157: LM, at the end of the Trecento, showing the influence of Sienese art; further bibliography // 1938/39, Pudelko, p. 238: LM, first years of the fifteenth century, with a new Sienese gracefulness in the style // 1954, Salmi, p. 45: a late work of LM, close to the miniatures in Bargello Cod. E 70 // 1958, Carli, p. 45, no. 157: LM // 1958, Levi D'Angonca, "Some New Attributions," p. 253: Matteo Torelli, with the closest parallels to the eglomisé *Madonna* in Turin and to miniatures in Bargello Cod. E70 // 1965, Bellosi, *Maestri*, [p. 7], reproduced in color: LM, around 1400 // 1965, Bellosi, "Da Spinello," p. 39: LM, close to the *Madonna Enthroned* in the Fitzwilliam Museum; in a style freed from the ideological pressures of a devotional severity // 1969, van Os, p. 141, note 193: workshop of LM // 1975, Boskovits, p. 354: LM, 1395-1400 // 1978, Torriti, p. 236, no. 157, reproduced in color: LM, just at the turn of the century or shortly before.

COMMENT: Lorenzo Monaco was responsible for the design of the Siena triptych, but his hand is discernible only in the central image of the Madonna in Glory. There are links with the drapery style and appliqué gold ornament of the Fitzwilliam *Madonna* (Fig. 15) and with the *Agony in the Garden* in the Accademia, Florence, most evidently in the figure of the sleeping Saint James (cf. Figs. 7 and 132). The facial types of the Baptist and Nicholas in the wings of the Siena triptych and of the Bishop Saint (Augustine?) in the crest of the center panel differ significantly, however, from Lorenzo's miniatures in the choir books from Santa Maria degli Angeli (Figs. 1-6) and from the Baptist and Zenobius in the Berenson *Madonna* (Fig. 16). The Gabriel and Virgin in the pinnacles of the wings are the ineffectual additions of a lesser assistant. Although Levi D'Ancona's (1958) ascription of the triptych to the miniaturist Matteo Torelli is not persuasive, her detection of similarities to works of Lorenzo's shop, to which she also attached Torelli's name, demonstrated that the master was assisted even in this early and intimate project. The resemblance in figure type of the Nicholas in the Siena triptych to the Zenobius of the Berenson panel indicates that a standard model, in this case of Cionesque stamp, was used in the workshop, to reappear with only slight variations in the Nicholas of the Berlin *Madonna* of around 1402 (Fig. 17). Longhi's (1928) recognition of alliances in the Siena triptych with the style of the Master of the Straus Madonna, which he also discerned in the Fitzwilliam *Madonna*, points up the interchanges between cognate shops active in Florence around 1400. As with the Fitzwilliam *Madonna*, the palette of the Siena triptych is dualistic, the transparent light blue of the central panel stemming from Agnolo Gaddi and the piquant reds and greenish white in the wings from the Cionesque tradition.

Contrary to Golzio's proposal (1931) that the work of Paolo di Giovanni Fei provided a direct model for the Siena triptych, the intermediary contribution of Don Silvestro dei Gherarducci must be taken into account, as in, for example, his intimate triptych in the Herrington Collection in Indianapolis, a work that reveals how deeply his stylistic roots lay in Cionesque and Sienese traditions (see Wagstaff, 1965, pp. 16-17, no. 11). H. W. van Os (1969), enlarging on Millard Meiss's definition of a "celestial version" of the Madonna of Humility (1951, p. 139), has observed that the apparitional Madonna in Glory placed on a cloud bank is specifically a later Trecento Florentine type, whereas in the Sienese tradition the Virgin is more likely to be surrounded with a seraphic aureole. An important exception is found in the work of the Florentine Master of Santa Verdiana, who represented the "celestial version" several times, with and without the aureole (e.g., see Boskovits, 1967, figs. 1, 4, and 5). The frequency with which the Master of Santa Verdiana depicted the Virgin on a cloud bank raises the possibility that this prolific artist of the generation immediately before Lorenzo Monaco provided the model for the central panel of the Siena triptych. Undeniably Sienese in origin, however, is the heavily crocketed frame of the triptych, which is comparable in type to portable tabernacles and triptychs by Paolo di Giovanni Fei (see Mallory, 1976, figs. 48 and 78). [ca. 1400]

Note: there is a modern copy of the Siena triptych in a private collection in Basel (photograph on deposit at the Kunsthistorisches Institut, Florence) in which the only significant modification from the original is the omission of the punched trefoil on the gold ground at the base of the center panel.

§ STUTTGART, Staatsgalerie Stuttgart, no. 2773

Madonna of Humility

FIG. 39

Panel: 43.8 x 22.2 cm. (painted surface)
Inscribed date: 1407 (ABANNO SUE INCARNATIONIS M CCCC VII)

CONDITION: The frame, although made of old wood, does not appear to be the original one, as there is a segment of exposed beard at the crest of the gilded surface, indicating where an earlier frame impinged. The rays emanating from the Virgin and Child were apparently cut into the gold ground when the panel was inserted into the new frame, judging by the fact these crude incisions cross the segment of original beard and also invade the punched ornamentation of the haloes.

HISTORY: Private collection, Milan; [Thos Agnew & Sons, London]; Staatsgalerie, Stuttgart, 1967.

LITERATURE: 1948, Zurich, *Kunstschätze*, p. 214, no. 609: Lorenzo Monaco // 1975, Boskovits, p. 354: LM.

COMMENT: The Stuttgart *Madonna* and the *Prophets* in the Metropolitan Museum of Art (Figs. 40-43) provide the principal evidence of Lorenzo Monaco's brief though strong attraction to sculptural dimensionality toward the middle of the first decade of the century, but the contradictory shallowness of the Virgin's extended arm and shawl, and of the Child implies an unusual tentativeness in execution or the intervention of an assistant. The close bonding of the Christ Child to the arc of the Virgin's shoulder is a variant on the design of the Infant in the Empoli and Berenson *Madonna of Humility* panels of 1404 and 1405 (Figs. 21, 38). The fringing of the Virgin's kerchief is a decorative feature used by Lorenzo Monaco and his shop only in a few works of around 1407: cf., Altenburg, Staatliches Lindenau-Museum, *Flight into Egypt* (Fig. 32); London, Courtauld Institute Galleries, *Visitation* (Fig. 29); Turin, Museo Civico, *Madonna of Humility* (Fig. 140). [1407]

TAVÈRNOLA (near Grizzana, Emilia), Parish Church

Madonna Enthroned

FIG. 160

Panel: 98.5 x 55 cm. (painted surface)
Inscription: (Christ Child) EGO SU(m)

CONDITION: In a restoration of 1966 by Ottorino Nonfarmale, the figures of the Virgin and Child were found to be in an excellent state of preservation. In contrast, the gold ground and the ornamented draperies that enclose the two figures had suffered from several extensive regildings and repaintings. These additions were removed and where the loss had reached the gesso ground a neutral tone was applied. The heavy nineteenth-century frame was retained. The picture is presently (1987) in deposit at the studio of Sig. Nonfarmale in Bologna, awaiting further conservation measures.

HISTORY: As Francesco Arcangeli observed (1966, n.p., with references), the panel would seem to be the one recorded at Tavèrnola and attributed to Lippo Dalmasio, first in 1783 and again in the mid-nineteenth century. Arcangeli conjectured that the picture may have come to Tavèrnola because a certain Ferdinando Romualdo, a member of the Mingarelli family of that town, was a Camaldolese monk housed in Florence at the monastery of Santa Maria degli Angeli.

LITERATURE: 1783, S. Calindri, *Dizionario corografico . . . storico dell'Italia*, vol. 5, . . . *territorio bolognese*, p. 166 (cited by Arcangeli): Lippo Dalmasio // 1957, *Guida d'Italia del Touring Club Italiano, Emilia e Romagna*, Milan, p. 426: Lorenzo Monaco // 1959, C. Brandi, *Corriere della Sera*, August 21, p. 3 (cited by Arcangeli): reports going to see the panel in the company of Giorgio Morandi, at the latter's invitation; notes the regilded ground and that the work is "quasi un Lorenzo Monaco" // 1966, Arcangeli (n.p.): among the finest pictures by Lorenzo Monaco; a late work aligning stylistically with the frescoes at Santa Trinita; further references // 1975, Boskovits, p. 354, LM, 1420-25 (first brought the picture to my attention).

COMMENT: Although he saw the picture in an unrestored state, Cesare Brandi (1959) discerned that the Tavèrnola *Madonna* falls just short of being a fully autograph work of Lorenzo Monaco. That the design was Don Lorenzo's is recognized in the finely orchestrated rhythms of the Virgin's mantle, which are directly reminiscent of the Annunciate Virgin in the altarpiece at Santa Trinita (Fig. 120). The long V-shaped folds of the mantle falling between the knees recall comparable passages in the standing Virgin of the *Visitation* in the Santa Trinita predella (Fig. 124), or the *Saint Jerome* in Amsterdam (Fig. 129). As with those works, in the Tavèrnola *Madonna* a delicate balance is maintained between surface linearism and palpable mass, a pivotal aspect of Don Lorenzo's later style. Comparison with the Edinburgh *Madonna Enthroned* (Fig. 158) underscores the fact that the calligraphic silhouette, the keynote of his style in the later 1410s and sounded with a special brilliance in the Accademia *Annunciation* (Fig. 79), has now been abandoned. The presence, or at least the guidance of the master's hand in the Tavèrnola panel is apparent in the luminosity of the Virgin's lapis blue mantle, where the refined *velatura* is superbly preserved. But the ill-proportioned, neckless Child is virtually a caricature of Lorenzo's type; further, the exaggerated drawing of the Virgins's hands has a close parallel in the Berlin *Madonna of Humility* (Fig. 161), and her features are akin to the Kansas City *Madonna of Humility* (Fig. 145), both works of the shop. The abundant surround of patterned drapery, even in its fragmentary state, recalls those earlier and later Madonnas of the workshop in which this elaborate element was introduced probably to meet a demand for a more profuse ornamentation than was found in Don Lorenzo's autograph works (e.g., Figs. 139, 145, and 162). In spite of its eroded condition, the Tavèrnola *Madonna* should be considered among the important late collaborations of Lorenzo Monaco and his shop. [ca. 1422-23]

TOLEDO (Ohio), Toledo Museum of Art, no. 45.30

Madonna of Humility

FIGS. 149, 150

Pinnacle (roundel): *Blessing Redeemer*

Panel: 87.4 x 52 cm. (painted surface); (roundel) 9.7 cm.
Inscription: (Christ Child) EGO

CONDITION: There are scattered areas of unskilled repainting in the face of the Virgin, and the brocaded floor pattern is streaked with old varnish. The gold ground is extensively worn. The entire frame is a replacement, probably of the mid-nineteenth century (see Comment below, with regard to the roundels in the pinnacle and base of the frame).

HISTORY: Earl of Orford, Wolverton, by 1854; [sold at Christie's, June 26, 1856, no. 235, as school of Fra Angelico]; Sir Francis Cook, 1st Bt., Doughty House, Richmond, Surrey, 1868; Cook Collection, Richmond, until 1945. As the frame is not original, the two scutcheons in the plinth with the device of the Mazzinghi family of Florence, do not identify the initial patronage of the panel.

LITERATURE: 1854, Waagen, vol. 3, p. 436: probably the picture attributed to Taddeo di Bartolo // 1903,

Crowe and Cavalcaselle, vol. 2, p. 302, note 1: Lorenzo Monaco // 1905, Sirén, p. 170: shop of LM // 1909, Berenson, p. 154; LM // 1913, Borenius, no. 14: LM // 1927, van Marle, vol. 9, p. 172, school of LM // 1932, Berenson, p. 301: LM, in great part (1963, vol. 1, p. 121) // 1938/39, Pudelko, p. 76, note 2: LM shop // 1972, Fredericksen and Zeri, p. 111: LM; the figures in the pinnacle and base are also ascribed to him // 1975, Boskovits, p. 354: LM, 1405-1410 // 1976, *Toledo Museum of Art*, pp. 99-100: workshop of LM; further bibliography.

COMMENT: The Toledo panel was painted in Don Lorenzo's shop around 1418 to 1420, during a period of intense activity in the production of devotional images of the Madonna and Child (see the Introductory Essay, Note 120). The principal model from the master's style was the *Annunciation* in the Accademia, Florence (Fig. 77). Passages of drapery are quoted from that work, but the florid line is perfunctory in comparison with the model, and the proportional relationship of Mother and Child is not well conceived. The *Man of Sorrows* (van Marle, 1934/35, fig. 22), formerly in the van Gelder Collection, Brussels (Uccle), would seem to have been executed by the painter of the Toledo panel from the evidence of the similarly wiry, attenuated forms and the spindly hands of the Virgin and the half-length Christ, which are from the same mold. González-Palacios (1970, p. 34) has persuasively related the van Gelder panel to the cutout *Crucifix* in Toulouse (Fig. 151), attributing both to Lorenzo Monaco. For compositional alliances among the Toledo, Brooklyn, and Philadelphia *Madonna of Humility* panels, see Catalogue I, Brooklyn (New York), Brooklyn Museum.

The head and features of the Child in the Toledo panel are rendered with a livelier modelling in light and shade than those of the Virgin, a distinction perhaps accountable in part to the insensitive retouchings of her face. The optical interest implied in the modelling of the Child's features is further observed in the treatment of the gold-brocaded floor pattern. In the areas that support the cushion and mantle the painted gold designs are accented with a punched texture, whereas a strip at the base of the panel contains the same pattern, but without the punched ornamentation. This contrast in texture simulates the varying effects of light as it falls upon the horizontal platform and the vertical riser.

The *Blessing Redeemer* (Fig. 150), inserted into the ogival tympanum of the neo-gothic frame, was very likely in the same position in the original framing of the picture. That the roundel issued from Don Lorenzo's workshop may be demonstrated by comparison with the God the Father in the cut miniature in the Musée Marmottan (Fig. 206), and with the conformation of the blessing hand of Christ in the central pinnacle of the *Coronation of the Virgin* for Santa Maria degli Angeli (Fig. 48). The graduated lighting of the face of the Redeemer is closely comparable to that of the Child in the main panel. The roundel in the base of the ornate frame, which represents a half-length Man of Sorrows in an internal quatrefoil, is from the earlier fifteenth century, but is not related to the stylistic tradition of Lorenzo Monaco. [ca. 1418-20]

TOULOUSE, Musée des Augustins, no. 401

Crucifix

FIG. 151

Cutout central panel of a *Crucifixion* group by Neri di Bicci
Panel: 111 x 73 cm.
Inscription: .Ī.Ñ.R̄.Ī.

CONDITION: Excepting two horizontal cracks in the proper left of the torso, the condition is sound. Damage at the apex of the halo is superficially repaired.

HISTORY: Bequeathed to the Musée des Augustins by Alexandre Dumège, an archaeologist and curator of the museum in the mid-nineteenth century, who died in 1862.

LITERATURE: 1864, George, p. 46, no. 53: Italian school, fifteenth century // 1920, Roschach, p. 175, no. 401: Italian school, fifteenth century // 1928, R. Offner (verbally), Lorenzo Monaco and Neri di Bicci (recorded on Frick Art Reference Library, photo. no. 703-24d) // 1928, van Marle, vol. 10, p. 545: the entire work attributed to Neri di Bicci // 1932, Berenson, p. 389: (under Neri di Bicci) the *Crucifix* attributed to LM (1963, vol. 1, p. 157) // 1970, González-Palacios, p. 34: LM, late period; associated with the crosses in Budapest, Monte San Savino, and Florence (San Giovannino dei Cavalieri), and to the *Man of Sorrows* once in the van Gelder Collection, Brussels // 1975, Boskovits, p. 355: LM, 1400-1405.

COMMENT: The small size of the *Crucifix* aligns it with the intimate type at Santa Maria delle Vertighe (Fig. 71), in contrast to the imposing crosses at San Giovannino dei Cavalieri and Santa Marta (Figs. 70 and 72). Unlike the Monte San Savino cross, which would seem to have served a processional function, the original broad base of the Toulouse panel, with its explicit reference to Calvary, suggests use on an auxiliary altar in a chapel or within a domestic setting. The application of the *Crucifix* to a later panel surface prevents determination as to whether it is painted on the back as well as the front, as are the the Monte San Savino cross and that in the Museo Horne (Fig. 163). See Catalogue I, Toledo, Museum of Art, *Madonna of Humility*. [ca. 1418-20]

TURIN, Museo Civico di Torino, Museo d'Arte Antica, no. V.O. 152-3024

Madonna of Humility with Saints John the Baptist and John the Evangelist (?)

FIG. 140

Verre églomisé: 20.3 x 13.5 cm. (glass surface); 29.5 x 23 (with frame)
Inscribed date: 1408 (ANNO D MCCCCVIII)

CONDITION: Two extensive cracks in the glass intrude upon the heads of the Virgin and Child and the cusps above the attendant saints. The inscription on the frame in coarse Roman capitals would seem to be a later addition.

HISTORY: Costabili Collection, Ferrara, by 1841 (family coat of arms on the reverse); Massimo d'Azeglio; bequeathed to the Museo Civico in 1890.

LITERATURE: 1841, Laderchi, vol. 4, p. 40, no. 396: Giottesque, early fifteenth century // 1905, Sirén, "Tre Madonnine," p. 248: notes that Suida brought the work to his attention; Lorenzo Monaco, but of lesser quality than two works of the same year—the Louvre triptych wings and the *Madonna with Four Saints* in the Uffizi (now Accademia, Florence, no. 470) // 1908, Suida, "Beiträge," p. 305: LM; reads the date as 1405 (1929, p. 392) // 1908, Toesca, p. 254: LM // 1909, Berenson, p. 154: LM (1932, p. 301; 1963, vol. 1, p. 121) // 1927, van Marle, vol. 9, p. 134: LM // 1938/39, Pudelko, p. 76, note 1: LM // 1958, Levi D'Ancona, "Matteo Torelli," pp. 252-53: Matteo Torelli, from the same phase of his work as the triptych in Siena // 1968, Degenhart and Schmitt, pt. 1, vol. 2, p. 269: LM circle // 1975, Boskovits, p. 354: LM // 1978, Pettenati, pp. xxvii, and 15-17; pl. VI in color: LM; considers inscription on the frame to be original; additional bibliography and technical analysis.

COMMENT: The stylistic contradictions between the figure of the Virgin and the accompanying saints are the result of an assistant turning for models to Don Lorenzo's *Madonna of Humility* panels from the middle of the first decade (e.g., Biblioteca Berenson, 1405; Fig. 38) and to images of saints by both Lorenzo and his workshop from the last years of the Trecento (e.g., the Siena triptych, Fig. 132, and the miniature of *Saint John the Evangelist*, Fig. 5). The Turin Virgin also bears some resemblance to the types found in the "Courtauld predella" (e.g., Fig. 32). The brocaded cloth of honor, the abundant fringing, and the leafy ornament in the spandrels lend a more decorative effect than is characteristic of Don Lorenzo's autograph works. [1408]

Note: A fragment of *verre églomisé* in the Louvre, with the *Madonna Enthroned and Two Saints*, has been attributed to the early style of Lorenzo Monaco by Silvana Pettenati (1978, p. 16). Also see Pettenati, "Vetri a oro del Trecento padano," *Paragone* 24, no. 275, 1973, p. 73, and fig. 51; Bellosi, 1985, pp. 21-22, and fig. 58 (attributed to Lorenzo Monaco, ca. 1400; additional bibliography). Miklós Boskovits attributes the fragment to Cenni di Francesco (1975, p. 291).

VADUZ, Castle, Collections of the Prince of Liechtenstein, no. 865

Madonna in Glory with Two Angels

FIG. 194

Panel: 67.5 x 36 cm. (with engaged frame)
Inscription: AVE GRATIA PLENA DMS TECUM

CONDITION: The gold ground has been extensively reworked, which accounts for the rigid contour of the right side of the Virgin's mantle, while two parallel fissures disrupt the articulation of her wrist and hand. Except for a few retouchings, the tempera surface is intact.

HISTORY: Acquired in Florence in 1900 by Prince Johannes II of Liechtenstein. The panel was part of the family's collections in Vienna and Mödling before being transferred to Vaduz Castle.

LITERATURE: 1908, Suida, "Beiträge," p. 305: Lorenzo Monaco // 1912, Suida, no. 12: LM // 1927, van Marle, vol. 9, p. 130: LM, around 1405 // 1929, Suida, p. 392: LM // 1932, Berenson, p. 300: LM, then in Mödling (1963, vol. 1, p. 121: in Vaduz). // 1938/39, Pudelko, p. 76, note 1: LM, 1408, contemporary with the *Madonna of Humility* in Turin // 1938, Stix and Strohmer, p. 91: shop of LM, with the master's collaboration; illustration (pl. 9) reversed // 1948, Lucerne, *Meisterwerke*, p. 18, no. 4: LM // 1972, G. Wilhelm, *Italienische Kunst des XIV. bis XVI. Jahrhunderts aus den Sammlungen des Fürsten von Liechtenstein*, Vaduz, p. 15, no. 16: LM // 1975, Boskovits, p. 355: LM, 1415-20 // 1980, Baumstark, no. 2: LM.

COMMENT: As with the *Madonna in Glory* panels in Siena and formerly in the Schaeffer Galleries, New York (Figs. 132 and 195), the iconography of the Madonna of Humility has been adapted here to what Meiss has called a "celestial version" of the subject (1951, p. 139). The Liechtenstein *Madonna* is a late collaboration of Lorenzo Monaco and the workshop associate who was importantly active in the design and execution of the San Benedetto Altarpiece (see Catalogue I, London, National Gallery). The collaborator's hand is most evident in the censing angels who are simply reduced versions of the angels kneeling below the dais of the London *Coronation of the Virgin* (Fig. 175) and those that appear in only slightly modified form in the *Assumption of the Virgin* fresco at Santa Trinita (Fig. 112). The same associate would seem to have been entirely responsible for the *Madonna of Humility* of 1415 at Sant'Ermete in Pisa (Fig. 146). But the design of the Virgin and Child in the Vaduz panel was the personal invention of Lorenzo Monaco, falling between the Brooklyn *Madonna of Humility* of circa 1418 to 1420 (Fig. 147) and the late work in the Bartolini Salimbeni Chapel or the *Madonna of Humility* in Copenhagen (Fig. 128). An uncommon note of shot rose and silver-gray in the angels' tunics recalls the palette of the Santa Trinita frescoes. The compact physical presence and the quietening of the calligraphy begin to approach the predella of the late *Annunciation* (e.g., Figs. 126-27) and the Copenhagen panel, although in the Liechtenstein picture the emotive key is lower. It is the absence of expressively lighted forms abetted by the hatching of the tempera that essentially differentiates the panel in Vaduz from the autograph late works of Lorenzo Monaco. [ca. 1420-22]

WASHINGTON (D.C.), National Gallery of Art, Samuel H. Kress Collection, no. 514 (Kress no. K1293)

Madonna of Humility

FIG. 143

Panel: 117 x 55 cm.
Inscribed date (on painted riser): 1413 (AVE G . . . M ANO.D.M. CCCC.XIII)
Inscription: (Christ Child) EGO . . . (lu)X M

CONDITION: The facial areas have suffered some abrasion (see Giraudon photograph, no. 6491, which also shows considerable damage to the gold ground). See Shapley, 1979, vol. 1, p. 274, for notice of conservation measures in 1940 and 1956.

HISTORY: Masson Collection, Amiens; [Contini-Bonacossi, Florence]; Samuel H. Kress, 1939; Samuel H. Kress Collection, National Gallery, Washington, 1941.

LITERATURE: 1905, Sirén, pp. 88-89: Lorenzo Monaco, suggesting comparisons with the *Coronation of the Virgin* altarpiece of 1413 // 1909, Sirén, p. 36: attributes to LM, but sees the elongated contours as not typical of the master's style // 1927, van Marle, vol. 9, p. 162: LM 1929, Suida, p. 392: LM // 1938/39, Pudelko, pp. 76-77: LM; creates the same poetic atmosphere expressed later in Masolino's representations of the Virgin; influence of Ghiberti, particularly the terra-cotta Madonnas // 1963, Berenson, vol. 1, p. 121: LM // 1966, Shapley, p. 89: LM; close in composition to the *Madonna* in the Monte Oliveto Altarpiece (Florence, Accademia, dated 1410); provides further bibliography and unpublished opinions (reprinted with additional bibliography in Shapley, 1979, vol. 1, p. 274) // 1972, Fredericksen and Zeri, p. 111: LM // 1975, Boskovits, p. 355: LM // 1980, Cole Ahl, p. 368: LM, about the time Fra Angelico was likely to have been apprenticed // 1984, J. Walker, *National Gallery of Art, Washington*, revised ed., New York, p. 76, no. 19 (in color): LM.

COMMENT: Comparison of the National Gallery's *Madonna of Humility* with the Uffizi *Coronation of the Virgin* of 1414, a contemporary work and the apogee of Lorenzo's art at mid-career, reveals dissimilarities that cannot be explained simply by assigning the picture to the workshop, as I once proposed (quoted by Shapley, 1966). The vivid contrast between the springing calligraphy of the Virgin's mantle and the Child's rectilinear tunic and sharply radial mantle reaches a degree of rhythmic disjuncture that is unique in works by Lorenzo Monaco or his shop. In such late collaborations as the *Madonna* panels in Edinburgh (Fig. 158) and Lugano (Fig. 159) the tubular forms of the drapery echo the larger rhythms of the Virgin. These standing Infants, however, seem conventional when confronted by the individuality of the Child in the earlier panel. Pudelko's (1938/39) analogy with Ghiberti is justified and even better observed in the *Transfiguration* relief of the North Door (designed by 1413), where the rigid tunic of Moses contradicts the dominant flow of calligraphic line (Krautheimer, 1956, pl. 37). A technique visible in the Kress panel that is foreign to Lorenzo Monaco is the modelling in light and shade of the Virgin's face and the entire head of the Child, with the features emerging from a structure of chiaroscuro. In the old Giraudon photograph mentioned above, these nuances of modelling are more clearly visible in spite of the disturbing abrasion of the faces. If seen in isolation, the head of the infant could be pronounced a work of the 1420s, worthy of Angelico and predictive of Filippo Lippi. The painter of the National Gallery *Madonna* would seem to have been a distinctive assistant to Lorenzo Monaco who used the design of the master for the principal contours of the Virgin but introduced an opposing rhythm and a less traditional technique. Pudelko's detection of a hint of Masolino's art and Cole Ahl's linking with Angelico (1938/39; 1980), indicate recognition of the presence of a progressive vision that anticipates the optical realism of the 1420s. [1413]

WASHINGTON, National Gallery of Art, Rosenwald Collection, no. 1950.1.8

Prophet

FIG. 209

Cut miniature from a choir book
Parchment: 13.1 x 12.9 cm.

HISTORY: Santa Maria Nuova, Florence, Cod. H 74 (see below, Levi D'Ancona, 1958, and Nordenfalk, Vikan, et al, 1975); Simkhovitch Collection; Rosenwald Collection (1949).

LITERATURE: 1958, Levi D'Ancona, "Some New Attributions," pp. 177 and 181: Lorenzo Monaco, ca. 1423-24, on the basis of comparison with the predella of the *Annunciation* at Santa Trinita; establishes the provenance of the miniature as Cod. H 74 in the Bargello // 1975, Nordenfalk, Vikan, et al., pp. 44-46, no. 13, fig. 132, and colorplate 3: close to LM, early 1420s; a comprehensive catalogue entry, with full bibliography // 1975, Boskovits, p. 355: LM, 1410-15.

COMMENT: The *Prophet* is among the miniatures of Cod. H 74 that were executed by an assistant on Lorenzo's designs. The weakness in the drawing of the drapery, especially perceptible in the lower half of the figure, the inarticulate hands, and the overall mildness of expression, when compared with the fervid *Prophets* executed by Lorenzo Monaco in the same manuscript (Fig. 99), separate this miniature from the master's autograph works. (See Catalogue I, Florence, Bargello, Cod. H 74.) [ca. 1420-22]

II
OTHER WORKS ASCRIBED TO LORENZO MONACO

AACHEN, Suermondt-Ludwig-Museum, no. 24

Prophet

Cut miniature, from a choir book
Parchment: 23 x 25 cm.

LITERATURE: 1958, Levi D'Ancona, "Some New Attributions," p. 186: tentatively attributed to a follower of Lorenzo Monaco under the supervision of the master; possibly early fifteenth century, between the *John the Evangelist* of Corale 1 in the Laurenziana and the *Pietà* of 1404 in the Accademia in Florence // 1975, Boskovits, pp. 337-38, and fig. 444: LM, 1390-95 // 1977, E. G. Grimme, *Suermondt-Ludwig-Museum Aachen, Miniaturen, Handzeichnungen, Aquarelle*, Cologne, 1977, no. 8, colorplate 6: LM circle (*in litteris*, 1985, expresses doubt with regard to attribution of 1977) // 1978, Levi D'Ancona, p. 225: Bartolomeo di Fruosino.

COMMENT: Judging only from a photograph provided by the Frick Art Reference Library (unnumbered), the miniature is by a later, somewhat remote imitator who reverted to and exaggerated the characteristics of Don Lorenzo's early book painting. Although the stolid figure is clearly derived from his miniatures of the 1390s (Laurenziana, Corali 1, 5, and 8; Figs. 1-5), the hatched strokes used to simulate luminous drapery surfaces are a coarsened version of the technique in miniatures by Lorenzo Monaco from more than a decade later (Laurenziana, Corale 3; Fig. 65). The figure and its decorative surround are less skillfully executed than the typical miniature productions of either Don Lorenzo or his associates in the traditions of the Santa Maria degli Angeli scriptorium; the painter obviously faltered in his attempt to accommodate the Prophet to the ill-shaped letter *T*.

AMSTERDAM, Rijksmuseum, no. A 4004

Head of the Virgin

FIG. 235

Panel: 31 x 24 cm.

LITERATURE: 1934/35, van Marle, p. 302: early work of Niccolò di Pietro Gerini, in a Giottesque vein // 1950, Gronau, p. 221: ascribed to the formative years of Lorenzo Monaco; strongly Sienese in feeling and drawing; close in style to the *Madonna Enthroned* in the Fitzwilliam Museum; part of a group of works comparable to the San Gaggio Altarpiece attributed to Lorenzo and dated ca. 1390-91 // 1954, Eisenberg, p. 146: refutes the attribution to LM; closer to Master of the Straus Madonna // 1958, Levi D'Ancona, "Matteo Torelli," p. 252: Matteo Torelli, along with such works as the Turin *Madonna* on glass of 1408 and the Siena triptych // 1964/65, Zeri, p. 11: confirms Gronau's attribution to LM; part of a group of works following the San Gaggio polyptych, which should be dated no earlier than 1394-95, including the Bologna *Maestà*, the Rijksmuseum *Madonna Enthroned*, the Assisi *Madonna of Humility*, and the San Diego *Madonna Enthroned* // 1968, B. Cole, (*in litteris*): observed the relationship of the Amsterdam *Head of the Virgin*, the Göttingen *Crucifixion*, and the Courtauld *Coronation*; not by LM // 1974, van Os and Prakken, pp. 73-74, no. 38: related to LM; from the last decade of the Trecento; the history of the panel and the iconographical tradition of the image are surveyed // 1975, Boskovits, p. 337: LM, 1390-95 // 1976, Amsterdam, *Paintings of the Rijksmuseum*, p. 393: milieu of LM; further bibliography.

COMMENT: The alliance of the Amsterdam panel with the stylistic milieu in which the San Gaggio Altarpiece is the key work (Gronau, 1950 and Zeri, 1964/65) is convincing, but as is argued elsewhere, the attribution of that polyptych and related works to Lorenzo Monaco is problematic (see Catalogue II, Florence, Accademia, *Saint Catherine*, and *Saint Caius*). Certain morphological and decorative aspects of the *Head of the Virgin*, which have not been emphasized in the attributions to Lorenzo Monaco, are foreign to his style but common to the elements of the San Gaggio Altarpiece and to the Cloisters *Intercession* (Fig. 234), a work from the same Cionesque culture, although probably not by the same hand. The long, fluttering line of the mantle, turning in parallel movement to reveal inner and outer faces of the cloth, is a rhythmic device unknown in Lorenzo's work, but commonly found in works of the "San Gaggio culture." The principal decorative motif in the gold brocading of the Virgin's tunic is a grid pattern with semicircular extensions, identical to the ornament on the tunic of the Virgin in the Courtauld *Coronation* (Fig. 228), but not within the ornamental vocabulary of Don Lorenzo or his shop. The tilt of the head and the features of the Virgin, with sharply pencilled brows, a flat, narrow nose, and slightly parted lips, are mirrored in the kneeling angel in the left background of the Courtauld *Coronation*. Also common to this group of works and to the *Madonna of Humility* in Assisi (Fig. 236) is the scallop and finial decoration of the mantle border. Cole (1968) convincingly associated the Göttingen *Crucifixion* (Fig. 233) with the Rijksmuseum *Virgin* and the Courtauld *Coronation*. The combination of a wide ornamental border with a scalloped pattern used in the Amsterdam, Assisi, and Göttingen panels also decorates the mantle of the *Madonna* in the Cionesque altarpiece of 1383 in Santi Apostoli in Florence (Fremantle, fig. 334). Whereas Gronau proposed that the expressive source of the Amsterdam *Virgin* is in Sienese painting of the earlier Trecento, with late echoes in Florence in the art of Agnolo Gaddi and the Straus Master, I would submit that emphasis should be given to an intermediate step—the mid-century lyricism of Nardo di Cione.

AMSTERDAM, Rijksmuseum, no. A 4005

Madonna Enthroned

FIGS. 237, 238

Canvas, transferred from panel: 150.5 x 78.5 cm.

LITERATURE: 1927, van Marle, vol. 9, p. 118: Lorenzo Monaco; an early work // 1929, Suida, p. 392: LM // 1932, Berenson, p. 298: LM, early (1963, vol. 1, p. 117) // 1938, Pudelko, p. 237, note 8: LM, before 1400; revival of a Giottesque type, with the influence of Spinello Aretino // 1950, Gronau, p. 221: LM, early 1390s; close analogies with the *Saint Catherine* in the Accademia, Florence, and the *Coronation of the Virgin* in the Gambier-Parry Collection (now London, Courtauld Institute Galleries), which were elements in the San Gaggio polyptych, attributed to LM; ca. 1390-91; a faint resemblance to the style of Spinello // 1957, Eisenberg, pp. 50-51: LM, early work // 1958, Levi D'Ancona, "Some New Attributions," p. 184, note 40: by a follower of LM around 1406-1410; the head of the Madonna bears a strong resemblance to the Monte Oliveto Altarpiece of these years // 1959, Levi D'Ancona, "Letter," p. 129: Matteo Torelli // 1964/65, Zeri, p. 11: LM, following on the San Gaggio polyptych, which cannot be dated before 1394-95; in a group of works including the *Maestà* in Bologna, the *Head of the Madonna* in the Rijksmuseum, the Assisi *Madonna of Humility*, and the San Diego *Madonna and Saints*, all from the years following the San Gaggio polyptych and in which here and there one begins to notice, alongside the master's hand, the hand of pupils and assistants // 1965, Bellosi, "Da Spinello," p. 37: LM, early; close to a group of works with characteristics of the Master of the Straus Madonna // 1974, van Os and Prakken, pp. 72-73, no. 37: related to LM, suggesting a date in the late Trecento; further literature and the provenance are recorded // 1976, Amsterdam, *Paintings of the Rijksmuseum*, p. 393: school of LM.

COMMENT: Contrary to my prior acceptance of the Amsterdam *Madonna* as an early work of Lorenzo Monaco (1957), I have come to see it as part of an expanding list of later Trecento pictures of various stylistic hues that have been dubbed "Lorenzo Monaco in his formative years." This *Madonna* cannot be directly aligned with Lorenzo's earliest works, most centrally the *Agony in the Garden* in the Accademia in Florence (Fig. 7), from the standpoint of pictorial structure, morphology, or decorative vocabulary. Nor does a retrospective view from such works of Lorenzo's early maturity as the Empoli triptych of 1404 (Fig. 21) or the Monte Oliveto Altarpiece of 1407-1410 (Fig. 22) help associate his name with the Amsterdam picture. The flat and angular drapery forms, noted by Levi D'Ancona (1958) to be indicative of the work of a follower, are not in the idiom either of Lorenzo or his shop, as Saskia Bos (van Os and Prakken, 1974) has observed. The lighted surfaces of projecting forms, a distinctive feature of Lorenzo's earliest works, are also missing. Of the wide range of stylistic cultures mentioned in the literature cited above, Gronau's (1950) and Zeri's (1964/65) suggestions of proximity to the milieu of the San Gaggio polyptych are the most convincing. But, as is discussed elsewhere (Catalogue II, Florence, Accademia, *Saints Catherine*, and *Saint Caius*), rather than confirming the attribution to Lorenzo Monaco, this alliance removes the work from his shop to a different, though cognate one of the last years of the Trecento. As in the Courtauld *Coronation* (Fig. 228) from the San Gaggio complex, the late-century revival of Giottesque space is reflected in the lightly constructed throne, with a recession that would have been even more spacious if the original paint and gold surface had not been narrowed, probably at the time of transfer from panel to canvas. The patterned background may have been added at the same moment to replace a defaced gilded surface, with the result of flattening the mass of the throne. The proposed analogies with the style of Spinello Aretino would seem to be premised on his exactly contemporary interest in representing an ample figure within a convincing spatial setting. But the concern for space and bulk of the painter of the Amsterdam picture is an overlay on a stylistic language that is essentially Cionesque. The formal and expressive inheritance is in the lineage from Nardo di Cione to the wide diffusion of Cionesque style in shops of the later Trecento, either still run by the long-surviving Jacopo di Cione or dependencies from that central current of the third quarter of the Trecento. More than thirty years after Nardo's *Madonna* of the 1360s in the New-York Historical Society (on loan to the Metropolitan Museum of Art; Meiss, 1951, fig. 11), the extended hand in the Amsterdam *Madonna* remains a slight variation on that focal passage in the earlier work. And the palette of royal blue, light green, yellow, dark coral red, and rose is favored in Cionesque painting. A midpoint in this path of survival and an immediate precursor of the Amsterdam *Madonna* is the Cionesque altarpiece of 1383 in Santi Apostoli, Florence (Boskovits, 1975, fig. 119, attributed to Jacopo di Cione). The sharp angles of flat drapery folds, the long uninterrupted silhouette extending from the crown of the Virgin's inclined head to the waist, the sharply pencilled brows, the small but full mouth, and the variety of ornamentation are all from similar molds. Cionesque decorative hallmarks are the garland of the halo and the cloth of honor heavily brocaded in gold and striped at the edge, an accessory used in the Amsterdam picture, the Santi Apostoli polyptych, and the Courtauld *Coronation*. Although the Rijksmuseum's *Madonna* and *Head of the Virgin* (Fig. 235) are by different hands—the latter even closer to the milieu of the San Gaggio polytpych—they both emerged from a prolific and widespread shop culture that was contemporary but not identifiable with the formative years of the art of Lorenzo Monaco. Bellosi's (1965) suggestion of a relationship between the Amsterdam *Madonna* and the style of the Master of the Straus Madonna signals an infusion of Cionesque forms into an important later Trecento artistic milieu whose sources have been defined too exclusively as Gaddesque.

AMSTERDAM, Rijksmuseum, no. A 4007

Annunciate Virgin

Panel (roundel): 23.5 cm.

LITERATURE: 1927, van Marle, vol. 9, p. 177, note 1: school of Lorenzo Monaco, revising his earlier attribution to Spinello Aretino (vol. 3, 1924, p. 606, note 1) // 1934, Amsterdam, *Italiaansche Kunst*, p. 88, no. 239: LM // 1934/35, van Marle, p. 304: LM // 1974, van Os and Prakken, pp. 75-76, no. 39, fig. 39: Lorenzo di Niccolò, adopting my verbal suggestion that the style is close to that master // 1975, Boskovits, p. 337: LM, 1415-20 // 1976, Amsterdam, *Paintings of the Rijksmuseum*, p. 353: Lorenzo di Niccolò.

COMMENT: The tondo is allied with the stylistic milieu of Lorenzo di Niccolò, although the schematism is more extreme than in the work of that master. The bulbous right hand recalls the supporting hand of the Virgin in Lorenzo di Niccolò's Terenzano triptych (Fremantle, fig. 815) and the features resemble Saint John the Evangelist in the same painter's *Madonna and Saints* polyptych from the Sacristy at Santa Croce (Fremantle, fig. 813) or the *Saint Ansanus* in the Acton Collection, Florence (no. 37).

ASSISI, Sacro Convento di San Francesco, Perkins Collection, no. 38

Madonna of Humility

FIG. 236

Panel: 84 x 58.9 cm.

LITERATURE: 1903, Toesca, p. 226: Lorenzo Monaco; relates the style to the Monte Oliveto triptych of 1406-1410 (then in the Uffizi) // 1905, Sirén, pp. 165-66: an early work of Lorenzo's shop, related to the *Agony in the Garden* in the Accademia, Florence, and the *Madonna Enthroned* in Bologna, also considered early shop works // 1906, Giglioli, p. 74: Cennino Cennini (by comparison with the *Madonna* of 1408, Fig. 138, then in the Uffizi) // 1927, van Marle, vol. 9, p. 177, note 1: school of LM // 1932, Berenson, p. 298: LM (1963, vol. 1, p. 117) // 1964/65, Zeri, p. 11: LM; youthful work following on the San Gaggio polyptych; along with the Assisi *Madonna* this group includes the *Madonna Enthroned* in Bologna and in the Rijksmuseum, the *Head of the Madonna* in the Rijksmuseum, and the San Diego *Madonna and Saints*; a group in which here and there may be seen the hand of pupils and assistants // 1973, Palumbo, p. 50, no. 38 (Perkins, no. 86), reproduced in color: LM, close to the *Madonna of Humility* of 1405 in the Berenson Collection and the *Madonna* of 1408 in the Accademia in Florence // 1975, Boskovits, p. 338: LM, 1400-1405.

COMMENT: The hybrid style of the Assisi *Madonna of Humility* poses problems of localization and dating which I am unable to resolve with any degree of certainty. The panel bridges two stylistic milieus—the shop of Lorenzo Monaco at the turn of the century and the culture of the San Gaggio Altarpiece, which is cognate but not ascribable to Lorenzo Monaco (see Catalogue II, Florence, Accademia, *Saint Catherine*, and *Saint Caius*). As was noted by Toesca (1903) and Giglioli (1906), the extended hand of the Virgin silhouetted against the ornamented tunic has the closest analogy in Lorenzo's Madonna of the Monte Oliveto Altarpiece (1407-1410) and in a shop work such as the *Madonna and Saints* of 1408, both in the Accademia, Florence (Figs. 23 and 138). The standing Christ Child in a salute of benediction is a favored motif in Lorenzo's stock of types, and the adoring angels have close replicas in three shop works—the *Madonna of Humility* in the Metropolitan Museum, New York and in Moscow (Figs. 141 and 142), and the *Madonna and Saints* (Fig. 152) in Prato; the bland and shallowly modelled features of the Assisi *Madonna* recall the Prato Saint Catherine. But similar beribboned angels also accompany the Virgin and Child in the Walters Gallery panel (Fig. 225), an example of the sharing of motifs in cognate shops of the later Trecento.

As Zeri observed (1964/65), there is a close stylistic kinship between the Assisi *Madonna* and the San Gaggio Altarpiece—to which there may be added the Christ in the Cloisters *Intercession* (Fig. 234). These affinities, I believe, outweigh the connection with the distinctive idiom of Lorenzo Monaco. The strict symmetry in the long, fluttering cascade of the Virgin's mantle from head to breast recalls the studied casualness in the fall of drapery in such works as the Accademia *Saint Catherine* (Fig. 227), the *Martyrdom of Saint Catherine* in Berlin (Fig. 230) (compare the mantle of the old man next to the executioner), or the Christ of the Cloisters *Intercession*. The angular fluting in the lower left portion of the Virgin's mantle in the Assisi panel may be compared with the drapery of Christ in the *Intercession*. The same formality nearing rigidity is seen in the heavily pocketed and radiating folds in the mantles of the Christ Child in the Assisi panel, the Accademia *Saint Catherine*, and the king of the Santa Barbara *Martyrdom of Saint Caius* (Fig. 232). An ornamental detail in the Assisi Madonna that is not found in works by Lorenzo Monaco or his shop is the gold drapery border composed of a double line, scallop, and finial, a combination of motifs seen in the *Intercession* and in such allied works as the Göttingen *Crucifixion* (Fig. 233) and the *Head of the Virgin* in the Rijksmuseum (Fig. 235). In this last work the fall of drapery closely resembles the same passages in the Assisi panel, a relationship observed by Zeri, who ascribes both pictures to Lorenzo Monaco.

A further connection of the Assisi *Madonna of Humility* to works in the milieu of the San Gaggio Altarpiece is discerned in the means of spatial construction. The steeply raked hexagonal dais and the frieze of heavy bosses along the riser are similar to the same elements in the Courtauld *Coronation* (Fig. 228) and the *Madonna Enthroned* in Amsterdam (Fig. 237). The weightless architectural forms in this cluster of pictures and in the *Martyrdom of Saint Caius* from the predella of the San Gaggio Altarpiece are like audibly movable stage properties in contrast to the ponderability of the throne in as diminutive a panel as Don Lorenzo's *Madonna* in Cambridge (Fig. 15).

AVIGNON, Musée du Petit Palais, no. 119

Saint Lawrence Enthroned, with Saints Ansanus and Margaret

FIG. 244

Panel: (Center) 162 x 66 cm.; (sides) 142 x 42 cm.
Inscribed date: (on base of central panel) MICHELE. DI. LORECO. VANI. RINGI. FECE. FARE. QUESTA MCCC [CVII] (see below, 1956, Cohn)

[Predella; Rome, Pinacoteca Vaticana: *Martyrdom of Saint Lawrence* (no. 215; 19 x 60 cm.; Fig. 245); *Martyrdom of Saint Ansanus* and *Saint Margaret Confronted by the Prefect Olibrius* (nos. 216 and 217; 19 x 39 cm.; Fig. 246)]

LITERATURE: 1883, Tauzia, no. 225: Lorenzo Monaco // 1883, Crowe and Cavalcaselle, vol. 2, p. 347: LM; note the lamb is a later addition (transformation of left lateral from Saint Ansanus into Saint Agnes observed earlier by Reiset, 1863, no. 72) // 1905, Sirén, pp. 166-67: shop of LM; the light palette not typical of Lorenzo's style; the Copenhagen *Annunciation* by the same hand // 1906, Schubring, p. 175: refutes association with painter of the Copenhagen panel // 1906, Sirén, "Notizie critiche," p. 328: links three-part predella in the Vatican with the Louvre altarpiece; attributes predella to school of Lorenzo Monaco // 1909, Bernardini, p. 91: Vatican predella attributed to LM school // 1927, van Marle, vol. 9, p. 174, fig. 118 (with modern frame and repainted left lateral): shop of LM; the drawing is too hard to permit an attribution to Lorenzo; the Vatican predella by a less able hand // 1929, Suida, p. 329: LM shop // 1932, Berenson, p. 300: LM; p. 301: the predella from the studio // 1933/34, Colasanti, p. 338: LM school; notes similarities in predella to the *Martyrdom of Saint Lawrence* by the Maestro del Bambino Vispo in the Colonna Collection, Rome, particularly in the pose of Saint Lawrence and in the figure of the executioner with the long prod // 1956, Cohn, p. 68: cites notice by Carlo Strozzi in the seventeenth-century *Sepoltuario Strozziano* that triptych is in the church of San Salvadore di Valle di Monteloro (Pontassieve) and inscribed with the date of 1407; transcribes inscription on base of central panel // 1958, Levi D'Ancona, "Matteo Torelli," pp. 252 and 254-55: Matteo Torelli, although somewhat different from his usual style; possibly the altarpiece commissioned in 1422 for the Chapel of Saint Lawrence in the Cathedral of Florence; Don Lorenzo could have turned over the commission to Matteo Torelli; does not comment on predella // 1963, Berenson, vol. 1, p. 120: studio of LM, 1407; Vatican predella also by the studio // 1971, Zeri, pp. 67-68: the triptych apparently by the same shop assistant to Lorenzo Monaco who painted a *Madonna of Humility* in the Metropolitan Museum (Fig. 141) // 1972, Boskovits, p. 46: LM; the predella by Bartolomeo di Fruosino // 1975, Boskovits, p. 351: LM, dated 1407 // 1977, Laclotte and Mognetti, no. 119: the triptych a collaborative work from shop of Lorenzo Monaco, based on master's design, although it is tempting to attribute the triptych, as well as the predella in the Vatican, to Bartolomeo di Fruosino, the Saint Margaret in particular approaching the style of the figures in the predella; the predella in a free style, closer to later works of Bartolomeo di Fruosino than to his miniatures of around 1407, the date of the Avignon altarpiece; additional bibliography // 1977, Bergeon and Mognetti, pp. 265-66: a full report on the restoration of the altarpiece in 1976, including regained identity of Saint Ansanus // 1977, Vertova, p. 164: LM; remarks on effective cleaning of the altarpiece // 1984, Bellosi, pp. 308-309: main register, workshop of LM; predella, "Maestro del Codice Squarcialupi."

COMMENT: Moving a hesitant step beyond Laclotte and Mognetti's temptation to attribute the Avignon triptych as well as the Vatican predella to Bartolomeo di Fruosino (1977), I propose with reservation that the entire altarpiece may be the work of that minor master, whose career would seem to have evolved both within and outside Don Lorenzo's workshop. The major obstacle to the attribution is the lack of a significant corpus of works by Bartolomeo di Fruosino other than his considerable production in miniature painting (see Mirella Levi D'Ancona's fundamental study of 1961). In the extensive documentation of Bartolomeo's career he is most frequently denoted as "dipintore" (Levi D'Ancona, 1962, pp. 45-48), which refers principally to his work as a painter of miniatures within the illuminated initials of choir books. Bartolomeo is known to have been a pupil of Agnolo Gaddi, having assisted him in the fresco project at the Cappella del Sacro Cingolo in Prato, although perhaps only in the decorative details; his association with Lorenzo Monaco may have begun in 1396, the year of Agnolo's death (Levi D'Ancona, 1961, pp. 85-87). The list of works on panel attributable to Bartolomeo has remained a short one. The documented *Crucifix* of 1411 is of the cutout type made popular by the workshop of Lorenzo Monaco (see Catalogue II, Florence, Accademia, no. 3147). Levi D'Ancona (1961, pp. 84 and 92) first ascribed to Bartolomeo the two lateral *Prophet* roundels atop Don Lorenzo's late *Annunciation* (see Catalogue I, Florence, Santa Trinita, Bartolini Salimbeni Chapel). The attribution of two *deschi da parto*, one in the Serristori Collection in Florence and the other belonging to the New-York Historical Society (Fig. 324), augmented our knowledge of the works on panel of secular subject matter (Levi D'Ancona, 1961, p. 84; Boskovits, 1972, p. 58, note 55; Watson, 1974, pp. 4-9). And finally, the Vatican predella has been added to this small corpus (Boskovits, 1972). From my limited study of the problem, I do not yet discern sufficient stylistic homogeneity within the group of works to which Luciano Bellosi has recently attached the name "Maestro del Codice Squarcialupi" to necessitate denial of Boskovits's attribution of the Vatican predella to Bartolomeo di Fruosino (Bellosi, 1984, p. 309).

Just as none of Bartolomeo's miniatures may be confounded with the style of Lorenzo Monaco or his closest assistants, the group of panels stands apart from the vast but essentially homogeneous production of Don Lorenzo's workshop. The Avignon triptych and its predella veer from the style of Lorenzo Monaco sufficiently to indicate either that they were created by an associate in the workshop who was reaching well beyond its confines for primary models, or that it was produced outside Don Lorenzo's immediate shop environment; presently, I favor the latter premise. The stylistic disparities that would seem to exist between the main register and the predella may largely be explained by the need for a higher degree of formality and precision in the saints' effigies in contrast to the freer style of the narrative scenes. The kinship of the Vatican predella and the Avignon triptych (noted by Laclotte and Mognetti, 1977), is demonstrable in several comparisons: the identical cranial structure of Saint Lawrence and the similar gesture in the shaping of the tonsure; the marked resemblance in stance and draping of the Prefect in the predella to Saint Margaret in the right lateral; the deep shelving of her mantle and that of the onlooker at the far right of the *Martyrdom of Saint Lawrence*. Analogies may also be drawn between the *Saint Lawrence* altarpiece and the work of Bartolomeo di Fruosino as a miniaturist, in which certain figures and scenes are nearly of predella scale: compare, for example, the mantles of the Saint Margaret in Avignon and of Saint Peter on fol. 36 of Corale 7 in the Laurenziana (dated 1406; see Levi D'Ancona, 1961, fig. 1); or, for a still closer parallel, the mantle of Simeon in the *Circumcision* (Fig. 247) on fol. 185 of Corale D in the Arcispedale di Santa Maria Nuova, Florence (see *Ghiberti, 'materia e ragionamenti,'* 1978, p. 305; dated ca. 1411 by Levi D'Ancona, 1961, p. 91). Echoes of the Saint Margaret remain in Bartolomeo's tortuous later style in the cascading drapery of the cardinal at the right in the scene of the *Consecration of the Church of Sant'Egidio*, on fol. 61v of a Missal in the Museo di San Marco (Inv. 557), dated 1421 (Chiarelli, pl. XVIII). And in the *Saint Egidius Enthroned*, fol. 35v of the same manuscript (Fig. 248), the insertion of the head into an encircling collar recalls the Saint Lawrence in the central panel at Avignon, and the cupbearer at the proper left of Saint Egidius and the Saint Margaret of the Vatican predella gather up their draperies identically with the right hand. The blond palette of the *Saint Lawrence* altarpiece closely matches that in the miniatures of Bargello, Cod. G 73 (e.g., fols. 35v and 38v, of ca. 1411; Levi D'Ancona, 1961, fig. 8); in the same fol. 35v there is the extreme stylization of the rocky landscape that is found in the Vatican predella (Fig. 246). The refinement of painting technique in the Avignon triptych would seem to run counter to Bartolomeo's cursory brush in such major miniatures as those of the San Marco Missal of 1421. But his earlier miniatures reveal a far tamer hand, perhaps under the closer scrutiny of Lorenzo Monaco, that was sufficiently disciplined to have rendered the three saints in the Avignon altarpiece (Levi D'Ancona, 1961, fig. 1; from Laurenziana Cor. 7, dated 1406).

If Bartolomeo di Fruosino did, indeed, paint the *Saint Lawrence* altarpiece of 1407, at forty years of age, he would have been by then an independent artist whose limited talent demanded close adherence to the styles of major contemporaries, initially Lorenzo Monaco. The parallelisms of the *Saint Lawrence Enthroned* and the *Saint James Enthroned* (Fig. 171) are too evident to require demonstration, and though the latter work is a product of Don Lorenzo's workshop, there is no reason to deny that the design was provided by the master. But the most fundamental impact of a contemporary artist on the style of Bartolomeo di Fruosino came not from Lorenzo Monaco, but from Gherardo Starnina. Without demonstrating the specific influence of Starnina, Levi D'Ancona (1961, p. 90) cited him among the several artists she deemed important to Bartolomeo's formation. The voluminous, deeply shelved, and sharply lighted mantle of Saint Margaret in the right lateral of the Avignon triptych shows a closer resemblance to the saints of Starnina's altarpiece in Würzburg (Fig. 285), painted before 1408, than to any work of Lorenzo Monaco. In Bartolomeo's miniature of the *Nativity* (Bargello, Cod. G 73, fol. 35v, ca. 1411; Levi D'Ancona, 1961, fig. 8) the model for the draperies of the Virgin and Joseph could have been the seated musical angels in the same Würzburg triptych (Fig. 294). The influence of Starnina's aggressive linearism is similarly recognizable in another *Nativity* miniature attributable to Bartolomeo, that on fol. 9v in Missal C of the Museo dell'Opera del Duomo in Prato (see Florence, *Codici miniati*, 1982, fig. on p. 217; reported on p. 215 as stolen from the manuscript). And the dependence of the Vatican predella on Starnina's *Martyrdom of Saint Lawrence* in the Colonna Collection, once in the predella of the Certosa altarpiece, completed no later than 1408, is further evidence of the link between major and minor master (Colasanti, 1933/34; Berenson, 1963, vol. 1, pl. 479). A chromatic parallel between the two artists is the pervasive apple green and light rose favored by Starnina in the Carmine frescoes and by the painter of the Avignon triptych, a color chord that is nowhere struck by Lorenzo Monaco. The art of Bartolomeo di Fruosino, as represented in his miniatures of the first decade of the Quattrocento and possibly by the *Saint Lawrence* altarpiece, which would be his earliest and most ambitious known effort on panel, should be viewed as cognate to Lorenzo Monaco insofar as both artists felt the impact of Starnina soon after the influential painter had returned from Spain. Given the stronger internal evolution of Don Lorenzo's art, he never mirrored the style of Starnina so directly as did Bartolomeo di Fruosino (see the Introductory Essay, Note 60).

An informative sidelight on the interconnection of later Trecento and early Quattrocento Florentine workshops is the observation by Klesse (p. 393) that the pattern of the cloth of honor in the Avignon triptych is found identically in a work by Agnolo Gaddi, and was also introduced by Lorenzo Monaco into the Berlin *Madonna with the Baptist and Saint Nicholas* (Fig. 17) and the Uffizi *Coronation of the Virgin* (Fig. 47). (Also see Catalogue I, New York, Metropolitan Museum, *Madonna of Humility*.)

BALTIMORE, Walters Art Gallery, no. 37.645

Madonna in Glory with Saints Paul and Peter
FIG. 225

Panel: 82.3 x 48 cm.

LITERATURE: 1932, Berenson, p. 298: Lorenzo Monaco, early (1963, vol. 1, p. 117) // 1939, Sandberg-Vavalà, p. 108: early LM; in the style of the Horne *Madonna* and the predella panels in Baltimore, Berlin, and Princeton // 1964/65, Zeri, p. 8 and fig. 14: LM; between a reconstructed polyptych of ca. 1390 and the San Gaggio Altarpiece of ca. 1394-95 // 1965, Bellosi, "Da Spinello," p. 37: approaches the idiom of the Master of the Straus Madonna // 1972, Fredericksen and Zeri, p. 111: LM // 1975, Boskovits, p. 338: LM, 1390-95 // 1976, Zeri, vol. 1, pp. 25-26: LM, immediately after 1390.

COMMENT: The analogies that have been cumulatively drawn by Sandberg-Vavalà (1939) and Zeri (1964/65) between the Walters *Madonna*, the Horne *Madonna* (Fig. 224), and the various elements of a dispersed polyptych are unequivocal. Zeri's recognition of the transitional nature of the Baltimore panel reinforces, in my view, the bridging of cognate workshops that is implied in Bellosi's opinion (1965) and further substantiates the clear parallels with Don Lorenzo's early *Madonna* in the Biblioteca Berenson (Fig. 16). The slack figural construction in the Walters *Madonna*, most apparent in the Saint Paul, marks the work as of lesser quality than the other pictures of the group. The pair of floating angels is a motif that will be found in slight variants in works from the shop of Lorenzo Monaco and from the culture of the San Gaggio Altarpiece (e.g., Figs. 141, 142, and 236). For further comment, see Catalogue II, Florence, Accademia, *Saint Jerome*; *Saint John the Baptist*. . . .

BALTIMORE, Walters Art Gallery, no. 37.688

Crucifixion of Saint Peter
FIG. 222

Panel: 25.4 x 40.7 cm.

LITERATURE: 1939, Sandberg-Vavalà, pp. 105-11: early style of Lorenzo Monaco, in the last years of the Trecento; associates the Baltimore panel with a *Nativity* in Berlin and a *Martyrdom of Saint Paul* in Princeton, to form a three-part predella // 1954, Eisenberg, p. 102: LM, 1390-95 // 1964/65, Zeri, p. 7: LM, ca. 1390; reconstructs the altarpiece // 1965, Bellosi, "Da Spinello," p. 37: approaches the idiom of the Master of the Straus Madonna // 1970, González-Palacios, p. 31: LM // 1972, Fredericksen and Zeri, p. 111: LM // 1975, Boskovits, p. 338: LM, 1395-1400 // 1976, Zeri, vol. 1, pp. 26-27: LM, 1390, or shortly after.

COMMENT: See Catalogue II, Florence, Accademia, *Saint Jerome*; *Saint John the Baptist*. . . .

BERLIN-DAHLEM, Staatliche Museen, Gemäldegalerie, no. 1063

Martyrdom of Saint Catherine of Alexandria
FIG. 230

Panel: 42.2 x 57 cm.

LITERATURE: 1950, Gronau, pp. 184-88: Lorenzo Monaco, ca. 1390-91; establishes the panel as a side element in a predella that once formed part of an altarpiece in the church of San Gaggio, outside Florence; provides a full bibliography of earlier attributions // 1954, Eisenberg, p. 143: rejects attribution to LM // 1958, Levi D'Ancona, "Some New Attributions," p. 187, note 58: refutes the attribution of the San Gaggio Altarpiece to Lorenzo Monaco // 1963, Berenson, vol. 1, p. 121: Lorenzo di Niccolò? // 1964/65, Zeri, pp. 8 and 11: confirms Gronau's attribution; revises the dating to ca. 1394-95 // 1965, Bellosi, "Da Spinello," p. 36: LM // 1975, Boskovits, p. 339: LM, 1390-95 // 1978, Berlin-Dahlem, *Catalogue*, p. 241, no. 1063: LM // 1979, Gealt, p. 153: follower of Agnolo Gaddi.

COMMENT: See Catalogue II, Florence, Accademia, *Saint Catherine of Alexandria*, and *Saint Caius*.

BERLIN-DAHLEM, Staatliche Museen, Gemäldegalerie, no. 1108

Last Supper
FIG. 231

Panel: 41 x 137 cm.

LITERATURE: 1950, Gronau, pp. 184-88: Lorenzo Monaco, ca. 1390-91; establishes the panel as the central element of a predella to an altarpiece once in the church of San Gaggio, outside Florence; provides a full bibliography of earlier attributions // 1954, Eisenberg, p. 143: rejects attribution to LM // 1958, Levi D'Ancona, "Some New Attributions," p. 187, note 58: denies the attribution of the San Gaggio Altarpiece to Lorenzo Monaco // 1963, Berenson, vol. 1, p. 121: Lorenzo di Niccolò? // 1964/65, Zeri, pp. 8 and 11: confirms Gronau's attribution to Lorenzo Monaco; revises the dating to ca. 1394-95 // 1965, Bellosi, "Da Spinello," p. 36: LM // 1975, Boskovits, p. 338: LM, 1390-95 // 1978, Berlin-Dahlem, *Catalogue*, pp. 241-42, no. 1108: LM // 1979, Gealt, p. 153: follower of Agnolo Gaddi.

COMMENT: See Catalogue II, Florence, Accademia, *Saint Catherine of Alexandria*, and *Saint Caius*; see also Rome, Biblioteca Vaticana, MS. Rossiano, 1192/a, no. 35.

BERLIN-DAHLEM, Staatliche Museen, Gemäldegalerie, no. 1113

Nativity
FIG. 221

Panel: 26.3 x 60.7 cm.

LITERATURE: 1905, Sirén, p. 137, note 1: Agnolo Gaddi, representing the milieu from which the art of Lorenzo Monaco arose // 1939, Sandberg-Vavalà, pp. 105-111: an early work of Lorenzo Monaco, from the last years of the Trecento; associates the panel with a *Crucifixion of Saint Peter* in the Walters Gallery, Baltimore, and a *Beheading of Saint Paul* at Princeton // 1954, Eisenberg, p. 120: LM, ca. 1390-95 // 1963, Berenson, vol. 1, p. 214: between Agnolo Gaddi and Lorenzo Monaco // 1964/65, Zeri, p. 7: LM, shortly after 1390; reconstructs the altarpiece to which the predella panel belonged (also see, 1976, vol. 1, pp. 26-27) // 1965, Bellosi, "Da Spinello," p. 37: approaches the idiom of the Master of the Straus Madonna // 1975, Boskovits, p. 338: LM, 1395-1400 // 1978, Berlin-Dahlem, *Catalogue*, p. 242, no. 1113: LM.

COMMENT: See Catalogue II, Florence, Accademia, *Saint Jerome*; *Saint John the Baptist*. . . .

BERLIN-DAHLEM, Staatliche Museen, Kupferstichkabinett, no. min. 682

Prophet (Isaiah or Jeremiah?)

Cut miniature from a choir book
Parchment: 14.5 x 14.5 cm.

LITERATURE: 1931, Wescher, p. 90 and fig. 75: Lorenzo Monaco // 1959, Levi D'Ancona, "Don Silvestro," p. 21: Don Silvestro dei Gherarducci, 1380-90 // 1975, Boskovits, p. 421: Don Silvestro, 1375-80.

COMMENT: Levi D'Ancona's attribution to Don Silvestro dei Gherarducci is definitive. The Berlin *Prophet* points up the importance of the grave, heavily bearded patriarchs of Nardo di Cione in the formation of the styles of Don Silvestro and Lorenzo Monaco, and the progression toward the earliest miniatures by Don Lorenzo in the mid-1390s (Figs. 1-5).

BRAUNSCHWEIG, Herzog Anton-Ulrich-Museum, no. 3

Saints Stephen, Lawrence, Francis, and *Anthony of Padua*

Panel: 37.5 x 14.5 cm. (each panel)

LITERATURE: 1906, Sirén, "Dipinti del Trecento," p. 86: Lorenzo Monaco // 1909, Berenson, p. 152 (not listed in later editions): LM, early // 1927, van Marle, vol. 9, pp. 174 and 176: shop of LM // 1938/39, Pudelko, p. 248, note 33: LM, perhaps the pilaster figures of the *Coronation of the Virgin* altarpiece in the National Gallery, London // 1950, Longhi, p. 47: Pseudo-Ambrogio di Baldese // 1950, Oertel, p. 48, nos. 69-72; nos. 69 and 70 illustrated: workshop of LM // 1969, Andriani, p. 90, no. 3: LM // 1970, González-Palacios, pp. 31-32: LM; close in style to the early *Madonna and Saints* in the Berenson Collection; very probably the pilasters of the Carmine Polyptych (see Catalogue II, Florence, Accademia, *Saint Jerome*; *Saint John the Baptist. . . .*) // 1975, Boskovits, p. 379: LM, 1395-1400.

COMMENT: Although I am unable to localize these panels within a specific Florentine workshop, the cultures of Bicci di Lorenzo and of the Pseudo-Ambrogio di Baldese (Longhi, 1950) in the first years of the fifteenth century offer the closest comparisons. The Braunschweig panels are not compatible stylistically with the various elements of the Carmine Polyptych.

BUDAPEST, Museum of Fine Arts, no. 7

Thebaid

Panel: 73.5 x 105 cm.

LITERATURE: 1908, Suida, "Studien," p. 208: Lorenzo Monaco; one half of the original work of which the Uffizi *Thebaid* is a copy // 1927, van Marle, vol. 9, p. 132: LM, from the first decade of the century // 1929, Suida, p. 392: LM // 1935, Procacci, p. 369, note 1: a copy of a section of the Uffizi panel by Gherardo Starnina // 1954, Pigler, p. 328: LM; in 1906 and 1913 catalogues listed as Tuscan, fourteenth to fifteenth centuries; 1937 catalogue as LM // 1957, E. Callmann, "A Quattrocento Jigsaw Puzzle," *Burlington Magazine* 99, p. 150: Florentine, first half of the fifteenth century // 1968, Pigler, p. 393: LM; additional bibliography // 1975, Callmann, p. 7 and fig. 12: Florentine, 1425-35.

COMMENT: Ellen Callmann's general label (1975) appropriately localizes the panel.

CAREGGI (FLORENCE), Sacristy of the Hospital

Crucifix

Panel: 212 x 170 cm.

LITERATURE: 1905, Sirén, p. 90: Lorenzo Monaco; the panel then located in the Convento delle Oblate, Florence // 1927, van Marle, vol. 9, p. 108, note 3: LM // 1932, Berenson, p. 299: shop of LM // 1936, Procacci, p. 41: notes Offner's observation that the panel is made up of the reverse surface of *Crucifix* no. 3147 in the Accademia, Florence // 1963, Berenson, vol. 1, p. 119: shop of LM; the back of Accademia 3147.

COMMENT: See Catalogue II, Florence, Accademia, *Crucifix*, no. 3147.

CHICAGO, Art Institute of Chicago, no. 1933.1032

Crucifixion

Panel: 50.9 x 23.5 cm.

LITERATURE: 1933, *Century of Progress Exhibition of Paintings and Sculpture*, Art Institute of Chicago, p. 16, no. 97: Gherardo Starnina (quoting van Marle's verbal attribution) // 1970, J. Maxon, *The Art Institute of Chicago*, New York, p. 24: Florentine, fourteenth century, rejecting a previous attribution to Bernardo Daddi (assumed when the panel was bought by Martin Ryerson in 1928) // 1972, Fredericksen and Zeri, pp. 111 and 571: tentatively attributed to Lorenzo Monaco // 1975, Boskovits, p. 340, fig. 457: LM, 1395-1400.

COMMENT: The eclectic nature of the style permits only a broad conjectural dating for this finely wrought panel. The roots are in the iconic formalities of Cionesque painting, but there is likewise evidence of the cognate miniaturist tradition of Santa Maria degli Angeli, most apparent in the accessory figures of the crest and base. The vivid physical presence of the kneeling male suppliant—the radiant nimbus seems to be a weak later addition—implies a dating in the first years of the fifteenth century, but the static form of the Christ is more in the mode of the later Trecento. The general label Florentine, circa 1400, would seem appropriate.

COPENHAGEN, Statens Museum for Kunst, no. 235

Annunciation, with Saint Benedict and a Praying Nun

FIG. 255

Panel: 29 x 102 cm.

LITERATURE: 1834, N. L. Høyen, *Dansk Ugeskrift*, vol. 5, p. 118: Lorenzo Monaco (based on the opinion of C. F. von Rumohr who presented the panel in 1833) // 1883, Crowe and Cavalcaselle, vol. 2, p. 346: LM // 1905, Sirén, pp. 167 and 191: school of LM, by the same shop assistant who executed the Louvre *Saint Lawrence* triptych (now Avignon) // 1906, Schubring, p. 175: denies Sirén's connection with the Louvre *Saint Lawrence* triptych // 1927, van

Marle, vol. 9, p. 177: school of LM // 1932, Berenson, p. 298: LM, studio // 1935, Pudelko, p. 84: Pseudo-Ambrogio di Baldese; related to the *Nativity* in Rome // 1951, Copenhagen, *Old Foreign Paintings*, p. 174: school of Lorenzo Monaco; reports restoration of horizontal crack through the panel // 1961, Olsen, p. 59: Florentine school, early fifteenth century; additional bibliography // 1963, Berenson, vol. 1, p. 117: studio of LM; companion to Tulsa *Saint Romuald* // 1966, Shapley, p. 89: studio of LM; associated with the Vatican *Nativity* and the Tulsa *Saint Romuald.*

COMMENT: See Catalogue II, Rome, Pinacoteca Vaticana, *Nativity*.

COPENHAGEN, Statens Museum for Kunst, Print Room

Multiplication of the Loaves; *Washing of the Feet*; *Christ's Farewell to His Mother and the Corruption of Judas*

Three preparatory drawings for choir book miniatures
Parchment: 31.6 x 23.1 cm.; 29.6 x 23.5 cm.; 15.2 x 36.3 cm. (for technical information, see citation below: Degenhart and Schmitt, 1968)

LITERATURE: 1946, Pouncey, p. 71: follower of Agnolo Gaddi // 1950, Gronau, p. 222: Lorenzo Monaco, showing an unmistakable affinity with the San Gaggio group of panels of ca. 1390-91 and close to the Nobili predella of 1387-88; earliest surviving examples of Lorenzo's work as a miniaturist, executed before he entered monastic life // 1954, Eisenberg, p. 171, note 148: refutes the attribution to LM // 1964/65, Zeri, p. 11: confirms Gronau's attribution to LM; immediately after 1390, contemporary with a dispersed polyptych by Don Lorenzo executed before the San Gaggio group but after the Nobili predella // 1968, Degenhart and Schmitt, pt. 1, vol. 1, pp. 263-64, nos. 156-58, and vol. 3, pl. 191 a, b, c: Florence, around 1400; deny the connection with the San Gaggio Altarpiece and do not see the drawings as by the same hand or as associable with Lorenzo's earliest miniatures; provide further bibliography and review all critical opinion on the three cuttings // 1975, Boskovits, p. 340: LM, 1390-95 // 1978, Bellosi and Bellini, p. xvii: LM.

COMMENT: The Copenhagen drawings are approached in the catalogue entry on the San Gaggio Altarpiece (see Catalogue II, Florence, Accademia, *Saint Catherine of Alexandria*, and *Saint Caius*).

DORTMUND, Cremer Collection (formerly)

Saint Jerome in Penitence

FIG. 219

Panel: 23 x 36 cm.

LITERATURE: 1929, *Sammlung Joseph Cremer, Dortmund*, Wertheim, Berlin, May 29, no. 128: style of Lorenzo Monaco // 1954, Eisenberg, pp. 83-85 and 102: LM, 1390-95; integrates the panel with a predella partially reconstructed by Sandberg-Vavalà (1939) // 1964/65, Zeri, p. 7: LM, shortly after 1390; reconstructs the altarpiece in which the former Cremer panel formed an element of the predella (also see Zeri, 1976, vol. 1, pp. 26-27) // 1974, Meiss, "Scholarship and Penitence," p. 135: LM? // 1975, Boskovits, p. 339: LM, 1395-1400.

COMMENT: See Catalogue II, Florence, Accademia, *Saint Jerome*; *Saint John the Baptist*. . . .

FLORENCE, Accademia, no. 3147

Crucifix

Panel (cutout): 280 x 190 cm.

LITERATURE: 1901, Pieraccini, p. 228: Lorenzo Monaco // 1905, Sirén, p. 89: mentions two Crosses in the Uffizi from Santa Maria Nuova, only one of which he considers to be by Lorenzo Monaco, thereby attributing to him either Accademia 3147 or 3153 // 1927, van Marle, vol. 9, p. 177, note 1: school of LM // 1932, Berenson, p. 299: LM // 1936, Procacci, p. 41: school of LM; notes Offner's unpublished observation that the Careggi *Crucifix* is an adaptation of the back of Accademia 3147 // 1961, Levi D'Ancona, p. 82, fig. 10: attributes Accademia 3147 to Bartolomeo di Fruosino and connects it with a document of 1411 that mentions a commission given to Bartolomeo for the painting of a cross for the refectory of Santa Maria Nuova; considers the model for Bartolomeo's work to be Don Lorenzo's Accademia 3153, of around 1410 // 1963, Berenson, vol. 1, p. 118: LM, front to Careggi // 1972, Boskovits, p. 58, note 55: a collaboration of LM and Bartolomeo di Fruosino // 1975, Boskovits, p. 343: designed by LM and executed by Bartolomeo; documented(?) 1411 // 1987, Bonsanti, p. 89 (listed as No. 3153): Lorenzo Monaco and Bartolomeo di Fruosino.

COMMENT: Mirella Levi D'Ancona's (1961) attribution of the design and execution to Bartolomeo di Fruosino is conclusive and the connection with the document of 1411, although less certain, is reasonable. The repainted condition of the Careggi *Crucifix*, once the back of Accademia 3147, makes a secure conclusion as to its date impossible, but the gross stylizations indicate an inept modern attempt to imitate the type of cutout cross of the early Quattrocento.

FLORENCE, Accademia, nos. 8605, 8604

Saint Catherine of Alexandria; and *Saint Caius*
FIGS. 227, 229

Panel: 225 x 72.5 cm. (each lateral)

LITERATURE: 1950, Gronau, pp. 183-88: partially reconstructs the altarpiece once in the church of San Gaggio outside of Florence, the elements comprising the Accademia *Saint Catherine of Alexandria* and *Saint Caius* as the left and right laterals of the main register, a *Coronation of the Virgin* in the Gambier-Parry Collection at Highnam Court (now London, Courtauld Institute Galleries) as the central gable, and two predella panels in Berlin, a *Last Supper* at the center and a *Martyrdom of Saint Catherine* at the left; attributes the group to Lorenzo Monaco, observing the mixture of Cionesque and Gaddesque stylistic ingredients; proposes a date ca. 1390-91, following the Nobili predella in the Louvre; the style is consistent with the Accademia *Agony in the Garden*; the central panel of the altarpiece may have been very similar to Don Lorenzo's *Madonna Enthroned* panels in Bologna or the Rijksmuseum // 1951, Procacci, p. 31, nos. 8604-8605: continues to attribute the panels to a master close to Lorenzo di Niccolò, as he had previously proposed in 1936 (p. 29), modifying Berenson's unqualified attribution to Lorenzo di Niccolò (1932, p. 302; 1963, vol. 1, p. 122) // 1954, Eisenberg, pp. 136-45: refutes the attribution of the San Gaggio Altarpiece to LM // 1958, Levi D'Ancona, "Some New Attributions," p. 187, note 58: denies the attribution of the San Gaggio Altarpiece to LM // 1964/65, Zeri, pp. 8 and 11: confirms Gronau's attribution to Don Lorenzo; revises the dating to ca. 1394-95, with a reconstructed polyptych of ca. 1390 providing a link between the Nobili predella and the San Gaggio Altarpiece // 1965, Bellosi, "Da Spinello," p. 36: LM // 1966, Zeri, pp. 150-51: adds to the predella a scene of the *Martyrdom of Saint Caius* in the Museum of Art at Santa Barbara, balancing the *Saint Catherine* panel in Berlin // 1970, González-Palacios, pp. 27-28: LM // 1973, Fenton, pp. 9-21: LM // 1975, Boskovits, p. 344: LM, 1390-95 // 1977, Fenton, figs. 1-3; proposes a revised reconstruction of the altarpiece (see Catalogue II, London, Courtauld Institute Galleries, *Coronation of the Virgin*) // 1979, Gealt, p. 155: follower of Agnolo Gaddi and Lorenzo Monaco // 1979, Levi D'Ancona, p. 476, note 42: refutes ascriptions to early LM grouped around the San Gaggio Altarpiece; tentatively proposes the name of Starnina for the altarpiece, but needs further study // 1987, Bonsanti, p. 93; colorplate of *Caius*, p. 89: *Caius* to LM; *Annunciatory Gabriel* in pinnacle to Lorenzo di Niccolò, with question mark; *Catherine* and *Annunciate Virgin* in pinnacle to Lorenzo di Niccolò.

COMMENT: The long list of attributions of the various elements of the San Gaggio Altarpiece, thoroughly reviewed in Gronau's study (1950, p. 188, note 25) and ranging through the entire complex of later Trecento Florentine shops, underscores the hybrid nature of the style. In the most extensive discussions of these panels—the essays by Hans Gronau (1950) and Federico Zeri (1964/65)—affinities with the style of Lorenzo Monaco are presented in general terms. A comparison that has been considered to be evidence of Lorenzo's authorship of the San Gaggio Altarpiece confronts the features of the Accademia *Saint Caius* (Fig. 229) with the miniature of *Saint Jerome* (Fig. 1) in a choir book dated 1394, in the Laurenziana. But there are essential morphological differences in the breadth of cranial structure, the shapes of eyes, the placement and drawing of ears, and the texture of hair. The expression of the *Caius* is blandly objective, while already in his earliest miniature Don Lorenzo endowed his iconic *Jerome* with a transfixing gaze; the seeming kinship of the *Caius* and *Jerome* may be explained by their common inheritance of Orcagnesque features. The lengthy and eloquent analyses of the elements of the San Gaggio polyptych do not, in my view, reconcile the differences in figure style, in palette, and in construction of a narrative scene between the *Martyrdom* panels in Berlin and Santa Barbara on the one hand

(Figs. 230 and 232) and the predella scenes of Lorenzo's *Agony in the Garden* on the other (Figs. 10 and 11). The virtuosic use of shot color and the daring chromatic juxtapositions, most notable in the Santa Barbara panel, are the work not of a novice but of a full-fledged master. And where in Don Lorenzo's subsequent work will we come upon what Roger Fry described as the "beautiful pale key" of the Courtauld *Coronation* in his sensitive analysis of the picture (1903, p. 126)? The deep recession beyond the picture plane impelled by oblique architectural forms and the inward thrust of geometrical floor patterns, observed in the Courtauld *Coronation* (Fig. 228), the Santa Barbara *Martyrdom of Caius*, and the Berlin *Last Supper* (Fig. 231), indicate that the illusion of space is a primary aspect of this painter's work. The less consistent early art of Lorenzo Monaco wavers between convincing spatial construction and the dominance of the picture plane (cf. Figs. 15, 18; and 16, 17).

An important monument of later Trecento Florentine painting that has close stylistic alliances with the San Gaggio polyptych is the *Intercession of Christ and the Virgin* (Fig. 234) in The Cloisters, New York, once on an altar in the Cathedral of Florence (see Zeri, 1971, pp. 56-60). God the Father at the crest of the composition bears the closest resemblance to disciples in the Berlin *Last Supper* (Fig. 231) and to the patriarchs in the Berlin *Martyrdom of Saint Catherine* (Fig. 230), while the abundant drapery of the kneeling Christ and the Virgin, gathered into dense parallel pleats or falling into cavernous shelves, equally abound in the same *Martyrdom* panel, in the Courtauld *Coronation*, and the Accademia *Catherine*. The long-fingered hands, whether in gestures of benediction or presentation, are identical and so omnipresent as to be a signature of the style. And yet, excepting Boskovits's attribution of the *Intercession* to Niccolò di Pietro Gerini and the Master of Santa Verdiana (1975, p. 412), Fahy's to Lorenzo di Niccolò (1978, pp. 380-381), and Gealt's to the School of Niccolò di Pietro Gerini and Lorenzo Monaco (p. 159), the critical consensus is that no name seems securely associable with the work, in spite of its importance in Florentine painting at the turn of the century. Zeri (1971, p. 59) considers the unknown artist to have been a late follower of Orcagna and the linear rhythms to be strongly reminiscent of the early Lorenzo Monaco. I would propose alternatively that the evident connections between the San Gaggio polyptych and the Cloisters *Intercession* mark these works as the products of the same stylistic milieu, which represents the principal late-century survival of the formalism of the Cioni, the admixture of Gerinesque elements, and an explicit Giottesque revival. Klesse (pp. 329 and 331) has noted that the heraldically confronted birds in the pattern of the cloth of honor in the Courtauld *Coronation of the Virgin* (Fig. 228) is a typically Orcagnesque decorative motif. Inevitably, in these later years of the century the model of Agnolo Gaddi would also have been influential, notably in the forms of landscape, in the attenuated architecture, and in the dense clustering of figures in narrative scenes.

The attempts to define the plot of Lorenzo's early art as a lineage from the Nobili Chapel altarpiece of 1387-88, to the Carmine Polyptych of circa 1390, to the San Gaggio Altarpiece of circa 1394-95 forms a sequence of works in which there are fundamental contradictions in style. These differences would not seem to be explained as the shifting choices of a young artist as he compounded his personal language out of the babel of later Trecento painting. Not until the Accademia *Agony in the Garden* of 1395-1400 is there, I believe, a comprehensive work attributable with certainty to the formative years of Lorenzo Monaco. As is observed in the Introductory Essay (p. 12), the reconstruction of those beginnings is seriously hampered by the loss of the Ardinghelli altarpiece for the Carmine, documented from 1398 to 1400. Finally, the various works considered to be collateral with the style of the San Gaggio polyptych and to be largely attributable to Lorenzo Monaco, are too heterogeneous to allow their unqualified connection with the elements of the San Gaggio Altarpiece. This group is made up of the following works: Bologna, *Madonna Enthroned* (Fig. 133); Amsterdam, *Madonna Enthroned* (Fig. 237) and *Head of the Virgin* (Fig. 235); Assisi, *Madonna of Humility* (Fig. 236); San Diego, *Madonna and Saints* (Fig. 239); Florence, Uffizi, Deposit (formerly Galleria Ferroni), *Crucifixion* (Fig. 240). Among these works I discern a specific connection with the San Gaggio panels only in the Assisi *Madonna* and in the two Rijksmuseum pictures. Bruce Cole (*in litteris*, 1968) has noted the close alliance of the *Crucifixion* in Göttingen (Fig. 233) with this same stylistic culture.

In defining the important milieu of which the San Gaggio Altarpiece is the central monument, there also comes into consideration a group of preparatory drawings for miniatures in the Print Room in Copenhagen, the Vatican Library, and the Cabinet des Dessins in Paris, all of which have been attributed to Lorenzo Monaco (see the individual entries in Catalogue II). There should be added to this group the large drawing of *Christ Giving the Keys to Saint Peter in the Presence of Saint Paul*, no. 58E in the Gabinetto Disegni e Stampe degli Uffizi (Bellosi and Bellini, 1978, fig. 5). Bellosi has justifiably withdrawn this important drawing from the corpus of works by Lorenzo di Bicci (1978, pp. 7-9, no. 5; with full bibliography), recognizing the close relationship to the Cloisters *Intercession*. Although Gronau's (1950) attribution of the Copenhagen drawings to Lorenzo is not persuasive, he was the first to discern the stylistic ties between the group of drawings and elements of the San Gaggio Altarpiece. Less convincing are the attempts to link the style with the Nobili predella (Gronau, 1950; Figs. 213, 216) and with the various panels of the Carmine Polyptych (Zeri, 1964/65; Figs. 215, and 217-223). The stylistic kinship of the Copenhagen drawings and those in Paris and the Vatican allies these latter sheets as well with the San Gaggio group. Degenhart and Schmitt (1968) observed that the Copenhagen drawings, and by extension those in Paris and the Vatican, are not all by the same hand. They represent, nonetheless, a stylistic modality that is closely identifiable with the San Gaggio Altarpiece and other panels in its orbit. Neither that cluster of works nor these various drawings would seem to be the first efforts of an artist searching for a formal language but are consistently formulated statements rooted in the conglomerate soil of later Trecento Florentine painting, the same soil from which the art of Lorenzo Monaco sprang in the last decade of the century. Given the existence of these drawings for miniatures in liturgical books, the question remains as to whether the works in the stylistic idiom of the San Gaggio group were produced within the confines of Santa Maria degli Angeli or were yet another intervention of secular painters in the vast artistic output of that Camaldolese center. For the focal work of this group—the San Gaggio Altarpiece—I would propose the following inclusive label: Cionesque/Gerinesque Master, 1390s; for the works within its orbit, Milieu of the San Gaggio Altarpiece, 1390s.

For further comment on the proposed reconstructions of the early style of Lorenzo Monaco, see the Notes to Essay, p. 53, Note 35 and the following entries in Catalogue II: Paris, Louvre, *Feast of Herod . . .*; Florence, Accademia, *Saint Jerome*; *Saint John the Baptist. . . .*

FLORENCE, Accademia, nos. 8705, 8708, 8709, 8704

Saint Jerome; *Saint John the Baptist*; *Saint Peter*; and *Saint Paul*

FIGS. 215, 218

Panel: 97 x 40 cm. (*Jerome* and *Paul*); 102 x 37 cm. (*Baptist*); 100 x 36 cm. (*Peter*)

LITERATURE: 1932, Procacci, pp. 155-56, note 3: by a master influenced by Orcagna // 1960, Longhi, p. 60: Florentine, late fourteenth century; probably by the same hand that painted the *Saint Peter* in the Gambier-Parry Collection (now, London, Courtauld Institute Galleries; Blunt, 1967, p. 19, no. 36, Bernardo Daddi, attr., following suggestion of John Shearman; see also, Boskovits, 1975, p. 243, note 201: Daddi) // 1964/65, Zeri, pp. 3-7, figs. 2-5: reconstructs an altarpiece composed of four *Saints*, then in deposit at Santa Maria, Quarto, but at one time in the Carmine, Florence, a *Madonna Enthroned*, in the Antinori Collection, Florence (now Toledo, Museum of Art), and five dispersed predella panels, as follows: *Saint Jerome in Penitence*, formerly in the Cremer Collection, Dortmund; *Saint John the Baptist Departing for the Wilderness*, Museums and Art Galleries, Leicester; *Nativity*, Staatliche Museen, Berlin-Dahlem; *Crucifixion of Saint Peter*, Walters Art Gallery, Baltimore; *Beheading of Saint Paul*, Art Museum, Princeton University; the Baltimore, Berlin, and Princeton panels had previously been integrated by Evelyn Sandberg-Vavalà (1939) and attributed to Lorenzo Monaco; (for the addition of the former Dortmund panel, see Eisenberg, 1954, pp. 83-85; accepting the attribution of the predella to Lorenzo Monaco); Zeri attributes the entire complex to Lorenzo Monaco dating it to the very beginning of the 1390s, that is, after the Nobili Chapel predella of 1387-88 (see Catalogue II, Paris, Louvre, *Feast of Herod . . .*) and before the San Gaggio Altarpiece of 1394-95 (see Catalogue II, Florence, Accademia, *Saint Catherine* and *Saint Caius*); the mixed influence of Agnolo Gaddi and earlier Giottesque painting are emphasized // 1965, Bellosi, "Da Spinello," p. 37: questions the attribution of the altarpiece to LM; observes stylistic traits of the earlier work of the Master of the Straus Madonna // 1970,

González-Palacios, pp. 28-29: LM // 1975, Boskovits, pp. 135, 338, and 345; figs. 451 and 453: LM, 1395-1400 // 1987, Bonsanti, p. 93: Florentine, end of the fourteenth century; *Saint Jerome* identified as *San Mosè*, using inscription on later frame.

COMMENT: [Note: Carmine Polyptych is used here as a convenient dubbing for a widely dispersed group of panels, but should not be identified with Don Lorenzo's lost altarpiece for the second Ardinghelli Chapel in the Carmine (see Documents 4A-4G and Notes to Essay, p. 50, Note 17).]

Federico Zeri's reconstruction of the Carmine Polyptych (1964/65) recovered an important monument in the history of Florentine painting toward the close of the Trecento. His unequivocal attribution of the altarpiece to Lorenzo Monaco and chronological placement of it between the Nobili Chapel predella (Figs. 213, 214, and 216; Zeri, 1964/65, I, figs. 6-11) and the San Gaggio Altarpiece (Figs. 227-232), to form a sequence of early works by the painter are, in my view, problematic. Within the series of works I discern the incipient traits of Don Lorenzo's mature style only in the Carmine Polyptych, but my stand on the attribution of this altarpiece and a group of allied panels, noted below and in separate entries in Catalogue II, has vacillated over the years and remains unresolved. Luciano Bellosi's brief observation (1965) that elements of the Carmine Polyptych approach the earlier work of the Master of the Straus Madonna (i.e., before 1400), is suggestive, but not a solution to the problem. The differences between the works of this still anonymous painter before and after the turn of the century are sufficiently wide to have prompted Ugo Procacci ("Opere inedite," 1933, pp. 224-30; 1951, p. 26) to posit a separate master for the magnificent *Annunciation* in the Accademia in Florence (Fig. 278), generally considered to be the pivotal work of the Master of the Straus Madonna. It is from this picture and the eponymous *Madonna* in Houston (Fig. 279) that certain analogies may be drawn with elements of the Carmine Polyptych. Bellosi observed the distinctive type of Child; the closely fitted shirt reveals an unusually muscular articulation of the shoulders and torso (cf. Figs. 217 and 279). Comparison of the Toledo *Madonna* with the Accademia *Annunciation* points up the similarity in the contours of the lower arm and hand of the Virgin and in the soft parallel pleats of her tunic. Ornamental motifs in textiles, drapery borders, and haloes, and the Cosmatesque inlays are distinctly alike in the Toledo and Accademia panels, but are not found within Don Lorenzo's vocabulary of ornament in any work that may be securely attributed to his hand. The halo ornamentation in the four Accademia *Saints*, however, reveals a range of motifs and a refinement of technique that will be a hallmark of Don Lorenzo's art, culminating in the *Coronation of the Virgin* of 1414 (Figs. 44-47).

In reconstructions of the Master of the Straus Madonna and of the early style of Lorenzo Monaco, I believe that frequently too exclusive an emphasis has been put on sources in the art of Agnolo Gaddi, with a resultant blurring of the decisive impact of the long-surviving Cionesque tradition, in particular the romantic lyricism and feminine grace of Nardo's art. Zeri's analyses of the Carmine Polyptych stressed Gaddesque elements and the Giottesque revival, and explicitly rejected the impact of a Cionesque idiom (p. 4). Yet, the secondary chromatic harmonies of the Accademia *Saints*, so eloquently characterized by Zeri, and the subtle passages of dark rose and violet in the Toledo *Madonna* are inevitable reminders of the sensibility of Nardo di Cione in the frescoes of the Strozzi Chapel at Santa Maria Novella. And from the standpoint of physiognomy, there could hardly be a closer resemblance than that between the Accademia *Saint Jerome* and the Saint Peter in the forefront of Jacopo di Cione's San Piero Maggiore *Coronation of the Virgin* (Fig. 299). A further bond between the *Madonna* in Toledo and the Accademia *Annunciation* is the airy spaciousness established by the gracile and finely drawn architecture. In the portentous throne of the Fitzwilliam *Madonna* (Fig. 15), Lorenzo Monaco constructed a vivid illusion of space, but in an obviously nostalgic reminiscence of Giotto combined with the weightier contemporary model of Spinello Aretino.

Zeri's alliance of the small *Madonna* panels in the Horne Museum (Fig. 224) and the Walters Art Gallery (Fig. 225) with the Toledo panel and its accompanying saints is definitive, and as he notes (p. 8), Evelyn Sandberg-Vavalà (1939, p. 108) had previously observed the stylistic ties between the Horne and Walters Madonnas and the predella panels in Berlin, Baltimore, and Princeton (Figs. 221-223). Identical ornamental patterns, again Cionesque in origin, in the three *Madonna* panels help to confirm their kinship. The varying sources and conjunctures within these works demonstrate the difficulty of precise attribution in a period of widespread artistic hybridization.

The attribution of the predella of the Carmine Polyptych is complicated by the fact that within the five panels there are wide variations in quality, which leads to the conjecture that more than one hand was at work in the series. Specifically, the panels in Baltimore, Princeton, and Leicester (Fig. 220) display considerably less refinement of technique and form than does the Berlin *Nativity* or the panel formerly in Dortmund, which are the most accomplished of the series and most clearly invite an attribution to Lorenzo Monaco. The connections with Don Lorenzo's *Agony in the Garden* (Fig. 7) were discerned by Sandberg-Vavalà (1939, pp. 106 and 111), who saw in that large panel the mingled Giottesque, Cionesque, and Gaddesque ingredients of the painter's early style. There is an unmistakable likeness in drapery forms, if not in facial type, between the sleeping Joseph of the Berlin picture and the Saint Peter in the *Betrayal* predella of the *Agony in the Garden* (Fig. 12), and the marginal Annunciation to the Shepherds will later be consistently included in Don Lorenzo's *Nativity* panels (e.g., Figs. 30 and 51). The precisely cut masses of rock (a textbook demonstration of Cennino Cennini's famous prescription for landscape) and the detail of the tree in the Berlin panel are closely matched in the Accademia *Agony*. An equally close comparison may be drawn with the steeply ascending cliffs and the vegetation in the *Ascension* miniature on fol. 86 of Corale 1 in the Laurenziana (book dated 1396; Fig. 243), a Gaddesque work with reminders as well of the style of Don Silvestro dei Gherarducci, or the same elements in that master's *Abraham and the Angels* miniature in London (Fig. 268). These landscape details depended on models that circulated among closely related workshops, their monumental prototype being in the Castellani Chapel at Santa Croce, above all in the fresco of *Saint Anthony Beaten by Devils and Christ Appearing to Saint Anthony*, painted in the 1380s by a contemporary of Agnolo Gaddi (see B. Cole, 1977, pp. 10-11, and pl. 17). There remains the difficulty in establishing a firm connection between the predella panels of the Carmine Polyptych and Don Lorenzo's two quatrefoils (Figs. 10-14) beneath the *Agony in the Garden*, painted in the second half of the 1390s. The stylistic differences between these two predellas are, in my view, difficult to reconcile within the less than half a decade that would seem to separate them. In turn, the few narrative predella panels that have been attributed to the Master of the Straus Madonna present contradictions as a group and do not jibe with the predella of the Carmine Polyptych. The stylistic range from the *Nativity* and *Adoration of the Magi* in a Milanese private collection and in Seattle (Bellosi, "Da Spinello," 1965, figs. 36-37; Fremantle, fig. 642) to the predella with the *Descent into Limbo and Legends of the Cross* in the "Martello Collection" and the National Gallery in Prague (Pujmanová, 1979, figs. 1 and 2; Boskovits, 1979, pp. 56-58, and 1985, pp. 107-111) indicates that the rubric Master of the Straus Madonna is an encompassing one. At the heart of this problem of attribution is the clear possibility of exchanges, or even collaborations, between the milieus of the Master of the Straus Madonna and of Lorenzo Monaco in his formative years, an elusive situation that continues to challenge attempts at precise attribution. Moreover, until there is forthcoming some degree of definition of the artistic beginnings of Gherardo Starnina within the stylistic welter of later Trecento Florentine painting, uncertainty prevails in the process of attaching labels to many pictures of the 1390s. For other clusters of works attributed to the early period of Lorenzo Monaco, see Catalogue II, Florence, Accademia, *Saint Catherine of Alexandria*, and *Saint Caius*; and Paris, Louvre, *Feast of Herod*. . . . Also see, Catalogue II, Leghorn (formerly), Larderel Collection, *Madonna with Four Saints*.

FLORENCE, Bargello (Museo Nazionale, Cod. C 71)

Annunciation; *Saint Stephen*; *Saint John the Evangelist*; *Saint Andrew*; *Saint Agnes*

Miniatures in an Antiphonary, fols. 2v, 95, 105, 210, 243v
Parchment: 54.5 x 37 cm. (size of page)

LITERATURE: 1932, Ciaranfi, p. 384, and fig. 12: by a precursor of Lorenzo Monaco, before 1412-13 // 1958, Levi D'Ancona, "Some New Attributions," pp. 185-86 and 189: the *Evangelist* is given to LM, 1390-94; the *Andrew* and *Agnes* are tentatively ascribed to him; the *Stephen* is assigned to a follower of Don Silvestro dei Gherarducci; the *Annunciation* is left unattributed because of the damaged condition; other miniatures are given to a follower of Don

Simone, to Rossello di Jacopo Franchi, and to a follower of Battista di Biagio Sanguigni // 1965, Bellosi, "Da Spinello," pp. 36-37: the entire sequence of miniatures ascribed to Lorenzo Monaco, after 1391; fig. 34 reproduces the *Annunciation* // 1975, Boskovits, pp. 242, note 196, and 345: fols. 95 and 105 attributed to LM, 1405-1410; other miniatures to Matteo Torelli // 1979, Levi D'Ancona, pp. 469, note 39, and 471-77; figs, 3, 4, and 8: the *Stephen* ascribed to Don Silvestro; the *Evangelist* to Don Lorenzo; the *Andrew* to the two painters in collaboration.

COMMENT: Though the damaged state of the *Annunciation* impedes attribution, it is apparent from what does survive that the miniature has no direct formal or expressive relationship to the art of Lorenzo Monaco, which is also true of the *Saint Stephen* (D'Ancona, 1914, vol. 1, pl. XLIIa). The *Saint Andrew* is possibly best understood as a later manifestation of the art of Don Silvestro, in which the older artist has absorbed some traits of the young Don Lorenzo (Levi D'Ancona, 1958, fig. 23; 1979, fig. 8), but the staccato and angular drapery, the brusque technique, and the summarily drawn hands preclude the latter's involvement. The *Evangelist* (D'Ancona, 1914, vol. 1, pl. XLIIb; Levi D'Ancona, 1979, fig. 3) bears some resemblance in pose and detail to the same figure in Laurenziana Corale 1 (fol. 33; Fig. 5). The planes of drapery, however, are flat and unmodulated, and the figure lacks the tension implied in the facial features; in the early years of his career Don Lorenzo had already produced the evocative miniatures in Corali 5 and 8 (Laurenziana; Figs. 1-6). A comparison may be drawn between the *Evangelist* of C 71 and the figure to the far right in the *Martyrdom of Saint Caius* in the Santa Barbara Museum of Art (Fig. 232), by a painter cognate to but distinctive from Lorenzo Monaco.

FLORENCE, Bargello (Museo Nazionale, Cod. G 73)

Twenty-eight miniatures in an Antiphonary (Sunday Diurnal)

Parchment: 50 x 36 cm. (size of page)

LITERATURE: 1932, Ciaranfi, p. 383, and fig. 11: identified as G 79; school of Lorenzo Monaco // 1958, Levi D'Ancona, "Some New Attributions," p. 190: Bartolomeo di Fruosino, possibly with the help of Don Lorenzo in four of the miniatures // 1961, Levi D'Ancona, pp. 83 and 88-89, and figs. 7 and 8: Bartolomeo di Fruosino, 1411, the year of payments to the painter for work in antiphonaries // 1972, Boskovits, p. 47: LM (preparation of the drawings), with later collaboration of Bartolomeo di Fruosino // 1984, Bellosi, p. 308: miniatures by Bartolomeo di Fruosino and the "Maestro del Codice Squarcialupi," the latter especially evident in the *Adoration of the Magi* (fol. 57).

COMMENT: The exclusion of Don Lorenzo's hand from the miniatures of this choir book (Levi D'Ancona, 1961; Bellosi, 1984), is justified and presents abundant evidence of secular involvement in the production of liturgical books for monastic use.

FLORENCE, Biblioteca Laurenziana, Cod. Cor. 7

Christ and David

Miniature in an Antiphonary, fol. 20
Parchment: 70 x 49.8 cm. (size of page)
Inscribed date of book: 1406 (fol. 123: COMPLETUM EST HOC OPUS ANNO DNI MCCCCVI)

LITERATURE: 1958, Levi D'Ancona, "Some New Attributions," pp. 176 and 189 and fig. 17: fol. 20 is given to Lorenzo Monaco, while the other three miniatures in the book (fols. 36, 72, and 95v) are attributed to Bartolomeo di Fruosino // 1975, Boskovits, p. 342: all miniatures are attributed to LM.

COMMENT: The blocky proportions of the figures, their naive relationship to the field of the letter, and the cursory execution, bring fol. 20 closer to the style of Bartolomeo di Fruosino, who was responsible for the three other miniatures of this book from Santa Maria Nuova ($F2^2$.J). The roughhewn hands are unknown in Don Lorenzo's work.

FLORENCE, Biblioteca Laurenziana, Cod. Cor. 13

Moses

Miniature in an Antiphonary, fol. 89
Parchment: 68.9 x 46.6 cm. (size of page)

LITERATURE: 1932, Ciaranfi, p. 301, note 1: close to Lorenzo Monaco, but not of his caliber; compares it with the *John the Evangelist* of Corale 1 (fol. 33) // 1958, Levi D'Ancona, "Some New Attributions," pp. 187 and 189, and fig. 25: by an assistant of LM, tentatively identified as Bartolomeo di Fruosino // 1975, Boskovits, p. 342: LM, 1395-1400.

COMMENT: Levi D'Ancona's provisory ascription to Bartolomeo di Fruosino satisfactorily removes the work from Don Lorenzo's immediate stylistic milieu. A cut miniature of *Saint Paul* in the Kupferstichkabinett, Berlin-Dahlem (no. 1232) has been identified by Levi D'Ancona as fol. 2v from this choir book, and attributed to Lorenzo Monaco, in collaboration with Matteo Torelli (1978, p. 231).

FLORENCE, Museo Horne, no. 14 (Soprintendenza, inv. no. 3231)

Madonna Enthroned, with Six Saints
FIG. 224

Panel: 113.5 x 62 cm.

LITERATURE: 1909, Sirén, p. 35: an early work of Lorenzo Monaco // 1927, van Marle, vol. 9, p. 33, note 1, Bicci di Lorenzo; p. 124: early LM, close to but not of the same level of quality as the Berlin *Madonna Enthroned* of 1400 [*sic*] // 1929, Suida, p. 392: LM // 1932, Berenson, p. 299: LM, early // 1938/39, Pudelko, p. 238: perhaps the earliest work of Lorenzo Monaco, showing a mixture of influences from Taddeo Gaddi, Spinello Aretino, and strong connections with Jacopo di Cione // 1939, Sandberg-Vavalà, p. 108: early LM, in the style of the Baltimore *Madonna* and the predella in Berlin, Baltimore, and Princeton // 1954, Eisenberg, p. 103: LM, 1390-95 // 1961, Gamba, p. 22, no. 14: Florentine, early fifteenth century // 1963, Berenson, vol. 1, p. 119: LM // 1964/65, Zeri, p. 8: LM, between the Nobili predella of 1387/88 and the reconstructed polyptych of ca. 1390 // 1965, Bellosi, "Da Spinello," p. 37: approaches the idiom of the Master of the Straus Madonna // 1966, Rossi, p. 139: Florentine, early fifteenth century // 1975, Boskovits, p. 345: LM, 1390-95.

COMMENT: The Horne *Madonna* is among the group of works attributed to the early style of Lorenzo Monaco by Sirén during the years following his circumscribed monograph of 1905. Juxtaposition of the Horne panel, the Rijksmuseum and San Diego *Madonna* panels (Figs. 237 and 239), and the former Ferroni *Crucifixion* (Fig. 240) shows the degree to which Lorenzo's name came to be attached to problematic works of varying idioms of the later Trecento and early years of the Quattrocento. The analogies drawn by Sandberg-Vavalà (1939) and Zeri (1964/65) between the Horne *Madonna* and the various elements of a polyptych dated by Zeri circa 1390 (Figs. 217-223), as well as with the *Madonna* in the Walters Gallery, Baltimore (Fig. 225), are definitive. Zeri observed the close kinship of the Saint Lucy of the Horne *Madonna* and the young Baptist in the Leicester panel (Fig. 220), but his comparison of the kneeling Saint Catherine with the Salome of the Louvre *Feast of Herod* (Fig. 213) is elusive. The Horne *Madonna* and the "Nobili predella" are not, in my view, links in the same chain.

The Horne *Madonna* evinces the survival of Cionesque style into the last years of the Trecento and its fusion with the language of Agnolo Gaddi. Pudelko (1938/39) and Sandberg-Vavalà (1939) emphasized the Cionesque quality of the palette in the Horne panel; the gentler spirit of Nardo rather than the severities of Orcagna pervades the image. More specifically, the Baptist is a direct descendant of Jacopo's version of the same saint in the *Coronation* of 1373 in the Accademia, Florence (Offner and Steinweg, sec. IV, vol. III, 1965, pl. VI). The heraldic birds in the textile pattern of the Horne panel are a favored motif of Cionesque ornament (see Klesse, p. 339).

For further comment, see Catalogue II, Florence Accademia, *Saint Jerome; Saint John the Baptist. . . .* With the closing of the Museo Horne after the flood of 1966, the panel was stored and then transferred in 1976 to the Cenacolo di Foligno for provisional exhibition. Since 1984 it has been at the Opificio delle Pietre Dure e Laboratori di Restauro in the Fortezza da Basso, Florence.

FLORENCE, Museo dell'Opera di Santa Croce

Madonna of Humility
FIG. 250

Fresco (detached): 110 x 118 cm.

LITERATURE: 1959, Florence, *III Mostra*, p. 10, no. 257: related to the stylistic idiom of Lorenzo Monaco // 1975, Boskovits, p. 346: LM, 1405-1410 // 1983, Becherucci, p. 177, no. 38, and pl. 156 (in color): LM circle, 1405-1410.

COMMENT: That the fresco is not a work of Don

Lorenzo's immediate milieu is apparent even through the veil of damage incurred in the flood of 1966 (Fig. 250, after restoration), the mild calligraphy of the Virgin's mantle being the lone reminder of the painter's personal style. The Child bears some resemblance to a type found in works of the circle of the Master of the Straus Madonna. There is also a tenuous link with the style of the fresco of the *Scourging of Saint Benedict* above the entrance to the Gianfigliazzi Chapel at Santa Trinita (Florence, Sopr. Gab. Fot. 24332).

The inclusion of the mandorla and crescent moon in the image of the *Madonna of Humility* is indicative of the Virgin as the Woman of the Apocalypse, a merging of iconographies that was considered by Meiss (1951, pp. 153-56, and figs. 133 and 135-37). He mentions a *Madonna of Humility* in the Museo di Santa Croce, in which stars appear in the Virgin's halo, one of the several symbols of the Woman of the Apocalypse (p. 155, note 106). The fragments of ornament that survive in the halo of the Virgin do not appear to contain a star motif, but there are vestiges of stars in the upper right arc of the mandorla. The vase with a stalk of lilies, included in the Santa Croce fresco, is also found in a panel by a Neapolitan follower of Simone Martini, in which the *Madonna of Humility* is given the second identity of the Woman of the Apocalypse (Meiss, 1951, fig. 133).

FLORENCE, Museo dello Spedale degli Innocenti, no. 247

Crucifixion with the Mourning Virgin and Saint John the Evangelist

Fresco (transferred to canvas): 155 x 114 cm.

LITERATURE: 1932, Berenson, p. 299: Lorenzo Monaco (1963, vol. 1, p. 119) // 1935, Calamandrei, p. 7, no. 29: school of Fra Angelico (then in the Refectory at Ognissanti) // 1952, Paatz, vol. 4, p. 429: Florentine, end of the fourteenth century // 1975, Boskovits, p. 346: LM, 1410-15 // 1977, Bellosi, p. 263, no. 247, pl. 283: LM, 1400-1404; close in style to the *Crucifixion* in Altenburg and the *Man of Sorrows* of 1404 in the Accademia, Florence; provides further bibliography.

COMMENT: This extensively obliterated fresco would appear to be by a retardataire Florentine working around 1415-20 who used as a principal model the *Crucifix with the Mourning Virgin and Saint John* at San Giovannino dei Cavalieri, Florence (Fig. 74). The rigid drapery forms and the facial type of the Saint John do not resemble Don Lorenzo's style or works from his shop.

FLORENCE, private collection

Crucifixion with the Adoring Saint Francis

Panel (dimensions not accessible)

LITERATURE: 1975, Boskovits, p. 346, fig. 455: Lorenzo Monaco, 1400-1405.

COMMENT: Although I know the picture only from a published illustration, the style seems but remotely suggestive of Lorenzo Monaco or of his shop, specifically in the figure of Christ and the landscape forms rising steeply at either side.

FLORENCE, Seminario Maggiore di Cestello

Crucifix

Panel (cutout): 121 x 83 cm.

LITERATURE: 1905, Sirén, p. 90: school of Lorenzo Monaco // 1927, van Marle, vol. 9, p. 177, note 1: school of LM // 1931, Golzio, p. 63: LM; similar to the cutout cross in the Horne Museum // 1933, Florence, *Mostra del Tesoro*, p. 87, no. 578: manner of LM // 1933/34, Gamba, p. 154: LM // 1941, Paatz, vol. 2, pp. 277 and 282, note 35: LM workshop; note the earlier location at the Florentine church of San Giovanni Battista della Calza.

COMMENT: The painter of the Cestello *Crucifix* worked in the milieus of Paolo Schiavo and Francesco d'Antonio, around 1425-30 (Florence, Sopr. Gab. Fot. 23252).

FLORENCE, Soprintendenza per i Beni Artistici e Storici, inv. no. 3227 (Accademia, Deposit)

Madonna and Child with Four Saints and Two Angels

FIG. 252

Panel: 105 x 55.5 cm.

LITERATURE: 1967, Vertova, p. 205: Lorenzo Monaco, 1395, showing strongly Giottesque traits //

1975, Boskovits, p. 344, pl. 145 (detail): LM, 1390–95.

COMMENT: This abraded panel would seem to be the work of an eclectic painter who adopted stylistic elements from later Cionesque painting, Agnolo Gaddi, and the Master of the Straus Madonna.

FLORENCE, Soprintendenza per i Beni Artistici e Storici, Deposit

Nativity; Adoration of the Magi

Fresco (detached; dimensions not accessible)

LITERATURE: 1909, Sirén, p. 33: Lorenzo Monaco, first decade of the fifteenth century; the basis for attributing to him the three frescoes in the former Convento delle Oblate (see Catalogue II, Florence, Soprintendenza, Deposit, *Agony in the Garden*, . . .). // 1927, van Marle, vol. 9, p. 122: LM, before 1400 // 1929, Suida, p. 392: LM // 1931, Golzio, p. 31: LM, similar to Oblate group // 1952, Paatz, vol. 4, pp. 22 and 48, note 89: style of LM, around 1400; record the physical setting of the frescoes.

COMMENT: The two frescoes, originally in the Convento delle Oblate at Santa Maria Nuova, part of which was transformed into the Archivio Notarile, may be aligned with works produced around 1395 to 1400 in the idiom of the elusive Ambrogio di Baldese (cf. Boskovits, 1975, pls. 114, 115, and fig. 372). (*Adoration of the Magi*, Alinari 29257.)

FLORENCE, Soprintendenza per i Beni Artistici e Storici, Deposit

Lamentation (fragment)

Fresco (detached): 100 x 150 cm. (approximate)

LITERATURE: 1905, Sirén, pp. 21-22: Lorenzo Monaco, around 1395 // 1909, Berenson, p. 153: LM, early (omitted from later editions) // 1927, van Marle, vol. 9, 122: LM, while still the unevolved pupil of Agnolo Gaddi // 1929, Suida, p. 392: LM // 1931, Golzio, p. 30: LM; very early and close to Agnolo Gaddi and to Sienese sources.

COMMENT: The *Lamentation* from the Casa del Mutilato, Santa Maria Nuova, was produced in the environment of Agnolo Gaddi, with an admixture of Gerinesque elements (Florence, Sopr. Gab. Fot. 25501).

FLORENCE, Soprintendenza per i Beni Artistici e Storici, Deposit

Agony in the Garden; Christ and the Sleeping Disciples; The Man of Sorrows with Episodes and Emblems of the Passion

Fresco (detached): 350 x 480 cm. (*Agony* and *Sleeping Disciples*); 250 x 460 cm. (*Man of Sorrows*)

LITERATURE: 1900, Berenson, p. 124: Lorenzo Monaco // 1905, Sirén, pp. 22-24: LM, around 1396 // 1909, Sirén, p. 33: revises the dating to the early fifteenth century on the basis of comparison with frescoes in the Archivio Notarile (now Soprintendenza, Deposit), which are also attributed to LM // 1927, van Marle, vol. 9, p. 122: LM, last decade of the Trecento // 1929, Suida, p. 392; LM // 1931, Golzio, pp. 31-32: LM, excepting the *Man of Sorrows*, which is by a pupil; as it is based on the *Man of Sorrows* panel of 1404, the fresco must date early in the fifteenth century // 1932, Berenson, p. 331: the *Agony* attributed to Mariotto di Nardo (p. 299, the entire cycle attributed to Don Lorenzo) // 1935, Procacci, p. 378: the *Agony* is by LM // 1938/39, Pudelko, p. 237: probably by Mariotto di Nardo; the attribution to Lorenzo Monaco has led to too much emphasis on the influence of Agnolo Gaddi on his early style // 1944, L. Venturi, p. 28: *Man of Sorrows* by LM // 1950, Gronau, p. 218, note 17: Mariotto di Nardo // 1952, Paatz, vol. 4, pp. 19-20 and 46, note 72: record the physical setting of the frescoes; perhaps by LM, around 1400 // 1956, Rosenthal, pp. 74-75: LM // 1957, Eisenberg, p. 51, note 9: Mariotto di Nardo // 1959, Florence, *III Mostra*, nos. 264-66 (*Man of Sorrows, Christ and the Sleeping Disciples*): LM // 1961, Procacci, pp. 55-56, and pls. 32 and 33: Florentine, beginning of the fifteenth century // 1963, Berenson, vol. 1, p. 119: LM // 1975, Boskovits, p. 393: Mariotto di Nardo, 1395-1400.

COMMENT: The frescoes are from the former Convento delle Oblate at Santa Maria Nuova. An attribution to Mariotto di Nardo and a dating in the last years of the Trecento most satisfactorily localize the three frescoes (also see Catalogue I, Florence, Accademia, *The Man of Sorrows with Episodes and Emblems of the Passion*). (Florence, Sopr. Gab. Fot. 11045, 11046, 113205.)

FLORENCE, Uffizi, Deposit (formerly Galleria Ferroni, no. 126)

Crucifixion

FIG. 240

Parchment, attached to panel: 24.5 x 16.5 cm.

LITERATURE: 1909, Sirén, p. 35: Lorenzo Monaco // 1927, van Marle, vol. 9, p. 168, note 3: LM // 1929, Suida, p. 392: LM // 1931, Golzio, p. 62: denies the attribution to LM // 1932, Berenson, p. 299: LM, early (1963, vol. 1, p. 119) // 1932, Berenson, "Quadri senza casa," p. 30: early LM, with the lingering influence of Spinello Aretino; closely related to the Horne and San Diego *Madonna* panels (1970, p. 139) // 1938/39, Pudelko, p. 248, note 35: denies the attribution to LM // 1954, Eisenberg, p. 103: LM, 1390-95 // 1958, Baldini, p. 22, no. 7: LM; provides a technical report on the removal of areas of repaint covering the decorative border which obscured the fact the *Crucifixion* was originally a miniature, probably from a choir book, affixed to a panel in recent times // 1964/65, Zeri, p. 11, note 14: early period of LM; related to a group of works following on the San Gaggio polyptych; the quality suggests the intervention of an assistant // 1975, Boskovits, p. 345: LM, 1395-1400 // 1979, Florence, *Gli Uffizi*, p. 346, no. P921: LM // 1986, Mosco, p. 106, no. 27 (entry by S. Melini Trkulija): LM, 1395-1400; the small size implies that it was not cut from a choir book.

COMMENT: See Catalogue II, San Diego, Museum of Art, *Madonna with Four Saints and The Man of Sorrows.*

FLORENCE, Santa Croce (predella of high altarpiece)

Death Riding a Bull

FIGS. 260, 261

Panel: 28 x 77 cm.

LITERATURE: 1842, Fantozzi, p. 205: a panel representing *Death on a Horse* [*sic*] is mentioned as lying beneath an *Enthroned Eternal Father* in the monastery of Santa Croce, dated 1408 // 1924, van Marle, vol. 3, p. 612: Niccolò di Pietro Gerini, along with the *Madonna and Saints* panel above it // 1930, Offner, sec. III, vol. II, pt. II, p. 194: Florentine, early fifteenth century // 1938/39, Pudelko, p. 77, note 6: Lorenzo Monaco, soon after 1415 // 1939, Sandberg-Vavalà, p. 107, note 13: refutes Pudelko's attribution to LM // 1962, Offner, sec. IV, vol. I, pp. 46-47: LM // 1974, L. White, p. 215 (passim for further bibliography on the subject) // 1975, Boskovits, p. 342: LM, 1408, using the date of the *Enthroned Saint James* with which it was probably once allied.

COMMENT: The panel became the center element of the predella of the conglomerate high altarpiece at Santa Croce when the various parts were assembled between 1869 and 1871 (see Marcucci, p. 112). This surely was the panel Fantozzi (1842) saw at Santa Croce beneath the *Saint James Enthroned* (Fig. 171), but there is no evidence that the two are by the same artist or were originally together. The date of 1408, inscribed on the *Saint James*, is not satisfactory for the *Death on a Bull*, nor would a panel 77 cm. in width, which according to Fantozzi was the only element of the predella, placed beneath a panel 95 cm. wide have been a probable combination. Furthermore, there is no iconographic basis for relating the *Enthroned Saint James* with the *Death on a Bull*. Rather than being by Lorenzo Monaco, the panel would seem to be by a painter who came under the influence of Don Lorenzo's later works, such as the three-part predella in the Accademia, Florence (Fig. 95), or the chiaroscuro drawing of the *Journey of the Magi* (Fig. 97) in the Berlin Print Room. The stilted rhythms of the horseman's tunic and cape are entirely unlike Lorenzo's handling of comparable passages, nor are the flattened shapes and the facial types of the fallen figures in his vocabulary of forms. As Evelyn Sandberg-Vavalà observed in denying the attribution to Don Lorenzo (1939), the panel lacks his "nervous virtuosity," which reaches fullest expression in the Berlin *Journey*.

From several standpoints, the style of *Death on a Bull* is reminiscent of the work of Giovanni Toscani, particularly the two cassone panels of the *Palii* in the Bargello and the Cleveland Museum of Art (*European Paintings before 1500*, Cleveland, 1974, figs. 45, 45a). The features of the horseman (Fig. 261) in the Santa Croce panel have a close double in the woman standing at the far right edge of the Baptistery in the Bargello cassone (Fremantle, fig. 1035), and the "schiacciato" effect of the figures stretched on the ground recalls the fallen horse in the Cleveland panel. The rounded contour and deep scalloping in the mantle of the stooped woman at the right of *Death on a Bull* is reminiscent of the head of the Virgin from the *Pietà* on the reverse of Giovanni Toscani's *Madonna and Saints* altarpiece in the Museo dello Spedale degli Innocenti (see Bellosi, 1977, fig. 49). The shape of the horse does not have an exact replica in any work by Giovanni Toscani, but there are several variants in his numerous depictions of horses, for example, in the Cleveland and Bargello panels, and the *Adoration of the Magi* (formerly New York, Schaeffer Galleries; see Bellosi, 1966, fig. 28). The nearest resemblance to the horse in *Death on a Bull* is in the steed at the far right of the Cleveland panel, where the minuscule head crowns a thick, bulbous neck. I propose a tentative attribution of the *Death on a Bull* to the workshop of Giovanni Toscani. The insistent, if relatively naive, calligraphy of the Santa Croce panel implies that it was produced several years prior to the Bargello and Cleveland cassoni, which Bellosi justifiably places at a late stage in the career of Giovanni Toscani, circa 1428 to 1429, when he most directly absorbed the influence of Masaccio (1966, pp. 53-54). The analogies between the Santa Croce panel and the *Pietà* of Giovanni Toscani's Innocenti altarpiece, which Bellosi localizes in the second decade of the Quattrocento (1977, p. 233), along with the implicit influence of Lorenzo Monaco's visionary later works, suggest a date circa 1420.

FLORENCE, San Firenze (Oratorio della Compagnia dei Neri)

Crucifix

Panel (cutout): 212 x 157 cm.

LITERATURE: 1931, Golzio, p. 248: probably by Lorenzo Monaco // 1933, Florence, *Mostra del Tesoro*, p. 81, no. 1050: style of LM // 1933, Offner, p. 169, pl. IA: Mariotto di Nardo // 1938, Pudelko, p. 248, note 35: school of LM // 1941, Paatz, vol. 2, p. 109: Florentine, around 1400 // 1975, Boskovits, p. 391: Mariotto di Nardo, 1385-90.

COMMENT: The ascription to Mariotto and a dating in the later Trecento are appropriate. The quietness of the loincloth, although now more static through loss of part of the projecting arabesque, places the work in an earlier phase of Mariotto's career. In contrast, the Christ in his *Trinity* altarpiece of 1416 (Florence, Santa Trinita; Fremantle, fig. 952) shows the direct influence of Don Lorenzo's calligraphy.

GÖTTINGEN, Universitätsmuseum, no. 65

Crucifixion, with the Virgin, Saint John the Evangelist, and Mary Magdalen

FIG. 233

Canvas, later attached to panel: 75 x 57.5 cm.

LITERATURE: 1914/15, Sirén, p. 108: Lorenzo Monaco, in the early period, showing the influence of Agnolo Gaddi and Niccolò di Pietro Gerini // 1924, Stechow, p. 213: Sienese, 1360s, with connections to the style of Bartolo di Fredi // 1926, Stechow, p. 22, no. 65: by a contemporary of LM, ca. 1400; shows the influence of Niccolò di Pietro Gerini // 1927, van Marle, vol. 9, p. 168, note 3: LM // 1929, Suida, p. 392: LM // 1932, Berenson, p. 300: LM, shop (1963, vol. 1, p. 110) // 1954, Eisenberg; pp. 126-27: not by LM; closer to Spinello Aretino // 1968, B. Cole (*in litteris*): observes the stylistic relationship between the Göttingen *Crucifixion* and the Rijksmuseum *Head of the Virgin*; the "San Gaggio idiom" is not LM // 1975, Boskovits, p. 347: LM, 1390-95.

COMMENT: The eclecticism of the work is evident from the variety of attributions since Sirén's initial notice. I propose that the stylistic milieu of the *Crucifixion* is the same that produced the *Intercession* in The Cloisters, New York (Fig. 234), and, as Cole first observed (1968), the various elements of the San Gaggio Altarpiece (Figs. 227-232). Formal elements common to this group are the following: the heavy pocketing and abundant cascading of mantles; the contour and placement of extended hands; the softness and transparency of the beards of Christ and God the Father, contrasted with the strongly accented locks falling to the shoulders; the squared-off hairline frequently found in the male coiffure; a heavy shadowing beneath elongated eyes; the ornamenting of drapery borders with a double gold line and scalloped pattern. The Rijksmuseum *Head of the Virgin* (1968, Cole) and the Assisi *Madonna of Humility* are from the same stylistic ambience (Figs. 235, 236). In the Cloisters *Intercession* and the Göttingen *Crucifixion* the use of a canvas support required simplification in the ornament of the gilded haloes. The painted patterns in the haloes of Christ in the *Crucifixion* and of Christ and God the Father in the *Intercession* are virtually identical; the other haloes were left unadorned. (For comment on this stylistic culture of the later Trecento, see Catalogue II, Florence, Accademia, *Saint Catherine of Alexandria*, and *Saint Caius*.)

HOUSTON, Museum of Fine Arts, Edith A. and Percy S. Straus Collection, nos. 44-567A and B

Saint Michael, and the Annunciatory Gabriel; Saint Francis, and the Annunciate Virgin

FIG. 257

Panel: 116 x 35.5 cm. (each panel)

LITERATURE: 1927, Golzio, p. 3: Lorenzo Monaco, ca. 1400 // 1927, van Marle, vol. 9, p. 150: LM, in the period of the Accademia *Annunciation*, around 1408 // 1931, Golzio, pp. 32 and 65, note 2: LM, first years of the fifteenth century // 1932, Berenson, p. 300: LM (1963, vol. 1, p. 119) // 1945, Houston, *Catalogue, Straus Collection*, pp. 12-13, no. 13: LM // 1958, Levi D'Ancona, "Matteo Torelli," pp. 252, 255, and 257: Matteo Torelli, in a later period after the frescoes in the Bartolini Chapel at Santa Trinita // 1972, Fredericksen and Zeri, p. 111: LM // 1975, Boskovits, p. 347: LM, 1410-15 // 1984, Bellosi, p. 311: related in style to miniatures by Don Lorenzo in Bargello Cod. E 70, which are no earlier than 1420.

COMMENT: The two panels, originally the wings of a triptych, were transformed into the inner faces of the doors of a tabernacle, or custodial, designed to enclose a work of sculpture. The tabernacle, now in the storage collections at Houston, would seem to date from the late nineteenth or early twentieth century and was acquired in Rome in 1925 by Percy S. Straus of New York. When the *Saint Michael* and *Saint Francis* were adapted to the tabernacle, ornamental strips of wood were added to the side of each panel to accommodate heavy hinges, the borders of the panels were carelessly repainted, and the spandrels between the main and upper registers were decorated with a geometrical pattern.

In addition to the attributions noted above, the following unpublished opinions have been recorded in the files of the Museum of Fine Arts: Adolfo Venturi, *in litteris*, 1925, to Lorenzo Monaco; Richard Offner, verbally, 1931, to Lorenzo Monaco; John Pope-Hennessy, verbally, 1970, to Rossello di Jacopo Franchi. Pope-Hennessy's attribution, although not generally accepted, appropriately removed the panels from the immediate environment of Lorenzo Monaco. The Houston *Saints* would seem to be the work of a provincial imitator of Lorenzo Monaco, painted probably no later than the mid-1420s, when his style continued to have some currency. *Saint Francis* is adapted from the Accademia *Annunciation* of around 1418 (Fig. 77); the cowl and the blousing of the cassock are verbatim copies of the same passages in that altarpiece, exhibiting a kind of exact replication that is unknown in the methods of Don Lorenzo's workshop. The spindly and indifferently proportioned *Saint Michael* does not exist among Lorenzo's types, although, as Levi D'Ancona observed (1958), the shape of the head and the facial features are somewhat reminiscent of the Saint Catherine in the Prato altarpiece (Fig. 152). A miniature of *Saint Michael* by a painter in the scriptorium at Santa Maria degli Angeli is related in type but not in style (see Catalogue I, Florence, Biblioteca Laurenziana, Cod. Cor. 5). The right pinnacle of the Monte Oliveto Altarpiece (Fig. 26) provided a partial source for the Annunciate Virgin in the Houston panel, but the miniaturistic Gabriel has no detectable model. The mixture of sources in the Houston panels bespeaks the methods of a provincial pasticheur, just as it underlies the forger's way of contriving an image. The atypical placement of the wound on Francis's left side is either an error in iconography or a matter of compositional necessity, as is true of the Saint Francis in a Cionesque panel formerly in the Finaly Collection in Florence (see Kaftal, 1952, fig. 439).

LEGHORN, Larderel Collection (formerly)

Madonna and Child with Four Saints

FIG. 226

Panel (dimensions not accessible)

LITERATURE: 1933, Offner, p. 170, note 14: Master of the Straus Madonna // 1963, Berenson, vol. 1, p. 119: Lorenzo Monaco // 1965, Bellosi, "Da Spinello," p. 40, fig. 40: LM, in the first years of the fifteenth century; notes that the gold ground and the haloes are not original // 1975, Boskovits, p. 347: LM, 1400-1405.

COMMENT: Offner's passing notice of the panel (1933), an astute if laconic recognition of its essential stylistic character, has gone unmentioned in subsequent literature. The Larderel *Madonna* is precious evidence of the close exchanges between the early shop of Lorenzo Monaco and the related but distinct stylistic culture centered around the Master of the Straus Madonna. As with Lorenzo's early *Madonna* in the Biblioteca Berenson (Fig. 16), the compositional type has a source in the Cionesque tradition. It is difficult to determine whether a common model for the Child was used by the painters of the Larderel and Berenson pictures or whether there was direct borrowing by one from the other. The fact that the facial features of the Saint Jerome in the Larderel picture are in the catalogue of Lorenzo's types makes it likely that a figure in the mold of the Saint Nicholas of the Berlin *Madonna* (Fig. 17) provided the source. Other aspects of the *Madonna* are more closely associated with the formal language of the Master of the Straus Madonna, for example, the extended hand of the Virgin with slender, sharply modelled fingers bent to a cupped shape, recalling the Horne and Baltimore *Madonna* panels (Figs. 224, 225), the heavy shadowing of the eye socket and the languorous expression of the elongated eye within this dark recess, and the lavish ornamentation of the Virgin's tunic. The bizarre script in the border of the Virgin's drapery, a mixture of pseudo-Cufic and barely legible Roman script, is virtually identical to the border of the robe of the *Saint Peter* in the Courtauld Institute Galleries in London, which Roberto Longhi (1960, p. 60) localized in later Trecento Florence (see Boskovits, 1975, p. 243, note 201 for a review of opinion on the panel; I am unable to concur with the present attribution to Bernardo Daddi). Until the interaction of these turn-of-the-century artistic circles gains clearer definition, the attribution of the former Larderel panel would seem to be weighted toward the important but still elusive later Trecento milieu of the Master of the Straus Madonna. For further comment, see Catalogue II, Florence, Accademia, *Saint Jerome; Saint John the Baptist*. . . .

LEICESTER, Leicestershire Museums and Art Galleries, no. 33 A 1959

Saint John the Baptist Departing for the Wilderness

FIG. 220

Panel: 22.8 x 35.6 cm.

LITERATURE: 1964/65, Zeri, p. 7: Lorenzo Monaco, shortly after 1390; reconstructs the altarpiece to which this predella panel belonged (see 1976, vol. 1, pp. 26-27) // 1965, Bellosi "Da Spinello," p. 37: approaches the idiom of the Master of the Straus Madonna // 1965, Gore, p. 18, no. 31: LM; the early date presumably explains the heavy-handed execution and the inelegance of the figure // 1975, Boskovits, p. 347: LM, 1395-1400.

COMMENT: See Catalogue II, Florence, Accademia, *Saint Jerome: Saint John the Baptist*. . . .

LONDON, British Museum, no. 1860-6-16-42

Annunciation, God the Father in Glory, and Five Prophets

Preparatory drawing for a miniature
Parchment: 39.8 x 32.5 cm. (for technical information, see citation below: Degenhart and Schmitt, 1968).

LITERATURE: 1946, Pouncey, pp. 71-72: Mariotto di Nardo // 1968, Degenhart and Schmitt, pt. 1, vol. 1, p. 264, no. 159, and vol. 3, pl. 192a: Florence, around 1400; from the Santa Maria degli Angeli school of miniaturists; related in style to drawings for miniatures in Copenhagen and Paris; provide technical information, provenance, and further bibliography // 1975, Boskovits, p. 347: Lorenzo Monaco, 1390-95 // 1978, Bellosi and Bellini, p. xvii: Mariotto di Nardo.

COMMENT: Pouncey (1946) noted the technical similarities of the British Museum drawing and those in Copenhagen, but denied their stylistic connection. The attribution to Mariotto di Nardo succeeded in placing this important sheet within an eclectic Cionesque and Gerinesque environment. Those stylistic labels, with a dating in the 1390s, would provide a more satisfactory ascription, given the lack of evidence that Mariotto ever painted miniatures in books.

LONDON, Brocklebank Collection

Saint Romuald; and *Saint Giles*

Panel: 31.1 x 12 cm. (each painted octagon)

LITERATURE: 1936, Evelyn Sandberg-Vavalà (*in litteris*): Lorenzo Monaco // 1955, H. Brocklebank, *A Turn or Two I'll Walk to Still My Beating Mind*, London, pp. 69 and 71: cites the attribution by Sandberg-Vavalà // 1952, Kaftal, col. 454: Jacopo di Cione (quoting R. Offner) // 1960, London, *Italian Art and Britain*, p. 106, no. 281: LM // 1975, Boskovits, p. 275 and fig. 370: "Ambrogio di Baldese."

COMMENT: The two *Saints* appear to be the work of a Cionesque painter, the *Romuald* closer to the style of Nardo di Cione and the *Giles* to Jacopo.

LONDON, Courtauld Institute Galleries, no. 70 (Gambier-Parry Collection, no. 116)

Coronation of the Virgin
FIG. 228

Panel: 183 x 153.5 cm.

LITERATURE: 1950, Gronau, pp. 183-88: Lorenzo Monaco, ca. 1390-91; suggests that the *Coronation* was the central gable of an altarpiece once in the church of San Gaggio, outside Florence; provides a list of previous attributions (p. 188, note 25), covering a wide range of Florentine Trecento painting (Giotto, Orcagna, Jacopo di Cione, Mariotto di Nardo, Agnolo Gaddi, Lorenzo di Niccolò) // 1954, Eisenberg, pp. 136-38: denies attribution to LM and connection with San Gaggio Altarpiece // 1958, Levi D'Ancona, "Some New Attributions," p. 187, note 58: denies the attribution of the San Gaggio Altarpiece to Lorenzo Monaco // 1963, Berenson, vol. 1, p. 123: Lorenzo di Niccolò, early // 1964/65, Zeri, pp. 8 and 11: confirms Gronau's attribution; revises the dating to ca. 1394-95 // 1965, Bellosi, "Da Spinello," p. 36: LM // 1967, Blunt, *Provisional Catalogue*, pp. 35-36, no. 116: LM; proposes that the *Coronation* was placed originally above a long rectangular panel depicting the Death of the Virgin, now lost; provides further bibliography // 1967, Blunt, "History," p. 115: LM // 1973, Fenton, pp. 10-11: LM // 1975, Boskovits, p. 237: LM, 1390-95 // 1977, Fenton, [p. 5] and figs. 1-3: proposes tentatively that the panel may originally have been greater in length, with the Death of the Virgin represented below the *Coronation* // 1979, Gealt, p. 158: follower of LM // 1983, London, *Early Italian Paintings*, pp. 25-26, no. 10, pl. 10 in color: LM; with provenance and bibliography // 1983, Sutton, p. 98: LM.

COMMENT: See Catalogue II, Florence, Accademia, *Saint Catherine of Alexandria*, and *Saint Caius*.

LONDON, National Gallery, No. 3089

Abraham and the Angels
FIG. 268

Cut miniature from a choir book
Parchment: 37 x 33 cm.

LITERATURE: 1925, *Catalogue*, National Gallery, London, p. 182: Lorenzo Monaco // 1932, Berenson, p. 300: LM? (1963, vol. 1, p. 120) // 1951, Davies, p. 243: denies the attribution to LM // 1959, Levi D'Ancona, "Don Silvestro," p. 22: Don Silvestro dei Gherarducci, in his last phase (i.e., 1390s) // 1961, Davies, pp. 312-13: while retaining the label "ascribed to Lorenzo Monaco," sees the attribution to Don Silvestro as more satisfactory, if not conclusive; presents an iconographic analysis // 1965, Bellosi, "Da Spinello," p. 39: LM, later 1390s // 1972, Boskovits, p. 56, note 39: LM, showing connections with the art of Don Silvestro // 1975, Boskovits, p. 348: LM, 1390-95 // 1978, Levi D'Ancona, p. 219: identifies provenance as fol. 146, Cod. Cor. 1, Biblioteca Laurenziana; changes attribution to Matteo Torelli.

COMMENT: The London miniature is a pivotal work in the corpus of miniatures and panels by Don Silvestro dei Gherarducci, as reconstructed by Mirella Levi D'Ancona (1959; more satisfactory than later attribution to Torelli). Close stylistic parallels may be drawn between the miniature and the lower section of the *Ascension* (Fig. 243) on fol. 86 of Corale 1 in the Laurenziana (book dated 1396), and the cut miniature in the Louvre representing the *Holy Women at the Tomb* (Fig. 269), attributed by Levi D'Ancona to Matteo Torelli (1958, "Matteo Torelli," p. 247, note 10; 1978, p. 220: *Ascension* also to Torelli). I tentatively propose that the Louvre miniature is the most developed example of Don Silvestro's work as a miniaturist, which Lorenzo Monaco may have referred to in designing the *Holy Women at the Tomb* of 1408 (Fig. 33).

LONDON, National Gallery, no. 4208

Baptism of Christ
FIG. 214

Panel: 31 x 21 cm.

LITERATURE: 1908, Sirén, p. 93: Agnolo Gaddi // 1932, Berenson, p. 238: Giottesque, after 1350, towards Lorenzo Monaco // 1936, Salvini, p. 185: late Gerinesque // 1951, Davies, p. 149: see 1961 ed. // 1961, Davies, p. 192, Florentine school; with further literature // 1964/65, Zeri, pp. 554-55: Lorenzo Monaco; integrated with the predella of the Nobili Chapel altarpiece for Santa Maria degli Angeli, documented 1387/88 // 1965, Bellosi, "Da Spinello," p. 36: LM // 1975, Boskovits, p. 348: LM, 1387/88 // 1977, B. Cole, p. 86: shop of Agnolo Gaddi.

COMMENT: See Catalogue II, Paris, Louvre, *Feast of Herod*. . . . Bellosi's (1965) view that the London Christ is virtually identical with Don Lorenzo's *Man of Sorrows* (Fig. 18) of 1404 in the Accademia, Florence, depends on resemblances of physical type rather than on formal aspects of draughtsmanship and modelling.

LONDON, private collection

Blessing Redeemer

Panel: 80 x 38 cm.

LITERATURE: 1938/39, Pudelko, p. 248, note 33: not wholly by Lorenzo's hand; perhaps from the period of the Monte Oliveto Altarpiece (1407-1410); may have been part of the altarpiece in Prato (the panel was then in the Loeser Collection, Florence) // 1975, Boskovits, p. 346: LM, 1405-1410, citing Brogi photograph 651/40.

COMMENT: The *Blessing Redeemer* would appear to be a work of the last years of the Trecento, produced within the same stylistic orbit as the various elements of the San Gaggio Altarpiece and the Cloisters *Intercession* (Figs. 227-232 and 234). Deeply shelved and cascading drapery, and rigidly symmetrical facial features typify the work of this artistic culture, which is contemporary with the early style of Lorenzo Monaco. The former Loeser panel anticipates Don Lorenzo's central pinnacles in the Monte Oliveto Altarpiece (Fig. 27), dated 1410, and the *Coronation of the Virgin* of 1414 (Fig. 48). The pinnacle bears no relationship to the Prato altarpiece (Fig. 152), a work from the shop of Lorenzo Monaco, circa 1412-14 (Pudelko, 1938/39).

MILAN, Saibene Collection

Crucifix

Panel (cutout): 47 x 36 cm.

LITERATURE: 1905, Sirén, p. 90: Lorenzo Monaco, within the years 1412-17; in the collection of Count Carlo Gamba, Florence // 1927, van Marle, vol. 9, p. 168, note 3: LM // 1929, Suida, p. 392: LM // 1970, González-Palacios, p. 34, fig. 37: LM; perhaps cut from a full panel; from a late moment in Don Lorenzo's career, when his art was approaching that of the young Fra Angelico // 1976, Boskovits, p. 34 and fig. 21: early work of Fra Angelico, with some reminiscence of cutout crosses by Lorenzo Monaco.

COMMENT: I had the opportunity to examine and measure the cross when it was in the collection of Count Gamba. The exaggerated modelling of the face and torso and the arbitrary twirl of the loincloth form an anachronistic alliance, which implies the work of an eclectic imitator of Lorenzo Monaco and Fra Angelico, active in the second quarter of the Quattrocento.

MILAN, private collection (formerly)

Piera degli Albizzi and Her Daughters

Panel: 28 x 22 cm.

LITERATURE: 1964/65, Zeri, p. 557 and fig. 12: Lorenzo Monaco; integrates with the predella of the Nobili Chapel altarpiece at Santa Maria degli Angeli, documented 1387/88 // 1965, Bellosi, "Da Spinello," p. 36: closer to Agnolo Gaddi, although from the same predella in which there are panels by Don Lorenzo // 1975, Boskovits, p. 349: LM, 1387/88 // 1977, B. Cole, pp. 85-86: shop of Agnolo Gaddi // 1979, Boskovits, p. 60, note 1: the panel was probably located originally in a pilaster of the altarpiece.

COMMENT: See Catalogue II, Paris, Louvre, *Feast of Herod*. . . .

NAPLES, Museo di Capodimonte, no. 956

Crucifix with the Kneeling Magdalen; and *Madonna and Blessing Christ Child with a Kneeling Donor*
FIG. 253

Panel: 13.5 x 21 cm. (overall size of the diptych)

LITERATURE: 1931/32, Quintavalle, p. 402, illus.: follower of Lorenzo Monaco // 1958, Molajoli, *Notizie di Capodimonte*, Naples, p. 33, no. 956: Arcangelo di Cola da Camerino // 1975, Boskovits, p. 350: LM, 1390-95; with further bibliography.

COMMENT: I am unable to propose either a place of origin or a cogent date for this provincial little work.

NEW YORK, Metropolitan Museum of Art (Robert Lehman Collection)

Christ in Judgment

Cut miniature
Parchment: 33 x 28 cm.

LITERATURE: 1927, H. Comstock, "The Robert Lehman Collection of Miniatures," *International Studio* 86, April 1927, p. 41, illus. p. 51: Lorenzo Monaco // 1957, Sterling, Laclotte, p. 113, no. 166: Florentine, early fifteenth century; influence of LM // 1959, Cincinnati, *Lehman Collection*, p. 31, and fig. 322: LM // 1978, Levi D'Ancona, p. 228: identifies the provenance as fol. 124, Cod. Cor. 7, Biblioteca Laurenziana (book dated 1406); notes that the miniature is restored; no attribution proposed.

COMMENT: The Lehman miniature appears to be the work of a miniaturist who was active at Santa Maria degli Angeli, but not directly associated with Lorenzo Monaco. The bust-length Christ approaches Don Lorenzo's style, whereas the resurrected are unknown among his physiognomic types. A similar composition is found on fol. 84v of Cod. E 70 in the Bargello (see Catalogue I, Florence). The miniature also resembles to a degree, especially in the organization of space, fol. 105 (*Saint Michael Slaying the Demons*) of Corale 5 in the Laurenziana. Jean Porcher (verbally; quoted in Sterling, Laclotte, 1957) noted that the ornament surrounding the initial letter is typically French, which led to the conjecture that the painter was an Italian working in Avignon or Bohemia. Levi D'Ancona's suggested provenance and mention of restoration (1978) would rule out the proposal and raise the question of authenticity with regard to the detailed ornament that surrounds the gold ground and foliate initial.

NEW YORK, Pierpont Morgan Library, no. 1981.78

The Man of Sorrows

Linen (cut out and laid down on paper): 9.7 x 8.2 cm.
Technique: Pen and brown ink, brown wash, touches of red, brown, and black tempera, some traces of gold.

LITERATURE: (Undated) notation at the Frick Art Reference Library: an attribution to Lorenzo Monaco proposed by M. J. Friedländer and E. Tietze-Conrat // 1960, Detroit, *Master Drawings*, no. 2, fig. 2: LM // 1962, Verdier and Miner, p. 23, no. 23: LM; with further bibliography // 1976, Scholz, p. 11, no. 3, fig. 3: LM; compared with the *Man of Sorrows* in the Accademia Carrara, Bergamo (Fig. 136).

COMMENT: This tiny icon is related to the art of Lorenzo Monaco only by dint of the fact that he and his workshop used a comparable iconography of The Man of Sorrows (Fig. 136). Neither the facial features nor the shapes of arms and torso have a resemblance to works by Don Lorenzo or his shop. I am able to propose only the general label of Tuscan, first quarter of the fifteenth century. The iconographic type had acquired a particular currency in Sienese painting of the Trecento (see Catalogue I, Bergamo, Accademia Carrara, *Man of Sorrows*). Verdier (1962) raised the question as to whether the drawing could in some way be related to the gold morse that Martin V commissioned in Florence from Ghiberti; but the sculptor described the subject of the morse as "Our Lord blessing" (see Krautheimer, 1956, p. 13). Verdier suggested, nonetheless, that the morse representing The Man of Sorrows included by Masolino in the figure of Saint Martin from the Santa Maria Maggiore Altarpiece (*John G. Johnson Collection*, 1966, p. 111) is a copy of Ghiberti's papal brooch.

NEW YORK, Frederick Stern Collection (formerly)

Hermogenes Destroying the Books of Sorcery

Panel: 30 x 21.6 cm.

LITERATURE: 1964/65, Zeri, p. 557 and fig. 9: Lorenzo Monaco; integrates with the predella of the Nobili Chapel altarpiece for Santa Maria degli Angeli, documented 1387/88 // 1975, Boskovits, p. 350: LM, 1387/88 // 1977, B. Cole, pp. 85-86: shop of Agnolo Gaddi // 1979, Boskovits, p. 60, note 1: the panel was probably located originally in a pilaster of the altarpiece.

COMMENT: See Catalogue II, Paris, Louvre, *Feast of Herod*. . . .

NORTHWICK PARK (GLOUCESTERSHIRE), Spencer-Churchill Collection (formerly)

Presentation of the Christ Child in the Temple

Panel: 31.1 x 39.3 cm.

LITERATURE: 1930, London, *Italian Art 1200-1900*, no. 65; 1931, London, *Commemorative Catalogue*, no. 48: Lorenzo Monaco // 1960, London, *Italian Art and Britain*, p. 103, no. 272: LM; further bibliography // 1960, Longhi, p. 60, no. 125: from the early period of Paolo Schiavo // 1973, Zeri, p. 364 and note 8; fig. 6: by an artistic personality parallel to Alvaro Pirez, but of higher quality, a phase of whose development took place in the Pisan region.

COMMENT: Federico Zeri's stylistic localization of the panel is persuasive, particularly the analogy he draws with the *Saint Jerome* in the Louvre (1973, p. 368, fig. 8).

PARIS, Musée Jacquemart-André, no. I 1559 (deposit)

Madonna and Child with Four Saints

Panel: 66 x 39.5 cm.

LITERATURE: 1970, González-Palacios, p. 31 and fig. 26: Lorenzo Monaco; by the same hand as the Louvre predella and the Horne and Antinori (now Toledo) *Madonna* panels // 1975, Boskovits, p. 351: LM, 1400-1405.

COMMENT: The panel is more justifiably identified with the stylistic culture of the Master of the Straus Madonna, as Alvar González-Palacios notes that he first observed, before deciding to include the picture in the corpus of early works of Lorenzo Monaco. But if certain formal similarities with the Toledo and Horne *Madonna* panels (Figs. 217, 224) are apparent, the quality of the Jacquemart-André panel is not at the level of those works. The ineptitude in drawing and in figural proportions, rather than suggesting the effort of a novice, reveals the hand of a lesser and perhaps provincial shop assistant working in a mixture of Cionesque and Gaddesque modes. In my view, comparison of the features of the Saint Stephen with those of the Saint Sebastian in the Pescia triptych (Fig. 134), proposed by González-Palacios, is elusive. The panel shows some relationship to the group of works associated with the nebulous name of Ambrogio di Baldese (see Boskovits, 1975, figs. 365-68).

PARIS, Louvre, no. 1302

Feast of Herod; Crucifixion; Saint James and the Sorcerer Hermogenes, and Martyrdom of Saint James

FIGS. 213, 216

Panel: 34 x 67 cm. (each panel)

LITERATURE: 1906, Sirén, "Notizie critiche," p. 327: Agnolo Gaddi // 1934, Salvini, p. 227: the central panel is by Agnolo Gaddi and the side panels are by the "Maestro Vaticano" // 1950, Gronau, pp. 217-18: Lorenzo Monaco, at the earliest stage of his career; the predella once formed part of the altarpiece of the Nobili Chapel at Santa Maria degli Angeli, which was dedicated in 1387 and first held masses in 1388 when the altarpiece was already in place; the style is strongly Gaddesque // 1954, Eisenberg, pp. 145-46: refutes the attribution to Lorenzo Monaco // 1958, Levi D'Ancona, "Some New Attributions," p. 187, note 58: denies the attribution to Lorenzo Monaco, proposing a date in the early fifteenth century with hints of a connection to the style of Battista di Biagio Sanguigni // 1963, Berenson, vol. 1, p. 68: Agnolo Gaddi, assisted // 1964/65, Zeri, pp. 554-58: confirms Gronau's attribution to Lorenzo Monaco and adds three further elements to the predella: *Baptism of Christ*, London, National Gallery; *Hermogenes Destroying the Books of Sorcery*, New York, Frederick Stern Collection; *Piera Al-*

bizzi and Her Daughters, Milan, Art Market; the Gaddesque nature of the style is emphasized; as Lorenzo would not have received the commission for the entire Nobili Chapel altarpiece at such an early age, the principal elements of the altarpiece, still undiscovered, may have been from the shop of Agnolo Gaddi // 1965, Bellosi, "Da Spinello," p. 36: LM // 1970, González-Palacios, p. 27: LM // 1973, Johnson and Muller, pp. 44-46: Muller notes a compositional relationship between the *Martyrdom of Saint James* and the Caius panel in the Santa Barbara Museum of Art // 1974, Bruce Cole (*in litteris*): see Cole, 1977 // 1975, Boskovits, p. 133 and p. 242, note 193: LM, working in the shop of Agnolo Gaddi; suggests with reservation that the predella was originally associated with the polyptych by Agnolo Gaddi in the Bode Museum, East Berlin // 1977, B. Cole, pp. 84-87, pls. 46-48: the three panels in Paris are from the Gaddi workshop, based on Agnolo's design; from the predella of the altarpiece by Agnolo now in the Bode Museum // 1979, Boskovits, p. 60, note 1: the New York and Milan panels cited above (Zeri, 1964/65) were probably originally located in the pilasters of the altarpiece.

COMMENT: Although Gronau's (1950) tracing of the Louvre predella to the Nobili Chapel at Santa Maria degli Angeli and Zeri's (1964/65) further reconstruction are incontestable, I would submit that Cole's (1974 and 1977) adherence to a more general attribution to the workshop of Agnolo Gaddi is preferable. The identification of the predella with the Bode Museum altarpiece, independently observed by Boskovits (1975) and Cole, reconstitutes the single major Gaddesque work known to have been at Santa Maria degli Angeli, where the visual environment was more deeply rooted in Cionesque and Gerinesque imagery (see Notes to Essay, p. 55, Note 44). For further comment on the reconstructions of Don Lorenzo's early activity, see Notes to Essay, p. 53, Note 35, and Catalogue II, Florence, Accademia, *Saint Catherine of Alexandria*, and *Saint Caius*; and Florence, Accademia, *Saint Jerome; Saint John the Baptist*. . . .

PARIS, Louvre, Cabinet des Dessins, no. R.F. 28970

Temptation of Christ

Preparatory drawing, probably for a choir book miniature

Parchment: 22.1 x 12.1 cm. (for technical information, see citation below: Degenhart and Schmitt, 1968)

LITERATURE: 1952, Paris, *Dessins florentins*, no. 36: Lorenzo Monaco; cites H. Gronau's opinion that the drawing is by LM and related to those in Copenhagen // 1968, Degenhart and Schmitt, pt. 1, vol. 1, p. 264, no. 160; vol. 3, pl. 192b: Florence, around 1400; from the Santa Maria degli Angeli school of miniaturists; does not relate to the "Nobili predella" (Louvre), as was implied by Gronau // 1975, Boskovits, p. 351: LM, 1390-95 // 1978, Bellosi and Bellini, p. xvii: LM.

COMMENT: The Louvre drawing is discussed in the catalogue entry on the San Gaggio Altarpiece (see Catalogue II, Florence, Accademia, *Saint Catherine of Alexandria*, and *Saint Caius*.

PESARO, Musei Civici, no. 33

Crucifixion

FIG. 249

Panel: 32 x 22 cm.

LITERATURE: 1929, L. Serra, *L'arte nelle Marche*, vol. 1, Pesaro, p. 305: Bolognese school, mid-fourteenth century // 1951, *Musei Civici, Pesaro*, p. 10, no. 33: Tuscan, fourteenth century // 1965, Bellosi, "Da Spinello," p. 39 and fig. 39: Lorenzo Monaco; once formed a diptych with the *Madonna Enthroned* in the Fitzwilliam Museum, Cambridge // 1975, Boskovits, p. 352: LM, 1390-95 // 1986, Mosco, p. 106, no. 27 (entry by S. Melini Trkulija): LM.

COMMENT: See Catalogue I, Cambridge, Fitzwilliam Museum, *Madonna Enthroned*.

PRINCETON, Art Museum, Princeton University, no. 36-23

Beheading of Saint Paul

FIG. 223

Panel: 25.7 x 40.5 cm.

LITERATURE: 1939, Sandberg-Vavalà, pp. 105-111: an early work of Lorenzo Monaco, from the last years of the Trecento; associates the panel with a *Nativity* in Berlin and a *Crucifixion of Saint Peter* in the Walters Art Gallery, Baltimore // 1954, Eisenberg, p. 102: LM, 1390-95 // 1964/65, Zeri, p. 7:

LM, shortly after 1390; reconstructs the altarpiece to which this predella panel belonged (see also 1976, vol. 1, pp. 26-27) // 1965, Bellosi, "Da Spinello," p. 37: approaches the idiom of the Master of the Straus Madonna // 1970, González-Palacios, p. 31: LM // 1972, Fredericksen and Zeri, p. 111: LM // 1975, Boskovits, p. 353: LM, 1395-1400 // 1977, Bauman, pp. 3-11: an iconographic study, with emphasis on the theme of the miraculous disappearance and return of the veil of Plautilla.

COMMENT: See Catalogue II, Florence, Accademia, *Saint Jerome; Saint John the Baptist. . . .*

RAVENNA, Galleria dell'Accademia, no. 191

Crucifixion with the Holy Family and Saint Lawrence

FIG. 251

Panel: 37 x 27 cm.

LITERATURE: 1898, Ricci, p. 10: Florentine school // 1900, A. Schmarsow, *Kunsthistorische Gesellschaft für photographische Publikationen*, vol. 6, p. 5, pl. 17: early work of Paolo Uccello // 1900, Berenson, p. 125: Lorenzo Monaco // 1905, Sirén, pp. 44-45: LM school, 1403-1405 // 1905, Ricci, p. 26: LM // 1927, van Marle, vol. 9, p. 176: follower of LM // 1932, Berenson, p. 301: LM, in great part (1963, vol. 1, p. 121) // 1936, Arfelli, p. 14: mainly LM // 1938/39, Pudelko, p. 248, note 35: by a remote follower of the school of Lorenzo Monaco // 1950, Pope-Hennessy, p. 167 (1969, p. 174): style of Lorenzo Monaco // 1959, Martini, p. 111, no. 191: LM, in the period of the Bartolini Chapel // 1965, Bellosi, *Maestri*, [p. 6]: LM // 1971, L. T. Tomasi, *L'Opera completa di Paolo Uccello*, Milan, p. 102, no. 88: from the early period of Antonio Vivarini // 1975, Boskovits, p. 353: LM, 1400-1405.

COMMENT: This *Crucifixion*, by an imitator of Lorenzo Monaco working around 1410 to 1415, is an additive assemblage of elements from works either by the master or his shop. The mourning women depend directly on the same personages in the Prague *Lamentation* (Fig. 36) of 1408, whereas the type of Christ reflects the heavier proportions of Lorenzo's cutout cross in the Accademia, Florence of around 1410 (Fig. 69), rather than the leaner forms of the Santa Maria delle Vertighe cross of circa 1415 (Fig. 71). The Saint John the Evangelist is a timid echo of the Thaddeus in the Monte Oliveto Altarpiece (Fig. 24) and the Saint Lawrence at the far right is a youthful descendant of Nicholas in the former Berlin *Madonna* of circa 1402 (Fig. 17).

ROCHESTER (NEW YORK), Geib Collection

Crucifix

Panel (cutout): 60 x 42 cm.

LITERATURE: 1934, Amsterdam, *Italiaansche Kunst*, p. 89, no. 243 (then the property of Douwes, Amsterdam): Lorenzo Monaco // 1934/35, van Marle, p. 304: LM.

COMMENT: This is the work of a provincial but contemporary imitator of the cutout crosses produced by Lorenzo Monaco and his shop. A similar cross in the collections of the Fogg Art Museum, attributed to Don Lorenzo's workshop, is by a different provincial hand (see Fredericksen and Zeri, p. 111).

ROME, Biblioteca Vaticana, MS. Rossiano, 1192/a, nos. 34-36

Entry into Jerusalem; Last Supper; and *Christ in the House of Mary and Martha*

Three preparatory drawings for choir book miniatures
Parchment: 31 x 43 cm.; 16.5 x 39 cm.; 16.5 x 25 cm.
(for technical information, see citation below: 1968, Degenhart and Schmitt)

LITERATURE: 1968, Degenhart and Schmitt, pt. 1, vol. 1, p. 265, nos. 161-63, and vol. 3, pl. 193 a, b, c: Florentine, first quarter of the fifteenth century; from the Santa Maria degli Angeli miniature school; related to but not by the same hand as the *Last Supper* in Berlin, which is close to the style of Lorenzo Monaco; further bibliography // 1975, Boskovits, p. 353: LM, 1390-95 // 1978, Bellosi and Bellini, p. xvii: LM.

COMMENT: The Vatican drawings are discussed in the catalogue entry on the San Gaggio Altarpiece (see Catalogue II, Florence, Accademia, *Saint Catherine of Alexandria*; and *Saint Caius*). A product of the same eclectic later Trecento milieu is the *Pentecost*, a fully executed cut miniature in the Rossiana MS. (no. 2) that Boskovits has attributed to Lorenzo Monaco and has dated from 1395 to 1400 (1975, p. 353, and fig. 142/c; confirmed in Bellosi and Bellini, 1978, p.

xvii). The clearly Cionesque character of this miniature allies it with the scriptorium at Santa Maria degli Angeli at a moment when Don Silvestro dei Gherarducci was the central personality. Neither the facial types nor drapery forms resemble Don Lorenzo's series of early miniatures for monastic choir books (Figs. 1-6).

ROME, Pinacoteca Vaticana, no. 194

Nativity

FIG. 256

Panel: 32 x 59 cm.

LITERATURE: 1906, Perkins, p. 121: Lorenzo Monaco, with acknowledgment that Berenson first proposed the attribution // 1906, Sirén, "Notizie critiche," p. 330: school of LM // 1909, Bernardini, p. 91: school of LM // 1913, *Guida della Pinacoteca Vaticana*, Rome, p. 35: manner of LM // 1915, Biagi, p. 228: follower of LM // 1927, van Marle, vol. 9, p. 176: school of LM // 1932, Berenson, p. 194: late studio of LM (1963, vol. 1, p. 121) // 1934, *Guida della Pinacoteca Vaticana*, Rome, p. 57: LM // 1935, Pudelko, p. 84: Pseudo-Ambrogio di Baldese; first associated with the *Annunciation with Saint Benedict* in Copenhagen // 1966, Shapley, p. 89: relates with *Saint Romuald* in Philbrook Art Center, Tulsa; the appearance of Saint Benedict and Saint Romuald in the predella suggest it was part of an altarpiece for Camaldolese use.

COMMENT: Pudelko's (1935) proposal that the Vatican *Nativity* and Copenhagen *Annunciation* (Fig. 255) once formed part of the predella of an altarpiece in San Pietro at Cedda (Poggibonsi, near Florence), ascribed to the Pseudo-Ambrogio di Baldese, is ruled out by the presence of the Annunciation within the pinnacles of that work (Fremantle, 1975, fig. 862). Works ascribed to the Pseudo-Ambrogio di Baldese (see Fremantle, figs. 856-73), a heterogeneous group, lack the refinement of form and technique of these panels, which would seem to be by a contemporary imitator of Lorenzo Monaco who selected stylistic features from different phases of the master's work. The mixture of the quatrefoil and octagonal shape in the framing system of the predella is indicative of this chronological range. Although Pudelko rightly observed that the Vatican *Nativity* depended directly on Lorenzo's scene in the predella of the Santa Trinita altarpiece (Fig. 125), the influence of the *Nativity* in the Uffizi *Coronation* predella was equally important, notably in the treatment of the cave and manger shed (Fig. 51). The advanced representation of interior space in the Copenhagen *Annunciation* recalls the developments in Don Lorenzo's work and that of his studio in the later 1410s and early 1420s, such as the predella of the London *Coronation* (Fig. 183) and the *Funeral of a Bishop Saint* (Fig. 193) in Nice, while the openings to corridors at either end of the *Annunciation* are direct adaptations from the altarpiece at Santa Trinita (Fig. 121). But the painter of this predella also knew stylistic developments in the generation of Fra Angelico, indicated by the light azure and pale rose chord in the *Nativity* and the modelling in a graduated chiaroscuro observed especially in the heads of Saint Benedict and Saint Romuald (Figs. 255 and 258).

See Catalogue II, Copenhagen, Statens Museum for Kunst, *Annunciation*; and Tulsa, Philbrook Art Center, *Saint Romauld*.

ROME, Pinacoteca Vaticana, no. 214

Meeting of Saint Anthony Abbot and Paul the Hermit

FIG. 259

Panel: 22.5 x 24.5 cm.

LITERATURE: 1906, Perkins, p. 123: Lorenzo Monaco // 1909, Bernardini, p. 91: close to LM; recalls the *Thebaid* in the Uffizi // 1915, Biagi, p. 231, fig. 2: LM, from the same period as the *Saint Benedict* panel in the Pinacoteca Vaticana // 1921, Sirén, p. 99: manner of LM // 1929, Suida, p. 392: LM // 1931, Golzio, p. 64: tentatively attributes to LM // 1932, Berenson, p. 301: LM, late work (1963, vol. 1, p. 121) // 1975, Boskovits, p. 353: LM, 1405-1410.

COMMENT: In this panel, probably of the 1420s, only the landscape elements are suggestive of Lorenzo Monaco, whereas the figure style and facial types have no parallels in his art, and the quatrefoil format is an anachronism.

ROME, Pinacoteca Vaticana (deposit), no. 569

Ascension of Christ
FIG. 241

Panel: 60.5 x 35.5 cm.

LITERATURE: 1906, Perkins, p. 121: notes Berenson's attribution to Lorenzo Monaco // 1906, Sirén, "Notizie critiche," p. 328: Giovanni da Milano // 1909, Bernardini, p. 91: manner of LM // 1912, Toesca, p. 226: anonymous Sienese // 1932, Berenson, p. 239: unidentified Florentine, close to early Lorenzo Monaco (1963, vol. 1, p. 216) // 1937, Meiss, p. 25, note 36: follower of LM // 1964/65, Zeri, p. 8, fig. 13: LM, early work //1965, Bellosi, "Da Spinello," p. 43, note 44: refutes attribution to Lorenzo Monaco // 1975, Boskovits, p. 353, fig. 449: LM, 1390-95.

COMMENT: In spite of the poor condition and areas of repainting, noted by Zeri (1964/65), I would propose that this *Ascension* is by an eclectic painter working in the first decade of the Quattrocento who had absorbed elements of the early style of Lorenzo Monaco, and of Mariotto di Nardo and Antonio Veneziano. A relationship with the manuscript tradition is recognized in the arrangement of figures, which shows some resemblance to an *Ascension* miniature in Cod. C at Santa Croce (fol. 3v), attributed by Boskovits to the so-called "Ser Monte" (1975, p. 233, note 128) and by D'Ancona (1914, vol. 1, pl. XXII) to Don Simone Camaldolese.

SAN DIEGO, San Diego Museum of Art, no. 46.18

Madonna with Four Saints and The Man of Sorrows
FIG. 239

Panel: 42.4 x 21.3 cm.

LITERATURE: 1932, Berenson, "Quadri senza casa," p. 28 (1970, p. 139): Lorenzo Monaco, demonstrating most clearly the Giottesque origins of his style; related closely to the Horne *Madonna* and the Ferroni *Crucifixion* // 1938/39, Pudelko, p. 237, note 8: LM; among the early works showing a close fusion of Sienese and Florentine styles (the location of the panel is noted as Berlin Art Market, 1927) // 1939, Sandberg-Vavalà, p. 108: LM in his formative Giottesque period, along with such works as the Accademia *Madonna and Saints* of 1408, the Horne and Berenson *Madonna* panels, and the Berlin-Baltimore-Princeton predella // 1947, *San Diego, Fine Arts Society*, p. 20, no. 19: LM; with listing of previous owners // 1950, Gronau, p. 218, note 17: LM, before the turn of the century // 1954, Eisenberg, p. 103: LM, 1390-95 // 1963, Berenson, vol. 1, p. 121: LM, early // 1964/65, Zeri, p. 11: LM, following on the San Gaggio Altarpiece; part of the group of early works for which the chronology must still be established and which show in varying degrees the hand of shop assistants: Bologna, *Maestà*; Rijksmuseum, *Madonna Enthroned* and *Head of the Madonna*; Assisi, Perkins Collection, *Madonna of Humility*; Florence, Ferroni Gallery, *Crucifixion* // 1965, Bellosi, *Maestri* [p. 4]: LM, in the earliest years // 1972, Muller, pp. 23-30: a technical report on the condition and conservation of the panel; emphasis is given to discovery of the coat of arms of the Alberti family, which lay under a later crest identified as that of the Lonati // 1972, Fredericksen and Zeri, p. 111: LM // 1975, Boskovits, p. 354: LM, 1395-1400.

COMMENT: Neither the composition nor morphology of the San Diego panel allows its inclusion within the stylistic orbit of Lorenzo Monaco. Comparison with early works by Don Lorenzo or his immediate shop (see Figs. 1-16 and 132-134) demonstrate the stylistic dissimilarity, which I do not believe can be explained as a matter of chronology. The San Diego panel bridges the stylistic cultures represented by such key works as the Carmine Polyptych (Figs. 215, 217-223) and the Rijksmuseum *Madonna Enthroned* (Fig. 237). In the San Diego picture, the Madonna afloat without visible support, and the strict layering of the accompanying saints, form a compositional type favored by Cionesque painters, with reminiscence of Nardo's New-York Historical Society *Madonna* (Meiss, 1951, fig. 11).

Closely related to the San Diego panel, as Berenson first noted (1932), is the small *Crucifixion* (Fig. 240) formerly in the Ferroni Gallery, but now in the Uffizi Deposit. In spite of superficial differences in type, there are the virtually identical facial features of John the Evangelist in the Ferroni picture and Paul in San Diego, or of the Magdalen in the former panel and Romuald in the latter, while the grief-stricken Virgins in the two pictures show a clear relationship. There are also notable resemblances in the shapes and modelling of the drapery of the Ferroni Evangelist and the San Diego Paul. From the same milieu as the San Diego and Ferroni pictures is the miniature of the *Ascension of Christ* on fol. 86 of Corale 1 in the Laurenziana (Fig. 243), painted under the direct influence of Don Silvestro dei Gherarducci. There is a kinship among the Ferroni Evangelist, the San Diego Paul, and the transfixed Apostles in the miniature, just as the rock forms have been cut from a common quarry. There may be inferred from the high-keyed palette of the San Diego panel that the painter also worked as a miniaturist. As the Ferroni *Crucifixion* was originally a miniature on vellum and only later transferred to panel, we may consider it to be a product of the Angeli workshop when Don Silvestro was a guiding force (see the Introductory Essay, p. 7). The San Diego *Madonna* and the Ferroni *Crucifixion* are important evidence of the variety of artistic activity in that monastic context, only one aspect of which was the idiom of Lorenzo Monaco. The association of the San Diego and Ferroni panels with Santa Maria degli Angeli is further confirmed by the discovery of the Alberti coat of arms on the former picture (Muller, 1972), as well as the principal role given Saint Romuald. The Alberti dedicated a chapel in the Camaldolese monastery in 1393 (see Paatz, vol. 3, 1952, pp. 109 and 123). A date in the mid-1390s would be appropriate for the San Diego panel, which could have served as a memento of the family's patronage of the Camaldolese Order. The Alberti's predilection for Cionesque works is indicated by the appearance of their coat of arms on the Zecca *Coronation of the Virgin* by Jacopo di Cione, in the Accademia, Florence, and on the *Coronation* altarpiece (Fig. 302) by Giovanni del Biondo in the Cathedral of Fiesole (Offner and Steinweg, sec. IV, vol. III, 1965, pl. VI, and sec. IV, vol. IV, 1967, p. 127, note 9).

SANTA BARBARA, Santa Barbara Museum of Art, no. 67.15

Martyrdom of Saint Caius

FIG. 232

Panel: 43.7 x 58.6 cm.

LITERATURE: 1966, Zeri, pp. 150-51: Lorenzo Monaco, 1394-95; integrates the panel into the predella of a partially reconstructed altarpiece once in the church of San Gaggio, outside Florence // 1972, Fredericksen and Zeri, p. 111: LM // 1973, Fenton, pp. 9-21: LM // 1973, Johnson and Muller, pp. 23-56: detailed analyses of physical aspects of the panel, the painting technique, and the compositional sources of the scene; Muller notes a compositional link with the Louvre *Martyrdom of Saint James* from the "Nobili predella" // 1977, Fenton: LM.

COMMENT: See Catalogue II, Florence, Accademia, *Saint Catherine of Alexandria*; and *Saint Caius*.

STOCKTON (CALIFORNIA), Haggin Museum, no. 72x-504

Madonna and Child with Saints Anthony Abbot and James Major

Panel: 100.3 x 52 cm.

LITERATURE: 1972, Fredericksen and Zeri, p. 220: Florentine, fourteenth century // 1975, Boskovits, p. 354, fig. 450: Lorenzo Monaco, 1395-1400.

COMMENT: The general attribution proposed by Fredericksen and Zeri is a useful label for this hybrid work, elements of which recall stylistic tendencies of the Master of the Straus Madonna, in particular the physiognomies and the athletic contours of the Child's shoulders. The type of Infant is, however, also reminiscent of the Assisi *Madonna of Humility* (Fig. 236), which lies closer to the culture of the San Gaggio Altarpiece. The adoring angels afloat above the Saints are a stock feature of numerous cognate works of the later Trecento (e.g., Figs. 141, 142, 225), but their soaring wings are reminiscent of the panel in the Fitzwilliam Museum (Fig. 15).

STUTTGART, private collection

Saint Thomas Aquinas

Panel: 46 x 27.2 cm.

LITERATURE: 1950, Oertel, no. 68, fig. 68: Lorenzo Monaco // 1950, H. Gronau, review of the Stuttgart exhibition, *Burlington Magazine*, LXXXXII, p. 325: Andrea di Bartolo, allied to the *Saint Michael* attributed by Berenson to Andrea di Bartolo ("Quadri senza casa," *Dedalo*, XI, 2, 1930/31, p. 348; 1970, p. 40, fig. 51).

COMMENT: The attribution to Andrea di Bartolo conclusively removed the panel from the context of Lorenzo Monaco and Florentine painting.

TOLEDO (OHIO), Toledo Museum of Art, no. 76.22

Madonna Enthroned
FIG. 217

Panel: 123.7 x 61 cm. (painted surface)

LITERATURE: 1964/65, Zeri, pp. 4-7, and figs. 1 and 11: Lorenzo Monaco, shortly after 1390; reconstructs the altarpiece for which the panel served as the central element (also, 1976, vol. 1, pp. 26-27) // 1965, Bellosi, "Da Spinello," p. 37: approaches the idiom of the Master of the Straus Madonna // 1970, González-Palacios, p. 30: LM // 1975, Boskovits, p. 349 and colorplate 6: LM, 1395-1400 // 1976, *Toledo Museum of Art*, pp. 98-99: LM.

COMMENT: See Catalogue II, Florence, Accademia, *Saint Jerome; Saint John the Baptist. . . .*

TULSA (OKLAHOMA), Philbrook Art Center, Kress Collection, no. 3360 (K 1047)

Saint Romuald
FIG. 258

Panel: 29.5 x 27 cm.

LITERATURE: 1953, W. Suida, *Paintings and Sculpture of the Samuel H. Kress Collection*, Philbrook Art Center, Tulsa, 1953: Lorenzo Monaco and assistants; related to Copenhagen *Annunciation* (citing Shapley information) // 1963, Berenson, vol. 1, p. 121: studio of Lorenzo Monaco; relates to Copenhagen *Annunciation* // 1966, Shapley, pp. 89-90: studio of Lorenzo Monaco; extensive catalogue entry, including the connections with the Copenhagen *Annunciation* and the Vatican *Nativity* // 1972, Fredericksen and Zeri, pp. 111 and 642: LM shop or Pseudo-Ambrogio di Baldese.

COMMENT: See Catalogue II, Copenhagen, Statens Museum for Kunst, *Annunciation*; and Rome, Pinacoteca Vaticana, *Nativity*. While the *Saint Romuald* has never been directly attributed to Lorenzo Monaco, its physical connection with the works in Copenhagen and Rome, both of which have been ascribed to him, necessitates inclusion of the panel in Catalogue II.

VENICE, Cini Collection (Fondazione Giorgio Cini)

Madonna of Humility
FIG. 254

Panel: 106 x 61 cm.

LITERATURE: 1975, Boskovits, p. 355: Lorenzo Monaco, 1405-1410.

COMMENT: The style of the picture comprises ingredients from the work of Lorenzo Monaco around 1405, the schematizations of Lorenzo di Niccolò, and elements from the vocabulary of the Master of the Straus Madonna. The eclecticism of the Cini *Madonna* exemplifies a late mediaeval craftsman's method of culling models from a variety of contemporary sources.

WASHINGTON, National Gallery of Art, Rosenwald Collection, no. 1958.8.105

Christ Giving the Keys to Saint Peter
FIG. 242

Cut miniature from a choir book
Parchment: 34.4 x 21.4 cm.

LITERATURE: 1956, Rosenthal, pp. 71-77: Lorenzo Monaco, slightly after 1395 // 1958, Levi D'Ancona, "Some New Attributions," p. 187: Trecentesque, but foreign to Lorenzo's early period or to his subsequent works // 1975, Nordenfalk, Vikan, et al, pp. 39-41, no. 11, fig. 11 a and b: Florence, ca. 1400; catalogued with full bibliography and provenance // 1975, Boskovits, p. 355: LM, 1390-95 // 1978, Levi D'Ancona, p. 229: identifies the provenance as fol. 134, Cod. Cor. 8, Biblioteca Laurenziana; Matteo Torelli, perhaps on a design by Lorenzo Monaco for the figure of Christ.

COMMENT: The tracing of the provenance (Levi D'Ancona, 1978) places the miniature within the Camaldolese environment of Santa Maria degli Angeli. The style shows alliances with the work of Don Silvestro and the earliest book painting by Lorenzo Monaco, so that a date circa 1400 would seem appropriate.

Appendix

UNKNOWN WORKS BY LORENZO MONACO CITED IN DOCUMENTS OR ASCRIBED IN PRE-NINETEENTH-CENTURY SOURCES

NOTE: As virtually all unidentifiable works ascribed to Lorenzo Monaco in sources after Vasari are derived from the *Vite*, only those later writers are cited who list previously unmentioned works or modify earlier notices.

SOURCES: Albertini, 1510; Billi, ca. 1516-30; Anonimo Gaddiano, ca. 1537-42; Vasari, 1550 and 1568; Fortunio, 1579; Bocchi, ed. Cinelli, 1677; Baldinucci, 1686; Farulli, 1710 and 1723; Richa, 1754 and 1755 (see the Bibliography for full citations; the pages cited for Vasari's notices of 1550 and 1568 are from the edition by Bettarini and Barocchi, vol. 2, Text).

Arezzo

San Pierino: a panel (Farulli, 1710, p. 31)

Camaldoli

Eremo: miniatures in choir books (Vasari, 1550, p. 304; the reference is to the monastery in the Casentino, not to the church and monastery of the Romiti di Camaldoli, outside Florence [cf. Ciaranfi, 1932, p. 285, note 2]; Vasari was active as a painter at the Badia di Camaldoli, and would have known works at the nearby Eremo [e.g., Vasari, 1568, p. 280]).

Florence

Certosa: some pictures (Vasari, 1568, p. 305)

Duomo: an altarpiece? (Document 17); miniatures in choir books (Farulli, 1723, p. 79)

Romiti di Camaldoli: many other works, i.e., other than a Crucifix and a Saint John (Vasari, 1568, p. 305; see Catalogue I, Florence, San Giovannino dei Cavalieri).

Santa Croce: a panel (Farulli, 1710, p. 31; see Catalogue I, Florence, Museo di Santa Croce, *Saint James Enthroned*)

Sant'Egidio: an altarpiece (Documents 16A-G; see Catalogue I, Florence, Uffizi, *Adoration of the Magi*)

San Jacopo sopr'Arno: a panel (Vasari, 1550 and 1568, p. 305; see Catalogue I, Florence, Accademia, *Crucifixion with the Lance and Sponge . . .*)

Santa Maria degli Angeli: many other works, i.e., other than the *Coronation of the Virgin* on the high altar (Albertini, Horne ed., p. 13; Billi [Strozziano], p. 361; Anonimo Gaddiano, p. 77; Vasari, 1550 and 1568, p. 304); a panel in the "stanza del Camarlingo," transferred from San Benedetto fuori della Porta a Pinti (Del Migliore, 1684, p. 332; for a suggested identification with a work of Zanobi Strozzi mentioned by Vasari, see Cohn, 1956, p. 45).

Santa Maria del Carmine: altarpiece for the Ardinghelli Chapel (Documents 4A-G; see the Introductory Essay, Note 5)

Santa Maria Nuova: a panel with Saints Cosmas and Damian (Document 7); panels (Document 14); miniatures in choir books (Documents 9A-D)

San Piero Maggiore: painted the chapel of the Fioravanti (Vasari, 1568, p. 305); panel in the Fioravanti Chapel (Bocchi, ed. Cinelli, p. 357); panel once in the Fioravanti Chapel (Richa, vol. 1, 1754, p. 142)

San Piero Scheraggio: high altarpiece (Albertini, Horne ed., pp. 16-17); panel (Vasari, 1550 and 1568, p. 305); a Madonna with Saints in the Sangalletti Chapel (Richa, vol. 2, 1755, p. 15)

Santa Trinita: Ardinghelli Chapel, portraits of Dante and Petrarch (Billi [Petrei], pp. 326-27, [Strozziano], p. 361; Anonimo Gaddiano, p. 77; Vasari, 1550 and 1568, pp. 304-305); Ardinghelli Chapel, frescoes and panel (Vasari, 1550 and 1568, p. 304; see the Introductory Essay, Note 17)

Vasari's collection: a drawing in chiaroscuro of the Theological Virtues (Vasari, 1568, p. 307; see Catalogue I, Berlin-Dahlem, Staatliche Museen, Kupferstichkabinett, *Visitation* and *Journey of the Magi*)

Pisa

San Michele (Camaldolese monastery): some panels (Vasari, 1550 and 1568, p. 305)

Rome

Papal Chapel: Missal for Pope Eugenius IV (Vasari, 1550, p. 305)

Unknown locations

A panel for Paolo and Francesco Banchini, carpenters (Document 10)

Pictures in many other places (Fortunio, p. 126)

Documents

NOTE: In the transcriptions of the documents, abbreviated words are completed, and some additional punctuation is provided.

1A [1391]
Florence, Archivio di Stato, *Conventi Soppressi 86* (*S. Maria degli Angeli di Firenze*), 95 (Registro Vecchio).

fol. 90v [December 10 and 11, 1391]: Don Lorenzo di Giovanni del popolo di San Michele de'Bisdomini di Firenze, che prima avea nome Piero, fece la sua professione in questo monastero a dì X di dicembre nel MCCCLXXXXI avendo prima compiuto l'anno del suo noviziato, in capitolo in domenica notte in presenza di tutto il convento, nelle mani di don Michele Ghiberti priore di questo monastero. E poi la mattina sequente si lesse la scritta della sua professione secondo l'usanza, in presenza del decto priore celebrante la messa e degli altri fratri e di molti secolari. E allora ricevette l'abito della chocolla dal decto priore. Era allora d'anni [*blank*] partissi dì [*blank*] di [*blank*] 13 [*blank*] tornocci morto.

1B [1391, 1392, 1396]
Florence, Archivio di Stato, *Conventi Soppressi 86* (*S. Maria degli Angeli di Firenze*), 96 (Registro Nuovo, Sec. XIV-XVI).

fol. 41v [December 10, 1391; September 21, 1392; February 26, 1395, n.s. 1396]: Don Lorenzo di Johanni del popolo di San Michele Bisdomini fece la sua professione a dì X di dicembre 1391, prima in capitolo e poi in chiesa alla messa del convento, nelle mani di don Michele Ghiberti nostro priore, in presentia degli altri frati. Partissi quinci a dì [*blank*] Fu ordinato a' IIII ordini minori di dicembre 1391, fra due volte, per decto vescovo de' Cipolloni et al subdiaconato dì 21 di settembre 1392, per decto messer Jacopo Altoviti vescovo di Fiesole, et al diaconato per messer frate Nofri dì 26 febraio 1395. Obiit die XXIIII Maii, hic sepultus.

DIGEST. Both documents are in the ledgers of monks resident at Santa Maria degli Angeli. Document 1A records Don Lorenzo's completion of the novitiate and his profession of simple vows. Notices of his departure from the monastery at some date before 1400 and the return of his body upon his death are appended in different hands. The cumulative notices in Document 1B, which are partially dependent on 1A, further record Don Lorenzo's entrance into minor orders, his elevation to the subdeaconate and deaconate, the incomplete date of his death, and his burial at the monastery. The truncated notation of his departure from Santa Maria degli Angeli ("partissi quinci a dì") is adapted from the appended notation in Document 1A.

PUBLICATION. Document 1A: Vasari, ed. Milanesi, vol. 2, 1878, p. 18, note 2; Sirén, 1905, p. 179, I. Document 1B: Sirén, 1905, p. 179, II.

2 [1394]
Florence, Archivio di Stato, *Diplomatico, S. Maria degli Angeli di Firenze*, 7 marzo 1393.

fol. [unnumbered parchment; March 7, 1393, n.s. 1394]: Donnus Laurentius Johannis

DIGEST. Don Lorenzo's name is the thirty-fourth of forty monks at Santa Maria degli Angeli who serve as witnesses to a notarial act. A total of forty is recorded as constituting two-thirds of the monks at the monastery. In the notarial act, ten proxies are elected from among the "conversi" (lay brothers) and granted power of attorney for five years in conjunction with various legal needs of the monastery (e.g., court appearances, financial transactions, rental of houses, leasing of land, etc.).

PUBLICATION. Levi D'Ancona, "Some New Attributions," 1958, p. 175, note 2 (cites the loose parchment leaf as fol. 161v); Gino Corti provided the above interpretation of the document.

3 [1396]
Florence, Archivio di Stato, *Accademia del Disegno*, 1 (*Compagnia dei Pittori, Statuti e Matricole*, 1340–ca. 1550).

fol. 14v [line 22]: Piero di Giovanni, popolo San Michele Bisdomini, LXXXXVI

DIGEST. A Piero di Giovanni from the parish of San Michele Visdomini is listed in the Company of Painters.

PUBLICATION. Gualandi, p. 187.

4A–E [1398, 1399, 1400]
Florence, Archivio di Stato, *Bigallo, 3*^{2} (*Libro 2° di stanziamenti*, 1395–1400).

4A. *fol. 93* [October 21, 1398]: Andree Johannis legniaiuolo, pro una tabula lignaminis cum civorio et aliis fornimentis ab eo empta pro altare capelle noviter facte in eclesia fratrum Sancte Marie del Carmino de Florentia, pro anima Chiari Ardinghelli, in totum florenos decem auri f. 10

4B. *fol. 96v* [November 18, 1398]: Andree Johannis legnaiuolo, pro quodam laborerio per eum noviter facto in quadam tabula alias ab eo empta pro altare cappelle noviter facte in eclesia Sancte Marie del Carmino pro anima Chiari Ardinghelli f. 11

4C. *fol. 100v* [January 3, 1398, n.s. 1399]: Dompno Laurentio Johannis predicto, ordinis fratrum Sancte Marie de Angnolis de Florentia, pro parte laborerii picture fiende per eum in tabula noviter empta pro cappella noviter facta pro anima Chiari Ardinghelli in eclesia Sancte Marie del Carmino de Florentia, florenos decem auri f.x

4D. *fol. 105v* [April 9, 1399]: Dompno Laurentio Johannis, ordinis fratrum Sancte Marie de Agnolis de Florentia, pro parte laborerii picture fiende per eum in tabula pro cappella noviter facta pro anima Chiari Ardinghelli in eclesia Sancte Marie del Carmino de Florentia, florenos decem auri f. x

4E. *fol. 129* [April 21, 1400]: Dompno Laurentio Johannis, ordinis fratrum Sancte Marie de Angiolis de Florentia, pro resto solutionis picture per eum facte in quadam tabula pro altare supradicte cappelle, florenos triginta quinque f. XXXV

4F. [1437]
Florence, Archivio di Stato, *Bigallo, 1668* (*Inventari*, 1436–1584).

fol. 3 [1437]:

Al nome di Dio MCCCCXXXVII

Aventario di chose hovero fornimento della chappella di Sa'Nicholò, posta nella chiesa di Santa Maria del Charmine di Firenze, lasciata per Chiaro d'Ardinghello del popolo di San Friano, chome apare per suo testamento fatto l'anno MCCCLXXVIII, roghato ser Nicholò di ser Zanobi Paghoni. In prima:

Uno dosale di lengno, dinanzi al'altare, dipinto e cho' sengno nostro.

Ancora una tavola al detto altare, bella e riccha, di mano di frate Lorenzo degli Angnoli e sengnata di nostro senengno [*sic*], ed eziandìo una predella apiè de' sopradetto altare.

Abiàne in chase la chiave, ed eziandìo n'ànno un'altra e detti frati.

Io frate Giovanni Martini, sindicho e procuratore del detto convento, cioè di S. Maria del Charmino (come del syndachato aparisce per mano di ser Cristophano notaio fiorentino, e per lui roghato a dì diciotto del mese di lulglio nel 1435) confesso avere avuto le sopra detta cosa [*sic*] e essere apresso al detto convento.

E per chiarezza di ciò, io mi sono soscritto di mia mano.

4G [1689]
Florence, Archivio di Stato, *Conventi soppressi, 113* (*Carmine di Firenze*), 13 (Libro de'padronati delle cappelle e sepolture della Chiesa della Beatissima Vergine Maria del Carmine di Firenze . . . fatto l'anno 1689), pp. 84–85: Oblighi della Cappella di S. Alberto.

p. 85: Dove è la Cappella de'Signori Marzichi vi era anticamente un altare dedicato a S. Niccolò Vescovo di Bari, che fu fatto d'un lascito di Chiaro d'Ardinghello, come per suo testamento rogato da ser Niccolò di ser Zanobi Maffei a'4 d'Agosto 1377 . . .

Quando fusse levato via quest'altare non se ne trova ricordo a'libri; si trova però la tavola di pittura all'anticha, che si conserva nell'Oratorio del Noviziato . . . L'altare è nominato in più luoghi nel libro vecchio delle sepolture, e ne'libri della Sagrestia.

DIGEST. Documents 4A–E record the payments for an altarpiece commissioned by the Compagnia del

Bigallo from the woodworker Andrea di Giovanni and from Lorenzo Monaco for one of the two chapels established by Chiaro Ardinghelli at the Carmine in Florence. Document 4F cites the altarpiece in an inventory of the chapel taken in 1437. Document 4G records that the altarpiece is relocated in an oratory at the Carmine; this notice of 1689 is the last mention of the work. See the Introductory Essay, Note 5; also see Note 17 for Vasari's mention of works by Lorenzo Monaco in the Ardinghelli Chapel at Santa Trinita.

PUBLICATION. Documents 4A-E: Cocchi, 1903, pp. 142-43 (partial); Poggi, 1904, pp. 237-38; Sirén, 1905, p. 181, VII. Documents 4F and 4G: Poggi, 1904, p. 201 (partial).

5 [1402]
Florence, Archivio di Stato, *S. Maria Nuova, 5043* (*Quaderno di Cassa K*, 1401-1404).

fol. 46 [March 14, 1401, n.s. 1402]: Don Lorenzo che sta in San Bartolo del Corso de' dare adì XIIII di marzo lire otto, ebbe per parte di [*blank*], portò ser Antonio di Bartoli L. VIII
Posto al quaderno L, a c. 4.

DIGEST. An unspecified record of payment to Don Lorenzo that mentions his being domiciled in the parish of San Bartolo del Corso (see Document 7).

PUBLICATION. Levi D'Ancona, 1962, p. 172.

6 [1402]
Florence, Archivio di Stato, *Accademia del Disegno, 1* (*Compagnia dei Pittori, Statuti e Matricole*, 1340-ca. 1550).

fol. 14v [line 17]: Piero di Giovanni pintore CCCCII

DIGEST. A Piero di Giovanni is listed in the Company of Painters.

PUBLICATION. Gualandi, p. 187.

7 [1406]
Florence, Archivio di Stato, *S. Maria Nuova, 4458* (*Uscita*, 1404-1406).

fol. 93v [November 10, 1406]: A don Lorenzo fue degli Angnoli e dipoi si riparava in San Bartolo del Corso, dì decto fiorini dieci d'oro per dipintura d'una tavola di Sancto Chosma e Damiano fiorini dieci d'oro, levati dal quaderno L di cassa, a c. IIII
f. X d'oro

DIGEST. Payment to Lorenzo Monaco for a panel painting of Saints Cosmas and Damian. Lorenzo is recorded as having been in the monastery of Santa Maria degli Angeli and having subsequently moved to the parish of San Bartolo del Corso (see Document 5).

PUBLICATION. Vasari, ed. Milanesi, vol. 2, 1878, p. 31 (cites document); Sirén, 1905, p. 182, IX; Levi D'Ancona, 1962, p. 172.

8A [1407]
Florence, Archivio di Stato, *Conventi Soppressi, 168* (*San Bartolommeo di Firenze* [*Monte Oliveto*]), 55 (*Memoriale*, 1391-1417).

fol. 63v [July 11, 1407]: Item richordo ch'io ebi da Bartolo Istadra [*sic*] per frate Giovanni Istrada
L. XV s. VIIII d. 8
ànne auto frate Lorenzo che dipignie la tavola di frate Giovanni Istrada, a dì XI di luglio
L. XV s. VIIII d. 8

8B [1411]
Florence, Archivio di Stato, *Conventi Soppressi, 168* (*San Bartolommeo di Firenze* [*Monte Oliveto*]), 81, (unnumbered miscellany of documents, XV-XVIII centuries).

fol. [unnumbered; June 20, 1411]: In nomine Domini amen
Item diede Bartholo e per lui da Nicholò di Giusto Covaregli e per frate Giovanni diede a frate Lorenzo dipintorore [*sic*], portò Checcho d'Antonio, a dì 20 di giugno 1411 fiorini 10 ____

DIGEST. Records of payment to Lorenzo Monaco for an altarpiece commissioned by Don Giovanni Strada for San Bartolomeo a Monte Oliveto (see the Introductory Essay, p. 17, and Catalogue I, Florence, Accademia, Monte Oliveto Altarpiece). Poggi (see below) recorded the date of Document 8A as 1406, whereas the two previous entries on the same page are from the year 1407 (observed by Gino Corti). The altarpiece is inscribed 1410.

PUBLICATION. Poggi, 1903, p. 58; Sirén, 1905, p. 182, VIII.

9A-B [1412]
Florence, Archivio di Stato, *S. Maria Nuova, 5046* (*Quaderno di Cassa N*, 1411-1414).

9A. *fol. 18v* [March 19 and 23, 1411, n.s. 1412; April 16 and September 21, 1412]: Pierozzo di Giovanni, fabro in Ghualfonda, de'dare adì XVIIII di marzo L. quatro, portò Sandro nostro, e sono per parte di ferri per l'interfanari

E dì XXIII di marzo L. sei s. dieci, per resto di X compassi L. 7 s. 10, e di 4 affibbiatoi di s. 20, e di XI chiovi grandi s. 15, e di 50 chiovi piccoli s. 25 piccioli, per tutto L. 16 s. 10, portò Giovanni d'esso Pierozzo dette L. sei s. dieci L. VI s. X

A frate Lorenzo degli Angnoli, che dipingnie, adì XVI d'aprile 1412, per miniatura di penello al'intefanari della chiesa, fiorini dieci d'oro, portò Buonchristiano di Benedecto in grossi f. X

A Giovanni decto, adì XXI di settembre 1412, per 20 bullette da libri s. 8 l'una, e per 100 a s. 1 l'una, e 100 a d. 2 l'una, e per 200 s. 18: somma L. 3 s. 13, portò lui L. III s. XIII

Posto in questo, a c. 40, che gl'interfanari deono dare

9B. *fol. 40v* [April 16, 1412]: Gli interfanari di chiesa deono dare levati in questo a c. 18 da Pierozo di Johanni, dati a lui per compassi L. 10 s. 10, ed a Johanni suo figlio per bullette L. 3 s. 13, ed a frate Lorenzo per mini, fior. dieci fior. X L. XIII s. III

A uscita segnata V, a c. 83, fior. 13 L. 2 s. 5

9C [1412]
Florence, Archivio di Stato, *S. Maria Nuova, 4463* (*Uscita*, 1410-1412).

fol. 83v [November 28, 1412]: A frate Lorenzo degli Angnoli, adì decto per cagione di miniare di penello gl' intefanari di chiesa fiorini dieci, e per bullette e compassi pe'detti interfanari lire quattordici soldi tre; levati dal quaderno segnato [N, c.] 40, da raxone d' essi interfanari f. XIII L. II s. V

9D [1413]
Florence, Archivio di Stato, *S. Maria Nuova, 4465* (*Uscita*, 1412-1413).

fol. 76 [December 7, 1413]: A frate Lorenzo di [*blank*] degli Angnoli, a dì VII di dicembre, per fighure che fecie ne'mini dello antifanari di chiesa fiorini due, portò Pippo di Bartolo, di soldi 80 per fiorino f. II d'oro

DIGEST. Payments for materials (compasses, nails, studs, and clasps) used in the making of choir books for Santa Maria Nuova, and for the illuminations and miniatures in these books commissioned from Lorenzo Monaco. For documented distinctions between the work of illuminators and miniaturists, see Catalogue I, Florence, Bargello, Cod. E 70.

PUBLICATION. Document 9A: unpublished. Document 9B: Levi D'Ancona, 1962, p. 172 (as fol. 90v). Documents 9C and 9D: Vasari, ed. Milanesi, vol. 2, 1878, p. 31 (cites documents); Sirén, 1905, p. 182, IX; Levi D'Ancona, 1962, p. 172.

10 [1412]
Florence, Archivio di Stato, *S. Maria Nuova, 4463* (*Uscita*, 1410-1412).

fol. 80v [June 20, 1412]: A Paolo e Francescho Banchini e fratelli lengniaiuoli, a dì decto, f. diciasette nuovi di zecha per parte di lengniame avemo da lloro più fae, al memoriale segnato E, a c. 23, e per loro a frate Lorenzo degli Agnoli in dì 9 di questo, per resto d'una tavola dipinse loro, levati dal quaderno segnato N, a c. 28 f. __ L. LXXIII s. II

DIGEST. Contrary to the interpretation by Milanesi and Sirén that the document concerns an altarpiece commissioned from Lorenzo Monaco for Santa Maria Nuova, the reference is to money paid by Santa Maria Nuova to the Banchini brothers for carpentry work, which was in turn paid by the Banchini to Lorenzo Monaco for a panel painting he executed for them. (I am grateful to Gino Corti for this explanation; for an alternative interpretation that the Banchini possibly served as dealers for Lorenzo's panel and, having sold it, paid the sum to the painter, see Gilbert, pp. 20-21.)

PUBLICATION. Vasari, ed. Milanesi, vol. 2, 1878, p. 31 (cites document); Sirén, 1905, p. 182, IX.

11 [1415]
Florence, Archivio di Stato, *Conventi Soppressi, 86* (*S. Maria degli Angeli di Firenze*), 95 (Registro Vecchio).

fol. 65 [January 29, 1414, n.s. 1415]: Memoria come adì 29 di gennaio 1414 vendemo a vita a don Lorenzo dipintore da siene[?] del nostro ordine una nostra casa con sporto posta qui dirimpetto a noi, a I° via, a II° la casa dove stette Luca di Geri, a III° messer maso delli albizi, a IIII° una altra casa nostra dove sta al presente [*blank*] coll'orto di dietro infino a' beni di messer Maso, come è disegnato per le sciepe[?] per f. 80, i quali avemo da llui contanti e doppo la sua morte torna a noi liberamente con ogni [ac]concime che ci avesse fatto su e dove non stesse don Lorenzo in Firenze siamo tenuti d'apigionarla e dare a lui la pigione. Ae da noi una scripta di questa sustantia.

DIGEST. A real estate transaction between Santa Maria degli Angeli and Lorenzo Monaco (see the Introductory Essay, p. 4).

PUBLICATION. Vasari, ed. Milanesi, vol. 9, 1885, p. 252; Sirén, 1905, p. 13, note 1, and pp. 180-181, III.

12 [1416]
Florence, Archivio di Stato, *Compagnie Soppresse, G XII, 192* (*Gesuiti*).

fol. [unnumbered; December 6, 1416]: Al nome de Dio amen, a dì 6 di dicienbre 1416

Sia chiaro e manifesto a qualunche persona vedarà o legiarà questa pre[se]nte scritta chome ogi questo presente dì scritto di sopra, messer Giovani Puci priore e retore e ghovernatore delo [s]pedale di sa[n]to Giovani di via di Sangallo chiamato lo spedale di messer Bonifazio Lupi, da l'una parte, e Piero di Nello dipintore, di chonchordia amendue chonmetono in voi frate Lorenzio di [*blank*] frate degli Angnioli, che per voi si vegha in luogho di grande servigio, quello che si viene di cierta dipintura à fato el detto mastro Piero ne'refetorio del detto spedale, e chosì lodiate e dichiariate sechondo che pare a voi, e quello per voi sarà lodato, l'uno e l'altro rimarano chontenti. E per chiarezia di ciò, ànno voluto che io ser Domenicho di Giovani abi fato questa scritta di mia propia mano, anno e dì detto, e mendune si sono soscriti qui di sotto di loro propia mano.

Io ser Giovanni Pucci priore del detto hospedale son contento a la sopra detta scritta e cossì vi priego.

Io Piell

Io Piero di Nello sono chontento alla sopra detta isscritta e cchosì vi priego.

Io frate Lorenzo di Giovanni stimo il sopraddetto lavorio il quale Piero di Nello à dipinto, f. XX a ongni sua spesa, cioè di cholori come d'azzurro, oro e ssimile chose appartinenti al dipingnere. Questo è quello mi pare si venga a cchoscienza. Frate Lorenzo.

DIGEST. Lorenzo Monaco estimates the value of a work by Pietro Nelli in the refectory of the hospital of San Giovanni (Spedale di Bonifazio); (see the Introductory Essay, p. 5, and Fig. 263).

PUBLICATION. Milanesi, 1872, p. 10; Pini and Milanesi, 1876 [unnumbered reproduction].

13 [1417]
Florence, Archivio di Stato, *Bigallo, 725* (*Debitori e Creditori*, 1413-1420; post-1966 flood call no.: CRIA, 7588).

fol. 187, right side [July 1, 1417]: Anbruogio di Baldese dipintore de'avere fiorini trentadua d'oro perchè dipinse la chapella de l'oratorio la quale si fecie stimare, chome si diliberò pe'chapitani, per una [*sic*] frate deli Agnioli e Marioto dipintore, la quale stima acietorono pe' le mani di ser Nofri di ser Pagholo Nemni a dì primo di luglio 1417 f. 32

DIGEST. Lorenzo Monaco and Mariotto (di Nardo?) estimate work by Ambrogio di Baldese.

PUBLICATION. Vasari, ed. Milanesi, vol. 2, 1878, p. 31 (cites document); Poggi, 1905, p. 48.

14 [1418]
Florence, Archivio di Stato, *S. Maria Nuova, 5049* (*Quaderno di Cassa* Q, 1418-1420).

fol. 11 [December 11, 1418]: Frate Lorenzo di Giovanni fue frate degli Agnoli, che dipignie tavole, de'dare a dì 11 di dicembre f. dieci, per noi da Vieri Ghuadagni, in questo a c. 174. f. X d'oro

DIGEST. Payment to Lorenzo Monaco for panels executed for Santa Maria Nuova.

PUBLICATION. Sirén, 1905, p. 183, IX; Levi D'Ancona, 1962, p. 172.

15 [1419]
Florence, Archivio di Stato, *Spedale di Bonifazio, 389* (*Debitori e Creditori A*, 1413-1419).

fol. 76, right side [January 1418, n.s. 1419]: Mastro Piero dipintore de'avere per la dipintura che fecie nella logia di nostra Donna e di tute quelle storie fiorini trentasei, e chosì fu lodato per frate Lorenzo dipintore f. 36 d'oro

E de'avere fiorini venti d'oro per la dipintura ch'à fata ne'rifetoro delo spedale dove si mangia, lodate pe' lo detto frate Lorenzo, a ongni sua spesa di cholori e stangnio e oro di tuta [*sic*] queste dipinture ch'a fate di fuori e dentro f. 20 d'oro

DIGEST. Lorenzo Monaco estimates works of the painter Pietro Nelli in the loggia and refectory of the Spedale di Bonifazio. Gino Corti has confirmed that the "Mastro Piero" is Pietro Nelli by observing that the painter's name is written on the left side of the same folio (Piero di Nello dipintore de' dare . . .).

PUBLICATION. Unpublished. The late Werner Cohn generously brought this document to my attention.

16A [1420]
Florence, Archivio di Stato, *S. Maria Nuova, 5049* (*Quaderno di Cassa Q*, 1418-1420).

fol. 217 [March 27, August 14, 1420]: Frate Lorenzo de'frati degli Angnoli de'avere a dì XXVII di marzo f. venti s. ventinove d. otto piccioli, per lui da Batista di Giovanni da Città di Castello, e per lui da Niccolò da Uzano e compagni, recò Alesandro d'Antonio Covoni nostro

f. XX L. I s. VIIII d. 8 piccioli

Ànne auto a dì XIIII d'aghosto 1420 f. quindici d'oro per sua lettera fatta dì 6 d'aghosto 1420, demo ad Isaù Martellini, portò Alexandro d'Antonio Covoni f. 15 d'oro

Posto al quaderno segnato R, a c. 170

E in questo, a c. 11

16B [1420, 1422]
Florence, Archivio di Stato, *S. Maria Nuova, 5050* (*Quaderno di Cassa R*, 1420-1422).

fol. 170 [March 27, 1420; August 8, 1422]: Frate Lorenzo de' frati degli Agnioli de'avere al quaderno segnato Q, a c. 217, f. 5 L. 1 s. 9 d. 8

f. V L. I s. VIIII d. 8

Ànne avuto adì 8 d'aghosto, posto de'avere in questo, a c. 218 f. V L. I s. VIIII d. 8

16C [1420]
Florence, Archivio di Stato, *S. Maria Nuova, 5049* (*Quaderno di Cassa Q*, 1418-20).

fol. 11 [October 31, 1420]: E dì 31 d'ottobre 1420, fiorini 8 lire 1, per pezzi M d'oro da Pietro di Francesco battiloro, messi a entrata segnata BB, a c. 66 ed a libro segnato D, a c. 152 f. VIII L. I

Posti al quaderno segnato E, a c. 3.

16D-G [1421, 1422]
Florence, Archivio di Stato, *S. Maria Nuova, 5050* (*Quaderno di Cassa R*, 1420-1422).

16D. *fol. 3* [January 22, 27, February 26, March 1, 19, 1420, n.s. 1421; May 31, 1421]: Frate Lorenzo di Giovanni fue frate degli Agnoli, de'dare al quaderno segnato Q, a c. XI, f. diciotto L. una, levati dal quaderno segnato Q di cassa, a c. 11 f. XVIII L. I

E dì 22 di giennaio 1420 ci scrisse avere avuto pezzi 500 d'oro da Piero di Francesco battiloro, per L. 3 s. 6 centinaio, sono a entrata CC, a c. 13

f. IIII s: X

E dì XXVII di giennaio decto f. due, portò Giannino di Bernardo dipintore, in grossi, disse Sandro nostro f. II

E dì 26 di febraio 1420 pezzi 500 d'oro ebbe da Piero sopra decto, L. 16 s. 10, a entrata da llui, a libro CC, a c. 13, ed a libro D, a c. 153 f. IIII s. X

E dì primo di marzo 1420 f. uno a Giannino di [*blank*], per sua lettera f. I

E dì XVIII di marzo 1420 f. sei portò Piero Piero [*sic*] di Antonio per sua cedola f. VI

E dì XXXI di maggio 1421 f. cinque, per lui a Giannino di Francesco, per la cedola di frate Lorenzo

f. V

Posto in questo, a c. 53, f. 40 L. 2.

16E. *fol. 53* [June 7, 16, and September 4, 1421; March 19, 1421, n.s. 1422; April 8, 24, and June 17, 30, 1422]: Frate Lorenzo di Giovanni fue frate degli Angnoli de'dare, levati in questo a c. 3, f. quaranta d'oro e L. due, sono per cagione della tavola dell'altare f. XL L. II

E dì VII di giugno 1421 f. sei e mezo, disse per azurro, disse venne da Vinegia, portò Piero d'Antonio per sua cedola, cioè L. 26 in grossi, vagliono

f. VI L. II

E dì XVI di giugno 1421 f. dieci, portò Piero d'Antonio in grossi di s. 80 f. X di grossi

E dì IIII di settembre 1421 f. tre, per lui a Giannino di Francesco, e f. uno portò Piero d'Antonio per sua cedola: somma f. IIII di grossi

E di XVIIII di marzo 1421 f. due, portò Piero d'Antonio per sua cedola f. II

E dì VIII d'aprile 1422 f. due, portò Piero decto per sua cedola f. II

E dì XXIIII d'aprile decto, f. due, portò Piero decto per sua lettera f. II

E dì XVII di giugno 1422 f. dieci per sua cedola, demo a Piero d'Antonio cioè f. dieci f. 10

E dì XXX di giugno 1422 f. o. L. quaranta nove s. dieci, per sua cedola, demo a Piero di Francescho battiloro, per 1500 pezzi d'oro, portò lui decto, sono di s. 78 d. 6 per fiorino f. XII L. II s. VIII

Posto in questo a c. 120, f. 88 L. 6 s. 8
sono f. LXXXVIII L. VI s. VIII

16F. *fol. 120v* [July 24, 31, August 7, 1422]: Frate Lorenzo de' frati degli Angnoli de'dare, levati in questo a c. 53, f. 88 L. 6 s. 8 piccioli f. 88 L. 6 s. 8

E dì 24 di luglio 1422 L. ventiquattro, per lui a Michele d'Angnolo dipintore, per sua cedola, sono f. 6 s. 6, di s. 79 per fiorino f. 6 L. __ s. VI

E dì 24 decto, di luglio, f. dieci, portò Piero d'Antonio sta co'llui, per sua cedola f. X

E dì 31 di luglio decto, mani ottanta di grossi, sono L. 88, portò Piero d'Antonio sta co'llui, vaglion, fu presente Franceschino di Johanni e Basilio di Simone f. XXII L. I s. II

E dì decto f. dieci, portò Franceschino di Johanni ed ècene cedola di sua mano f. X d'oro

E dì 7 d'aghosto 1422 f. quarantasei, per noi da Cosimo e Lorenzo de'Medici, in questo a c. 214, e per frate Lorenzo a [*blank*] f. XLVI

E dì decto L. due s. tre d. otto piccioli, portò Piero d'Antonio, sono per resto di ciò dee avere da noi
L. II s. III d. VIII

Posti in questo, a c. 218, f. 182, L. 9, s. 19, d. 8

16G. *fol. 218v* [August 7, 1422]: Frate Lorenzo di Johanni degli Angnioli de'avere a dì 7 d'aghosto f. 28 per legname d'una tavola per l'altare di Sancto Egidio, e per la ingiessatura f. 7, e per la dipintura f. 144: somma f. 179; a uscita CC, a c. 102 f. 179 d'oro

E de'avere, levati in questo a c. 170, f. 5 L. 1 s. 9 d. 10 piccioli

Ànne avuto, levati in questo a ca. 120, f. 182 L. 9 s. 19 d. 8, sono f. 182 L. I s. 19 d. 8

DIGEST. Documents 16A-16G constitute a sequence of payments for an altarpiece, clearly of major importance, for the church of Sant'Egidio, a dependency of Santa Maria degli Angeli. For comment on the proposed identification of this altarpiece, see Catalogue I, Florence, Uffizi, *Adoration of the Magi*. Two painters who were apparently assistants in Don Lorenzo's workshop are mentioned in the documents: Giannino di Bernardo (16D) and Michele d'Agnolo (16F). Sirén (1905, p. 163) stated that three other names in this series of documents—Piero d'Antonio, Giannino di Francesco, and Franceschino di Giovanni—are also those of assistants in the workshop, but the lack of the word "dipintore" after their names makes this observation conjectural.

PUBLICATION. Documents 16A-16C: Levi D'Ancona, 1962, pp. 172-73. Documents 16D-16G: Vasari, ed. Milanesi, vol. 2, 1878, p. 32 (cites documents); Sirén, 1905, pp. 183-84, X.

17 [1422]
Florence, Archivio di Stato, *Arte della Lana, 152* (*Partiti, Atti e Sentenze*, January 1421, n.s. 1422–April 1422).

fol. 36v. [March 3, 1421, n.s. 1422]:
Die III Martii

Compositio facta cum illis de Corsinis super negotiis cappelle.

Item supra dicti domini Consules ut supra in sufficienti numero more solito collegialiter congregati, viso testamento condito per Reverendum in Christo patrem dominum Petrum de Corsinis cardinalem Portuensem in sua ultima voluntate sub anno Domini M CCCC III et de mense ottobris dicti anni. Et viso legato per dictum dominum Petrum facto in dicto suo testamento de construendo unam cappellam in ecclesia cathedrali florentina et circa translationem sui corporis de Avinione ad dictam ecclesiam florentinam et sui corporis et seu ossium sepulturam [*omissis*]

fol. 37: Item quod dicti heredes faciant et seu fieri facere teneantur et debeant dictam cappellam infra decem otto menses proxime futuros et pro dicta cappella et ornatione ipsius faciant et seu fieri facere teneantur et debeant infra dictum terminum unam tabulam altaris pictam manu fratris de Angelis vel alterius ydonei et seu melioris pictoris, et unam tabulectam super altare sine columpnis. Et predicta omnia fiant et fieri debeant honorabiliter et sufficienter et prout et sicut deliberabitur per eosdem dominos Consules vel per eorum in offitio successores.

DIGEST. A contract between the Corsini family and the Arte della Lana that includes the commissioning of an altarpiece for the Cathedral of Florence, which is to be executed either by Lorenzo Monaco or by a painter who is equal or superior to him (see the Introductory Essay, p. 5, and Note 12).

PUBLICATION. Unpublished, excepting an Italian précis of the original Latin document (Vasari, ed. Milanesi, vol. 2, 1878, p. 25, note 2).

18A [1407]
Florence. Archivio di Stato, *Arte del Cambio, 104.*

fol. 5 [May 11, 1407]: Bartholomeo et Salimbene di Lionardo di Bartolomeo Bartolini Salimbeni, popolo di Sancta Trinita di Firenze, l'anno MCCCCVII comperorono per loro et per chi e' nominassino, uno podere con casa da lavoratore et terre lavoriate, vignate et fructate, posto nel popolo di San Piero a Ponte, luogo decto alla Strada overo el podere della Cappella de'Bartolini, da primo via, da II ser Bartholomeo di ser Guido da Pratovecchio, da III la via de'Mulattieri, da IIII e beni della chiesa di San Piero a Ponte. Tienlo a pigione Giovanni di Francesco Tornaquinci.

E decti Bartholomeo et Salimbene nominorno in comperatori di decto podere e consoli del'Arte del Cambio, con prohibitione d'alienatione. Le rendite et fitto se hanno a dare al monisterio di Sancta Trinita stando sotto l'ordine di Valembrosa, tractone le spese per mantenere gli edifitii et podere predecto, per honorare una cappella di decti Bartholomeo et Salimbene, posta in decta chiesa et intitolata nella Vergine Maria. Lo abbate è obbligato ogni dì farvi dire una messa et ogni anno el dì della Nuntiata farvi una festa con quello numero di preti pare a'consoli che pe'tempi saranno, et con dieci libbre di cera, et uno rinovale ogni anno per la festa del mese d'agosto, con 8 preti almeno et 10 libbre di cera.

E fu roghato sotto dì 11 di maggio 1407 ser Cristofano da lLaterina.

18B [1434 or 1435]
Florence, Archivio di Stato, *Arte del Cambio, 105* (*Ricordi di Testamenti . . .*, 1399-1464).

fol. 5v [March 1434, or n.s. 1435?] Nel MCCCCXXXIIII di mese di marzo venne a notitia a decti Consoli decto governo che prima l'avevano governato loro, che disseno avevano convertite le rendite de' decti beni in fare ornare decta chappella, che nel dì della decta compra non era ridocta a perfectione da dirvi messa. Et del decto mese di marzo si cominciò per la decta arte del chambio ad allogare decti beni.

DIGEST. Document 18A records the provision of funds for the maintenance and liturgical use of the Bartolini Salimbeni Chapel at Santa Trinita in Florence. The brothers Bartolomeo and Salimbene Bartolini Salimbeni cede the supervision of the chapel to the Arte del Cambio (see Catalogue I, Florence, Santa Trinita, Bartolini Salimbeni Chapel, *Life of the Virgin*). Document 18B records that the governing body of the Arte del Cambio does not find that the decoration of the Bartolini Salimbeni Chapel has been sufficiently completed to permit the celebration of mass.

PUBLICATION. Document 18A: unpublished (cited by San Luigi, pp. 268-69). Document 18B: Sirén, 1905, p. 185, XI.

Bibliography

Ackerman, J. S. "On Early Renaissance Color Theory and Practice." In *Studies in Italian Art and Architecture 15th through 18th Centuries.* Edited by H. A. Millon. Cambridge, Massachusetts, and London, 1980, pp. 11-44. [*Studies in Italian Art History*, I, American Academy in Rome.]

Albertini, F. *Memoriale di molte statue et picture sono nella inclyta cipta di Florentia. . . .* Florence, 1510. Facsimile ed., Florence, 1932. Reprinted by H. P. Horne, Letchworth, 1909.

Amerio, R. "Lorenzo Monaco." In *Encyclopedia of World Art.* Vol. 9. New York and London, 1964, cols. 337-40.

Amsterdam. *Italiaansche Kunst in Nederlandsch Bezit.* Stedelijk Museum, Amsterdam, 1934.

Amsterdam. *All the Paintings of the Rijksmuseum,* Amsterdam, 1976.

Andriani, G. *Herzog Anton-Ulrich Museum,* Braunschweig, 1969.

Angelelli, A. "La Pinacoteca Fornari di Fabriano." *Rivista marchigiana illustrata* 5, 1908, pp. 196-98.

Anonimo Gaddiano. "Cod. Magliabechiano" XVII, 17. MS., Biblioteca Nazionale, Florence; ca. 1537-1542. Edited by C. von Fabriczy, "Il Codice dell'Anonimo Gaddiano nella Biblioteca Nazionale di Firenze." *Archivio storico italiano,* ser. 5. vol. 12, 1893, pp. 15-94 and 275-334. Reprinted Farnborough, 1969.

Antal, F. *Florentine Painting and its Social Background.* London, 1947.

Arfelli, A. *La Galleria dell'Accademia di Belle Arti di Ravenna.* Rome, 1936.

[Artaud de Montor]. *Peintres primitifs. Collection de tableaux rapportée de l'Italie et publiée par M. le Chevalier Artaud de Montor. . . .* Paris, 1843.

Arcangeli, F. *Dipinti restaurati del territorio di Grizzana.* Bologna, 1966.

Baldani, R. *La pittura a Bologna nel secolo XIV: Documenti e studi.* Bologna, 1909.

Baldini, U. "Note brevi su inediti toscani." *Bollettino d'arte* 37, 1952, pp. 254-55, and 40, 1955, pp. 79-83.

——. *Mostra di opere d'arte restaurate: VIII esposizione.* Florence, 1955.

——. *Itinerario del Museo della Collegiata.* Empoli, 1956.

——. *Dodici capolavori restaurati, Mostra di opere d'arte restaurate: IX esposizione.* Florence, 1958.

——. *L'Opera completa dell'Angelico.* Milan, 1970.

——. "Contributi all'Angelico: il trittico di San Domenico di Fiesole e qualche altra aggiunta." In *Scritti di storia dell'arte in onore di Ugo Procacci.* Vol. 1, Florence, 1977, pp. 236-46.

Baldinucci, F. *Notizie de'professori del disegno da Cimabue in qua.* Vol. 2. Florence, 1686.

Bandera Viani, M. C. *Fiesole: Museo Bandini.* Bologna, 1981.

Bauman, G. C. "The Miracle of Plautilla's Veil in Princeton's Beheading of St. Paul." *Record of the Art Museum, Princeton University* 36, 1977, pp. 3-11.

Baumstark, R. *Meisterwerke der Sammlungen des Fürsten von Liechtenstein: Gemälde.* Zurich, 1980.

Baxandall, D. "A Lorenzo Monaco Madonna." *Scottish Art Review* 11, no. 1, 1967, pp. 6-7.

Becherucci, L. *I Musei di Santa Croce e di Santo Spirito a Firenze.* Milan, 1983.

Becker, F. *Herzoglich Sachsen-Altenburgisches Museum (Lindenau-Stiftung): Beschreibender Katalog der Gemäldesammlung.* Altenburg, 1898.

Beissel, S., S.J. *Fra Giovanni Angelico da Fiesole, sein Leben und seine Werke.* Freiburg i.B., 1905.

Bellosi, L. *I Maestri del colore: Lorenzo Monaco.* Milan, 1965.

——. "Da Spinello Aretino a Lorenzo Monaco." *Paragone* 16, no. 187, 1965, pp. 18-43.

——. "Il Maestro della Crocifissione Griggs: Giovanni Toscani." *Paragone* 17, no. 193, 1966, pp. 44-58.

——. "La mostra di affreschi staccati, al Forte Belvedere." *Paragone* 17, no. 201, 1966, pp. 73-79.

——. "Note brevi alle illustrazioni." *Paragone* 18, no. 203, 1967, pp. 84-91.

Bellosi, L. *Il Museo dello Spedale degli Innocenti a Firenze.* Florence, 1977.
——. "Ipotesi sull'origine delle terracotte quattrocentesche." In *Jacopo della Quercia fra Gotico e Rinascimento, Atti del Convegno di Studi.* Florence, 1977, pp. 163-79.
——. "Un trittico molto insolito." In *Itinerari, Contributi alla storia dell'arte in memoria di Maria Luisa Ferrari.* Edited by A. Boschetto. Vol. 1, Florence, 1979, pp. 61-65.
——. "Due note in margine a Lorenzo Monaco miniatore: il 'Maestro del Codice Squarcialupi' e il poco probabile Matteo Torelli." In *Studi di storia dell'arte in memoria di Mario Rotili.* Vols. 1 and 2, Naples, 1984, pp. 307-314, and pls. 138-44.
——. "Su alcuni disegni italiani tra la fine del Due e la metà del Quattrocento." *Bollettino d'arte* 70, 1985, pp. 1-42.
Bellosi, L., and F. Bellini. *I disegni antichi degli Uffizi: I tempi del Ghiberti.* Florence, 1978.
Bellosi, L., G. Cantelli, and M. L. Moriondo. *Arte in Valdichiana dal XIII al XVIII secolo.* Cortona, 1970.
[Benedict]. *The Rule of Saint Benedict, in Latin and English, with Notes.* Edited and translated by T. Fry, O.S.B. et al. Collegeville, Minnesota, 1980.
Berenson, B. *The Florentine Painters of the Renaissance.* New York and London, 1896.
——. *The Florentine Painters of the Renaissance.* 3d ed. New York and London, 1909.
——. "Un nuovo Lorenzo Monaco." *Rivista d'arte* 6, 1909, pp. 3-6.
——. *Catalogue of a Collection of Paintings and Some Art Objects.* Vol. 1, *Italian Paintings.* Philadelphia, 1913.
——. "Notes on Tuscan Painters of the Trecento in the Städel Institut at Frankfurt." *Städel-Jahrbuch* 5, 1926, pp. 17-29.
——. *Studies in Mediaeval Painting.* New Haven, 1930.
——. *Italian Pictures of the Renaissance.* Oxford, 1932.
——. "Fra Angelico, Fra Filippo e la cronologia." *Bollettino d'arte* 26, 1932/33, pp. 1-22 and 49-66.
——. "Quadri senza casa, il Trecento fiorentino-IV." *Dedalo* 12, 1932, pp. 5-34.
——. *Pitture italiane del Rinascimento.* Milan, 1936.
——. *The Drawings of the Florentine Painters.* 3 vols. Chicago, 1938. Rev. Italian ed., Milan, 1961.
——. *Italian Pictures of the Renaissance, Florentine School.* Edited by N. Mariano, L. Vertova Nicolson, and M. Rinehart. 2 vols. London, 1963.
——. *Italian Pictures of the Renaissance, Central Italian and North Italian Schools.* Edited by L. Vertova. 3 vols. London, 1968.
——. *Homeless Paintings of the Renaissance.* Edited by H. Kiel. Bloomington and London, 1970.
Bergeon, S., and E. Mognetti. "La restauration des primitifs italiens du Musée du Petit Palais d'Avignon: Quelques problèmes rencontrés." *Revue du Louvre* 27, 1977, pp. 264-70.
Berlin-Dahlem. *Staatliche Museen Preussischer Kulturbesitz: Catalogue of Paintings, 13th to 18th Century.* 2d rev. ed., translated by L. B. Parshall. Berlin, 1978.
Berliner, R. "Arma Christi." *Münchner Jahrbuch der bildenden Kunst* 6, 1955, pp. 35-152.
Bernardini, G. "La nuova Galleria Vaticana." *Rassegna d'arte* 9, 1909, pp. 89-94.
Berti, L. *Masaccio.* Milan, 1964.
——. *Il Museo di Palazzo Davanzati a Firenze.* Venice, 1970.
Biagi, L. "Note su alcuni quadri della Pinacoteca Vaticana." *L'Arte* 18, 1915, pp. 228-31.
Białostocki, J., and M. Walicki. *Europäische Malerei in polnischen Sammlungen, 1300-1800.* Cracow, 1957.
Billi, A. "Cod. Magliabechiano" XIII, 89 (Petrei) and XXV, 636 (Strozziano). MS., Biblioteca Nazionale, Florence, ca. 1516-1530. Edited by C. von Fabriczy, "Il libro di Antonio Billi e le sue copie nella Biblioteca Nazionale di Firenze." *Archivio storico italiano*, ser. 5, vol. 7, 1891, pp. 299-368. Reprinted Farnborough, 1969.
Blunt, A. "Thomas Gambier Parry: a great art collector." *Apollo* 81, no. 38, 1965, pp. 288-95.
——. *Provisional Catalogue, The Gambier-Parry Collection, Courtauld Institute of Art, University of London.* London, 1967.
——. "The History of Thomas Gambier Parry's Collection." *Burlington Magazine* 109, 1967, pp. 112-16.
Bocchi, F. *Le bellezze della città di Firenze.* Edited by G. Cinelli. Florence, 1677.
Bonsanti, G. *La Galleria della Accademia Firenze, Guida e catalogo completo.* Florence, 1987.
Borenius, T. *A Catalogue of the Paintings at Doughty House, I.* London, 1913.
——. "Treasures from the Rothermere Collection—I." *Apollo* 22, no. 130; 1935, pp. 185-90.

Borsook, E. *The Mural Painters of Tuscany*. 2d ed. Oxford, 1980.
Boskovits, M. *Early Italian Panel Paintings*. Budapest, 1966.
——. "Der Meister der Santa Verdiana." *Mitteilungen des Kunsthistorischen Institutes in Florenz* 13, 1967, pp. 31-60.
——. "Mariotto di Nardo e la formazione del linguaggio tardo-gotico a Firenze negli anni intorno al 1400." *Antichità viva* 7, no. 6, 1968, pp. 21-31.
——. "Su Don Silvestro, Don Simone e la 'scuola degli Angeli,' " *Paragone* 23, no. 265, 1972, pp. 35-61.
——. *Pittura fiorentina alla vigilia del Rinascimento, 1370-1400*. Florence, 1975.
——. *Un'Adorazione dei Magi e gli inizi dell'Angelico*, Bern, 1976.
——. "In margine alla bottega di Agnolo Gaddi." *Paragone*, 30, no. 355, 1979, pp. 54-62.
——. *A Critical and Historical Corpus of Florentine Painting*. Sec. III, vol. IX, Florence, 1984.
——. *The Martello Collection, Paintings, Drawings, and Miniatures from the XIVth to the XVIIIth Centuries*. Florence, 1985.
Botto, C. "Note e documenti sulla chiesa di S. Trinita in Firenze." *Rivista d'arte* 20, 1938, pp. 1-22.
Brandi, C. *La Regia Pinacoteca di Siena*. Rome, 1933.
——. *Mostra d'arte italiana a Palazzo Venezia*. Rome, 1945.
Brigstocke, H. *Italian and Spanish Paintings in the National Gallery of Scotland*. Edinburgh, 1978.
Brizio, A. M. Review of V. Golzio, *Lorenzo Monaco*. In *L'Arte* 35, 1932, pp. 339-40.
Brown, A. T. "Non-Narrative Elements in Tuscan Gothic Frescoes." Ph.D. diss., The University of Michigan, 1980.
Burckhardt, J. *Der Cicerone*. Basel, 1855. Ed. by H. Wölfflin, Stuttgart, 1933.
Byam, Shaw, J. *Paintings by Old Masters at Christ Church, Oxford*. London, 1967.
Cämmerer-George, M. *Die Rahmung der toskanischen Altarbilder im Trecento*. Strassburg, 1966.
Calamandrei, P. G. *Le opere d'arte in Ognissanti*. Florence, 1935.
Callmann, E. "Thebaid Studies." *Antichità viva* 14, no. 3, 1975, pp. 3-22.
Carli, E. *Guida della Pinacoteca di Siena*. Milan, 1958.
Carocci, G. *Il Valdarno da Firenze al mare*. Bergamo, 1906.
Castelfranchi Vegas, L. *International Gothic Art in Italy*. Translated by B. D. Phillips, revised by D. T. Rice. Leipzig, 1966.
Castellazzi, G. *La Basilica di S. Trinità: I suoi tempi ed il progetto del suo restauro*. Florence, 1887.
Chiappelli, A. *Pagine d'arte antica fiorentina*. Florence, 1905.
Chiarelli, R. *I codici miniati del Museo di S. Marco a Firenze*. Florence, 1968.
Christiansen, K. *Gentile da Fabriano*. Ithaca, 1982.
——. "Early Renaissance Narrative Painting in Italy." *Metropolitan Museum of Art Bulletin* 41, no. 7, 1983, pp. 3-48.
Ciaranfi, A. M. "Lorenzo Monaco miniatore." *L'Arte* 35, 1932, pp. 285-317 and 379-99.
——. "Lorenzo Monaco." In *Enciclopedia italiana*. Vol. 21, Rome, 1934, p. 502.
Ciatti, M. "Appunti e documenti per la storia della miniatura a Prato nel Quattrocento." In *La miniatura italiana tra Gotico e Rinascimento*. Vol. 2, Florence, 1975, pp. 509-33.
Cincinnati. *The Lehman Collection, New York*. Cincinnati Art Museum, 1959.
Cleveland. *Gothic Art, 1360-1440*. Cleveland Museum of Art, 1963.
Cocchi, A. "La Cappella Ardinghelli del Carmine." *Miscellanea d'arte* 1, 1903, pp. 142-43.
Cockerell, S. C. *Principal Pictures in the Fitzwilliam Museum*. London, 1912.
Cohn, W. "Notizie storiche intorno ad alcune tavole fiorentine del '300 e '400." *Rivista d'arte* 31, 1956, pp. 41-72.
——. "Due tondi sconosciuti della pala di San Pancrazio di Bernardo Daddi." *Bollettino d'arte* 42, 1957, pp. 176-78.
——. "Zur Ikonographie der Glasfenster von Orsanmichele." *Mitteilungen des Kunsthistorischen Institutes in Florenz* 9, 1959, pp. 1-12.
Colasanti, A. "Quadri fiorentini inediti." *Bollettino d'arte* 27, 1933/34, pp. 337-50.
Cole, B. *Agnolo Gaddi*. Oxford, 1977.
——. *Masaccio and the Art of Early Renaissance Florence*. Bloomington and London, 1980.
Cole, D. E. "Fra Angelico: His Role in Quattrocento Painting and Problems of Chronology." Ph.D. diss., University of Virginia, 1977.
Cole Ahl, D. "Fra Angelico: A New Chronology for the 1420s." *Zeitschrift für Kunstgeschichte* 43, 1980, pp. 360-81.
——. "Fra Angelico: A New Chronology for the 1430s." *Zeitschrift für Kunstgeschichte* 44, 1981, pp. 133-58.

Colnaghi, D. E. *A Dictionary of Florentine Painters from the 13th to the 17th Centuries*. Edited by P. G. Konody and S. Brinton. London, 1928.

Conti, A. "Quadri alluvionati, 1333, 1557, 1966." *Paragone* 19, no. 215, 1968, pp. 3-22.

Copenhagen. *Royal Museum of Fine Arts, Catalogue of Old Foreign Paintings*. Copenhagen, 1951.

Cornell, H. "The Iconography of the Nativity of Christ." *Uppsala Universitets Årsskrift*, 1924, pp. 1-101.

Cornu, S. *Catalogue des tableaux, des sculptures de la Renaissance et des majoliques du Musée Napoléon III*. Paris, 1862.

Covi, D. A. "Lettering in Fifteenth Century Florentine Painting." *Art Bulletin* 45, 1963, pp. 1-17.

Cracow. *La peinture italienne des XIVe et XVe siècles: Exposition des musées et des collections polonaises avec concours de la Galerie Nationale de Prague et du Musée de l'Art à Bucarest*. Edited by A. Różycka-Bryzek. Musée National de Cracovie, Galerie Czartoryski, Cracow, 1961.

Crowe, J. A., and G. B. Cavalcaselle. *A New History of Painting in Italy*. Vols. 1 and 2. London, 1864.

——. *Storia della pittura in Italia*. Vols. 1 and 2. Florence, 1883.

——. *A New History of Painting in Italy*. Edited by L. Douglas. Vols. 1 and 2. London, 1903.

D'Achiardi, P. *I quadri primitivi della Pinacoteca Vaticana*. Rome, 1929.

Dami, L. "Tesori d'arte ignorati o inediti, Una tavola di Lorenzo Monaco." *Il Marzocco* 18, 26 October 1913, p. 1.

D'Ancona, P. *La miniatura fiorentina*. 2 vols. Florence, 1914.

——. *La miniature italienne*. Paris, 1925.

Davanzati, Don B. "Istoria della Venerabile Basilica della Sant.^ma Trinità di Firenze." MS., Library of the Monastery of Santa Trinita, Florence. 1740.

Davies, M. "Lorenzo Monaco's 'Coronation of the Virgin' in London." *Critica d'arte* 29, 1949, pp. 202-210.

——. *The Earlier Italian Schools, National Gallery Catalogues*. London, 1951. 2d ed., rev. 1961.

Davisson, D. D. "The Advent of the Magi: A Study of the Transformations in Religious Images." Ph.D. diss., The Johns Hopkins University, 1971.

——. "The Iconology of the S. Trinita Sacristy, 1418-1435: A Study of the Private and Public Functions of Religious Art in the Early Quattrocento." *Art Bulletin* 57, 1975, pp. 315-34.

De Benedetti, M. "The Casino Rospigliosi and Private Collection of Prince Pallavicini in Rome." *Apollo* 16, no. 94, 1932, pp. 141-48.

De Benedictis, C. "Su un affresco di Spinello Aretino: Vicende di una committenza." In *Scritti di storia dell'arte in onore di Federico Zeri*. Vol. 2, Milan, 1984, pp. 55-59.

Degenhart, B. "Zur Ausstellung der Sammlung Otto Lanz in Rijksmuseum von Amsterdam." *Pantheon* 27, 1941, pp. 34-40.

Degenhart, B., and A. Schmitt. *Corpus der italienischen Zeichnungen, 1300-1450*. Pt. 1, vols. 1-4. Berlin, 1968.

Delécluze, E.-J. *Saggio intorno a Leonardo da Vinci*. Edited by C. Pini and G. Milanesi. Siena, 1844.

Della Santa, M., ed. and trans. *Vita di San Romualdo*. Arezzo, 1963.

Del Migliore, F. L. *Firenze, città nobilissima*. Florence, 1684.

De Ricci, S. *Description raisonnée des peintures du Louvre*. Vol. 1, *Ecoles étrangères, Italie et Espagne*. Paris, 1913.

Detroit. *Master Drawings of the Italian Renaissance*. Detroit Institute of Arts, 1960.

Devisse, J., and M. Mollat. *L'image du noir dans l'art occidental*. 2 vols. Paris, 1979.

Donati, Don G. G. *L'Ordine Camaldolese*. Arezzo, 1964.

Donop, L. von. *Verzeichnis der gräflich Raczynskischen Kunstsammlungen in der Königlichen National-Galerie*. Berlin, 1886.

Douglas, L. *Fra Angelico*. London, 1900.

Dubler, E. *Das Bild des heiligen Benedikt bis zum Ausgang des Mittelalters*. Erzabtei St. Ottilien, 1953.

Earp, F. R. *A Descriptive Catalogue of the Pictures in the Fitzwilliam Museum*. London, 1902.

Eisenberg, M. "The Origins and Development of the Early Style of Lorenzo Monaco." Ph.D. diss., Princeton University, 1954.

——. "A Crucifix and a Man of Sorrows by Lorenzo Monaco." *Art Quarterly* 18, 1955, pp. 44-49.

——. "Un frammento smarrito dell'*Annunciazione* di Lorenzo Monaco nell'Accademia di Firenze." *Bollettino d'arte* 41, 1956, pp. 333-35.

——. "An Early Altarpiece by Lorenzo Monaco." *Art Bulletin* 39, 1957, pp. 49-52

——. "Letter to the Editor." *Art Bulletin* 41, 1959, p. 127.

——. "The *Coronation of the Virgin* by Mariotto di Nardo." *Minneapolis Institute of Arts Bulletin* 55, 1966, pp. 9-24.

——. "Some Monastic and Liturgical Allusions in an Early Work of Lorenzo Monaco." in *Monasticism and the Arts.* Edited by T. G. Verdon and J. Dally. Syracuse, 1984, pp. 271-89.

Eisler, C. *The Seeing Hand: A Treasury of Great Master Drawings.* New York, 1975.

Emiliani, A. *La Pinacoteca Nazionale di Bologna.* Bologna, 1967.

Fahy, E. "Some Early Italian Pictures in the Gambier-Parry Collection." *Burlington Magazine* 109, 1967, pp. 128-39.

——. "A Madonna by Spinello Aretino." *Bulletin of the Cleveland Museum of Art* 65, 1978, pp. 261-67.

——. "On Lorenzo di Niccolò." *Apollo* 108, no. 202, 1978, pp. 374-81.

——. "Babbott's Choices." *Apollo* 115, no. 242, 1982, pp. 238-43.

Fantozzi, F. *Nuova guida ovvero descrizione storico-artistico-critica della città e contorni di Firenze.* Florence, 1842.

Farulli, Don G. *Istoria cronologica del nobile et antico Monastero degli Angioli di Firenze.* Lucca, 1710.

——. *Teatro storico del Sacro Eremo di Camaldoli.* Lucca, 1723.

Fehm, S. A., Jr. *Luca di Tommè, A Sienese Fourteenth-Century Painter.* Carbondale and Edwardsville, 1986.

Fenton, J. "The Martyrdom of Pope Caius." *Archivero I,* Santa Barbara Museum of Art, 1973, pp. 9-21.

——. "The Martyrdom of Pope Caius." *Gallery Notes, Santa Barbara Museum of Art* 2, 1977 (unpaginated).

Ferri, P. N. *Catalogo dei disegni esposti al pubblico nel corridoio del Ponte Vecchio nella R. Galleria degli Uffizi.* Florence, 1881.

——. *Catalogo riassuntivo della Raccolta di disegni . . . R. Galleria degli Uffizi in Firenze.* Rome, 1890.

Florence. *Mostra del Tesoro di Firenze Sacra.* Convento di San Marco, Florence, 1933.

——. *Mostra delle opere del Beato Angelico nel quinto centenario della morte (1455-1955).* Florence, 1955.

——. *III Mostra di affreschi staccati.* Florence, 1959.

——. *Gli Uffizi, Catalogo generale.* Florence, 1979.

——. *Codici liturgici miniati dei Benedettini in Toscana.* Centro d'Incontro della Certosa di Firenze, Florence, 1982.

——. *Iconografia di San Benedetto nella pittura della Toscana.* Centro d'Incontro della Certosa di Firenze, Florence, 1982.

Follini, V., and M. Rastrelli. *Firenze antica e moderna illustrata.* 8 vols. Florence, 1789-1802.

Fortunio, A. *Historiarum Camaldulensium.* Venice, 1579.

Fossi Todorow, M. *L'Italia dalle origini a Pisanello (I disegni dei maestri).* Milan, 1970.

Fredericksen, B. B., and F. Zeri. *Census of Pre-Nineteenth-Century Italian Paintings in North American Public Collections.* Cambridge, Massachusetts, 1972.

Fremantle, R. *Florentine Gothic Painters.* London, 1975.

Freytag, C. "Italienische Skulptur um 1400: Untersuchungen zu den Einflussbereichen." *Metropolitan Museum Journal* 7, 1973, pp. 5-36.

Friedländer, M. J. *Die Sammlung Richard von Kaufmann, Berlin.* Vol. 1, *Die italienische Gemälde.* Berlin, 1917.

Frizzoni, G. *La Galleria Morelli in Bergamo.* Bergamo, 1892.

——. *L'arte in Bergamo e l'Accademia Carrara.* Bergamo, 1897.

——. "Ricordi di un viaggio artistico oltralpe." *L'Arte* 5, 1902, pp. 290-301.

Fry, R. E. "Florentine Painting of the Fourteenth Century." *The Monthly Review* 3, June, 1901, pp. 112-34.

——. "Pictures in the Collection of Sir Hubert Parry, at Highnam Court, near Gloucester—I." *Burlington Magazine* 2, 1903, pp. 117-31.

Gabelentz, H.-C. von der. *Italienische Malerei der Vor- und Frührenaissance im Staatlichen Lindenau-Museum Altenburg.* Altenburg, 1955.

Gamba, C. *Catalogo illustrato della Fondazione Horne.* Florence, 1921.

——. "La Mostra del Tesoro di Firenze Sacra, La pittura." *Bollettino d'arte* 27, 1933/34, pp. 145-63.

——. *Il Museo Horne a Firenze.* Florence, 1961.

Gardner von Teuffel, C. "Lorenzo Monaco, Filippo Lippi und Filippo Brunelleschi: die Erfindung der Renaissancepala." *Zeitschrift für Kunstgeschichte* 45, 1982, pp. 1-30.

——. "From Polyptych to Pala: Some Structural Considerations." In *La pittura nel XIV e XV secolo, Il contributo dell'analisi tecnica alla storia dell'arte.* Edited by H. W. van Os and J.R.J. van Asperen de Boer. Bologna, 1983, pp. 323-44.

Gaye, G. *Carteggio inedito d'artisti dei secoli XIV, XV, XVI.* Vol. 2. Florence, 1840.

Gealt, A. M. "Lorenzo di Niccolò." Ph.D. diss., Indiana University, 1979.

George, M. *Catalogue, Musée des Augustins*. Toulouse, 1864.

Gerevich, T. *A Krakòi Czartoryski-Képtàr Olasz Mesterei*. Budapest, 1918.

[Ghiberti]. *Lorenzo Ghiberti, 'materia e ragionamenti.'* Museo dell'Accademia e Museo di San Marco, Florence, 1978.

——. *Lorenzo Ghiberti nel suo tempo, Atti del Convegno Internazionale di Studi*. 2 vols. Florence, 1980.

Giabbani, A., O.S.B. *L'eremo, vita e spiritualità eremitica nel monachismo Camaldolese primitivo*. Brescia, 1945.

Giglioli, O. *Empoli artistica*. Florence, 1906.

——. *Catalogo delle cose d'arte e di antichità d'Italia*. Rome, 1933.

Gilbert, C. "Peintres et menuisiers au début de la Renaissance en Italie." *Revue de l'art* 37, 1977, pp. 9-28.

Giolli, R. "Opere d'arte ignote o poco note." *Rivista d'arte* 8, 1912, pp. 25-29.

Glaser, C. "The Louvre Coronation and Early Angelico." *Gazette des beaux-arts*, 6th ser., vol. 22, 1942, pp. 149-64.

Goetz, H. "Oriental Types and Scenes in Renaissance and Baroque Painting—I." *Burlington Magazine* 73, 1938, pp. 50-62.

Goldner, G. R. *Niccolò and Piero Lamberti*. New York, 1978.

Golzio, V. "Lorenzo Monaco e una sua nuova opera." *Corriere d'Italia* 22, no. 220, Rome, 16 September 1927, p. 3.

——. *Lorenzo Monaco*. Rome, 1931.

González-Palacios, A. "Indagini su Lorenzo Monaco." *Paragone* 21, no. 241, 1970, pp. 27-36.

Goodison, J. W., and G. H. Robertson. *Fitzwilliam Museum, Cambridge, Catalogue of Paintings*. Vol. 2, *Italian Schools*. Cambridge, 1967.

Gore, St. J. *The Art of Painting in Florence and Siena from 1250 to 1500*. Wildenstein, London, 1965.

Grassi, R. *Descrizione storica e artistica di Pisa*. Pisa, 1837.

Gronau, H. "The Earliest Works of Lorenzo Monaco—I and II." *Burlington Magazine* 92, 1950, pp. 183-88 and 217-22.

Gualandi, M. *Memorie originali italiane risguardanti le belle arti*. Ser. 6. Bologna, 1845.

Guasti, G. *I quadri della Galleria . . . del Comune di Prato*. Prato, 1888.

Harck, F. "Quadri di maestri italiani in possesso di privati a Berlino." *Archivio storico dell'arte* 2, 1889, pp. 204-214.

Hatfield, R. "The Compagnia de' Magi." *Journal of the Warburg and Courtauld Institutes* 33, 1970, pp. 107-61.

——. *Botticelli's Uffizi "Adoration."* Princeton, 1976.

Hautecoeur, L. *Musée National du Louvre, Catalogue des peintures*. Vol. 2, *Ecole italienne et école espagnole*. Paris, 1926.

Hibbard, H. *The Metropolitan Museum of Art*. New York, 1980.

Hills, J.G.P. "Studies in the Use of Light in Central Italian Painting: Cavallini to Masaccio." Ph.D. thesis, Courtauld Institute of Art, University of London, 1976.

Horster, M. *Andrea del Castagno*. Ithaca, 1980.

Houston. *The Edith A. and Percy S. Straus Collection*. Museum of Fine Arts, Houston, 1945.

Howett, J. "Two Panels by the Master of the St. George Codex in The Cloisters." *Metropolitan Museum Journal* 11, 1976. pp. 5-102.

Ishinabe, M. "La Maestà di Simone Martini e la diffusione del Bambino stante e benedicente nell'arte italiana." *Antichità viva* 19, no. 1, 1980, pp. 7-13.

Jacobus da Voragine. *Leggenda aurea. Volgarizzamento toscano del Trecento*. Edited by A. Levasti. 3 vols. Florence, 1924-26.

——. *The Golden Legend of Jacobus de Voragine*. Translated and edited by G. Ryan and H. Ripperger. 2 vols. London and New York, 1941.

Janson, H. W. *The Sculpture of Donatello*. 2 vols. Princeton, 1957. 2d ed., 1 vol., Princeton, 1963.

Jarves, J. J. *Descriptive Catalogue of "Old Masters" collected by James Jackson Jarves, to Illustrate the History of Painting from A.D. 1200 to the Best Periods of Italian Art*. Cambridge, Massachusetts, 1860.

John G. Johnson Collection. Catalogue of Paintings. Philadelphia, 1941.

John G. Johnson Collection. Catalogue of Italian Paintings. Philadelphia, 1966.

Johnson, B. B., and N. E. Muller. "A Study of Technical Aspects and Stylistic Sources of the Martyrdom of Pope Caius by Lorenzo Monaco." *Archivero I*, Santa Barbara Museum of Art, 1973, pp. 23-56.

Jones, R. "Palla Strozzi e la Sagrestia di Santa Trinita." *Rivista d'arte* 37, ser. 4, vol. 1, 1984, pp. 9-106.

Kaftal, G. *Iconography of the Saints in Tuscan Painting*. Florence, 1952.

Kehrer, H. L. *Die Heiligen drei Könige in Literatur und Kunst.* 2 vols. Leipzig, 1908-1909.

Khvoshinsky, B., and M. Salmi. *I pittori toscani dal XIII al XVI secolo.* 2 vols. Rome, 1914.

Kiel, H., and D. Neri. *Paesaggi inattesi.* Milan, 1952.

Klesse, B. *Seidenstoffe in der italienischen Malerei des 14. Jahrhunderts.* Bern, 1967.

Krautheimer, R. *Lorenzo Ghiberti.* Princeton, 1956. 2d printing with corrections. 2 vols. Princeton, 1970.

Kreytenberg, G. "Giovanni Fetti und die Porta dei Canonici des florentiner Domes." *Mitteilungen des Kunsthistorischen Institutes in Florenz* 20, 1976, pp. 128-58.

——. "La prima opera del Ghiberti e la scultura fiorentina del Trecento." In *Lorenzo Ghiberti nel suo tempo. Atti del Convegno Internazionale di Studi.* Vol. 1, 1980, pp. 59-78.

——. "The Unexpected Apostle." *Burlington Magazine* 123, 1981, pp. 3-7.

Krohn, M. *Italienske billeder i Danmark.* Copenhagen, 1910.

Kultzen, R. *Alte Pinakothek München, Katalog V: Italienische Malerei.* Munich, 1975.

Laclotte, M. *De Giotto à Bellini: Les primitifs italiens dans les musées de France.* Orangerie des Tuileries, Paris, 1956.

Laclotte, M., and E. Mognetti. *Inventaire des collections publiques françaises 21: Avignon - Musée du Petit Palais, Peinture italienne.* 2d ed. Paris, 1977.

Laderchi, C. *Descrizione della Quadreria Costabili.* Ferrara, 1841.

Ladis, A. *Taddeo Gaddi.* Columbia, Missouri, and London, 1982.

Lafenestre, G. and E. Richtenberger. *La peinture en Europe: Florence.* Paris, n.d. [1895].

Lanzi, L. *Storia pittorica della Italia.* 2d ed. Vol. 1, Bassano, 1795.

Larner, J. *Culture and Society in Italy 1290-1420.* London, 1971.

Lazareff, V. "Una Madonna di Lorenzo Monaco a Mosca." *L'Arte* 27, 1914, pp. 124-26.

Levi D'Ancona, M. *The Iconography of the Immaculate Conception in the Middle Ages and Early Renaissance.* College Art Association of America, New York, 1957.

——. "Some New Attributions to Lorenzo Monaco." *Art Bulletin* 40, 1958, pp. 175-91.

——. "Matteo Torelli." *Commentari* 9, 1958, pp. 244-58.

——. "Letter to the Editor." *Art Bulletin* 41, 1959, pp. 128-29.

——. "Don Silvestro dei Gherarducci e il 'Maestro delle Canzoni,' " *Rivista d'arte* 32, 1959, pp. 3-37.

——. "Bartolomeo di Fruosino." *Art Bulletin* 43, 1961, pp. 81-97.

——. *Miniatura e miniatori a Firenze dal XIV al XVI secolo.* Florence, 1962.

——. "I corali di S. Maria degli Angeli, ora nella Biblioteca Laurenziana, e le miniature da essi asportate." In *Miscellanea di studi in memoria di Anna Saitta Revignas.* Florence, 1978, pp. 213-35.

——. "Arte e politica: L'Interdetto, gli Albizzi e la miniatura fiorentina del tardo Trecento." In *La miniatura italiana in età romanica e gotica, Atti del I Congresso di Storia della Miniatura Italiana.* Florence, 1979, pp. 461-87.

Lindberg, H. *To the Problem of Masolino and Masaccio.* 2 vols. Stockholm, 1931.

Lloyd, C. *A Catalogue of the Earlier Italian Paintings in the Ashmolean Museum.* Oxford, 1977.

Loeser, C. "Ueber einige italienische Handzeichnungen des berliner Kupferstichkabinetts." *Repertorium für Kunstwissenschaft* 25, 1902, pp. 348-59.

Logan Berenson, M. "Dipinti italiani a Cracovia." *Rassegna d'arte* 15, 1915, pp. 1-4.

London. *Exhibition of Italian Art 1200-1900.* Royal Academy of Arts, London, 1930.

——. *A Commemorative Catalogue of the Exhibition of Italian Art held in the Galleries of the Royal Academy, Burlington House, London, January-March, 1930.* Edited by Lord Balniel and K. Clark, 2 vols. London, 1931.

——. *Italian Art and Britain.* Winter Exhibition, Royal Academy of Arts, London, 1960.

——. *Early Italian Paintings and Works of Art, 1300-1480.* Matthiesen, London, 1983.

Longhi, R. "Ricerche su Giovanni di Francesco." *Pinacotecha* 1, 1928, pp. 34-48.

——. "Fatti di Masolino e di Masaccio." *Critica d'arte* 25/26, 1940, pp. 145-91. Reprinted in *Opere complete di Roberto Longhi.* Vol. 8, pt. 1, Florence, 1975, pp. 3-65.

——. "Primitivi italiani a Stoccarda." *Paragone* 1, no. 7, 1950, pp. 46-48.

——. "Uno sguardo alle fotografie della Mostra 'Italian Art and Britain' alla Royal Academy di Londra." *Paragone* 11, no. 125, 1960, pp. 59-61.

——. "Una 'riconsiderazione' dei primitivi italiani a Londra." *Paragone* 16, no. 183, 1965, pp. 8-16.

Lucerne. *Meisterwerke aus den Sammlungen des Fürsten von Liechtenstein*. Lucerne, 1948.

Madsen, K. *A Collection of Paintings Exhibited in the Danish Museum of Fine Art*. Copenhagen, 1920.

Maginnis, H.B.J. "A Lorenzettian Crucifix in Cortona." *RACAR* 7, 1981, pp. 59-61.

Mallory, M. "Toward a Chronology for Paolo di Giovanni Fei." *Art Bulletin* 46, 1964, pp. 529-36.

——. *The Sienese Painter Paolo di Giovanni Fei*. New York, 1976.

Mancinelli, F., and E. Nahmad. *Musei Vaticani: Pinacoteca*. Florence, 1981.

Marchese, V. *Memorie dei più insigni pittori, scultori ed architetti Domenicani*. Vol. 1. Florence, 1854.

Marchini, G. *Le vetrate italiane*. Milan, 1955.

——. *La Galleria Comunale di Prato*. Florence, 1958.

——. *Filippo Lippi*. Milan, 1975.

Marcucci, L. *Gallerie Nazionali di Firenze: I dipinti toscani del secolo XIV*. Rome, 1965.

Mark, P. *Africans in European Eyes: The Portrayal of Black Africans in Fourteenth and Fifteenth Century Europe*. Syracuse, New York, 1974.

Marle, R. van. *The Development of the Italian Schools of Painting*. Vol. 3. The Hague, 1924; Vol. 9. The Hague, 1927; Vol. 10. The Hague, 1928.

——. "La pittura all'Esposizione d'arte antica italiana di Amsterdam." *Bollettino d'arte* 28, 1934/35, pp. 293-313.

Martindale, A. "Italian Art and the International Gothic Style." *Apollo* 76, no. 4, 1962, pp. 277-82.

Martini, A. *La Galleria dell'Accademia di Ravenna*. Venice, 1959.

Mauceri, E. *La Regia Pinacoteca di Bologna*. Bologna, 1931.

Meditations on the Life of Christ. Translated and edited by I. Ragusa and R. B. Green. Princeton, 1961.

Meiss, M. "A Dugento Altarpiece at Antwerp." *Burlington Magazine* 71, 1937, pp. 14-25.

——. "Light as Form and Symbol in Some Fifteenth-Century Paintings." *Art Bulletin* 27, 1945, pp. 175-81.

——. "Italian Primitives at Konopiště." *Art Bulletin* 28, 1946, pp. 1-16.

——. "Four Panels by Lorenzo Monaco." *Burlington Magazine* 100, 1958, pp. 191-98.

——. "Letter to the Editor: Four Panels by Lorenzo Monaco." *Burlington Magazine* 100, 1958, p. 359.

——. "Notes on Three Linked Sienese Styles." *Art Bulletin* 45, 1963, pp. 47-48.

——. *Painting in Florence and Siena after the Black Death*. 2d ed. New York, 1964.

——. *French Painting in the Time of Jean de Berry: The Late Fourteenth Century and the Patronage of the Duke*. 2 vols. London, 1967.

——. *French Painting in the Time of Jean de Berry: The Boucicaut Master*. London, 1968.

——. *The Great Age of Fresco: Discoveries, Recoveries, and Survivals*. New York, 1970.

——. *French Painting in the Time of Jean de Berry: The Limbourgs and Their Contemporaries*. 2 vols. New York, 1974.

——. "Scholarship and Penitence in the Early Renaissance: The Image of St. Jerome." *Pantheon* 32, 1974, pp. 134-40.

Mendelsohn, H. *Fra Filippo Lippi*. Berlin, 1909.

Micheletti, E. *Masolino da Panicale*. Milan, 1959.

Middeldorf, U. "Die Ausstellung kirchlicher Kunst im Kloster von S. Marco in Florenz." *Pantheon* 11, 1933, pp. 194-97.

Milanesi, G. *Memoria intorno a Pietro Nelli*. Florence, 1872.

——. *Catalogue des tableaux, meubles et objets d'art formant la Galerie de M. le Chev. Toscanelli*. Florence, 1883.

Milliken, W. M. "Miniatures by Lorenzo Monaco and Francesco del Cherico." *Bulletin of the Cleveland Museum of Art* 37, 1950, pp. 43-46.

Mittarelli, G. B., and D. A. Costadoni. *Annales Camaldulenses*. Vol. 6. Venice, 1761.

Montebello, G.-P. de. "Four Prophets by Lorenzo Monaco." *Metropolitan Museum of Art Bulletin* 25, no. 4, 1966, pp. 155-68.

Moreni, D. *Notizie istoriche dei contorni di Firenze*. Vol. 6. Florence, 1795.

Moriondo, M. *Arezzo, Mostra d'arte sacra*. Arezzo, 1950.

Mosco, M., et al. *La Maddalena tra sacro e profano*. Milan and Florence, 1986.

Muller, N. E. "Examination and Conservation of an Altarpiece attributed to Lorenzo Monaco." *Fine Arts Gallery of San Diego, Annual Report*, 1972, pp. 23-30.

——. "Three Methods of Modelling the Virgin's Mantle in Early Italian Painting." *Journal of the American Institute for Conservation* 17, 1978, pp. 10-18.

Munich. *Bayerische Staatsgemäldesammlungen: Alte Pinakothek*. Munich, 1983.

Murray, P. *An Index of Attributions made in Tuscan Sources before Vasari*. Florence, 1959.

——. "Trecento and Quattrocento; a notable show in London." *Apollo* 81, no. 38, 1965, pp. 282-87.

Nocioni, Padre T. A. *La Basilica di S. Trinita in Firenze*. Florence, 1980.

Nordenfalk, C., G. Vikan, et al. *Mediaeval and Renaissance Miniatures from the National Gallery of Art*. Washington, D.C., 1975.

Norris, C. "The Disaster at Flakturm Friedrichshain; a Chronicle and List of Paintings." *Burlington Magazine* 94, 1952, pp. 337-46.

Oertel, R. "Wandmalerei und Zeichnung in Italien." *Mitteilungen des Kunsthistorischen Institutes in Florenz* 5, 1940, pp. 217-314.

——. *Frühe italienische Tafelmalerei*. Württembergischen Staatsgalerie, Stuttgart, 1950.

——. *Frühe italienische Malerei in Altenburg*. Berlin, 1961.

Offner, R. *Italian Primitives at Yale University*. New Haven, 1927.

——. *Studies in Florentine Painting*. New York, 1927. Reprinted with introductory essay by B. Cole, New York, 1972.

——. "The Mostra del Tesoro di Firenze Sacra—II." *Burlington Magazine* 63, 1933, pp. 166-78.

——. *A Critical and Historical Corpus of Florentine Painting*. Sec. III, Vols. I-VII; and Sec. IV, Vols. I-II. New York, 1930-62.

Offner, R., and K. Steinweg. *A Critical and Historical Corpus of Florentine Painting*. Sec. IV, Vols. III-VI. New York, 1965-79.

Offner, R. *A Critical and Historical Corpus of Florentine Painting: A Legacy of Attributions*. Edited by H.B.J. Maginnis. New York, 1981.

Olcott-Heywood, L. *Guide to Siena*. Siena, 1903.

Olschki, L. "Asiatic Exoticism in Italian Art of the Early Renaissance." *Art Bulletin* 26, 1944, pp. 95-106.

Olsen, H. *Italian Paintings and Sculpture in Denmark*. Copenhagen, 1961.

——. "Italienske malerier fra det 15. og 16. Århundrede i Thorvaldsens Museum." *Meddelelser fra Thorvaldsens Museum*, 1965, pp. 51-63.

Orlandi, S., O.P. *Beato Angelico*. Florence, 1964.

Os, H. W. van. "Schnee in Siena." *Nederlands Kunsthistorisch Jaarboek* 19, 1968, pp. 1-50.

——. *Marias Demut und Verherrlichung in der sienesischen Malerei*. The Hague, 1969.

——. "Andrea di Bartolo's Madonna of Humility." *M, A Quarterly Review of The Montreal Museum of Fine Arts* 6, no. 3, 1974, pp. 19-27.

——. "Discoveries and rediscoveries in early Italian painting." *Arte cristiana* 71, 1983, pp. 69-80.

——. *Sienese Altarpieces 1215-1460, Form, Content, Function*. Vol. 1: 1215-1344. Groningen, 1984.

Os, H. W. van, and M. Prakken. *The Florentine Paintings in Holland, 1300-1500*. Amsterdam, 1974.

Ottino della Chiesa, A. *Accademia Carrara*. Bergamo, 1955. 2d ed., 1967.

Paatz, W., and E. Paatz. *Die Kirchen von Florenz*. 6 vols. Frankfurt a.M., 1940-1954.

Padoa Rizzo, A. "Sul polittico della Cappella Ardinghelli in Santa Trinita, di Giovanni Toscani." *Antichità viva* 21, no. 1, 1982, pp. 5-10.

Pagnani, A. *Storia dei Benedettini Camaldolesi*. Sassoferrato, 1949.

——. *Vita di S. Romualdo abbate*. Camaldoli (Poppi), 1967.

Palumbo, G. *Collezione Federico Mason Perkins*. Sacro Convento di San Francesco, Assisi, 1973.

Panczenko, R. "Cultura umanistica di Gentile da Fabriano." *Artibus et historiae* 8, 1983, pp. 27-75.

Panofsky, E. *Early Netherlandish Painting*. 2 vols. Cambridge, Massachusetts, 1964.

Paolucci, A. *Il Museo della Collegiata di S. Andrea in Empoli*. Florence, 1985.

Paris. *Exposition de l'art italien de Cimabue à Tiepolo*. Petit Palais, Paris, 1935.

——. *Dessins florentins du Trecento et du Quattrocento*. Musée du Louvre, Paris, 1952.

Parronchi, A. *Studi su la dolce prospettiva*. Milan, 1964.

Pasadena. *Selected Paintings at the Norton Simon Museum, Pasadena, California*. Introduced by F. Herrmann. London, 1980.

Perkins, F. M. "Pitture senesi negli Stati Uniti." *Rassegna d'arte senese* 1, 1905, pp. 74-78.

——. "Note su alcuni quadri del 'Museo Cristiano' nel Vaticano." *Rassegna d'arte* 6, 1906, pp. 106-108.

——. "Nuovi appunti sulla Galleria delle Belle Arti di Siena." *La Balzana* 2, 1928, pp. 143-61.

Peters, C. T. "Rossello di Jacopo Franchi: Portrait of a Florentine Painter, ca. 1376-1456." Ph.D. diss., Indiana University, 1981.

Pettenati, S. *I vetri dorati graffiti e i vetri dipinti del Museo Civico di Torino*. Turin, 1978.

Pieraccini, E. *Catalogue da la Galerie des Offices à Florence*. Florence, 1901.

——. *Catalogo della R. Galleria degli Uffizi*. Florence, 1907.

Pigler, A. *A Régi Képtár katalógusa—Orszagos Szép-*

művészeti Múzeum. Budapest, 1954. Revised German ed., Budapest, 1968.
Pillsbury, E. P. *Florence and the Arts: Five Centuries of Patronage*. Cleveland Museum of Art, Cleveland, 1971.
Pini, C. *Catalogo delle tavole dell'antica scuola senese . . . esistenti nell'I. e R. Istituto di Belle Arti di Siena*. Siena, 1842.
Pini, C., and G. Milanesi. *La scrittura di artisti italiani, secoli XIV-XVII*. Vol. 1. Rome, 1876.
Pittaluga, M. *Filippo Lippi*. Florence, 1949.
Platt, D. F., and F. Newlin Price. *The Collection of Frank Lusk Babbott*. New York, 1934.
Plehn, A. L. *Farbensymmetrie und Farbenwechsel*. Strassburg, 1911.
Podestà, A. "Mostra di capolavori salvati dalla guerra." *Emporium* 106, November-December 1947, pp. 107-113.
Poggi, G. "La chiesa di S. Bartolommeo a Monte Oliveto." *Miscellanea d'arte* 1, 1903, pp. 57-64.
——. "La Compagnia del Bigallo." *Rivista d'arte* 2, 1904, pp. 189-202 and 235-38.
——. *Il Bigallo*. Florence, 1905.
Pope-Hennessy, J. *Sassetta*. London, 1939.
——. *Paolo Uccello*. London, 1950. 2d ed., 1969.
——. *Fra Angelico*. London, 1952. 2d ed., Ithaca, 1974.
——. *Italian Gothic Sculpture*. London, 1955. 2d ed., 1972.
——. "The Interaction of Painting and Sculpture in Florence in the Fifteenth Century." *Journal of the Royal Society of Arts* 117, 1969, pp. 406-424.
——. *The Study and Criticism of Italian Sculpture*. New York, 1980.
——. "Some Italian Primitives." *Apollo* 118, no. 257, 1983, pp. 10-15.
Popham, A. E. *Italian Drawings Exhibited at the Royal Academy, Burlington House*. London, 1931.
Porçal, P. "Letter to the Editor." *Art Bulletin* 58, 1976, p. 474.
Posse, H. *Die Gemäldegalerie des Kaiser-Friedrich-Museums, Königliche Museen zu Berlin*. Vol. 1, *Die romanischen Länder*. Berlin, 1909.
Pouncey, P. "An Initial Letter by Mariotto di Nardo." *Burlington Magazine* 88, 1946, pp. 71-72.
Poznań. *Muzeum Narodowe w Poznaniu, Galeria Atanazego Raczyńskiego*. Poznań, 1981.
Preiser, A. *Das Entstehen und die Entwicklung der Predella in der italienischen Malerei*. Hildesheim and New York, 1973.
Previtali, G. *La fortuna dei primitivi, dal Vasari ai neoclassici*. Turin, 1964.
Procacci, U. "L'incendio della Chiesa del Carmine del 1771." *Rivista d'arte* 14, 1932, pp. 141–232.
——. "Opere inedite alla Mostra del Tesoro di Firenze Sacra." *Rivista d'arte* 15, 1933, pp. 224-44.
——. "Gherardo Starnina." *Rivista d'arte* 15, 1933, pp. 151-90; 17, 1935, pp. 333-84; 18, 1936, pp. 77-94.
——. *La Galleria dell'Accademia di Firenze*. Rome, 1936. 2d ed., 1951.
——. *Mostra di opere d'arte trasportate a Firenze durante la guerra e di opere d'arte restaurate*. Florence, 1947.
——. *Sinopie e affreschi*. Milan, 1961.
——. *The Great Age of Fresco: Giotto to Pontormo*. New York, 1968.
Pudelko, G. "The Minor Masters of the Chiostro Verde." *Art Bulletin* 17, 1935, pp. 71-89.
——. "The Maestro del Bambino Vispo." *Art in America* 26, 1938, pp. 47-63.
——. "The Stylistic Development of Lorenzo Monaco." *Burlington Magazine* 73, 1938, pp. 237-48; and 74, 1939, pp. 76-81.
Pujmanová, O. "Italian Primitives in Czechoslovak collections." *Burlington Magazine* 119, 1977, pp. 536-50.
——. "Lorenzo Monaco v Národní Galerii v Praze." *Umění* 25, 1977, pp. 35-43.
——. "Dvě Florentské Desky z Pražské Národní Galerie." *Umění* 27, 1979, pp. 229-35.
Quandt, J. G. von, and H. W. Schulz. *Beschreibung der im neuen Mittelgebäude des Pohlhofs befindlichen Kunstgegenstände*. Altenburg, 1848.
Quintavalle, A. "Tavolette del tardo Trecento e del Quattrocento nella Pinacoteca del Museo Nazionale di Napoli." *Bollettino d'arte* 25, 1931-32, pp. 397-404.
Ragghianti Collobi, L. *Il Libro de'Disegni del Vasari*. 2 vols. Florence, 1974.
Ramirez di Montalvo, A. "Catalogo dei Disegni scelti della R. Galleria di Firenze." MS., Gabinetto Disegni e Stampe, Florence, 1849.
Reinach, S. *Répertoire de peintures du moyen-âge et de la Renaissance*. 6 vols. Paris, 1905-1923.
Reiset, M. F. *Notice des tableaux du Musée Napoléon III*. Paris, 1863.
Ricci, C. *La Galleria di Ravenna*. Ravenna, 1898.
——. *Raccolte artistiche di Ravenna*. Bergamo, 1905.
Richa, G. *Notizie artistiche delle chiese fiorentine*. 9 vols. Florence, 1754-1761.

Richter, J. P. *Catalogue of Pictures at Locko Park*. London, 1901.

Ridderbos, H.N.B. *Saint and Symbol, Images of Saint Jerome in early Italian Art*. Groningen, 1984.

Ridolfi, E. "La galleria dell'Arcispedale di S. Maria Nuova." In *Le gallerie nazionali italiane, Notizie e documenti*. Vol. 4, Rome, 1899, pp. 162-86.

Righi, G., and E. Landi. "Il contributo del Vasari alla storia della miniatura italiana." In *Il Vasari Storiografo e Artista, Atti del Congresso Internazionale nel IV Centenario della Morte*. Florence, 1974, pp. 395-403.

Rigoni, C. *Catalogo della R. Galleria degli Uffizi*. Florence, 1888 and 1891.

Rio, A.-F. *De l'art chrétien*. 2d ed. Vol. 1. Paris, 1861.

Robb, D. M. "The Iconography of the Annunciation in the Fourteenth and Fifteenth Centuries." *Art Bulletin* 18, 1936, pp. 480-526.

Robert, P., O.S.B. "Camaldules (Ordre des)." In *Dictionnaire de spiritualité ascétique et mystique, Doctrine et histoire*. Vol. 2. Paris, 1937, cols. 50-60.

Roditi, E. "The Destruction of the Berlin Museums." *Magazine of Art* 42, 1949, pp. 306-311.

Roschach, E. *Catalogue des collections de peinture du Musée de Toulouse*. Toulouse, 1920.

Rosenthal, E. "Una pittura di Lorenzo Monaco scoperta recentemente." *Commentari* 7, 1956, pp. 71-77.

Rosini, G. *Storia della pittura italiana*. Vol. 2. Pisa, 1848.

Rossi, F. *Mostra di arte sacra dalle diocesi di Firenze, Fiesole, e Prato*. Palazzo Strozzi, Florence, 1961.

——. *Il Museo Horne a Firenze*. Milan, 1966.

Rossi, F. *Accademia Carrara, Bergamo*. Bergamo, 1974.

Roth, A. G. *Die Gestirne in der Landschaftsmalerei des Abendlandes*. Bern, 1945.

Różycka-Bryzek, A. "Nowe artybucje kilku obrazów włoskich w Zbiorach Czartoryskich." *Biuletyn Historii Sztuki* 22, 1960, pp. 213-15.

——. "L'esposizione della pittura italiana del Trecento e Quattrocento nel Museo Nazionale a Cracovia-Galleria Czartoryski." *L'Arte* 27, 1962, pp. 115–19.

Ruda, J. *Filippo Lippi Studies, Naturalism, Style and Iconography in Early Renaissance Art*. New York and London, 1982.

Ruskin, John. *Mornings in Florence*. Orpington (Kent), 1875-1876. 2d ed., New York, 1889.

Russoli, F. *La Raccolta Berenson*. Milan, 1962.

——. "The Princes Pallavicini." In *Great Family Collections*. Edited by D. Cooper. New York, 1965, pp. 123-44.

Saalman, H. *The Church of Santa Trinita in Florence*. New York, 1966.

Salles, G. A., and D. Lion-Goldschmidt. *Adolphe Stoclet Collection*. Vol. 1, *Selection of the Works Belonging to Madame Féron-Stoclet*. Brussels, 1956.

Salmi, M. "Italia sconosciuta: Monte San Savino." *Emporium* 56, no. 336, 1922, pp. 351-60.

——. *La miniatura fiorentina gotica*. Rome, 1954.

——. *Italian Miniatures*. New York, 1954.

——. "Lorenzo Ghiberti e la pittura." In *Scritti di storia dell'arte in onore di Lionello Venturi*. Vol. 1, Rome, 1956, pp. 223-37.

——. *Il Beato Angelico*. Spoleto, 1958.

Salvini, R. "In margine ad Agnolo Gaddi." *Rivista d'arte* 16, 1934, pp. 205-228.

——. *L'arte di Agnolo Gaddi*. Florence, 1936.

Salvini, R., and L. Traverso. *The Predella from the XIIIth to the XVIth Centuries*. London, 1960.

San Diego, Fine Arts Society of, A Catalogue of European Paintings, 1300-1870. San Diego, 1947.

San Luigi, Ildephonso di. *Istoria genealogica delle famiglie de'Salimbeni di Siena e de'Marchesi Bartolini Salimbeni di Firenze*. In *Raccolta di tutte le prose fiorentine (Delizie degli eruditi toscani)*. Vol. 25. Florence, 1786.

Sandberg-Vavalà, E. *La croce dipinta italiana*. Verona, 1929.

——. "Early Italian Paintings in the Collection of Frank Channing Smith, Jr." *Worcester Art Museum Annual* 3, 1937/38, pp. 23-44.

——. "Reconstruction of a Predella." *Art in America* 27, 1939, pp. 105-11.

——. *Uffizi Studies, The Development of the Florentine School of Painting*. Florence, 1948.

——. *Studies in the Florentine Churches—I, Pre-Renaissance Period*. Florence, 1959.

Savelli, D. *Il Convento di S. Maria degli Angeli a Firenze*. Florence, 1983.

Schiller, G. *Ikonographie der christlichen Kunst*. 5 vols. Gütersloh, 1966-1980.

——. *Iconography of Christian Art*. Translated by J. Seligman. Vol. 1. London, 1971; vol. 2. London, 1972.

Schmarsow, A. *Masaccio Studien*, Kassel, 1895.

——. "Meister des XIV und XV Jahrhunderts im Lindenau-Museum zu Altenburg, II. Florentiner

Trecentisten." In *Festschrift zu Ehren des Kunsthistorischen Instituts in Florenz*. Leipzig, 1897, pp. 162-77.

——. "Maîtres italiens à la Galerie d'Altenburg et dans la collection A. de Montor." *Gazette des beaux-arts*, 3d period, 20, 1898, pp. 494-510.

Scholz, J. *Master Drawings, 1350-1800, from the Janos Scholz Collection*. New York, 1976.

Schubring, P. Review of O. Sirén, *Lorenzo Monaco*. In *Kunstchronik* 40, new series, 1906, pp. 174-75.

Seymour, C., Jr. *Sculpture in Italy, 1400 to 1500*. Harmondsworth, 1966.

——. *Early Italian Paintings in the Yale University Art Gallery*. New Haven and London, 1970.

——. *Jacopo della Quercia Sculptor*. New Haven, 1973.

Seymour, C., Jr., and H. Swarzenski. "A Madonna of Humility and Quercia's Early Style." *Gazette des beaux-arts*, ser. 6, vol. 30, 1946, pp. 129-52.

Shapley, F. R. *Paintings from the Samuel H. Kress Collection: Italian Schools, XIII-XV Century*. London, 1966.

——. *Catalogue of the Italian Paintings, National Gallery of Art, Washington*. 2 vols. Washington, D.C., 1979.

Shearman, J. "Developments in the Use of Colour in Tuscan Painting of the Early Sixteenth Century." 2 vols. Ph.D. diss., University of London, 1957.

——. "Le rovine dell'arte fiorentina." *Paragone* 18, no. 203, 1967, pp. 13-33.

Shell, C. "Giovanni dal Ponte and the Problem of Other Lesser Contemporaries of Masaccio." Ph.D. diss., Harvard University, 1958.

——. "Francesco d'Antonio and Masaccio." *Art Bulletin* 47, 1965, pp. 465-69.

Shorr, D. C. "The Mourning Virgin and Saint John." *Art Bulletin* 22, 1940, pp. 61-69.

——. *The Christ Child in Devotional Images in Italy during the XIV Century*. New York, 1954.

Sirén, O. "Italian Pictures in Sweden—I." *Burlington Magazine* 5, 1904, pp. 439-51.

——. "Di alcuni pittori fiorentini che subirono l'influenza di Lorenzo Monaco." *L'Arte* 7, 1904, pp. 337-55.

——. *Don Lorenzo Monaco (Zur Kunstgeschichte des Auslandes. XXXIII)*. Strassburg, 1905.

——. "Tre Madonnine nel Fitzwilliam Museum di Cambridge." *Rivista d'arte* 3, 1905, pp. 245-52.

——. "Notizie critiche sui quadri sconosciuti nel Museo Cristiano Vaticano." *L'Arte* 9, 1906, pp. 321-35.

——. "Dipinti del Trecento in alcuni musei tedeschi di provincia." *Rassegna d'arte* 6, 1906, pp. 81-87.

——. *Giottino und seine Stellung in der gleichzeitigen florentinischen Malerei*. Leipzig, 1908.

——. "Trecento pictures in American Collections—III." *Burlington Magazine* 14, 1908/1909, pp. 325-26.

——. "Early Italian Pictures, in the University Museum, Göttingen." Pt. 2, *Burlington Magazine* 26, 1914/15, pp. 107-114.

——. *A Descriptive Catalogue of the Pictures in the Jarves Collection Belonging to Yale University*. New Haven, 1916.

——. *Giotto and Some of His Followers*. 2 vols. Cambridge, Massachusetts, 1917.

——. "Alcune note aggiuntive a quadri primitivi nella galleria vaticana." *L'Arte* 24, 1921, pp. 97-102.

Sirén, O., and M. W. Brockwell. *Catalogue of a Loan Exhibition of Italian Primitives in Aid of the American War Relief*. Kleinberger Galleries, New York, 1917.

Sommerard, E. du. *Catalogue . . . Musée des Thermes et de l'Hôtel de Cluny*. Paris, 1861 and 1883.

Soulier, G. *Les influences orientales dans la peinture toscane*. Paris, 1924.

Spencer, J. "Spatial Imagery of the Annunciation in Fifteenth Century Florence." *Art Bulletin* 37, 1955, pp. 273-80.

Stechow, W. "Italienische Bilder des XIV und XV Jahrhunderts in der Gemäldesammlung der Universität Göttingen." *Zeitschrift für bildenden Kunst* 58, 1924/25, pp. 209-219.

——. *Katalog der Gemäldesammlung der Universität Göttingen*. Göttingen, 1926.

Sterling, C., M. Laclotte, et al. *Exposition de la Collection Lehman de New York*. Musée de l'Orangerie, Paris, 1957.

Stiavelli, C. *L'arte in Val di Nievole*. Florence, 1905.

Stinger, C. L. "Ambrogio Traversari and the 'Tempio degli Scolari' at S. Maria degli Angeli in Florence." In *Essays Presented to Myron P. Gilmore*. Edited by S. Bertelli and G. Ramakus. Vol. 1, Florence, 1978, pp. 271-86.

Stix, A., and E. V. Strohmer. *Die Fürstlich Liechtensteinsche Gemäldegalerie in Wien*. Vienna, 1938.

Straelen, H. van. *Studien zur florentiner Glasmalerei des Trecento und Quattrocento (Lebensräume der Kunst, V)*. Wattenscheid, 1938.

Stubblebine, J. H. *Duccio di Buoninsegna and His School*. 2 vols. Princeton, 1979.

Sturgis, R., Jr. *Manual of the Jarves Collection*. New Haven, 1868.

Suckale, R. "Arma Christi." *Städel-Jahrbuch*, new ser., 6, 1977, pp. 177-208.

Suida, W. "Beiträge zum Oeuvre bekannter Maler-II. Don Lorenzo Monaco." *Monatshefte für Kunstwissenschaft* 1, 1908, pp. 305-307.

——. "Studien zur Trecentomalerei-VI." *Repertorium für Kunstwissenschaft* 31, 1908, pp. 199-214.

——. *Oesterreichische Kunstschätze*. Vol. 2. Vienna, 1912.

——. "Lorenzo Monaco." In U. Thieme and F. Becker. *Allgemeines Lexikon der bildenden Künstler*. Vol. 23, Leipzig, 1929, pp. 391-93.

——. *S. H. Kress Collection: Italian Art*. Seattle Art Museum, Seattle, 1952.

Sutton, D. "Piety and Restraint, Two Centuries of Italian Painting in London." *Apollo* 118, no. 257, 1983, pp. 94-99.

Sweet, F. A. "The Collection of Frank Lusk Babbott." *Brooklyn Museum Quarterly* 21, no. 4, 1934, pp. 86-89.

Szabó, G. *The Robert Lehman Collection, The Metropolitan Museum of Art*. New York, 1975.

——. *Masterpieces of Italian Drawing in the Robert Lehman Collection, The Metropolitan Museum of Art*. New York, 1983.

Tarani, Don F. *Cenni storici e artistici della chiesa di S. Trinita e suo restauro*. Florence, 1898.

Tartuferi, A. "Due croci dipinte poco note del Trecento fiorentino." *Arte cristiana* 72, 1984, pp. 3-12.

Tauzia, B. de. *Notice des tableaux exposés dans les galeries du Musée National du Louvre*. Vol. 1, *Ecoles d'Italie et d'Espagne*. Paris, 1878 and 1883.

Thompson, C., and H. Brigstocke. *Shorter Catalogue, National Gallery of Scotland*. Edinburgh, 1970.

Toesca, P. "Ricordi di un viaggio in Italia." *L'Arte* 6, 1903, pp. 225-50.

——. "Nuove opere di Lorenzo Monaco." *L'Arte* 7, 1904, pp. 171-74.

——. "Vetri italiani a oro con graffiti del XIV e XV secolo." *L'Arte* 11, 1908, pp. 247-61.

——. *La pittura e la miniatura nella Lombardia*. Milan, 1912.

——. *Monumenti e studi per la storia della miniatura italiana: La collezione di U. Hoepli*. Milan, 1930.

——. *Il Trecento*. Turin, 1951.

Toledo Museum of Art, European Paintings. Toledo, Ohio, 1976.

Tolnay, C. de. "The Music of the Universe: Notes on a Painting by Bicci di Lorenzo." *Journal of the Walters Art Gallery* 6, 1943, pp. 83-104.

——. "Remarques sur la *Sainte Anne* de Léonard." *Revue des arts* 6, no. 3, 1956, pp. 161-66.

Torriti, P. *La Pinacoteca Nazionale di Siena, I dipinti dal XII al XV secolo*. Genoa, 1977.

Valentiner, W. R. *Italian Gothic Painting*. Detroit, 1944.

Vasari, Giorgio. *Le opere di Giorgio Vasari pittore e architetto aretino*. Edited by G. Montani and G. Masselli. Pt. 1. Florence, 1832.

——. *Le Vite de' più eccellenti pittori, scultori e architetti*. Edited by V. Marchese, C. Pini, C. Milanesi, and G. Milanesi. Vol. 2. Florence, 1846.

——. *Le Vite de' più eccellenti pittori, scultori ed architettori: Le opere di G. Vasari*. Edited by G. Milanesi. Vols. 1 and 2. Florence, 1878.

——. *Le Vite de' più eccellenti pittori, scultori e architettori, nelle redazioni del 1550 e 1568*. Edited by R. Bettarini and P. Barocchi. Vol. 2, Text and Commentary. Florence, 1967 and 1969.

Vasaturo, N. *Chiesa di Santa Trinita*. Florence, 1973.

Venturi, A. *La Galleria Crespi in Milano*. Milan, 1900.

——. *Storia dell'arte italiana: Pittura del Quattrocento*. Vol. 7, pt. 1. Milan, 1911.

——. "Esposizione dei primitivi italiani a Bruxelles." *L'Arte* 25, 1922, pp. 161-69.

——. *Studi del vero*. Milan, 1927.

Venturi, L. *Pitture italiane in America*. Milan, 1931.

——. *Italian Paintings in America*. 3 vols. Milan, 1933.

——. "Reconstruction of a Painting by Andrea del Castagno." *Art Quarterly* 7, 1944, pp. 23-32.

Verdier, P., and D. Miner. *The International Style, The Arts in Europe around 1400*. Walters Art Gallery, Baltimore, 1962.

Vertova, L. "Lorenzo Monaco." In *Kindlers Malerei Lexikon*. Vol. 4, Zurich, 1967, pp. 204-205.

——. "A New Museum is Born." *Burlington Magazine* 119, 1977, pp. 158-67.

Vienna. *Europäische Kunst um 1400*. Kunsthistorisches Museum, Vienna, 1962.

Volpe, C. "Per il completamento dell'altare di San Lorenzo del Maestro del Bambino Vispo." *Mitteilungen des Kunsthistorischen Institutes in Florenz* 17, 1973, pp. 347-55.

——. "La pittura gotica." In *La Basilica di S. Petronio*

in Bologna. Vol. 1, Bologna, 1983, pp. 254-65, and pls. 223-38.

Waadenoijen, J. van. "A Proposal for Starnina: exit the Maestro del Bambino Vispo?" *Burlington Magazine* 116, 1974, pp. 82-91.

——. "Ghiberti and the Origin of his International Style." In *Lorenzo Ghiberti nel suo tempo. Atti del Convegno Internazionale di Studi*. Vol. 1, Florence, 1980, pp. 81-87.

——. *Starnina e il gotico internazionale a Firenze*. Florence, 1983.

Waagen, G. F. *Treasures of Art in Great Britain*. 3 vols. London, 1854.

Wackernagel, M. *Der Lebensraum des Künstlers in der florentinischen Renaissance*. Leipzig, 1938.

——. *The World of the Florentine Renaissance Artist*. Translated by A. Luchs. Princeton, 1981.

Wagstaff, S. *An Exhibition of Italian Panels and Manuscripts from the Thirteenth and Fourteenth Centuries in Honor of Richard Offner*. Wadsworth Atheneum, Hartford, 1965.

Watson, P. "A *Desco da Parto* by Bartolomeo di Fruosino." *Art Bulletin* 56, 1974, pp. 4-9.

Wehle, H. B. *A Catalogue of Italian, Spanish and Byzantine Paintings*. The Metropolitan Museum of Art, New York, 1940.

Wescher, P. "Florentinische Buchminiaturen im berliner Kupferstichkabinett." *Jahrbuch der preuszischen Kunstsammlungen* 50, 1929, pp. 96-104.

——. *Beschreibendes Verzeichnis der Miniaturen, Handschriften und Einzelblätter des Kupferstichkabinetts der Staatlichen Museen, Berlin*. Leipzig, 1931.

White, J. *Art and Architecture in Italy, 1250-1400*. Baltimore, 1966.

——. "Paragone: Aspects of the Relationship between Sculpture and Painting." In *Art, Science, and History in the Renaissance*. Edited by C. S. Singleton. Baltimore, 1967, pp. 43-109.

——. *The Birth and Rebirth of Pictorial Space*. 2d ed. New York and London, 1972.

White, L., Jr. "Indic Elements in the Iconography of Petrarch's *Trionfo della Morte*." *Speculum* 49, 1974, pp. 201-21.

Wilkins, D. "Maso di Banco and Cenni di Francesco: A Case of Late Trecento Revival." *Burlington Magazine* 111, 1969, pp. 83-84.

Wixom, W. "The Hours of Charles the Noble." *Bulletin of the Cleveland Museum of Art* 52, 1965, pp. 50-83.

Wohl, H. *The Paintings of Domenico Veneziano, ca. 1410-1461, A Study in Florentine Art of the Early Renaissance*. New York and London, 1980.

Zeri, F. "Sul problema di Nicolò Tegliacci e Luca Tomè." *Paragone* 9, 1958, pp. 3-16.

——. "Un'apertura per Giovanni Bonsi." *Bollettino d'arte* 49, 1964, pp. 224-28.

——. "Investigations into the Early Period of Lorenzo Monaco—I and II." *Burlington Magazine* 106, 1964, pp. 554-58; and 107, 1965, pp. 3-11.

——. "Italian Primitives at Messrs Wildenstein." *Burlington Magazine* 107, 1965, pp. 252-56.

——. "Aggiunta a una primizia di Lorenzo Monaco." *Bollettino d'arte* 51, 1966, pp. 150-51.

——. "Sul catalogo dei dipinti toscani del secolo XIV nelle Gallerie di Firenze." *Gazette des beaux-arts*. 6th period, 71, 1968, pp. 65-78.

——. *Italian Paintings: A Catalogue of the Collection of The Metropolitan Museum of Art, Florentine School*. With E. E. Gardner. New York, 1971.

——. "Qualche appunto su Alvaro Pirez." *Mitteilungen des Kunsthistorischen Institutes in Florenz* 17, 1973, pp. 361-70.

——. *Italian Paintings in the Walters Art Gallery*. 2 vols. Baltimore, 1976.

Zeri, F., and F. Rossi. *La Raccolta Morelli nell'Accademia Carrara*. Milan, 1986.

Index

Note: Throughout the index Roman numerals I and II refer to the sections of the Catalogue in which works are considered: I—Lorenzo Monaco and his workshop; II—other ascriptions to Lorenzo Monaco. Works from Catalogue I are denoted in the index as follows: LM, LM/Shop, Shop LM; works from Catalogue II are denoted attr. LM, with an alternative attribution included when appropriate.

Index

ADDENDUM

AFTER THIS BOOK had reached a final stage of production, there came to my attention an important panel by Lorenzo Monaco in a European private collection. The subject and ownership of the work presently may not be divulged. This picture has proved to be a stylistic bridge from the Trecento to the Quattrocento, heretofore an undefined moment in the evolution of Don Lorenzo's work.

The newly emerged panel leads me to conclude that the Accademia *Agony in the Garden* (Fig. 7) and two works in its orbit, the Fitzwilliam *Madonna Enthroned* (Fig. 15) and the Berenson *Madonna and Child with Saints John the Baptist and Zenobius* (Fig. 16), must be dated later in the 1390s than I had proposed. This shift in chronology has opened a span of years in the 1390s that will accommodate the Carmine Polyptych, a work whose attribution I had left explicitly unresolved (see Catalogue II, pp. 186-88, and Figs. 215 and 217-23). I would now remove the question marks from the attribution of the various components of the altarpiece and, by implication, the works in its milieu (Figs. 224 and 225), and propose their inclusion in Catalogue I, with a dating toward the mid-1390s, immediately preceding Don Lorenzo's early choir book miniatures (Figs. 1-6). Thus, in contrast to the view expressed on page 3 of the Introductory Essay, Lorenzo Monaco would seem to have been a painter of both panels and books from the outset of his career. The eclecticism of Don Lorenzo's style in the works produced throughout the 1390s reinforces the view that virtually every strain of Florentine Trecento painting met at Santa Maria degli Angeli.

The wider interval of time now allotted between the Carmine Polyptych and the Accademia *Agony in the Garden* helps explain the degree of technical and stylistic maturation from the earlier to the later work. Two such extensive accomplishments on panel provide a substantial basis for Don Lorenzo's receiving so important a commission as the altarpiece for the second Ardinghelli Chapel at the Carmine, just at the moment of his emergence from Santa Maria degli Angeli to establish a workshop outside the monastery (see pp. 4, 12, and 48, note 5). Could that major commission, in fact, have impelled his secession from the Angeli workshop? The loss of the Ardinghelli altarpiece, apparently in the fire of 1771 at the Carmine, obliterated important evidence of Don Lorenzo's art at the threshold of the Quattrocento.

I would hope to enlarge on these observations, should permission eventually be secured to publish the work noted at the beginning of this addendum. In Miklós Boskovits's catalogue of the early Italian pictures in the Gemäldegalerie, Berlin-Dahlem, which postdates the completion of this book, the literature on the Carmine Polyptych is extensively reviewed and an illustrated reconstruction presented (*Frühe italienische Malerei*, translated from the Italian and edited by Erich Schleier, Berlin [West], 1988, no. 37, pp. 96-99; figs. 147-48 and colorplate VIII). The fact that Boskovits reverses the chronological progression from the Carmine Polyptych to the San Gaggio Altarpiece as first postulated by Federico Zeri, and places the latter work at a moment before Don Lorenzo's entrance into Santa Maria degli Angeli (i.e., before 1391; p. 96), suggests that stylistic parallels and progressions between these two altarpieces need further demonstration (see Catalogue II, pp. 184-86).

In 1988, the *Saint Jerome in Penitence*, an element of the Carmine Polyptych predella formerly in the Cremer Collection, Dortmund, emerged at a Sotheby's auction (*Old Master Paintings*, London, 6th July 1988, no. 8, illustrated in color; to Colnaghi).

Ann Arbor, June 1989 Marvin Eisenberg

Illustrations

1. Lorenzo Monaco, *Saint Jerome*, fol. 138, Cod. Cor. 5, Biblioteca Laurenziana, Florence. (Cat. I)

2. Lorenzo Monaco, *Tobit*, fol. 20, Cod. Cor. 5, Biblioteca Laurenziana, Florence. (Cat. I)

3. Lorenzo Monaco, *King David*, fol. 34, Cod. Cor. 8, Biblioteca Laurenziana, Florence. (Cat. I)

4. Lorenzo Monaco, *Saint Romuald*, fol. 76, Cod. Cor. 8, Biblioteca Laurenziana, Florence. (Cat. I)

5. Lorenzo Monaco, *Saint John the Evangelist*, fol. 33, Cod. Cor. 1, Biblioteca Laurenziana, Florence. (Cat. I)

6. Head of *Saint Romuald*, detail of Fig. 4.

7. Lorenzo Monaco, *Agony in the Garden*, Accademia, no. 438, Florence. (Cat. I)

8. *Christ*, detail of Fig. 7.

9. *Saints James and John the Evangelist*, detail of Fig. 7.

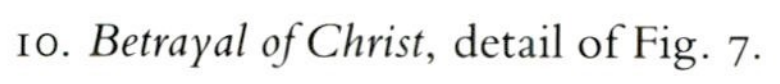

10. *Betrayal of Christ*, detail of Fig. 7.

11. *Stripping of Christ*, detail of Fig. 7.

12. *Saint Peter and Malchas*, detail of Fig. 10.

13. *Sorrowing Virgin and Saint John the Evangelist*, detail of Fig. 11.

14. *Christ and Judas*, detail of Fig. 10.

15. Lorenzo Monaco, *Madonna Enthroned*, Fitzwilliam Museum, Cambridge. (Cat. I)

16. Lorenzo Monaco, *Madonna and Child with Saints John the Baptist and Zenobius*, Biblioteca Berenson, Florence. (Cat. I)

17. Lorenzo Monaco, *Madonna and Child with Saints John the Baptist and Nicholas*, formerly Kaiser-Friedrich-Museum, Berlin. (Cat. I)

18. Lorenzo Monaco, *The Man of Sorrows with the Virgin, Saint John the Evangelist, and Episodes and Emblems of the Passion*, Accademia, no. 467, Florence. (Cat. I)

19. *Head of Christ*, detail of Fig. 18.

20. Lorenzo Monaco, *Madonna of Humility with Four Saints*, Museo della Collegiata, Empoli. (Cat. I)

21. *Madonna of Humility*, detail of Fig. 20.

22. Lorenzo Monaco, *Monte Oliveto Altarpiece*, Accademia, no. 468, Florence. (Cat. I)

23. *Madonna and Child*, detail of Fig. 22.

24. *Saints Thaddeus and Benedict*, detail of Fig. 22.

25. *Annunciatory Gabriel*, detail of Fig. 22.

26. *Annunciate Virgin*, detail of Fig. 22.

27. *Blessing Redeemer*, detail of Fig. 22.

28. *Malachi*, detail of Fig. 22.

29. Lorenzo Monaco, *Visitation*, Courtauld Institute Galleries, London. (Cat. I)

30. Lorenzo Monaco, *Nativity*, Metropolitan Museum of Art, 1975.1.66, New York. (Cat. I)

31. Lorenzo Monaco, *Adoration of the Magi*, Courtauld Institute Galleries, London. (Cat. I)

32. Lorenzo Monaco, *Flight into Egypt*, Staatliches Lindenau-Museum, Altenburg. (Cat. I)

33. Lorenzo Monaco, *Agony in the Garden* and *Holy Women at the Tomb*, Louvre, Paris. (Cat. I)

34. Lorenzo Monaco, *Lamentation*, National Gallery, Prague.
(Cat. I)

35. *Calvary and Jerusalem*, detail of Fig. 34.

36. *Lamentation*, detail of Fig. 34.

37. *Mourner*, detail of Fig. 34.

38. Lorenzo Monaco, *Madonna of Humility*, Biblioteca Berenson, Florence. (Cat. I)

39. Lorenzo Monaco (and Workshop?), *Madonna of Humility*, Staatsgalerie, Stuttgart. (Cat. I)

40. Lorenzo Monaco, *Moses*, Metropolitan Museum of Art, no. 65.14.3, New York. (Cat. I)

41. Lorenzo Monaco, *Abraham*, Metropolitan Museum of Art, no. 65.14.1, New York.

42. Lorenzo Monaco, *Noah*, Metropolitan Museum of Art, no. 65.14.2, New York.

43. Lorenzo Monaco, *David*, Metropolitan Museum of Art, no. 65.14.4, New York.

44. Lorenzo Monaco, *Coronation of the Virgin Altarpiece*, Uffizi, Florence. (Cat. I)

45. *Adoring Saints*, detail of Fig. 44.

46. *Adoring Saints*, detail of Fig. 44.

47. *The Virgin*, detail of Fig. 44.

48. *Blessing Redeemer*, detail of Fig. 44.

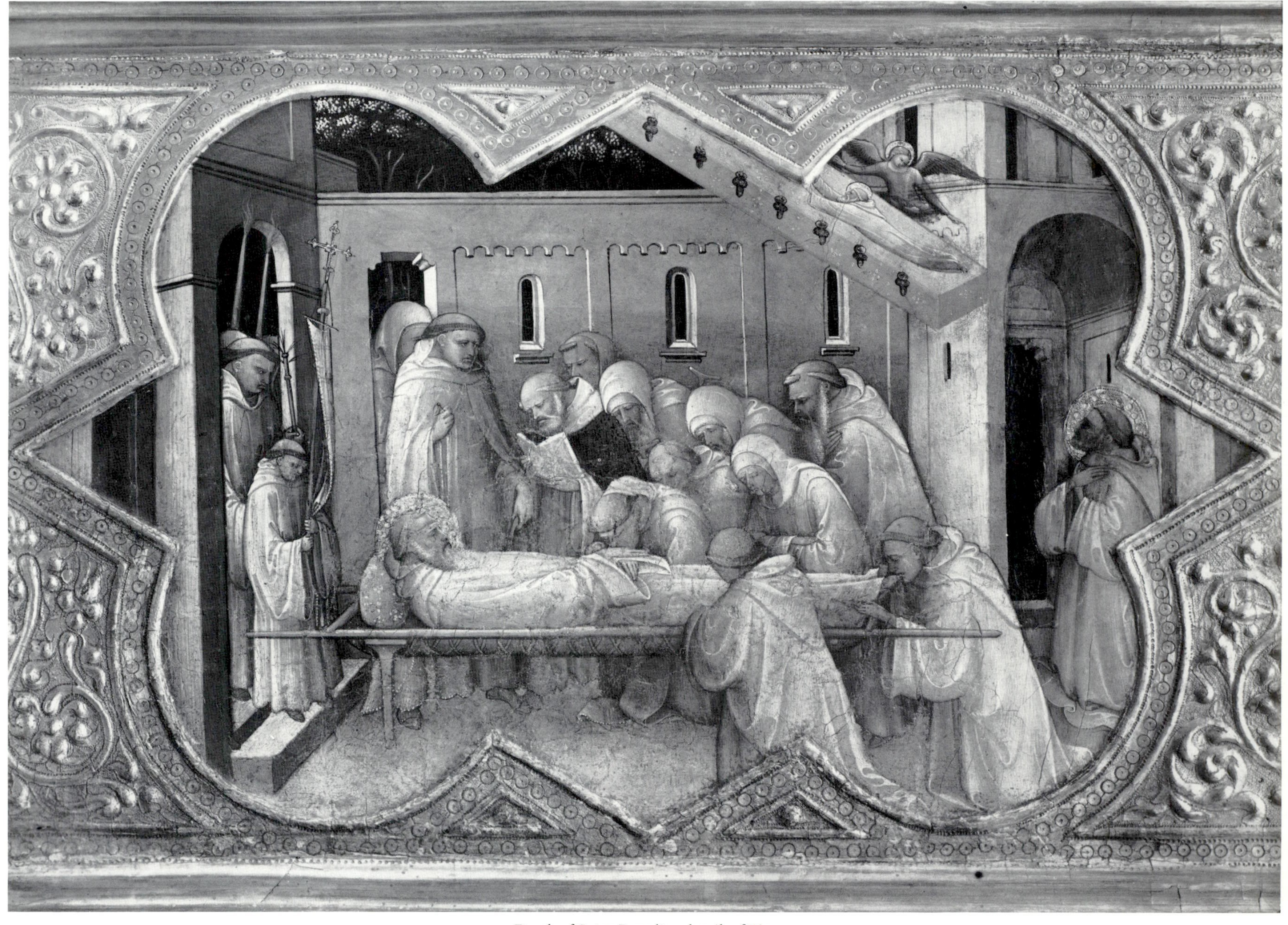

49. *Death of Saint Benedict*, detail of Fig. 44.

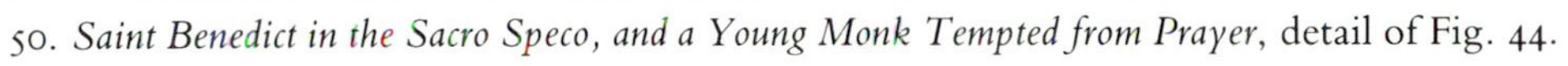

50. *Saint Benedict in the Sacro Speco, and a Young Monk Tempted from Prayer,* detail of Fig. 44.

51. *Nativity*, detail of Fig. 44.

52. *Adoration of the Magi*, detail of Fig. 44.

53. *Annunciation to the Shepherds*, detail of Fig. 51.

54. *Saint Maurus Rescuing Saint Placidus*, detail of Fig. 57.

55. *Retinue of the Magi*, detail of Fig. 52.

56. *Saint Benedict and Saint Scholastica*, detail of Fig. 57.

57. *Rescue of Saint Placidus and Saint Benedict's Visit to Saint Scholastica*, detail of Fig. 44.

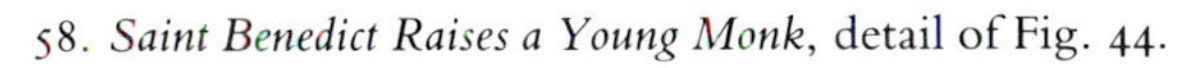

58. *Saint Benedict Raises a Young Monk*, detail of Fig. 44.

59. *Annunciatory Gabriel*, detail of Fig. 44.

60. *Annunciate Virgin*, detail of Fig. 44.

61. Workshop of Lorenzo Monaco, *Abraham*, detail of Fig. 44.

62. Lorenzo Monaco and Workshop, *Daniel*, detail of Fig. 44.

63. Lorenzo Monaco, *Saint Benedict Enthroned* (detail), Gabinetto Disegni e Stampe, Uffizi, Florence. (Cat. I)

64. Lorenzo Monaco, *Prophet*, fol. 46v, Cod. Cor. 3, Biblioteca Laurenziana, Florence. (Cat. I)

65. Lorenzo Monaco, *Prophet*, fol. 65v, Cod. Cor. 3, Biblioteca Laurenziana, Florence. (Cat. I)

66. Lorenzo Monaco, *Prophet*, fol. 96v, Cod. Cor. 3, Biblioteca Laurenziana, Florence.

67. Lorenzo Monaco, *Prophet*, fol. 35, Cod. Cor. 3, Biblioteca Laurenziana, Florence.

68. Lorenzo Monaco, *Prophet*, fol. 86v, Cod. Cor. 3, Biblioteca Laurenziana, Florence.

69. Lorenzo Monaco, *Crucifix* (before restoration), Accademia, no. 3153, Florence (Cat. I)

70. *Crucifix*, detail of Fig. 74.

71. Lorenzo Monaco, *Crucifix*, Santa Maria delle Vertighe, Monte San Savino. (Cat. I)

72. Lorenzo Monaco, *Crucifix*, Convento di Santa Marta, Florence. (Cat. I)

73. *Head of Christ*, detail of Fig. 74.

74. Lorenzo Monaco, *Crucifix with the Mourning Virgin and Saint John the Evangelist* (before restoration), San Giovannino dei Cavalieri, Florence. (Cat. I)

75. *Mourning Virgin*, detail of Fig. 74.

76. Lorenzo Monaco and Workshop, *Mourning Saint John the Evangelist*, detail of Fig. 74.

77. Lorenzo Monaco, *Annunciation with Four Saints*, Accademia, no. 8458, Florence. (Cat. I)

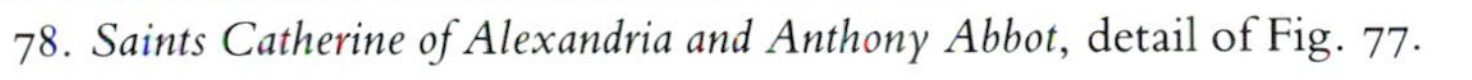

78. *Saints Catherine of Alexandria and Anthony Abbot*, detail of Fig. 77.

79. *Annunciation*, detail of Fig. 77.

80. *Christ Logos*, detail of Fig. 77.

81. Lorenzo Monaco, *Isaiah*, Richard L. Feigen Collection, New York. (Cat. I)

82. Lorenzo Monaco, *Adoration of the Magi*, Uffizi, Florence. (Cat. I)

83. *Virgin and Child, and the Manger*, detail of Fig. 82.

84. *Retinue of the Magi*, detail of Fig. 82.

85. *David*(?), detail of Fig. 82.

86. *Retinue of the Magi*, detail of Fig. 82.

87. *Retinue of the Magi*, detail of Fig. 82.

88. Lorenzo Monaco, *Noli Me Tangere*, Museo di San Marco, Florence. (Cat. I)

89. Lorenzo Monaco, *Resurrection*, Museo di San Marco, Florence.

90. Lorenzo Monaco, *Holy Women at the Tomb*, Museo di San Marco, Florence.

91. *Holy Women*, detail of Fig. 90.

92. Lorenzo Monaco, *Saint Nicholas Rescuing a Storm-tossed Ship*, Accademia, no. 8617, Florence. (Cat. I)

93. *Shrine of Saint Nicholas at Bari*, detail of Fig. 92.

94. Lorenzo Monaco, *Nativity*, Accademia, no. 8616, Florence. (Cat. I)

95. Lorenzo Monaco, *Legend of Saint Onuphrius*, Accademia, no. 8615, Florence. (Cat. I)

96. Lorenzo Monaco, *Visitation*, Kupferstichkabinett, Staatliche Museen, Berlin-Dahlem. (Cat. I)

97. Lorenzo Monaco, *Journey of the Magi*, Kupferstichkabinett, Staatliche Museen, Berlin-Dahlem. (Cat. I)

98. *Magi*, detail of Fig. 97.

99. Lorenzo Monaco, *Prophet*, fol. 21, Cod. H 74, Bargello, Florence. (Cat. I)

100. Lorenzo Monaco, *Prophet*, fol. 63, Cod. H 74, Bargello, Florence.

101. Lorenzo Monaco, *Prophet*, fol. 95v, Cod. H 74, Bargello, Florence.

102. Bartolini Salimbeni Chapel (before restoration), Santa Trinita, Florence. (Cat. I)

103. Bartolini Salimbeni Chapel (before restoration), Santa Trinita, Florence.

104. Lorenzo Monaco and Workshop, *Expulsion of Joachim and Annunciation to Joachim*, Bartolini Salimbeni Chapel, Santa Trinita, Florence.

105. Lorenzo Monaco and Workshop, *Meeting of Joachim and Anna,* Bartolini Salimbeni Chapel, Santa Trinita, Florence.

106. Lorenzo Monaco, *Birth of the Virgin*, Bartolini Salimbeni Chapel, Santa Trinita, Florence.

107. Lorenzo Monaco and Workshop, *Presentation of the Virgin*, Bartolini Salimbeni Chapel, Santa Trinita, Florence.

108. *Midwife*, detail of Fig. 106.

109. Lorenzo Monaco, *Betrothal of the Virgin*, Bartolini Salimbeni Chapel, Santa Trinita, Florence.

110. Detail of Fig. 109.

111. Lorenzo Monaco and Workshop, *Dormition of the Virgin*, Bartolini Salimbeni Chapel, Santa Trinita, Florence.

112. Workshop of Lorenzo Monaco, *Assumption of the Virgin* (before restoration), Bartolini Salimbeni Chapel, Santa Trinita, Florence.

113. Lorenzo Monaco, *Four Prophets*, Bartolini Salimbeni Chapel, Santa Trinita, Florence.

114. Lorenzo Monaco (and Workshop?), *Miracle of the Snow*, Bartolini Salimbeni Chapel, Santa Trinita, Florence.

115. *David*, detail of Fig. 113.

116. *Malachi*, detail of Fig. 113.

117. *Micah*, detail of Fig. 113.

118. Lorenzo Monaco, *Saint Bartholomew*, Bartolini Salimbeni Chapel, Santa Trinita, Florence.

119. Lorenzo Monaco and Workshop, *Saint John the Baptist*, Bartolini Salimbeni Chapel, Santa Trinita, Florence.

120. Lorenzo Monaco, *Annunciation Altarpiece*, Bartolini Salimbeni Chapel, Santa Trinita, Florence. (Cat. I)

121. *Annunciation*, detail of Fig. 120.

122. Detail of Fig. 121.

123. *Annunciate Virgin*, detail of Fig. 121.

124. *Visitation*, detail of Fig. 120.

125. *Nativity*, detail of Fig. 120.

126. *Adoration of the Magi*, detail of Fig. 120.

127. *Flight into Egypt*, detail of Fig. 120.

128. Lorenzo Monaco, *Madonna of Humility*, Thorvaldsens Museum, Copenhagen. (Cat. I)

129. Lorenzo Monaco, *Saint Jerome in His Study*, Rijksmuseum, Amsterdam. (Cat. I)

130. *Lectern*, detail of Fig. 129.

131. Lorenzo Monaco, *Saint Anthony Abbot*, fol. 52v, Cod. E 70, Bargello, Florence. (Cat. I)

132. Lorenzo Monaco and Workshop, *Madonna in Glory, with Saints John the Baptist and Nicholas,* Pinacoteca, Siena. (Cat. I)

133. Lorenzo Monaco and Workshop, *Madonna Enthroned*, Pinacoteca, Bologna. (Cat. I)

134. Workshop (or Imitator?) of Lorenzo Monaco, *Madonna and Child with Saints Peter and Sebastian*, Museo Civico, Pescia. (Cat. I)

135. Lorenzo Monaco and Workshop, *Crucifixion with the Virgin and Saint John the Evangelist*, Metropolitan Museum of Art, no. 1975.1.67, New York. (Cat. I)

136. Workshop of Lorenzo Monaco, *The Man of Sorrows*, Accademia Carrara, Bergamo. (Cat. I)

137. Workshop of Lorenzo Monaco, *Crucifixion with the Virgin and Saint John the Evangelist*, Seattle Art Museum, Seattle. (Cat. I)

138. Workshop of Lorenzo Monaco, *Madonna and Child with Four Saints*, Accademia, no. 470, Florence. (Cat. I)

139. Workshop of Lorenzo Monaco, *Madonna of Humility*, San Martino a Gangalandi, Lastra a Signa. (Cat. I)

140. Workshop of Lorenzo Monaco, *Madonna of Humility with Saints John the Baptist and John the Evangelist*(?), Museo Civico, Turin. (Cat. I)

141. Workshop (or Imitator?) of Lorenzo Monaco, *Madonna of Humility with Two Angels*, Metropolitan Museum of Art, no. 09.91, New York. (Cat. I)

142. Workshop of Lorenzo Monaco, *Madonna of Humility*, Pushkin State Museum of Fine Arts, Moscow. (Cat. I)

143. Lorenzo Monaco and Workshop, *Madonna of Humility*, National Gallery of Art, Washington. (Cat. I)

144. Workshop of Lorenzo Monaco, *Madonna of Humility*, Louvre, Paris. (Cat. I)

145. Workshop of Lorenzo Monaco, *Madonna of Humility*, Nelson-Atkins Museum of Art, Kansas City. (Cat. I)

146. Workshop of Lorenzo Monaco, *Madonna of Humility with Eight Angels*, Sant'Ermete, Pisa. (Cat. I)

147. Lorenzo Monaco and Workshop, *Madonna of Humility*, Brooklyn Museum, Brooklyn. (Cat. I)

148. Workshop of Lorenzo Monaco, *Madonna of Humility*, John G. Johnson Collection, Philadelphia. (Cat. I)

149. Workshop of Lorenzo Monaco, *Madonna of Humility*, Toledo Museum of Art, Toledo. (Cat. I)

150. *Blessing Redeemer*, detail of Fig. 149.

151. Workshop of Lorenzo Monaco, *Crucifix* (*Virgin, Saint John, and Magdalen* by Neri di Bicci), Musée des Augustins, Toulouse. (Cat. I)

152. Workshop of Lorenzo Monaco, *Madonna Enthroned, with Saints Catherine of Alexandria, Benedict, Giovanni Gualberto, and Agatha*, Galleria Comunale, Prato. (Cat. I)

153. Workshop of Lorenzo Monaco, *Saints Catherine of Alexandria and John the Baptist*, National Museum, Cracow. (Cat. I)

154-155. Workshop of Lorenzo Monaco, *Saints John the Evangelist and Catherine of Alexandria; Saint John the Baptist and a Bishop Saint*, Museo della Collegiata, Empoli. (Cat. I)

156. Workshop of Lorenzo Monaco, *Madonna Enthroned* (before restoration), Museo della Collegiata, Empoli. (Cat. I)

157. Workshop of Lorenzo Monaco, *Annunciation*, Private collection (formerly Féron-Stoclet Collection, Brussels). (Cat. I)

158. Lorenzo Monaco and Workshop, *Madonna Enthroned*, National Gallery of Scotland, Edinburgh. (Cat. I)

159. Lorenzo Monaco and Workshop, *Madonna Enthroned*, Thyssen-Bornemisza Foundation, Lugano. (Cat. I)

160. Lorenzo Monaco and Workshop, *Madonna Enthroned*, Parish Church, Tavèrnola. (Cat. I)

161. Workshop of Lorenzo Monaco, *Madonna of Humility*, formerly Kaiser-Friedrich-Museum, Berlin. (Cat. I)

162. Workshop of Lorenzo Monaco, *Madonna Enthroned*, Rijksdienst Beeldende Kunst, The Hague. (Cat. I)

163. Workshop of Lorenzo Monaco, *Crucifix*, Museo Horne, Florence. (Cat. I)

164. Workshop of Lorenzo Monaco, *Crucifix*, Museum of Fine Arts, Budapest. (Cat. I)

165. Lorenzo Monaco and Workshop, *Crucifix*, San Giuseppe, Florence. (Cat. I)

166. Detail of Fig. 165 (before 1966).

167. Workshop of Lorenzo Monaco, *Crucifixion*, Accademia, no. 2141, Florence. (Cat. I)

168. Workshop of Lorenzo Monaco, *Mourning Virgin*, Accademia, no. 2140, Florence. (Cat. I)

169. Lorenzo Monaco and Workshop, *The Man of Sorrows*, Museo dello Spedale degli Innocenti, Florence. (Cat. I)

170. Workshop of Lorenzo Monaco, *Mourning Saint John the Evangelist*, Accademia, no. 2169, Florence. (Cat. I)

171. Workshop of Lorenzo Monaco, *Saint James Enthroned* (unrestored), Museo dell'Opera di Santa Croce, Florence. (Cat. I)

172. Workshop of Lorenzo Monaco, *Saint Peter*, Alte Pinakothek, Munich. (Cat. I)

173. Workshop of Lorenzo Monaco, *Crucifixion with Saints Francis, Benedict, and Romuald*, Staatliches Lindenau-Museum, Altenburg. (Cat. I)

174. Workshop of Lorenzo Monaco, *Crucifixion with God the Father, the Mourning Virgin, and Saint John the Evangelist*, Yale University Art Gallery, New Haven. (Cat. I)

175. Lorenzo Monaco and Workshop, *Coronation of the Virgin*, National Gallery, London. (Cat. I)

176. Workshop of Lorenzo Monaco, *Six Kneeling Saints*, Gabinetto Disegni e Stampe, Uffizi, Florence. (Cat. I)

177. Lorenzo Monaco, *Coronation of the Virgin*, detail of Fig. 44.

178. Detail of Fig. 175.

179. Detail of Fig. 177.

180. Lorenzo Monaco and Workshop, *Annunciate Virgin*, Norton Simon Museum, Pasadena. (Cat. I)

181. *Head of the Virgin*, detail of Fig. 180.

182. *Head of Christ*, detail of Fig. 175.

183. Lorenzo Monaco and Workshop, *Saint Benedict Admitting Saints Maurus and Placidus into the Order*, National Gallery, London. (Cat. I)

184. Lorenzo Monaco and Workshop, *Rescue of Saint Placidus and Saint Benedict's Visit to Saint Scholastica*, National Gallery, London. (Cat. I)

185. Lorenzo Monaco and Workshop, *Adoration of the Magi*, National Museum, Poznań. (Cat. I)

186. Lorenzo Monaco and Workshop, *A Young Monk Tempted from Prayer and Saint Benedict Raises a Young Monk*, Pinacoteca Vaticana, Rome. (Cat. I)

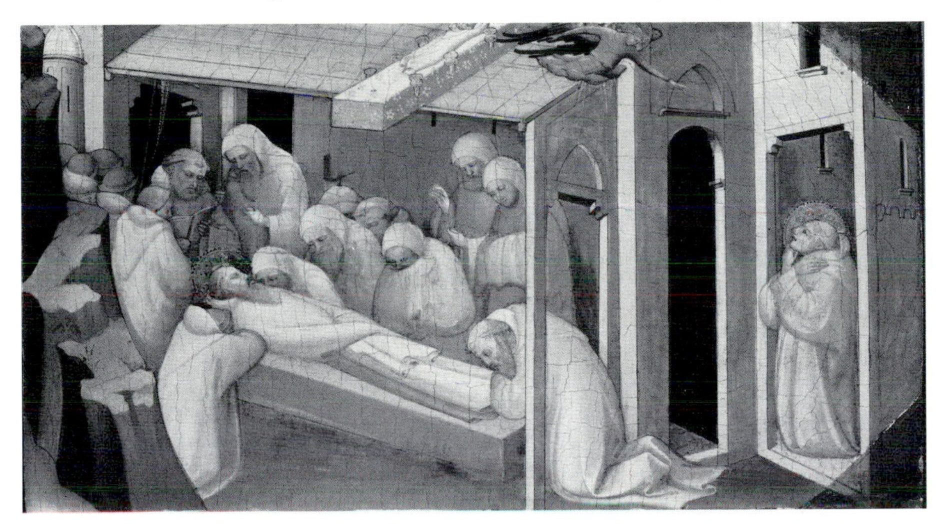

187. Lorenzo Monaco and Workshop, *Death of Saint Benedict*, National Gallery, London. (Cat. I)

188. *Retinue of the Magi*, detail of Fig. 185.

189. *Virgin and Child and Adoring Magus*, detail of Fig. 185.

190. Lorenzo Monaco and Workshop, *Stigmatization of Saint Francis*, Rijksmuseum, Amsterdam. (Cat. I)

191. Workshop of Lorenzo Monaco, *Funeral of Saint Francis*, Galleria Pallavicini, Rome. (Cat. I)

193. Lorenzo Monaco and Workshop, *Funeral of a Bishop Saint*, Musée des Beaux-Arts, Nice. (Cat. I)

192 (at left). Lorenzo Monaco and Workshop, *Crucifixion with the Virgin and Saints John the Evangelist and Francis*, Museo Bandini, Fiesole. (Cat. I)

194. Lorenzo Monaco and Workshop, *Madonna in Glory with Two Angels*, Liechtenstein Collection, Vaduz. (Cat. I)

195. Workshop of Lorenzo Monaco, *Madonna in Glory with Six Saints*, formerly Schaeffer Galleries, New York. (Cat. I)

196. Workshop of Lorenzo Monaco, *Saint Benedict in the Sacro Speco*, National Gallery, London. (Cat. I)

197. Lorenzo Monaco(?), *Scenes from the Early Life of the Baptist*, Otto Manley Collection, Scarsdale, New York. (Cat. I)

198. Workshop of Lorenzo Monaco (Bartolomeo di Fruosino?), *Joachim*, detail of Fig. 104.

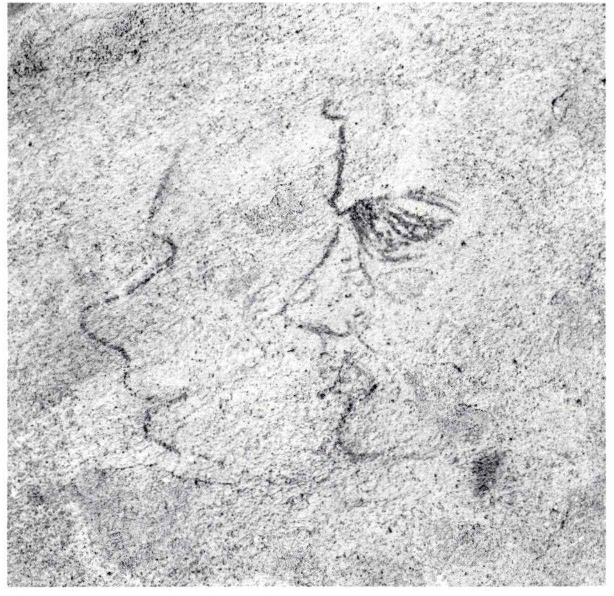

199. Workshop of Lorenzo Monaco, *Sketches in sinopia*, detail of Fig. 104.

200. Workshop of Lorenzo Monaco, *Baldachin above Saint Paul*, detail of Fig. 103.

201. Bartolomeo di Fruosino, *Isaiah*, detail of Fig. 121.

202. Workshop of Lorenzo Monaco (Bartolomeo di Fruosino?), *Saints in Pilasters*, detail of Fig. 121.

203. Workshop of Lorenzo Monaco, *Saint Paul*, fol. 163, Cod. Cor. 8, Biblioteca Laurenziana, Florence. (Cat. I)

204. Lorenzo Monaco and Workshop, *Saint John the Baptist* (detail), Kupferstichkabinett, Staatliche Museen, Berlin-Dahlem. (Cat. I)

205. Workshop of Lorenzo Monaco, *Christ in Glory* (detail), Kupferstichkabinett, Staatliche Museen, Berlin-Dahlem. (Cat. I)

206. Lorenzo Monaco and Workshop, *God the Father, with the Crucifix*, Musée Marmottan, Paris. (Cat. I)

207. Workshop of Lorenzo Monaco, *Prophet* (detail), Cleveland Museum of Art, Cleveland. (Cat. I)

208. Workshop of Lorenzo Monaco, *Pentecost*, Detroit Institute of Arts, Detroit. (Cat. I)

209. Lorenzo Monaco and Workshop, *Prophet*, National Gallery of Art, Washington. (Cat. I)

210. Workshop of Lorenzo Monaco, *Madonna and Child*, fol. 74v, Cod. E 70, Bargello, Florence. (Cat. I)

211. Workshop of Lorenzo Monaco(?), *Virgin and Child*, Gabinetto Disegni e Stampe, Uffizi, Florence. (Cat. I)

212. Workshop of Lorenzo Monaco(?), *Virgin and Child*, Gabinetto Disegni e Stampe, Uffizi, Florence. (Cat. I)

213. Workshop of Agnolo Gaddi, *Feast of Herod*, Louvre, Paris. (Cat. II)

214. Workshop of Agnolo Gaddi, *Baptism of Christ*, National Gallery, London. (Cat. II)

215. Lorenzo Monaco(?), *Saints Jerome and John the Baptist*, Accademia, Florence. (Cat. II)

216. Workshop of Agnolo Gaddi, *Saint James and Hermogenes; Martyrdom of Saint James*, Louvre, Paris. (Cat. II)

217. Lorenzo Monaco(?), *Madonna Enthroned*, Toledo Museum of Art, Toledo. (Cat. II)

218. Lorenzo Monaco(?), *Saints Peter and Paul*, Accademia, Florence. (Cat. II)

219. Lorenzo Monaco(?), *Saint Jerome in Penitence*, formerly Cremer Collection, Dortmund. (Cat. II)

220. Lorenzo Monaco(?), *The Baptist Departing for the Wilderness*, Leicestershire Museums and Art Galleries, Leicester. (Cat. II)

221. Lorenzo Monaco(?), *Nativity*, Staatliche Museen, Berlin-Dahlem. (Cat. II)

222. Lorenzo Monaco(?), *Crucifixion of Saint Peter*, Walters Art Gallery, Baltimore. (Cat. II)

223. Lorenzo Monaco(?), *Beheading of Saint Paul*, Art Museum, Princeton University, Princeton. (Cat. II)

224. Milieu of the Carmine Polyptych, *Madonna Enthroned, with Six Saints*, Museo Horne, Florence. (Cat. II)

225. Milieu of the Carmine Polyptych, *Madonna in Glory with Saints Paul and Peter*, Walters Art Gallery, Baltimore. (Cat. II)

226. Circle of the Master of the Straus Madonna, *Madonna and Child with Four Saints*, formerly Larderel Collection, Leghorn. (Cat. II)

227. Cionesque/Gerinesque Master, 1390s, *Saint Catherine of Alexandria*, Accademia, Florence. (Cat. II)

228. Cionesque/Gerinesque Master, 1390s, *Coronation of the Virgin*, Courtauld Institute Galleries, London. (Cat. II)

229. Cionesque/Gerinesque Master, 1390s, *Saint Caius*, Accademia, Florence. (Cat. II)

230. Cionesque/Gerinesque Master, 1390s, *Martyrdom of Saint Catherine of Alexandria*, Staatliche Museen, Berlin-Dahlem. (Cat. II)

231. Cionesque/Gerinesque Master, 1390s, *Last Supper*, Staatliche Museen, Berlin-Dahlem. (Cat. II)

232. Cionesque/Gerinesque Master, 1390s, *Martyrdom of Saint Caius*, Santa Barbara Museum of Art, Santa Barbara. (Cat. II)

233. Milieu of the San Gaggio Altarpiece, *Crucifixion*, Universitätsmuseum, Göttingen. (Cat. II)

234. Milieu of the San Gaggio Altarpiece, *Intercession of Christ and the Virgin*, The Cloisters, Metropolitan Museum of Art, New York. (Cat. II)

235. Milieu of the San Gaggio Altarpiece, *Head of the Virgin*, Rijksmuseum, Amsterdam. (Cat. II)

236. Milieu of the San Gaggio Altarpiece(?), *Madonna of Humility*, Sacro Convento di San Francesco, Assisi. (Cat. II)

237. Milieu of the San Gaggio Altarpiece, *Madonna Enthroned*, Rijksmuseum, Amsterdam. (Cat. II)

238. *Head of the Virgin*, detail of Fig. 237.

239. Later Cionesque, 1390s, *Madonna with Four Saints and The Man of Sorrows*, San Diego Museum of Art, San Diego. (Cat. II)

240. Later Cionesque, 1390s, *Crucifixion*, Uffizi, Deposit, Florence. (Cat. II)

241. Eclectic Florentine, ca. 1400-1405, *Ascension of Christ*, Pinacoteca Vaticana, Rome. (Cat. II)

242. Later Orcagnesque, 1390s, *Christ Giving the Keys to Saint Peter* (detail), National Gallery of Art, Washington. (Cat. II)

243. Santa Maria degli Angeli Workshop, 1390s, *Ascension of Christ*, fol. 86, Cod. Cor. 1, Biblioteca Laurenziana, Florence. (Cat. II)

244. Imitator of Lorenzo Monaco (Bartolomeo di Fruosino?), *Saint Lawrence Enthroned, with Saints Ansanus and Margaret*, Musée du Petit Palais, Avignon. (Cat. II)

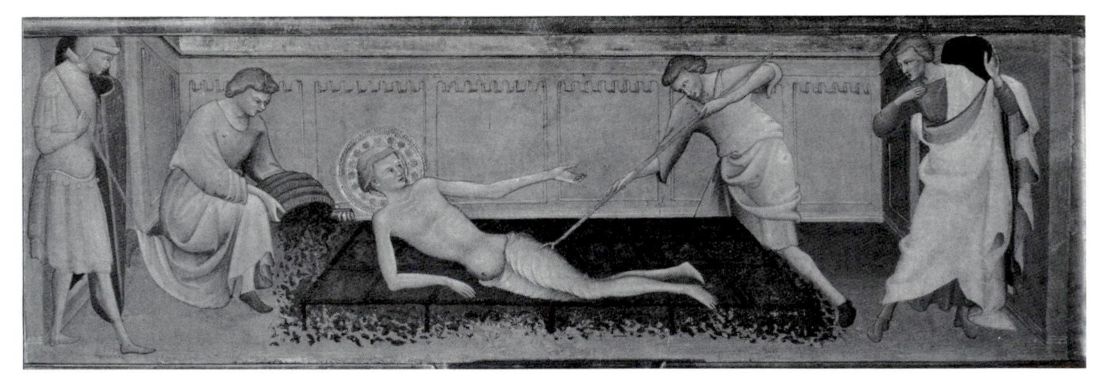

245. Imitator of Lorenzo Monaco (Bartolomeo di Fruosino?), *Martyrdom of Saint Lawrence*, Pinacoteca Vaticana, Rome. (Cat. II)

246. Imitator of Lorenzo Monaco (Bartolomeo di Fruosino?), *Saint Margaret and the Prefect*, Pinacoteca Vaticana, Rome. (Cat. II)

247. Bartolomeo di Fruosino, *Circumcision*, fol. 185, Cor. D, Arcispedale di Santa Maria Nuova, Florence.

248. Bartolomeo di Fruosino, *Saint Egidius Enthroned* (detail), fol. 35v, Missal, Inv. 557, Museo di San Marco, Florence.

249. Remote Follower of Spinello Aretino, *Crucifixion*, Musei Civici, Pesaro. (Cat. II)

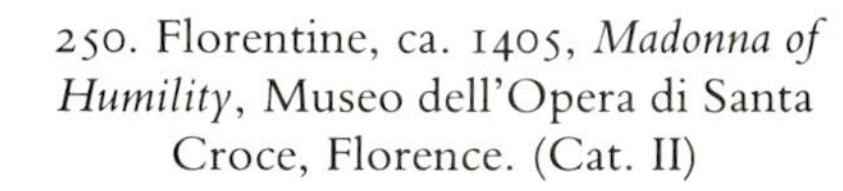

250. Florentine, ca. 1405, *Madonna of Humility*, Museo dell'Opera di Santa Croce, Florence. (Cat. II)

251. Imitator of Lorenzo Monaco, *Crucifixion with the Holy Family and Saint Lawrence*, Accademia, Ravenna. (Cat. II)

253. Provincial Tuscan or Emilian(?), *Crucifix with the Kneeling Magdalen; Madonna with a Donor*, Museo di Capodimonte, Naples. (Cat. II)

252. Eclectic Florentine, 1390s, *Madonna and Child with Four Saints and Two Angels*, Accademia (Deposit), Florence. (Cat. II)

254. Imitator of Lorenzo Monaco, *Madonna of Humility*, Cini Collection, Venice. (Cat. II)

255. Imitator of Lorenzo Monaco, *Annunciation with Saint Benedict and a Praying Nun*, Statens Museum for Kunst, Copenhagen. (Cat. II)

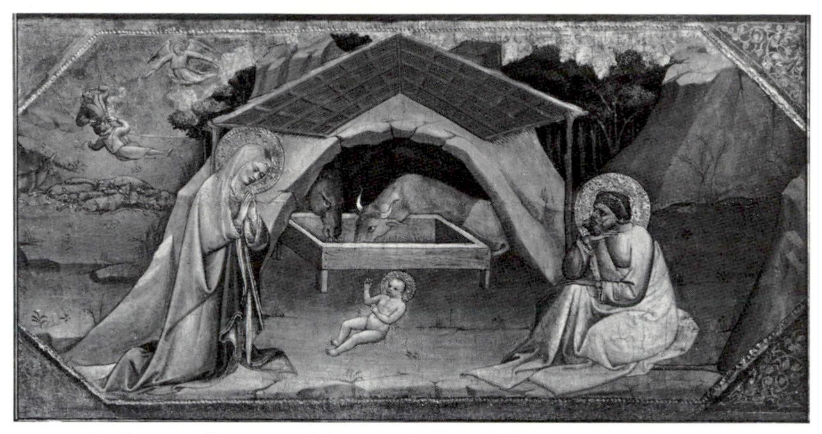

256. Imitator of Lorenzo Monaco, *Nativity*, Pinacoteca Vaticana, Rome. (Cat. II)

257. Imitator of Lorenzo Monaco, *Saint Michael and the Annunciatory Gabriel; Saint Francis and the Annunciate Virgin*, Museum of Fine Arts, Houston. (Cat. II)

258. Imitator of Lorenzo Monaco, *Saint Romuald*, Philbrook Art Center, Tulsa. (Cat. II)

259. Imitator of Lorenzo Monaco, *Meeting of Saint Anthony Abbot and Paul the Hermit*, Pinacoteca Vaticana, Rome. (Cat. II)

260. Workshop of Giovanni Toscani(?), *Death Riding a Bull*, Santa Croce, Florence. (Cat. II)

261. *Horseman*, detail of Fig. 260.

262. *Santa Maria degli Angeli and Saint Benedict*, fol. 17v, Codex Rustici, Biblioteca del Seminario Maggiore di Cestello, Florence.

263. Estimate of a work by Pietro Nelli, Archivio di Stato, Florence (see Document 12).

264. Don Silvestro dei Gherarducci, *Saint Mark*, fol. 68v, Cod. Cor. 2, Biblioteca Laurenziana, Florence.

265. Nardo di Cione, *Five Saints* (detail), Alte Pinakothek, Munich.

266. Jacopo di Cione, *Madonna of Humility*, National Gallery of Art, Washington.

267. Don Silvestro dei Gherarducci, *Madonna of Humility*, Accademia, Florence.

268. Don Silvestro dei Gherarducci, *Abraham and the Angels* (detail), National Gallery, London.

269. Don Silvestro dei Gherarducci(?), *Holy Women at the Tomb* (detail), Louvre, Paris.

270. Workshop of the Cioni, *Saint Peter*, Private collection.

271. Agnolo Gaddi, *Discovery and Testing of the True Cross* (detail), Choir, Santa Croce, Florence.

272. Agnolo Gaddi, *Return of the Sticks and Stones* (detail), Castellani Chapel, Santa Croce, Florence.

273. Taddeo Gaddi, *Annunciation to the Shepherds*, Baroncelli Chapel, Santa Croce, Florence.

274. Niccolò di Piero Lamberti, *Martyrdom of Saint James*, Orsanmichele, Florence.

275. Niccolò di Piero Lamberti(?), *Madonna della Rosa* (detail), Orsanmichele, Florence.

276. Taddeo Gaddi, *Saint John the Evangelist*, from the *Tree of Bonaventura*, Museo dell'Opera di Santa Croce, Florence.

277. Spinello Aretino, *Adoration of the Magi*, Galleria Nazionale, Parma.

278. Master of the Straus Madonna, *Annunciation*, Accademia, Florence.

279. Master of the Straus Madonna, *Madonna and Child*, Museum of Fine Arts, Houston.

280. Luca di Tommè, *Adoration of the Magi* (detail), Thyssen-Bornemisza Foundation, Lugano.

281. Spinello Aretino, *Coronation of the Virgin*, Accademia, Florence.

282. Agnolo Gaddi, *Seth and the Angel,* detail of *Death of Adam,* Choir, Santa Croce, Florence.

283. Spinello Aretino, *Annunciatory Gabriel,* detail of *Annunciation,* San Francesco, Arezzo.

284. Lorenzo Ghiberti, *Annunciation* (detail), North Door, Baptistery, Florence.

285. Gherardo Starnina, *Saints Margaret and Andrew,* Martin von Wagner Museum, Würzburg.

286. Gherardo Starnina, *Mary Magdalen, and Saint Lawrence with donor*, Staatliche Museen zu Berlin, Berlin (DDR).

287. Gherardo Starnina, *Saint Benedict*, Santa Maria del Carmine, Florence.

288. *Saint Benedict*, detail of Fig. 287.

289. *Saint Benedict*, detail of Fig. 290.

290. Gherardo Starnina, *Saint Benedict*, Nationalmuseum, Stockholm.

291. Lorenzo Ghiberti, *Adoration of the Magi*, North Door, Baptistery, Florence.

292. Lorenzo Ghiberti, *Agony in the Garden*, North Door, Baptistery, Florence.

293. Lorenzo Ghiberti, *Virgin and Infant Christ*, detail of the *Nativity*, North Door, Baptistery, Florence.

294. Gherardo Starnina, *Musical Angels*, detail of *Madonna and Saints*, Martin von Wagner Museum, Würzburg.

295. Filippo Brunelleschi, *Prophets*, from the *Altar of San Jacopo*, Cathedral, Pistoia.

296. Lorenzo di Giovanni d'Ambrogio, *Prophet*, Porta della Mandorla, Cathedral, Florence.

297. Donatello, *Saint John the Evangelist*, Museo dell'Opera del Duomo, Florence.

298. Jacopo della Quercia, *Silvestri Madonna*, Museo del Duomo, Ferrara.

299. Jacopo di Cione, *Coronation of the Virgin*, National Gallery, London.

300. Orcagna, *Tabernacle* (detail), Orsanmichele, Florence.

301. Lorenzo Ghiberti, *Saint John the Baptist*, Orsanmichele, Florence.

302. Giovanni del Biondo, *Coronation of the Virgin*, Cathedral, Fiesole.

303. Spinello Aretino, *Death of Saint Benedict*, Sacristy, San Miniato, Florence.

304. Spinello Aretino, *Raising of the Young Monk*, Sacristy, San Miniato, Florence.

305. Workshop of Nardo di Cione, *Saint Romuald's Vision of Saint Apollinaris*, from the *Trinity Altarpiece*, Accademia, Florence.

306. Master of the Rinuccini Chapel, *Rescue of Saint Placidus*, from the *Saint Bernard Altarpiece*, Accademia, Florence.

307. Giovanni del Biondo, *Saint Benedict Restores Life to a Young Monk*, Art Gallery of Ontario, Toronto.

308. Follower of Pietro Lorenzetti, *The Miraculous Reading*, from the *Beata Umiltà Altarpiece*, Uffizi, Florence.

309. Lorenzo Ghiberti, *Crucifixion*, North Door, Baptistery, Florence.

310. Mariotto di Nardo, *Charity of Saint Nicholas*, Santa Maria Maggiore, Florence.

311. Lorenzo Ghiberti, *Way to Calvary* (detail), North Door, Baptistery, Florence.

312. Lorenzo Ghiberti, *Betrayal of Christ* (detail), North Door, Baptistery, Florence.

313. Lorenzo Ghiberti, *Prophet*, North Door, Baptistery, Florence.

314. Lorenzo Ghiberti, *Pentecost* (detail), North Door, Baptistery, Florence.

315. Bartolo di Fredi, *Adoration of the Magi*, Pinacoteca, Siena.

316. Fra Angelico and Lorenzo Monaco, *Descent from the Cross*, Museo di San Marco, Florence.

317. Spinello Aretino, *Marriage of Saint Catherine, and Six Saints* (detail), Sercialli Chapel, Santa Trinita, Florence.

318. Leonardo di Giovanni, *The Baptist Departing for the Wilderness*, Silver Altar, Museo dell'Opera del Duomo, Florence.

319. Master of the Saint Nicholas Legend, *Miracle of the Drowned Child and the Golden Chalice*, Castellani Chapel, Santa Croce, Florence.

320. Taddeo Gaddi, *Expulsion of Joachim and Annunciation to Joachim*, Baroncelli Chapel, Santa Croce, Florence.

321. Nardo di Cione, *Christ of the Last Judgment*, Strozzi Chapel, Santa Maria Novella, Florence.

322. Giotto, *Moorish Guardsmen*, detail of the *Fire Ordeal Before the Sultan*, Bardi Chapel, Santa Croce, Florence.

323. Pietro Lorenzetti, *Honorius IV Granting the Habit to the Carmelites*, Pinacoteca, Siena.

324. Bartolomeo di Fruosino, *Scene in a Birth Chamber*, New-York Historical Society, New York.

325. Donatello, *Saint George and the Dragon*, Bargello (from Orsanmichele), Florence.

326. Rossello di Jacopo Franchi, *Saint Stephen Enthroned, with Angels*, fol. 48v, Cod. D, Museo dell'Opera del Duomo, Prato.

327. Lorenzo di Niccolò, *Madonna Enthroned*, San Leonardo in Arcetri, Florence.

328. Lorenzo di Niccolò, *Madonna Enthroned*, San Lorenzo a Collina, Mezzomonte.

329. Andrea di Giusto, *Madonna with Four Saints, Annunciation, and predella*, Galleria Comunale, Prato.

330. Francesco d'Antonio, *Madonna Enthroned, with Saints Lawrence and Giovanni Gualberto*, Fitzwilliam Museum, Cambridge.

331. Francesco d'Antonio, *Annunciation*, San Francesco, Figline.

332. Masolino, *Madonna of Humility*, Alte Pinakothek, Munich.

333. Masolino, *Man of Sorrows with the Virgin and Saint John the Evangelist* (detail), Museo della Collegiata, Empoli.

334. Fra Angelico, *Madonna Enthroned*, Museo di San Marco, Florence.

335. Fra Angelico, *Crucifixion* (pinnacle of the *Madonna and Saints Altarpiece*; before restoration), Museo Diocesano, Cortona.

336. Sandro Botticelli, *Annunciation* (before restoration), Uffizi, Florence.

337. Sandro Botticelli, *The Ascent to Mercury, Paradiso VI* (detail), Staatliche Museen, Berlin (DDR).